C000143266

1 MONTH OF
FREE
READING

at

www.ForgottenBooks.com

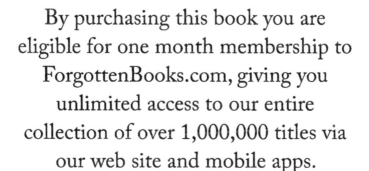

By purchasing this book you are
eligible for one month membership to
ForgottenBooks.com, giving you
unlimited access to our entire
collection of over 1,000,000 titles via
our web site and mobile apps.

To claim your free month visit:

www.forgottenbooks.com/free913637

* Offer is valid for 45 days from date of purchase. Terms and conditions apply.

ISBN 978-0-266-94502-4
PIBN 10913637

This book is a reproduction of an important historical work. Forgotten Books uses
state-of-the-art technology to digitally reconstruct the work, preserving the original format
whilst repairing imperfections present in the aged copy. In rare cases, an imperfection in
the original, such as a blemish or missing page, may be replicated in our edition. We do,
however, repair the vast majority of imperfections successfully; any imperfections that
remain are intentionally left to preserve the state of such historical works.

Forgotten Books is a registered trademark of FB &c Ltd.
Copyright © 2018 FB &c Ltd.
FB &c Ltd, Dalton House, 60 Windsor Avenue, London, SW19 2RR.
Company number 08720141. Registered in England and Wales.

For support please visit www.forgottenbooks.com

THE

LAW REPORTS.

Exchequer Division.

REPORTED BY

JAMES M. MOORSOM and ALEXANDER MORTIMER,
BARRISTERS-AT-LAW;

AND

IN THE COURT OF APPEAL

BY

CHARLES MARETT, WILLIAM MILLS, AND
HENRY HOLROYD, BARRISTERS-AT-LAW.

EDITED BY

JAMES REDFOORD BULWER, Q.C.

VOL. II.

FROM MICHAELMAS SITTINGS, 1876, TO TRINITY SITTINGS, 1877,
BOTH INCLUSIVE.
XL VICTORIA.

LONDON:
Printed for the Incorporated Council of Law Reporting for England and Wales
BY WILLIAM CLOWES AND SONS,
DUKE STREET, STAMFORD STREET; AND 14, CHARING CROSS.
PUBLISHING OFFICE, 51, CAREY STREET, LINCOLN'S INN, W.C.
1877.

COPY OF THIS
CPS ON .

a.54772

JUL 12 '901

JUDGES

OF

THE EXCHEQUER DIVISION

OF

THE HIGH COURT OF JUSTICE.

XL VICTORIA.

The Right Hon. Sir FITZROY KELLY, Lord Chief
  Baron, President.
Sir ANTHONY CLEASBY, Knt.
Sir CHARLES EDWARD POLLOCK, Knt.
Sir JOHN WALTER HUDDLESTON, Knt.
Sir HENRY HAWKINS, Knt.

ATTORNEY GENERAL:

Sir JOHN HOLKER, Knt.

SOLICITOR GENERAL:

Sir HARDINGE STANLEY GIFFARD, Knt.

JUDGES

OF

THE COURT OF APPEAL.

XL VICTORIA.

Lord CAIRNS, Lord Chancellor.

Sir ALEXANDER JAMES EDMUND COCKBURN, Bart.,
Lord Chief Justice of England.

Sir GEORGE JESSEL, Master of the Rolls.

Lord COLERIDGE, Lord Chief Justice of the
Common Pleas.

Sir FITZROY KELLY, Lord Chief Baron of the
Exchequer.

Sir WILLIAM MILBOURNE
JAMES,

Sir GEORGE MELLISH,

Sir RICHARD BAGGALLAY,

Sir GEORGE WILSHERE
BRAMWELL,

Sir WILLIAM BALIOL BRETT,

Sir RICHARD PAUL AMPHLETT,

Sir HENRY COTTON,

} Ordinary Judges
of Court of
Appeal.

The Mode of Citation of the Volumes in the *Three Series* of the LAW REPORTS, commencing January 1, 1876, will be as follows :—

In the First Series,
1 Ch. D.

In the Second Series,

| 1 Q. B. D. | 1 Ex. D. |
| 1 C. P. D. | 1 P. D. |

In the Third Series,
1 App. Cas.

TABLE OF CASES REPORTED

IN THIS VOLUME.

TABLE OF CASES CITED.

A.

B.

J.

K.

L.

M.

CASES

DETERMINED BY THE

EXCHEQUER DIVISION

OF THE

HIGH COURT OF JUSTICE

AND BY THE

COURT OF APPEAL

ON APPEAL FROM THE EXCHEQUER DIVISION

XL VICTORIA.

[IN THE COURT OF APPEAL.]

NICHOLS *v.* MARSLAND.

1876
Deo. 1.

Water stored—Liability of Owner for Escape of Water—Vis major or Act of God proximate Cause of Damage—Maxim Sic utere tuo ut alienum non lædas.

One who stores water on his own land, and uses all reasonable care to keep it safely there, is not liable for damage effected by an escape of the water, if the escape be caused by the act of God, or vis major ; e.g., by an extraordinary rainfall, which could not reasonably have been anticipated, although, if it had been anticipated, the effect might have been prevented.

On the defendant's land were ornamental pools containing large quantities of water. These pools had been formed by damming up with artificial banks a natural stream which rose above the defendant's land and flowed through it, and which was allowed to escape frcm the pools successively by weirs into its original course. An extraordinary rainfall caused the stream and the water in the pools to swell so that the artificial banks were carried away by the pressure, and the water in the pools, being thus suddenly let loose, rushed down the course of the stream and injured the plaintiff's adjoining property. The plaintiff having brought an action against the defendant for damages, the jury found that there was no negligence in the maintenance or construction of the pools, and that the flood was so great that it could not reasonably have been anticipated, though if it had been anticipated the effect might have been prevented :—

Held, affirming the judgment of the Court of Exchequer, that this was in substance a finding that the escape of the water was caused by the act of God, or vis major, and that the defendant was not liable for the damage.

Rylands v. *Fletcher* (Law Rep. 3 H. L. 330) distinguished.

APPEAL from a judgment of the Court of Exchequer (Kelly, C.B., Bramwell and Cleasby, BB.), making absolute a rule to enter the verdict for the defendant. The facts are fully set out in the report of the case in the Court below. (1) For the present purpose they are sufficiently stated in the judgment.

June 13, 14. *Cotton, Q.C.* (*McIntyre, Q.C.*, and *Coxon*, with him), for the plaintiff, appellant. Assuming the jury to be right in finding that the defendant was not guilty of negligence, and that the rainfall amounted to vis major, or the act of God, still the defendant is liable because she has, without necessity and voluntarily for her own pleasure, stored on her premises an element which was liable to be let loose, and which, if let loose, would be dangerous to her neighbours. One who keeps a mischievous animal, with knowledge of its propensities, is bound to keep it secure at his peril, and if he does not, is liable for the damage caused, though innocent of negligence: *May* v. *Burdett.* (2) The House of Lords has decided that water is in the same category: *Rylands* v. *Fletcher.* (3) So, though a railway company, when authorized by statute to use locomotives, is not liable for the damage done by sparks of fire, if they have taken all reasonable precautions and are not guilty of negligence: *Vaughan* v. *Taff Vale Ry. Co.* (4), yet they are liable when not expressly authorized by statute: *Jones* v. *Festiniog Ry. Co.* (5) These authorities were all discussed in *Madras Ry. Co.* v. *Zemindar of Carvatenagarum* (6), where the defendant was held not liable on the ground that it was

(1) Law Rep. 10 Ex. 255.

(2) 9 Q. B. 101, 112 ; 16 L. J. (Q.B.) 64, 67.

(3) Law Rep. 1 Ex. 265, 279 ; affirmed Law Rep. 3 H. L. 330, 339, 340.

(4) 5 H. & N. 679 ; 29 L. J. (Ex.) 247.

(5) Law Rep. 3 Q. B. 733.

(6) Law Rep. 1 Ind. App. 364, 385.

1876
———
NICHOLS
v.
MARSLAND.

his duty to maintain the reservoirs on his premises. The present defendant was under no such duty. Even if she be considered innocent of wrong doing, why should the plaintiff suffer for the defendant's voluntary act of turning an otherwise harmless stream into a source of danger? But for the defendant's embankments, the excessive rainfall would have escaped without doing injury. The fact of the embankments being so high caused the damage. They ought to have been much higher or less, or the weirs ought to have been much larger and kept in order. Even if vis major does excuse from liability, the vis major must be the sole cause of the damage, which it was not here. Such a storm as this occurs periodically, and may be foreseen, and is therefore not the act of God or vis major in the sense that it excuses from liability.

Gorst, Q.C., and *Hughes* (*Dunn* with them), for the defendant, cited *Carstairs* v. *Taylor* (1); *McCoy* v. *Danbey* (2); *Tennent* v. *Earl of Glasgow.* (3)

Cur. adv. vult.

Dec. 1. The judgment of the Court (Cockburn, C.J., James and Mellish, L.JJ., and Baggallay, J.A.) (4), was read by

MELLISH, L.J. This was an action brought by the county surveyor (5) of the county of Chester against the defendant to recover damages on account of the destruction of four county bridges which had been carried away by the bursting of some reservoirs. At the trial before Cockburn, C.J., it appeared that the defendant was the owner of a series of artificial ornamental lakes, which had existed for a great number of years, and had never previous to the 18th day of June, 1872, caused any damage. On that day, however, after a most unusual fall of rain, the lakes overflowed, the dams at their end gave way, and the water out of the lakes carried away the county bridges lower down the stream. The jury found that there was no negligence either in the construction or the maintenance of the reservoirs, but that if the flood could have been anticipated, the effect might have been pre-

(1) Law Rep. 6 Ex. 217.

(2) 20 Penn. St. R. 85.

(3) 1 Court of Session Cases, 3rd series, 183.

(4) Archibald, J., who was a member of the Court when the case was argued, died before judgment was delivered.

(5) Under 43 Geo. 3, c. 59, s. 4.

vented. (1)　Upon this finding the Lord Chief Justice, acting on the decision in *Rylands* v. *Fletcher* (2) as the nearest authority applicable to the case, directed a verdict for the plaintiff, but gave leave to move to enter a verdict for the defendant. The Court of Exchequer have ordered the verdict to be entered for the defendant, and from their decision an appeal has been brought before us.

The appellant relied upon the decision in the case of *Rylands* v. *Fletcher*. (2)　In that case the rule of law on which the case was decided was thus laid down by Mr. Justice Blackburn in the Exchequer Chamber (3) :—" We think the true rule of law is that the person who for his own purposes brings on his lands and collects and keeps there anything likely to do mischief if it escapes, must keep it at his peril, and if he does not do so, is primâ facie answerable for all the damage which is the natural consequence of its escape.　He can excuse himself by shewing that the escape was owing to the plaintiff's default; or perhaps that the escape was the consequence of vis major, or the act of God; but as nothing of the sort exists here it is unnecessary to inquire what excuse would be sufficient." It appears to us that we have two questions to consider :—First, the question of law, which was left undecided in *Rylands* v. *Fletcher* (2), can the defendant excuse herself by shewing that the escape of the water was owing to vis major, or, as it is termed in the law books, the " act of God?" And, secondly, if she can, did she in fact make out that the escape was so occasioned ?

Now, with respect to the first question, the ordinary rule of law is that when the law creates a duty and the party is disabled from performing it without any default of his own, by the act of God, or the King's enemies, the law will excuse him; but when a party by his own contract creates a duty, he is bound to make it good notwithstanding any accident by inevitable necessity.　We can see no good reason why that rule should not be

(1) The judgment of the Court below, read by Bramwell, B., states the finding thus: " In this case I understand the jury to have found that all reasonable care had been taken by the defendant, that the banks were fit for

all events to be anticipated, and the weirs broad enough; that the storm was of such violence as to be properly called the act of God, or vis major."

(2) Law Rep. 3 H. L. 330.

(3) Law Rep. 1 Ex. at p. 279.

applied to the case before us. The duty of keeping the water in and preventing its escape is a duty imposed by the law, and not one created by contract. If, indeed, the making a reservoir was a wrongful act in itself, it might be right to hold that a person could not escape from the consequences of his own wrongful act. But it seems to us absurd to hold that the making or the keeping a reservoir is a wrongful act in itself. The wrongful act is not the making or keeping the reservoir, but the allowing or causing the water to escape. If, indeed, the damages were occasioned by the act of the party without more—as where a man accumulates water on his own land, but, owing to the peculiar nature or condition of the soil, the water escapes and does damage to his neighbour—the case of *Rylands* v. *Fletcher* (1) establishes that he must be held liable. The accumulation of water in a reservoir is not in itself wrongful; but the making it and suffering the water to escape, if damage ensue, constitute a wrong. But the present case is distinguished from that of *Rylands* v. *Fletcher* (1) in this, that it is not the act of the defendant in keeping this reservoir, an act in itself lawful, which alone leads to the escape of the water, and so renders wrongful that which but for such escape would have been lawful. It is the supervening vis major of the water caused by the flood, which, superadded to the water in the reservoir (which of itself would have been innocuous), causes the disaster. A defendant cannot, in our opinion, be properly said to have caused or allowed the water to escape, if the act of God or the Queen's enemies was the real cause of its escaping without any fault on the part of the defendant. If a reservoir was destroyed by an earthquake, or the Queen's enemies destroyed it in conducting some warlike operation, it would be contrary to all reason and justice to hold the owner of the reservoir liable for any damage that might be done by the escape of the water. We are of opinion, therefore, that the defendant was entitled to excuse herself by proving that the water escaped through the act of God.

The remaining question is, did the defendant make out that the escape of the water was owing to the act of God? Now the jury have distinctly found, not only that there was no negligence in the construction or the maintenance of the reservoirs, but that the

(1) Law Rep. 3 H. L. 330.

flood was so great that it could not reasonably have been anticipated, although, if it had been anticipated, the effect might have
been prevented; and this seems to us in substance a finding that
the escape of the water was owing to the act of God. However
great the flood had been, if it had not been greater than floods
that had happened before and might be expected to occur again,
the defendant might not have made out that she was free
from fault; but we think she ought not to be held liable because she did not prevent the effect of an extraordinary act of
nature, which she could not anticipate. In the late case of
Nugent v. *Smith* (1) we held that a carrier might be protected from
liability for a loss occasioned by the act of God, if the loss by no
reasonable precaution could be prevented, although it was not absolutely impossible to prevent it.

It was indeed ingeniously argued for the appellant that at any
rate the escape of the water was not owing solely to the act of
God, because the weight of the water originally in the reservoirs
must have contributed to break down the dams, as well as the extraordinary water brought in by the flood. We think, however, that
the extraordinary quantity of water brought in by the flood is in
point of law the sole proximate cause of the escape of the water.
It is the last drop which makes the cup overflow.

On the whole we are of opinion that the judgment of the Court
of Exchequer ought to be affirmed.

Judgment affirmed. (2)

Solicitors for plaintiff: *Philpot & Son, for Potts & Roberts,
Chester.*

Solicitor for defendant: *E. Byrne, for Brocklehurst & Co.,
Macclesfield.*

---

(1) 1 C. P. D. 423.

(2) The question whether the rule
should be made absolute for a new
trial, on the ground that the verdict
was against the evidence, was reserved
for future discussion, if the plaintiff
should desire it.

[IN THE COURT OF APPEAL.]

LLOYD *v.* LEWIS.

1876
Nov. 22.

Practice—Award—Signing Judgment—Judicature Act, 1873 (36 & 37 *Vict.
c.* 66), *s.* 22—*Order XL., Rule* 3.

A verdict having been taken, subject to a reference, before the Judicature Act
came into operation, the arbitrator to have power to direct a verdict for either
party, the award was not made until after the Act came into operation :—

Held, that judgment on the award could be signed without obtaining an order
of the Court or of a judge.

Semble, per Brett, J.A., that where the award, made under a reference since
the Act, is final and conclusive on the parties, judgment may be signed on the
award, though no direction to that effect is given in the order of reference or in
the award ; and it is not necessary to set down the action on motion for judgment
under Order XL., Rule 3.

AT the trial of this cause at the Carmarthen Assizes on the 23rd
of July, 1875, a verdict was taken by consent for the plaintiff
for the amount claimed, subject to a reference of the cause and
all matters in difference to an arbitrator, who was empowered to
direct that a verdict should be entered for the plaintiff, or for the
defendant, or a nonsuit. On the 24th of July, 1876, the arbitrator
published his award, directing the verdict to be entered for the
plaintiff for 175*l.* 1*s.* 4*d.*

The postea was entered by the associate in the usual form, dated
the 22nd of July, 1875, the first day of the assizes, and judgment
was signed upon production of the postea.

A summons was taken out by the defendant to set aside the
judgment, and an order was made by Field, J., at chambers,
setting aside the judgment, on the ground that a motion for
judgment ought to have been made. The plaintiff moved the
Divisional Court to rescind this order; and the motion was, on
the 19th of September, refused by Field, J., and Huddleston, B.,
sitting as vacation judges.

The plaintiff appealed.

B. T. Williams, Q.C., and *Anstie,* for the plaintiff. This reference was made under the old system, and the subsequent proceedings are in accordance. The judgment was set aside because the

1876

LLOYD
v.
LEWIS

Court thought the case came within Order XL., Rule 3, and that as the order of reference did not in terms direct judgment to be entered, the action must be set down on motion for judgment. There is already a verdict for the plaintiff, and orders of reference never contain an express direction to the arbitrator to order judgment to be entered. That was understood, and this rule applies only to cases where the referee under the new system makes a report, on which the decision of the Court must be obtained. Sect. 22 of the Act of 1873 provides that causes begun before are to go on as if the Act had not been passed: *Cruikshank v. Floating Baths Co.* (1) What would be the use of setting down such a cause? No opposition could be made, and the order would be of course.

Bucknill for the defendant. The practice is clearly altered, and the plaintiff ought to have applied in chambers, or have moved for judgment. The defendant would then have had an opportunity of shewing that the award was defective and ought to be sent back to the arbitrator. The matter was not fully heard until after the Act came into operation, and judgment must be obtained under the new system.

MELLISH, L.J. In this case an action was tried at the summer assizes of 1875, and a verdict was taken for the plaintiff, subject to a reference in the usual terms. The award was not made until long after the Judicature Act came into operation, and the effect of the award is to give a verdict for the plaintiff for a certain amount. On that the plaintiff signed judgment. An order was made by the judge in chambers setting aside that judgment, and that order was affirmed by the Divisional Court of the Long Vacation. The first question is, whether the plaintiff was, under these circumstances, entitled to sign judgment according to the old practice. Now, in the first place, reference was made to Order XL., Rule 3; but it is plain that this order does not apply to this case, and can only apply to cases where the trial took place after the Act came into operation. Then our attention was called to the 22nd section of the Judicature Act, 1873, and, no doubt, looking at it literally, it makes a distinction between those cases which

(1) 1 C. P. D. 260.

have been fully heard and those which have not been fully heard. If they have been fully heard, judgment is to be signed under the old system, if not, either under the new or the old, and what has been argued is, that this is a case under the new system, and that the plaintiff ought to have got an order at chambers before he could proceed under the new system. But the object of the order of reference appears plainly that the successful party should be at liberty to sign judgment. The parties might have finished the arbitration before the Long Vacation, and before the Judicature Act came into operation, and there could have been no intention that the arbitrator should have less power over it because the Act had come into operation. The principle is, that when the award is obtained the parties are in the same position as if that was the original verdict. What would be the object of adding to the reference that the successful party may sign judgment, or that it is to be in the power of the arbitrator to give that direction? When the decision of the arbitrator has been given, it is absurd that an unnecessary additional expense should be put upon the parties. When, therefore, the postea was entered and taken to the proper officer to sign judgment, the parties were in the same position as if the Act had not been passed.

BRETT, J.A. In my opinion one canon of construction which we ought to apply to the Judicature Act is, that the law and the ordinary administration of the law are to be preserved, but that useless expenses are to be cut away. There was here a trial at nisi prius, and a verdict was taken for the plaintiff, subject to a reference made under the old form. The arbitrator heard the case, and maintained the verdict for the plaintiff, but diminished the amount claimed. Then it is said, that after this proceeding it was necessary that the plaintiff should either take out a summons at chambers for directions how to proceed, or should set down the action for judgment. I do not in the least retract what I said in *Cruikshank* v. *Floating Baths Co.* (1), that there are, since the Judicature Act, references of different sorts, some like those which were usual in Chancery where the referee is to report to the Court, when the decision of the referee may be reviewed by the Court;

(1) 1 C. P. D. 260.

but there is nothing in the Judicature Act which prevents the use of the old form of reference making the decision of the arbitrator final as to law and as to fact. This is not a reference under the Judicature Act, but one which might have been made after that Act came into operation. The decision of the arbitrator was final, and could not be reviewed. The suggestion made by the defendant in this case is crotchety and uselessly technical. The order could be only in one way, and judgment must be signed according to the decision of the arbitrator. It is clearly not within Order XL., Rule 3, which relates only to references under the Act. Many orders have been drawn up in this form, and it has always been considered that judgment could at once be signed on the award. It is a necessary implication from this order that the parties had consented to such a course. I therefore have very little doubt that whether this order of reference was before the Judicature Act, or after it, and whether it says in specific terms that judgment is to be signed or does not say so, consent that judgment shall be signed is to be implied, and, in my opinion, it is not necessary to insert this in the order. I think that the judgment was properly signed. Suggestions of this crotchety nature ought not to be countenanced; and the decision of the Vacation Court was wrong, and ought to be reversed.

AMPHLETT, J.A. I am of the same opinion.

Judgment for the plaintiff.

Solicitors for plaintiff: *Vizard, Crowder, & Co., for W. Howell, Llanelly.*

Solicitor for defendant: *Stretton.*

BENNETT, Trustee, &c. v. GAMGEE and Another.

Bankruptcy or Liquidation—Pending Action by Debtor—Trustee declining to continue Action—Fresh Action by Trustee—Common Law Procedure Act, 1852, s. 142.

1876
Nov. 22.

Where the trustee of a liquidating debtor elects, under the Common Law Procedure Act, 1852, s. 142, not to continue a pending action commenced by the debtor, such election is not a bar to a subsequent action by the trustee in his representative capacity founded on the same cause of action.

DEMURRER to a statement of defence.

The plaintiff sued as trustee of the estate and effects of David Foster and William Lockwood, liquidating debtors, on an agreement made between them (before the liquidation proceedings) and the defendants for the purchase by the latter of the Britannia Foundry. The statement of claim set out the agreement, and alleged as breach the non-payment by the defendants of 2500*l.* deposit.

The defendants delivered a statement of defence, the effect of which was, that David Foster and William Lockwood sued the defendants for the same causes of action as in the claim alleged : that during the pendency of that action Foster and Lockwood presented their petition for liquidation, and the plaintiff was appointed trustee; that subsequently, in accordance with the provisions of the Common Law Procedure Act, 1852, s. 142 (1), he was called on to elect whether he would continue that action and give security for the costs thereof, which he declined; that the defendants thereupon obtained leave to plead the liquidation proceedings in bar, which they did; and the plaintiffs, Foster and Lockwood, confessed the truth of the matters stated in such plea, and prayed judgment for their costs of suit, and thereupon such

(1) 15 & 16 Vict. c. 76, s. 142: "The bankruptcy or insolvency of the plaintiff in any action which the assignees might maintain for the benefit of the creditors shall not be pleaded in bar to such action, unless the assignees shall decline to continue and give security, for the costs thereof, upon a judge's order to be obtained for that purpose, within such reasonable time as the judge may order, but the proceedings may be stayed until such election is made; and in case the assignees neglect or refuse to continue the action and give such security within the time limited by the order, the defendant may, within eight days after such neglect or refusal, plead the bankruptcy."

1876

BENNETT
v.
GANGES.

costs were taxed at 134*l.* 2*s.*, which the defendants paid. The defendants averred that these proceedings estopped Foster and Lockwood, and the plaintiff as their trustee, from bringing the present action.

To this statement of defence the plaintiff demurred.

H. Lush (*Waddy*, Q.C., with him), for the plaintiff. Before the Common Law Procedure Act, 1852, a plea of bankruptcy was a good plea in bar to the action by the bankrupt, but did not estop a trustee from bringing a separate action: *Kinnear* v. *Tarrant* (1); and there is nothing in s. 142 to take away this right from the trustee. [He was then stopped.]

Herschell, Q.C. (*S. Woolf* with him), contrà. The trustee takes no more rights than the bankrupt had where the contract and breach were by the bankrupt, and he takes subject to all rights and equities against the bankrupt. It cannot have been contemplated that the defendants, having been called on to pay the costs of the first action, should be harassed by further litigation in respect of the same matter. It is no doubt true, that for the purpose of carrying out the principles of the bankruptcy laws the trustee may have rights independent of, or differing from, those of the bankrupt; as, for instance, where the latter has fraudulently released a debt, the trustee would not be bound, though the bankrupt would be; but that is not the case here, where, for the purpose of this action, the debtors and their trustee are one. The onus of deciding once for all in the interest of the creditors is thrown on the trustee. If he declines to go on, and the bankruptcy is pleaded, there is a final ending, not merely of the action, but of the cause of action: *Newington* v. *Levy*. (2) If there is a final ending of the cause of action, namely, the breach of contract as between the parties between whom the contract was made, it must be argued, in order to support this action, that there is a separate cause of action in the trustee; but the bankruptcy confers no fresh cause of action, it simply vests in the trustee that which already exists, if he chooses to avail himself of it; if he does not elect to do so, then the cause of action remains in the bankrupt and is put an end to with the action.

(1) 15 East, 622.   (2) Law Rep. 5 C. P. 607; Law Rep. 6 C. P. 180.

H. Lush, in reply.

KELLY, C.B. I think that the plaintiff is entitled to the judgment of the Court. The question is whether a right to recover in a separate action, as well as a right to continue an action commenced by the insolvent debtors, has accrued to their trustee in respect of a right of action which had accrued to the debtors themselves. Are these one and the same right? In my opinion they are very different.

The defendants do not set up that there has not been a breach of contract and a consequent right to recover independently of the question of insolvency, but the argument is, that on the election of the trustee not to continue the action, the right of action remained in the debtors, and was extinguished by the judgment in their action, and the trustee could take no further proceedings.

The debtors having become insolvent after the cause of action accrued, their trustee, according to the provisions of the Common Law Procedure Act, 1852, was called upon to elect whether he would continue the action brought by them or no. The trustee elected not to proceed, and the debtors then admitted their insolvency, and the question is whether, because in consequence of this the defendants may be liable to some costs, they are to be permitted to stop the trustee from recovering in a fresh action. If the contention for the defendants is right, the trustee might be prevented from recovering, for the general benefit of the creditors, money undoubtedly due to the debtors, and the defendants would be exonerated from paying it because certain costs may have been incurred by them in the former action.

I find nothing in the Act or in the law to enable the defendants to evade their liability, and I think, therefore, that the demurrer must be allowed.

CLEASBY, B. I am of the same opinion. I do not think that the defendants have set up any answer to the plaintiff's claim. This is an action of debt by the trustee of two liquidating debtors, and we must, for the purpose of considering the case, treat the debt as existing. It is said, however, that the action is barred because the trustee elected not to continue an action for the same debt brought by the debtors before the proceedings in liquidation, in which action the defendants, on the then plaintiffs going into liquidation, pleaded that fact, on which the plaintiffs confessed the plea and got judgment, under the 22nd and 23rd rules of Trinity Term, 1853, for their costs, which the defendants paid. No doubt that would be a bar to a further action by the same plaintiffs, because, the cause of action having been the subject of a judgment, there would be a complete answer to further proceedings. In *Newington* v. *Levy* (1) it is decided that the effect of a confession of a plea containing a defence arising after the commencement of the action is to make a final ending of the cause of action. But on what ground can this confession be said to be a bar to the trustee? His action has not been the subject of a judgment, and if it is barred it must be on the ground of some new effect to be given to the decision of the trustee in electing not to continue the action which has been ended by the confession of the plea. To this present action there is no satisfaction, no set off, and no judgment pleaded, but it is said that because the plaintiff has not chosen to take advantage of what had been done when he was appointed, the debt is barred. I can see no authority for this. It has been again and again said that the position of a trustee is not that he merely represents the bankrupt so as simply to stand in his shoes, but that the position of the two is very different. In *Heilbut* v. *Nevill* (2) I pointed out that the assignees were not suing as representing the bankrupt, but as assignees of the estate under the bankrupt laws. That makes the real difference between the position of the plaintiff if he had chosen to continue the action of the liquidating debtors, on which he would have been bound by all their acts, and his position here, where he is entitled to say that he sues under the authority of the bankrupt laws. I see no authority for the defendants' contention, and no sufficient reason for adopting it, and our judgment must be for the plaintiff.

Judgment for the plaintiff.

Solicitor for plaintiff: *Charles Butcher, for Henry Patteson, Sheffield.*

Solicitors for defendants: *Michael Abrahams & Roffey.*

(1) Law Rep. 5 C. P. 607; Law Rep. 6 C. P. 180.
(2) Law Rep. 5 C. P. 478.

[IN THE COURT OF APPEAL.]

1875.
Dec. 11.

BORROWMAN AND OTHERS v. DRAYTON.

Contract of Sale—Construction—Cargo.

The plaintiffs sold to the defendant "a cargo of from 2500 to 3000 barrels (seller's option) American petroleum .... to be shipped from New York .... and vessel to call for orders off coast for any safe floating port in the United Kingdom, or on the Continent between Havre and Hamburg, both inclusive (buyer's option)." The plaintiffs chartered a vessel, on which were placed 3000 barrels of petroleum, and a bill of lading was signed making them deliverable to the plaintiffs; but as this quantity did not constitute a full cargo, 300 additional barrels were placed on board, which were marked with a different mark, and for which a separate bill of lading was signed. The plaintiffs gave notice to the defendant of the shipment of the 3000 barrels, and were ready to order the vessel from its port of call to any port of delivery within the contract, and there to deliver to the defendant the 3000 barrels and to take the 300 barrels themselves, or to deliver to the defendant at any such port 2750 barrels as the mean between 2500 and 3000, but the defendant refused to accept either the 3000 barrels or any other quantity. The plaintiffs having brought an action for non-acceptance:—

Held, affirming the decision of the Exchequer Division, that, on the true construction of the contract, "cargo" meant the entire load of the vessel which carried it; that the defendant was therefore not bound to accept part of a cargo; and that the action was not maintainable.

THIS was an action for breach of contract in refusing to accept a cargo of 3000 barrels of petroleum sold by the plaintiffs to the defendant. At the trial before Kelly, C.B., at the London sittings after Hilary Term, 1875, the facts stated in the judgment were proved. The plaintiffs were nonsuited, with leave to move to enter a verdict for them on the ground that the defendant was not justified in refusing the plaintiffs' offer, the amount of damages to be settled by an arbitrator, the Court to draw inferences of fact. A rule nisi accordingly was obtained, and was on the 11th day of November, 1875, discharged by the Exchequer Division (Kelly, C.B., Cleasby and Amphlett, BB.), for reasons substantially the same as those which appear in the judgment of the Court of Appeal. From this decision the plaintiffs appealed.

June 13, 1876. *Morgan Howard, Q.C.,* and *Tindal Atkinson,* for the plaintiffs, appellants. The Exchequer Division held, that upon a contract to buy "a cargo of from 2500 to 3000 barrels (seller's option) of petroleum," the defendant was not liable for refusing to accept 3000 barrels, on the ground that the vessel not being filled with the 3000 barrels carried 300 additional barrels for the seller; and they were partly influenced by *Kreuger* v. *Blanck* (1), where it was held that a "cargo" meant a whole cargo and not part of a cargo. There, however, the whole freight of the vessel was at the buyer's risk as soon as shipped, the contract being a "cost freight and insurance" one. In the present case the 3000 barrels were at the seller's risk till weighed and delivered to the buyer. Moreover, in that case the timber for the buyer had to be measured out of the whole cargo at the uncontrolled discretion of the seller, and there were no separate marks or bill of lading; but here a separate bill of lading was made out for the 300 barrels, they were marked separately, and the buyer having an option as to the port of discharge might obviate any disadvantage supposed to arise from the 300 barrels being brought into the market. It is suggested by the defendant that the margin of 500 barrels given by the contract was given to enable the seller to find a vessel of the right capacity. But it was really given to allow for the large leakage which always takes place in the carriage of petroleum. Supposing "cargo" means the whole cargo, that is only where the ship is named in the contract. The defendant has suffered no damage, for he gets a full equivalent, and this was the view of Blackburn, J., in *Ireland* v. *Livingston* (2), where he said, "If necessary I should advise your Lordships to reconsider the decision of the Court of Exchequer in *Kreuger* v. *Blanck*." (1) At the most the defendant can only bring a cross action. It cannot have been intended to be a condition precedent that the vessel should carry no other goods. If the defendant's contention is right, the seller could not ship any other goods in the same vessel, even those of a different sort, and such as would not come into competition with the buyer's goods.

Benjamin, Q.C., and *English Harrison (W. G. Harrison* with

(1) Law Rep. 5 Ex. 179.   (2) Law Rep. 5 H. L. at p. 410.

them), for the defendant. Their arguments sufficiently appear
from the judgment.

Tindal Atkinson replied.

1876

BORROWMAN
v.
DRAYTON.

Cur. adv. vult.

Dec. 1. The judgment of the Court (1) (Cockburn, C.J., James
and Mellish L.JJ., and Baggallay, J.A.,) was delivered by

MELLISH, L.J. This was an appeal from a judgment of the
Exchequer Division, discharging a rule to enter a verdict for the
plaintiffs. The action was brought by the plaintiffs against the
defendant on account of the defendant having refused to accept
3000 barrels of petroleum which he had agreed to purchase from
the plaintiffs, and the question to be determined is, whether, according to the true construction of the contract between the
parties, the defendant was entitled to refuse to buy those 3000
barrels on the ground that 300 other barrels of petroleum formed
part of the cargo of the *Lindesnaess*, so that the 3000 barrels did
not constitute the entire cargo.

The contract between the plaintiffs and the defendant was made
on the 13th of December, 1873, and was as follows :—

> Sold this day, for Borrowman, Phillips, & Co., to John B. Drayton & Co., a
> cargo of from 2500 to 3000 barrels (seller's option) United States American
> refined petroleum, crown diamond brand, of good merchantable quality, without
> any guarantee as to test, but having American certificate, standard white, burning
> test not under 120° Fah., at one shilling and three farthings per gallon weighed
> 8lbs. delivered. To be shipped from New York during the last half of February
> next, and vessel to call for orders off coast for any safe floating port in the United
> Kingdom or on the Continent between Havre and Hamburg both inclusive (buyer's
> option). In case of vessel being ordered to the Continent, buyers are to pay the
> extra freight, including insurance. On arrival of vessel at port of discharge, the
> oil is to be landed at a public wharf, and weighed on landing, and tared for average,
> real average tare to be arrived at by taring one in every twenty barrels as they
> come from the ship. Buyers agree to pay landing and all other charges, including
> fire insurance, for which they are to be allowed five shillings per ton on the gross
> weight. In event of vessel coming to United Kingdom, payment to be made at
> landing weights in 14 days from last day of landing, by cash, less 2½ % discount,
> or cash against delivery order, if required, allowing interest at five per cent. per
> annum, or bank rate if over, for unexpired portion of prompt, if to the Continent,
> three-fourths of gross amount of invoice to be paid in exchange for shipping docu-
> ments on arrival of vessel at port of call, less interest at five per cent. per annum,

---

(1) Archibald, J., who was a mem-   argued, died before judgment was
ber of the Court when the case was   delivered.

or bank rate if over, for unexpired portion of prompt, and remaining fourth to be
paid on the prompt say 14 days from last day of landing, by cash, less 2½ % dis-
count. Should any dispute arise out of this contract, the same to be settled by
arbitration in London in the usual way. Particulars of shipment to be declared
so soon as ascertained. Should vessel be lost, contract to be void, as also for any
portion that may not arrive. Destination to be given within 48 hours after ship's
arrival at port of call.

Rose & Wilson, Brokers.

On the 11th of February, 1874, the plaintiffs' principals,
Sawyer, Wallace, & Co., of New York, chartered the *Lindesnaess*
to convey the petroleum. (1)   3000 barrels of petroleum were
placed on board the *Lindesnaess* at New York, and a bill of lading
signed making them deliverable to the order of Sawyer, Wallace,
& Co., but as this quantity did not constitute a full cargo, 300
additional barrels of petroleum were placed on board. They were
marked with a different mark, and a separate bill of lading was
signed for them.

The plaintiffs gave notice to the defendant of the shipment of
the 3000 barrels, and were ready to order the ship from its port
of call to any port of delivery within the contract, and there
to deliver to the defendant the 3000 barrels, and to take the
300 additional barrels themselves, or to deliver to the defendant
at any such port a quantity of 2750 barrels. (2)   But the
defendant refused to receive either the 3000 barrels, or any other
quantity.

The question is, were the plaintiffs, under those circumstances,
ready and willing to deliver to the defendant a cargo of from 2500
to 3000 barrels of petroleum within the contract?

We are of opinion that they were not.   The whole cargo of the

(1) By the charterparty, dated the
11th of February, 1874, the vessel was
chartered to carry about 3000 round
barrels of petroleum from New York
to Queenstown or Falmouth "for
orders, thence to a safe port in the
United Kingdom, or to a safe port on
the Continent between Havre and
Hamburg, both included, or to a safe
direct port as above, orders to be given
on signing bills of lading; one port
only to be used, or as near thereunto
as she can always float with safety."

The charterers to provide a full and
complete cargo of refined petroleum in
customary sized barrels. The bills of
lading to be signed without prejudice
to the charterparty. The charterer's
liabilities to cease as soon as the cargo
was shipped, but the vessel to have a
lien on the cargo for all freight, dead
freight and demurrage. Vessel to go
consigned to charterers' friends at port
of discharge.

(2) As the mean between 2500 and
3000 barrels.

Lindesnaess consisted of 3300 barrels, and therefore was in excess of the quantity ordered, and the plaintiffs cannot succeed unless the defendant was bound to accept a part of a cargo. We, however, are of opinion that an agreement to sell a cargo is, according to the plain and natural meaning of the words, an agreement to sell the entire quantity of goods loaded on board a vessel on freight for a particular voyage.

By the terms of the contract the seller engages to deliver to the buyer a cargo of petroleum of from 2500 to 3000 barrels at sellers' option. We think that effect must be given to the term " cargo,". as distinguished from the specified quantity, as, if the parties had intended otherwise, it would have been enough to specify the quantity without introducing the term "cargo" at all.

Now, generally speaking, the term " cargo," unless .there is something in the context to give it a different signification, means the entire load of the ship which carries it, and it may fairly be assumed that when one man undertakes to sell and another to buy a cargo, the subject-matter of the contract is to be the entire load of the ship. And that such must have been the sense in which the term " cargo " is used in this contract is materially strengthened by the agreement that the vessel shall proceed to a port of discharge to be determined, within certain limits, by the buyer, shewing plainly that what was contemplated was that the vessel and its entire cargo were to be at his disposal. There are various reasons why a purchaser may wish to buy the whole quantity of goods loaded on board a particular vessel. Such a contract gives him the complete control of the vessel. It enables him to select he port of discharge, to appoint the place in the port at which the discharge is to take place, to be free from the inconvenience of other persons' goods being unloaded at the same time with his own, and from the competition arising from other persons' goods being ready for sale, at the same place, and at the same time, with his.

It may be said that in this particular case the plaintiffs were ready to give the defendant the same advantages, or nearly the same advantages, as if the 3000 barrels had formed the entire cargo. We think, however, that though the refusal to accept the petroleum, looking to the offers made by the plaintiffs, may, under

1876
BORROWMAN
*.
DRAYTON.

the circumstances, have been an unhandsome proceeding on the part of the defendant, the latter, in point of law, was not bound to accept it; nor can we enter into the question whether what the plaintiffs offered was or was not a fair equivalent for what they contracted to do, or whether the defendant would or would not have suffered any substantial damage from not getting the entire cargo. It may be that the real reason why the defendant refused to receive the 3000 barrels was that the price of petroleum had fallen. Still, we think he was entitled, in point of law, to say, "The thing which you offered me was not the thing I agreed to buy, and, therefore, I will not take it."

It was argued that even though an agreement to buy the cargo of a particular named ship should amount to an agreement to buy the whole cargo, yet that an agreement to buy a cargo of from 2500 to 3000 barrels of petroleum, no particular ship being named, would be satisfied by sending a quantity of from 2500 to 3000 barrels in any one ship, although the ship might be filled up with other goods. We do not agree with this. We think that the reason why the precise quantity of petroleum to be sent is not fixed, and the seller has a margin of 500 barrels, is that he may have no difficulty in chartering a ship of the requisite size, and that he was not entitled without the defendant's consent to place any additional cargo on board the ship.

Judgment affirmed.

Solicitors for plaintiffs: *Mercer & Mercer.*
Solicitors for defendant: *Johnson, Upton, & Budd.*

[IN THE COURT OF APPEAL FROM INFERIOR COURTS.]

1876
Nov. 23.

DENNY, Appellant; THWAITES, Respondent.

Jurisdiction of Justices—Wilful or malicious Injury to Property—Surveyor of Highways—Removal of Obstruction and Nuisance to Highway—24 & 25 Vict. c. 97, s. 52.

The respondent was the occupier of a residence which communicated with an adjoining highway by means of a gateway; an enclosed drain and brickwork were put down at the gateway for the purpose of convenient access to the respondent's residence, and also for the purpose of allowing the free passage of water running by the side of the highway. The drain and brickwork, with the earth covering the same, formed a nuisance and obstruction to the highway. The appellant, being surveyor of highways for the parish within which the respondent's residence was situate, took up and removed the drain and the brickwork, and in so doing damaged them. The appellant having been charged upon an information before justices with committing damage, injury, and spoil upon the respondent's property, against the provisions of 24 & 25 Vict. c. 97, s. 52, they found that the appellant acted bonâ fide, but that he did not do the act complained of under a fair and reasonable supposition that he had a right to do it, and they convicted him of the offence charged :—

Held, that the conviction was wrong, and that the information ought to have been dismissed; for the appellant was not a private individual, but the surveyor of highways having a control over, and an interest in, the drains laid for carrying off the water, and that in dealing bonâ fide with the drains he was not guilty of wilful or malicious damage.

Semble, that, as the appellant, according to the finding of the justices, acted bonâ fide, they ought, upon the facts stated, also to have found that he acted under a fair and reasonable supposition that he had a right to do what was complained of in the information.

White v. *Feast* (Law Rep. 7 Q. B. 353) distinguished.

Case stated by four justices of the peace for the county of Norfolk, under 20 & 21 Vict. c. 43.

At a petty session holden at Mundford on the 4th of January, 1876, an information and complaint was preferred by the respondent, the Rev. William Thwaites, against the appellant, charging, under s. 52 of 24 & 25 Vict. c. 97 (1), that he, with R. Jarred, on

(1) By 24 & 25 Vict. c. 97, s. 52, "Whosoever shall wilfully or maliciously commit any damage, injury, or spoil to or upon any real or personal property whatsoever, either of a public or private nature, for which no punish- ment is hereinbefore provided, shall, on conviction thereof before a justice of the peace, at the discretion of the justice, either be committed to the common gaol or house of correction, there to be imprisoned only, or to be imprisoned

the 29th of December, 1875, at the parish of Northwold, did aid and abet Thomas Jackson, Edward Jackson, T. Bell, and W. Ellinor, in wilfully committing damage, injury, and spoil to and upon certain real property of a private nature, being the property of the said William Thwaites, to wit, certain draining pipes and a pathway, by removing the pipes, breaking one of them, and digging up the pathway where the said pipes were laid, thereby doing damage and injury to an amount not exceeding 5*l.*

At the hearing the following facts appeared from the evidence given on behalf of the respondent in support of the complaint.

Before the year 1874 a gateway led from a highway to certain allotments situate at Whittington, an outlying district within the parish of Northwold. At this gateway was a four-inch wooden tunnel for water to pass. Some years previously the highway had been under the management of the trustees of a turnpike trust. About 1872 the gateway was made wider, and then the respondent gave two pieces of four-inch iron pipe to put in at each end of the wooden tunnel. In 1874 a church and a vicarage were built upon the allotments, and the gateway then formed the entrance to the vicarage. About that time, under the direction of the architect of the works, the wooden tunnel and four-inch iron pipes were removed, and instead of them some new six-inch pipes were laid down; a grating was put in flush with the gutter or drain at one end of the new pipes, and some brick-work was built at the other end. The respondent was the vicar. The appellant and O.

---

and kept to hard labour for any term not exceeding two months, or else shall forfeit and pay such sum of money not exceeding five pounds as to the justice shall seem meet, and also such further sum of money as shall appear to the justice to be a reasonable compensation for the damage, injury, or spoil so committed, not exceeding the sum of five pounds; which last-mentioned sum of money shall, in the case of private property, be paid to the party aggrieved . . . and if such sums of money, together with costs (if ordered) shall not be paid either immediately after the conviction, or within such period as the justice shall at the time of the conviction appoint, the justice may commit the offender to the common gaol or house of correction, there to be imprisoned only, or to be imprisoned and kept to hard labour, as the justice shall think fit, for any term not exceeding two months, unless such sums and costs be sooner paid; provided that nothing herein contained shall extend to any case where the party acted under a fair and reasonable supposition that he had a right to do the act complained of."

Jarred sent to the respondent the following notice, dated the 23rd of November, 1875:—

"We, the highway surveyors for the parish of Northwold, request the road at the vicarage to be re-instated to its former level, and the watercourse by its side and in front of the said entrance be laid open as before, within ten days from this date : on your failing to do so, we shall send our own men to do it, and charge you with the expense."

The respondent did not comply with this notice. Upon the 29th of December the appellant, Jarred, and four men, took up the pipes, brickwork, and grating; in so doing, one of the pipes was broken.

For the appellant, witnesses were called to shew that the new pipes and the grating, with the earth covering them, formed an obstruction dangerous to the public using the highway, and that he bonâ fide believed he had a right to remove it.

It was admitted that the appellant was one of the surveyors of the parish of Northwold, comprising the outlying district of Whittington, and it was agreed by both parties that there were not fifteen feet from more than one part of the brickwork, grating, drain, or tunnel, to the centre of the highway.

The justices were of opinion, and found that, for many years there had been a drain or gutter by the side of the highway in question, and that it had formerly been under the control and management of the trustees of the turnpike trust, and afterwards of the surveyors of Northwold; that parts of the brickwork grating and pipes forming the tunnel under the gateway leading from the public road to the respondent's residence, not being in some places fifteen feet from the centre of the road, were encroachments upon the highway, and as such were obstructions and dangerous to the free passage thereof; that the appellant unlawfully and wilfully caused the digging up, breakage, and removal of the brickwork, grating, and pipes; that their jurisdiction was not ousted by the mere bonâ fide belief of the appellant that he had a right to do the act complained of; that the appellant, in order to obtain the removal of the encroachment or obstruction complained of, had a legal remedy by taking proceedings under 5 & 6 Wm. 4,

c. 50, s. 69 (1), or by indictment; and that the property in the
brickwork, grating, and pipes, and in the road next the respondent's residence was in the respondent sufficiently to support the
charge; and that the appellant did not do the acts complained of
under a fair and reasonable supposition that he had a right to do
them. The justices convicted the appellant, and adjudged him to
pay a penalty of 1s., and also to pay to the respondent the sum of
£2, being a reasonable compensation for the damage and injury
committed, and the sum of £4 1s. 6d. for costs, and in default of
paying these sums, to be committed to Norwich Castle for the
space of one day.

The questions of law stated for the opinion of the Court were

(1) By 5 & 6 Wm. 4 c. 50, s. 67,
"the said surveyor, district surveyor,
or assistant surveyor, shall have power
to make, scour, cleanse, and keep open
all ditches, gutters, drains, or watercourses, and also to make and lay such
trunks, tunnels, plats, or bridges, as he
shall deem necessary, in and through
any lands or grounds adjoining or lying
near to any highway, upon paying the
owner or occupier of such lands or
grounds, provided they are not waste or
common, for the damages which he
shall sustain thereby, to be settled and
paid in such manner as the damages
for getting materials in inclosed lands
or grounds are herein directed to be
settled and paid": i.e., in s. 54.

Sect. 68 : "If any owner, occupier,
or other person shall alter, obstruct, or
in any manner interfere with any such
ditches, gutters, drains, or watercourses,
trunks, tunnels, plats or bridges, after
they shall have been made by or taken
under the charge of such surveyor or
district surveyor, and without his
authority and consent, such owner,
occupier, or other person shall be liable
to reimburse all charges and expenses
which may be occasioned by reinstating
and making good the work so altered,
obstructed, or interfered with, and shall

also forfeit any sum not exceeding
three times the amount of such charges
and expenses."

Sect. 69: "If any person shall en-
croach by making, or causing to be
made, any building, hedge, ditch, or
other fence on any carriage-way or
cart-way within the distance of fifteen
feet from the centre thereof, every
person so offending shall forfeit, on
conviction, for every such offence any
sum not exceeding 40s.; and the surveyor who hath the care of any such
carriage-way or cart-way, shall, and he
is hereby required to, cause such building, hedge, ditch, or fence to be taken
down or filled up at the expense of the
person to whom the same shall belong;
and it shall and may be lawful for the
justices at a special sessions for the
highways, upon proof to them made
upon oath, to levy as well the expenses
of taking down such building, hedge,
or fence, or filling up such ditch as
aforesaid, as the several and respective
penalties hereby imposed, by distress
and sale of the offender's goods and
chattels, in such manner as distresses
and sales for forfeitures are authorized
and directed to be levied by virtue of
this Act."

1876

DENNY
v.
THWAITES.

(1.) whether the appellant was justified by the provisions of 5 & 6 Wm. 4, c. 50, ss. 67, 68, or had he any other authority to cause the digging-up, breaking, and removal of the brickwork, grating, and pipes: (2.) whether the mere fact that the appellant acted under a bonâ fide belief that he had a right to do the act complained of, was sufficient to oust the jurisdiction of the justices: (3.) whether the property in the brickwork, grating, and pipes, or in the said road, was sufficiently in the respondent to support the charge against the appellant or not.

If the Court should be of opinion, with reference to the points raised in the foregoing questions, that the appellant was properly and legally convicted, then the conviction was to remain in full force and effect; but if the said Court should be of a contrary opinion, then the information and complaint was to be dismissed with costs to the appellant.

The case was signed by the four justices, but one of them stated that he did not agree to all the above findings. (1)

Nov. 17, 18.   *C. G. Merewether*, for the appellant. The conviction is wrong. The Court may look at the case as a whole, and may say upon all the facts whether the appellant was "properly and legally convicted." The Court is not bound by the finding of the justices that the appellant did not act under a reasonable supposition of right; for it is admitted that he was acting bonâ fide. In his capacity as surveyor the appellant who represented the public was justified in what he did: *Bagshaw* v. *Buxton Local Board* (2); and he stood in a different position from a private person, who, for doing what was complained of, perhaps might be convicted under 24 & 25 Vict. c. 97, s. 52: *White* v. *Feast*. (3)

A. L. Smith, for the respondent. The conviction is right. The justices have found, following the very words of the 52nd section of 24 & 25 Vict. c. 97, that the appellant did not act under a fair and reasonable supposition of right, and the question is not whether the weight of the evidence is in favour of that finding,

(1) In the case as stated by the justices the evidence given by the parties respectively at the hearing was set out at length, and it contained copies of several letters written by the respondent, but the above are the only facts necessary to be here inserted.

(2) 1 Ch. D. 220.

(3) Law Rep. 7 Q. B. 353.

but whether the appellant was legally convicted. The animus of the appellant was purely a question for the justices, and they having decided that he acted malo animo, this Court is bound to uphold the conviction. Moreover, before the appellant acted as he did, he ought to have put in force against the respondent the 69th section of the Highway Act. A surveyor acting independently of this statutory authority acts at his peril: *Keane* v. *Reynolds.* (1)

Merewether, in reply. *Keane* v. *Reynolds* (1) is only an authority that the appellant would be liable civilly, and *Mill* v. *Hawker* (2) is to the same effect; but to make him criminally liable is very different, and would be a step beyond all previous authorities. Even civilly a surveyor has greater privileges than a private person, for he is entitled to notice of action. (3) At all events it is a doubtful question whether the appellant had or had not authority by virtue of his office to remove the drain and the brickwork, per Blackburn, J., in *Mill* v. *Hawker* (4): and this ground is sufficient to avoid the conviction, for the justices have jurisdiction only when the law has been clearly ascertained.

Cur. adv. vult.

Nov. 23. The judgment of the Court (Mellor, J., Cleasby, B., ahd Grove, J.), was delivered by

CLEASBY, B. This case raises a question of liability to prosecution under the 52nd section of 24 & 25 Vict. c. 97 (Malicious Injury to Property). The facts are stated and evidence set out at great length in the case. It is sufficient to say that the appellant was the surveyor of highways for a certain district, that he or his predecessor had put down a pipe of certain dimensions under the access from the highway to a dwelling-house, that certain persons, for improving the access to the house, had taken up this pipe and constructed a brick culvert of larger dimensions, thereby raising the level of the access, and that the effect of this was to raise the

---

(1) 2 E. & B. 748.

(2) Law Rep. 9 Ex. 309; affirmed Law Rep. 10 Ex. 92.

(3) By 5 & 6 Wm. 4, c. 50, s. 109; see *Selmes v. Judge,* Law Rep. 6 Q. B. 724.

(4) Law Rep. 10 Ex. 92, at p. 96.

1876

DENNY

v.

THWAITES.

highway opposite to such an extent as to interfere with the convenient use of the highway by the public, and so occasion a nuisance. The appellant gave notice to the respondent, who was the owner and occupier of the dwelling house, to abate the nuisance, which could not be done without removing the culvert, and upon this notice not being complied with, caused the ground to be broken up and the culvert to be taken up, and the culvert, in doing this, was broken and much damaged.

The respondent therefore took proceedings under s. 52, treating this as a wilful or malicious injury to his property, and the magistrates convicted the appellant.

Under this conviction the magistrates might have committed the appellant to prison with hard labour for two months, or have fined him 5*l*., besides awarding compensation not exceeding 5*l*. If the damage had been above 5*l*. the offence would have been a misdemeanor, and the punishment might have been two years' imprisonment with hard labour. (1)

The magistrates have found as a fact that the appellant did not act under a fair and reasonable supposition that he had a right to do the act complained of, in the terms of s. 52. And the questions put to the Court are: first, whether the appellant was justified in doing the act complained of; secondly, whether the mere fact of his acting bonâ fide was a sufficient answer to the complaint; and, thirdly, whether the property in the brickwork, grating, and pipes was sufficiently in the respondent to support the charge.

Upon the first question, viz. whether the appellant was justified; it was urged on behalf of the respondent that surveyors had no right to abate the nuisance until it had been found to be a nuisance to a highway by a competent authority, and the case of *Keane* v. *Reynolds* (2) was referred to. On the other hand, it was contended that the surveyor who represented the public stood in a different

---

(1) By 24 & 25 Vict. c. 97, s. 51: "Whosoever shall unlawfully and maliciously commit any damage, injury, or spoil to or upon any real or personal property whatsoever, either of a public or private nature, for which no punishment is hereinbefore provided, the damage, injury, or spoil being to an amount exceeding five pounds, shall be guilty of a misdemeanor, and being convicted thereof, shall be liable, at the discretion of the Court, to be imprisoned for any term not exceeding two years, with or without hard labour."

(2) 2 E. & B. 748.

position from a private individual, and that several authorities, if they did not shew that he had such a right, shewed at all events that it was a doubtful matter. Reference was made to the judgment in *Keane* v. *Reynolds* (1), in which it was said that a person acts at his peril (which means according as it turns out to be a highway or not) who abates a nuisance without a conviction, and also to a passage in the judgment of Blackburn, J., in *Mill* v. *Hawker* (2), in which he treats the matter as doubtful, and declines to express an opinion upon it. And chief reliance was placed upon the judgment of the Master of the Rolls in *Bagshaw* v. *Buxton Local Board* (3), in which that learned judge expresses a clear opinion that a surveyor who represents the public has a right to remove such an obstruction. Without in any way dissenting from the opinion of the Master of the Rolls, we think it sufficient for the decision of this case that this is not an ordinary case of removing an obstruction, but it is the case of removing one of the drains or tunnels placed on the side of the highway instead of the ordinary gutter, which was so constructed as to interfere with the use of the road by the public. By s. 67 of the Highway Act (5 & 6 Wm. 4, c. 56) the surveyor is empowered to make and cleanse all drains and ·to make and lay such tunnels as he may think necessary; and by s. 68 if any person alters or interferes with such drains, tunnels, &c., he is liable to the cost of restitution and a penalty. The surveyor has in general the sole control over the drains, &c., by the side of the highway, and if the drain or tunnel is constructed so as to affect the use of the highway, he would be authorized to alter it.

There might be special circumstances under which a private owner might have an exclusive right to a particular drain, but such circumstances do not exist in the present case. A drain of proper size had been laid by the surveyor, and afterwards this had been taken up by the adjoining owner and a larger drain inserted, which caused the nuisance. It was certainly competent to the surveyor bonâ fide to remove this nuisance, and restore the original culvert, without coming within the peril of a conviction for a wilful or malicious damage, injury, or spoil to property.

(1) 2 E. & B. 748.   (2) Law Rep. 10 Ex. 92, at p. 96.
(3) 1 Ch. D. 220, at p. 224.

This decision does not in any way conflict with the case of *White* v. *Feast* (1), where it was held that in the case of a private person doing wilful damage to property, mere bona fides is not of itself a protection from the penalty of the statute. The decision follows from the words of s. 52.

The ground of our decision is that the appellant is not a private individual, but the surveyor of highways having a control over and an interest in the drains laid for carrying off the water, and that in dealing bonâ fide with the drains he was not guilty of wilful or malicious damage. We only add, as regards the third question, that the owner of the adjoining land only had a qualified property in the drains, &c., subject to the exercise by the surveyor of his control over them.

We think it right to add that though the magistrates have found that the appellant did not act under a fair and reasonable supposition that he was justified, we think it so clear that if he acted bonâ fide he did act under such fair and reasonable supposition, that if it had been necessary to decide the case on that ground we should certainly have remitted the case to the magistrates for further consideration. The finding referred to appears, from a statement made before us and not contradicted, to have been inserted in a casual manner, and it is not surprising that the magistrates were not unanimous as to the findings.

According to the terms of the reference to us the information and complaint are dismissed with costs.

My Brothers Mellor and Grove agree in this conclusion.

Judgment for the appellant.

Solicitor for appellant : *T. M. Wilkin.*
Solicitor for respondent : *C. O. Humphreys.*

(1) Law Rep. 7 Q. B. 353.

1876
Nov. 16.

[IN THE COURT OF APPEAL FROM INFERIOR COURTS.]

WOOD AND OTHERS v. BEARD.

*Landlord and Tenant—Construction of Demise—Lease void for Uncertainty—
Tenancy from Year to Year—Statute of Frauds, s. 2—8 & 9 Vict. c. 106,
ss. 2, 3.*

By a written instrument not under seal, and dated the 28th of February, 1872,
W. purported to demise a messuage to the defendant as tenant from year to year,
for so long as he should keep the rent paid, and as W. should have " power to let
the said premises ;" the rent reserved by the instrument was less than two-thirds
of the annual value of the messuage.   The defendant entered and paid rent
quarterly :—

Held, that the instrument was void as a lease, first, on the ground of uncertainty ; secondly, on the ground that, not being within the terms of s. 2 of the
Statute of Frauds, it ought to have been under seal pursuant to 8 & 9 Vict.
c. 106, ss. 2 & 3.

Held, further, that the only estate vested in the defendant was a tenancy from
year to year.

Browne v. Warner (14 Ves. 156, 409) and *In re King's Leasehold Estates* (Law
Rep. 16 Eq. 521) distinguished.

CASE stated upon appeal from the county court of Kent, holden
at Gravesend.

1. This is an action commenced in the above county court on
the 29th of March, 1876, to recover possession of a tenement
under 19 & 20 Vict. c. 108, ss. 50, 51.

2. By the particulars of demand the plaintiffs claimed possession
of the house and premises known as No. 167, Windmill Street,
Gravesend, with the outbuilding belonging thereto, known formerly
as a skittle ground, in the rear of the said house, the defendant's
interest, as tenant of the premises to George Wood deceased,
being alleged in the particulars to have been determined by a
notice to quit, and also to have expired.

4. The action came on for trial on the 25th of April, 1876,
when the plaintiffs put in an agreement under hand only between
the defendant and the said George Wood deceased, which had been
previously admitted and was as follows :—

"An agreement made this 28th day of February, 1872, between
George Wood, of Milton-next-Gravesend, Kent, brewer, of the one

part, and Alfred John Beard, of Gravesend, Kent, of the other part: The said George Wood doth hereby agree to let, and the said Alfred John Beard to hire and take as tenant from year to year, from the 25th day of March, 1872, the house and premises known as No. 167, Windmill Street, Gravesend, with the outbuilding belonging thereto, known formerly as a skittle ground, in the rear of the said house, at the yearly rental of 16*l.* payable quarterly. And the said George Wood doth hereby agree to let the said Alfred John Beard remain as tenant of the above-named premises, so long as he, the said Alfred John Beard, keeps his rent paid, and he, the said George Wood, has power to let the said premises. Also the said George Wood doth likewise agree not to raise or increase the rental of the said house and premises during the tenancy of the said Alfred John Beard. Also the said Alfred John Beard doth agree to make all purchases of ale, beer, and porter (disposed or consumed on the said premises) at the public-house attached known by the sign of the Rose and Crown Tavern. And the said Alfred John Beard doth further agree to pay all rates and taxes, with the exception of the land and property tax. Witness the hands of the said parties the day and year first above written.

" Alfred John Beard,

" per pro   George Wood,

" George Wood, junr.

" Witness, George Smith, clerk to Mr. George Wood, brewer."

5. With the exception of the said agreement, there was no evidence as to what the interest or estate of the said George Wood in the premises was.

6. On the 24th of September, 1875, defendant was served with a notice to quit of that date, signed by the said George Wood deceased, to the following effect:—" To Mr. Alfred John Beard, of 167, Windmill Street, Gravesend. I hereby give you notice to quit and deliver up possession of the house, with the outbuildings thereto and premises, with the appurtenances, situate at 167, Windmill Street, in the parish of Gravesend, in the county of Kent, which you hold of me as tenant thereof, on the 25th day of March next."

7. The said George Wood died on the 12th of December, 1875.

8. All rent due by the defendant to the testator, George Wood, was paid by the defendant quarterly up to the 29th of September, 1875, and no rent had been accepted by the plaintiffs after that date; though it was admitted that a tender of the same as it became due at Christmas, 1875, and Lady Day, 1876, had been duly made by the defendant but refused by the plaintiffs.

9. The said George Wood, by his will dated the 31st of December, 1874, gave, devised, and bequeathed all and singular his real and personal estate (with some exceptions not applying to this case), unto the three plaintiffs, George Wood, William Browne Ferris, and Edward Hilder, their heirs, executors, administrators, and assigns, and appointed the three plaintiffs executors of his will.

10. The will was proved in the principal registry of the Court of Probate on the 12th of January, 1876, by the plaintiffs William Browne Ferris and Edward Hilder, the plaintiff George Wood having renounced probate thereof.

11. On the 27th of March, 1876, the defendant was served with a notice of that date signed by the three plaintiffs to the following effect:—" To Mr. Alfred John Beard. We hereby demand of and require you forthwith to quit and deliver up possession of the house and premises known as No. 167, Windmill Street, Gravesend, with the outbuilding belonging thereto, known formerly as a skittle-ground, in the rear of the said house, which were held by you under a tenancy from the late Mr. George Wood, deceased, and which tenancy has expired and been determined;" but the defendant refused to give up possession.

12. The plaintiffs also proved by three witnesses, one a surveyor and auctioneer, and the other two house agents and auctioneers, that the annual value of the premises was from 40l. to 42l. and no more, and also proved that in the present parochial valuation list for the purposes of the poor-rate, the premises were assessed at 28l. as the gross annual value and 23l. net rateable value; and that they were assessed at the same sums in the valuation list for January, 1871, when the defendant unsuccessfully appealed to the assessment committee against that assessment on the ground that it was beyond the gross annual value; also that the premises were at first occupied by the defendant as dining-rooms, but recently

were underlet by him as a provision store, and had been shut up
and unoccupied for the then last six weeks.

13. It was contended on behalf of the defendant, that the defendant was entitled under the agreement to hold as long as he
kept his rent paid, and the said George Wood had power to let;
that it was incumbent on the plaintiffs to prove that the defendant
had not kept his rent paid and that the power to let had ceased,
and that they had not done so; that even if the lease were void at
law, the Court could give effect to it as a Court of Equity; that
the agreement was definite (videlicet) for as long as the defendant
kept his rent paid, and George Wood had power to let, and that
the notice to quit was given before the death of the said George
Wood the testator.

14. It was contended on behalf of the plaintiffs, first, that
whether by the first part of the agreement or by payment of rent,
the defendant became a tenant from year to year, such tenancy
was only a tenancy from year to year determinable by the usual
half-year's notice, and had been determined by the first notice to
quit; secondly, that the first part of the agreement distinctly
stipulated for a tenancy from year to year, and that the subsequent
clause, being inconsistent with this, was to be rejected as repugnant;
thirdly, that the document was void as a lease under the Statute
of Frauds and 8 & 9 Vict. c. 106, from not being under seal,
either because it was for more than three years, or that two-thirds
of the rack-rent was not reserved; and that the defendant had not
given any notice of any counter-claim to have a lease under the
equitable jurisdiction of the Court; fourthly, that the agreement
was void for indefiniteness, vagueness, and uncertainty; fifthly,
that it expired on the death of the said George Wood, and that the
second notice of the 27th of March had been served since his
death.

15. The judge decided that the term and interest of the defendant had not expired or been determined by the plaintiffs by a legal
notice to quit; that the defendant was tenant from year to year,
and for so long as he paid his rent and the testator, George Wood,
had power to let, and that the defendant paid or tendered all his
rent as it became due, and there was no evidence that the power
of the said testator, George Wood, to let had ceased before the

notice to quit dated the 24th of September, 1875, was given to the defendant. The judge gave judgment of nonsuit against the plaintiffs, with leave to them to appeal if such leave were necessary.

16. The questions for the opinion of the Divisional Court of the High Court of Justice were, first, whether or not the tenancy of the defendant had expired or been determined by a legal notice to quit before the commencement of the action; secondly, whether or not the tenancy of the defendant had been determined by the demand of possession dated 27th March, 1876, made by the plaintiffs; thirdly, whether the defendant was entitled under the agreement to hold so long as he kept his rent paid and the testator, George Wood, had power to let; fourthly, whether or not the tenancy of the defendant was binding on the plaintiffs, and continued so long as the defendant kept his rent paid and they had power to let.

Nov. 9, 10.   *H. Matthews, Q.C.* (*Laxton* with him), for the plaintiffs. First, since the nature of George Wood's title does not appear upon the face of the instrument mentioned in the fourth paragraph, he must be taken to have been seised in fee: *Cuthbertson* v. *Irving* (1); and the defendant, in effect, claims a freehold estate created out of that seisin, namely, a tenancy for life subject to the terms of the instrument; for a tenancy for life is valid although its existence depends upon the fulfilment of a condition, and although it may be determinable at will: Co. Lit. 42a; but this estate is void, for, since 8 & 9 Vict. c. 106, ss. 2, 3, no freehold interest can be conveyed without deed. Secondly, if the instrument amounts to a lease not exceeding three years it has expired by effluxion of time; if it amounts to a lease for more than three years, it would have been void by the Statute of Frauds, ss. 1, 2, if not in writing, the rent being less than two-thirds the full improved value of the messuage; and now it is void pursuant to 8 & 9 Vict. c. 106, s. 3, it not being under seal. Thirdly, the words of the instrument, "so long as the said Alfred John Beard keeps his rent paid and the said George Wood has power

(1) 4 H. & N. 742; 28 L. J. (Ex.) 306; in Ex. Ch. 6 H. & N. 135; 29 L. J. (Ex.) 485.

to let the said premises," are repugnant to the demise from year to year and introduce an uncertainty, and therefore must be rejected: *Say* v. *Smith* (1); *Doe* d. *Warner* v. *Browne* (2); *Fitz-Maurice* v. *Bayley.* (3) Fourthly, the only interest vested in the defendant was a tenancy from year to year to be implied from payment of rent quarterly, and this interest has been determined by the notice to quit mentioned in the sixth paragraph.

Rolland, for the defendant. First, the instrument is not void for uncertainty; the maxim applies, Id certum est quod certum reddi potest, and the plaintiffs were bound to shew at least that the power of George Wood to let had ceased before the notice to quit was given on the 24th of September, 1875: it is probable that he was only tenant from year to year, and that the words were introduced to provide for the determination of his own interest. *Weld* v. *Baxter* (4) shews that the demise is not evidence of seisin in fee. Secondly, it follows from the reasoning in *Davis* v. *Waddington* (5) and *Ashworth* v. *Hopper* (6) that an estate of freehold was not granted to the defendant, and therefore no deed was required upon that ground. Thirdly, even if the instrument were invalid as a demise, the defendant may hold under its terms, "so far as they are not at variance with the species of tenancy which the law under the circumstances creates," per Maule, J., in *Berrey* v. *Lindley.* (7) Fourthly, at all events, if the instrument fails to carry out the intention of the parties, the defendant would in equity be entitled to the grant of a lease: *Lester* v. *Foxcroft* (8); *Browne* v. *Warne* (9); *In re King's Leasehold Estates.* (10) And now, by the Supreme Court of Judicature Act, 1873, ss. 24, 91, a county court has power to give the same amount of relief as might have been formerly granted by the Court of Chancery.

Matthews, Q.C., replied.

Cur. adv. vult.

Nov. 16. The following judgments were delivered:—

CLEASBY, B. This was an action to recover the possession of a

(1) 1 Plowd. 269.
(2) 8 East, 165.
(3) 9 H. L. C. 78.
(4) 1 H. & N. 568; 26 L. J. (Ex.) 112.
(5) 7 Man. & Gr. 37.
(6) 1 C. P. D. 178.
(7) 3 Man. & Gr. 498, at p. 514.
(8) 1 W. & T. (L. C. in Eq.) 768.
(9) 14 Ves. 156, 409.
(10) Law Rep. 16 Eq. 521.

house which had been let by one George Wood to the defendant. On the 24th of September, 1875, Wood had served a notice to quit on the 25th of March following, and the question was whether, after the expiration of that notice, the defendant had any interest in the premises.

The demise was by writing under the hand of Wood without seal, and purported to let the premises to the defendant as tenant from year to year from the 25th of March, 1872, and for so long as he continued to pay the rent and Wood had power to let; and there was a stipulation that the defendant should procure all the beer, &c., sold or consumed on the premises from a public house of Wood. It is set out at length in the case. The question was, having regard to the Statute of Frauds and the statute 8 & 9 Vict. c. 106, s. 3, what is the effect of the instrument, and what interest did the defendant take under it?

It will be observed that the stipulation, that the defendant shall not be disturbed in his tenancy so long as he pays his rent, has this qualification—so long as the landlord has power to let. These words, which put a qualification upon the interest intended to be created, cannot be rejected as of course. The plaintiffs relied upon the case of *Doe* d. *Warner* v. *Browne* (1), where it was held that a similar lease, so far as it created an interest beyond a tenancy from year to year, was void. This was before the statute of Victoria, which made a deed necessary for all leases exceeding three years, and rested upon this, that the interest created was a freehold one, so far as it was greater than a tenancy from year to year.

The learned counsel for the defendant distinguished the present case on the ground that the continuance of the term did not wholly depend upon the will and act of the lessee, as in the case cited, in which case the uncertain interest would be a freehold one; but this was a qualification which introduced the will of the lessor, namely, his capacity to let depending, not necessarily upon his capacity at the time of the agreement, but capacity afterwards acquired; and it was suggested that the lessor might be, and indeed was, tenant from year to year himself. And, further, it was contended for the defendant that, whatever the legal interest

(1) 8 East, 165.

of the lessee might be, he acquired, at all events, an equitable right to an extension of the term. And for this the decision of Lord Eldon was referred to when the same case came before him as that reported in 8 East, upon a bill for a specific performance by granting a formal lease. The case is reported 14 Ves.; and it appears that Lord Eldon overruled a demurrer to the bill for want of equity (p. 156), and that an injunction against the action was allowed, though what became of the suit, and whether the injunction was continued, did not appear. (1)   It should be noticed that the agreement in that case contained a clause that the tenant was to receive 40l. on a change of tenancy, and upon this Lord Eldon relied, upon both occasions when the case was before him, as shewing that a lease was necessary to carry into effect the intention of the parties. There is no such clause in the present agreement.

Various other authorities were referred to, and, among others, particularly the case *In re King's Leasehold Estates* (2), in which a person holding under a similar agreement was held entitled to compensation beyond his yearly tenancy, when the property was compulsorily taken.

These authorities do not apply to the present case, by reason of the additional condition, " so long as the lessor has power to let." It appears to me that this clause (which, as before observed, cannot be rejected as necessarily unmeaning, and the meaning of which can only be arrived at by conjecture) introduces an uncertainty, which makes it impossible to give effect to the lease as conferring any particular estate. This objection equally applies, whether the legal or equitable estate of the defendant is considered.

Another objection was that, in addition to the rent, there was in this case a further consideration for the lease, namely, the procuring all the beer, &c., at the public-house of Mr. Wood, and that the other evidence shewed that less than two-thirds of the value was reserved, so that the case was taken out of the 2nd section of the Statute of Frauds, and though not within the 1st section of the Statute of Frauds, being in writing, the lease was void at law, by virtue of the statute of 8 & 9 Vict. c. 106, for not being under seal. It followed from this that the only legal estate of the defendant was that derived from the entry under the agreement or from the

(1) 14 Ves. 409.   (2) Law Rep. 16 Eq. 521.

1876

WOOD
v.
BEARD.

yearly payment of rent, namely, a tenancy from year to year, and that the lease being void, there was nothing to give the defendant any equitable estate beyond his legal tenancy.

It is unnecessary to consider other objections; but it seems clear that, if the defendant was entitled to any lease beyond the lease from year to year, the lease should contain a clause of forfeiture upon non-payment of rent and non-performance of covenants. In a lease from year to year, such a clause is unnecessary, because the landlord can always put an end to the tenancy by a six months' notice. But if a lease were granted, it is by no means clear that it ought not to be in such a form as would make the discontinuing the use of the premises as a dining-room, and letting them as a provision store, followed by their being shut up, a forfeiture of the lease. This only shews, further, how undefined and uncertain the interest of the defendant was, except so far as it was an interest as tenant from year to year.

As I think the only interest of the defendant was terminated by the legal notice to quit (which is an answer to the first question), it is unnecessary to say what would be the effect of the demand of possession after Mr. Wood's death, if the notice had been inoperative. I do not think that a question arises in the present case what would be the result of a proper application for a specific performance of the agreement, as there is no counter-claim; and the only question is, whether, upon the agreement as it stands without explanation, there is a defence to the action.

GROVE, J. I agree with the judgment delivered by my Brother Cleasby. I have only to add that the question as to the defendant's right in equity to the grant of a lease does not arise before us, as he has not given any notice of a counter-claim; and, as to this point, I express no opinion.

Judgment reversed.

Solicitors for plaintiffs: *Walker, Son, & Field, for E. W. Bewley, Gravesend.*

Solicitor for defendant: *Thomas Sismey, for Alfred Tolhurst, Gravesend.*

1876
Nov. 23.

[IN THE COURT OF APPEAL FROM INFERIOR COURTS.]

SCOTT, Appellant; LEGG, Respondent.

Metropolitan Building Act, 1855 (18 & 19 Vict. c. 122), s. 27, r. 4, s. 28, r. 2—
Addition to Building—Union of Buildings.

By the Metropolitan Building Act, 1855, s. 27, rule 4, every warehouse or other building used for the purposes of trade or manufacture, containing more than 216,000 cubic feet, shall be divided by party walls. By s. 28, rule 2, no buildings shall be united, if when so united they will be in contravention of the Act. Within the limits of the Act the respondent added to a building previously erected a new building without separating them by party walls; the addition was made by taking down one of the external walls of the old building, and then erecting the new building against the old one; the addition contained less than 216,000 cubic feet, but the two buildings taken together contained more than 216,000 cubic feet:—

Held, that the buildings had been united in contravention of the statute, and must be separated by a party wall.

SPECIAL case stated pursuant to the Metropolitan Building Act, 1855 (18 & 19 Vict. c. 122), ss. 106 and 107.

A complaint was preferred by the respondent against the appellant, under s. 46 of the above-mentioned statute, charging that the appellant did complete the covering-in of a new building erected and united to the then present building, namely, the Anchor Brewery, Mile End Road, without a party wall, the buildings so united exceeding the cubical contents allowed by the Metropolitan Building Act above mentioned, and as required by s. 27, rule 4, and s. 28, rule 2, thereof. (1)

(1) By the Metropolitan Building Act, 1855 (18 & 19 Vict. c. 122), s. 3, " ' Builder ' shall apply to and include the master builder or other person employed to execute or who actually executes any work upon any building."

Sect. 7 : " With the exemptions hereinbefore mentioned, this Act shall apply to all new buildings ; and whenever mention is herein made of any building, it shall, unless the contrary appears from the context, be deemed to imply a new building."

Sect 9 : " Any alteration, addition, or other work made or done for any purpose, except that of necessary repair not affecting the construction of any external or party wall, in, to, or upon any old building, or in, to, or upon any new building after the roof has been covered in, shall, to the extent of such alteration, addition, or work, be subject to the regulations of this Act; and whenever mention is hereinafter made of any alteration, addition, or work in, to, or upon any building, it shall, unless the contrary appears from the context, be deemed to

1876

Scott
v.
Legg.

Upon the hearing of the complaint before a metropolitan police magistrate the following facts were proved by the respondent and admitted by the appellant:—

The appellant, the builder as defined by s. 3 of the Metropolitan Building Act, 1855, was also the clerk of the works to Messrs. Charrington, Head, & Co., of the Anchor Brewery, Mile End Road; and the respondent is the district surveyor under the Metropolitan Building Act, 1855, of the hamlet of Mile End Old Town.

The Anchor Brewery, to which the new building was an addition, was an old building erected long before the passing of the above Act, in itself containing a greater number of cubic feet than that specified in s. 27, rule 4, and was not divided by party walls. The addition, which was roofed in, and which the appellant was making to the front of the old building, taken by itself, contained less than the before-mentioned number of cubic feet; but the old and new buildings taken together greatly exceeded that amount.

It was contended by the respondent that a party wall should be made between the old and new buildings, because the old and new buildings were so united as to contravene s. 28, rule 2, of the above Act, and were, taken together, of larger cubical contents than that specified in s. 27, rule 4.

It was contended by the appellant, first, that by s. 9 the operation of the said Act as to alterations, additions, or other work made or done for any purpose in, to, or upon any old building was confined to the extent of such alterations, additions, or other works so made or done; secondly, that the enactment of s. 27 as to party walls was by s. 7 confined to new buildings which exceeded the cubical contents mentioned in s. 27, rule 4; thirdly, that in the present case a new building having been added to an old building, they did not come within s. 28, which applied to the uniting of new buildings to each other.

---

imply an alteration, addition, or work to which this Act applies."

Sect. 27, rule 4: "Every warehouse or other building used either wholly or in part for the purposes of trade or manufacture, containing more than two hundred and sixteen thousand cubic feet, shall be divided by party walls in such manner that the contents of each division thereof shall not exceed the above-mentioned number of cubic feet."

Sect. 28, rule 2: "No buildings shall be united if when so united they will, considered as one building only, be in contravention of any of the provisions of this Act."

The magistrate made an order on the appellant, commanding him to erect a proper party wall, so as to divide the new building from the old one, on the ground that the addition of the new building to the old building was a uniting of them within s. 28, rule 2, and that, therefore, the buildings taken together were in contravention of s. 27, rule 4.

The questions of law for the opinion of the Court were, first, whether s. 28, rule 2, contemplated the union of a new with an old building, and whether, even if it should so contemplate a union, an addition such as appeared by the foregoing case was within the said section of the statute; secondly, whether the defendant was rightly convicted under s. 27, rule 4.

If the Court should be of opinion that the said order was legally and properly made, and was valid, and the appellant was liable, then it was to stand; but if the Court should be of opinion otherwise, then the said complaint was to be dismissed.

Nov. 18. *Benjamin, Q.C.* (*Scott* with him), for the appellant; *Meadows White* (*Biron* with him), for the respondent.

The arguments are sufficiently noticed in the judgment of the Court.

Cur. adv. vult.

Nov. 23. The judgment of the Court (Cleasby, B., and Grove, J.) was delivered by

CLEASBY, B. The question in this case was whether an addition made to an old building after the passing of the Metropolitan Building Act (18 & 19 Vict. c. 122) required to be separated by a party-wall in order to comply with the Act.

By the 27th section, any warehouse or building used for the purpose of trade, containing more than 216,000 cubic feet, must be divided by party walls, so that no part contains a greater cubic measurement; this only applies to new buildings; old buildings are not affected by the Act. By the 9th section any addition to an old building is, to the extent of such addition, to be subject to the regulations of the Act.

The addition made by the appellant contained by itself less than 216,000 cubic feet. It was made by taking down one of the external walls of an old building, which contained more than the contents

mentioned and was not subject to the Act, and building it up to a
certain distance, so that the old building and addition contained,
of course, much more than the measurement named.

If the addition had contained more than the above contents, it
was not disputed that it must comply with the Act, and have one
or more party walls; but it was contended that, as, taken by itself,
it contained less, the 9th section did not apply, and that there
were no words in the Act which, fairly read, could include such a
case. If the case had rested on the 9th section only, I should have
felt great difficulty in holding that it extended to anything beyond
the addition itself.

But the main reliance of the respondent was placed on the 28th
section, 2nd subsection, by which it is provided that no buildings
shall be united if, when so united, they shall be in contravention
of the provisions of the Act. It was powerfully urged, on behalf
of the appellant, that this was intended to meet a different state
of things from the present, namely, the making into one of two
separate buildings whether new or old, and that it would be
straining the language beyond what could be intended to make it
apply to so different a subject as the addition to a former building.
The answer to this argument is that the case comes within the
mischief intended to be prevented, and that the following consequences will ensue from holding the rule not to be applicable to
additions to old buildings. A man might have a building of less
than the specified dimensions, and he might add a new building,
also of less than those dimensions; and the two together, containing perhaps 400,000 cubic feet, would require no partition,
though no such building existed before the passing of the Act.
Also, if one wall of the brewery should be taken down and
200,000 feet added, the owners might afterwards take down the
three other walls and make further additions to the same extent,
each under the specified dimensions, and so add 800,000 cubic feet
without any partitions. It is certain this could not have been
intended. It seldom happens that the framer of an Act of Parliament or the legislature has in contemplation all the cases which are
likely to arise, and the language therefore seldom fits every possible
case. Whenever the case is clearly within the mischief, the words
must be read so as to cover the case if by any reasonable construc-

tion they can be read so as to cover it, though the words may point more exactly to another case; this must be done rather than make such a case a casus omissus under the statute. We think that the words may be read as including not only the uniting buildings already constructed, but the adding a new building to an old one, and so uniting them together.

The appeal is therefore dismissed, and of course with costs.

My Brother Grove agrees in this judgment.

Judgment for the respondent.

Solicitors for appellant: *Loxley & Morley.*
Solicitor for respondent: *William Wyke Smith.*

BULLOCK *v.* DUNLAP.

1876
Nov. 15.

1876
SCOTT
v.
LEGG.

Constable in Possession of stolen Goods—Metropolitan Police—Action for Detinue pending Application to a Magistrate—2 & 3 Vict. c. 71, s. 29.

The plaintiff having been indicted for stealing goods and acquitted, a metropolitan police constable, within a reasonable time after coming into possession thereof, applied to a magistrate, under s. 29 of 2 & 3 Vict. c. 71, to make an order with respect to the goods. The magistrate adjourned the hearing to a future day. After the application and before the day of hearing arrived the plaintiff brought an action against the constable to recover the goods:—

Held, that the constable was protected by s. 29, and that the action could not be maintained.

WRIT issued on the 10th of April, 1876. The statement of claim alleged as follows: The plaintiff being, in October, 1875, in possession of a diamond ring and diamond pin as his own property, a metropolitan police constable arrested him upon a charge of stealing them, and took them from him. The plaintiff was afterwards taken before a metropolitan police magistrate, committed for trial, indicted, tried upon the charge, and acquitted. The constable delivered the jewelry to the defendant as his superior officer and as a superintendent of the metropolitan police, and the defendant converted it to his own use, and detains it from the plaintiff. The plaintiff claims a return of the jewelry, or its value, and damages for its detention and conversion.

The statement of defence, dated the 11th of May, 1876, alleged

as follows (inter alia):—After the plaintiff had been acquitted as
alleged the jewelry was in the lawful possession of the defendant as
a constable within 2 & 3 Vict. c. 71, s. 29, and the defendant being
ignorant who was the rightful owner thereof, before the commencement of this action and within a reasonable time after he became
possessed thereof, duly applied to a magistrate then having jurisdiction in that behalf under s. 29 of 2 & 3 Vict. c. 71, to make an
order for the delivery of the jewelry to the party who should
appear to be the rightful owner, or such other order as to such
magistrate should seem meet. The magistrate entertained and
heard evidence in support of the application, and the plaintiff appeared before him and gave evidence in support of his claim. The
magistrate afterwards adjourned the hearing of the application to
a day which has not yet expired. The application is still pending
before the magistrate, and no order has been made by him under
s. 29. The defendant as such constable, and in the performance
of his duty in that behalf, and not otherwise, detained and still
detains the jewelry till an order has been made under s. 29.

Demurrer to so much of the statement of defence as is above
set out, and joinder therein.

Talfourd Salter, Q.C. (*L. Glyn* with him), for the plaintiff. The
defendant must rely on s. 29 (1) as affording him an absolute pro-

---

(1) By s. 29 of 2 & 3 Vict. c. 71
(An Act for regulating the Police
Courts in the Metropolis), it is enacted
"that if any goods or money charged
to be stolen or fraudulently obtained
shall be in the custody of any constable
by virtue of any warrant of a justice,
or in prosecution of any charge of
felony or misdemeanor in regard to
the obtaining thereof, and the person
charged with stealing or obtaining possession as aforesaid shall not be found,
or shall have been summarily convicted
or discharged, or shall have been tried
and acquitted, or if such person shall
have been tried and found guilty, but
the property so in custody shall not have
been included in any indictment upon
which he shall have been found guilty,
it shall be lawful for any magistrate to
make an order for the delivery of such
goods or money to the party who shall
appear to be the rightful owner thereof,
or, in case the owner cannot be ascertained, then to make such order with
respect to such goods or money as to
such magistrate shall seem meet : Provided always that no such order shall
be any bar to the right of any person
or persons to sue the party to whom
such goods or money shall be delivered,
and to recover such goods or money
from him by action at law, so that
such action shall be commenced within
six calendar months next after such
order shall be made."

tection. But the circumstances do not bring him within that section. If, indeed, the defendant before action brought had obtained a magistrate's order to deliver the goods to the party who appeared to be the rightful owner, or any "such order as to such magistrate should seem meet," he might perhaps have been protected by s. 29. But the magistrate has made no order, and has adjourned the application. The reason is not stated in the pleadings, but it is no doubt for the very purpose that this action may be tried. If, therefore, the action is stayed or judgment given for the defendant on demurrer there is a deadlock, and the plaintiff has no means of ascertaining his rights. The defendant must bring himself strictly within the statute, and nothing short of an " order " before action will protect. There is evidence for a jury of a "conversion": *Pillot* v. *Wilkinson.* (1) A refusal to make an order under s. 40 does not bar the right of action: *Dover* v. *Child.* (2)

Sir H. Giffard, S.G. (F. M. White with him), for the defendant. Sect. 29 assumes that the constable should have a reasonable time to make inquiry and apply to a magistrate, and as soon as he has applied s. 29 protects him. Independently of statute every person coming into possession of another's goods is entitled to detain them for a reasonable time in order to ascertain the real owner: *Vaughan* v. *Watt.* (3)

T. Salter, Q.C., replied.

CLEASBY, B. (4) I think the statement of defence is a good defence to the action, and that the defendant is entitled to judgment.

The case turns entirely upon s. 29 of 2 & 3 Vict. c. 71. What was the object of that section? It was to protect a person who is placed by virtue of his office in possession of the property of some other person to which he has no title himself. That is always a dangerous position for a man to be in, because, although he may take time to make up his mind what to do, he is eventually bound by what he does, and makes himself responsible if he does not deliver the property to the right person. The object of

---

(1) 2 H. & C. 72; 32 L. J. (Ex.) 201.

(2) 1 Ex. D. 172.

(3) 6 M. & W. 492.

(4) Sitting alone as a Divisional Court.

this section obviously was to protect a constable from that difficulty and to enable him to go to the magistrate and say, "Tell me what I am to do with these goods which do not belong to me, and to whom I am to deliver them." The section says it shall be lawful for the magistrate to make the order; and the person who obeys that order would be protected in obeying it without any reference to the title of the person claiming. That being so, under the circumstances of this case which comes within the Act, the defendant applies to the magistrate to know what he is to do with these goods. The application is not disposed of at the time, and the magistrate may indicate some idea in his own mind that the plaintiff, that is, the person who has been tried, is not the person to whom he ought to order the goods to be delivered up. It seems to be almost admitted that it would be impossible for him to maintain an action before the constable has had a reasonable time to apply to a magistrate. That being so, what difference can it make, the matter being in the hands of the magistrate, that some time elapses before he gives his decision? Is it possible to hold, in construing a clause of an Act of Parliament which is made for the protection of an officer, that he becomes responsible for the way in which the judge to whom he is to apply deals with the case, the matter being within the judge's jurisdiction? A magistrate may say, "I cannot dispose of this case now—I shall require some further consideration upon it, and proper persons to attend before me again." I cannot but presume that a judge is influenced by right motives, and will deal with the case properly as long as it is pending before him.

That being so, it appears to me that the defendant has done all that the Act calls upon him to do, to render up possession. Therefore he cannot be responsible because he is not able before the commencement of this action to relieve himself from the possession of these goods.

Judgment for the defendant.

Jan. 24, 1877. Against this judgment the plaintiff appealed, and the Court (Cockburn, C.J., Mellish, L.J., and Brett, J.A.) dismissed the appeal.

Solicitors for plaintiff: *Fisher & Co.*
Solicitors for defendant: *Ellis & Ellis.*

1876
Dec. 7.

In re ARTHUR HEAVENS SMITH.

Imprisonment for Debt—Debtors Act, 1869 (32 & 33 *Vict. c.* 62)—*Crown Debt —Costs of Appeal to House of Lords—Estreated Recognizance.*

. The appellant in an appeal to the House of Lords in a Chancery suit had, in conformity with the practice in such appeals, entered into a recognizance for the payment of the respondents' costs if unsuccessful. The appeal was unsuccessful, and the appellant making default in payment of respondents' costs, the recognizance was estreated, and the appellant was arrested under process from the Court of Exchequer :—

Held, that the appellant was a debtor to the Crown in respect of such costs, and therefore that the Debtors Act, 1869, did not apply to the case, and the appellant was not entitled to be discharged from custody.

A WRIT of habeas corpus had been obtained to bring up one Arthur Heavens Smith, a prisoner in the county prison of Gloucester, under process issuing out of the Court of Exchequer upon an estreated recognizance. It appeared that the prisoner had been the appellant in an appeal to the House of Lords in a Chancery suit, and had, in conformity with the practice in such appeals, entered into a recognizance to the Crown for the payment of the respondents' costs of the appeal if unsuccessful. The House of Lords gave judgment in the respondents' favour, and the appellant had not paid their costs. The recognizance was consequently estreated, and the appellant was arrested under process, as before mentioned.

Channell, on behalf of the prisoner, moved for his discharge from custody. The Debtors Act, 1869, not expressly mentioning the Crown, it must be admitted that that Act does not bind the Crown. But it is contended that this debt, though in form a Crown debt, is not so in substance, and that, therefore, the power of imprisoning in respect of such debt was taken away by the Act. It is only where the Crown is really and substantially interested that the Act does not apply. See *Magdalen College Case* (1) ; *Rex* v. *Wright.* (2) The recognizance is a mere security for the costs of the respondents.

[LORD COLERIDGE, C.J. Suppose, what would now in practice

(1) 11 Co. Rep. 66 b.   (2) 1 A. & E. 434.

1876
Re Smith.

be a monstrous supposition, but might not have been so absurd in the times gone by, that the Crown refused to hand the money over to the respondents, how could it be compelled to do so?]

The statute 3 & 4 Wm. 4, c. 99, ss. 34–36, enables the parties interested in the case of any forfeited recognizances, if the commissioners of the treasury refuse to pay over the money to them, to apply to the Court of Exchequer, who may order payment. The Crown is only in the nature of a trustee for the respondents. It is the invariable practice to pay over these sums of money to the party really interested, and by 3 & 4 Wm. 4, c. 99, which binds the Crown, such payment may now be enforced.

C. S. C. Bowen, for the Crown. The Crown has no interest in this matter, except that the practice may be settled in accordance with law. It is contended, however, that this is a Crown debt in law. The recognizance is taken in the name of the Queen, and the money is due to her. It is true, of course, that in practice the Crown hands over the money to the party whose costs are so secured, but there is no legal obligation to do so. The statute 3 & 4 Wm. 4, c. 99 has made no difference in this respect. The petition to the barons of the Exchequer provided for by that Act is made to them by virtue of the ancient functions of the Court of Exchequer, in relation to the charge of the royal purse and revenues. In this matter they only represent the Crown. There is no pecuniary obligation on the part of the Crown.

Pritchard appeared for the respondents in the House of Lords.
Channell in reply.

Lord Coleridge, C.J. I think this is clearly a Crown debt in law, and that consequently the Debtors Act, 1869, does not apply, and the power of imprisonment continues.

Pollock, B., concurred.

Rule to discharge the prisoner refused.

Solicitors for applicant: *Milne, Riddle, & Mellor.*
Solicitor for Crown: *Solicitor to the Treasury.*
Solicitor for respondent: *R. J. Child.*

[IN THE COURT OF APPEAL.]

1876
Nov. 10.

THE MAYOR, ALDERMEN, AND CITIZENS OF THE CITY OF WOR-
CESTER, Appellants; THE ASSESSMENT COMMITTEE OF THE
DROITWICH POOR LAW UNION, Respondents.

*Poor-rate—Mode of rating Property occupied by a public Body for public Pur-
poses—Rateable Value ascertained by actual Profit—Occupier subject to
statutory Restrictions.*

Where land is used for a public purpose, and the occupiers thereof are prevented
by statute from deriving the full pecuniary benefit which it is capable of producing, the land is to be rated to the poor with reference to the amount of profit
actually made, and not with reference to the amount which might be earned by
the occupiers if they were not subject to restrictions.

The local board of health for W. erected and occupied works for the purpose
of supplying the inhabitants thereof with water. The works were situate within
the parish of C. In order to benefit the inhabitants of W., the local board made
the scale of charges so low, as to leave a profit far less than would have accrued
to a company carrying on the works as a commercial undertaking. In adopting
the scale of charges above mentioned, the local board intended to carry out those
provisions of the Public Health Act, 1848, the object of which was to insure a
supply of water at a low price for sanitary purposes. The assessment committee
of the D. union, within which the parish of C. was situate, by a valuation list
assessed the local board at a rateable value of 1400*l.*, based upon the amount
which might have been earned by a trading company carrying on the waterworks
for their own benefit; the local board claimed to be assessed at a rateable value
of 540*l.*, based upon the profit actually earned by them:—

Held, affirming the judgment of the Court of Appeal from Inferior Courts, that
the assessment at 1400*l.* was wrong, and that the local board were liable to be
assessed at 540*l.* only; for, under the provisions of the Public Health Act, 1848,
they could not make rates of an amount more than sufficient to enable them to
maintain the waterworks, and they could be lawfully assessed only with reference
to the profit actually earned.

Special case stated by order of Blackburn, J., bearing date
July 25, 1874, under 12 & 13 Vict. c. 45, s. 11.

1. The appellants are the mayor, aldermen, and citizens of the
city of Worcester, who, being the council of the said city, are the
local board of health and urban sanitary authority for the said city.

2. The respondents are the assessment committee of the Droitwich Union, in which the whole of the parish of Claines is situated,
but which parish is partly in the city and partly in the county of
Worcester.

1876

CORPORATION
OF
WORCESTER
v.
DROITWICH
ASSESSMENT
COMMITTEE.

3. In the year 1849 the Public Health Act, 1848 (11 & 12 Vict. c. 63), was applied to the city of Worcester, and the appellants became the local board of health for the city.

4. In 1856 the appellants, in pursuance of the powers conferred by the before-mentioned statute, and for the purpose of supplying the sanitary requirements of the city, purchased certain land in that part of the parish of Claines which is situated within the municipal boundary of the city of Worcester, but which forms part of the Droitwich poor-law union, and is for poor-law purposes distinct and separate from the city of Worcester.

5. On the land thus purchased the appellants erected waterworks and a reservoir, which, with certain mains and pipes, extending throughout the city of Worcester for the supply of water to the inhabitants, cost 30,000l.

6. On the 2nd of March, 1858, the appellants duly fixed a rate of 4d. in the pound per annum on the net annual value of the dwelling-houses and premises supplied with water for domestic use, cleanliness, and drainage, and an additional charge for water used for trade and other special purposes, and also a certain scale for water supplied by meter. In fixing the above-mentioned rate, the appellants took into consideration, not so much the profit to be made out of the water as a commercial speculation, as its value as a sanitary agent in preserving the health of the said city, and the necessity of bringing the supply within the reach of the poorest class of inhabitants, and in order to induce the inhabitants to discontinue the private sources of supply; and they accordingly fixed a price which has left but little profit above the actual cost of supply, but which has effected the object they had in view by promoting the general use of the water throughout the city.

7. The price which the appellants actually charge for household supply is only 4d. in the pound per annum upon the net annual value, and for houses the net annual value of which does not exceed 8l. per annum, they only charge two-thirds of that amount; and when the rent of the houses includes the parochial rates, which is almost universally the case in the dwellings of the labouring class, the charge is only one-half, or 2d. in the pound per annum on the rateable value. Thus, a house let at 10l. per annum, the rateable value of which would be about 8l., gets an unlimited

1876

CORPORATION
OF
WORCESTER
v.
DROITWICH
ASSESSMENT
COMMITTEE.

supply of water for 1s. 9d. per annum if the tenant pays the rates, and for 1s. 4d. per annum if the landlord pays them, while a house, the rateable value of which is 20l. per annum, gets all the water required for domestic purposes for 6s. 8d. per annum, and warehouses, shops, and offices, of the same rateable value, at 3s. 4d. per annum.

8. The appellants have also a scale of charges for water supplied (not by meter) for trade purposes, e.g., to fishmongers, 10s. per annum; greengrocers, 4s. per annum; livery stables, 1s. per annum for each stall; washerwomen, 4s. per annum.

9. The charges for supply by meter range from 3d. per 1000 gallons for the largest quantities, and going up to 7d. per 1000 gallons when the supply is less than 20,000 gallons per quarter, and this is the maximum charge. The above charges are to be taken as below those that would be charged by the appellants if they were an ordinary trading body.

10. In 1866, the existing waterworks proving insufficient, the appellants purchased additional land at Barbourne, in the parish of Claines, and between the years 1867 and 1871 expended 18,000l. in enlarging the then existing works. The said further sum of 18,000l. and the former sum of 30,000l. were raised by mortgage of the general district rates of the city of Worcester, repayable by annual instalments, extending over thirty years. The interest and instalments of principal payable in the year ending the 31st of August, 1873, amounted to 2976l. Of the said sum of 48,000l. the sum of 37,250l., or thereabouts, has been expended in the parish of Claines.

13. On the 22nd of October, 1873, a new valuation list or supplemental valuation list for the parish of Claines was approved by the assessment committee of the Droitwich Union. The gross estimated rental of the waterworks and land of the appellants was therein stated to be 1750l., and the rateable value 1400l.

14. On the 17th of December, 1873, notice of objection and appeal against the said valuation list was served on the overseers and on the assessment committee, the principal and main ground of objection being that the appellants were over-assessed or rated in respect of the gross estimated rental of the waterworks and land occupied by them in the parish of Claines.

1876

Corporation
of
Worcester
v.
Droitwich
Assessment
Committee.

15. The appellants failed to obtain any relief from the assessment committee, and they have appealed to the court of quarter
sessions against the poor-rates based on the said valuation list
made on the 22nd of October, 1873, their principal ground of
such appeal, and the only one now raised, being the same as
above stated.

16. By the accounts of the local board of health, which are
annually audited, printed, and circulated in accordance with the
Municipal Corporation Act, the Public Health Act, 1848, and the
Local Government Act, 1858, it appears, as the fact is, that the
whole net income derived from the said waterworks during the
eight years previous to such appeal averaged about 651l. per
annum, without any deduction having been made for rates, taxes,
expenses of management, collection of water-rate, depreciation of
plant and machinery, and other matters which in making out a
commercial account would have been allowed for.

Paragraphs 17 and 18 stated respectively the contentions for
the appellants and the respondents, and are set out in the judgment
of the Court of Appeal delivered by Mellish, L.J., as hereinafter
mentioned.

19. If the Court should be of opinion that the contention of the
appellants is right, then the said rate is to be amended, and so
much of the said valuation list as refers to the lands and works in
question is to be cancelled; and the income that the appellants
have actually received for the same shall be taken as the annual
value thereof, and the said assessment shall stand at 600l. as the
gross estimated value of the said land and works, and 540l. as the
rateable value thereof as aforesaid.

20. If the Court should be of opinion that the contention of the
respondents is right, then the assessment of 1750l., as the gross
estimated value, and 1400l. as the rateable value, is to stand.

22. The Court is to have power to draw inferences.

Feb. 5.   In the Court of Appeal from Inferior Courts.

G. M. Dowdeswell, Q.C. (*E. J. Castle* with him), for the corporation of Worcester. The question is whether a municipal body
performing a public duty in erecting and maintaining waterworks,
and restricted as to the amount of their charges, ought to be

assessed at the same amount as a private company who are free from any restriction as to the amount which they may earn. It is submitted that the corporation are clearly limited as to the amount of their charges. The waterworks were constructed under the Public Health Act, 1848, s. 75 (1), and ss. 76, 77, and 78 of

(1) By the Public Health Act, 1848 (11 & 12 Vict. c. 63), s. 75, " the local board of health may provide their district with such a supply of water as may be proper and sufficient for the purposes of this Act, and for private use to the extent required by this Act; and for those purposes, or any of them, the said local board may from time to time, with the approval of the general board of health, contract with any person whomsoever, or purchase, take upon lease, hire, construct, lay down, and maintain such waterworks, and do and execute all such works, matters, and things as shall be necessary and proper; and any waterworks company may contract with the local board of health to supply water for the purposes of this Act in any manner whatsoever, or may sell and dispose of or lease their waterworks to any local board of health willing to take the same; and the said local board may provide and keep, in any waterworks constructed or laid down by them under the powers of this Act, a supply of pure and wholesome water, and the water so supplied may be constantly laid on at such pressure as will carry the same to the top story of the highest dwelling house within the district supplied."

Sect. 76: " If upon the report of the surveyor it appear to the local board of health that any house is without a proper supply of water, and that such a supply of water can be furnished thereto at a rate not exceeding two pence per week, the said local board shall give notice in writing to the occupier, requiring him, within a time to be specified therein, to obtain such supply, and to do all such works as may be necessary for that purpose. And if such notice be not complied with, the said local board may, if they shall think fit, do such works, and obtain such supply accordingly, and make and levy water-rates upon the premises, not exceeding in the whole the rate of two pence per week, in manner hereinafter provided, as if the owner or occupier of the premises had demanded a supply of water and were willing to pay water-rates for the same; and the expenses incurred by them in doing such works as last aforesaid shall be private improvement expenses, and be recoverable as such in the manner hereinafter provided."

Sect. 77: " The local board of health may, if they shall think fit, supply water from any waterworks purchased or constructed by them under this Act to any public baths or wash-houses, or for trading or manufacturing purposes, upon such terms and conditions, as may be agreed upon between the said local board and the persons desirous of being so supplied."

Sect. 78: " The local board of health may cause all existing public cisterns, pumps, wells, reservoirs, conduits, aqueducts, and works used for the gratuitous supply of water to the inhabitants to be continued, maintained, and plentifully supplied with water, or they may substitute, continue, maintain, and plentifully supply with water other such works equally convenient; and the said local board may, if they shall think fit, construct any number of new cisterns, pumps, wells, conduits, and works for the gratuitous supply of any public

1876

CORPORATION
OF
WORCESTER
v.
DROITWICH
ASSESSMENT
COMMITTEE.

that statute specify the purposes for which the water may be supplied. The intention of the legislature clearly was that a local board of health should confer a benefit upon the inhabitants of their district by a proper supply of water. It would be quite inconsistent with the object of the Act that the local board should derive any pecuniary advantage from the supply of water; and, therefore, they can only levy such rates as will enable them to pay the expenses of keeping the works in operation. The decisions in *Mersey Docks* v. *Cameron* (1) and *Jones* v. *Mersey Docks* (1) have established that property is not exempt from rateability merely because it is occupied for public objects; and it is admitted for the purposes of the present case that the waterworks are to some extent liable to be rated; but the corporation of Worcester contend that as they are restricted by statute from earning the same profit which a trading company might have earned, they are rateable only in respect of the income actually derived from their occupation, which they are willing to take without further question as the proper basis for estimating their liability; and *Mayor*

---

baths or wash-houses established otherwise than for private profit or supported out of any poor or borough rates."

Sect. 88 relates to the mode of making special and general district rates.

Sect. 93: "Whenever and so long as any premises are supplied with water by the local board of health for the purposes of domestic use, cleanliness, or drainage, they shall make and levy, in addition to any other rate, a water-rate upon the occupier, except as hereinafter provided; and the rate so made shall be assessed upon the net annual value of the premises, ascertained in the manner hereinbefore prescribed with respect to the said special and general district rates."

Sect. 94: "The said water-rate shall be payable in advance; and whenever any person supplied with water under the provisions of this Act neglects to pay the water-rate due from him upon

demand, the local board of health may prevent the water from flowing into the premises of the defaulter in such manner as they may think fit, and may recover the arrears due, together with the expenses of stopping the supply, in the manner hereinafter provided with respect to the recovery of rates made under the authority of this Act: provided always that the stopping or cutting off any supply of water by the said local board under this enactment shall not relieve any person from any penalty or liability to which he would have been otherwise subject."

The Public Health Act, 1848, is repealed by s. 343 of the Public Health Act, 1875 (38 & 39 Vict. c. 55); but the sections of the latter statute, commencing at the 51st, contain enactments similar to those above set out.

(1) 11 H. L. C 443; 35 L. J. (M.C.) 1.

of *Liverpool* v. *Overseers of Wavertree* (1) is a clear authority in their favour. Moreover, it is a general principle of the law of rating that property must be assessed at its actual value, and not at the value which it might acquire if it were used in a different manner; thus, before the Rating Act, 1874, if the lessor of land reserved the right to kill the game thereon, the lessee was not rateable in respect thereof: *Reg.* v. *Thurlstone.* (2)

[FIELD, J. *Reg.* v. *Thurlstone* (2) seems hardly consistent with

1876

CORPORATION
OF
WORCESTER
v.
DROITWICH
ASSESSMENT
COMMITTEE.

(1) In the Court of Queen's Bench.

January 23, 1875.

The Mayor of Liverpool, &c., Appellants; The Overseers of Wavertree, Respondents.

CASE stated under 12 & 13 Vict. c. 45, s. 11.

By virtue of certain statutes the appellants were empowered to supply water for domestic and other purposes, within certain limits, including therein the borough of Liverpool. Pursuant to their statutory powers they maintained waterworks in the township of Wavertree. By the Liverpool Corporation Waterworks Act, 1862 (25 & 26 Vict. c. cvii.), s. 59, the corporation of Liverpool were to estimate and fix the amount of money necessary for defraying the costs, charges, and expenses payable out of the Liverpool water account for the year then current, and were to fix the rate in the pound at which the domestic water-rent was to be charged at such an amount as, regard being had to the several sources of revenue, would be sufficient in the aggregate to meet the estimated expenses payable out of the water account for the current year. The corporation were limited by the said Act from receiving any more money from the consumers than was requisite to pay the above-mentioned expenses, and in this respect their income differed from that of an ordinary trading company, inasmuch as it did not necessarily represent the full value of the use and enjoyment of the water to the consumers. One of the questions for the opinion of the Court was whether, in arriving at the gross annual value of the appellants' waterworks, the respondents ought to ascertain the gross receipts which the appellants might derive if they were a trading company earning a profit by water supply, and then make the statutory and proper deductions from the figure so obtained, or whether they were limited to the actual receipt.

L. Williams, for the appellants, was stopped.

Gully, for the respondents.

BLACKBURN, J. I think it clear that the appellants are right. The whole question turns on the rule given by the Parochial Assessment Act, which says the occupier is rateable at what a tenant from year to year will give as the rent, who takes the land subject to the same restrictions as those under which the appellants hold it. Now the tenant would only give such a rent as the restrictions imposed by statute would enable him to earn; and the rateable value is to be based upon that rent.

LUSH, J., concurred.

Judgment for the appellants.

(2) 1 E. & E. 502; 28 L. J. (M.C.) 106. *Reg.* v. *Thurlstone* appears to have been doubted by Cockburn, C.J., and Lush, J., in *Reg.* v. *Battle Union*, Law Rep. 2 Q. B. 8.

1876

CORPORATION
OF
WORCESTER
*.
DROITWICH
ASSESSMENT
COMMITTEE.

the decision in *Reg.* v. *Rhymney Ry. Co.* (1); but *Staley* v. *Overseers of Castleton* (2) clearly shews that the rateable value is to be based upon the actual value for the time being.]

It is plain from the facts stated that no person or company would carry on the waterworks as a commercial speculation under the restrictions imposed upon the corporation, and this exempts the present case from the rule laid down in *Reg.* v. *London and North Western Ry. Co.* (3), that if several persons are willing to hire land of itself almost worthless, that is a circumstance which may be taken into account in enhancing its rateable value. *Alison* v. *Monkwearmouth* (4) is not in point for the present case; and, moreover, it seems hardly consistent with *Sunderland* v. *Sunderland.* (5)

Henry Matthews, Q.C. (*A. R. Jelf* with him), for the assessment committee. If the argument on behalf of the corporation were valid, it might have been successfully contended that they are not rateable at any amount in respect of the waterworks; but it is clear that they are rateable, for they have a beneficial occupation: *Reg.* v. *Longwood* (6); *Reg.* v. *Kentmere* (7); *Mayor of Manchester* v. *Overseers of Manchester* (8); and they are only trustees for the inhabitants of Worcester, who will really bear the burden of the assessment: *Reg.* v. *Longwood* (9), per Coleridge, J., and *Mayor of Liverpool* v. *Overseers of West Derby.* (10) The corporation are liable to be assessed to the same extent as a trading company.

Dowdeswell, Q.C., in reply.

> *Cur. adv. vult.*

Feb. 11. The judgment of the Court (Cleasby, B., and Field, J.) was delivered by

CLEASBY, B. The question in this case is not the rateability of

---

(1) Law Rep. 4 Q. B. 276.

(2) 5 B. & S. 505; S. C. 33 L. J. (M.C.) 178.

(3) Law Rep. 9 Q. B. 134.

(4) 4 E. & B. 13; 23 L. J. (M.C.) 177.

(5) 18 C. B. (N.S) 531; 34 L. J. (M.C.) 121.

(6) 13 Q. B. 116.

(7) 17 Q. B. 551.

(8) 17 Q. B. 859; S. C. sub. nom. *Reg.* v. *Mayor of Manchester*, 21 L. J. (M.C.) 160.

(9) 17 Q. B. 871, at p. 881.

(10) 6 E. & B. 704; 25 L. J. (M.C.) 112.

1876

CORPORATION
OF
WORCESTER
v.
DROITWICH
ASSESSMENT
COMMITTEE.

a public body in respect of premises occupied by them for public purposes. That question has been for some time settled; and it is not disputed that the appellants, who are the local board of health of Worcester, are liable to be rated in respect of waterworks erected and occupied by them for the purpose of supplying the inhabitants with water. The question is, whether the rateable occupation is to be measured by the profits actually derived from the occupation, or by the profits which might be derived from it by a person or a company who occupied the works solely for the purpose of profit; the fact being that the corporation having in view the benefit of the inhabitants, have made the scale of rates so low as to leave a profit only of 600l. upon the rates actually received, after deducting the expenses connected with the providing the water, collection, &c., upon which amount they contend they ought to be rated: whereas the respondents contend that a trading company with the same powers of rating might have realised a net profit of 1750l., on which amount they say the rate ought to have been made.

It seems to us that the respondents cannot maintain the rate which they contend for; and that the restrictions which are put by law upon a public body as to the profits derivable from the occupation of waterworks or gasworks, or other property of that description, must be regarded in considering the profitable occupation by that body. For example, if the local board was prohibited from charging more than 2d. a week on a dwelling-house, and the waterworks were so complete and the demand so great that a private trading company would be able to charge 6d. a house, we should feel no doubt whatever that the local board, whose duty it was not to let to a trading company, but themselves to occupy, could only be rated upon the occupation and the rate which they were compelled to charge. This is not the present case, but only an illustration of a restriction put by law upon the value of the occupation, and the effect of it could not be disputed, and, indeed, was hardly disputed in the course of the argument. The hypothetical tenant, subject to no restriction, cannot represent the real occupier, who is by law subject to restrictions.

This conclusion would be well supported by the cases of *Reg.*

1876
———
CORPORATION
OF
WORCESTER
v.
DROITWICH
ASSESSMENT
COMMITTEE.

v. *Metropolitan Board of Works* (1) and *Metropolitan Board of Works* v. *Overseers of West Ham* (2), and is fairly borne out by the opinion of Wightman, J., and Crompton, J., in *Reg.* v. *Long-wood.* (3)

We were also referred during the argument to another case, *Mayor of Liverpool* v. *Overseers of Wavertree* (4), and it may be said to have been there expressly so decided.

The only question, therefore, is, whether a public body exercising their powers properly for the benefit of the inhabitants, and making their rates bonâ fide for that purpose, and so regulating their conduct by the restriction, as it may be called, of acting in obedience to the Act of Parliament, can be properly represented for the purpose of rating by a hypothetical tenant acting under no such restriction. We are of opinion that they cannot. They only acquire the right to the rates by the Act of Parliament for the purpose of carrying the objects of the Public Health Act properly into effect, and the profitable occupation which they in fact have is the only one which they can properly have, and it would be strange to rate them, not in respect of what they can properly enjoy and do enjoy, but in respect of what they cannot properly enjoy and do not enjoy. We adopt the language of Lush, J., in the before-cited case of *Metropolitan Board of Works* v. *Overseers of West Ham* (5), that the proper mode of estimating the profitable occupation is to take it as it actually is.

No distinction was attempted to be made between the money derivable from the rates properly so called and that derived from agreements with tradesmen and manufacturers. The question above discussed was the only one argued before us, and it appears to us, for the reasons above given, that the contention of the appellants is right, and that as the sum of 600*l.* properly represents the value of the profits actually had, the gross estimated rental ought to be reduced to that sum, and the rateable value to 540*l.*

June 22.   In the Court of Appeal.

A. R. Jelf, for the assessment committee of the Droitwich Union.

(1) Law Rep. 4 Q. B. 15.
(2) Law Rep. 6 Q. B. 193.
(3) 17 Q. B. 871, at p. 883.

(4) See note, ante, p. 55.
(5) Law Rep. 6 Q. B. 193, at pp. 197, 198.

J. J. Powell, Q.C., and *E. J. Castle,* were for the corporation of Worcester.

The arguments were similar to those urged in the Court below. The following additional authorities were cited: *Reg.* v. *Justices of Hull* (1); *Commissioners of the Leith Harbour and Docks* v. *Inspector of the Poor.* (2)

Cur. adv. vult. (3)

1876

CORPORATION
OF
WORCESTER
v.
DROITWICH
ASSESSMENT
COMMITTEE.

Nov. 10. The judgment of the Court (James and Mellish, L.JJ., and Baggallay, J.A.), was delivered by

MELLISH, L.J. The question to be determined in this case is, on what principle the corporation of Worcester are to be assessed to the poor-rate in respect of a certain reservoir and waterworks situate within the Droitwich Union, which were erected and are maintained by the corporation under the provisions of the Public Health Act, for the purpose of supplying the city of Worcester with water.

The corporation, as is stated in the 17th paragraph of this case, contend that the provisions of the Public Health Act contain the only authority for them to charge a water rate on consumers of water, and that such a rate only is authorized by the statute as might be reasonably expected to be necessary to defray the expenses incident to the water supply, and that they have no authority by the said Act or otherwise to receive any more money from the consumers than is required to pay the above-mentioned expenses: and, further, that as the inhabitants have, on the faith of the existing rates, adopted the water supply of the corporation and suffered their private resources to fall into disuse, without special causes it would be a breach of good faith to alter such rates: and that, therefore, the corporation are only rateable for the rent which a tenant from year to year would give for the land subject to the existing rates, and the same restrictions (if any) as those under which the corporation hold it, and not that which a tenant entirely unfettered might give.

On the other hand, the assessment committee of the Droitwich

(1) 4 E. & B. 29; S. C. sub nom. *Reg.* v. *Cooper,* 23 L. J. (M.C.) 183.
(2) Law Rep. 1 H. L., Sc. 17.

(3) Quain, J., was present during the argument, but died before the delivery of the judgment.

1876

CORPORATION
OF
WORCESTER
v.
DROITWICH
ASSESSMENT
COMMITTEE.

Union, as is stated in the 18th paragraph of this case, contend that it is right to rate the corporation, in respect of the
waterworks in Claines (as directed by s. 1 of 6 & 7 Wm. 4, c. 96),
at an amount based upon the rent which a tenant would give, with
liberty to raise the price of water as he might think proper, so far
as not restricted by law; that there were no restrictions by law in
the present case, and that the fact, that the corporation in fixing
their rates looked only to the benefit of the inhabitants and ratepayers of the city of Worcester, only transfers the advantage and
benefit of the property from themselves to those inhabitants and
ratepayers for whom they are trustees, and that it would be unfair
that the inhabitants and ratepayers of the city of Worcester should
enjoy this advantage and benefit at the expense of the parish of
Claines and the rest of the Droitwich Union.

It has been held by the Divisional Court of Appeal that the
contention of the corporation is right, and we are of opinion that
their decision ought to be affirmed.

There are two questions to be considered: first, are the corporation, according to the true construction of the Public Health Act,
prevented from charging for the use of the water a larger sum
than the sum they actually require for the maintenance and
repair of the waterworks? and, secondly, if they are, can they be
rated as occupiers in respect of profits which the law does not allow
them to earn?

Now, with respect to the first question, we think that the corporation, in making a water-rate under s. 93 of the Public Health
Act, are bound to make an estimate of the sum they actually
require for the maintenance of their waterworks, and cannot
legally levy a larger sum by a water-rate than the sum they so
require. The 94th section makes the water-rate payable in
advance, and enables the supply of any person who neglects to
pay it to be cut off, and we think it cannot have been intended
that the corporation should charge any person more than his fair
share of the sum which is required to maintain the waterworks.
There is nothing in the case to prove that the 651l., which is
stated to be on the average of eight years the whole net income
the corporation have derived from the waterworks, was not the
whole sum they required for the maintenance of the waterworks.

1876

CORPORATION
OF
WORCESTER
v.
DROITWICH
ASSESSMENT
COMMITTEE.

The question, then, is, whether, in applying the rule given by the Parochial Assessment Act, the Court is to consider what rent a tenant from year to year would give for the reservoir and waterworks who was subject to the same restrictions the corporation are subject to, or what rent a tenant from year to year would give who was subject to no such restriction, and we are of opinion that the hypothetical tenant is to be a tenant subject to the restrictions. The case of *Corporation of Liverpool* v. *Overseers of Wavertree* (1) is directly in point, and we are of opinion that case was correctly decided. Blackburn, J., there says, "The whole question turns on the rule given by the Parochial Assessment Act, which says the occupier is rateable at what a tenant from year to year will give as the rent who takes the land subject to the same restrictions as those under which the tenant holds it." This decision seems to us to be right on principle. An occupier of land is not rateable in respect of the whole profit derived from the land, but only in respect of the profit which he himself derives from the land. If there be a common in the possession of the lord of the manor, he is not rateable in respect of the profits derived by the commoners from the common, although in rating the lands of the commoners the fact of their lands being rendered more valuable by reason of the occupiers being entitled to a right of common is taken into account. So in the present case, the rent, and therefore the rateable value, of every house in Worcester is increased by reason of the occupier being entitled to cheap water from the waterworks of the corporation, and if the corporation in respect of the reservoir and waterworks were rated at the profit which a tenant under no restriction could get from the waterworks, the same profit would be rated twice over. If the waterworks were transferred to a tenant who was under no restriction as to the price he charged for water, the rateable value of the waterworks would be increased, but there would be a corresponding diminution of the rateable value of the premises supplied with the water. We may also observe that the reservoir by itself, without the power of connecting the reservoir with the houses by pipes running through the streets, is probably worth nothing, and certainly is not worth 651*l.* a year; and it is the same Act of Parliament which gives the

(1) See note, ante, p. 55.

1876

CORPORATION
OF
WORCESTER
v.
DROITWICH
ASSESSMENT
COMMITTEE.

power to lay the pipes and therefore creates the value of the reservoir, which contains the restrictions on the amount of profit which the occupiers of the reservoir can earn. Even in the case of the reservoirs of Public Companies, established by Act of Parliament to supply towns with water, in estimating the rateable value of the reservoirs the Court only considers the amount of profit which the terms of their Act enable the company to earn, not the profits which the company might earn if Parliament had enabled the company to establish waterworks without restriction as to the price to be charged to consumers. So, also, in rating a railway, or any other work made under an Act of Parliament, the calculation must always commence with the profits which are actually earned according to the terms of the Act of Parliament, not with the profits which might be earned if the company was unlimited in its charges. It follows, therefore, that according to the contention of the assessment committee, the corporation are rateable in respect of their reservoir at a higher sum than a waterworks company established by Act of Parliament would be rateable, and are rateable on an assumption which not only is not true, but which cannot be true, that a tenant is in possession of a reservoir with the monopoly of the supply of a particular town with water, and is unlimited in respect of his charges.

Judgment affirmed.

Solicitors for Mayor, &c., of Worcester: *Church, Sons, & Clarke,* for *Thomas Southall, Worcester.*

Solicitors for Assessment Committee: *Tucker & Lake.*

[CROWN CASE RESERVED.]

THE QUEEN v. KEYN.

1876
Nov. 11, 13.

*Jurisdiction — Central Criminal Court — Admiralty — Territorial Waters —
Offence within Three Miles of English Coast — Manslaughter — 15 Ric. 2,
c. 3 — 28 Hen. 8, c. 15 — 39 Geo. 3, c. 37 — 4 & 5 Wm. 4, c. 36, s. 22 — 7 & 8
Vict. c. 2.*

The prisoner was indicted at the Central Criminal Court for manslaughter.
He was a foreigner and in command of a foreign ship, passing within three miles
of the shore of England on a voyage to a foreign port; and whilst within that
distance his ship ran into a British ship and sank her, whereby a passenger on
board the latter ship was drowned. The facts of the case were such as to amount
to manslaughter by English law :—

Held, by the majority of the Court (Cockburn, C.J., Kelly, C.B., Bramwell,
J.A., Lush and Field, JJ., Sir R. Phillimore, and Pollock, B.; Lord Coleridge,
C.J., Brett and Amphlett, JJ.A., Grove, Denman, and Lindley, JJ., dissenting),
that the Central Criminal Court had no jurisdiction to try the prisoner for the
offence charged.

By the whole of the majority of the Court, on the ground that, prior to 28 Hen.
8, c. 15, the admiral had no jurisdiction to try offences by foreigners on board
foreign ships, whether within or without the limit of three miles from the shore
of England; that that and the subsequent statutes only transferred to the Common Law Courts and the Central Criminal Court the jurisdiction formerly possessed by the admiral; (and that, therefore, in the absence of statutory enactment,
the Central Criminal Court had no power to try such an offence.)

By Kelly, C.B., and Sir R. Phillimore, also, on the ground that, by the principles
of international law, the power of a nation over the sea within three miles of
its coasts is only for certain limited purposes; and that Parliament could not,
consistently with those principles, apply English criminal law within those
limits.

Held, contrà, by Lord Coleridge, C.J., Brett and Amphlett, JJ.A., Grove,
Denman, and Lindley, JJ., on the ground that the sea within three miles of the
coast of England is part of the territory of England; that the English criminal
law extends over those limits; and the admiral formerly had, and the Central
Criminal Court now has, jurisdiction to try offences there committed although on
board foreign ships.

By Lord Coleridge, C.J., and Denman, J., on the ground that the prisoner's
ship having run into a British ship and sank it, and so caused the death of a passenger on board the latter ship, the offence was committed on board a British
ship, and, therefore, the Central Criminal Court had jurisdiction.

Case stated by Pollock, B.

Ferdinand Keyn was tried at the April sittings of the Central
Criminal Court for the manslaughter of Jessie Dorcas Young.

On the part of the prosecution it was proved that Jessie Dorcas

Young was a passenger by a British steamer called the *Strathclyde*, from London to Bombay, and that when off Dover the *Strathclyde* was run into by a steamer called the *Franconia*, whilst she was under the command and immediate direction of the prisoner'; whereby the *Strathclyde* was sunk, and Jessie Dorcas Young was drowned.

The *Franconia* was a German vessel, carrying the German flag. She sailed from Hamburg with the prisoner, who is a German, in command, and a crew of seventy-three,' nearly all of whom were Germans, and a French pilot. She was carrying the mail from Hamburg to St. Thomas in the West Indies, and put into Grimsby to take on board an English pilot, whose duty it was to conduct her down channel as far as the South Sand light; after which she would proceed to and touch at Havre, where she would land the English pilot and the French pilot, whose duty it was to conduct her from off Dungeness to Havre; and thence go to St. Thomas.

The *Franconia* had performed the same voyage six times.

The point at which the *Strathclyde* was run down by the *Franconia* was one mile and nine-tenths of a mile S.S.E. from Dover pier-head, and within two and a half miles from Dover beach.

At the close of the case for the prosecution, the counsel for the prisoner objected that the Court had no jurisdiction. The learned judge, without expressing any opinion, ruled that the Court had jurisdiction.

Witnesses were called for the prisoner. The jury found him guilty.

The question for the opinion for the Court for Crown Cases Reserved was whether the Central Criminal Court had jurisdiction.

May 6, 13. The case was argued before Kelly, C.B., Sir R. Phillimore, Lush, Field, and Lindley, JJ., and Pollock, B., by *Benjamin, Q.C.* (*Cohen, Q.C., Phillimore,* and *Stubbs* with him), for the prisoner; and by *Sir H. Giffard, S.G.* (*Poland, C. Bowen,* and *Straight* with him), for the prosecution.

The Court being divided, the case was directed to be re-argued.

June 16, 17, 21, 22, 23. The case was again argued before Cockburn, C.J., Lord Coleridge, C.J., Kelly, C.B., Sir R. Phillimore,

Bramwell, Pollock, and Amphlett, BB., Lush, Brett, Grove, Denman, Archibald (1), Field and Lindley, JJ.

The arguments and the authorities cited sufficiently appear from the judgments.

Cur. adv. vult.

Nov. 11, 13. The following judgments were delivered :—

SIR R. PHILLIMORE. The prisoner was indicted at the Central Criminal Court for the manslaughter of Jessie Dorcas Young on the high seas, and within the jurisdiction of the Admiralty of England.

The deceased was a passenger on board the *Strathclyde*, a British steam-vessel bound from London to Bombay.

This vessel, when at a distance of one mile and nine-tenths of a mile S.S.E. from Dover pier-head, and within two and a half miles from Dover beach, was run into by the *Franconia*, a German steamer, in consequence of which she sank, and the deceased woman was drowned.

The *Franconia* was carrying the German mails from Hamburg to St. Thomas in the West Indies.

The prisoner, being the officer in command of the *Franconia*, was convicted of manslaughter, but a question of law was reserved for this Court of Criminal Appeal. An objection was taken on the part of the prisoner that, inasmuch as he was a foreigner, in a foreign vessel, on a foreign voyage, sailing upon the high seas, he was not subject to the jurisdiction of any Court in this country. The contrary position maintained on the part of the Crown is that, inasmuch as at the time of the collision both vessels were within the distance of three miles from the English shore, the offence was committed within the realm of England, and is triable by the English Court. The case has been most ably conducted on both sides, and the Court has derived very great assistance from the arguments of counsel.

Before I consider the principal question, whether the offence committed on board the foreign vessel be triable here, it may be well to take notice of a subsidiary contention put forward on behalf of the Crown, namely, that the person injured was on

(1) Archibald, J. died after the argument, and before judgment was delivered : see post, p. 238.

board an English ship at the time when she received the injury which was the immediate and direct result of the collision, and that in fact the offence was committed on board an English ship. It seems expedient to deal with this contention in the first place, because, if it be valid, the inquiry as to the juris-diction of the English Court over a foreign ship would be unneces-sary. I am of opinion that this contention cannot be sustained. Looking at the facts stated by the learned judge who tried the case, as well as the indictment, it appears that the prisoner had no intention to injure the *Strathclyde* or any person on board of her. He was guilty of negligence, and want of nautical skill, and of presence of mind in the management of his vessel, and thereby caused the collision, but the act by which the woman died was not his act, nor was it a consequence immediate or direct of his act. He never left the deck of his own ship, nor did he send any missile from it to the other ship; neither in will nor in deed can he be considered to have been on board the British vessel. He can no more be considered by intendment of law to have been on board the British vessel than he would have been if his bad navigation had caused the *Strathclyde* to impale herself upon the *Franconia*, and so to sink. The jurisdiction of the English Court, therefore, cannot be founded on this contention.

The administration of the criminal law of England was formerly distributed among two tribunals; the Court of oyer and terminer took cognizance of offences committed in the body of a county, the Court of the Lord High Admiral of those committed on the sea.

A *divisum imperium* existed with respect to rivers and arms of the sea within the body of a county; each Court claimed concur-rent jurisdiction over these waters.

Two statutes were passed for the purpose of reconciling these claims and for restricting the Court of the admiral to the high seas.

The first of these two statutes, namely, the statute of 13 Rich. 3, c. 5, entitled "What things the admiral and his deputy shall meddle," enacts that,—

"Forasmuch as a great and common clamour and complaints hath been often-times made before this time, and yet is, for that the admirals and their deputies hold their sessions within divers places of this realm, as well within franchise as without, accroaching to them greater authority than belongeth to their office, in prejudice of our lord the king, and the common law of the realm, and in diminishing of divers franchises, and in destruction and impoverishing of the common people, it is accorded and assented, that the admirals and their deputies shall not meddle from henceforth of anything done within the realm, but only of a thing done upon the sea."

By 15 Rich. 2, c. 3, entitled "In what places the admiral's jurisdiction doth lie," it is

"Declared, ordained and established, that of all manner of contracts, pleas, and quarrels, and all other things rising within the bodies of the counties, as well by land as by water, and also of wreck of the sea, the admiral's Court shall have no manner of cognizance, power, nor jurisdiction; but all such manner of contracts, pleas, and quarrels, and all other things rising within the bodies of counties, as well by land as by water, as afore, and also wreck of the sea, shall be tried, determined, discussed, and remedied by the laws of the land, and not before nor by the admiral nor his lieutenant in anywise; nevertheless, of the death of a man, and of a maihem done in great ships, being and hovering in the main stream of great rivers, only beneath the bridges of the same rivers nigh to the sea, and in none other places of the same rivers, the admiral shall have cognizance."

This adjustment of jurisdiction continued until the 28 Hen. 8, c. 15, which transferred the jurisdiction to commissioners of oyer and terminer under the great seal, among whom was included the judge of the Admiralty Court, and ultimately this jurisdiction became regulated by the statutes 4 & 5 Wm. 4, c. 36, and 7 & 8 Vict. c. 2, by the former of which statutes the Central Criminal Court was established.

The jurisdiction which now exists over offences committed at sea is that which was once possessed by the Court of the admiral.

The county extends to low-water mark, where the "high seas" begin; between high and low-water mark, the Courts of oyer and terminer had jurisdiction when the tide was out, the Court of the admiral when the tide was in.

There appears to be no sufficient authority for saying that the high sea was ever considered to be within the realm, and, notwithstanding what is said by Hale in his treatises de Jure Maris and Pleas of the Crown, there is a total absence of precedents since the reign of Edward III., if indeed any existed then, to support the doctrine that the realm of England extends beyond the limits of counties.

I am not aware of any instance, none was cited to us, of the exercise of criminal jurisdiction over a foreign vessel for an offence

1876
THE QUEEN
v.
KEYN.
Sir R. Phillimore.

committed when she was not within a port or harbour of the inland
waters of the realm.

Various statutes have been passed from time to time empowering
what may be called inland authorities, such as justices of the peace,
coroners, and the Lord Warden of the Cinque Ports, to try offences
committed at sea. Some clauses in the Merchant Shipping Act it
may be necessary to refer to hereafter; but it may be stated here
that no statute will be found to authorize the exercise of the
criminal jurisdiction over a foreign vessel not in one of our ports
or inland waters.

It being, then, in my opinion, clear that the jurisdiction to try
this prisoner was not derived from the common law, or the statute
law, or the law of the High Court of Admiralty, what law did
render the English Court competent for this purpose?

As I understand the contention on behalf of the Crown, the
answer is, international law; in other words, by the consent of all
civilized states, England has become entitled to include within her
realm a marine league of sea, and therefore has jurisdiction over a
foreign vessel within that limit.

It is, indeed, a most grave question whether, if this statement of
international law were correct, nevertheless an Act of Parliament
would not be required to empower the Court to exercise jurisdiction; but, waiving this consideration for the present, it becomes
important in this view of the question to consider the sources from
which we are to derive this doctrine of international law.

Too rudimental an inquiry must be avoided; but it must be
remembered that the case is one primæ impressionis, of the
greatest importance both to England and to other states; and the
character of it in some degree necessitates a reference to first
principles.

In the memorable answer, pronounced by Montesquieu to be
réponse sans réplique, and framed by Lord Mansfield and Sir
George Lee, of the British to the Prussian Government,

"The law of nations is said to be founded upon justice, equity, convenience,
and the reason of the thing, and confirmed by long usage."

It is more especially to this usage, as evidencing the consent of
nations, that great judges, such, among others, as Lord Stowell and

1876

Tʜᴇ Qᴜᴇᴇɴ
v.
Kᴇᴛɴ.

Sɪʀ R. Pʜɪʟʟɪᴍᴏʀᴇ.

Chancellor Kent, and great jurists of all countries, have continually referred.

"It has been contended," Lord Stowell says, "that such a sentence is perfectly legal, both on principle and authority. It is said that on principle the security and consummation of the capture is as complete in a neutral port as in the port of the belligerent himself. On the mere principle of security it may perhaps be so, but it is to be remembered that this is a matter not to be governed by abstract principles alone; the use and practice of nations have intervened, and shifted the matter from its foundations of that species; the expression which Grotius uses on these occasions (placuit gentibus) is, in my opinion, perfectly correct, intimating that there is a use and practice of nations to which we are now expected to conform": *The Henrick and Maria.* (1)

With respect to "justice, equity, convenience, and the reason of the thing," one particular class of authority has been much relied upon in the arguments of counsel, namely, the treatises of learned writers on law, and it is perhaps in this case especially important to assign a proper, and not an extravagant, value to these digests of the principles of public and international jurisprudence.

"All writers upon the law of nations unanimously acknowledge it," was a fact that weighed greatly with Lord Stowell in the case of the *Maria*, which established the belligerent's right of search.

Mr. Wheaton says:—

"Text writers of authority, shewing what is the approved usage of nations, or the general opinion respecting their mutual conduct, with the definitions and modifications introduced by general consent," are placed as the second branch of international law": Elem. of Int. Law, vol. i. p. 59.

Lord Mansfield, deciding a case in which ambassadorial privileges were concerned, said that he remembered a case before Lord Talbot, in which he

"Had declared a clear opinion that the law of nations was to be collected from the practice of different nations and the authority of writers. Accordingly he argued and determined from such instances and the authority of Grotius, Barbeyrac, Bynkershoek, Wiquefort, &c., there being no English writer of eminence upon the subject."

Chancellor Kent says:—

"In cases where the principal jurists agree the presumption will be very great in favour of the solidity of their maxims, and no civilized nation that does not arrogantly set all ordinary law and justice at defiance will venture to disregard the uniform sense of the established writers of international law"; Kent's Com. vol. i. p. 19.

(1) 4 C. Rob. 54, 55.

1876

THE QUEEN

v.

KEYN.

Sir R. Phillimore.

Ortolan (Dipl. de la Mer. l. 1, p. 74) has some very sensible remarks on this subject, which he thus concludes :—

"Ces publicistes ont non-seulement fourni, pour la gestion des affaires extérieures, une branche de droit international, qui supplée aux lacunes des autres et avertit de leurs vices, mais ils ont même contribué puissamment à la formation et à l'amélioration graduelle du droit international positif."

It is also the opinion of a very learned living jurist (Dr. Franz von Holzendorf, Encycl. der Rechtsw. IV. Das Europäische Völkerrecht, p. 935), that the usage and practice of international law is in great measure founded upon the tardy recognition of principles which have been long before taught and recommended by the voice of wise and discerning men, and that thus the fabric of international jurisprudence has been built up.

Of course the value of these responsa prudentum is affected by various circumstances; for instance, the period at which the particular work was written, the general reputation of the writer, the reception which his work has met with from the authorities of civilized states, are circumstances, which, though in no case rendering his opinion a substitute for reason, may enhance or derogate from the consideration due to it.

With these preliminary observations, I proceed to inquire what is the nature and extent of the jurisdiction over the high seas, which international law confers upon or concedes to the sovereign of the adjacent territory.

Whatever may have been the claims asserted by nations in times past—and perhaps no nation has been more extravagant than England in this matter—it is at the present time an unquestionable proposition of international jurisprudence, that the high seas are of right navigable by the ships of all states. Whether the reasons upon which this liberty of navigation rests be, as some jurists say, that the open sea is incapable of continuous occupation and insusceptible of permanent appropriation, or, as other jurists say, that the use of it is inexhaustible, and, therefore, common to all mankind; or, whether it rests upon both these, or upon other reasons also, it is unnecessary to inquire. This liberty of navigation is a fact recognised by all civilized states.

An important corollary of this proposition is that the merchant

1876

THE QUEEN
v.
KEYN.

Sir R. Phillimore.

vessel (with ships of war we are not now concerned) on the open sea is subject only to the law of her flag, that is, the law of the state to which she belongs.

The next proposition, though it be of an elementary kind, to which attention should be drawn, is, that every state is entitled to exclusive dominion over its own territory, that is, not only over the soil and over all subjects, but over all foreigners commorant therein.

"When," says Marshall, C.J., " private individuals of one nation spread themselves through another as business or caprice may direct, mingling indiscriminately with the inhabitants of that other, or when merchant vessels enter for the purposes of trade, it would be obviously inconvenient and dangerous to society, and would subject the laws to continual infraction, and the government to degradation, if such individuals or merchants did not owe temporary and local allegiance, and were not amenable, to the jurisdiction of the country": *Schooner Exchange* v. *McFaddon and Others.* (1)

The question as to dominion over portions of the seas inclosed within headlands or contiguous shores, such as the King's Chambers, is not now under consideration. It is enough to say that within this term "territory" are certainly comprised the ports and harbours, and the space between the flux and reflux of tide, or the land up to the furthest point at which the tide recedes. But it is at this point that the difficulty presented by the case before us begins, and here the following questions present themselves for solution:—

1. Is a state entitled to any extension of dominion beyond low-water mark?

2. If so, how far does this territory, or do these territorial waters, as they are usually called, extend?

3. Has a state the same dominion over these territorial waters as over the territory of her soil and in her ports, or is it of a more limited character and confined to certain purposes?

With respect to the first of these questions the answer may be given without doubt or hesitation, namely, that a state is entitled to a certain extension of territory, in a certain sense of that word, beyond low-water mark.

With respect to the second question, the distance to which the territorial waters extend, it appears on an examination of the

(1) 7 Cranch's Rep. (U.S.) 145.

1876

THE QUEEN
v.
KEYN.

Sir R. Phillimore.

authorities that the distance has varied (setting aside even more extravagant claims) from 100 to 3 miles, the present limit.

Grotius may be said to be the first accredited writer who introduced the principle of limiting the dominion to the distance to which protection could reach it from the shore :—

"Videtur autem imperium in maris portionem eadem ratione acquiri, qua imperia alia, id est, ut supra diximus, ratione personarum et ratione territorii. Ratione personarum, ut si classis, qui maritimus est exercitus, aliquo in loco maris se habeat ratione territorii, quatenus ex terra cogi possunt, qui in proxima maris parte versantur, nec minus quam si in ipsa terra reperirentur ": Grotius de Jure Belli et P., l. 2, cap. iii. s. 13, s. 2.

Bynkershoek, adopting this principle, pronounced "potestatem terræ finiri ubi finitur armorum vis " or (De Dom. Maris, c. 2) "quousque tormenta exploduntur," a phrase constantly repeated by subsequent jurists, but he carried the idea of dominium still further:—

"Etenim transitum, quamvis inermem et innoxium, a domino recte prohiberi omnino est dicendum, licet rursus contradicat ó Μέγας (de J. B. et P. l. 2, c. 13, n. 12) . . . . de terra marique illud ipse negat, sed nullo jure. Nemo, me invito, re mea recte utitur fruitur, alia est humanitatis, alia juris regula, est longum esset id argumentum digne persequi. Sub conditione navigatio prohibebitur, quum maris usus, cætera concessus, in hac vel illa specie negetur; ut si quis piscari velit, si eo vel eo transmittere, si hac illacve merces portare, si non salutare, vel non eo, quo imperatum est, modo, si non vectigal solvere, ut quæ ejus generis sunt sexcenta hæc enim recte imperat, qui imperat mari, seu extero, seu proximo": Bynk. De Dom. Maris, c. iv.

Wolff, writing later, in 1749 A.D., says (Jus Gentium, &c., s. 128):—

"Partes maris a gentibus, quæ idem accolunt, occupari possunt, quousque dominium in iisdem tueri possunt. Idem intelligitur de finibus et fretis. Etenim in istiusmodi maris partibus prope littora usus, qui in piscatione et collectione rerum in mari nascentium, non in sola navigatione consistit, semper innoxius, cum mare regionibus maritimis vicem munimenti præbeat, ac ideo intersit accolarum, ne cuilibet ibidem cum armatis navibus versari liceat."

Vattel (1), who borrowed largely from Wolff, and whom he often merely abridged, says :—

"It is not easy to determine to what distance a nation may extend its rights over the sea by which it is surrounded. Bodinus pretends that according to the common right of all maritime nations the prince's dominion extends to the distance of thirty leagues from the coast. But this exact determination can only

---

(1) Vattel's Law of Nations, book i. chap. xxiii. sec. 289.

be founded on a general consent of nations, which it would be difficult to prove. Each state may on this head make what regulation it pleases, so far as respects the transactions of the citizens with each other, or their concerns with the sovereign; but between nation and nation all that can reasonably be said is, that in general the dominion of the state over the neighbouring sea extends as far as her safety renders it necessary and her power is able to assert it."

But this author draws an important distinction between the authority of a state over what has been called the maritime belt and the port or harbour. He says (1):—

" The shores of the sea incontestably belong to the nation that possesses the country of which they are a part, and they belong to the class of public things. If civilians have set them down as things common to all mankind (res communes), it is only in regard to their use, and we are not thence to conclude that they considered them as independent of the empire; the very contrary appears from a great number of laws." Observe what follows: " Ports and harbours are manifestly an appendage to, and even a part of, the country, and consequently are the property of the nation. Whatever is said of the land itself will equally apply to them, so far as respects the consequences of the domain and of the empire."

When Azuni wrote in 1796 his "Systema dei Principii del Diritto Maritimo," he complained that the limit was still undecided (sempre combattuto e non ancora deciso), and hoped the three miles distance would be agreed upon, as "without doubt" it was the greatest distance cannon shot could ever be made to reach: vol. i., 67–68.

Since this period, the three-mile belt of water has been adopted in treaties and conventions, though a longer distance is still claimed for purposes of protecting the revenue against smuggling. Chancellor Kent says (2):—

"It is difficult to draw any precise or determinate conclusion, amidst the variety of opinions, as to the distance to which a state may lawfully extend its exclusive dominion over the sea adjoining its territories, and beyond those portions of the sea which are embraced by harbours, gulfs, bays, and estuaries, and over which its jurisdiction unquestionably extends. All that can reasonably be asserted is, that the dominion of the sovereign of the shore over the contiguous sea extends as far as is requisite for his safety, and for some lawful end. A more extended dominion must rest entirely upon force and maritime supremacy. According to the current of modern authority, the general territorial jurisdiction extends into the sea as far as cannon-shot will reach, and no farther, and this is generally calculated to be a marine league; and the Congress of the United

---

(1) Vattel's Law of Nations, book i. chap. xxiii. sec. 290.

(2) Kent's Com. vol. i. pp. 28, 29 (ed. 1844).

1876

THE QUEEN
v.
KEYN.

Sir R. Phillimore.

States have recognised this limitation by authorizing the district courts to take cognizance of all captures made within a marine league of the American shores. The executive authority of this country in 1793 considered the whole of Delaware Bay to be within our territorial jurisdiction, and it rested its claim upon those authorities which admit that gulfs, channels, and arms of the sea belong to the people with whose lands they are encompassed. It was intimated that the law of nations would justify the United States in attaching to their coasts an extent into the sea beyond the reach of cannon-shot.

"Considering the great extent of the line of the American coasts, we have a right to claim, for fiscal and defensive regulations, a liberal extension of maritime jurisdiction, and it would not be unreasonable, as I apprehend, to assume for domestic purposes connected with our safety and welfare, the control of the waters on our coasts, though included within lines stretching from quite distant headlands, as, for instance, from Cape Ann to Cape Cod, and from Nantucket to Montauk Point, and from that point to the capes of the Delaware, and from the south cape of Florida to the Mississippi. It is certain that our Government would be disposed to view with some uneasiness and sensibility, in the case of war between other maritime powers, the use of the waters of our coast, far beyond the reach of cannon-shot, as cruising ground for belligerent purposes."

Mr. Wheaton says (s. 188) (1):—

"The reasons which forbid the assertion of an exclusive proprietary right to the sea in general, will be found inapplicable to the particular portions of that element included in the above designations.

"(1.) Thus, in respect to those portions of the sea which form the ports, harbours, bays, and mouths of rivers of any state where the tide ebbs and flows, its exclusive right of property as well as sovereignty in those waters may well be maintained consistently with both the reasons above mentioned, as applicable to the sea in general. The state possessing the adjacent territory, by which these waters are partially surrounded and inclosed, has that physical power of constantly acting upon them, and at the same time of excluding at its pleasure the action of any other state or person which, as we have already seen, constitutes possession. These waters cannot be considered as having been intended by the Creator for the common use of all mankind any more than the adjacent land which has already been appropriated by a particular people. Neither the material nor the moral obstacle to the exercise of the exclusive rights of property and dominion exists in this case. Consequently the state within whose territorial limits these waters are included has the right of excluding every other nation from their use,"—a very important test of dominium, I may observe in passing. The writer continues,—"The exercise of this right may be modified by compact, express or implied; but its existence is founded upon the mutual independence of nations, which entitles every state to judge for itself as to the manner in which the right is to be exercised subject to the equal reciprocal rights of all other states to establish similar regulations in respect to their own waters." The learned writer, having thus spoken of contiguous

_____

(1) Wheaton's International Law (Dana), pp. 188-190.

1876

THE QUEEN
v.
KEYN.

Sir R. Phillimore.

waters, continues (s. 189): "It may perhaps be thought that these considerations do not apply with the same force to those portions of the sea which wash the coasts of any particular state, within the distance of a marine league, or as far as a cannon-shot will reach from the shore. The physical power of exercising an exclusive property and jurisdiction, and of excluding the action of other nations within these limits, exists to a certain degree; but the moral power may perhaps seem to extend no further than to exclude the action of other nations to the injury of the state by which this right is claimed. It is upon this ground that is founded the acknowledged immunity of a neutral state from the exercise of acts of hostility by one belligerent power against another, within those limits. This claim has, however, been sometimes extended to exclude other nations from the innocent use of the waters washing the shores of a particular state in peace and in war; as, for example, for the purpose of participating in the fishery, which is generally appropriated to the subjects of the state within that distance of the coasts. This exclusive claim is sanctioned both by usage and convention, and must be considered as forming a part of the positive law of nations."

In the valuable Traité des Prises Maritimes, published during the Crimean War (1855) (vol. i., p. 93), it is stated that the "portée du canon" is recognised as the true limit of territorial waters. Lastly, Massé, in his recent edition of Le Droit Commercial dans ses rapports avec le Droit des Gens, observes:—

That a state has not "la pleine propriété de la mer littorale: il a seulement juridiction sur cette partie de la mer: 'Quamvis in mare non sit territorium,' dit Roccus (cent. 2, resp. 3, n. 10) 'tamen in eo jurisdictio exercetur (3):' ou plutôt la propriété est grévée d'une servitude naturelle au profit de tous les peuples navigateurs. Cependant il en est autrement pour la pêche, qui ne peut être faite que par les habitants du littoral." He then says:—"C'est, du reste, un point fort difficile à décider en théorie pure, que celui de savoir quelle est l'étendue de la mer littorale."

He proceeds to examine the different theories upon the subject, and concludes by adopting that of the cannon-shot or three-miles distance, but admits that a greater distance is claimed by some nations.

The third question, though touched upon in the preceding citations, remains to be substantively considered; it is one of much importance, viz., whether, admitting that the state has a dominion over three miles of adjacent water, it is the same dominion which the possessor has over her land and her ports, or is it of a more limited character—limited to the purpose of protecting the adjacent shore, for which it was granted, and not extending to a general sovereignty over all passing vessels, and therefore not improbably called ligne de respect? Pando, the Spanish jurist

1876

THE QUEEN
v.
KEYN.

Sir R. Phillimore.

(following the authority and adopting almost the very words of Martens), observes (Elementos del Derecho Internacional, p. 155):—

" But we ought not to carry beyond certain limits what a writer calls the *línea de respecto.* The meaning of this conventional phrase is that we should not do within this line anything that the government of the country has a right to prevent, as being an attempt on the property and security of the nation."

An authority relied upon by the counsel for the Crown was Loccenius de Jure Maritimo, chap. iv. (De imperio Maris, s. 5.) That author observes that some learned jurists have claimed a jurisdiction of two days' journey from the coasts, others sixty miles, others one hundred ; and then he proceeds,—

" Alii strictius et brevius determinant ; præsertim si mare interjacens eousque se non extendat : nimirum ut unicuique juxta sua littora competat dominium ; extra ea, quatenus classe locum occupavit, vel quousque ejus territorium juxta mare porrigitur. . . . . Communiter tamen delictum in mari particulari perpetratum in illa civitate vel republica puniri solet, ad cujus jurisdictionem mare spectat, cujusque portui locus ille maris propinquior est. . . . Sed si crimen in mari inter duas urbes æqualiter distantes commissum sit, ejus cognitio ad utramque per concursum jurisdictionis pertinebit ; quia delictum commissum est in confinio, quod est commune utriusque civitatis. Si vero eadem pars maris ad plures pertineat, illi omnes poterunt cognoscere ; ita tamen ut sit præventioni locus. Prævenire autem dicitur, qui delinquentem cepit in mari, licet alius judex prius eum citarit. . . . ."

Surely the extravagance of these propositions according to recognised modern international law carries with them their own refutation.

It is right to mention here that the authority of Heineccius was properly cited by the counsel for the Crown as supporting his proposition. The passage is,—

" Extori, qui in territorio nostro sunt, sunt subditi temporarii ; ita qui in mari nostro navigant. Hinc nullum est dubium quin puniri a Belgis possit, qui in mari hoc australi piraticam exercuit, vel homicidium commisit, quamvis sit exterus." (1)

Another authority relied upon was Casaregis ; that writer gives his opinion boldly :—

" Eandem prorsus jurisdictionem, qua princeps in terrestri suo territorio potitur, etiam habet in mari eidem suo terrestri territorio adjacente ; *nam totum illud mare, quod suo territorio usque ad centum milliaria,* non interruptum ab jurisdictione alterius vicini principis, adjacet, non minus reputatur suum proprium territorium, quam tota terra in qua ipse regit ut dominatur. . . . ."

(1) Heineccius, lib. ii. cap. iii. sec. xii. ad Grotium.

1876

THE QUEEN
v.
KEYN.

Sir R. Phillimore.

" Ideoque in vim talis jurisdictionis potest Princeps Gabellas et Vectigalia in mari suo, suisque portubus imponere, easque à vehentibus merces per mare suum exigere . . . .; inibique navigationes permittere, vel prohibere, vel alias quascumque leges statuere, etsi adversus præscripta factum fuerit ; naves arrestare, ut merces confiscare valet . . . ."

Casaregis then proceeds to state pretty broadly the extent of jurisdiction over foreigners in their territorial waters :—

" Potest insuper omnes, ut *quoslibet delinquentes in navibus,* vel navigiis existentibus in illius portubus, *vel ejus mari dicto suo territorio adjacente* punire, quinimmo capitaneus, seu magister navis, vel cujuslibet navigii *tales delinquentes* eidem principi, vel ejus judici præsentare ut per eum juxta illius leges puniantur . . .

" Pariterque pro debitis civilibus ad instantiam creditorum potest naves sequestrari, vel arrestari facere . . . ."

With all respect for the opinion of Casaregis I must express my dissent from these propositions of international law ; they may be the logical and legitimate conclusions from the premiss that the adjacent waters are as much, and in as unlimited a sense, territory as the land, but if so, they prove the error of the premiss.

The learned American writer, Mr. Bishop, appears also to think that this jurisdiction is exclusive and absolute, susceptible of no limitation not imposed by itself, and that over these waters foreign vessels have no right to pass if the implied licence under which they do so be withdrawn by the state : Criminal Law, I., sect. 76.

A much juster description of the authority appears to me to be given by Lord Stowell (1) :—

" Thirdly, it is an observation of law that the passage of ships over territorial portions of the sea or external water is a thing less guarded than the passage of armies over land, and for obvious reasons. An army, in the strictest state of discipline, can hardly pass into a country without great inconvenience to the inhabitants ; roads are broken up, the price of provisions is raised, the sick are quartered on individuals, and a general uneasiness and terror is excited ; but the passage of two or three vessels or of a fleet over external waters may be neither felt nor perceived. For this reason the act of inoffensively passing over such portions of water, without any violence committed there, is not considered as any violation of territory belonging to a neutral state ; permission is not usually required ; such waters are considered as the common thoroughfare of nations, though they may be so far territory as that any actual exercise of hostility is prohibited therein."

The same principle is laid down in the case of the *United States* v. *Kessler* (2), heard before the Circuit Court of the United States,

(1) *The Twee Gebroeders,* 3 C. Rob. 352.　　(2) 1 Baldwin's Rep. pp. 15, 17.

1876   Pennsylvania. The defendant was indicted for robbery and piracy

THE QUEEN   on the high seas, on board a brig called *L'Eclair*, a foreign vessel,

KEYN.   belonging exclusively to French owners, and sailing under the

Sir R. Phillimore.   French flag. Mr. Brewster, the counsel for the defendant, said

that he had no evidence to offer. He stated his ground of
defence :—

"1. That the evidence had not made out a case of general piracy, but that the
defendant, if guilty of anything, is guilty of a piracy, made so by the Acts of
Congress.

"2. That the power to define and punish piracy, given to Congress by the constitution, does not extend to any vessel under any flag but that of the United
States, although the offender be a citizen of the United States; that this being a
French vessel, and the defendant a mariner on board of her, he had, for the time
being, expatriated himself, and if guilty of any offence, can be punished only by
the laws of France; that there is no evidence that the defendant is a citizen of
the United States; that the vessel was not scuttled, nor the robbery committed
within a marine league of the coast of the United States, and, if they were, yet
the Acts of Congress do not make such acts piracy; that the indictment is imperfect and insufficient; there is no averment that the vessel was American; it
is necessary to aver that the defendant is an American citizen, and that the
owners were Americans."

It was holden by the Court that the piracy was not piracy in
the international sense, but by the Acts of Congress; and with
regard to the second question, as to the offence having been committed within a marine league of the coast, and therefore within
the territory of the United States, the learned judge (Judge
Hopkinson) expressed himself as follows:—

"It is my duty to go on one step further on this subject; you will remark that
this point becomes important to the prosecution only on account of the foreign
ownership of this brig. Had she been American, then, the crime being committed
on the high seas, it would have been immaterial whether it was within or without
the marine league of the coast, either of this or any other country; but it is
argued that although we may not have jurisdiction of an offence committed on
the high seas on board of a foreign vessel at a greater distance than three miles
from the shore, yet if it be within that distance we obtain a right to try and
punish it. I am not of this opinion. The jurisdiction of this Court is derived
wholly from the Acts of Congress on this subject. The description of the place
to which or over which it extends is the high seas. If, then, the space within
the marine league is not comprehended within this description, this Court has no
jurisdiction over it; if it be comprehended, as it certainly is, then it is so because
it is a part of the high seas in all respects and to all purposes the same as any
other part of the high seas. Nothing is added to the jurisdiction of the courts of
the United States by reason of the offence having been committed within this
distance of their coast, nothing is taken from it by reason of its having been com-

mitted within the jurisdictional limits of a foreign government, within a marine league of the shore, if done on the high seas, which are held to be any waters on the sea coast, without the boundaries of low-water mark. It follows from these principles that if this Court has no power under the Act of Congress to try and punish this offence committed on board of a foreign vessel on the ocean, it acquires no such power because she was within a marine league of our coast when the offence was committed. The principle on which nations claim this extension of their authority and jurisdictional rights for a certain distance beyond their shores is to protect their safety, peace, and honour from invasion, disturbance, and insult. They will not have their strand made a theatre of violence and bloodshed by contending belligerents. Some distance must be assumed. It varies by different jurists from one league to thirty, and again as far as a cannon will carry a ball. Such limits may be well enough for their object, but would be extraordinary boundaries of the judicial power and jurisdiction of a court of law.

"It is my opinion that whether this offence was committed within or without a marine league from the coast of the United States is of no importance to the question of the jurisdiction of this Court to hear and determine it :" *United States* v. *Kessler.* (1)

The following case deserves for several reasons attentive consideration. The judge, Sir John Nicholl, had been Queen's Advocate during a great part of the French Revolution; he was well versed in international law, and had a high judicial reputation.

In the case of *Rex* v. 49 *Casks of Brandy* (2), he observed:

"Again, it is said that there is no instance where the Admiralty has set up a claim; but is there any instance where notice has been given to the Admiralty that the goods have been picked up and brought in from a considerable distance beyond low-water mark? These goods were picked up floating at sea, and carried either to Poole or Weymouth, and was it not the duty of the lord, or his steward, to give notice where goods had been brought in from beyond low-water mark; for as to the right of the lord extending three miles beyond low water, it is quite extravagant as a jurisdiction belonging to any manor. As between nation and nation the territorial right may, by a sort of tacit understanding, be extended to three miles, but that rests upon different principles, viz., that their own subjects shall not be disturbed in their fishing, and particularly in their coasting trade and communications between place and place during war; they would be exposed to danger if hostilities were allowed to be carried on between belligerents nearer to the shore than three miles; but no person ever heard of a land jurisdiction of the body of a county which extended to three miles from the coast."

So Merlin, in his article on "Mer," (3) says:—

"De toutes les choses qui sont communes aux hommes, il n'y en a point dont l'usage ait plus d'étendue et soit plus universel que celui des mers, puisqu'il est

1876

THE QUEEN
v.
KEYN.

Sir R. Phillimore.

---

(1) 1 Baldwin's Rep. pp. 34, 35.   (2) 3 Hagg. Ad. pp. 289, 290.
(3) Merlin, Rep. de Juris, vol. x. p. 135.

1876

THE QUEEN
v.
KEYN.
Sir R. Phillimore.

naturellement propre à toutes les nations. D'où il suit, qu'aucun souverain n'a droit de s'attribuer l'empire de la mer.

"Mais la liberté d'user de la mer doit avoir des bornes, pour prévenir les inconvéniens qui auraient lieu si chacun en usait selon ses vues particulières : en effet, chaque souverain, étant bien fondé à défendre le commerce étranger dans ses possessions, et les garantir d'insulte" [observe the reason of the jurisdiction conceded],—"peut empêcher qu'on n'en approche qu'à une certaine distance.

"Ce principe établi, il n'a plus été question que de convenir, entre les souverains, de la distance jusqu'à laquelle s'étendrait leur domination respective ; et c'est à quoi ont pourvu les traités de paix et de commerce, qui ont fixé cette distance à deux lieues de la côte. Ainsi, au-delà de cette distance, la navigation doit absolument être libre, et par conséquent être exempte de toute visite de la part des commandans des garde-côtes ; mais, en deçà, on est suspect de commerce clandestin et prohibé ; c'est pourquoi on est sujet à être visité, et même à voir confisquer les marchandises et la navire, à moins qu'il n'y ait preuve qu'on n'a excédé la distance déterminée, que par force majeure."

The privilege of the three-mile belt, therefore, is granted, according to this author, for the purposes of self-defence against attacks in war and smuggling in peace.

So M. Ortolan (1), in his chapter on "Mer territoriale," observes that the right of the state to the adjacent sea

"Est fondé sur son droit de défense ;" she cannot close these waters as she may close her ports, "le droit qui existe sur la mer territoriale n'est pas un droit de propriété ; on ne peut pas dire que l'État, propriétaire des côtes, soit propriétaire de cette mer." He further says, "On sent que l'espace maritime soumis ainsi, non pas à un droit de propriété, mais à la souveraineté d'un État, doit être nécessairement renfermé dans d'étroites limites. C'est à ce régime complet que répondent expressément la dénomination de mer territoriale, et la limite commune de la plus forte portée du canon." (2)

Bluntschli (3) seems to recognize the distinction in principle between the passing and the, so to speak, commorant ship. He says :

"Les navires qui pénétrent dans les eaux d'un État étranger, jettent l'ancre dans un port étranger, remontent un fleuve, une rivière, etc., sont soumis à la souveraineté de l'État étranger, tant qu'ils restent sur le territoire maritime de ce dernier." His note is : "Les navires étrangers, comme les voyageurs étrangers, ne peuvent pas se soustraire à la souveraineté de l'État où ils se trouvent. Cette souveraineté se fait sentir, aussi bien sur la mer dépendant du territoire, que sur la terre ferme ; il n'existe aucun motif d'accorder des immunités aux navires étrangers. L'État étranger exerce donc la police sur tous les navires mouillés dans le port, et ses tribunaux sont compétents pour connaître des procès civils, comme aussi des délits

---

(1) Diplo de la Mer, vol. i. pp. 174, 175.　　(2) Diplo de la Mer, vol. i. p. 177.
(3) Le Droit International Codifie, livre iv. §§ 319, 322.

1876

THE QUEEN
v.
KEYN.

Sir R. Phillimore.

ou contraventions des matelots étrangers, lorsque le navire se trouve dans les eaux qui dépendent du territoire :" § 319.

"Les navires qui se bornent à longer les côtes d'un Etat, dans la partie de la mer qui fait partie du territoire de ce dernier, sont soumis temporairement à la souveraineté de cet État, en ce sens, qu'ils doivent respecter les ordonnances militaires, ou de police, prises par lui pour la sûreté de son territoire et de la population côtière." And his note to this is : " V. art. 302 et 310.—La juridiction de l'État riverain ne s'étend, sur la 'mer voisine,' que dans la mesure jugée nécessaire par la police et les autorités militaires. Le navire est, sous tous les autres rapports, aussi libre que s'il se trouvait en pleine mer, c'est-à-dire qu'il est regardé comme une partie flottante des territoires de l'État dont il dépend :" § 322.

The authority of Kaltenborn, which is certainly respectable, he writes in 1851, is directly in favour of the exemption of the passing vessel from the law of the state. [Endlich muss wohl davon als befreit ansehen die bloss vorübersegelnden Schiffe.] He differs from Heffter, inasmuch as Heffter applies the same exemption to vessels forced into port by stress of weather. Heffter appears to have changed his opinion to a certain extent on the question, but in the French edition of 1873, he expressly exempts from the territorial jurisdiction "les navires ne faisant que traverser les eaux qui coulent en avant d'un port :" Droit Inter. § 72, v. 3. This author appears to have had in his mind the passage in the Digest, l. v. t. l. xix. :

"Nam ubi sic venit, ut confestim discedat, et quasi a viatore, vel eo qui transvehebatur vel eo qui παρέπλει, emit, durissimum est, quotquot locis quis navigans vel iter faciens delatus est, tot locis se defendere."

The sound conclusions which result from the investigation of the authorities which have been referred to appear to me to be these :—

The consensus of civilised independent states has recognised a maritime extension of frontier to the distance of three miles from low-water mark, because such a frontier or belt of water is necessary for the defence and security of the adjacent state.

It is for the attainment of these particular objects that a dominium has been granted over this portion of the high seas.

This proposition is materially different from the proposition contended for, namely, that it is competent to a state to exercise within these waters the same rights of jurisdiction and property which appertain to it in respect to its lands and its ports. There is one obvious test by which the two sovereignties may be distinguished.

1876

THE QUEEN
v.
KEYN.

Sir R. Phillimore.

According to modern international law, it is certainly a right incident to each state to refuse a passage to foreigners over its territory by land, whether in time of peace or war. But it does not appear to have the same right with respect to preventing the passage of foreign ships over this portion of the high seas.

In the former case there is no jus transitus; in the latter case there is.

The reason of the thing, that is, the defence and security of the state, does not require or warrant the exclusion of peaceable foreign vessels from passing over these waters; and the custom and usage of nations has not sanctioned it.

Consequences fraught with mischief and injustice might flow from the opposite doctrine, which would render applicable to a foreign vessel while in itinere from one foreign port to another, passing over these waters, all the criminal law of the adjacent territory. No single instance has been brought to our notice of the practical exercise by any nation of this jurisdiction.

The authorities cited in order to shew that a foreign vessel is subject to the laws of the foreign port which she enters appear to me inapplicable to the present case.

A foreign merchant vessel going into the port of a foreign state subjects herself to the ordinary law of the place during the period of her commorancy there; she is as much a subditus temporaneus as the individual who visits the interior of the country for the purposes of pleasure or business.

It may be that the foreign state, influenced by considerations of public policy or by treaty obligations, chooses to forego the exercise of her law over the foreign vessel and crew, or exercises it only when they disturb the peace and good order of the port. This is the course which France has usually pursued; an illustration of it is furnished by the case cited from Dalloz (Juris Gen. 1859, "Cour de Cassation," pp. 88, 89), the result of which is correctly stated in the marginal note.

"Les bâtiments de commerce étrangers, stationnant dans un port français, sont soumis à la juridiction territoriale pour ce qui concerne les délits entre étrangers et notamment entre gens de l'équipage, dont la répression n'intéresse pas exclusivement la discipline et l'administration intérieure du bord : C. Nap. 3 ;. Av. Cons. d'Et. 20 Nov. 1806."

1876

THE QUEEN
v.
KEYN.

Sir R. Phillimore.

"Il en est ainsi, surtout, lorsque ces délits sont de nature à compromettre la tranquillité du port, ou lorsque l'intervention de l'autorité locale a été réclamée."

I cannot entertain any doubt that in this country a foreign sailor, complaining of the ill-treatment of his master on board a foreign ship in an English port, would be entitled to the protection of an English court of justice.

If, indeed, as has been contended, there be no difference between the jurisdiction by the adjacent state over vessels in ports and over passing and commorant vessels, then the whole criminal law of England was applicable to the crew and those on board the German vessel, so long as she was within a marine league of the English shore.

The consequences of such a position of law appear to me, especially in the absence of any precedent, sufficient to render it untenable.

There is yet another argument, already partially adverted to, which appears to me entitled to great weight in an English court of justice.

Upon the subject of the three-miles belt of territorial water, Parliament has frequently legislated. It might perhaps be not impertinently asked, why, if these waters are territorial in the same sense as the land, and those who traverse them are already subject to the law. But, passing by this observation, it will be found on examination of the statutes that the provisions in them are either framed exclusively for British subjects and ships, or that they relate to the protection and peace of the state.

The statutes are as follows :—

By the existing Customs Consolidation Act, 16 & 17 Vict. c. 10, and section 212, it is enacted that, "If any ship or boat belonging wholly or in part to Her Majesty's subjects, or having half the persons on board subjects of Her Majesty, shall be found or discovered to have been within four leagues of that part of the coast of the United Kingdom which is between the North Foreland, on the coast of Kent, and Beachy Head, on the coast of Sussex, or within eight leagues of any other part of the coast of the United Kingdom ; or if any foreign ship or boat having one or more subjects of Her Majesty on board, shall be found or discovered to have been within three leagues of the coast of the United Kingdom, or if any foreign ship or boat shall be found or discovered to have been within one league of the coast of the United Kingdom, or if any ship or boat shall be found or discovered to have been within one league of the Channel Islands, any such ship or boat so found or discovered, having on board or in any manner attached thereto, or having had on board or in any manner attached thereto, or conveying

1876

THE QUEEN
v.
KEYN.

Sir R. Phillimore.

or having conveyed in any manner, any spirits, &c., &c., then and in every such case the said spirits, &c. &c., and also the ship or boat, shall be forfeited."

By 33 & 34 Vict. c. 90 (Foreign Enlistment Act), it is enacted, s. 2, "This Act shall extend to all the dominions of Her Majesty, including the adjacent territorial waters."

Sect. 14: "If, during the continuance of any war in which Her Majesty may be neutral, any ship, goods, or merchandize, captured as prize of war within the territorial jurisdiction of Her Majesty, in violation of the neutrality of this realm, or captured by any ship which may have been built, equipped, commissioned, or despatched, or the force of which may have been augmented, contrary to the provisions of this Act, are brought within the limits of Her Majesty's dominions by the captor, or any agent of the captor, or by any person having come into possession thereof, with knowledge that the same was prize of war so captured as aforesaid, it shall be lawful for the original owner of such prize, or his agent, or for any person authorized in that behalf by the government of the foreign state to which such owner belongs, to make application to the Court of Admiralty for seizure and detention of such prize, and the Court shall, on due proof of the facts, order such prize to be restored."

By 17 & 18 Vict. c. 104, part IX., s. 502, it is enacted, "The ninth part of this Act shall apply to the whole of Her Majesty's dominions."

Ib., Part X., s. 517: "The tenth part of this Act shall in all cases, where no particular country is mentioned, apply to the whole of Her Majesty's dominions."

Sect. 527: "Whenever any injury has, in any part of the world, been caused to any property belonging to Her Majesty or to any of Her Majesty's subjects, by any foreign ship, if at any time thereafter such ship is found in any port or river of the United Kingdom, or within three miles of the coast thereof, it shall be lawful for the judge of any Courts of record in the United Kingdom, or for the judge of the High Court of Admiralty, or, in Scotland, the Court of Session, or the sheriff of the county within whose jurisdiction such ship may be, upon its being shewn to him by any person applying summarily that such injury was probably caused by the misconduct or want of skill of the master or mariners of such ship, to issue an order directed to any officer of customs or other officer named by such judge, requiring him to detain such ship until such time as the owner, master, or consignee thereof, has made satisfaction in respect of such injury, or has given security, to be approved by the judge, to abide the event of any action, suit, or other legal proceeding that may be instituted in respect of such injury, and to pay all costs and damages that may be awarded thereon; and any officer of customs or other officer to whom such order is directed shall detain such ship accordingly."

By 18 & 19 Vict. c. 91, s. 21 (Merchant Shipping Act Amendment): "If any person, being a British subject, charged with having committed any crime or offence on board any British ship on the high seas or in any foreign port or harbour, or if any person, not being a British subject, charged with having committed any crime or offence on board any British ship on the high seas, is found within the jurisdiction of any Court of justice in Her Majesty's dominions, which would have had cognizance of such crime or offence if committed within the limits of its ordinary jurisdiction, such Court shall have jurisdiction to hear and try the case as if such crime or offence had been committed within such limits."

The foreign ship is not mentioned in this section, which is

1876

THE QUEEN
v.
KEYN.

Sir R. Phillimore.

therefore applicable only to British ships, because it is an established principle as to the construction of a statute that it should be construed, if the words will permit, so as to be in accordance with the principles of international law.

By 25 & 26 Vict. c. 63, s. 54 (the Merchant Shipping Acts, &c., Amendment): "The owners of any ship, whether British or foreign, shall not, in cases where all or any of the following events occur, without their actual fault or privity" (here the different events are specified) "be answerable in damages in respect of loss of life or personal injury, either alone or together, with loss or damage to ships, boats, goods, merchandise, &c., to an aggregate amount exceeding 15*l.* for each ton of their ship's tonnage; nor in respect of loss or damage to ships, goods, merchandise, &c., whether there be in addition loss of life or personal injury or not, to an aggregate amount exceeding 8*l.* for each ton of the ship's tonnage," &c.

Then in the same section there are two other provisions made concerning the measurement of foreign ships.

By 36 & 37 Vict. c. 85, s. 16 (Merchant Shipping Acts Amendment), it is enacted, "In every case of collision between two vessels, it shall be the duty of the master or person in charge of each vessel, if and so far as he can do so without danger to his own vessel, crew, and passengers (if any), to stay by the other vessel until he has ascertained that she has no need of further assistance, and to render to the other vessel, her master, crew, and passengers (if any) such assistance as may be practicable and as may be necessary in order to save them from any danger caused by the collision; and also to give to the master or person in charge of the other vessel the name of his own vessel, and of her port of registry, or of the port or place to which she belongs, and also the names of the ports and places from which and to which she is bound.

"If he fails so to do, and no reasonable cause for such failure is shewn, the collision shall, in the absence of proof to the contrary, be deemed to have been caused by his wrongful acts, neglect, or default."

So far the statute applies to all vessels, and then follows a section making the offence criminal, but especially confining it to the navigation of British vessels:—

"Every master and person in charge of a British vessel who fails, without reasonable cause, to render such assistance or give such information as aforesaid shall be deemed guilty of a misdemeanor, and if he is a certificated officer an inquiry into his conduct may be held, and his certificate may be cancelled or suspended."

Then the statute continues with a provision as to civil actions applicable to all vessels:—

Sect. 17: "If in any case of collision it is proved to the Court before which the case is tried that any of the regulations for preventing collision contained in

1876

THE QUEEN
v.
KEYN.

Sir R. Phillimore.

or made under the Merchant Shipping Acts, 1854 to 1873, has been infringed, the ship by which such regulation has been infringed shall be deemed to be in fault, unless it is shewn to the satisfaction of the Court that the circumstances of the case made departure from the regulation necessary."

We are now in effect and substance asked to extend the criminal jurisdiction confined by this statute to the masters of British vessels to the master of a foreign vessel.

Upon the whole, I am of opinion that the Court had no jurisdiction over this foreigner for an offence committed on board a foreign ship on the high seas, though within three miles of the coast; that he is governed by the law of the state to which his flag belongs; and that the conviction cannot be sustained.

Lindley, J.

LINDLEY, J.　In order to determine this case it is necessary to consider,—1. Whether that part of the high seas which adjoins the English coasts (and which for convenience may be called its coast waters) is subject to the criminal law of England: If it is, then—2. Whether that law applies to foreigners when on board a foreign ship sailing over such coast waters; and if it does, to what extent.

The distance seawards from the shores of England to which its criminal law extends is not declared in any statute and has never been authoritatively decided.　The question must therefore be investigated upon principle.

It is laid down in English law books of the highest authority that the seas adjoining the English coast are part of the realm of England, and are subject to the dominion of the Crown. (1)　Indeed there is considerable authority (2) for saying that those seas are to some distance part of the property of the Crown, subject to the right of the public freely to navigate them; but it is not necessary for the purposes of this case to affirm this proposition to its full extent.　It is sufficient to shew that the English criminal law extends over the seas in question.

Lord Hale, in his Pleas of the Crown, expressly treats the sea adjoining the coast, though it may be high sea, as within the

(1) Co. Lit. 206a, b; Hale de Jure Maris, pt. i. c. 4; Com. Dig. Prerog. b. 1.

(2) Hale, ubi supra; Gammel v. Commissioners of Woods, &c., 3 Macq. 419;

Gann v. Free Fishers of Whitstable, 11 H. L. C. 192; Foreman v. Same, Law Rep. 4 H. L. 266; see also 21 & 22 Vict. c. 109, s. 2, as to mines below low-water mark.

1876

THE QUEEN
v.
KEYN.

Lindley, J.

King's realm of England. (1)   He further says, "Special commissions to hear and determine offences upon the coast, Secundum legem et consuetudinem regni Angliæ, did often issue." (2)

In this passage he uses the word "coast;" but it is plain from the context that he does not mean by "coast" the land next the sea, but the sea next the land.

It further appears from the same writer that the Court of Admiralty had jurisdiction to deal with certain crimes committed on the high seas out of the bodies of counties; and since 38 Edw. III., and until Lord Hale's time, no other court in England took cognizance of crimes there committed.   The jurisdiction thus exercised does not appear to have been limited as regards distance from the shore.

By the statute 28 Hen. 8, c. 15, which was passed in order to remedy certain defects in the practice and procedure of the Court of Admiralty in criminal cases, it was enacted (s. 1) :—

" That all treasons, felonies, robberies, murders, and confederacies hereafter to be committed in or upon the sea, or in any other haven, river, creek, or place where the Admiralty or admirals have or pretend to have power, authority, or jurisdiction, shall be inquired, tried, heard, determined, and judged in such shires and places in the realm as shall be limited in the king's commission or commissions, to be directed for the same in like form and condition as if any such offence or offences had been committed or done in or upon the land:" and (s. 2) " that such persons to whom such commission or commissions shall be directed, or four of them at the least, shall have full power and authority to inquire if such offences and every of them by the oaths of twelve good and lawful inhabitants in the shire, limited in their commission in such manner and form as if such offences had been committed upon the land within the same shire; and that every indictment found and presented before such commissioners of any treasons, felonies, robberies, murders, manslaughters, or such other offences, committed or done in or upon the seas, or in or upon any haven, river, or creek, shall be good and effectual in the law."

I do not understand this statute as extending the jurisdiction of the commissioners appointed under this statute, either over a larger district or over a larger or different class of persons than there was jurisdiction over before.   But the statute shews that, both as regards distance from the shore and as regards persons, the jurisdiction to punish crimes on the high seas was as wide as it could be; and the statute did extend the jurisdiction of the com-

(1) See vol. i. p. 154, and vol. ii. pp. 12–15, Wilson's ed.
(2) Vol. ii. p. 15.

1876

THE QUEEN
*.
KEYN.
Lindley, J.

missioners over offences not triable before. The statute is, in fact, an express legislative enactment that the crimes there specified if committed on the seas are to be tried and punished according to English law, and the crime of manslaughter is one of those mentioned in this statute.

By 39 Geo. 3, c. 37, this enactment was in effect extended to all offences committed upon the high seas out of the body of any county. This statute again assumes that, as regards geographical limits, and persons within those limits, the jurisdiction of the commissioners appointed to try offences on the high seas was as wide as it could be; and the statute again extended that jurisdiction as regards the offences triable by commissioners.

The joint effect of these two statutes was, in my opinion, to make the criminal law of England applicable over the high seas so far as it was competent for Parliament so to make it. Provision was made for the appointment of commissioners to carry these enactments into operation; and in practice the Court of Admiralty exercised the jurisdiction thus created.

Similar general language is used in those more modern statutes which have transferred to the Central Criminal Court (1), and to the judges of assize (2), the jurisdiction of the above-mentioned commissioners and of the Admiralty over crimes committed on the high seas.

Those statutes however have not extended the criminal law to persons or places not previously subject to it. The statutes speak of offences on the high seas and other places within the jurisdiction of the Admiralty. Unless, therefore, it can be shewn that prior to the passing of these last-mentioned statutes the prisoner could have been properly convicted, according to the law of England, by commissioners appointed under the older statutes, that is, by the Court of Admiralty, his conviction cannot be supported.

It is necessary, therefore, to fall back on the jurisdiction of the Court of Admiralty as recognised in and as declared and extended by 28 Hen. 8, c. 15, and 39 Geo. 3, c. 37. In other words, it is necessary to consider what limits there were to such jurisdiction as regards offences committed on the high seas.

(1) 4 & 5 Wm. 4, c. 36, s. 22.
(2) 7 & 8 Vict. c. 2; see also 24 & 25 Vict. c. 100, s. 68.

The jurisdiction is assumed throughout to have been as extensive as it could be. The question therefore is, how extensive could it be?

This brings us at once to the consideration of the limits of the legislative power of this country and of the jurisdiction of its Courts, and there being no other limit than that set by international law, those limits must be sought for amongst the recognised authorities on that branch of jurisprudence. Here, however, a fresh difficulty presents itself; for there are no treaties and there is no established practice bearing directly on the subject under consideration. But there are, in my opinion, certain general principles sufficiently well established to afford a basis for the decision of the case before us.

The controversy between Grotius in his Mare Liberum and Selden in his Mare Clausum has been observed upon by almost every writer on international law since their day; and the result has been that whilst the extravagant propositions contended for by each of these celebrated men have been long ago exploded, it appears to me to be now agreed by the most esteemed writers on international law that, subject to the right of all ships freely to navigate the high seas, every state has full power to enact and enforce what laws it thinks proper for the preservation of peace and the protection of its own interests, over those parts of the high seas which adjoin its own coasts and are within three miles thereof. But that beyond this limit, or, at all events, beyond the reach of artillery on its own coasts, no state has any power to legislate save over its own subjects and over persons on board ships carrying its flag.

This general principle is based on various grounds, and is made subject to various exceptions, as will be seen by reference to the authorities referred to below; but in the above general result and to this limited extent all modern writers appear to agree; and Mr. Bishop in his well-known work is, I think, right in his statement (made with express reference to criminal law), that "the sea adjoining the coast is within the territorial sovereignty which controls the adjacent shores." (1)

The contention of Mr. Benjamin, that the high seas adjoining the land are not to all legal intents and purposes the same as the

(1) Bishop, Crim. Law, § 104, 5th ed.

land, appears to me to be well founded; for those seas are subject
to a freedom of passage which land is certainly not; and but for
the statutes above referred to, or some other enactment or evidence
shewing that offences on the high seas were punishable by English
law, I should not hold that the criminal law applicable to the land
had any application beyond it.

I am, however, unable to assent to Mr. Benjamin's further contention, viz., that the dominion of a state over the seas adjoining
its shores exists only for certain definite purposes for which such
dominion has been conceded to it by other nations; i. e., the protection of its coasts from the effects of hostilities between other
nations which may be at war, the protection of its revenue and of
its fisheries, and the preservation of order by its police. On the
contrary, I think the weight of authority is entirely in favour of a
general dominion for all purposes consistent with peaceful navigation.

In support of this proposition numerous authorities ancient and
modern may be referred to. Amongst them, the most important
are the following : *The Leda* (1), in which the United Kingdom was
held to include three miles from its shore. The judgment of Vice-
Chancellor Wood, in *General Iron Screw Co.* v. *Schurmanns* (2),
which shews that the right of Parliament to legislate over an area
of three miles from the shore is not open to doubt; and that
in construing any Act of Parliament the question is, whether
it was meant to operate over the whole of that territory within
which there is the right to legislate; Wheaton's Elements of International Law, part ii. ch. 4, ss. 6–10, pp. 233 et seq. et ed. 6,
and part ii. ch. 2, ss. 2 and 13, pp. 113, 174; Kent's International Law, p. 115, Abdy's ed.; Kent's Commentaries, vol. i. p. 28,
&c., which, I think, correctly states the result of the authorities on
this point; Manning's Law of Nations, p. 119, Amos' edition. This
writer restricts the dominion over the three miles to definite purposes, but he cites no authorities for such restriction, and other
writers do not so restrict it; Phillimore's International Law, vol. i.
ch. 4, s. 154, and ch. 8, s. 196, &c.; Marten's Précis du droit des
Gens, book 4, ch. iv. ss. 152–4 (vol. i. p. 399, &c., and see especially p. 402, Verge's ed. of 1864, and book 2, ch. i. ss. 40, 41;

(1) Swa. Adm. 40.   (2) 1 J. & H. 193, et seq.

vol. i. p. 144, same edition); Ortolan, Diplomatie de la Mer, vol. i. book 2, ch. viii. see particularly p. 157, ed. 4; Hautefeuille, Des droits et des devoirs des nations neutres, vol. i. tit. ch. 3 (pp. 82, &c., ed. 2), and tit. 6, s. 1 (p. 287, &c., see particularly p. 297); Heffter Le droit international pub. de l'Europe (Bergson's French translation), book 1, s. 75, p. 149, &c., and s. 79, p. 161, &c.; Bluntschli, Droit international codifié, 2nd French edition, ss. 302, 319, 322.   Indeed, from the time of Bynkerschoek, downwards, the principle here referred to has been in process of establishment; and there being such a concurrence of opinion amongst writers on international law, and no treaty or practice, or indeed, opinion, expressed to the contrary, it appears to me that the rule, to the limited extent above mentioned, ought to be judicially treated as now established, the more so as such rule has been already judicially acted upon by the civil tribunals of this country in the cases to which I have already referred: see Lord Mansfield's observations in 3 Burr. 1471.

The right of every vessel to pass over the high seas adjoining the English coast has more than once been judicially recognised by the highest Court in the realm (see *The Whitstable Fishery Cases* referred to above; see also *The Twee Gebroeders* (1)) and cannot be denied, so long as there is no law expressly prohibiting it. No general words in any statute can properly be construed so as to interfere with or restrict such right unless it be abused.

The conviction of the prisoner in this case in no way diminishes the right of foreigners to sail peaceably along the English coast waters; that right is not questioned by the prosecution and is conceded to the fullest extent.

For these reasons I have arrived at the conclusion that, speaking generally and subject to such exception, if any, as can be established, the general language of the statutes, 28 Hen. 8, c. 15, and 39 Geo. 3, c. 37, may properly be construed as having made punishable by English law all offences committed within the conventional limit of three miles from our shores.

Nevertheless, if these statutes had already been judicially construed in such a way, as to shew that they had no general application to the English coast waters as part of our maritime territory,

_____
(1) 3 C. Rob. 336.

1876

THE QUEEN
v.
KEYN.

Lindley, J.

1876

THE QUEEN
v.
KEYN.
Lindley, J.

I should unhesitatingly adopt that construction; but, in truth, no interpretation involving this point has ever yet been put upon them.

We have now to consider for the first time what construction ought to be put upon them, and having regard to their objects and to the inconveniences which will follow if they are not construed as widely as is consistent with their language, and with established principles, I am clearly of opinion that they ought to be construed as widely as they properly can; and in expressing this opinion, I do not overlook the fact that Parliament, when making it penal to abandon a ship in the event of a collision, expressly confined this enactment to the masters of British ships (36 & 37 Vict. c. 85, ss. 16 and 17).

Having thus arrived at the conclusion that, by virtue of the statutes 28 Hen. 8, c. 15, and 39 Geo. 3, c. 37, the criminal law of England was extended over the waters adjoining the coast to as great a distance as the rules of international law allow, and that this distance is now at least three miles from the coast, I proceed to inquire to what persons within these geographical limits the law is applicable. I answer, to all persons who cannot be shewn to be excepted from its operation. Criminal laws exist for the protection of all persons within the limits to which they apply; and this protection cannot be secured unless all persons, whether native or foreign, within such limits are punishable if they infringe such law: see Heffter, s. 36; *People* v. *McLeod*. (1)

Foreigners on board British ships are subject to the criminal law of this country, in respect of offences committed on board those ships: see *Reg.* v. *Sattler* (2), where the ship was on the high sea, and not within the territorial waters of any other state; *Reg.* v. *Anderson* (3), where the ship was in the territorial waters of France; see also *Reg.* v. *Lesley*. (4) So foreigners in foreign ships are punishable by English law for crimes committed on board in English rivers: *Cunningham's Case*. (5)

It is said, indeed, that in the absence of clear evidence of intention to the contrary, a general statute is not to be construed to

(1) 1 Hill, N. Y. at p. 406.
(2) Dears. & B. Cr. C. 525.
(3) Law Rep. 1 Cr. C. 161.
(4) Bell, Cr. C. 220, 234.
(5) Bell, Cr. C. 72.

extend to foreigners; and this is quite true of foreigners out of the limits to which the statute is geographically applicable, but it is not true of foreigners within those limits. In fact, this rule of construction is only another mode of expressing the more general rule, that statutes are to be so construed as to apply only to those persons and places which are within the dominion of the legislative power: see Maxwell on Statutes, p. 123.

Reference was made in the course of the argument to the case of *The Saxonia* (1), in support of the proposition that, in the absence of express words, a statute ought not to be construed so as to affect a foreign ship even in English waters. But when the case is looked at, it will be seen that the decision only was that the statutory enactments there in question (i.e. 17 & 18 Vict. c. 104, ss. 291, 295–298) were confined to British ships; and it is, I think, quite consistent with that case to hold that criminal laws, applicable generally over a given sea area, are applicable to everything within that area, unless there be some special exemption in its favour.

It is, however, argued that a foreign ship in its passage over the high seas is subject, and subject only, to the law of the country to which the ship belongs; that such a ship is part of the territory of that country, and that the laws of no other country apply to it; and it is further contended that this proposition is true, not only with respect to the conduct of those on board, inter se, but also with respect to their conduct towards other persons.

This contention renders it necessary to investigate the doctrine that a merchant ship is part of the territory of the country whose flag she bears.

It is obvious that she is not so in point of fact; and it is easy to shew that the doctrine holds good to a very limited extent indeed. First, It is admitted that a foreign merchant ship, which enters the ports, harbours, or rivers of England, becomes subject to English law, her so-called territoriality does not in that case exclude the operation of English law: *Cunningham's Case.* (2)

Secondly, It is conceded that, even in time of peace, the territoriality of a foreign merchant ship, within three miles of the coast of any state, does not exempt that ship or its crew from the

(1) 15 Moo. P. C. 262.   (2) Bell, Cr. C. 72.

1876

THE QUEEN
v.
KEYN.
Lindley, J.

operation of those laws of that state which relate to its revenue or fisheries.

Thirdly, In time of war the so-called territoriality of a ship of one of the belligerents does not subject it to invasion or capture within three miles of a neutral coast.

Fourthly, In time of war the so-called territoriality of a neutral merchant ship does not exempt it from invasion in search of contraband of war.

Fifthly, In time of war this country has invariably denied that the territoriality of a neutral merchant ship protected enemy's goods on board; and although England has agreed with some nations that in future free ships shall make free goods (unless contraband of war), England resolutely maintains the old doctrine against all other nations.

In all these cases the territoriality of the ship becomes an unmeaning phrase, and care must be taken not to be misled by it, and not to allow the general assertion that a ship is part of the territory whose flags she bears to pass unchallenged, and to be made the basis of a legal argument.

When, indeed, a ship is out at sea in waters which are not the territorial waters of any state, it is right that those on board her should be subject to the laws of the country whose flags she bears; for otherwise they would be subject to no law at all. To this extent a ship may be said to be part of the territory of the country of her flag: see Man. Law of Nations, pp. 117–255; but so to speak of her is to employ a metaphor, and this must never be lost sight of.

Again, for some purposes at all events, a ship may remain subject to the laws of her own state even when in the territorial waters of another state. In *Reg.* v. *Anderson* (1) a foreigner was tried and convicted in England for a manslaughter committed by him when on board a British ship in the Garonne. It was held, that though he might have been properly tried and convicted in France, the jurisdiction of the English Courts over him was not thereby ousted. The so-called territoriality of a ship may give jurisdiction to the state whose flag she bears, without exempting her from the jurisdiction of the state whose waters she enters.

(1) Law Rep. 1 Cr. C. 161.

1876

THE QUEEN
v.
KEYN.

Lindley, J.

It is, however, said that the criminal law of a state does not apply to those on board a foreign ship merely passing through its waters, and we were referred to an American decision of *United States* v. *Kessler* (1), and to a note in Russell on Crimes, vol. i. p. 155, in support of this proposition. Reference was also made to the French law, according to which such crimes are not punishable unless they affect persons other than the crew and passengers of the vessel: see Wheaton's Elem. 6th ed. p. 154, &c., and *Reg.* v. *Anderson.* (2) The case of *United States* v. *Kessler* (1) was a case of robbery on board a foreign ship, and persons not on board were not affected; moreover, the robbery was in fact committed when the ship was on the ocean and not when she was within three miles of the coast. The note in Russ. vol. i. p. 155, is a note to *Cunningham's Case* (3), which turned on a technical point of venue. The ship in that case was an American ship in the sea (i.e., in the British Channel), but in the body of the county of Glamorgan; a crime was committed on board; the venue was laid in Glamorganshire, and the prisoner was convicted. He was not indicted for an offence committed on the high seas under 7 & 8 Vict. c. 2. The note referred to is as follows:—

"As the offence in this case was committed on a foreign vessel it could not have been tried as an Admiralty offence."

I can, however, find no decision in this country or elsewhere to the effect that a crime committed on board a foreign ship, whilst navigating the coast waters of another state, is not punishable by the laws of that state. But inasmuch as all persons on board are under the protection of the laws of the country to which the ship belongs, it may be that crimes on board such ships, and affecting no one except their own passengers and crew, may form an exception to the general rule that a crime is punishable by the law of the country or geographical area in which it is committed.

But even assuming this exception to be established, there is neither principle nor authority for extending the exception to cases where persons on board foreign ships commit offences against other people.

The reason for the exception (if any exception there be) does not

(1) Baldwin's Rep. p. 15.   (2) Law Rep. 1 Cr. C. 161.
(3) Bell, Cr. C. 72.

1876
THE QUEEN
v.
KEYN.
Lindley, J.

extend to such cases; and so to extend it would, in my judgment, be most unreasonable and most injurious to the interests of all civilized states. The French law draws the distinction clearly between the two classes of cases; and whilst the French criminal Courts refuse to exercise any jurisdiction where no one is injured except persons subject to the law of the flag of the foreign ship, they naturally claim jurisdiction and exercise it where injuries are sustained by other persons.

Indeed the concession made on all hands that a ship in territorial waters is subject to the regulations of police and safety of the state whose shores are washed by them, appears to me to be a concession of the whole principle for which it is necessary for the Crown to contend. The object of police laws and the object of criminal laws are precisely the same, viz. the preservation of peace and order, and the punishment more or less severe of those who disturb it. The boundaries between police law and criminal law are not set by any general principle, but depend simply on what is considered expedient; and it is entirely discretionary with each legislative power to say what offences committed within the limits of its dominion shall be dealt with summarily by the police, and what shall be tried more deliberately and be punished more severely.

If any state chooses to extend its own criminal laws, in addition to its police laws, to offences committed on the high seas within its dominion, there is no principle of international law which forbids the application of such criminal laws to foreigners, who, whilst passing through the territorial waters of that state in foreign ships, injure persons over whom that state has thrown its protection.

It appears to me that the statute law of this country, construed with reference to established doctrines of international law, has placed under the protection of our criminal law all persons on the high seas within three miles of the English shores; and conceding that it is doubtful whether those laws apply to cases where offences are committed on foreign ships traversing those seas, and no one, save their passengers or crew, are concerned in or suffer from what is done on board, I am unable to come to the conclusion that other persons in those waters are deprived of the protection thrown around them, when they are injured by the passengers or crew of a foreign passing ship.

A contrary doctrine would be most injurious and startling in its consequences; for, if such doctrine were to prevail, it would follow that, although crimes amounting by the law of nations to piracy might be punished in England if committed by a foreigner on the high seas, this country would be powerless to punish a foreigner for any less crime than piracy by the law of nations, although committed within a few yards of low-water mark, provided only he were on board a passing foreign ship when he committed the crime. He might, according to this doctrine, wilfully run down a boat, recklessly injure others to any extent, and yet not be punishable by our criminal law as distinguished from our police law. Indeed, I do not see why he should not be free from punishment by English criminal law, even if when on board his ship he shot and murdered some one off it; for such a crime is not necessarily piracy by the law of nations. That he might be apprehended and sent to his own country for trial is scarcely an equivalent for trial on the spot, where the witnesses are, and means of proof are readily accessible. It is no answer to this observation to say that the cases I have put would be punishable by the law of England as piracy; for the argument to which I am addressing myself is that the criminal law of England, as distinguished from the law of nations relating to piracy, has no application to foreigners in the situation supposed. Nor do I feel the force of the observation that the crime of which the prisoner in this case has been convicted is treated as manslaughter or homicide by the law of England alone. The question whether he is amenable to the criminal law of England in no way depends upon how he is to be treated by that law if amenable to it.

On the other hand, it is said that the consequences of upholding this conviction will be inconvenient and absurd. It is said to be absurd that a child born in a foreign ship passing through English waters should be treated as a native-born English subject. I am, however, by no means prepared to admit this to be a consequence of the limited principles on which I have sought to shew that this conviction is right; and even if such consequence were to follow, it would rather be the law of allegiance than the criminal law which would deserve to be called absurd. Again, it is said to be absurd to expect foreigners to know the laws of all countries along whose shores they sail; and that it would be cruel to punish them for infringing those laws when ignorant of them. But this observation, though forcible when urged against the doctrine that whatever takes place on board a coasting ship is cognizable by the shore authorities, loses all its force when urged against the rule that those on board such ship are to conduct themselves so as not to injure other people, and that if they fail in this respect they are punishable by the law of the land near which they are sailing.

Lastly, it is urged that the jurisdiction contended for by the Crown has never been exercised, and this apparently is the fact. On the other hand, no case appears ever to have arisen for its exercise.

So far as precedent is concerned, the case before us is quite new. It must, therefore, be decided on principle; and the absence of any precedent either way is by no means conclusive against the existence of the jurisdiction. To say that the Admiralty had no criminal jurisdiction over persons on board foreign ships on the high seas, even though close to our shore, is simply to assert the proposition which has to be considered. And I have endeavoured to shew that its jurisdiction was general over the English coast waters; and that there is no principle or authority for holding it to have been restricted to the extent contended for on behalf of the prisoner. The question does not, I think, turn on any of those technical distinctions taken in the older cases between the limits of the jurisdiction of the several Courts of this country; but upon the broad consideration of English and international law; and for the reasons I have given I am of opinion that this conviction ought to be affirmed.

In the view thus taken it becomes unnecessary to consider whether the conviction can be supported on the ground that the offence of the prisoner was committed on board the *Strathclyde*, and not on board the *Franconia*. The case of the *United States* v. *Davis* (1) is an authority in support of the conviction on this ground also, but I am not satisfied on this point; I prefer to rest my judgment upon the broader ground that the waters around the

(1) 2 Sumner, 482.

coasts of England are under the protection of English law, and
that all persons, whether English or foreign, who recklessly navigate those waters and thereby cause others to lose their lives, are
punishable by the criminal law of this country.

DENMAN, J. The question in this case of manslaughter is
whether the Central Criminal Court, by virtue of the Act of 4 &
5 Wm. 4, c. 36, s. 22, had jurisdiction to try the prisoner, Ferdinand
Keyn, a foreigner.

The prisoner was tried upon an indictment in which the venue
was laid in the Central Criminal Court. It contained two counts,
one of which alleged a felonious killing and slaying " upon the
high seas." The other omitted those words.

It was suggested upon the argument that this case was consistent with the possibility of the deceased having jumped over-
board from alarm, and so perished. All I will say as to this
suggestion is, that I do not feel at liberty to adopt it in any sense
inconsistent with a death by manslaughter. If there were any
real doubt upon the question whether the deceased's death was
immediately caused by the wrongful act of the prisoner, under
such circumstances as to constitute the offence of manslaughter,
subject only to the question of jurisdiction, I should have desired
that the case should be more fully stated; but I think it clear that
the only point intended to be decided by us is whether, assuming
the verdict of the jury to be right, and manslaughter to have
been committed somewhere, this is a case where the offence of
manslaughter was committed by such a person, under such circumstances, and in such a place, as to give the Central Criminal
Court jurisdiction. I can only read the case as stating that the
prisoner, by his negligence in continuing to navigate a vessel
which was "under his immediate direction" in a wrong and
dangerous course, caused her to strike and sink the *Strathclyde*,
and so committed manslaughter by drowning, subject only to the
question whether such manslaughter was "an offence committed"
within the jurisdiction of the Admiralty now exercised by the
Central Criminal Court.

The question then is, whether, where the foreign captain of a
foreign ship so negligently manages his ship that she cuts into a

British ship with her own stem, makes a hole in her, and sinks her, and a passenger is thereby drowned in the sea from the foundering of the ship, all happening on the high seas within three miles of the shore of England, the foreign captain (being afterwards in England) is liable to be tried for manslaughter in the Central Criminal Court, and to be convicted upon either count of an indictment such as the present. I am of opinion that he is so liable.

The first ground upon which I consider that this liability exists is that upon which it was last placed by the Solicitor General in his learned and exhaustive argument.

The Central Criminal Court has, by s. 22 of 4 & 5 Wm. 4, c. 36, jurisdiction to inquire of, hear, and determine any offence or offences committed or alleged to have been committed on the high seas or other places within the jurisdiction of the Admiralty of England.

A doubt has been expressed in the course of this case whether the words " within the jurisdiction of the Admiralty of England " apply to the words " offences committed," or to the words " other places." I am strongly inclined to think the latter, but it does not appear to me important for the purposes of this case to decide this, or to hold that they may not apply to both; for in the present case the offence charged, viz. manslaughter, is one which is clearly within the jurisdiction of the Admiralty, so far as its nature is concerned: see *Reg.* v. *Anderson* (1), and it was clearly committed upon the high seas, and therefore within the area of Admiralty jurisdiction, in the sense that if it had been committed by one British subject in one British ship running down another British ship and so drowning another British subject, the Admiralty, and not the common-law tribunal, would have had jurisdiction.

If this be so, the first question seems to be reduced to this, Does the 4 & 5 Wm. 4, c. 36, s. 22, apply to a case of a manslaughter by running down a British ship on the high seas and drowning its crew and passengers (such running down and drowning being all completed on the high seas), whether the running down and drowning be caused by a foreign ship or not, and whether a foreigner or an Englishman be the person charged?

(1) Law Rep. 1 Cr. C. 161.

This question appears to me to turn mainly upon the question, where is the "offence committed?" and in deciding this question, I think we are bound to decide according to the principles of English law.

One principle of English law about which there has been no dispute in this case is that a British ship, as regards criminal offences committed on board of her, is to be treated as British territory, at all events so long as she is upon the high seas, and is as much subject to and under the protection of our law as any other part of the Queen's dominions, though the tribunal, administering the law relating to offences committed on a British ship while on the high seas, is a different one from that which tries offences committed within the body of a county.

If the offence of manslaughter is committed by a foreigner on board an English ship on the high seas, such foreigner is liable to be tried and convicted in the Central Criminal Court exercising the jurisdiction of the Court of Admiralty. This is clearly established by numerous authorities, of which *Reg.* v. *Anderson* (1), cited above, is the most recent.

If, then, in the present case the offence of which the prisoner was convicted was an offence committed on board a British ship on the high seas, I apprehend the jurisdiction to try was indisputable, subject only to the question whether a foreigner is exempt by reason of being on board a foreign ship himself, while committing the offence on board the British ship.

It was argued that the offence was not committed on board a British ship, because the offence of manslaughter is of a complex character, consisting of an act of negligence, and of death the result of that negligence; and that, inasmuch as in the present case the act of negligence was completed on board a German ship and there ended, the offence, at all events as to one material ingredient of it, was there committed, and so there was no jurisdiction to try a foreigner as for an offence committed on board a British ship and so on British territory. In support of this view the case of *Lacy*, cited in *Bingham's Case* (2), was much relied on. In my opinion that case only proves that where the mortal stroke is given on the high seas, and the death occurs within the

(1) Law Rep. 1 Cr. C. 161.   (2) 2 Co. Rep. 93a.

1876

THE QUEEN
v.
KEYN.

Denman, J.

body of a county, neither the Admiralty nor the judges who try offences committed within the body of the county had at common law jurisdiction to try, and therefore the jurisdiction given to the Central Criminal Court would not apply to such a case. Mr. Benjamin, in his admirable argument, admitted that such was the whole effect of that case.

But that decision or dictum (for it seems to me to be no more (1),) appears to be wholly inapplicable to the present case, for in the present case the whole offence, of whatever elements it may consist, was clearly committed on the high seas. The negligence, the mortal stroke, and the resulting death all took place out of the body of any county, and on the high seas. But it was argued on behalf·of the prisoner that this is not sufficient, for that in the present case the negligence which caused the death, though on the high seas, was wholly and completely confined to acts done by a foreigner, being upon a foreign ship; that such negligence is one of the main ingredients of the manslaughter of which he has been found guilty, and that, therefore, upon the principle of *Lacy's Case* (2), the Admiralty had no jurisdiction to try the prisoner.

I think this objection is completely answered by the case which was cited by the Solicitor General, *Combes' Case* (3), stated in East's P. C. p. 367, as follows:—

" Where one standing on the shore shot another standing in the sea who afterwards died on board a ship, all the judges held that the trial must be in the Admiralty Court, and not at common law."

The report in Leach shews that the case was one of murder. The deceased was a sailor on board a boat which had run aground on a sand-bank about 100 yards from the shore; and the prisoner, a smuggler, being on the shore firing at other sailors who were endeavouring to push off the boat, struck and killed the deceased, who died in the boat, or possibly on board the ship to which he belonged, at sea. The case was argued twice by counsel, before all the judges but one, upon the question whether the prisoner had been properly tried by the Admiralty tribunal, or whether he ought not to have been tried at common law. They were all of

(1) See 1 Leon. 270.   (2) 2 Co. Rep. 93a.
(3) 1 Lea. Cr. C. 388.

opinion that the prisoner was tried by a competent tribunal, and the prisoner was executed pursuant to the sentence. This case appears to me to be a strong authority for the Crown to this extent, viz., that if the present case had been one of murder and not of manslaughter, if the prisoner, instead of negligently causing his ship to strike the *Stratholyde*, had purposely and of malice aforethought done the same act, the mortal stroke in contemplation of law would have been given where it actually took effect, which having been on board a British ship on the high seas and the death also on the high seas, there could have been no question whatever as to the jurisdiction of the Central Criminal Court to try the offence as one committed on the high seas, and within the jurisdiction of the Admiralty transferred to that Court. Then does the circumstance that the offence here alleged was manslaughter and not murder make any difference as regards the question of jurisdiction? It is said that it does. The decision in *Combes' Case* (1) was alleged to be supportable on the ground that in the case of murder the intention is presumed to accompany the act, and so the shot which takes effect on the high seas must be presumed to be accompanied thither by the intention with which it is fired, and both there together to operate. I agree that this is the principle upon which *Combes' Case* (1) is founded and I think that such a presumption is one of good sense and sound law. But I fail to see any true principle upon which a distinction can be drawn between a case of murder and a case of manslaughter, so far as the jurisdiction to try is concerned, on the ground that in the one case there is an intention to kill accompanying the stroke and operating at the place where it takes effect, and that in the other case there is no such intention. In my opinion, the negligence operates just as much as the intention at the spot where the violence is done, and though death is an ingredient of either offence equally, and, therefore, if death had not occurred within the Admiralty jurisdiction, *Lacy's Case* (2), but for a subsequent statute, would have applied, I can find no case nor authority of text-writers on English criminal law which furnishes any ground for saying that where the stroke or collision which causes the death and the death itself both occur within a certain jurisdiction,

(1) 1 Lea. Cr. C. 388.   .   (2) 1 Leon. 270.

1876

THE QUEEN
v.
KEYN.

Denman, J.

and the case is one either of manslaughter or murder, the mere fact that in the one case there is intention to kill, and in the other case only recklessness causing a killing by precisely the same instrument, makes any difference as to the liability of the prisoner to be tried for " an offence committed within the jurisdiction."

My Brother Grove during the argument pointed out one consequence of such a distinction, which I must confess appears to me to be almost conclusive against it. Suppose murder in this case had been charged, and clear jurisdiction admitted on all hands to try for murder if malice ' prepense were proved, and the jury thinking malice prepense not proved, but negligence established, had found the prisoner guilty of manslaughter, would the Court be bound to set aside the conviction on the ground of negligence only, and not malice, having been proved, though, if intention to kill had been established, it would have held the jurisdiction established? Again, can it be maintained that if a foreigner passing by in his boat fired deliberately at a person on a British ship and killed him he would be triable, but that if he recklessly fired, and killed the same person he would not be triable? It seems to me that this distinction would be contrary to English law, which alone we are to administer, and that it could not be so held without practically overruling *Combes' Case* (1), by which we ought to abide.

Upon a question of venue, I can find no trace of any authority for saying that there is any such distinction. I must confess that it appears to me impossible to read the case of *United States* v. *Davis*, in 2 Sumner, p. 482, without coming to the conclusion that Story, J., had never heard or thought of the distinction in question, which of itself appears to me to be a very strong argument against its existence. That was a case of manslaughter, and Story, J., says:

" I say the offence was committed on board of the schooner; for, although the gun was fired from the ship *Ross*, the shot took effect, and death happened on board of the schooner, and the act was, in contemplation of law, done where the shot took effect."

The same view of the law seems to have been entertained by the law officers of the Crown in the year 1725, when our Attorney

(1) 1 Lea. Cr. C. 388.

1876

THE QUEEN
v.
KEYN.

Denman, J.

and Solicitor General, Sir Phillip Yorke and Sir Clement Wearg, advised that a manslaughter committed by firing a gun from a fort in Barbadoes, and unlawfully, though not intentionally, killing a person on board a ship two miles off at sea, was not triable in any court of common law, but either in the Admiralty Court at Barbadoes, or by a special commission under 11 & 12 Wm. 3, c. 7 (See Forsyth's Cases and Opinions on Constitutional Law, p. 219).

I therefore feel bound to look at this case exactly as though it were one of murder caused by intentionally running down the *Strathclyde*, so far as the question of jurisdiction is concerned. In such case, would not the charge have been one of an offence committed on British territory, i.e., a British ship on the high seas, by a foreigner, having in contemplation of law entered the British ship, and there committed the offence afterwards completed by the death of the deceased, within the jurisdiction of the Admiralty? I think it would.

The case of *Combes*, already referred to, was a case of the trigger pulled ashore, the man killed in a boat at sea. The bullet sent from the shore having done the mischief at sea, it was held that the prisoner had "committed the offence at sea." That was a case of murder; but the case of *United States* v. *Davis* (1), which was a case of manslaughter, was decided upon the same principle; and it appears to me that the principle is sound and reasonable. Applying that principle to the present case, I can see no reason for drawing any distinction between the case of propelling a bullet from a gun and that of striking with the further end of a spear, or directing the prow of a ship so as to strike either a person or a vessel containing a number of living beings.

Can a ship, directed by its captain against the hull of another ship, and there inflicting an injury which sends it to the bottom in a few minutes, and drowns its crew and passengers, be more appropriately said to be inflicting the mortal stroke at any place than where she makes the hole, through which the water rushes, which sends the ship to the bottom and drowns those on board? And if, as in this case, she penetrates the skin of the other vessel some feet, must it not be held that the person under whose immediate direction she is does the mischief which is most entitled to be

(1) 2 Sumner, 482.

1878

THE QUEEN
v.
KEYN.

Denman, J.

called the "mortal stroke" on board the ship which is sunk? I think it must.

But it is argued that the law which gives our Courts jurisdiction to try offences upon the high seas cannot be held to apply to this case, because the prisoner was a foreigner on his own ship, and therefore not amenable to our criminal law.

I am of opinion, however, that the law which makes foreigners liable for the violation of our criminal law for offences committed by them when bodily on our soil, whether there by their own desire or not, is not so restricted as to leave them unpunishable because they may have been on a foreign ship at the time of the commission of the offence. By way of illustration: suppose that a foreigner in a foreign ship, lying on the sea in deep water, were to commit a burglary by thrusting a hooked stick through the window of some building adjoining the sea, and thus, and thus only, break in and steal goods and chattels. I think that in such a case, if he were to be afterwards on shore, our Courts would have jurisdiction to try him, and that if they tried him, they must hold that, though he was a foreigner in a foreign ship on the high seas, he was not the less a foreigner breaking, entering, and stealing in the county of S., and therefore liable to be tried and punished there.

It is argued that there would be hardship in trying a foreigner, who knows not our laws, for an act which might be regarded quite differently, and triable by totally different rules, and punishable by a different punishment, in his own country.

But I do not think that this argument ought to prevail. It might be thought hard to try a foreigner for manslaughter committed by gross negligence in driving furiously and recklessly along the road to the nearest town immediately after being shipwrecked on our coast, or immediately after having fallen from a balloon, but I conceive it would be no legal answer to such a charge to plead, however truly, that the prisoner was a foreigner, and that in his own country manslaughter was only a civil offence. I can indeed easily conceive cases in which a jury might acquit a foreigner, though they would have convicted an Englishman, doing the same acts, of manslaughter, as, for instance, if it were established that the death had happened through a bonâ fide ignorance of our rule of the road; but any defence analogous to this must

1876

THE QUEEN
v.
KEYN.

Denman, J.

be taken to have been disposed of, so far as it would have been applicable to this case by the verdict of the jury, and in the absence of any such defence, I apprehend that the case of a person, who does a criminal act directly causing injury or death to persons on board a British vessel on the high seas, must be dealt with precisely in the same way (though by a different tribunal) as that of a person committing the same offence in England; and that there is no more reason for reading our criminal statutes as excluding foreigners in the one case than in the other.

The conclusion that the prisoner did commit the offence of manslaughter on a British ship is, I think, inevitable from the considerations and from the authorities above applied to the case. He being in command of his ship, which is found to have been under his immediate direction, so directed her as to cause her bow to penetrate the *Strathclyde* and make a large hole in her through which the water rushed in. I am of opinion that the making of that hole was his negligent act done within British jurisdiction, just as much as if he had personally boarded the vessel and staved her in with a hammer, and that by doing that act, followed as it was by the immediate sinking of the vessel and drowning of the deceased, he was liable to be tried for a manslaughter committed on the high seas within the jurisdiction of the Central Criminal Court.

I have felt bound to write fully upon this point, though it occupied a comparatively small part of the argument, because, in my opinion, it is one of vast importance to the security of British seamen and of persons of all nations sailing in British ships, and therefore entitled to the protection of our laws, throughout the world. I can see no ground for curtailing the generality of our criminal law in such a case as this, or for applying different principles from those which would be applicable to a manslaughter on land. I cannot see that it would in any way interfere with the free navigation of the high seas, for I see no inconsistency between perfect freedom of navigation and a power on the part of each nation to punish those who kill its own subjects, or those of other countries enjoying its hospitality on board its ships, by running them down, whether through design or negligence. On the contrary, I think that the real freedom as well as the safety of navi-

1876

THE QUEEN
v.
KEYN.

Denman, J.

gation would be impaired if we were to place such a limit upon the jurisdiction of our criminal Courts.

With regard to the other point in the case which was so ably and elaborately argued by counsel, I am of opinion that the jurisdiction is also made out, on the ground that a foreigner committing manslaughter in the course of navigation of a foreign ship *within three miles* of the coast is subject to our jurisdiction, but I do not think it necessary to write separately upon this point, as I entirely agree with the judgment which will be read by Sir Baliol Brett.

One argument which was used for the prisoner was that the absence of any proof of the exercise of such a jurisdiction was strongly against it. I admit that there is some force in the observation, but I do not think it goes so far as was contended for. Cases of criminal negligence in the management of vessels on the high seas are happily very rare; cases of death by such negligence still rarer; cases in which either public opinion or the feelings of relatives would be such as to lead to a prosecution rarest of all. There are, to my mind, sufficient reasons to account for the absence of any user upon the subject. The comparatively modern invention of steam navigation is of itself almost enough to account for the absence of any authority in ancient times, inasmuch as it is far more difficult to establish a clear case of criminal negligence against the captain of a sailing ship than against one directing a steamship on its course. But I can see no reason whatever for holding that a foreigner, who drives his own ship into a British ship and kills its crew by negligence, is less responsible to British law than a foreigner would be, who brought his ship within range of the Isle of Wight and shot or lanced to death upon a pier one of its inhabitants, and who afterwards landed upon the island and was brought to trial at Winchester assizes; in which case, for the reasons already given, he would, I think, be punishable by the criminal law of this country when found at the bar of the proper tribunal.

For these reasons I think that the conviction was right.

Grove, J.

GROVE, J. In this case, the defendant, master of and on board a foreign ship, the *Franconia*, ran into a British ship, the *Strathclyde*, and by such act British subjects on board the last-named ship were drowned off Dover, within three miles of the land. The defendant was indicted for the manslaughter of one of the persons so drowned, it being alleged that he was guilty of culpable or criminal negligence, and he was convicted at the Central Criminal Court.

For the purpose of this case the Court must assume the culpable negligence by the defendant, and that it caused the death; the question reserved is, had the Court jurisdiction to try the case by virtue of its Admiralty jurisdiction transferred to it by statute 4 & 5 Wm. 4, c. 36, s. 22, the defendant being a foreigner, commanding a foreign ship, and the offence not being committed on British soil or within a British port or river?

It was contended by the counsel for the Crown. 1st. That the belt of sea extending to the distance of three miles from the shore was British territory, and that an offence committed within it was within the criminal law of this country. 2ndly. That a person sailing or swimming within this belt of water in the Queen's peace is entitled to the protection of her law from aggressive or reckless acts causing personal injury, whether done by foreigners or by British subjects; this is, in fact, a limitation of the first point. 3rdly. That the offence was committed on board a British ship, such ship being struck and submerged by the blow, and the death, and immediate consequence of it, and the impinging of the foreign vessel being in the nature of a trespass on a British ship. These propositions were severally denied by the counsel for the defendant; if either of them is well founded the conviction is right, if no one of them is sustainable it is wrong.

I am of opinion that the conviction is right, and that our judgment should be for the Crown.

The proposition that a belt or zone of three miles of sea surrounding or washing the shores of a nation,—what is termed territorial water,—is the property of that nation, as a river flowing through its land would be, or, if not property, is subject to its jurisdiction and law, is not in its terms of ancient date; but this defined limit, so far at least as a maritime country like England is concerned, is rather a restriction than an enlargement of its earlier claims, which were at one time sought to be extended to a general dominion on the sea, and subsequently over the channels between

1876

THE QUEEN
v.
KEYN.
Grove, J.

it and other countries, or, as they were termed, the narrow seas. The origin of the three-mile zone appears undoubted. It was an assumed limit to the range of cannon, an assumed distance at which a nation was supposed able to exercise dominion from the shore.

I forbear from reiterating the terms used by the numerous publicists quoted by the learned counsel in the arguments on this case. The principal authorities may be conveniently arranged as follows :—

1st. Those who affirm the right in what are generally termed territorial waters to extend at least to the distance at which it can be commanded from the shore or as far as arms can protect it.

2ndly. Those who, assigning the same origin to the right, recognised it as being fixed at a marine league or three geographical miles from the shore.

3rdly. Those who affirm the right to be absolute and the same as over an inland lake, or, allowing for the difference of the subject-matter, as over the land itself.

4thly. Those who regard the right as qualified: And the main if not only qualification that seems to me fairly deducible from the authorities is, that there is a right of transit or passage, and as incident thereto possibly a right of anchorage when safety or convenience of navigation requires it, in the territorial waters for foreign ships.

Puffendorff, Bynkershoek, Casaregis, Mozer, Azuni, Kluber, Wheaton, Hautefeuille, and Kaltenborn, though not all placing the limit of territorial jurisdiction at the same distance from the shore, none of them fix it at a smaller distance than a cannon-shot, or as far off as arms can command it; they also give no qualification to the jurisdiction, but seem to regard it as if, having regard to the difference of land and water, it were an absolute territorial possession. Chancellor Kent seems also to recognise an exclusive dominion. Hautefeuille speaks of the power of a nation to exclude others from the parts of the sea which wash its territory, and to punish them for infraction of its laws, and this as if it were dealing with its land dominion. Wheaton, Calvo, Halleck, Massey, Bishop, and Manning give the limit as a marine league, or three miles. Heffter mentions this limit, but says it may be

1876

The Queen
v.
Keyn.
Grove, J.

extended. Ortolan, Calvo, and Massè put the right as one of jurisdiction and not of property, but do not limit it further than that the former writer says that the laws of police and surety are there obligatory, and Massè also writes of police jurisdiction. Bluntschli says the territorial waters are subject to the military and police authorities of the place. Faustin Helie speaks of crimes in these waters coming within the jurisdiction of the tribunals of the land to which they belong. Unless these words " military, police, and surety " be taken to impose a limit, no limit to the jurisdiction of a country over its territorial waters beyond a right of passage for foreign ships is mentioned, as far as I could gather from the numerous authorities cited, except by Mr. Manning, who confines it (though not by words expressly negativing other rights) to fisheries, customs, harbours and lighthouses, dues, and protection of territory during war. Grotius, Ortolan, Bluntschli, Schmaltz, and Massè consider there is a right of peaceable passage for the ships of other nations, and Vattel says that it is the duty of nations to permit this, but seems to think that, as a matter of absolute right, they may prohibit it.

Such are the conclusions of the principal publicists, most of whom are of very high authority on questions of international law.

The result of them is to shew that, as in the case of many other rights, a territorial jurisdiction over a neighbouring belt of sea had its origin in might, its limits being at first doubtful and contested, but ultimately by a concession or comity of nations it became fixed at what was for a long time the supposed range of a cannon shot, viz. three miles distance.

In addition to the authority of the publicists, this three-mile range, if not expressly recognised as an absolute boundary by international law, is yet fixed on, apparently without dispute, in Acts of Parliament, in treaties, and in judgments of courts of law in this country and America.

The Merchant Shipping Act, 17 & 18 Vict. c. 104, s. 527, provides for injury to property by giving power to detain a foreign ship when within three miles of the coast. The Customs Act, 3 & 4 Wm. 4, c. 53, legislates for foreign vessels within one league of the coast. The 59 Geo. 3, c. 38, s. 2, sanctions fishing and drying fish by British subjects within three miles of the coast. The 33 & 34 Vict. c. 90, s. 52, a foreign enlistment Act, extends "to all the dominions of Her Majesty, including the adjacent territorial waters."

The Congress of the United States has authorized the district courts to take cognizance of all captures made within a marine league of the American shores.

In many treaties, e.g. those mentioned by the Lord Chief Justice, of 1786–1787 and 1794, the cannon-shot range is fixed on as a zone protected from hostilities when the country which this belt adjoins is neutral.

It is true that this may be explained as a mutual concession, though I should incline to regard the concession rather as a disclaimer of rights beyond this belt; at all events it shews that this limit has been fixed on or assumed as internationally separable from the parts of the high seas beyond it.

In many cases in the law courts cannon-shot range on this three-mile belt has been recognised. The charge of Sir Leoline Jenkins, in 1683, goes beyond this, and extends the dominion of the Crown to what were called the four seas. In the case of *The Twee Gebroeders* (1) it was held that a vessel lying within the three miles could not by her boats make a good capture beyond this distance. So in the case of *The Brig Anne*, a vessel, having anchored and taken in provisions within the three miles, was seized under an Act of Congress which laid an embargo on vessels within the limits and jurisdiction of the United States; Story, J., saying, "The *Anne* was certainly in a place within the jurisdiction of the United States." In *Gammell* v. *The Lord Advocate* (2) the right of the Crown to the bed of the sea within the three miles is recognised by Lord Wensleydale, and to some extent by Lord Cranworth. In the case of *The Leda*, the words "United Kingdom" were held by Dr. Lushington to include three miles from the shore. So in the case of *Whitstable Fishers* v. *Gann* (3), an anchorage case, Erle, C.J., says, "The soil of the sea shore to the extent of three miles from the beach is vested in the Crown," and

(1) 3 C. Rob. 162.   (3) 11 C. B. (N.S.) 337; 13 C. B.
(2) 3 Macq. 419–465.   (N.S.) 353; 11 H. L. 192.

this is quoted with approval by Lord Chemsford in the same case on appeal in the House of Lords.

Chancellor Kent recognises *Bruce's Case* (1), but although the occurrence is treated as within territorial waters, yet, as it took place in Milford Haven, it may be said this was within a port. Some belt of sea must, as a necessary protection, be within the control of the country which it washes. There are parts of the coast where the cliffs are such that the tide at low water hardly, if at all, leaves their base uncovered, and if there were no jurisdiction over any part of the water in such places hostile gun-boats might hover within pistol-shot of the land.

The result of the authorities on international law, of the concessions of nations, and of decided cases is admitted by the learned counsel for the defendant to prove that there is a jurisdiction for certain purposes in tribunals of the country within the three miles. Is then this jurisdiction limited, and, if so, to what extent?

I do not find in any of the authorities cited an express limitation of jurisdiction, as by words to the effect that such and such rights exist and no other, or any express assertion that there is no criminal jurisdiction within the territorial waters. Manning goes the nearest to this, for he does say that for some limited purposes a special right of jurisdiction and even of dominion is conceded to a state, in respect of the part of the ocean immediately adjoining its own coast line. If this statement were borne out by the general current of authority, or even by a few writers of eminence, or by authoritative decision, it would have great weight; but I do not find that it is so supported.

The limitation for which, as I have said, there is no doubt considerable authority, is that of a right of passage, and this may,—and I will assume it for the purpose of my judgment in this case,—go so far as to exclude from English jurisdiction anything which may happen within the foreign ship, between members of its crew or even passengers who trust themselves for the time being to the government of the commander of the ship.

As we claim for this nation that a British ship is British territory wherever it be, I concede for the present that foreigners may rightly claim for their ships the same privilege, except when

(1) 2 Lea. Cr. C. 1093.

restricted by special legislation, e.g., customs laws, &c. But, assuming fully this right of passage through the territorial waters,
it seems to me that the very exception involves a right within a
right, a serviency quâ the rights conceded, but dominion ultra
those ; it seems to me also that a right of passage cannot be other
than a right to be properly exercised, with due regard to the
safety of the subjects of the nation over whose territorial waters
the right is used. If the lives or limbs of such subjects are
jeopardized, it would be an idle dominion which cannot protect
them against injury, or punish for it if committed.

If the dominion be absolute, such seems to me a necessary conclusion; and even if the words "police and surety" or "military
and police authorities" be taken to impose a further limitation
than that of a right of passage, still the limited rights could
not be protected if reckless navigation were permitted to endanger those rightfully enjoying them, or if the persons guilty of
injury to them were not punishable by the tribunals of the
country having this police or military jurisdiction. Police without this protection would be impotent and useless. It may be
said complaint may be made to the tribunals of the country to
whom the offender is a subject, but resort to such remedies, in
addition to the enormous difficulties of procuring evidence, want
of power to compel attendance of witnesses, and expense, assumes
that the offender returns to his own country, which he may not
do, and gives in this respect no meaning to the jurisdiction over
the limited area for police and surety; for this resort to the
country of the accused could be had if the offence were committed
anywhere on the high seas.

It is true that there is no case expressly in point either way
with that now before the Court. If there had been a case of
recognised authority, this case would probably not have been
argued. This, though by no means a conclusive argument either
way, is rather an argument in favour of the defendant than
against him. It may, however, be remarked that collisions were
not frequent until late years, when the great increase in the
number of ships navigating the ocean has given rise to them.
The loss of human life, except from murder or piracy, was not
thought so much of in former times as at present, and unless there

were something directly calling in question the jurisdiction, the limit of territorial water would not be likely to be narrowly watched. Still, I am far from undervaluing the argument.

As I have come to the conclusion that there is jurisdiction in such a case as the present, there arises the question whether it is necessary that there should be special legislation to enable our tribunals to deal with a foreigner guilty of such offence.

If the matter were one of police regulation merely, such as that the vessel should pass between certain buoys, should exhibit certain lights, be liable to customs requirements, &c., I should be of opinion that special legislation would be requisite; but I cannot see that it is for murder, mayhem, or manslaughter, any more than it would be if the offence were committed within a port or haven. The criminality of and punishment for such offence is a part of the common law of the realm, not originated by statutory legislation. If the locality where the offence is committed is within the realm, a statute is unnecessary, if not, it is ultra vires. The learned counsel for the defendant, if I rightly understand him, admitted that a foreigner would be liable for murder committed within the three-mile belt. His words were, "If a man intentionally fires at a man, I should not contest it might be murder, whether I carry that admission too far or not."

It certainly would seem a strong proposition to contend for that, if a foreigner from the motive of pure individual malice should intentionally shoot down the master of a fishing-smack peacefully and rightfully casting his net in English waters, or a dredger for oysters, or an officer civil or military in the execution of his duty there, such murder should not be cognizable by English tribunals without a special statute: see *Coombes' Case.* (1) Manslaughter may come within a hair's breadth of murder; it may be a nice and difficult question to decide; and is the offender's life to be forfeited if his act is on one side of the line? But if there be, say, provocation enough to reduce the homicide, though intentional, to what we call manslaughter, is he to be acquitted altogether?

So, if a foreigner in a foreign ship, with malice prepense, runs his ship at a fishing-boat or a swimmer, and so kills a British

(1) 1 Lea. Cr. C. 388.

1876

THE QUEEN
v.
KEYN.

Grove, J.]

subject, is it punishable as murder by our tribunals; while, if he
produce the same result by the most gross and culpable negligence, it is not within their jurisdiction? If this be so, a foreign
vessel might run riot among our fishing boats with impunity.
Nor is this simply an argument ab inexpediente. Admitting a
right to these waters for purposes of police and safety, which is, I
think, fairly supported by the authorities, it seems to me that the
existing laws for the protection of life and limb are a necessary
adjunct to such right. The case of *The Twee Gebroeders* (1) is
an authority for there being a jurisdiction over ships lying within
the three miles.

I cannot see any sufficient distinction between the rights and
immunities of a ship availing itself of a right of passage, and a ship
at anchor within the same district; in the latter case the ship is
availing itself of the soil which, to give the country a right of
interference, must be assumed to be a part of the territory of that
country; if so, the water over that soil must, it seems to me, also
belong to that territory: cujus est solum ejus est usque ad cælum
is a maxim of general application; the ship using the soil for
anchorage, which is incident to safe navigation, is no more availing
itself of the protection of that country and subjecting itself to its
laws, than when passing over that soil and availing itself of a
water highway, which may be a channel overlooked by the cliffs of
the adjacent country.

In *Gann* v. *Whitstable Fishers* (2) Lord Westbury says:

"The right to anchor is a necessary part of the right of navigation, because it
is essential for the full enjoyment of that right."

Although on the high seas generally the Admiralty may not
have jurisdiction over foreigners, except when specified, as in the
Merchant Shipping Act, yet in *Bruce's Case* (3), cited apparently
with approval by Kent, the judges agree that the Admiralty had
concurrent jurisdiction with the Courts of common law in such
waters as Milford Haven; and whether this be considered a port

(1) 3 C. Rob. 162.
(2) 11 H. L. 208.
(3) 2 Lea. C. C. 1093; Kent's Com.
vol. i. p. 366, 367; *R.* v. *Cunningham*,
Bell, Cr. C. 80, per Cockburn, C. J.;

see also Sir Leoline Jenkins' Charge;
see also 11 & 13 C. B. (N.S.) 413; 11
H. L. 192–218; and *Coombes' Case*,
1 Lea. Cr. C. 388.

or not, if, as is not denied, the Courts of common law have juris-   1876
diction over a foreigner committing an offence within a port or   The Queen
haven, the Admiralty must have, according to this case, concurrent   Keyn.
jurisdiction, and if so, then, assuming I am right as to an offence   Grove, J.
committed by a foreigner (not on board, on the rigging, or within
the hull of a foreign ship, but outside the ship on a British subject
in the Queen's peace), being within the jurisdiction of the Crown,
if within the three-mile belt, then it seems to me the case is
parallel, and the Admiralty must in the same right have jurisdiction over it; and if so, the Central Criminal Court, to which the
Admiralty jurisdiction has been given, must also have it.

I have therefore come to the conclusion that as, in this case, the
offence, although committed by a foreigner in a foreign ship, is
committed dehors the vessel upon a British subject in the Queen's
peace, within the three-mile belt, the Court which tried this case
had jurisdiction, and that the conviction should be affirmed.

This being the conclusion at which I have arrived, it is unnecessary for me to give an opinion on the last question, viz., whether
this offence was an offence committed on board of a British ship.

AMPHLETT, J.A. The prisoner is a foreigner, and committed   Amphlett, J. A.
the offence of which he has been convicted while captain on board
a foreign vessel passing along the open sea, within a little less
than two miles of the English coast, and the question is, whether,
under the circumstances stated in the case, the Admiralty formerly,
and now the Central Criminal Court, to which the jurisdiction of
the Admiralty has been transferred by statute, was competent to
try him.

The following propositions may, I think, be considered as established, both on principle and by authority, and were not, in fact,
disputed during the argument before us :—

1. That a foreigner committing an offence of any kind, even
against an Englishman, on foreign territory cannot be tried for it
in an English court.

2. That a foreigner committing a criminal offence while on
English territory, is equally amenable to English law as a subject,
except so far, if at all, as he may be exempted therefrom by convention or by some established rule of the law of nations.

1876

THE QUEEN

v.

KEYN.

Amphlett, J.A.

Neglecting, then, for the moment, any such case of exemption, the question we have to decide resolves itself into this, viz., whether the locality of the offence was within English territory, or, what for the present purpose appears to me the same thing, within the dominion or sovereignty of England? If it was, I think that, as a necessary attribute of sovereignty, it was the right and duty of the sovereign to enforce order and security to life and property in such territory, and that, so far as necessary, the law of England would in the absence of any other law attach thereto without the necessity of legislation.

I am unable to see any difficulty about venue. The locality not being within the body of any county, the offence was not cognizable under the ordinary commissions of oyer and terminer; but, assuming the locality to have been English territory on the high seas, it was, in my judgment, clearly within the former jurisdiction of the Admiralty. For example, it being established that, by the law of nations, a merchant ship was to be considered as a floating part of the territory of the country to which she belonged, crimes by foreigners, committed on board of an English ship, were held to be cognizable by the English Courts, without any Act of Parliament to that effect: see *Anderson's Case.* (1)

Now there are two grounds on which it was contended for the Crown that the offence was committed on English territory:—

1. Because, by international law, every maritime nation is entitled to have, as an extension of its territory, such a part of the adjacent sea as may be necessary for its own security, and which, after some fluctuations, had been settled by general consent to extend to a distance of a marine league, or three miles from low-water mark.

2. Because, the death of the party injured through the criminal negligence of the prisoner having occurred on board an English vessel, the offence was in law committed there, and therefore, by the law of nations, on English territory.

I will first dispose of the second ground, which of course is quite independent of the three-mile zone, and if valid would justify the conviction of the prisoner had the offence been committed in the middle of the ocean. Now, according to the decision in *R. v.*

(1) Law Rep. 1 Cr. C. 261.

Coombes (1), the crime must be, for the purpose of determining the venue, held to have been committed on the English ship where the death occurred ; but that doctrine, founded as it is upon a convenient fiction, and binding no doubt upon a British subject, does not decide the question before us, which is, whether a foreigner who committed the offence while he was de facto outside the English territory, could be made amenable to English law. With some doubt I have come to the conclusion that he could not. I can find no authority for saying that a state has any jurisdiction to punish a foreigner who at the time of the commission of the offence was not within the territory, and consequently not owing it any allegiance.

The first ground on which the argument for the Crown was based, viz., the right of maritime states to a zone of three miles over the adjacent seas, remains to be considered.

We know historically that from the earliest times maritime states have claimed dominion over adjacent seas, and often to an outrageous extent. England claimed dominion over the whole of the narrow seas, even to the extent of excluding, if it thought proper, foreign ships from passing over them, and other countries were not far behind England in that respect. These extravagant claims, however, have been long since abandoned, and the freedom of the high seas for the inoffensive navigation of all nations is firmly established, and England and most, if not all, maritime states have been content to limit the claim to advance their frontier seaward to the extent of three miles. That limited extent, however, of maritime territory has been in modern times with remarkable unanimity recognized by the English Courts.

In *Reg.* v. 49 *Casks of Brandy* (2) Sir John Nichol, in deciding against the claim of the lord of a manor to wreck beyond low-water mark, said :

"As between nation and nation the territorial right may by a sort of tacit understanding be extended to three miles; but that rests upon different principles, viz., that their own subjects shall not be disturbed in their fishing, and particularly in their coasting trade and communications between place and place during war, &c., but no person ever heard of a land jurisdiction of the body of a county which extended three miles from the coast."

---

(1) 1 Lea. Cr. C. 388.   (2) 3 Hag. Adm. Rep. 247.

1876·

THE QUEEN
v.
KEYN.

Amphlett, J.A.

In *The Twee Gebroeders* (1) Sir W. Scott speaks of the sea within three miles of the coast of Friedland as "waters belonging to Prussia."

In *The Leda* (2) Dr. Lushington decided that where one of the Merchant Shipping Acts spoke of disputes arising with respect to salvage "in the United Kingdom," those words meant "the land of the United Kingdom and three miles from the shore."

In the *General Iron Screw Co.* v. *Schurmanns* (3) it was decided that the limitation upon the liability of a shipowner in case of a collision under one of the Merchant Shipping Acts applied to a case of damage done to a foreign ship within three miles of the English coast, though foreign ships are not mentioned in the Act, and Lord Hatherley, in the course of his judgment, says:

> " "As to the question how far our legislature could properly affect the rights of foreign ships within the limits of three miles from the coast of this country there can be no possible doubt that the water below low-water mark is part of the high seas. But it is equally beyond question that for certain purposes every country may by the common law of nations legitimately exercise jurisdiction over that portion of the high seas which lies within the distance of three miles from its shores."

Afterwards he says:

> "Authorities have been cited to the effect that every nation has the right to use the high seas even within the distance of three miles from the shore of another country, and it was contended that it was not legitimate to interfere with foreigners so using this portion of the common highway, except for the bonâ fide purposes of defence, protection of the revenue, and the like.
>
> "It is not questioned that there is a right of interference for defence and revenue purposes, and it is difficult to understand why a country having this kind of territorial jurisdiction over a certain portion of the high road of nations should not exercise the right of settling the rules of the road in the interests of commerce. An exercise of jurisdiction for such a purpose would be at least as beneficial as for purposes of defence and revenue."

In *Gammel* v. *Commissioners of Woods and Forests* (4) Lord Wensleydale, in discussing the distance to which the exclusive right of the Crown (affirmed in that case) in the salmon fishery on the coast of Scotland extended, says,

> "That it would be hardly possible to extend fishing seaward beyond the distance of three miles, which by the acknowledged law of nations belongs to the coast of the country."

---

(1) 3 Rob. Adm. 162.   (3) 1 J. & H. 180.

(2) Swa. Adm. 42.   (4) 3 Macq. 465.

In this last case it would appear to have been decided by the House of Lords that not only was the three-mile zone within the territory of England, but that the actual property therein was vested in the Crown; and that view seems to have been adopted by the legislature, for in the Act of 21 & 22 Vict. c. 119, which was passed for the purpose of defining the rights of the Crown and the Duchy of Cornwall to mine and minerals under land between high and low-water mark and below low-water mark adjacent to the county of Cornwall, it was by the 2nd section enacted, that all mines and minerals lying below low water under the open sea adjacent to, but not being part of, the county of Cornwall were, as between the Crown and the duchy, vested in her Majesty in right of her Crown "as part of the soil and territorial possessions of the Crown." Moreover, the right of this country to legislate for foreign ships within the zone of three miles from the coast has been exercised by Parliament in the Customs Act (16 & 17 Vict. c. 117), ss. 212, 218, and 236, the Merchant Shipping Act (17 & 18 Vict. c. 104), s. 517, and the Foreign Enlistment Act (32 & 33 Vict. c. 90), s. 24, which were fully brought to our notice in the argument, and it may be pertinently asked, what right could Parliament have to legislate at all for foreign ships within the zone unless it was considered to be English territory?

It is true that neither the Parliament, in the Acts to which I have referred, nor our Courts in modern times, have claimed any right to interfere with the inoffensive passage of a foreign vessel over the zone, and I think it may be conceded that it would be at variance with the established law of nations to do so, unless under special circumstances the security of the state required it; and it may be conceded that, so far as regards internal discipline and acts done on board with no consequences beyond the vessel, the law of the flag would be respected and our criminal law would not attach.

But to extend this exemption, however, from the law of the territory to acts of criminal negligence, by which persons outside the vessel are killed or injured, appears to me to be highly unreasonable and, so far as I know, absolutely without authority.

The assumption by the legislature and in judicial decisions that the three-mile zone is English territory ought, perhaps, to be

1876

THE QUEEN
v.
REYN.

Amphlett, J.A.

binding upon us in an English court of justice without more; but, passing that by, I will proceed to shew that that assumption is in accordance with and fully warranted by international law.

To ascertain that law it is most important in this and all other cases to consult the published opinions of eminent jurists of different countries, for although, as has been justly said, those writers cannot make the law, still if there is found a practical unanimity or a great preponderance of opinion among them, it would afford weighty, and in many cases, conclusive evidence that their statement of the law had been received with the general consent of the civilized nations of the world.   Chancellor Kent, in his Commentaries, vol. i. p. 19, says:—

"In cases where the principal jurists agree the presumption will be very great in favour of the solidity of their maxims; and no civilized nation that does not arrogantly set all ordinary law and justice at defiance will venture to disregard the uniform sense of the established writers on international law."

See other authorities to the same effect, collected and discussed by Sir Robert Phillimore, in his Commentaries on International Law, 2nd ed. vol. i. pp. 61–66.

Both sides, therefore, very properly called our attention to the opinions of almost every accredited writer on international law who has dealt with this question of maritime territory.

As, however, some of my learned Brothers, whose judgments I have had the privilege of seeing, have stated and discussed these writings in detail, I do not think it necessary or right to go over the same ground, or to do more than state briefly the general conclusions I have myself derived from them.

These conclusions are as follows :—

1. That all these writers, and, as far as I can see, with complete unanimity, acknowledge the right of a maritime state to an extension of their territory over some portion of the adjacent sea.

2. That, although there is found a great variety of opinion among these writers as to the distance to which such maritime territory should be allowed, not one of them puts such distance at less than three miles.

3. That all the earlier writers, including Grotius, the vigorous advocate of the free navigation of the high seas, and many of the later writers, maintained that within the zone of three miles the state

1876

THE QUEEN
v.
KEYN.

Amphlett, J.A.

had, without qualification, a proprietary, as well as a territorial, right, so that it might at its pleasure exclude foreign ships from passing along the same; but that others of the later writers contended that the state had a territorial, but not a proprietary, right over the zone, or that, at all events, the innocent use of the zone by foreign ships for the purpose of navigation could not without wrong be interfered with.

4. That not one of the last-mentioned writers maintained that the sovereign state had no jurisdiction to prevent what I may call external wrong committed by them on board a foreign vessel within the zone. Indeed the writers most relied upon for the defence, such as Ortolan and Calvo, I think, imply, if they do not say, the contrary, for while arguing against the right of the maritime state to exclude foreign ships from the zone, they all appear to me to admit in substance that they have the right to make laws of "police and surety."

Does not that necessarily imply that the maritime state may not only make, but enforce, laws against such acts of criminal negligence as are charged against the prisoner in this case, and how can they be adequately enforced but by attaching to them penal consequences?

According to the meaning attributed to some of these writers by the counsel for the prisoner, a foreigner may come on the high seas close to our shores, and so long as he steers clear of acts of piracy, he may injure and insult our people, destroy their property, and endanger the navigation with impunity. Cases might be put without number of intolerable wrongs which might be thus committed in the zone against the dignity, honour, and security of the state, and if it be the fact that any of those writers have maintained that such wrongs are not punishable by the state on whose territory they are committed, they are at variance in that respect with an enormous majority of other writers of the first eminence, and may, I think, be safely put aside.

It is no sufficient answer to say that a foreigner so acting would be punishable by the law of his own country. For it may be that he does not belong to any civilised country, or that the law of the country to which he belongs has made no provision for the punishment of an outrage upon the subject of another state out of their

1876

THE QUEEN
v.
KEYN.

Amphlett, J.A.
own dominions. Indeed until a comparatively recent period our own law contained no such provision.

Nor is it any answer to say that the same evils might arise on the ocean beyond the zone. Our immediate shores would at least be protected by extending our frontier to that distance, nor would any collision such as has happened in this case be so likely to occur.

It is said that no precedent can be found for the exercise by the Court of Admiralty of criminal jurisdiction over a foreigner on board of a foreign vessel, but it must be remembered that the jurisdiction is only claimed in respect of crimes committed against a person outside the vessel, and where such vessel is within the zone. Such a case must be rare, and very probably was never under the consideration of any Court before.

For these reasons I think that the Central Criminal Court had jurisdiction to try the prisoner for the offence with which he was charged, and that the conviction, therefore, ought to be confirmed.

Brett, J.A.

BRETT, J.A. The prisoner was at the Central Criminal Court convicted of manslaughter, that is to say, he was found to have been guilty of acts and their results which amount, according to the law of England, to the crime of manslaughter. The prisoner was a German subject.

The question reserved is, whether the Court which tried him had jurisdiction so to do. All are agreed that it had none, unless by reason of the locality in which the crime was committed. It was committed on the open sea, but within three miles of the coast of England. It is suggested that it was also committed on board an English ship. In either case it is urged it was committed in a locality or place subject to the criminal law of England, and to the jurisdiction of the Central Criminal Court. It was argued on the one side that the open sea within three miles of the coast of England is a part of the territory of England as much and as completely as if it were land a part of England; that the criminal law of England, unless expressly restricted, applies to every crime, by whomsoever committed, within the territory of England; that there is no express restriction as to the crime in question; that the criminal law, therefore, is to be applied to the present case. It was further argued that at all events the crime was committed on board an English ship, and, therefore, although by a foreigner, it is by statute to be tried according to the criminal law of England. It was answered that the open sea within three miles of the coast of England is not in any sense a part of the territory of England or within the jurisdiction of the Crown of England; that if it be within the jurisdiction of the Crown, so that the Sovereign or Parliament of England might, by constituting a Court to do so, have properly taken cognizance of the crime, yet no such Court has been constituted, and, therefore, the Central Criminal Court had no jurisdiction. It was further argued that even though the open sea within three miles be a part of the territory of England, yet the crime was committed on board a foreign ship, and, therefore, could not be tried in England.

The questions raised by these arguments seem to me to be: First, is the open sea within three miles of the coast a part of the territory of England as much and as completely as if it were land a part of England? Secondly, if it is, has the Central Criminal Court any jurisdiction to try alleged crimes there committed, by whomsoever committed? Thirdly, can the crime be properly said to have been committed on board of an English ship so as thereby to give jurisdiction to an English Court, although the sea in question be not a part of England? Fourthly, can it be properly said to have been committed on board of the German ship; and if so, is jurisdiction thereby ousted from an English Court, although the sea in question be a part of English territory? As to the first part, the argument does not deny that it is an axiom of law that the criminal law of England runs everywhere within England, so as to be applicable to every crime by whomsoever therein committed. If the three miles of open sea are a part of the territory of England, it was not denied,—nay it was expressly admitted,—that unless there be an exception in favour of a crime committed on board of a foreign passing ship, and this crime was committed on board of such a ship, the criminal law of England might of right be applied to the crime. What was denied upon this hypothesis, as to the three miles of open sea, was that the Central Criminal Court, or indeed any Court hitherto

constituted by the sovereign authority, had had jurisdiction given
to it to apply the criminal law to such a case. The great question
argued was, whether the three miles of open sea next the coast
are or are not a part of the territory of England, meaning thereby
a territory in which its law is paramount and exclusive. Before
examining this proposition, I should wish to observe that the
question what is or is not a part of the realm is, in my opinion, not
in general a question for judges to decide. Their duty as to the
administration of the criminal law is to administer it, as between
the Crown and all persons within the realm, with regard to any
crime alleged to have been committed within the realm, and as
between the Crown and all the Queen's subjects, with regard to
any crime alleged to have been committed by any subject of the
Queen anywhere. What are the limits of the realm should in
general be declared by Parliament. Its declaration would be conclusive, either as authority or as evidence. But in this case of
the open sea there is no such declaration, and the question is in
this case necessarily left to the judges, and to be determined on
other evidence or authority. Such evidence might have consisted
of proof of a continuous public claim by the Crown of England,
enforced, when practicable, by arms, but not consented to by other
nations. I should have considered such proof sufficient for English
judges. In England it cannot be admitted that the limits of
England depend on the consent of any other nation. But no such
evidence was offered. The only evidence suggested in this case
is, that by the law of nations every country bordered by the sea is
to be held to have, as part of its territory, meaning thereby a
territory in which its law is paramount and exclusive, the three
miles of open sea next to its coast; and, therefore, that England
among others has such territory. The question on both sides has
been made to depend on whether such is or is not proved to be the
law of nations. On the one side it is said there is evidence and
authority on which the Court ought to hold that such is the law
of nations; on the other side it is said there is no such evidence or
authority. The evidence relied on for the Crown is an alleged
common acquiescence by recognized jurists of so many countries,
as to be substantially of all countries, and declarations of statesmen, and similar declarations of English judges in court in the

course of administering law. On the other side it is said that the declarations cited of the judges were opinions only, and not decisions; that there is no common acquiescence of jurists to the alleged effect, or declarations of statesmen; and that if there were, such acquiescence or declarations are not sufficient; that there should be acquiescence by governments declared in treaties or evidenced by acts of government. It is admitted that there is no such acquiescence by any general treaty or by unequivocal acts of many, if of any, governments. Main reliance is placed by the one side on the alleged common agreement of jurists. Their acquiescence or agreement in fact is denied by the other side, and, further, their authority is denied, if such acquiescence or agreement is held to exist.

It seems, therefore, necessary to determine, first, what is the authority of a common agreement or acquiescence of jurists; secondly, is there any such acquiescence or agreement with regard to three miles of open sea adjacent to countries? thirdly, if there is, what is the exact purport of such agreement. As to the first, the propositions in respect of which the testimony of jurists may be accepted, and the grounds of accepting their testimony, are stated by Grotius:—

"As the laws of each state are made with regard to its own particular advantage, so the *consent of all* states, or of the greater number, may *well make laws common between them all.* And it seems that in fact such laws have been made, which tend to the advantage, not of each state in particular, but of the whole assemblage of such states. These are what are called the law of nations as distinguished from the law of nature": Introduction, s. 18.

That is to say, that there is in fact a law of nations, enacted, as it were, by common consent. Again, he says:

"I have used in favour of this law the testimony of philosophers, historians, poets, and even of orators; not that they are to be indiscriminately relied on, &c., but because where many persons in different ages and countries concur in the same statement, it (i.e. the sentiment or proposition) must be referred to some general cause. In the subject now in question, this cause must be either a just deduction from the principles of natural justice or universal consent. The first discovers to us the natural law, the second the law of nations. In order to distinguish these two branches of the same science, we must consider not merely the terms which authors have used to define them (for they often confound the terms natural law and law of nations), but the nature of the subject in question. For if a certain maxim, which cannot fairly be inferred from admitted principles, is nevertheless found to be everywhere observed, there is reason to conclude that it derives its origin from positive institution:" s. 41.

This latter citation seems to me to assert that the testimony of writers and statesmen is to be received, and that if they, being of different nations and living at different times, have agreed to a common proposition which is not unreasonable, such agreement may be received as evidence of a common consent of nations, forming thereby a law of nations:—

"To form an useful library (says Martens, Introduction, s. 8), for the studying of the positive law of nations, the following classes of books are indispensably necessary." He then enumerates treaties, history, &c., and lastly, he says, " And above all, all the regular treatises on this science."

Wheaton (c. 1, s. 11) is still more distinct:—

"The various sources of international law," he says, are these: (1.) Text-writers of authority shewing what is the approved usage of nations, or the general opinion respecting their mutual conduct, with the definitions and modifications introduced by general consent. Without wishing to exaggerate the importance of these writers, or to substitute in any case their authority for the principles of reason, it may be affirmed that they are generally impartial in their judgment. They are witnesses of the sentiments and usages of civilized nations, and the weight of their testimony increases every time that their authority is invoked by statesmen, and every year that passes without the rules laid down in their works being impugned by the avowal of contrary principles."

Kent (Lecture 1, p. 2), says:

"The most useful and practical part of the law of nations is, no doubt, in-stituted on positive law, founded on usage, consent, and agreement." At p. 16:—
" Grotius, therefore, went purposely into the details of history and the usages of nations ; and he resorted to the works of philosophers, historians, orators, poets, civilians, and divines for the materials out of which the science of public morality should be formed ; proceeding on the principle that when many men at different times and places unanimously affirmed the same thing for truth, it ought to be ascribed to some universal cause."

He then cites Puffendorf and Vattel as authorities for the proposition he has in hand. And then, at p. 18, he says:

" We now appeal to more accurate, more authentic, more precise, and more commanding evidence of the rules of public law, by a reference to the decisions of those tribunals to whom in every country the administration of that branch of jurisprudence is specially intrusted, &c." "But in the absence of higher and more authoritative sanctions, the ordinances of foreign states, the opinions of eminent statesmen, and the writings of distinguished jurists are regarded as of great con-s'deration on questions not settled by conventional law. In cases where the

1876

THE QUEEN
v.
KEYN.

Brett, J.A.

principal jurists agree, the presumption will be very great in favour of the solidity of their maxims; and no civilized nation that does not arrogantly set all ordinary law and justice at defiance will venture to disregard the uniform sense of the established writers on international law."

Story in his Treatise on the Conflict of Laws (s. 3), says, after stating the use among commercial nations of a system of international justice,

" The system thus introduced for the purposes of commerce has gradually extended itself to other objects, &c. New rules, resting on the basis of general convenience and an enlarged sense of national duty, have from time to time been promulgated by jurists and supported by courts of justice, by a course of judicial reasoning which has commanded almost universal confidence, respect, and obedience without the aid either of municipal statutes, or of royal ordinances, or of international treaties."

This is a strong assertion of the respect due to the propositions of great jurists, though they may not have been adopted either in legislation or treaties. And Phillimore, summing up all these, says, in chap. 5 :

" The next and only other source of international law is the consent of nations. This consent is expressed in two ways, (1.),'it is openly expressed by being embodied in positive conventions or treaties; (2.), it is tacitly expressed by long usage, practice, and custom." And in chap. 6 :—"Such being the influence of usage upon international law, it becomes of importance to ascertain where the repositories and what the evidence may be of this great source of international law."

He then enumerates history, treaties, proclamations or manifestoes, marine ordinances, the decisions of prize courts. And then in chap. 7 :—

" The consent of nations is further evidenced by the concurrent testimony of great writers upon international jurisprudence."
(Citing Ortolan, b. 1, c. iv. t. i. p. 74):—
" The works of some of them have become recognized digests of the principles of the science, and to them every civilized country yields great, if not implicit, homage." In the note he says : "The English Courts of common law, and English commentators on that law, both in cases of public and private international law, have been in the habit of referring to other works of those foreign authors as containing evidence of the law to be administered in England." " Lord Mansfield," he says, " in fact built up the fabric of English commercial law upon the foundation of the principles contained in the works of foreign jurists. In the Admiralty and Ecclesiastical Courts these works have always been referred to as authorities." Speaking of Grotius, he says:—" He may be almost said to have himself laid the foundation of that great pillar of international law, the authority of international jurists."

1876

THE QUEEN
v.
KEYN.

Brett, J.A.

Such are the views expressed in the treatises of recognised writers. The same opinion seems to be affirmed in judgments of the greatest judges. Lord Stowell, in *The Maria* (1), says:—

"If authority is required, I have authority, I mean, &c., Baron Puffendorf." Again:—"All writers upon the law of nations unanimously acknowledge it." And, again:—"Vattel is here to be considered, not as a lawyer merely delivering an opinion, but as a witness asserting the fact, the fact that such is the existing practice of modern Europe."

Lord Stowell then cites as authorities for the proposition he is enunciating, Valin, Vattel, and other known writers. I have cited these specific statements from this one judgment of Lord Stowell, but I think that a perusal of his judgments throughout his judicial career, and of those of Dr. Lushington, will shew that neither of those great masters ever treated of or decided a disputed proposition of international law without citing and relying on, as authority and evidence, the expressed opinions of recognised writers on the law of nations. In *Triquet* v. *Bath* (2) Lord Mansfield says upon this very point, and in order to justify his own reliance on the writers:—

"I remember a case before Lord Talbot of *Buvot* v. *Barbut*, in which Lord Talbot declared a clear opinion, that the law of nations in its full extent was part of the law of England, and that the law of nations was to be collected from the practice of different nations and the authority of writers. And accordingly he argued and determined from such instances, and the authority of Grotius, Barbeyrac, Bynkershoek, Wiquefort, &c., there being no English writers of eminence upon the subject. I was counsel in the case, says Lord Mansfield, and have a full note of it. I remember, too, Lord Hardwicke's declaring his opinion to the same effect."

Here, therefore, we have the opinions and practice of Lord Talbot, Lord Hardwicke, Lord Mansfield, Lord Stowell, and Dr. Lushington.

As to the opinions of statesmen, I will cite only that of Sir James Mackintosh, because, if any can be decisive, his must be. In his Discourse upon the Study of the Law of Nature and the Law of Nations, he says:

"What we at the present time call the law of nations is become, as to many points, as precise and certain as positive law; the principles of it are more parti-

---

(1) 1 C. Rob. at p. 351.   (2) 3 Burr. 1478.

1876

THE QUEEN
v.
KEYN.

Brett, J.A.

cularly established in the writings of those who have treated on the science which I am about to treat." Speaking of Grotius he says: "His mind was not so servile and stupid as that he used the opinions of poets and orators, of historians and philosophers, as the decisions of judges without appeal. He cites them, as he himself says, as witnesses, whose unanimous consent or agreement, strengthened moreover by their differences on almost all other points, is conclusive proof of the general agreement of mankind upon the great rules of duty and the fundamental principles of morality."

This passage is styled by Hallam as "a noble defence of Grotius," whom he himself styles as "the founder of the modern law of nations": Literature of Europe, part iii. c. 4, s. 3.

And Phillimore again, citing this, says (at p. 62):

"In truth, a reverence for the opinion of accredited writers upon public and international law has been a distinguishing characteristic of statesmen in all countries, and perhaps especially of those who have deserved that appellation in this kingdom. It has been felt and eloquently expressed by them, that though these writers were not infallible, nevertheless the methodized reasonings of the great publicists and jurists formed the digest and jurisprudence of the Christian world."

And in chap. 8 (Recapitulation of Sources of International Law) he says:

"The sources, then, from which international jurisprudence is derived are these," &c., &c. He then enumerates many, and among them this: "The universal consent of nations, both as expressed by positive compact or treaty, and as implied by usage, custom, and practice; such usage, custom, and practice being evidenced in various ways: by precedents recorded in history, by being embodied and recorded in treaties, in public documents of states, in the decisions of international tribunals, in the works of eminent writers upon international jurisprudence."

And he cites a remarkable adhesion to the same view by a great American statesman. In Mr. Webster's letter of the 28th of March, 1843, to the British Government, that statesman says:

"If such well-known distinction exists, where are the proofs of it? What writers of authority on the public law, what adjudications in Courts of Admiralty, what public treaties recognise it?"

These authorities seem to me to make it clear that the consent of nations is requisite to make any proposition a part of the law of nations. Their consent is to be assumed to the logical application to given facts of the ethical axioms of right and wrong. Such an application is the foundation of every system of law, including necessarily the law of nations. Their consent must be proved by sufficient evidence to any other asserted proposition of international law. The question is, what is to be considered sufficient

proof of such consent. On the one side, it is said, that among
other heads of evidence of such consent the writings of recognised
jurists of different nations are to be received, and that a common
consent of them all, or of substantially all of them, to a reasonable
proposition may be accepted as proof of the common consent of
nations, though the proposition has not yet been brought, for the
purposes of action, before the governments of nations. On the
other side, it is said, that the propositions of such writers are
theories, not binding unless and until they have been adopted by
governments; and that such adoption must be shewn by some express declarations of governments, or by some acts of governments.
If the latter be true, it is obvious that there can be no law on any
particular point until it has arisen in fact for the treatment of
governments; it cannot be raised by them and decided by antici-
pation, because there is no common tribunal or legislature. Yet
the latter contention is, as I understand, approved by high authority among us.

It is in deference to the weight of that authority that I have so
elaborated the citations from great writers, judges, and statesmen.
And I feel obliged to say that, in my opinion, the long list of great
authorities to which I have referred and the constant practice of
the English International Court, nay, I think, of all English Courts,
shew that it is considered that all countries have recognised that
the consent of them all, as sovereigns, may and should be inferred
in favour of a reasonable proposition from a common consent to it
of all, or of such a considerable number as to amount substantially
to all, recognised writers on international law, although there be
no other evidence of their sovereign assent.

The next questions are whether there is, by reason of such or
other evidence, proof of a common consent of nations to any propositions, and if to any, to what proposition, with regard to the
three miles of open sea which are adjacent to any country. And,
first, let us consider the writers. It seems to me that Grotius
assents to a right to the adjacent sea, and to the proposition that
such right is a territorial right. It will be necessary hereafter to
consider the sense in which that term "territorial" is used by the
writers :—

"Videtur autem imperium in maris portionem eadem ratione acquiri, qua
imperia alia, id est ut supra diximus, ratione personarum et ratione territorii.

Ratione personarum ut si classis, qui maritimus est exercitus, aliquo in loco maris se habeat : ratione territorii quatenus ex terra cogi possunt qui in proxima maris parte versantur, nec minus quam si in ipsa terra reperirentur."

This seems to me to admit a territorial right in a country over the adjacent sea. It does not explicitly determine the limits of that sea ; but it states, as the principle of limitation, the distance from land over which compulsion could be exercised from the land. There is no real difference, as it seems to me, between this and the proposition of Bynkershoek. The more general principle enunciated by him is—

"Unde dominium maris proximi non ultra concedimus quam e terra illi imperari potest."

That is the same as the principle of Grotius. In order to carry this principle into practice, he lays down the other :

"Quare omnino videtur rectius eo potestatem terræ extendi quousque tormenta exploduntur."

And then further to shew that he is adapting the practical application of his principle to the times in which he lived, he says :

"Loquor autem de his temporibus, quibus illis machinis utimur; alioquin generaliter dicendum esset, potestatem terræ finiri ubi finitur armorum vis."

He gives the dominion of the adjacent sea to the adjacent land, and defines the limit of such sea to be the distance of a cannon shot from the land. I do not think it useful to cite the words on this point of all the other writers. It is not, as I understand, denied that all, or substantially all, agree that there is a right of some kind over the adjacent open sea, and that none deny the extent of a marine league or three miles, although some claim more. As to the nature of that right, Puffendorf speaks of it as—

"An accessory to the land as much as the ditch of a town is accessory to the town."

I apprehend his meaning to be, that it is a part of the town, that is, a part of the territory of the town. Wolff is still more express. Speaking of the adjacent sea, he says :

"Quoniam partes maris occupatæ ad territorium illius gentis pertinent, quæ eas occupavit, quale jus Rector civitatis in suo territorio habet, tale etiam ipsi competit in partibus maris occupatis. Per consequens, qui in iis versantur iisdem legibus subsunt quam qui in terris habitant aut commorantur, etiam peregrini admissi."

This is to say that the adjacent sea is "territory," and that a consequence of its being territory is that the country has its ordinary jurisdictions over all who are within that territory. Hubner calls this sea "an accessory." Moser says it is under the sovereignty of the adjacent land. Hautefeuille calls them "territorial waters," and declares that they are the property of the nation, and that consequently the nation has over them all the rights of sovereignty without exception. Ortolan has a chapter (chap. viii.) headed "De la mer Territoriale." He admits that there is a right in the adjacent country over the adjacent territorial water. As to its extent, he says :

"La règle que donne Bynkershoek : Terræ potestas finitur ubi finitur armorum vis, est aujourd'hui la règle du droit des gens, et depuis l'invention des armes à feu cette distance a ordinairement été considérée comme de trois milles." As to the kind of jurisdiction, he says (p. 157) : "Ce n'est pas seulement la défense générale du pays et de ses intérêts publics contre toutes les attaques dont il pourrait être l'objet; c'est aussi la défense de ses nationaux, de ses habitants, de toute personne même étrangère, qui y résident, dans leur sûreté, dans leur propriété, dans leurs intérêts individuels contre les délits de toute sorte qui pourraient y porter atteinte. Chargé de cette défense publique et particulière sur tout cet espace, l'État a le droit de faire les règlements, les lois nécessaires à ce but, et d'employer la force publique pour les y faire exécuter. Ainsi les lois de police et de sûreté y sont obligatoires. En un mot, l'État a sur cet espace non la propriété, mais un droit d'empire; un pouvoir de législation, de surveillance et de juridiction, conformément aux règles de la juridiction internationale."

A right of sovereignty which gives a right of legislation, in order to protect the rights of property and to ensure the individual safety of all, even strangers, against offence of every kind, is, I think, as complete a sovereign right as any nation has on land. It is true that Ortolan denies that the nation has a right of property in this territorial sea :

"Ainsi, le droit qui existe sur la mer territoriale n'est pas un droit de propriété; on ne peut pas dire que l'État, propriétaire des côtes, soit propriétaire de cette mer."

But this assertion, it must be observed, is made as a conclusion from a previous chain of reasons. Therefore, it says, the right is not a right of property. The previous reason is, the want of power properly to refuse a free passage to ships passing with harmless intent. The conclusion is not, to English lawyers, a

satisfactory result of such a cause. There may be a right of property, subject to a prescriptive accorded free right of way. I
cannot but think, therefore, that substantially all the foreign jurists
are in accord in asserting that, by the common consent of all
nations, each which is bordered by an open sea has over the three
adjacent miles of it a territorial right. And the sense in which
they all use that term seems to me to be fully explained by
Vattel (lib. i. c. 18, s. 205). He says:

"Lorsqu'une nation s'empare d'un pays qui n'appartient encore à personne, elle
est censée y occuper l'empire, ou la souveraineté, en même temps que le domaine."
"Tout l'espace dans lequel une nation étend son empire forme le ressort de sa juridiction et s'appelle son territoire." At lib. ii. s. 84:—" L'empire, uni au domaine,
établit la juridiction de la nation dans le pays qui lui appartient, dans son territoire."

This seems plain; sovereignty and dominion necessarily give or
import jurisdiction, and do so throughout the territory. Applying this to the territorial sea (at lib. 1, c. 23, s. 295) he says:

"Quand une nation s'empare de certaines parties de la mer, elle y occupe
l'empire aussi bien que le domaine, etc. Ces parties de la mer sont de la juridiction du territoire de la nation; le souverain y commande, il y donne des lois
et peut réprimer ceux qui les violent; en un mot, il y a tous les mêmes droits
qui lui appartiennent sur la terre," etc.

It seems to me that this is in reality a fair representation of the
accord or agreement of substantially all the foreign writers on
international law; and that they all agree in asserting that, by the
consent of all nations, each, which is bordered by open sea, has a
right over such adjacent sea as a territorial sea, that is to say, as a
part of its territory; and that they all mean thereby to assert that
it follows, as a consequence of such sea being a part of its territory,
that each such nation has in general the same right to legislate
and to enforce its legislation over that part of the sea as it has
over its land territory. With its own consent, given to all other
nations in the same way as they have consented to its right of
territory, consent from which neither it nor they can rightly
depart without the consent of all, there is for all nations a free
right of way to pass over such sea with harmless intent; but such
a right does not derogate from the exercise of all its sovereign
rights in other respects. As to the extent of this territory, it is
impossible to say that all writers have been always agreed as to its

1876
THE QUEEN
v.
KEYN.
Brett, J.A.

boundary seaward. Some nations have in the olden times claimed more than the three miles. The reasonings of some writers would now give more than three miles; but no nation is, I think, shewn to claim less than three miles, and all nations and writers yield to three miles at least. If that be so, as I think it is, it may properly be said that all are agreed as to three miles. If one claims a debt of 1000*l.* and the other admits a debt of 500*l.*, they are agreed that there is a debt of 500*l.*, though they are in dispute as to the other 500*l.* Let us now proceed to the American and English writers. Wheaton (c. 4, s. 10) says:

" The controversy how far the open sea or main ocean beyond the immediate boundary of the coasts may be appropriated by one nation to the exclusion of others, &c., can hardly be considered open at this day. We have already seen that by the generally approved usage of nations, which forms the basis of international law, the maritime territory of every nation extends (1), to the ports, harbours, bays, &c.; (2) to the distance of a marine league, or as far as a cannon shot will reach from the shore, along all the coasts of the state." And afterwards —" The reasons which forbid the assertion of an exclusive proprietary right to the sea in general will be found inapplicable to the particular portions of that element included in the above designations."

In these passages the same expressions are used as are used by the foreign writers, namely, " maritime territory," and, as a paraphrase, " an exclusive proprietary right."

The passage in Kent (s. 2, p. 29) is said to be indistinct. I think it will be seen that the only portions of the received propositions which he declares to be indistinct are those which relate to the distance. I think he shews that he is clearly of opinion that for some distance there is an exclusive dominion. This meaning is certainly attributed to Kent by Sir R. Phillimore, who cites this passage of Kent among other authorities in support of the following statement:—

" Though the open sea be thus incapable of being subject to the rights of property or jurisdiction, yet reason, practice, and authority have firmly settled that a different rule is applicable to certain portions of the sea. And, first, with respect to that portion of the sea which washes the coast of an independent state, &c., the rule of law may be now considered as fairly established, namely, that this absolute property and jurisdiction does not extend, unless by the specific provisions of a treaty, or an unquestionable usage, beyond a marine league, &c. In the sea, out of reach of cannon shot, says Lord Stowell, universal use is presumed. This (i.e. the reach of cannon shot or a marine league) is the limit fixed to absolute property and jurisdiction."

In *The Maria* (1), Lord Stowell says :

1876

THE QUEEN
v.
KEYN.

Brett, J.A.

" It might likewise be improper for me to pass over entirely without notice, as another preliminary observation, though without meaning to lay any particular stress on it, that the transaction in question took place in the British Channel close upon the British coast, a station over which the crown of England has from pretty remote antiquity always asserted something of that special jurisdiction which the sovereigns of other countries have claimed and exercised over certain parts of the seas adjoining to their coasts."

This is not precise, but it could not have been written by Lord Stowell in such a judgment if he had intended to reject the proposition which asserts jurisdiction over the adjacent open sea within some limit of distance. His view of the law, however, cannot be doubted. In *The Twee Gebroeders* (2) the Prussian consul claimed restitution of four Dutch ships seized by an English man-of-war; on a suggestion by the consul that the seizure was made within the protection of the Prussian territory, Lord Stowell, in giving judgment, said :

" This ship was taken on a voyage to Amsterdam, which was then under blockade. A claim has been given for the Prussian government, asserting the capture to have been made within the Prussian territory. It has been contended that, although the act of capture itself might not have taken place within the neutral territory, yet that the ship to which the capturing boats belonged was actually lying within the neutral limits. The first fact to be determined is the character of the place where the capturing ship lay, whether she was actually stationed within those portions of land and water, or of something between water and land, which are considered to be within Prussian territory. She was lying within the eastern branch of the Eems, within what I think may be considered as a distance of three miles at most from East Friesland. I am of opinion that the ship was lying within those limits in which all direct operations are by the law of nations forbidden to be exercised. No proximate acts of war are in any manner to be allowed to originate on neutral ground, and I cannot but think that such an act as this, that a ship should station herself on neutral territory and send out her boats on hostile enterprises, is an act of hostility much too immediate to be permitted. The capture cannot be maintained."

This case seems to me to be of immense importance in the present discussion. The very ground of decision is, that the capturing ship was stationed within neutral territory. The only reason why she was held to be so was, that the three miles of sea was the territory of Prussia. The ground of that last decision is not that the water was intra fauces or otherwise. It is only on the ground that the ship was within three miles of the coast. Here,

(1) 1 C. Rob. 352.   (2) 3 C. Rob. 162.

1876

THE QUEEN
v.
KEYN.

Brett, J.A.

therefore, we have a claim based on this principle made by a government, an opinion of Lord Stowell, and a judicial decision by him in an international court.

In the case of *The Leda* (1) Dr. Lushington held that s. 330 of the Merchant Shipping Act, 1864, which is limited in terms to the United Kingdom, "applied to the three miles of open sea round England."

"What," he says, "are the limits of the United Kingdom? The only answer I can conceive to that question is, the land of the United Kingdom and three miles from the shore."

In the *General Iron Screw Colliery Co.* v. *Schurmanns* (2), there had been a collision between a British ship of the plaintiffs and a Dutch ship, two miles and a half off Dungeness. The British ship had in the Admiralty Court been held solely to blame. The plaintiffs, her owners, filed a bill in Chancery to declare a limitation of her liability according to the provisions of the Merchant Shipping Act. It was admitted that, unless there was reciprocity, that is to say, that unless the statute might, in like case, have been relied on by the foreign ship, it could not be relied on against her. The question therefore argued was, whether the statute applied to the locality of the collision, and therefore would have applied to the foreign ship. It was argued for the plaintiffs that the ninth part of the statute is general, and therefore applies to the whole of Her Majesty's dominions. The statute must, therefore, be taken, it was said, to extend as far as jurisdiction could be asserted consistently with the law of nations. It has long been the settled law of nations that each country may exercise jurisdiction over the sea within three miles of the shore. The answering argument was: "The fallacy of the argument for the plaintiffs lies in the assumption that a country has by the law of nations a general territorial jurisdiction to the distance of three miles from its coast. The question as to jurisdiction and territorial jurisdiction, that is to say, jurisdiction on the ground of the locality being the territory of England, was precisely raised by the facts and arguments. Lord Hatherley's judgment is:—

"With respect to foreign ships, I shall adhere to the opinion which I expressed

(1) Swa. Adm. 40.   (2) 1 J. & H. 180.

1876

THE QUEEN
v.
KEYN.

Brett, J.A.

in *Cope* v. *Doherty* (1), that a foreign ship meeting a British ship on the open ocean cannot properly be abridged of her rights by an act of the British legislature. Then comes the question how far our legislature could properly affect the rights of foreign ships within the limits of three miles from the coast of this country. There can be no possible doubt that the water below low-water mark is part of the high sea. But it is equally beyond question, that for certain purposes every country may, by the common law of nations, exercise jurisdiction over that portion of the high seas which lies within three miles from its shores."

He cites *The Leda,* and holds that the statute does apply to foreign as well as to British ships within the three miles. I can see no principle on which this application of the British statute can be founded other than the principle that a British statute in general terms is applicable to every part of British territory. The foundation of the judgment therefore is, that the three miles of high sea or open sea next to the coast is a part of the British territory, and by citing *The Leda* the learned judge shewed that he so intended.

In *Free Fishers of Whitstable* v. *Gann* (2), Erle, C.J., says:

"The soil of the sea shore to the extent of three miles from the beach is vested in the Crown."

In *Gann* v. *Free Fishers of Whitstable* (3) this was not denied, though it was held that no toll can be taken for the mere fact of a ship anchoring, as part of her process of navigating through the three miles. Lord Chelmsford says:

"The three-miles limit depends upon a rule of international law, by which every independent state is considered to have territorial property and jurisdiction in the seas which wash their coast within the assumed distance of a cannon shot from the shore."

And in *Gammell* v. *Commissioners of Woods and Forests* (4) it was held that salmon fishing in the open sea around the coast belongs to the Crown. Lord Wensleydale, at p. 465, says:

"It may be worth while to observe that it would be hardly possible to extend it seaward beyond the distance of three miles, which by the acknowledged law of nations belongs to the coast of the country, is under the dominion of the country by being within cannon range, and so capable of being kept in perpetual possession."

These expressions of great lawyers are, no doubt, not binding authority, but they disclose an intimate acquaintance with the writers, using their very terms of art, and shew that these judges

(1) 4 K. & J. 367.   (3) 2 H. L. C. 192.
(2) 11 C. B. (N.S.) 387.   (4) 3 Macq. 419.

acquiesced in the authority and the law of those writers. And the full meaning of so learned a judge as Lord Wensleydale is to be gathered from the passage in Co. Litt., s. 439. The section is:

> "In the same manner it seemeth where a man is out of the realm, &c., if such a one be disseised," &c. The comment is—"Out of the realm, id est, extra regnum, as much as to say as out of the power of the King of England, as of his crown of England; for if a man be upon the sea of England he is within the kingdom or realm of England, and within the liegeance of the King of England as of his crown of England. And yet altum mare is out of the jurisdiction of the common law, and within the jurisdiction of the Lord Admiral," &c.

Once let it be fixed what is the sea of England—and this is high authority that such sea is within the kingdom, and realm, and dominion of the sovereign,—that is to say, once agree that the three miles are the sea of England, and then it follows that the rights of England within that sea are as if it were land territory, and are the same as in any other part of the kingdom, and realm, and dominion of the sovereign. The decision in *The Saxonia* (1) is not to the contrary. The statute, in the part of it in question, is in express terms confined to British ships, that is to say, to ships owned to a given extent by British subjects. In America there is the great authority of Mr. Justice Story. In the brig *Ann* (2), the case was that by statute a certain embargo was laid on all ships and vessels in the ports and places within the limits and jurisdiction of the United States, that is to say, an embargo against their sailing out of or away from such limits.

The *Ann* had arrived from Alexandria in Columbia off the port of Newburyport. She anchored between two and three miles from Newburyport bar, which, that is to say, the bar, as the case states, is the limit of the port of Newburyport, and about the same distance from the neighbouring land. She afterwards sailed for Jamaica. The question made was whether, by sailing from her anchorage off Newburyport for Jamaica, she had broken a statutory embargo, which question depended on whether she was within the United States when at anchor off Newburyport. Story, J., said:

> "As the *Ann* arrived off Newburyport, and within three miles of the shore, it is clear that she was within the acknowledged jurisdiction of the United States. All the writers upon public law agree that every nation has exclusive jurisdiction

---

(1) 15 Moo. P. C. 262.   (2) 1 Gallison, 62.

1876

The Queen
v.
Keyn.
Brett, J.A.

to the distance of a cannon shot or marine league over the waters adjacent to its shores, and this doctrine has been recognised by the Supreme Court, &c. Indeed, such waters are considered as a part of the territory of the sovereign."

It is clear that he held that, because the brig was within the territory of the United States when anchored in the open sea off Newburyport, but within three miles of the shore, and because she sailed from the territory of the United States for Jamaica, she broke the embargo, and was liable to forfeiture. In this case, as in the case of *The Leda*, there is a judicial decision, the foundation of which is the affirmation of the proposition, that the open sea, adjacent to a sovereign country, is, for a distance of three miles, a part of the territory of that country, and that it is so by virtue of a consent of all nations. I cited a passage from Vattel (lib. 1, c. 18, s. 205) to shew what is, in the view of the foreign jurists, the extent of the sovereign jurisdiction consequent upon the national ownership of territory. I will add the view of Marshall, C.J. In *The Exchange*, he says: (1)

"The jurisdiction of the nation within its own territory is necessarily exclusive and absolute. It is susceptible of no limitation not imposed by itself. Any restriction upon it, deriving validity from an external source, would imply a diminution of its sovereignty to the extent of the restriction, and an investment of that sovereignty to the same extent in that power which could impose such restriction. All exceptions, therefore, to the full and complete power of a nation within its own territories must be traced up to the consent of the nation itself. They can flow from no other legitimate source."

There remains one more piece of evidence. It is stated in Wheaton, at p. 344, thus:

"In the negotiations which preceded the signature of the Treaty of Intervention of the 15th of July, 1840, the closing of the straits of the Dardanelles in the hands of Turkey was objected to by Russia. It was replied on the part of the British Government, that its opinion respecting the navigation of these straits by the ships of war of foreign nations rested upon a general and fundamental principle of international law." Every state is considered as having territorial jurisdiction "over the sea which washes its shores as far as three miles from low-water mark; and consequently any strait, which is bounded on both sides by the territory of the same sovereign, and which is not more than six miles wide, lies within the territorial jurisdiction of that sovereign."

And the treaty was concluded in accordance with that proposition. And as further, and to my mind the strongest of all evidence of what kind of right is recognised by all nations to be

(1) 7 Cranch, 136.

in these three miles of adjacent open sea, I cite the admitted rules
as to neutrality—not merely the rights given to the adjacent
state, but the duties imposed on such state. Such a duty has
hitherto invariably been founded on an abuse or improper use of
the territory of the neutral state. To found such duty on any other
ground would be abnormal. To found it on territory is to act on
the universal rule. The fact, therefore, of such duty being universally vouched in respect of the three miles of sea, is, as it seems
to me, the strongest evidence that such sea is universally treated
as a part of the territory of the adjacent state.

After citing this long list of authorities, I make the following
observations. I have done so because it seems to me that the
whole question depends entirely upon authority. There is no
reason, founded on the axiomatic rules of right and wrong, why the
three miles should or should not be considered as a part of the
territory of the adjacent country. They may have been so treated
by general consent; they might equally well have not been so
treated. If they have been so treated by such consent, the authority for the alleged ownership is sufficient. The question is,
whether such a general consent has in this case been proved by
sufficient evidence. I have cited the assertions of a large number
of writers, recognised as able writers on international law, of different countries and different periods. I have cited assertions of
statesmen, and opinions of great judges, and the decisions of some
judges, and the assertion made on behalf of a great government. As
there is no common court of nations, and no common legislature,
none of these are, in the usual sense, binding on this Court. As
the opinions of the judges are manifestly founded on the opinions
of the writers, I think the principal evidence is that of the writers.
I have already said that, in my opinion, a general consent of recognised writers of different times and different countries to a
reasonable proposition is sufficient evidence of a general consent
of nations to that proposition. Such a general consent establishes
the proposition as one of international law. In this case I think
there is a general consent to a proposition with regard to the
three miles of open sea adjacent to the shores of sovereign states.
I do not think that such general consent, as to a distance of three
miles, is impeached by shewing that there has been a difference

as to a claim by some with regard to a greater distance than three miles. The question is, what is the proposition to which such general consent as to the three miles is given? The dispute is whether, by the consent of all, certain limited rights are given to the adjacent country, such as a right that the waters should be treated as what is called a neutral zone, or whether the water is, by consent of all, given to the adjacent country as its territory, with all rights of territory, it being agreed by such country with all others, that all shall have a free right of navigation or way over such waters for harmless passage and some other rights. If the first be true, it is impossible, according to the reasoning of Vattel and Marshall, C.J.,—which reasoning, I think, is irresistible —that it can be properly said that the adjacent country has any proprietary right in the three miles, or any dominion, or any sovereignty, or any sovereign jurisdiction. If the latter be correct, the adjacent country has the three miles, as its property, as under its dominion and sovereignty. If so, that three miles are its territorial waters, subject to its rights of property, dominion, and sovereignty. Those are all the rights, and the same rights which a nation has, or can have, over its land territory. If, then, such be its rights over the three miles of sea, that sea is as much a part of its country or territory as its land.

Considering the authorities I have cited, the terms used by them, wholly inconsistent, as it seems to me, with the idea that the adjacent country has no property, no dominion, no sovereignty, no territorial right; and considering the necessary foundation of the admitted rights and duties of the adjacent country as to neutrality, which have always been made to depend on a right and duty as to its territory, I am of opinion that it is proved that, by the law of nations, made by the tacit consent of substantially all nations, the open sea within three miles of the coast is a part of the territory of the adjacent nation, as much and as completely as if it were land a part of the territory of such nation. By the same evidence which proves this proposition, it is equally proved that every nation which possesses this water territory has agreed with all other nations that all shall have the right of free navigation to pass through such water territory, if such navigation be with an innocent or harmless intent or purpose. This right of free navi-

extent of that jurisdiction is not touched by that dispute. The statute 13 Rich. 2, c. 5, does not in any way restrict the jurisdiction of the admiral on the sea not within a county. The admirals and their deputies, it says, "shall not meddle from henceforth with anything done within the realm of England, but only with things done upon the sea." This is evidently pointed at the same dispute. It recognises the jurisdiction of the admiral in respect of things done upon the sea. The term "realm," therefore, by the context means that part of the realm which is within counties. And so 15 Rich. 2, c. 3, is a declaration against an alleged jurisdiction of the admiral "within the bodies of counties either by land or water." The exception, therefore, in that statute as to death or mayhem done in great ships, &c., applies also to such crimes committed in such ships, though they are within the body of a county. The Commentary of Lord Coke says so.

"This latter clause gives the admiral further jurisdiction in case of death and mayhem, but in all other happening within the Thames or in any other river, port, or water which are within any county of the realm, &c., by express words of this Act of Parliament, the admiral or his deputy hath now jurisdiction."

This statute therefore does not define, or restrain, or limit any jurisdiction which the admiral had of things done on the seas. And the Commentary seems to me to assume that the admiral already had jurisdiction in respect of death and mayhem done and caused on the seas. I do not, of course, mean to say that it suggests that he had jurisdiction to administer the law of England in respect of things done to which the law of England was not applicable, but it does seem to me that it assumes that he had jurisdiction to administer the law of England to everything done on the seas to which the law of England was properly applicable.

The administration of the whole law of England is assumed to be divided between the land Courts and the admiral's Court. He cites, but with a wrong reference, as acknowledging the jurisdiction of the admiral, a statute of Elizabeth in these terms:—

"All and every such of the said offences before mentioned as hereafter shall be done on the main sea, or coast of the sea being no part of the body of any county, &c."

So that, says Lord Coke, by the judgment of the whole parliament the jurisdiction of the Lord Admiral is wholly confined to the "main sea," or "coasts of the sea being no parcel of the body of any county of this realm."

I cannot help thinking that the mention, both in the statute and the Commentary, of both the main sea "and the coasts of the sea," which latter must refer to sea no part of a county, i.e. to sea which is below low-water mark and which is open sea, is pregnant with an assumption by Lord Coke that there is a difference between the open sea, called the main sea, and the open sea on the coast. And in the case of *The Admiralty* (1) Lord Coke says:

"Upon which book I observe, &c. This proves directly that then the admiral had jurisdiction to adjudge things done upon the sea from whence no pais may come; and this did not begin then, but, without question, so long as there has been trade and traffic (which is the life of every land), there was marine jurisdiction to redress depredations, piracies, murders, and other offences upon the sea, &c.; and this does appear by the said Beresford, C.J., who speaketh in the voice of the Court, where he says that the King willeth that the peace be as well kept upon the sea as upon the land, and it is not possible that peace should be kept without jurisdiction of justice."

This is a strong assertion, that the jurisdiction of the sovereign authority, whatever that was, that is, to whatever it was applicable, to preserve peace, was, in respect of things done upon the sea, given to the Lord High Admiral. I think that the cases cited by Lord Hale are consistent with the supposition that those which were criminal cases were cases of piracy, and therefore that they cannot be relied on as judicial decisions of the point now in question; but still, I think that the opinion of Lord Hale himself is of great weight, and that in favour of the view that either the Admiralty or the Queen's Bench had criminal jurisdiction in respect of treasons and felonies done on those seas which were claimed to be the seas of England, and that such jurisdiction existed on the ground of the locality of the crime. If so, such jurisdiction extended to the crime by whomsoever there committed, for that is the meaning of jurisdiction by reason of locality. The charge of Sir Leoline Jenkins is unfortunately open to the remark that it is declamatory, and therefore inexact. Yet it is a statement of the law upon the very point of the jurisdiction of the Admiralty over crimes made by one of the most learned of English civilians and international lawyers. It is reported by

(1) 12 Co. Rep. 79, 80.

1876

THE QUEEN
v.
KEYN.
Brett, J.A.

Curteis as an authority for, and judicial exposition of, the law. It certainly seems to me to claim for the admiral no less than all the jurisdiction over the sea as to criminal offences which the sovereign might properly exercise. It claims, no doubt, also something more. But the excess of the claim does not seem to me to derogate from the authority of the view of this great lawyer, that the King had deputed to the admiral all the administration of criminal law in respect of crimes committed on the seas which the King could properly depute.

Considering, therefore, the presumption to be in favour of the constitution of a court to administer the criminal law, which it was the first duty of the sovereign to administer, and considering that all the authorities which speak of that Court speak of its jurisdiction without any terms of restriction, I think it is proved that the admiral's court was authorized by the sovereign authority to administer the criminal law in respect of all cases happening on . the seas outside of counties to which the criminal law of England might properly be applied, and therefore to all offences, by whomsoever committed, which are committed within the three miles adjacent to the coast. There are no words of restriction in the statutes through which the jurisdiction of the admiral is transferred to the Central Criminal Court. The phraseology of 9 Geo. 4, c. 31, s. 32, is of the largest capacity, and the crime of manslaughter is one mentioned at s. 9 in the Act.

It follows, therefore, in my opinion, that the Central Criminal Court has jurisdiction to try all crimes made cognizable in general terms by English law which may be committed by British subjects on any part of the sea, or which may be committed by any foreigner on board any British ship in any part of the sea, or which may be committed by any foreigner or British subject in any ship, British or foreign, on the open sea within three miles of the coast of Great Britain.

As to the question of whether the criminal offence charged in this case, namely, the offence of manslaughter, was committed on board of the foreign ship or on board of the British ship, I agree entirely with the Lord Chief Justice that it was not committed on board of either. There was no jurisdiction, therefore, given in respect of a complete offence committed locally within the British

ship. If there had been a complete offence within the foreign
ship, there would have been no exemption on that ground from
liability to English law. The only jurisdiction in respect of
locality which arises is that which arises from the fact of the
foreign ship having been within the territory of Great Britain.
Because she was, I am of opinion that the Central Criminal Court
had jurisdiction to try the case, and that the prisoner was legally
convicted.

BRAMWELL, J.A. I am of opinion that this conviction should
be quashed. The question is whether the case is within the
jurisdiction of the Admiralty. The first ground on which it is
said that it is, is that the matter occurred within three miles of
the English shore, it being admitted as to this point that if it had
occurred beyond that distance there would be no jurisdiction. As
no statute has given jurisdiction on that ground it follows that the
Admiralty, if it has that jurisdiction now, always has had it. Now
there is no case, no doctrine, no trace of opinion by judge or writer
that the Admiralty ever had a criminal jurisdiction in matters
occurring within a distance of three miles which it would not
have had they occurred beyond that distance.

One great argument in support of the claim of jurisdiction is,
that unless it exists, British subjects might be run down or otherwise injured, within a few yards of the British shore, with impunity
as far as British criminal law is concerned. The answer to which
is, that even though the Crown is right on this point the same
thing is true of a few yards distant from the three miles. I am
not influenced, on the other hand, by the argument that an act
done on a foreign ship by one foreigner on another passing within
the three miles would be the subject of our criminal law if the
Crown is right on this point, and that a child born in such a case
would be British. It may or may not be so. But the same
consequence would follow if the foreign ship were in a British
port. It is true that in that case it would have sought our hospitality, and not be exercising a right of navigation. But I can
see no great difference between a ship sailing inside or outside
Plymouth Breakwater. If such consequences follow logically,
they do not seem to me to preclude the possibility of what the

1876

THE QUEEN
v.
KEYN.

Bramwell, J.A.

Crown contends for. I am influenced by what the Solicitor General said we ought not to be influenced by, viz. the possible consequence of our decision, or rather that which would flow from it, if in favour of the Crown on this point. The right we should claim we must concede to other countries, and so admit that whatever laws they thought fit to make bound our ships when within three miles of their shores; and as to our own shores in our remote colonies, that we were as responsible for all that took place within three miles of our shores, as if it had taken place on land. No doubt if the law is so, we ought to declare it, regardless of consequences. But if it is a measuring cast which opinion is right, I think we ought to leave it to the legislature, and not make a law ourselves with imperfect powers. On the ground, then, that no such jurisdiction as now claimed has ever been claimed before, I hold that none exists. This may be a very narrow-minded view of the matter—my excuse for it is that I believe it is right.

As to the authorities, I can only say that there is none which suggests such a criminal jurisdiction as now claimed.

There is another remark I wish to make on this head. As a rule, where the sovereign has jurisdiction there is allegiance, permanent, as subject or citizen, or temporary, as being within the territory. In such case there is a corresponding duty of protection. Do any of those exist in this case?

As to the other point, that the offence was committed on a British ship, it seems to me enough to say that the offence of manslaughter consists of an act, and its result—death. Here the act was on the Prussian ship, the result, death, was in the water. It is said, suppose there was an indictment for murder, would not the Admiralty have jurisdiction if the act was wilful, and if it had, would not a conviction for manslaughter be possible? I say, No. If the act was wilful it is done where the will intends it should take effect; aliter when it is negligent. The same argument might be used as to a murder in mid-Atlantic.

Kelly, C.B.

KELLY, C.B. I have had the advantage of considering with great attention the judgment to be delivered by the Lord Chief Justice of England, and I have participated in the preparation of

the judgment of the judge of the Admiralty Court, Sir Robert
Phillimore, and which may, therefore, be taken to be his judgment
and my own; and thus, agreeing substantially with both, it is unnecessary that I should say more than to observe expressly and
emphatically that, inasmuch as it cannot be disputed, that the high
seas, that is to say, all the whole seas of the world below low-water
mark, are open to the whole world, and that the ships of every
nation are free to navigate them, I hold that no one nation has
the right to exercise criminal jurisdiction over the ships of other
nations, or the subjects of other nations within such ships, navigating the high seas, that is, passing through the high seas (without
casting anchor or stopping) between one foreign port and another,
unless by treaty, or express agreement, or unless by some uniform,
general, and long-continued usage, evidenced by the actual exercise of such jurisdiction acquiesced in by the nation or nations
affected by it; whereas not one single instance of the exercise of
such a jurisdiction is to be found in the history of the world from
the beginning of time; and it appears to me indisputable that no
authorities of any number of writers upon international law, even
if they were (which they are not) express and uniform to the same
effect, can take away or impose conditions upon the right to the
free navigation of the high seas by all the nations of the world, or
bring the people of all nations within the criminal jurisdiction of
England without their assent.

The limited jurisdiction exercised within three miles, or some
other space or distance, for some purposes has been established and
sanctioned by a long-continued actual exercise of it by the one
nation, acquiesced in by all others against or in respect of whom it
has been claimed. But the right to seize and try in England for
an offence committed on the high seas by a foreign commander of
a foreign vessel on a foreign voyage, can, in my opinion, no more
exist than the right to seize and try in England any foreigner for
an act done in his own country, a foreign territory, which act may
happen to constitute a criminal offence by the law of England.

LORD COLERIDGE, C.J. I have had the advantage of reading
and considering the judgments which have been already delivered,
and that also which will be delivered after mine by the head of

1876

THE QUEEN
v.
KEYN.

Lord Coleridge,
C.J.

this Court. I assent without qualification to the reasoning upon
the first point of my Brothers Brett and Lindley; upon the
second, to the reasoning of my Brother Denman; although upon
the second point I admit that I do not feel free from doubt. In an
ordinary case, therefore, I should content myself with simply expressing my assent, referring to those judgments for the reasons of it;
but in this case it seems fit that I should indicate shortly the train
of reasoning by which this conclusion has been arrived at. I agree
in thinking it clear that unless the place where the offence was
committed was part of the realm of England locally, or unless the
offence itself was committed on board a British ship, whether the
British ship was locally within the realm of England, or without
it, the conviction cannot stand.

But, first, I think the offence was committed within the realm
of England; and if so, there was jurisdiction to try it. Whether
there was any jurisdiction, and, if there were, what particular Court
was to exercise it, are two separate questions; and I am here
concerned only with the former. Now the offence was committed
much nearer to the line of low-water mark than three miles; and
therefore, in my opinion, upon English territory. I pass by for
the moment the question of the exact limit of the realm of England beyond low-water mark. I am of opinion that it does go
beyond low-water mark; and if it does, no limit has ever been
suggested which would exclude from the realm the place where this
offence was committed. But for the difference of opinion upon
the Bench, and for the great deference which is due to those who
differ from me, I should have said it was impossible to hold that
England ended with low-water mark. I do not of course forget
that it is freely admitted to be within the competency of Parliament to extend the realm how far soever it pleases to extend it
by enactments, at least so as to bind the tribunals of the country;
and I admit equally freely that no statute has in plain terms,
or by definite limits, so extended it. But, in my judgment, no Act
of Parliament was required. The proposition contended for, as I
understand, is that for any act of violence committed by a foreigner
upon an English subject within a few feet of low-water mark,
unless it happens on board a British ship, the foreigner cannot
be tried, and is dispunishable. As I understand the proposition,

it follows, further, that even if the English subject be an officer of the Crown, and the violence is committed by the foreigner in resisting the English officer in the execution of duties which the penal or police laws of the country compel him to perform, laws to which it is admitted this country has for a series of years subjected her coast waters, still the consequence is the same, and the act of resistance, though resulting in the death of the officer, unless it takes place on board a British ship, cannot be made the subject of any criminal proceeding in any Court of the country where the officer has been outraged. This it is said has always been the law, and it is the law now. The argument ab inconvenienti is perhaps not one which sound logic recognises; and a startling conclusion does not always shew that the premises from which it follows are untenable. But the inconvenience here is so grave, and the conclusion so startling, as to make it reasonable, I think, to say that the burden of proof lies heavy upon those who disregard the inconvenience, and maintain the conclusion.

Now my Brothers Brett and Lindley have shewn that by a consensus of writers, without one single authority to the contrary, some portion of the coast waters of a country is considered for some purposes to belong to the country the coasts of which they wash. I concur in thinking that the discrepancies to be found in these writers as to the precise extent of the coast waters which belong to a country (discrepancies, after all, not serious since the time at least of Grotius) are not material in this question; because they all agree in the principle that the waters, to some point beyond low-water mark, belong to the respective countries, on grounds of sense if not of necessity, belong to them as territory or sovereignty, in property, exclusively, so that the authority of France or Spain, of Holland or England, is the only authority recognised over the coast waters which adjoin these countries. This is established as solidly as, by the very nature of the case, any proposition of international law can be. Strictly speaking, international law is an inexact expression, and it is apt to mislead if its inexactness is not kept in mind. Law implies a law-giver, and a tribunal capable of enforcing it and coercing its transgressors. But there is no common law-giver to sovereign states; and no tribunal has the power to bind them by decrees or coerce them if they trans-

1876
THE QUEEN
v.
KEYN.
Lord Coleridge,
C.J.

gress. The law of nations is that collection of usages which civilized states have agreed to observe in their dealings with one another. What these usages are, whether a particular one has or has not been agreed to, must be matter of evidence. Treaties and acts of state are but evidence of the agreement of nations, and do not in this country at least per se bind the tribunals. Neither, certainly, does a consensus of jurists; but it is evidence of the agreement of nations on international points; and on such points, when they arise, the English Courts give effect, as part of English law, to such agreement.

Regarding jurists, then, in the light of witnesses, it is their competency rather than their ability which most concerns us. We find a number of men of education, of many different nations, most of them quite uninterested in maintaining any particular thesis as to the matter now in question, agreeing generally for nearly three centuries in the proposition that the territory of a maritime country extends beyond low-water mark. I can hardly myself conceive stronger evidence to shew that, as far as it depends on the agreement of nations, the territory of maritime countries does so extend. For myself I must add that, besides their competency, I have the greatest respect and admiration for the character and abilities of such of these writers as I am personally familiar with. It is not difficult in the works of a voluminous writer, or indeed of any writer, nay, even in the reported judgments of great judges, to find statements exaggerated or untenable, beliefs which lapse of time has shewn to be unwise, prejudices which must always have been foolish. But these things do not detract from the just authority of distinguished men, and, if the matter were to be determined for the first time, I should not hesitate to hold that civilized nations had agreed to this prolongation of the territory of maritime states, upon the authority of the writers who have been cited in this argument as laying down the affirmative of this proposition.

But it is not now to be done for the first time. For from the two judgments to which I have already had occasion to refer it sufficiently appears that a number of English judges, of the very highest authority, have themselves accepted and acted upon the authority of these jurists. Lord Talbot, Lord Hardwicke, Lord

Mansfield, Lord Stowell, and Dr. Lushington, form altogether a
bódy of judges sufficient to support the authority of the writers
upon whom they relied.

Furthermore, it has been shewn that English judges have held
repeatedly that these coast waters are portions of the realm. It
is true that this particular point does not seem ever distinctly to
have arisen. But Lord Coke, Lord Stowell, Dr. Lushington, Lord
Hatherley, L.C., Erle, C.J., and Lord Wensleydale (and the cata-
logue might be largely extended) have all, not hastily, but in writing,
in prepared and deliberate judgments, as part of the reasoning
necessary to support their conclusions, used language, some of them
repeatedly, which I am unable to construe, except as asserting, on
the part of these eminent persons, that the realm of England,
the territory of England, the property of the State and Crown of
England over the water and the land beneath it, extends at least
so far beyond the line of low water on the English coast as to include the place where this offence was committed. I should only
waste time if I were to go through again the cases which my
learned Brothers have so fully and so accurately examined. It is,
I presume, competent for the Court to overrule those cases; but
at least it must be admitted that they decide as much as this. It
is, perhaps, referring to weaker authorities in order to support
stronger ones; but I will add that the English and American text
writers, and two at least of the most eminent American judges,
Marshall and Story, have held the same thing.

Further—at least in one remarkable instance—the British Parliament has declared and enacted this to be the law. In the
present reign two questions arose between Her Majesty and the
Prince of Wales as to the property in minerals below high-water
mark around the coast of Cornwall. The first question was as to
the property in minerals between high and low-water mark around
the coasts of that county; and as to the property in minerals below
low-water mark won by an extension of workings begun above low-
water mark. This was referred by Lord Chancellor Cranworth on
the part of Her Majesty, and by Lord Kingsdown, the then Chancellor of the Duchy, on the part of the Prince of Wales, to the
arbitration of Sir John Patteson. His decision led to the passing
of an Act of Parliament, and a further question as to the minerals

below low-water mark was referred by Lord Selborne, then Sir
Roundell Palmer, the Queen's Attorney General, and Sir William
Alexander, the Attorney General to the Prince of Wales, to the
arbitration of Sir John Coleridge. All the proceedings in both
references were in writing; and by the kindness of Viscount Port-
man, the present Lord Warden of the Stannaries, I have been
furnished with copies of the whole of them. As might be expected from the known characters of the persons who drew and
settled all the statements in both cases, the greatest learning and
ability were displayed in them; most of the authorities cited
before us are cited in the arguments on behalf of the Crown and
the Prince of Wales, and some others of considerable importance
not cited to us are cited there. The whole argument on the part
of the Crown was founded on the proposition that the fundus
maris below low-water mark, and therefore beyond the limits of
the county of Cornwall, belonged in property to the Crown. The
Prince was in possession of the disputed mines; he had worked
them from land undoubtedly his own; and, therefore, unless the
Crown had a right of property in the bed of the sea, not as first
occupier—for the Prince was first occupier, and was in occupation,
—the Crown must have failed. The argument on behalf of the
Duchy was twofold: first, that all which adjoined and was connected
with the county of Cornwall passed to the Dukes of Cornwall under
the terms of the original grant to them at the time of the creation of the Duchy; and, therefore, that even if the bed of the
sea elsewhere belonged to the Crown, it had passed from the Crown
to the Duke in the seas adjacent to Cornwall; secondly, that the
bed of the sea did not belong to the Crown, and that the Prince
was entitled, as first occupier, to the mines thereunder. I pass by,
as not relevant to the present inquiry, the argument as to the
property in the soil between high and low water, and I omit
Sir John Patteson's decision on that point in favour of the Duchy
as not material. On the second point he thus expressed himself:—

"I am of opinion, and so decide, that the right to the minerals below low-
water mark remains and is vested in the Crown, although those minerals may
be won by workings commenced above low-water mark and extended below it."

And he recommended the passing of an Act of Parliament to

give practical effect to his decision, so far as it was in favour of
the Crown.

The Act of Parliament accordingly was passed, the 21 & 22
Vict. c. 109, a public Act.   By s. 2 it is not merely enacted, but
declared and enacted as follows :—

> " All mines and minerals lying below low-water mark under the open sea
> adjacent to but not being part of the County of Cornwall are, as between the
> Queen's Majesty, in right of her Crown, on the one hand, and His Royal Highness
> Albert Edward Prince of Wales and Duke of Cornwall, in right of his Duchy of
> Cornwall, on the other hand, vested in Her Majesty the Queen in right of her
> Crown as part of the soil and territorial possessions of the Crown."

A subsequent question was raised as to minerals in the beds of
estuaries below low-water mark, but, so to speak, intra fauces
Cornubiæ; and this question, which arose after the death of Sir
John Patteson, was referred for decision to Sir John Coleridge.
This decision was substantially in favour of the Prince, and the
arguments in the former case were repeated before him; but as he
had to decide the matter after the passing of the Act of Parliament,
and in truth as to the construction to be placed upon its clauses,
it is not material to refer in detail to the words of his judgment
and award.

It is true, that the particular question between Her Majesty and
the Prince of Wales, which arose in respect of the bed of the sea
adjacent to the county of Cornwall, could not, as far as I know,
arise in respect of the bed of the sea adjacent to any other county.
But it might well arise between Her Majesty and private persons
all round the British Islands.   The sovereign stands in no more
peculiar relation to Cornwall than she does to Kent.   There is no
reason, legal or otherwise, as far as I am aware, why the bed of
the sea " adjacent to but not part of the county of Cornwall "
should be, and why the bed of the sea adjacent to, but not part of
the county of Kent, where this offence was committed, should *not*
be, " part of the soil and territorial possession of the Crown " in the
words of the Act of Parliament.   Parliament did but apply to a
particular case, in order to settle a question between the two
highest persons in the state, that which is and always has been
the law of this country.   We have therefore it seems the express

and definite authority of Parliament for the proposition that the realm does not end with low-water mark, but that the open sea and the bed of it are part of the realm and of the territory of the sovereign. If so it follows that British law. is supreme over it, and that the law must be administered by some tribunal. It cannot, for the reasons assigned by my Brother Brett, be administered by the judges of oyer and terminer; it can be, and always could be, by the Admiralty, and if by the Admiralty, then by the Central Criminal Court.

I do not feel much pressed by the undoubted fact that no record can be found of the exercise of this particular authority. Cases of collision are not often the subject of criminal inquiry, they do not often happen within local limits so as to raise this particular question. If they were cases of wanton violence they would in former days, I conceive, have been very summarily disposed of. Sometimes, no doubt, the fact that a jurisdiction has never been exercised is a strong argument against the existence of the jurisdiction; but the force of this argument varies with circumstances; and though undoubtedly it is a matter to be considered, it does not, I think, in this case outweigh the arguments which establish its existence. On the whole, therefore, I am of opinion on the first point that the conviction is right.

I am of the same opinion, though with some doubt, upon the second, i.e., that the offence was committed on board an English ship. If this had been murder it would, as I understand the law, be clear that the offence was so committed. I need cite no further authority than the case of *Reg.* v. *Armstrong* (1), decided in 1875 by my lamented Brother Archibald. I think I follow, and I am sure I feel the weight of, the reasoning which has brought the Lord Chief Justice to the opposite conclusion on this point. But on the whole, though not without some hesitation, I concur in the reasoning of my Brother Denman, and I think the same rule should apply in manslaughter which applies in murder. And on the second point, therefore, I am of opinion that the conviction was right and should be affirmed.

(1) 13 Cox, Cr. C. 184.

Cockburn, C.J. The defendant has been convicted of the offence
of manslaughter on the high seas, on a trial had at the Central
Criminal Court, under the statute 4 & 5 Wm. 4, c. 36, s. 22, which
empowers the judges sitting there to hear and determine offences
"committed on the high seas and other places within the jurisdiction of the Admiralty of England." The facts were admittedly
such as to warrant the conviction, if there was jurisdiction to try
the defendant as amenable to English law. Being in command
of a steamship, the *Franconia*, and having occasion to pass the
Strathclyde, a British ship, the defendant brought his ship unnecessarily close to the latter, and then, by negligence in steering,
ran into the *Strathclyde* and broke a hole in her, in consequence
of which she filled with water and sank, when the deceased, whose
death the accused is charged with having occasioned, being on
board the *Strathclyde*, was drowned.

That the negligence of which the accused was thus guilty,
having resulted in the death of the deceased, amounts according
to English law to manslaughter can admit of no doubt. The
question is, whether the accused is amenable to our law, and
whether there was jurisdiction to try him?

The legality of the conviction is contested, on the ground that
the accused is a foreigner; that the *Franconia*, the ship he commanded, was a foreign vessel, sailing from a foreign port, bound on
a foreign voyage; that the alleged offence was committed on the
high seas. Under these circumstances, it is contended that the
accused, though he may be amenable to the law of his own
country, is not capable of being tried and punished by the law of
England.

The facts on which this defence is based are not capable of being
disputed; but a twofold answer is given on the part of the prosecution:—1st. That, although the occurrence on which the charge
is founded took place on the high seas in this sense, that the
place in which it happened was not within the body of a county,
it occurred within three miles of the English coast; that, by the
law of nations, the sea, for a space of three miles from the coast, is
part of the territory of the country to which the coast belongs;
that, consequently, the *Franconia*, at the time the offence was
committed, was in English waters, and those on board were there-

fore subject to English law. 2ndly. That, although the negligence of which the accused was guilty occurred on board a foreign vessel, the death occasioned by such negligence took place on board a British vessel; and that, as a British vessel is in point of law to be considered British territory, the offence, having been consummated by the death of the deceased in a British ship, must be considered as having been committed on British territory.

I reserve for future consideration the arguments thus advanced on the part of the Crown, and proceed, in the first instance, to consider the general question—how far, independently of them, the accused, having been at the time the offence was committed a foreign subject, in a foreign ship, on a foreign voyage, on the high seas, is amenable to the law of England.

Now, no proposition of law can be more incontestable or more universally admitted than that, according to the general law of nations, a foreigner, though criminally responsible to the law of a nation not his own for acts done by him while within the limits of its territory, cannot be made responsible to its law for acts done beyond such limits :—

"Leges cujusque imperii," says Huber de Conflictu legum, citing Dig. de jurisdictione, l. ult., "Vim habent intra terminos ejusdem reipublicæ, omnesque ei subjectos obligant, nec ultra." "Extra territorium jus dicenti impune non paretur" is an old and well-established maxim. "No sovereignty," says Story (Conflict of Laws, s. 539), "can extend its process beyond its own territorial limits, to subject either persons or property to its judicial decisions. Every exertion of authority of this sort beyond this limit is a mere nullity, and incapable of binding such persons or property in any other tribunals." "The power of this country," says Dr. Lushington in the case of The Zollverein (1), "is to legislate for its subjects all the world over, and as to foreigners within its jurisdiction, but no further."

This rule must, however, be taken subject to this qualification, namely, that if the legislature of a particular country should think fit by express enactment to render foreigners subject to its law with reference to offences committed beyond the limits of its territory, it would be incumbent on the Courts of such country to give effect to such enactment, leaving it to the state to settle the question of international law with the governments of other nations.

(1) 1 Sw. Adm. 96.

1876

Tʜᴇ Qᴜᴇᴇɴ
ᴠ.
Kᴇʏɴ.

Cockburn, C.J.

The question of express legislation will be dealt with hereafter. For the present I am dealing with the subject with reference to the general law alone.

To the general rule to which I have referred there is one exception—that of a foreigner on board the ship of another nation. But the exception is apparent rather than real; for by the received law of every nation a ship on the high seas carries its nationality and the law of its own nation with it, and in this respect has been likened to a floating portion of the national territory. All on board, therefore, whether subjects or foreigners, are bound to obey the law of the country to which the ship belongs, as though they were actually on its territory on land, and are liable to the penalties of that law for any offence committed against it.

But they are liable to that law alone. On board a foreign ship on the high seas, the foreigner is liable to the law of the foreign ship only. It is only when a foreign ship comes into the ports or waters of another state that the ship and those on board become subject to the local law. These are the established rules of the law of nations. They have been adopted into our own municipal law, and must be taken to form part of it.

According to the general law, therefore, a foreigner who is not residing permanently or temporarily in British territory, or on board a British ship, cannot be held responsible for an infraction of the law of this country. Unless, therefore, the accused, Keyn, at the time the offence of which he has been convicted was committed, was on British territory or on board a British ship, he could not be properly brought to trial under English law, in the absence of express legislation.

Moreover, while the accused is thus on general principles exempt from being subject to our criminal law in respect of an offence committed on a foreign ship on the high seas, if we proceed to look at the matter in a more technical point of view, with reference to jurisdiction, equal difficulties will be found to stand in the way of the prosecution.

The indictment on which the defendant has been convicted alleges the offence to have been committed on the high seas, and it is admitted that the place in which it occurred cannot in any sense be said to have been within the body of a county. The case,. therefore, if the indictment can be maintained, must necessarily fall within what would formerly have been the jurisdiction of the admiral—a jurisdiction now transferred, but transferred unaltered, to the common-law Courts. It becomes, therefore, necessary to inquire more particularly into the character and extent of the Admiralty jurisdiction.

From the earliest period of our legal history, the cognizance of offences committed on the high seas had been left to the jurisdiction of the admiral. And the reason is obvious. By the old common law of England, every offence was triable in the county only in which it had been committed, as from that county alone the "pais," as it was termed—in other words, the jurors by whom the fact was to be ascertained—could come. But only so much of the land of the outer coast as was uncovered by the sea was held to be within the body of the adjoining county. If an offence was committed in a bay, gulf, or estuary, inter fauces terræ, the common law could deal with it, because the parts of the sea so circumstanced were held to be within the body of the adjacent county or counties; but, along the coast, on the external sea, the jurisdiction of the common law extended no further than to low-water mark. But, as from the time when ships began to navigate the sea, offences would be committed on it which required to be repressed and punished, while the common law jurisdiction and procedure was inapplicable to such offences, as not having been committed within the boundary of any county, the authority of the Crown in the administration of justice in respect of such crimes was left to the admiral, as exercising the authority of the sovereign upon the seas.

Even the office of coroner could not, for the like reason, be executed by the coroner of a county in respect of matters arising on the sea. An inquest could not be held by one of these officers on a body found on the sea. Such jurisdiction could only be exercised by a coroner appointed by the admiral.

A similar difficulty existed as to wrongs done on the sea, and in respect of which the party wronged was entitled to redress by civil action, till the anomalous device of a fictitious venue, within the jurisdiction of the common-law Courts, and which those Courts 1876

THE QUEEN
v.
KEYN.

Cockburn, C.J. did not allow to be disputed, was resorted to, and so the power of trying such actions was assumed.

It is true that in Hale's Pleas of the Crown (vol. ii. p. 12) it is stated that prior to the 35 Edw. III. the Court of King's Bench

"Most certainly had, usually, cognizance of treasons and felonies done on the narrow seas, though out of the boundaries of counties, and it was presented and tried by men of the adjacent counties; so that," says the writer, "even in these cases of felonies or treasons committed on the narrow seas, the King's Bench, or special commissions of oyer and terminer, secundum legem et consuetudinem regni angliæ, had a concurrent jurisdiction with the Court of Admiralty."

In proof of this eight cases are cited, of which one had occurred in the time of Edward I., four in that of Edward II., and three in that of Edward III.

The original editor of Hale's work has given us in a note from the records the details of the cases referred to by the author, from which it appears that of these eight cases, four were in the nature of a civil remedy, and, as it would seem, were properly within the jurisdiction of the Court of King's Bench; four were cases of piracy, which may have been dealt with on the principle that piracy is triable anywhere and everywhere. Moreover, as to two of the latter cases, it is doubtful whether the offence was not committed within the body of a county, and therefore triable at common law.

The earliest case, in the 34 Edw. I. was of a peculiar character. A ship of certain merchants of Lincoln, richly laden, had been plundered by subjects of the Count of Hainault, in Zealand, for which satisfaction had been demanded of the count in vain. Therefore a writ was directed, at the suit of the merchants, to the bailiffs of Lynn, to seize all the goods of the merchants of Hainault at Lynn, and keep them till the Lincoln merchants had received satisfaction, or till further order. The bailiffs returned nulla bona infra ballivam suam. One of the Lincoln merchants traversed the return, alleging that the bailiffs had levied 31l. 17s. of the Hainault merchants, but had re-delivered the same without warrant, which appearing, the bailiffs were ordered to pay that amount, or appear coram rege in octavis trinitatis ubicunque, &c. Subsequently, the Count of Hainault, by his messengers, acknow-

ledged in the English Parliament that he was indebted to the
English merchants in the sum of 954*l*., of which 74*l*. was allotted
to Walter Le Ken, one of them ; whereupon a writ was directed at
his suit to the sheriffs to levy that amount of certain Hainault
merchants at Yarmouth, arrested by consent of the said count, and
to bring the money into Chancery to satisfy the said Le Ken,
which was accordingly done. It is plain that all this was in the
nature of a civil remedy, and as the case, not having happened on
the high seas, was not within the jurisdiction of the admiral, and
the remedy was by civil process within the realm, the matter
appears to have been rightly within the jurisdiction of the King's
Bench.

Another case was a civil action brought by the mayor and corporation of Grimsby against certain persons for loading and
unloading their ships at a place within four leagues of Grimsby,
instead of bringing them to Grimsby, whereby the corporation had
lost their customs and dues. This, too, was a matter of which the
Court might well take cognizance. In a third instance, precepts
had been issued, in the 19 Edw. II., to the sheriffs of several counties, to attach certain persons for having, during a truce between
the King and the Count of Flanders, plundered, with armed force,
a Flemish ship in the waters of Tyne, and for having taken goods
to the value of 2000 marks, and divided the spoil among themselves. Several persons were thereupon arrested by the sheriff of
Northumberland, and brought coram rege, where they were impleaded by the King's attorney for having part of the goods. " Et
dicunt quod nihil ceperunt, &c., et de hoc ponunt se super patriam."
Whereupon the King's attorney joined issue with them, and the
Court bailed them de die in diem quousque, &c. It is plain that
here again we have only a proceeding in the nature of civil process
to satisfy a claim for compensation in damages for a pecuniary loss.
Moreover, as the wrong complained of had occurred in the waters
of Tyne, it must have been committed inter fauces terræ, and
therefore was within the jurisdiction of the common law.

In the 26 Edw. III., John Solandere impleaded several persons
de placito transgressionis, per billam, for entering his ship, super
costerum maris de North'lenn, in Norfolk, beating and wounding

1876

THE QUEEN
v.
KEYN.

Cockburn, C.J.

him, and plundering the ship, which they then left in a helpless condition, by reason of which it was lost; and he recovered 360 marks against them for the damages sustained thereby. Here, again, from the nature of the suit and the recovery of damages, it is plain that this, too, was in the nature of a civil proceeding. I have not succeeded in making out what place is meant by " North'lenn." But as it is stated to have been on the coast, the wrongs complained of may have occurred inter fauces terræ.

Of the remaining four cases, two were clearly cases of piracy, which may have been deemed common ground. But in neither of these cases does the proceeding appear to have originated in the Court of King's Bench. In one of them, in 18 Edw. II., several persons had been indicted for piracy before the admiral, and the indictment having been returned into Chancery, a writ had been issued to the sheriff of Gloucestershire to attach the said persons, and, auditâ querelâ, to do justice to the merchants whose goods had been plundered, detaining, nevertheless, the offenders in prison till delivered in course of law. The sheriff neglecting to execute the writ, the matter was brought, it does not appear how, into the King's Bench. "Processus totius negotii prædicti," says the record, "was brought coram rege;" after which, it appearing that the offenders had been indicted at common law as well as before the admiral, a capias issued to the sheriff to bring them coram rege ubicumque, &c., to answer for the said crime. The statement of the case is very confused, nor does it appear what further became of it.

In another case, which occurred in 25 Edw. III., an indictment for piracy had been found, "coram vice comite et custodibus pacis in comitatu Linc.;" and the indictment having been removed into the King's Bench, ad respondendum, it appeared that the defendants had been already tried in the county of Lincoln, and acquitted. Judgment was therefore given " ut eant quieti."

In the two remaining cases, it is by no means clear that the offence was not committed within the body of a county. In the 8 Edw. II. a mandate is said to have issued to the Constable of Dover and Warden of the Cinque Ports to take into custody several persons for entering, vi et armis, a ship from Flanders,

1876

· THE QUEEN
v.
KEYN.

Cockburn, C.J.

laden with cloth, binding the merchants, and taking the cloth; and to have them coram rege, ad respondendum. But it is not said that the offence had been committed on the high seas. It may have taken place inter fauces terræ, or even in harbour. ·

In the 27 'Edw. III. the coroner of London delivered coram rege,

"Quasdam cognitiones coram ipso factas, by several persons who confessed that they had feloniously entered a ship near Feversham, thrown the men in it into the sea, plundered it, and then sunk it; that they had then gone from Waxering, usque ad forlongg de Tenet—which from another part of the case appears to have been an old form of Thanet—and having feloniously entered another ship there, stripped it of what goods were on board, and killed all that were on it except two women, fornicaverunt cum illis, and then flung them into the sea." After which, "Four of these criminals being brought coram rege, and being asked what they had to say why judgment should not pass against them, said nothing, whereupon they were condemned to be drawn and hanged."

Upon what ground this offence was held to be within the jurisdiction of the Court of King's Bench, is not stated. Possibly the place where the offence was committed may have been considered to be within the fauces terræ, Feversham being situated on a navigable creek, a mile from the sea; in which case the Court would have had jurisdiction; murder, robbery, and rape, not being less within the common law, because committed on the sea, if occurring within the body of a county. But the greater probability is that the offence was treated as piracy. Indeed, that this must have been so seems clear from the fact that the criminals were condemned to be drawn as well as hanged, this having been, at that time, the punishment for piracy, as a species of treason in levying war against the King's subjects or allies; as appears from the case mentioned by Lord Coke, in which certain Normans and Englishmen having been engaged in common in piracy, the Normans, then owing no allegiance to the crown of England, were simply sentenced to be hanged, as guilty of piracy, the Englishmen to be drawn and hanged, as guilty of treason. For murder, robbery, or rape, the punishment was hanging only.

At all events, it appears that the Court of King's Bench, in dealing with cases occurring below low-water mark, and therefore dehors the limits of any county, was deemed to be exceeding its lawful authority. For Lord Hale informs us that "this jurisdiction of the Common Law Courts in cases of felonies and treasons, and other crimes committed upon the seas, was interrupted by a special order of the King and his council, in the 35 Edw. III., and by a supersedeas issued shortly after ;" " since which," says Lord Hale, " I have not observed that the King's Bench or Courts of common law have proceeded criminally in cases of crimes of this. nature committed on the high sea." The probability is that the exercise of this jurisdiction was looked upon as a usurpation of authority, which it was thought necessary to restrain. Certain it is that from.that time to this no such jurisdiction has ever been exercised or claimed by the Courts of common law. There cannot possibly be a question that, in respect of any offences committed on the sea, out of the body of a county, the jurisdiction was formerly exclusively in the Admiralty, and is at the present time, in the courts to which the Admiralty jurisdiction has been transferred. Upon this all authorities on criminal law are entirely agreed.

But if Edward III. and his council were careful to prevent the Courts of common law from encroaching on the province of the admiral, it appears from the statutes of Richard II. that they were equally so in preventing any usurpation of authority by the admiral on the domain of the common law.

In the reign of the latter king arose the dispute as to the jurisdiction of the admiral, who, not content with the authority exercised in the previous reign, now asserted a claim to jurisdiction in respect of matters arising not only on the sea, but in the inland tidal waters of England, as also in respect of matters of contract though made on the land, if at all connected with the sea, a usurpation which gave rise to complaints on the part of the Commons, the procedure in the Courts of Admiralty having been that of the civil law, which appears to have been distasteful to the people. Accordingly, by the statute 13 Ric. 2, c. 5, it is provided—

" That the admirals and their deputies shall not meddle from henceforth with anything done within the realm of England, but only with things done upon the sea, according to that which hath been duly used in the time of the noble King Edward, grandfather of King Richard the Second."

Two years later it was thought necessary still more expressly to

1876

THE QUEEN
v.
KEYN.

Cockburn, C.J.

declare the limits of the admiral's jurisdiction. Accordingly, by statute 15 Ric. 2, c. 3, it was enacted—

"That the Court of the Admirall hath no manner of conusance, power, nor jurisdiction of any manner of contract, plea, or querell, or of any other thing done, or rising within the bodies of the counties, either by land or by water, and also of wrecks of the sea; but all such manner of contracts, pleas, and querels, and all other things rising within the bodies of the counties, as well by land as by water, as is aforesaid, and also wrecks of the sea, shall be tried, determined, discussed, and remedied by the laws of the land, and not before, nor by the Admirall or his Lieutenant, in no manner."

At the same time it was deemed expedient to give the admiral concurrent jurisdiction with the common law, in respect of murder and mayhem committed in ships at the mouths of great rivers. The statute accordingly proceeds :—

"Neverthelesse of the death of a man, and of a mayhem done in great ships, being and hovering in the main stream of the great rivers, only beneath the points of the same rivers, and in no other place of the same rivers, the Admirall shall have conusance."

Upon this footing the criminal law has remained ever since. Whatever of the sea lies within the body of a county is within the jurisdiction of the common law. Whatever does not, belonged formerly to that of the Admiralty, and now belongs to the Courts to which the jurisdiction of the admiral has been transferred by statute; while in the estuaries or mouths of great rivers, below the bridges, in the matter of murder and mayhem, the jurisdiction is concurrent. On the shore of the outer sea the body of the county extends so far as the land is uncovered by water. And so rigorous has been the line of demarcation between the two jurisdictions, that, as regards the shore between high and low-water mark, the jurisdiction has been divided between the Admiralty and the common law according to the state of the tide. Such was the law in the time of Lord Coke; and as regard offences such it is still. As regards civil matters the jurisdiction of the admiral has been extended to inland seas by statute 3 & 4 Vict. c. 65.

We must, therefore, deal with this case as one which would have been under the ancient jurisdiction of the admiral. But the jurisdiction of the admiral, though largely asserted in theory, was never, so far as I am aware—except in the case of piracy, which, as the pirate was considered the communis hostis of mankind, was triable anywhere—exercised, or attempted to be exercised, in respect of offences, over other than English ships. No instance of any such exercise, or attempted exercise, after every possible search has been made, has been brought to our notice. Nor, for the reason already given, could such jurisdiction be so exercised consistently with legal principle. And though, by 25 Hen. 8, c. 15, the trial of offences previously within the jurisdiction of the admiral was transferred to commissioners to be appointed by commission from the King, under which the trial was to be held in such county as the commission should direct, and, " according to the common course of the laws of the realm, used for such offences when done upon the land within the realm," it is, I think, beyond dispute, that all that was effected by this statute or by those that have succeeded it, as regards jurisdiction, was a transfer of the criminal jurisdiction of the admiral, such as it was, to Courts proceeding according to the ordinary procedure of the common law—not an extension of it. The statute created no new offence, effected no extension of jurisdiction. It simply transferred the jurisdiction of the admiral, talem qualem, to the Common Law Courts, to be exercised according to the procedure of the common law. As to this the received authorities are, as I shall have occasion more fully to shew hereafter, entirely agreed. The Central Criminal Court Act, 4 & 5 Wm. 4, c. 36, which gives power to try " offences committed on the high seas and other places within the *jurisdiction of the Admiralty of England,*" has, obviously, carried the matter no further. If the admiral had not jurisdiction as to offences committed on foreign ships, the commissioners, to whom the jurisdiction was transferred by the statute, must be equally without it.

Any doubt which could possibly exist as to the want of jurisdiction of the admiral, in respect of offences committed on the high seas on other than British ships, is conclusively disposed of by the decision of the judges in the cases of *Reg.* v. *Serva and Others* (1), and of *Reg.* v. *Lewis.* (2) I fully admit that these cases will not apply to the present case if the second contention on the part of the Crown should succeed, and the offence should be held to have been committed on board a British ship. At present I am

(1) 1 Den. Cr. C. 104. (2) 1 Dears. & B. Cr. C. 182.

1876
The Queen
v.
Keyn.
Cockburn, C.J.
dealing with the subject on the assumption that that position, to which I shall advert more fully hereafter, cannot prevail.

In *Reg.* v. *Serva* (1), the prisoners had been tried for murder under an Admiralty Commission, and had been found guilty. The facts were shortly these. A Brazilian vessel, named the *Felicidade*, had been taken by H.M. ship *Wasp*, off the coast of Africa, as being fitted out and intended for the slave trade. A prize crew having been put on board the captured ship, under the command of a lieutenant, the latter was ordered to proceed in chase of another Brazilian vessel, the *Echo*, then just sighted from the *Wasp*, and supposed to be carrying slaves. This vessel having been overtaken and captured, and being found to contain a cargo of slaves, possession of her was taken, and a midshipman, with eight men, was put on board. The prisoner, Serva, who had been the captain of the *Echo*, with twelve other Brazilians, rose upon the Englishmen, and succeeded in killing them all. On the trial, it was contended for the prisoners, first, that certain formalities required by the existing treaties for the capture of vessels engaged in the slave trade not having been complied with, the capture of both vessels had been illegal; and that, consequently, the detention of Serva and his associates had been unlawful; for which reason, their act in killing those who were forcibly detaining them, though it might be manslaughter, would not amount to murder. Secondly, that the *Echo*, having been illegally captured and taken possession of, was not thereby converted into a British ship, but retained her original nationality; for which reason, as the jurisdiction of the Admiralty was confined to offences committed on board British ships, there was an absence of jurisdiction in respect of the offence for which the accused were on their trial. These points having been reserved by the judge on the trial for the consideration of the judges, eleven out of thirteen judges, before whom the case was argued, were of opinion that the conviction was wrong, on the ground that it had not been shewn that the possession of the vessel was lawful, without which there could be no jurisdiction in a British court to try the prisoners for an offence committed on board of it. The two dissentient judges, while admitting the principle that, to give jurisdiction to a British Court, it was necessary that the crime

(1) 1 Den. Cr. C. 104.

should have been committed on board a British ship, differed only in this, that they thought that the ship was at the time in the lawful possession of the Queen's officers, and that, consequently, an act committed on board of it must be taken to have been committed on board a ship of Her Majesty. On the general principle of law as to jurisdiction, the judges were unanimous. The case is, therefore, decisive on the point that by the law of England an English Court of justice has no authority to try a foreigner accused of having committed an offence on a foreign vessel not within British waters.

In *Reg.* v. *Lewis* (1) the prisoner was tried for manslaughter. He and the deceased were foreigners, and the injuries of which the deceased had died were inflicted on board a foreign ship on the high seas, but the death took place at Liverpool. The prisoner was convicted, but, on a case reserved, the conviction was held to be wrong. It was sought to be upheld under 9 Geo. 4, c. 31, s. 8, which provides that, if a person has been feloniously stricken on the high sea and dies on the land, the offence may be tried in the county in which the death shall happen. But it was held that the statute could not apply to foreigners in respect of acts done out of British territory.

In the course of the discussion, Coleridge, J., says:

" Before coming to the construction of the statute, we must consider whether we have any right to legislate here for foreigners on board ships upon the high seas. How can we say whether one foreigner wounding another, on the high seas, commits a felony ? Suppose by the law of a state the murder of a subject was not a capital offence, should we have power to say that, when committed on the high seas by a foreigner, we had the right to make it capital ?"

And Willes, J., in delivering the judgment of the Court, said:

" The 8th section of 9 Geo. 4, c. 31, was obviously intended to prevent a defeat of justice which, without it, might have arisen, from the difficulty of trial, in cases of homicide where the death occurs in a different place from that at which the blow causing it was given, and that section ought not, therefore, to be construed as making a homicide cognizable in the courts of this country by reason only of the death occurring here, unless it would have been so cognizable in case the death had ensued at the place where the blow was given, which the homicide, in this particular case, would have been by the 7th section, if the offender had been a British subject, but not otherwise. In the present case the injury which caused the death was inflicted by one foreigner upon another on board a foreign

(1) 1 Dears. & B. Cr. C. 182.

1876

THE QUEEN
v.
KEYN.
Cockburn, C.J.

vessel upon the high seas; and, consequently, if death had then and there followed, no offence cognizable by the law of this country would have taken place.
The 8th section of 9 Geo. 4, c. 31, therefore, is inapplicable, and, unless it be
applicable, the conviction cannot be sustained. It must, therefore, be quashed,
and the prisoner discharged."

In a series of important cases in the American courts, the decisions have proceeded on the same principle. In *Palmer's Case* (1),
and in the cases of *United States* v. *Howard* (2), *United States* v.
Klintock (3), *United States* v. *Kessler* (4), and *United States* v.
Holmes, referred to in the latter case, the question was, whether
an Act of Congress, enacting that "any person committing the
crime of robbery, in or upon any ship or vessel on the high seas,
should be guilty of piracy," applied to robbery committed on other
than American ships, and it was uniformly held that it did not,
even though the offence had been committed by an American
citizen.

In the last of these cases it was contended that the offence,
having been committed within a marine league of the American
shore, was within the Act of Congress; but Mr. Justice Hopkinson,
in giving judgment, says:

"I am not of this opinion. The jurisdiction of this Court is derived wholly
from the Acts of Congress on this subject. The description of the place to which
or over which it extends is the high seas. If, then, the space within the marine
league is not comprehended within this description, this Court has no jurisdiction
over it; if it be comprehended, as it certainly is, then it is so because it is a part
of the high seas, in all respects and to all purposes, the same as any other part of
the high seas. Nothing is added to the jurisdiction of the Courts of the United
States by reason of the offence having been committed within this distance of
their coast; nothing is taken from it by reason of its having been committed
within the jurisdictional limits of a foreign government, within a marine league
of the shore, if done on the high seas, which are held to be any waters on the sea
coast, without the boundaries of low-water mark. It follows from these principles
that if this Court has no power under the Act of Congress to try and punish this
offence committed on board of a foreign vessel on the ocean, it acquires no such
power because she was within a marine league of our coast when the offence was
committed. The principle on which nations claim this extension of their authority and jurisdictional rights for a certain distance beyond their shores is to protect
their safety, peace, and honour from invasion, disturbance, and insult. They will
not have their strand made a theatre of violence and bloodshed by contending
belligerents. Some distance must be assumed. It varies by different jurists from

---

(1) 3 Wheat. 610.   (3) 5 Wheat. 144.
(2) 3 Wash. C. C. R. 340.   (4) Bald. 15.

1876

THE QUEEN
v.
KEYN.

Cockburn, C.J.

one league to thirty, and again as far as a cannon will carry a ball. Such limits may be well enough for their object, but would be extraordinary boundaries of the judicial power and jurisdiction of a court of law. It is my opinion that, whether this offence was committed within or without a marine league from the coast of the United States is of no importance to the question of the jurisdiction of this Court to hear and determine it."

These decisions are conclusive in favour of the accused in the present case, unless the contention, on the part of the Crown, either that the place at which the occurrence, out of which the present inquiry has arisen, was, though on the high seas, yet within British waters, by reason of its having been within three miles of the English shore; or that, the death of the deceased having occurred in a British ship, the offence must be taken to have been there committed, so as in either case to give jurisdiction to the Admiralty, or the Courts substituted for it, shall prevail. These questions it becomes, therefore, necessary carefully to consider.

On entering on the first, it is material to have a clear conception of what the matter in controversy is. The jurisdiction of the admiral, however largely asserted in theory in ancient times, being abandoned as untenable, it becomes necessary for the counsel for the Crown to have recourse to a doctrine of comparatively modern growth, namely, that a belt of sea, to a distance of three miles from the coast, though so far a portion of the high seas as to be still within the jurisdiction of the admiral, is part of the territory of the realm, so as to make a foreigner in a foreign ship, within such belt, though on a voyage to a foreign port, subject to our law, which it is clear he would not be on the high sea beyond such limit. It is necessary to keep the old assertion of jurisdiction and that of to-day essentially distinct, and it should be borne in mind that it is because all proof of the actual exercise of any jurisdiction by the admiral over foreigners in the narrow seas totally fails, that it becomes necessary to give to the three-mile zone the character of territory in order to make good the assertion of jurisdiction over the foreigner therein.

Now, it may be asserted without fear of contradiction that the position that the sea within a belt or zone of three miles from the shore, as distinguished from the rest of the open sea, forms part of the realm or territory of the Crown is a doctrine unknown to the ancient law of England, and which has never yet received the sanction of an English criminal Court of justice. It is true that from an early period the kings of England, possessing more ships than their opposite neighbours, and being thence able to sweep the Channel, asserted the right of sovereignty over the narrow seas, as appears from the commissions issued in the fourteenth century, of which examples are given in the 4th Institute, in the chapter on the Court of Admiralty, and others are to be found in Selden's Mare Clausum, Book 2. At a later period still more extravagant pretensions were advanced. Selden does not scruple to assert the sovereignty of the King of England over the sea as far as the shores of Norway, in which he is upheld by Lord Hale in his treatise De jure maris: Hargrave's Law Tracts, p. 10.

In the reign of Charles II. Sir Leoline Jenkins, then the judge of the Court of Admiralty, in a charge to the grand jury at an Admiralty sessions at the Old Bailey, not only asserted the King's sovereignty within the four seas, and that it was his right and province "to keep the public peace on these seas"—that is, as Sir Leoline expounds it, "to preserve his subjects and allies in their possessions and properties upon these seas, and in all freedom and security to pass to and fro on them, upon their lawful occasions," but extended this authority and jurisdiction of the King

"To preserve the public peace and to maintain the freedom and security of navigation all the world over; so that not the utmost bound of the Atlantic Ocean, nor any corner of the Mediterranean, nor any part of the South or other seas, but that if the peace of God and the King be violated upon any of his subjects, or upon his allies or their subjects, and the offender be afterwards brought up or laid hold of in any of His Majesty's ports, such breach of the peace is to be inquired of and tried in virtue of a commission of oyer and terminer as this is, in such county, liberty, or place as His Majesty shall please to direct—so long an arm hath God by the laws given to his vicegerent, the King."

To be sure, the learned civilian, as regards these distant seas, admits that other sovereigns have a concurrent jurisdiction, which, however, he by no means concedes to them in these so-called British seas. In these the refusal by a foreign ship to strike the flag and lower the topsail to a King's ship he treats as amounting to piracy.

Venice, in like manner, laid claim to the Adriatic, Genoa to the

Ligurian Sea, Denmark to a portion of the North Sea. The
Portuguese claimed to bar the ocean route to India and the Indian
Seas to the rest of the world, while Spain made the like assertion
with reference to the West.

All these vain and extravagant pretensions have long since given
way to the influence of reason and common sense. If, indeed,
the sovereignty thus asserted had a real existence, and could now
be maintained, it would of course, independently of any question
as to the three-mile zone, be conclusive of the present case. But
the claim to such sovereignty, at all times unfounded, has long
since been abandoned. No one would now dream of asserting
that the sovereign of these realms has any greater right over the
surrounding seas than the sovereigns on the opposite shores; or
that it is the especial duty and privilege of the Queen of Great
Britain to keep the peace in these seas; or that the Court of Admiralty could try a foreigner for an offence committed in a foreign
vessel in all parts of the Channel. No writer of our day, except
Mr. Chitty in his treatise on the prerogative, has asserted the
ancient doctrine. Blackstone, in his chapter on the prerogative in
the Commentaries, while he asserts that the narrow seas are part
of the realm, puts it only on the ground that the jurisdiction of
the Admiralty extends over these seas. He is silent as to any
jurisdiction over foreigners within them. The consensus of jurists,
which has been so much insisted on as authority, is perfectly
unanimous as to the non-existence of any such jurisdiction. Indeed,
it is because this claim of sovereignty is admitted to be untenable
that it has been found necessary to resort to the theory of the
three-mile zone. It is in vain, therefore, that the ancient assertion
of sovereignty over the narrow seas is invoked to give countenance
to the rule now sought to be established, of jurisdiction over the
three-mile zone. If this rule is to prevail, it must be on altogether
different grounds. To invoke as its foundation, or in its support,
an assertion of sovereignty which, for all practical purposes, is,
and always has been, idle and unfounded, and the invalidity of
which renders it necessary to have recourse to the new doctrine,
involves an inconsistency, on which it would be superfluous to
dwell. I must confess myself unable to comprehend how, when
the ancient doctrine as to sovereignty over the narrow seas is

adduced, its operation can be confined to the three-mile zone. If the argument is good for anything, it must apply to the whole of the surrounding seas.   But the counsel for the Crown evidently shrank from applying it to this extent.   Such a pretension would not be admitted or endured by foreign nations.   That it is out of this extravagant assertion of sovereignty that the doctrine of the three-mile jurisdiction, asserted on the part of the Crown, and which, the older claim being necessarily abandoned, we are now called upon to consider, has sprung up, I readily admit.   Let me endeavour to trace its origin and growth.

With the celebrated work of Grotius, published in 1609, began the great contest of the jurists as to the freedom of the seas.   The controversy ended, as controversies often do, in a species of compromise.   While maintaining the freedom of the seas, Grotius, in his work De Jure Belli et Pacis, had expressed an opinion that, while no right could be acquired to the exclusive possession of the ocean, an exclusive right or jurisdiction might be acquired in respect of particular portions of the sea adjoining the territory of individual states.   Thus, he says (lib. ii., cap 2, s. 13):

"Videtur autem imperium in maris portionem eadem ratione acquiri, qua imperia alia; id est, ut supra diximus, ratione personarum et ratione territorii. Ratione personarum, ut si classis, qui maritimus est exercitus, aliquo in loco maris se habeat; ratione territorii, quatenus ex terra cogi possunt qui in proxima maris parte versantur, nec minus quam si in ipsa terra reperirentur."

This, however, must be taken with some qualification, for in another place he says:

"Illud certum est, etiam qui mare occupaverit navigationem impedire non posse inermem et innoxiam, quando nec per terram talis transitus prohiberi potest, qui et minus esse solet necessarius et magis noxius."

Other writers adopted a similar principle, but with very varying views as to the extent to which the right might be exercised. Albericus Gentilis extended it to 100 miles; Baldus and Bodinus to sixty. Loccenius (De Jure Maritimo, ch. iv. s. 6) puts it at two days' sail; another writer makes it extend as far as could be seen from the shore.   Valin, in his Commentary on the French Ordonnances of 1681 (ch. v.), would have it reach as far as bottom could be found with the lead-line.

Puffendorf, whose work, De Jure Naturæ et Gentium, was first

published in 1672, treats the sea adjacent to the land as an accessory to the latter:

" Putaverim citra absurditatem dici posse, partes maris, in quantum rationem
munimenti, adeoque appendicis duntaxat habent, absque peculiari actu corporali
cœpisse subire dominium ejus populi, cujus littoribus prætexuntur, postquam
inter gentes armatarum usus navium innotuit. Nam hoc intuitu mare sese habet,
tanquam accessorium terræ, sicut fossæ, vel etiam proximæ uligines et paludes
censentur accessio urbis " (lib. iv. c. 2, s. 8).

As to the distance to which the sea is to be thus treated as
accessory to the land, Puffendorf himself expresses no opinion,
contenting himself with referring to that of Baldus and Bodin, that
it should extend to sixty miles.

Even Casaregis, writing as late as 1740, after the three-mile
theory had been propounded by Bynkershoek, asserts (Discursus
de Commercio, s. 136) that the sovereign possessing the coast has
an equal sovereignty over the sea to an extent of 100 miles, and
criminal jurisdiction over all offenders, and has not only the power
of imposing tolls and dues on passing ships, but also that of prohibiting ships from passing through his waters.

Differing altogether from these writers as to the extent of
maritime sovereignty, Bynkershoek, an advocate, like Grotius, for
the mare liberum, and who entered the lists against Selden as to
the dominion of England in the so-called English Sea, in his
treatise De Dominio Maris, published in 1702, follows up the idea
of Grotius as to a limited dominion of the sea from the shore:

" Existimem itaque," he says, " eousque possessionem maris proximi videri
porrigendam, quousque continenti potest haberi subditum; eo quippe modo,
quamvis non perpetuo navigetur, recte tamen defenditur et servatur possessio jure
quæsita: neque enim ambigendum est eum possidere continuo, qui ita rem tenet,
ut alius eo invito tenere non possit. Unde dominium maris proximi non ultra
concedimus, quam è terra illi imperari potest; et tamen, eousque, nulla siquidem
sit ratio, cur mare, quod in alicujus imperio est et potestate, minus ejusdem esse
dicamus, quam fossam in ejus territorio."

After combating the doctrine of a mare clausum as regards the
sea at large, and enumerating these inconsistent opinions, which
he seems little disposed to respect, Bynkershoek continues :

" Hinc videas priscos juris magistros, qui dominium in mare proximum ausi
sunt agnoscere, in regundis ejus finibus admodum vagari incertos." " Quare omnino
videtur rectius," he adds, after disposing of the foregoing opinions,
" Eo potestatem terræ extendi, quousque tormenta exploduntur; eatenus quippe,

cum imperare, tum possidere videmur. Loquor autem de his temporibus; quibus illis machinis utimur; alioquin generaliter dicèndum esset, potestatem terræ finiri, ubi finitur armorum vis; etenim hæc, ut diximus, possessionem tuetur."

We have here, for the first time, so far as I am aware, a suggestion as to a territorial dominion over the sea, extending as far as cannon-shot would reach—a distance which succeeding writers fixed at a marine league, or three miles. Prior to this, no one had suggested such a limit. The jurisdiction, assumed in the Admiralty commissions, or exercised by the Court of King's Bench in the time of the Edwards, was founded on the King's alleged sovereignty over the whole of the narrow seas; it had no reference whatever to any notion of a territorial sea. To English lawyers the idea of this limited jurisdiction was utterly unknown. With Selden and Hale, they stood up stoutly for the King's undivided dominion over the four seas. No English author makes any distinction, as regards the dominion of the Crown, between the narrow seas as a whole and any portion of them as adjacent to the shore. The doctrine was equally unknown to the Scotch lawyers. Craig, writing at the outset of the seventeenth century, while he allots part of the sea to the shore it adjoins, gives no limit as to distance :—

"Quod ad mare attinet, licet adhuc ita omnium commune sit, ut in eo navigari possit, proprietas tamen ejus ad eos pertinere hodie creditur ad quos proximus continens; adeo ut mare Gallicum id dicatur quod litus Galliæ alluit, ut ei propius est quam ulli alii continenti. Sic Anglicum, Scoticum, Hibernicum, quod propius Angliæ, Scotiæ, et Hiberniæ est. Ita ut reges inter se quasi omnia maria diviserint, et quasi ex mutuâ partitione alterius id mare censeatur quod alteri propinquius et commodius est; in quo si delictum aliquod commissum fuerit, ejus sit jurisdictio qui proximum continentem possideat: isque suum illud mare vocat:" Jus Feudale, lib. 1, s. 13, p. 140.

Even to our times the doctrine of the three-mile zone has never been adopted by the writers on English law. To Blackstone, who in his Commentaries treats of the sea with reference to the prerogative, as also to his modern editor, Mr. Stephen, it is unknown; equally so to Mr. Chitty, whose work on the prerogative is of the present century. It was not till the beginning of this century that any mention of such a doctrine occurs in the courts of this country. But to the continental jurists, the suggestion of Bynkershoek seemed a happy solution of the great con-

1876

THE QUEEN
v.
KEYN.

Cockburn, C.J.

troversy as to the freedom of the sea; and the formula, potestas finitur ubi finitur armorum vis, was a taking one; and succeeding publicists adopted and repeated the rule which their predecessor had laid down, without much troubling themselves to ascertain or inquire whether that rule had been recognised and adopted by the maritime nations who were to be affected by it.

Wolff in his Jus Gentium, published in 1749, argues that, as the use of the sea adjoining the shore, and which consists in fishing and the collection of such things as the sea produces, is not inexhaustible, nor the use of such sea for navigation always innocuous, and as the sea affords protection to the adjacent country, and it is to the interest of the inhabitants that armed ships should not be allowed to pass, there is no reason why it should not be subjected to the dominion of the state, or why others should not be excluded from it. It is therefore, he contends, beyond doubt that the inhabitants of the shore may occupy the adjoining sea so far as they can maintain their dominion, and that it thus becomes their territory. Hence he concludes:

"Quoniam partes maris occupatæ ad territorium illius gentis pertinent, quæ eas occupavit, quale jus Rector civitatis in suo territorio habet, tale etiam ipsi competit in partibus maris occupatis. Per consequens, qui in iis versantur iisdem legibus subsunt, quam qui in terris habitant, aut commorantur, etiam peregrini admissi."

On the same ground he ascribes to the state full legislative power over the sea in question, which shall be binding upon all who may come within it: chap. i. § 128–132.

Hubner, whose work De la Saisie des Bâtimens Neutres was published in 1759, contrasting the parts of the sea which wash the coast of maritime countries with the open sea, says of the former, but in general terms, and with reference to Bynkershoek's doctrine,

"It is clear that these parts of the sea belong to the master of the country, as accessory to the land. First, because it is in his power to take possession, and maintain it by means of forts and batteries which he can erect on the shore; secondly, because these waters serve as a rampart to the land."

Vattel (Droit des Gens, § 288) states the law thus:

"A nation may appropriate to itself things, the free and common use of which would be hurtful or dangerous to it. This is a reason why powers extend their dominion over the sea as far as they can protect their right. It is of importance to the safety and welfare of the state that it should not be free to all the world

1876

THE QUEEN
v.
KEYN.

Cockburn, C.J.

to come so near to its possessions, especially with ships of war, which may impede the access of commercial nations, and disturb their navigation." "These parts of the sea," he goes on to say, "thus subject to a nation, are comprised within its territory. No one can navigate therein against its will." "But then, he continues, "the nation cannot refuse access to ships not suspected, or making innocent use of its waters, without a violation of its duty." "It is true it is for the nation to judge of what it shall do in the particular case. If it determines wrongly, it errs, but the others must put up with it."

Coming to the question of distance, Vattel lays it down as most consistent with reason that the dominion of the state over the adjacent sea should extend "as far as is necessary for its safety, or it can make its power respected."

To this somewhat vague rule he afterwards gives more precision :

"Now-a-days," he says, " all the extent of sea which is within reach of cannon-shot from the shore is considered as forming part of the territory. For this reason a vessel taken under the cannon of a neutral fortress is not a good prize."

In the great French work, the Répertoire de Jurisprudence, published in 1777, in the article " Mer," the writer, after saying that no sovereign has the right of attributing to himself the empire of the seas, goes on to say that as every sovereign is entitled to forbid foreign commerce in his possessions and to protect these possessions from insult, he may prevent their being approached within a certain distance. This principle being settled, it remains, the writer continues, to determine this distance, which, he says, " has been fixed by treaties of peace and commerce at *two* leagues from the coast." What the treaties are which are thus referred to is not stated.

Moser, writing in 1778 (Versuch des neuesten Europäischen Völkerrechts, vol. v. p. 486), asserts the same principle, but puts the distance differently.

" The sea," he says, "which borders on the coast of a country is indisputably according to the law of nations, under the sovereignty of the adjacent land, so far as a cannon-shot will reach."

Lampredi, writing in the same year, while he concedes the right of property in the adjacent waters, makes the limit depend on convenience :

" Nobis visum est singulas gentes eam partem circa littus suum occupare posse, cujus usus necessarius, quamque tuendis littoribus et territorio necessarium arbitrantur ": Public. Jur. Theor., vol. ii. p. 65.

The part so occupied he assimilates absolutely to the land :

"Maris pars, quam gens occupavit, veluti ejus territorium habetur, atque adeo est in ejus imperio et dominio. Quapropter quisquis in mari versatur occupato, sive indigena sive peregrinus sit, imperio gentis subjicitur, legibusque imperantis tenetur, quibus vel cives generatim, vel præsertim personæ et res maritimæ reguntur": Ib. p. 7.

Galiani, in his work De' Doveri de' Principi Neutrali, published in 1782, says that it is "Cosa ricevutissima" to consider the belt of open sea which washes the shore as belonging to, and, as it were, incorporated with, the land and forming part of it. At the same time he observes that the opinion as to the extent of this territorial sea has differed in various epochs. He seems at first prepared to extend it as far as the magistrates can, by the fear of the powers confided to them, cause their decrees to be obeyed. But further on he seems disposed to fix this at cannon-range, or the three-mile distance.

But as though an element of uncertainty should not be wanting, he proceeds to argue that, while for fixing tolls, or restricting the freedom of passage to foreign ships, or for customs purposes, this should be the limit, on the other hand, if the purpose is the benevolent one of enforcing the observance of its neutrality and preventing belligerent cruisers from carrying on their operations within its waters, the limit may be extended by the state to double the distance.

Martens, who wrote in 1778, after speaking of straits and bays, continues :

"So a nation may assert an exclusive right to the neighbouring portions of the sea capable of being maintained from the shore. At this day all European nations agree that, as a rule, straits, bays, gulfs, and the neighbouring sea belong to the master of the coast, to the extent, at least, of a cannon-shot from the shore. In a number of treaties, the wider range of three leagues has even been adopted."

M. Rayneval (Institutions du Droit de la Nature et des Gens, liv. 2, ch. ix. § 10) makes the horizon the boundary of the territorial sea—à rule obviously very difficult, if not incapable of application where the coast of one country can be seen from that of another.

Schmalz, a professor of law at the University of Berlin, writing at the beginning of the present century—I am citing from the French translation, ch. ii. p. 144—says:

"The parts of the sea which bathe the coast have always been considered to be the property of the country which they bound." "In Europe, the opinion of jurists who have treated the matter philosophically, has been systematically adopted. According to this principle the sea should belong to the continent as far as the defence of the shore can extend, of which a cannon-shot was to be taken as the measure. At a later period the distance has been fixed arbitrarily at three marine leagues."

This, it will be observed, would make the distance three times greater than other writers fix it at. According to this author, this alleged property in the sea carries with it criminal jurisdiction in respect of offences committed on it; the right to levy tolls, in consideration of providing for the general peace and security; and, with the exception of the freedom of navigation, which he holds cannot be withheld, the right of excluding foreigners from all use whatsoever of the sea.

Azuni, writing in 1805 (Droit Maritime de l'Europe, vol. i. p. 252, s. 14), adopts the view of Galiani, as

"Offering the most just and only rule for fixing the extent of the territorial sea, a point always contested, and not as yet decided, at least not fixed, as it ought to be, on the basis of solemn treaty between the maritime powers." "Till such an agreement shall have been come to publicly," adds Azuni, "everything will depend on arbitrary usage, and the stronger will give the law to the weaker."

This is not very encouraging, but the author goes on to prescribe as the safest limit the space to which a shot from a cannon can be carried, the extreme range of which he estimates at three miles. He, too, following Galiani, thinks the distance may be extended when the purpose is one of benevolence and peace. As regards the degree of dominion which the state is entitled to exercise, he says:

"Any nation which occupies a part of the adjacent sea has the right of sovereignty as well as the domain over it: in other words, the same right that it has over the land." "It may legitimately prohibit the navigation of its territorial waters to foreigners, without infringing on general liberty, or offending against the law of nations."

Klüber (Droit des Gens Modernes, Part II., tit. ii, § 130, published in 1881), says:

"To the maritime territory (Seegebiet) of a state belong the maritime districts or waters capable of exclusive possession, over which the state has acquired, whether by occupation or convention, and maintained sovereignty. Among these must be reckoned the parts of the ocean which adjoin the continental territory of the state, at all events, according to the generally received opinion, to the extent of the space which can be reached by cannon-shot from the shore " (Mare proximum—vicinum—nächst angränzendes Meer).

Wheaton, whose work on the Elements of International Law, appeared in 1836, concurs with the writers who had preceded him respecting the formula of Bynkershoek, laying it down that,

" By the generally-approved usage of nations, which forms the basis of international law, the maritime territory of every state extends (among other things) to the distance of a marine league, or as far as a cannon-shot will reach from the shore, all along the coasts of the state." In the French edition of his work he adds : " Dans ces limites les droits de propriété et de juridiction sont absolus, et excluent ceux de toutes les autres nations."

Pascal Fiore, an Italian jurist, in his work on International Law, published in 1865 (vol. i. p. 370), says :

" Every nation has a dominium utile on the sea which washes its shores, in the interest of its preservation. It exercises, besides, a right of jurisdiction and police, in the interest of its defence. Upon this all publicists and treaties agree. International conventions have always regarded a territorial sea as the property of the state. " But the publicists," continues this author, " are not agreed as to the extent of the territorial sea, and the limit of the use (domaine utile) which the state may exercise."

This, he says, must be determined " by the necessity of the case and the nature of the particular right claimed." Thus the right of fishing, that of levying tolls for the maintenance of the navigation, that of the defence of the coast, may come into question. As regards the latter, the writer seems to think that it should extend to the point at which " the state has the means of making its will respected and causing its rights of sovereignty to be acknowledged." " According to this principle, the zone of jurisdiction would increase with the perfection of artillery." But, whatever the right of the sovereign, M. Fiore denies him the power of interfering with the passage of vessels which do not compromise the safety of his territory.

MM. Pistoye and Duverdy, in their Traité des Prises Maritimes (tit. 2, chap. iii. vol. i. p. 93), write as follows :—

" While no human power can possess and govern the sea at large, those portions of it which border on the coast may be, and are, brought under the power and sovereign dominion of the nations they adjoin. From the coast, each power can, in a given zone, measured by the range of a cannon-shot, impose its laws and

1876

THE QUEEN
v.
KEYN.

Cockburn, C.J.

enforce obedience to them. There is not, it is true, bodily possession of the waves, which from their perpetual flow and movement, render any action of this kind upon them impossible; but there is a direct and constant domination, which places these territorial waters under the immediate police of the local government, in the same manner as each state is master of the rivers, lakes, and channels which pass through its territory."

" There has been much discussion," these writers continue, "as to the extent of this territorial sea; but the principle upon which its appropriation rests, serves also to determine its bounds, and it must be acknowledged that the range of cannon from the shore is the only real and true limit of the sea in question. No measure, however, has been generally agreed upon between different nations as to the distance which cannon range may be supposed to cover. But the eyes of experienced sailors and officers employed upon the coast may be trusted to to judge how far a given spot is within the distance."

No writer has carried the doctrine of the territorial sea further than M. Hautefeuille, in his two works, the Histoire des Origines, des Progrès et des Variations du Droit Maritime, and his treatise, Des Droits et Devoirs des Nations Neutres. In the first, at p. 197, he explains the foundation of the doctrine:

"While," he says, "the high sea cannot be possessed exclusively by any people, because it cannot be brought or kept under the power of man, the part of the sea which touches the coast may easily be defended by the riparian, may be kept under his subjection by force, and held in his possession. With a few instruments of war, a few cannons, he, in fact, commands this area; he can shut out foreign vessels, or admit only such as he pleases."

Next, taking the same ground as had been previously taken by Wolff, M. Hautefeuille argues that the products of the sea are not inexhaustible, and that the pursuit of them requires to be kept under proper regulation; while the people in possession of the shore are deeply interested in possessing the adjoining waters also, in order to protect themselves against pirates. Hence the distinction between these waters and the open sea; hence the former may be possessed and considered as an accessory to the shores they wash. In the second work he asserts that—

" These territorial waters are the property of the nations possessing the shores, and, consequently, that these nations have within such waters all the rights of sovereignty without exception, as though it were on so much land. They can, therefore," he asserts, " prohibit the vessels of all other nations, or of any particular nation, from navigating these waters; or they may prohibit the navigation for particular purposes, as, for instance, the coasting trade. They may limit the number of ships of war that shall be allowed to enter or to anchor in these waters, even in open roadsteads. They may subject merchant vessels, not only to search in respect of customs-dues, but also to tolls for anchorage, lights, buoys, and the

1876

THE QUEEN
v.
KEYN.

Cockburn, C.J.

like. In a word, they may make whatever regulations it appears to them expedient to make with a view to their own interest. Foreigners entering this reserved territory must submit to the law of the sovereign in all that concerns their relations with the land and its inhabitants, as though they were on the land. The limit of the territorial sea is fixed by the principle from which its territorial character arises. It extends as far as the sea can be commanded from the shore, but no further."

Very different is the view of another modern French writer on international law, M. Ortolan, as to the degree of dominion which may be exercised over the territorial sea. While he asserts the existence of such a sea, he denies any right of property in it, or of absolute dominion over it. To determine this question, says M. Ortolan (Diplomatie de la Mer, liv. ii. c. 8),

" It is necessary to refer to the principles on which the particular rule as to this portion of the sea is founded, and to the nature of the rights which the nation owning the coast can claim over it." " It signifies little," he continues, " that the bottom of the sea is manifestly a continuation of the coast. As soon as there is sufficient depth for navigation, nations are entitled, as of right, to the use of the sea as a means of communication, nor can it be legitimately denied to them. While the nation owning the coast is entitled to refuse access to its land territory, it cannot assert a right to prevent ships from passing in front of its shores, or to declare the territorial sea closed, as it might do in respect of one of its ports. It cannot impose tolls on passing vessels as in a water belonging to itself, except as a fair indemnity for works for the benefit of the navigation or for special services rendered. To act contrary to these rules would be to act in contradiction to the essential destination of the sea, and to derive an advantage from it which no one has a right to. And though the nation might have the means of compulsion, this would not make its proceedings the more lawful. The right, then, to the territorial sea is not a right of property; it cannot be said that the state, which is the proprietor of the land, is also proprietor of this sea."

To make this good, M. Ortolan refers to the grounds on which the doctrine of the territorial sea rests, namely, the protection of the country as regards safety, prosperity, and individual interests, against offences of every kind by which these may be affected. With a view to this defence the state is entitled to make the necessary laws and regulations, and to employ force to insure their execution. " Les lois de police et de sûreté," says the author, " y sont obligatoires." Whether he thereby means to imply that other laws would not be so is left uncertain. " En un mot," concludes M. Ortolan, " l'État a sur cet espace, non la propriété, mais un droit d'empire; un pouvoir de législation, de surveillance et de juridiction, conformément aux règles de la juridiction interna-

1876

THE QUEEN
v.
KEYN.

Cockburn, C.J.
tionale." What is to be understood by laws of " police et sûreté"
is very uncertain, and what the rules are to which he here refers,
and whether any and what limitation would be thereby imposed on
the rights attaching to territorial dominion he fails to inform us.

As regards distance, M. Ortolan would fix it at the extreme range
of cannon-shot according to the improvement of artillery, as varying with the age.

A still later author, M. Calvo (Droit International, liv. v. §§
199–201), takes the same view as to the absence of any right of
property in the territorial belt, but would concede a much larger
and more exclusive dominion to the state to whom the belt
belongs.

" To facilitate the defence of the coasts," he says, " the general practice of
nations, sanctioned by numerous treaties, has drawn, at a certain distance from
the land, an imaginary line, as the extreme limit of the maritime frontier of each
country. Whatever comes within that line falls ipso facto within the jurisdiction of the state which commands it, and is entitled territorial sea." At the
same time he goes on to say that " the publicists are far from being agreed
as to the extent of this sea ; and that to solve the question in a rational and practical
manner, it is necessary to bear in mind that nations have not a right of property
in the territorial sea (*que les états n'ont pas sur la mer territoriale un droit de
propriété*) but only a right of surveillance and jurisdiction in the interest of their
own defence, or the protection of their fiscal interests. It is therefore in the
nature of things that this right should extend as far as its existence can be justified, but should terminate where all fear of real danger, or its public usefulness, or
the possibility of defence, ceases."

Where this point is to be found the author fails to tell us.

" Hence it follows," says M. Calvo, " on principle, that the territorial sea can
only comprehend the space capable of being defended from the shore, or of serving
as a place from which to attack it. Since the invention of fire-arms, an extent of
three miles has been generally given to this zone. Within it the exercise of the
territorial jurisdiction is absolute and incontestable, and excludes the rights of
every other nation."

On the other hand, Professor Heffter, in his highly-esteemed
work, the Public International Law of Europe (§ 75), after asserting, as incontestable, the right of maritime nations, both for the
defence of their territory against unexpected attack, and the protection of their commercial interests and customs-laws, to establish
an active surveillance and a police on their coasts and the parts
adjoining, and to take all necessary measures to close the access
to their territory to those whom they may not choose to receive,

or who do not conform to the established regulations, goes so far as to ascribe to the particular state the power of fixing, according to circumstances, the limit to which its right shall extend. Adverting to the generally received rule, which fixes the limits of the dominion over the adjoining sea at three miles, he is disposed to think, with Vattel, that this dominion extends as far as is necessary for the safety of the state, and the latter can enforce its power; or even that the principle of Rayneval may be adopted, which makes the horizon the boundary of the territorial sea. "The range of cannon-shot affords," he thinks, "no invariable basis, and the distance may be fixed, at all events provisionally"—what he means by this is by no means clear—"by the law of each state." He concedes to the state the power of making regulations relative to the use of the territorial waters, as, for instance, in respect of fishing and "the right of jurisdiction;" but what he includes under the latter term he omits to explain. On the other hand, he is wholly silent as to any territorial right of property in the waters in question.

Professor Bluntschli, in his work Das Moderne Völkerrecht (§§ 307-9), while he states that the open sea is free to all nations and individuals for navigation and fishing, affirms that portions of the sea are subject to a limited jurisdiction ("einer beschränkten Gebietshoheit"). Amongst these he enumerates the sea which washes the shore, on the ground that the close connection of such parts of the sea with the land and state justifies an extension of the territorial jurisdiction of the latter; for which reason such part of the sea is considered as accessory to the land, the power and protection of the latter extending over it. In the opinion of this author

"The safety and order of the state is so manifestly interested in this particular that the usual measure of the cannon-shot is not always to be considered as sufficiently extensive in the case of gulfs and bays." "As incidental to this limited jurisdiction," says M. Bluntschli (Article 310), "the state is entitled to extend measures necessary for the protection of its territory and its laws to these portions of the sea; and to make regulations of police with reference to navigation and fishing; but it is not entitled in time of peace to deny the right of passage, or the use of these waters for navigation, or to exact tolls in respect of them."

But the writer draws a distinction between ships commorant on the territorial waters of a state and ships merely passing through

1876

THE QUEEN
v.
KEYN.

Cockburn, C.J.

them. After laying it down, that foreign ships within the territorial waters of a state are subject to its laws, he goes on to say :

"Ships which confine themselves to passing along the coasts of a state, in the
part of the sea which forms a portion of its territory, are subject for the time to
the sovereignty of such state, in this sense, that they are bound to respect the
military and police regulations adopted by it for the safety of its territory and of
the population of the coast." "The jurisdiction of the adjoining state extends
over the neighbouring sea only as far as is deemed necessary by the police and
military authorities. In all other respects the ship is as free as if it were on the
high seas, that is to say, it is considered as a floating portion of the country to
which it belongs." (§ 322.)

Thus, according to this author, it is only with regard to matters
of police and military regulation, that the jurisdiction of a state
over its littoral sea extends.

An American writer on International Law, Mr. Halleck (ch. vi.
§ 13), after speaking of ports, bays, and mouths of rivers as
national territory, within the limits of which the rights of property and territorial jurisdiction are absolute, and exclusive of
those of every other state, goes on to say that—

"The general usage of nations superadds to this maritime territory an exclusive
territorial jurisdiction over the sea for the distance of one marine league, or the
range of a cannon-shot along all the shores or coasts of a state." He adds,
that "even beyond this limit states may exercise a qualified jurisdiction for fiscal
and defensive purposes, that is, for the execution of their revenue laws, and to
prevent hovering on their coasts."

He observes that "it is necessary to distinguish between *maritime territory* and *territorial jurisdiction*," which he proposes to do
in a subsequent chapter, and, indeed, does with respect to vessels
in a foreign port; but he is silent as to how far the law of the
local state is applicable to vessels passing along or anchoring in
its external waters.

A writer of our own country, Mr. Manning, in his Law of
Nations (p. 119), lately edited by a distinguished jurist, Mr.
Amos, thus limits the purposes as to which this right may be
exercised :—

"For some limited purposes a special right of jurisdiction, and even (for a few
definite purposes) of dominion, is conceded to a state in respect of the part of the
ocean immediately adjoining its own coast line. The purposes for which this
jurisdiction and dominion have been recognised are—(1) the regulation of fisheries ;
(2) the prevention of frauds on customs laws ; (3) the exaction of harbour and
lighthouse dues ; and (4) the protection of the territory from violation in time

of war between other states. The distance from the coast line to which this qualified privilege extends has been variously measured—the most prevalent distances being that of a cannon-shot or of a marine league from the shore."

We have here a total silence as to any criminal jurisdiction over foreigners.

Chancellor Kent, whose opinion we should have been so much disposed to respect, also leaves the matter in doubt.

"It is difficult," he says, "to draw any precise or determinate conclusion, amidst the variety of opinions, as to the distance to which a state may lawfully extend its exclusive dominion over the sea adjoining its territories, and beyond those portions of the sea which are embraced by harbours, gulfs, bays, and estuaries, and over which its jurisdiction unquestionably extends. All that can be reasonably asserted is, that the dominion of the sovereign of the shore over the contiguous sea extends as far as is requisite for his safety, and for some lawful end. A more extended dominion must rest entirely upon force and maritime supremacy. According to the current of modern authority, the general territorial jurisdiction extends into the sea as far as cannon-shot will reach, and no farther; and this is generally calculated to be a marine league. And the congress of the United States have recognised this limitation by authorizing the district courts to take cognizance of all captures made within a marine league of the American shores."

Three or four other learned authors remain to be noticed, who, although not professing to treat of international law, have nevertheless incidentally touched on this subject, and whose opinions may be deserving of attention.

The subject is discussed by M. Massé, in his recent work, Le Droit Commercial dans ses rapports avec le Droit Civil, of which the last edition appeared in 1874 (book ii. tit. ii. ch. i. art. 105). After giving the usual reasons for conceding the right to the territorial sea, he continues:—

"Every nation has, therefore, a right of police and of jurisdiction over the part of the sea which borders on its coasts, and makes, in some sort, a part of its territory. It can, consequently, subject all ships that come within the extent of the territorial sea to its customs and navigation laws; but this right is not so absolute as that the nation whose coast the sea adjoins can prohibit navigation for the purposes of commerce. This can only be denied to ships of war. So that, to speak truly, in all that concerns navigation, a people has not the full right of property over the littoral sea. It has only jurisdiction over it. 'Quamvis in mari non sit territorium,' says Roccus (cent. 2, resp. 3, n. 10), 'Tamen in eo jurisdictio exercetur;' or rather the right of property is burdened with a natural servitude for the general benefit of navigation. It is otherwise in respect of the right of fishing, which is confined to the inhabitants of the coast."

M. Massé then goes into the question of distance; and after repeating and rejecting the views of the earlier publicists, adopts the reasoning usually followed, and fixes the distance at three miles, as being the range of cannon-shot. At the same time he observes that this logical rule is not always followed, as nations sometimes fix their own limits at a greater distance, which is binding upon those who recognise the right. Thus, France subjects all vessels to its customs-laws to a distance of five leagues.

Von Kaltenborn, in his Private Maritime Law of Europe, observes that, since the time of Bynkershoek, that is to say for a period of 200 years, the rule has been gaining ground, both in theory and practice, that the littoral sea so far as cannon-shot will reach (quousque mare e terrâ imperari potest), belongs to the maritime territory (Seegebiet) of a nation. With regard to distance, the writer contents himself with repeating the opinions of his predecessors, but expresses none of his own.

Another writer, Mr. Bishop, in his Commentaries on Criminal Law, an elaborate and learned work, published in 1865, says (book iv. c. 5, § 74):

" A nation bordering on the sea can hold actual possession of it as far from the shore as cannon-balls will reach, while dominion to this extent is necessary for the safety of the inhabitants, who might otherwise, being neutral, be cut down in in time of war by the artillery of the belligerents contending on the water. And so much of ocean, the authorities agree, is within the territorial sovereignty which controls the adjacent shores. A cannon-shot is, for this purpose, estimated at a marine league, which is a little short of three and a half of our English miles, or exactly 3·4517. But the rule of computing a cannon-shot as a marine league for this purpose was established before the late improvements in guns and gunnery ; and, in reason, the distance would seem now to require extension, though the author is not able to refer to any sufficient authority shewing the extension to have been actually made in the law of nations."

A fourth author, Signor Foramiti, in a short but very able treatise, entitled L'Avvocato Marittimo, after dividing the sea into mare vasto and mare territoriale, says :

" The waters which bathe the coast and shores of a state form its natural boundary ; for the more effectual protection and defence of which the general usage of nations allows an imaginary line to be traced upon the sea at a convenient distance from the shore, and adapting itself to the formation of the latter, which line must be considered as the artificial maritime boundary of the state."

This line the author, adopting the language of Martens, calls " Linea di rispetto," and fixes at the usual distance of three miles:

" Every ship," he continues, " which is found within this line must be considered as in the waters of the state of which it bounds the sovereignty and jurisdiction, and those on board must conduct themselves as though they were on the shore, doing nothing which the government has a right to prohibit as prejudicial to the property or safety of the nation."

Whether, if the contrary should happen, they will be within the criminal law of the country, the author does not proceed to tell us.

From the review of these authorities we arrive at the following results. There can be no doubt that the suggestion of Bynkershoek, that the sea surrounding the coast to the extent of cannon-range should be treated as belonging to the state owning the coast, has, with but very few exceptions, been accepted and adopted by the publicists who have followed him during the last two centuries. But it is equally clear that, in the practical application of the rule, in respect of the particular of distance, as also in the still more essential particular of the character and degree of sovereignty and dominion to be exercised, great difference of opinion and uncertainty have prevailed, and still continue to exist.

As regards distance, while the majority of authors have adhered to the three-mile zone, others, like M. Ortolan and Mr. Halleck, applying with greater consistency the principle on which the whole doctrine rests, insist on extending the distance to the modern range of cannon—in other words doubling it. This difference of opinion may be of little practical importance in the present instance, inasmuch as the place at which the offence occurred was within the lesser distance; but it is, nevertheless, not immaterial as shewing how unsettled this doctrine still is. The question of sovereignty, on the other hand, is all-important. And here we have every shade of opinion.

One set of writers, as, for instance, M. Hautefeuille, ascribe to the state territorial property and sovereignty over the three miles of sea, to the extent of the right of excluding the ships of all other nations, even for the purpose of passage—a doctrine flowing immediately from the principle of territorial property, but which is too monstrous to be admitted. Another set concede territorial property and sovereignty, but make it subject to the right of other nations to use these waters for the purpose of navigation. Others again, like M. Ortolan and M. Calvo, deny any right of territorial property, but concede "jurisdiction;" by which I understand them to mean the power of applying the law, applicable to persons on

the land, to all who are within the territorial water, and the power
of legislating in respect of it, so as to bind every one who comes
within the jurisdiction, whether subjects or foreigners. Some, like
M. Ortolan, would confine this jurisdiction to purposes of " safety
and police "—by which I should be disposed to understand measures
for the protection of the territory, and for the regulation of the
navigation, and the use of harbours and roadsteads, and the maintenance of order among the shipping therein, rather than the
general application of the criminal law.

Other authors,—for instance, Mr. Manning,—would restrict the
jurisdiction to certain specified purposes in which the local state
has an immediate interest, namely, the protection of its revenue
and fisheries, the exacting of harbour and light dues, and the protection of its coasts in time of war.

Some of these authors,—for instance, Professor Bluntschli,—make
a most important distinction between a commorant and a passing
ship. According to this author, while the commorant ship is subject
to the general law of the local state, the passing ship is liable to
the local jurisdiction only in matters of " military and police regulations, made for the safety of the territory and population of the
coast." None of these writers, it should be noted, discuss the
question, or go the length of asserting that a foreigner in a foreign
ship, using the waters in question for the purpose of navigation
solely, on its way to another country, is liable to the criminal law
of the adjoining country for an offence committed on board.

Now, when it is remembered that it is mainly on the statements
and authority of these writers, and to opinions founded upon them,
that we are called upon to hold that foreigners on the so-called
territorial sea are subject to the general law of this country, the
discrepancy of opinion which I have been pointing out becomes
very material. Looking to this, we may properly ask those who
contend for the application of the existing law to the littoral sea
independently of legislation, to tell us the extent to which we are
to go in applying it. Are we to limit it to three miles, or to
extend it to six? Are we to treat the whole body of the criminal
law as applicable to it, or only so much as relates to "police and
safety"? Or are we to limit it, as one of these authors proposes,
to the protection of fisheries and customs, the exacting of harbour

1876

THE QUEEN
v.
KEYN.

Cockburn, C.J.

and light dues, and the protection of our coasts in time of war? Which of these writers are we to follow? What is there in these conflicting views to guide us, in the total absence of precedent or legal sanction, as to the extent to which we may subject foreigners to our law? What is there in them which authorizes us to assume not only that Parliament can of right deal with the three-mile zone as forming part of our territory, but also that, by the mere assent of other nations, the sea to this extent has become so completely a part of our territory as to be subject, without legislation, to the whole body of our existing law, civil and criminal.

But it is said that, although the writers on international law are disagreed on so many essential points, they are all agreed as to the power of a littoral state to deal with the three-mile zone as subject to its dominion, and that consequently we may treat it as subject to our law. But this reasoning strikes me as unsatisfactory; for what does this unanimity in the general avail us when we come to the practical application of the law in the particular instance, if we are left wholly in the dark as to the degree to which the law can be legitimately enforced? This unanimity of opinion that the littoral sea is, at all events for some purposes, subject to the dominion of the local state, may go far to shew that, by the concurrence of other nations, such a state may deal with these waters as subject to its legislation. But it wholly fails to shew that, in the absence of such legislation, the ordinary law of the local state will extend over the waters in question—which is the point which we have to determine.

Not altogether uninfluenced, perhaps, by the diversity of opinion to which I have called attention, the argument in support of the prosecution presents itself—not without some sacrifice of consistency—in more than one shape. At one time it is asserted that, for the space of three miles, not only the sea itself, but the bed on which it rests, forms part of the territory or realm of the country owning the coast, as though it were so much land; so that the right of passage and anchorage might be of right denied to the ships of other nations. At another time it is said that, while the right is of a territorial character, it is subject to a right of passage by the ships of other nations. Sometimes the sovereignty is asserted, not as based on territorial right, but simply as

1876

The Queen
v.
Keyn.

Cockburn, C.J.
attaching to the sea, over which it is contended that the nation owning the coast may extend its law to the foreigner navigating within it.

To those who assert that, to the extent of three miles from the coast, the sea forms part of the realm of England, the question may well be put, when did it become so? Was it so from the beginning? It certainly was not deemed to be so as to a three-mile zone, any more than as to the rest of the high seas, at the time the statutes of Richard II. were passed. For in those statutes a clear distinction is made between the realm and the sea, as also between the bodies of counties and the sea; the jurisdiction of the admiral being (subject to the exception already stated as to murder and mayhem) confined strictly to the latter, and its exercise " within the realm" prohibited in terms. The language of the first of these statutes is especially remarkable:

" The admirals and their deputies shall not meddle from henceforth with any-thing done *within the realm of England, but only with things done upon the sea.*"

It is impossible not to be struck by the distinction here taken between the realm of England and the sea; or, when the two statutes are taken together, not to see that the term " realm," used in the first statute, and ." bodies of counties," the term used in the second statute, mean one and the same thing. In ʾthese statutes the jurisdiction of the admiral is restricted to the high seas, and, in respect of murder and mayhem, to the great rivers below the bridges, while whatever is within the realm, in other words, within the body of a county, is left within the domain of the common law. But there is no distinction taken between one part of the high sea and another. The three-mile zone is no more dealt with as within the realm than the seas at large. The notion of a three-mile zone was in those days in the womb of time. When its origin is traced, it is found to be of comparatively modern growth. The first mention of it by any writer, or in any court of this country, so far as I am aware, was made by Lord Stowell, with reference to a question of neutral rights, in the first year of the present century, in the case of *The Twee Gebroeders*. (1) To this hour it has not, even in theory, yet settled into certainty.

(1) 3 C. Rob. 162.

For centuries before it was thought of, the great landmarks of our judicial system had been set fast—the jurisdiction of the common law over the land and the inland waters contained within it, forming together the realm of England, that of the admiral over English vessels on the seas, the common property or highway of mankind.

But I am met by authority, and, beyond question, ancient authority, may be found in abundance for the assertion that the bed of the sea is part of the realm of England, part of the territorial possessions of the Crown. Coke, commenting on s. 439 of Littleton, says, in explaining the words "out of the realm":

"If a man be upon the sea of England, he is within the kingdom or realme of England, and within the ligeance of the King of England, as of his crowne of England. And yet *altum mare* is out of the jurisdiction of the common law, and within the jurisdiction of the lord admirall."

So Lord Hale, no doubt, in his work De Jure Maris, speaks of the narrow seas, and the soil thereof, as "part of the King's waste, demesnes, and dominions, whether in the body of a county or not." But this was said, not with reference to the theory of the three-mile zone, which had not then been thought of, but (following Selden) to the wild notion of sovereignty over the whole of the narrow seas. This pretension failing, the rest of the doctrine, as it seems to me, falls with it. Moreover, Hale stops short of saying that the bed of the sea forms part of the realm of England, as a portion of its territory. He speaks of it under the vague terms of "waste," "demesnes," or "dominions." He carefully distinguishes between the parts of the sea which are within the body of a county and those which are not.

It is true that, in his later work on the Pleas of the Crown, Lord Hale, speaking in the chapter on Treasons (vol. i. p. 154), of what is a levying of war against the King "within the realm," according to the required averment in an indictment for that offence, instances the hostile invasion of the King's ships (" which," he observes, "are so many royal castles"); and this, he says, "is a levying of war within the realm;" the reason he assigns being that "the narrow seas are of the ligeance of the Crown of England," for which he cites the authority of Selden. Here, again, we have Lord Hale blindly following "Master Selden," in asserting that the narrow seas owe allegiance to the Crown of England. A hostile attack by a subject on a ship of war on the narrow seas would, I need scarcely say, be a levying of war against the sovereign, but it could not now be said to be high treason as having been done within the realm.

Blackstone (Comm. vol. i. p. 110) says that "the main or high seas" (which he afterwards describes as beginning at low-water mark) "are part of the realm of England"—here Mr. Stephen, feeling that his author was going too far, interposes the words "in one sense"—"for thereon," adds Blackstone, "our Courts of Admiralty have jurisdiction; but they are not subject to the common law." This is, indeed, singular reasoning. Instead of saying that, because these seas are part of the realm of England, the Courts of Admiralty have jurisdiction over them, the writer reverses the position, and says, that because the Admiralty has jurisdiction these seas are part of the realm—which certainly does not follow. If it did, as the jurisdiction of the Admiralty extended, as regards British ships, wherever the sea rolls, the entire ocean might be said to be within the realm.

But to what, after all, do these ancient authorities amount? Of what avail are they towards establishing that the soil in the three-mile zone is part of the territorial domain of the Crown? These assertions of sovereignty were manifestly based on the doctrine that the narrow seas are part of the realm of England. But that doctrine is now exploded. Who at this day would venture to affirm that the sovereignty thus asserted in those times now exists? What English lawyer is there who would not shrink from maintaining—what foreign jurist who would not deny—what foreign government which would not repel such a pretension? I listened carefully to see whether any such assertion would be made; but none was made. No one has gone the length of suggesting, much less of openly asserting, that the jurisdiction still exists. It seems to me to follow that when the sovereignty and jurisdiction from which the property in the soil of the sea was inferred is gone, the territorial property which was suggested to be consequent upon it must necessarily go with it.

But we are met here by a subtle and ingenious argument. It is said that although the doctrine of the criminal jurisdiction of the admiral over foreigners on the four seas has died out, and can no longer be upheld, yet, as now, by the consent of other nations, sovereignty over this territorial sea is conceded to us, the jurisdiction formerly asserted may be revived and made to attach to the newly-acquired domain. I am unable to adopt this reasoning. Ex concessis, the jurisdiction over foreigners in foreign ships never really existed, at all events, it has long been dead and buried, even the ghost of it has been laid. But it is evoked from its grave and brought to life for the purpose of applying it to a part of the sea which was included in the whole, as to which it is now practically admitted that it never existed. From the time the jurisdiction was asserted to the time when the pretension to it was dropped, it was asserted over this portion of the sea as part of the whole to which the jurisdiction was said to extend. If it was bad as to the whole indiscriminately, it was bad as to every part of the whole. But why was it bad as to the whole? Simply because the jurisdiction did not extend to foreigners in foreign ships on the high seas. But the waters in question have always formed part of the high seas. They are alleged in this indictment to be so now. How, then, can the admiral have the jurisdiction over them contended for if he had it not before? There having been no new statute conferring it, how has he acquired it?

To come back to the subject of the realm, I cannot help thinking that some confusion arises from the term "realm" being used in more than one sense. Sometimes it is used, as in the statute of Richard II., to mean the land of England, and the internal sea within it, sometimes as meaning whatever the sovereignty of the Crown of England extended, or was supposed to extend, over.

When it is used as synonymous with territory, I take the true meaning of the term "realm of England" to be the territory to and over which the common law of England extends—in other words, all that is within the body of any county—to the exclusion of the high seas, which come under a different jurisdiction only because they are not within any of those territorial divisions, into which, among other things for the administration of the law, the kingdom is parcelled out. At all events, I am prepared to abide by the distinction taken in the statutes of Richard II. between the realm and the sea. For centuries our judicial system in the

1876

Thᴇ Qᴜᴇᴇɴ
v.
Kᴇʏɴ.

Cockburn, C.J.
administration of the criminal law has been divided into two distinct and independent branches, the one having jurisdiction over
the land and any sea considered to be within the land; the other
over the sea external to the land. No concurrent assent of nations,
that a portion of what before was treated as the high sea, and as
such common to all the world, shall now be treated as the territory
of the local state, can of itself, without the authority of Parliament, convert that which before was in the eye of the law high
sea into British territory, and so change the law, or give to the
Courts of this country, independently of legislation, a jurisdiction
over the foreigner where they had it not before. The argument
in support of the contrary appears to me, I must say, singularly
inconsistent with itself. According to it the littoral sea is made
to assume what I cannot help calling an amphibious character.
At one time it is land, at another it is water. Is it desired to
apply the law of the shore to it, so as to make the foreigner subject to that law?—it becomes so much territory. Do you wish to
keep it within the jurisdiction of the admiral—as you must do to
uphold this indictment?—it is made to resume its former character as part of the high seas. Unable to follow this vacillating
reasoning, I must add that, to my mind, the contention that the
littoral sea forms part of the realm or territory of Great Britain is
fatal to the argument which it is intended to support. For, if the
sea thus becomes part of the territory, as though it were actually
inter fauces terræ, it seems to follow that it must become annexed
to the main land, and so become part of the adjoining county, in
which case there would be an end to the Admiralty jurisdiction.
The littoral sea cannot be land for one purpose and high sea for
another. Nor is anything gained by substituting the term "territory" for land. The law of England knows but of one territory
—that which is within the body of a county. All beyond it is the
high sea, which is out of the province of English law as applicable
to the shore, and to which that law cannot be extended except
by legislation.

It does not appear to me that the argument for the prosecution
is advanced by reference to encroachments on the sea, in the way
of harbours, piers, breakwaters, and the like, even when projected
into the open sea, or of forts erected in it, as is the case in the

1876

THE QUEEN
v.
KEYN.

Cockburn, C.J.

Solent. Where the sea, or the bed on which it rests, can be physically occupied permanently, it may be made subject to occupation in the same manner as unoccupied territory. In point of fact, such encroachments are generally made for the benefit of the navigation; and are therefore readily acquiesced in. Or they are for the purposes of defence, and come within the principle that a nation may do what is necessary for the protection of its own territory. Whether, if an encroachment on the sea were such as to obstruct the navigation to the ships of other nations, it would not amount to a just cause of complaint, as inconsistent with international rights, might, if the case arose, be deserving of serious consideration. That such encroachments are occasionally made seems to me to fall very far short of establishing such an exclusive property in the littoral sea as that, in the absence of legislation, it can be treated, to all intents and purposes, as part of the realm.

Again, the fact, adverted to in the course of the discussion, that in the west of England mines have been run out under the bed of the sea to beyond low-water mark, seems to me to avail but little towards the decision of the question of territorial property in the littoral sea. But for the Act of 21 & 22 Vict. c. 109, to which our attention has been specially directed, I should have thought the matter simple enough. Between high and low-water mark the property in the soil is in the Crown, and it is to be assumed that it is by grant or licence from the Crown, or by prescription, which presupposes a grant, that a mine is carried beneath it. Beyond low-water mark the bed of the sea might, I should have thought, be said to be unappropriated, and, if capable of being appropriated, would become the property of the first occupier. I should not have thought that the carrying one or two mines into the bed of the sea beyond low-water mark could have any real bearing on a question of international law like the present.

But the Act just referred to, and the circumstances out of which it arose, have been brought impressively to our attention by the Lord Chief Justice of the Common Pleas, as shewing that, according to parliamentary exposition, the bed of the sea beyond low-water mark is in the Crown. I cannot help thinking that, when the matter comes to be looked at a little more closely, it will be found that the facts by no means warrant this conclusion. The Duchy of Cornwall, which is vested in His Royal Highness the Prince of Wales, extends, as is known, to low-water mark. Mines existing under the bed of the sea within the low-water mark having been carried out beyond it, a question was raised on the part of the Crown as to whether the minerals beyond the low-water mark, and not within the county of Cornwall, as also those lying under the sea-shore between high and low-water mark within the county of Cornwall, and under the estuaries and tidal rivers within the county, did not belong to the Crown. The matter having been referred to Sir John Patteson, his decision as to the mines and minerals below low-water mark was in favour of the Crown; with reference to the others, in favour of the duchy. Not having had the advantage of seeing Sir John Patteson's award, I am unaware whether the precise grounds on which his decision proceeded are stated in it, but the terms in which it was framed may be gathered with perfect precision from the recitals of the Act of Parliament which, by arrangement, was passed shortly afterwards to give statutory effect to the award. From the recitals in the preamble to the Act it appears that the award was very carefully, I may say cautiously, drawn. After stating the matter in dispute, and the reference to Sir John Patteson, the preamble goes on to recite that the arbitrator had decided,

" "First, that the right to all mines and minerals lying under the sea-shore between high and low-water marks within the said county of Cornwall, and under estuaries and tidal rivers, and other places, even below low-water mark, being in and part of the said county, is vested in His Royal Highness as part of the soil and territorial possessions of the Duchy of Cornwall. Secondly, that the right to all mines and minerals lying below low-water mark, under the open sea adjacent to, but not being part of, the county of Cornwall, is vested in Her Majesty the Queen in right of her Crown, although such minerals may or might be won by workings commenced above low-water mark and extended below it."

The difference between the two parts of this recital is at once apparent. When dealing with that which is within low-water mark, the award declares the right to the mines and minerals under the sea-shore to be vested in His Royal Highness "as part of the soil and territorial possessions of the Duchy of Cornwall." But when the learned arbitrator comes to deal with the mines and minerals below low-water mark, he stops short of saying that these

mines and minerals belong to Her Majesty by virtue of any owner- 1876
ship in the soil. He confines himself to awarding that the right
to such mines and minerals is vested in Her Majesty "in right of
her Crown." What the grounds were on which this decision was
based I can only conjecture. Sir John Patteson may have held,
on the authority of Collis (p. 58), that a subject cannot have any
ownership in the soil below low-water mark—and, though standing
next to the Throne, the Prince of Wales is still a subject—and
that, as between the Crown and a subject, as regards property in
or under the open sea, the Crown had the better right. Or the
decision may have been founded on the peculiar constitution o
the Duchy of Cornwall, which is settled by Act of Parliament and
occasionally reverts to the Crown. I cannot help thinking that if
the arbitrator had proceeded on the ground that the bed of the
sea below low-water mark belonged to the Crown, he would have
said so, as he had just before done with reference to the soil above
low-water mark. It is true that, when we come to the enacting
part of the statute, that which had been left unsaid by Sir John
Patteson is supplied. The mines and minerals beyond low-water
mark are enacted and declared to be in the Queen, in right of her
Crown, as part of the soil and possessions of the Crown, just as the
mines and minerals within low-water mark are stated to be vested
in the Prince of Wales as Duke of Cornwall, in right of the Duchy
of Cornwall, as part of the soil and possessions of the duchy. But
it is expressly declared that this is to be taken to be so only "as
between the Queen in right of her Crown, and the Prince of Wales
in right of the Duchy of Cornwall," and the rights of all other
persons are expressly preserved. I am surprised, I own, that we
should be asked to look on this piece of legislation as a parliamentary recognition of the universal right of the Crown to the
ownership of the bed of the sea below low-water mark. This was
a bill for the settlement of the question as to the right to particular
mines and minerals between the Crown and the duchy, a measure
in which both the royal personages particularly concerned and
their respective advisers concurred, and in which no other person
whatever was interested. To what member of Parliament, even
the most eccentric, could it possibly have occurred to raise an
objection to it on the ground that it involved an assertion of the

THE QUEEN
v.
KEYN.

Cockburn, C.J.

Queen's right of property in the bed of the sea? To whom would
it occur that, in passing it, Parliament was asserting the right of
the Crown to the bed of the sea over the three-mile distance,
instead of settling a dispute as to the specific mines which were
in question? With the most unfeigned respect for my learned
colleague, I cannot but think that he has attached to this piece
of legislation a degree of importance to which it is by no means
entitled.

It thus appearing, as it seems to me, that the littoral sea beyond
low-water mark did not, as distinguished from the rest of the high
seas, originally form part of the territory of the realm, the question again presents itself, when and how did it become so? Can
a portion of that which was before high sea have been converted
into British territory, without any action on the part of the British
Government or legislature—by the mere assertions of writers on
public law—or even by the assent of other nations?

And when in support of this position, or of the theory of the
three-mile zone in general, the statements of the writers on international law are relied on, the question may well be asked, upon
what authority are these statements founded? When and in what
manner have the nations, who are to be affected by such a rule as
these writers, following one another, have laid down, signified
their assent to it? to say nothing of the difficulty which might be
found in saying to which of these conflicting opinions such assent
had been given.

For, even if entire unanimity had existed in respect of the important particulars to which I have referred, in place of so much
discrepancy of opinion, the question would still remain, how far
_ne law as stated by the publicists had received the assent of the
civilized nations of the world. For writers on international law,
however valuable their labours may be in elucidating and ascertaining the principles and rules of law, cannot make the law. To be
binding, the law must have received the assent of the nations who
are to be bound by it. This assent may be express, as by treaty or
the acknowledged concurrence of governments, or may be implied
from established usage,—an instance of which is to be found in the
fact that merchant vessels on the high seas are held to be subject
only to the law of the nation under whose flag they sail, while in

1876

THE QUEEN
v.
KEYN.

Cockburn, C.J.

the ports of a foreign state they are subject to the local law as well
as to that of their own country.   In the absence of proof of assent,
as derived from one or other of these sources, no unanimity on the
part of theoretical writers would warrant the judicial application
of the law on the sole authority of their views or statements.
Nor, in my opinion, would the clearest proof of unanimous assent
on the part of other nations be sufficient to authorize the tribunals
of this country to apply, without an Act of Parliament, what would
practically amount to a new law.   In so doing we should be un-
justifiably usurping the province of the legislature.   The assent of
nations is doubtless sufficient to give the power of parliamentary
legislation in a matter otherwise within the sphere of international
law; but it would be powerless to confer without such legislation
a jurisdiction beyond and unknown to the law, such as that now
insisted on, a jurisdiction over foreigners in foreign ships on a
portion of the high seas.

When I am told that all other nations have assented to such an
absolute dominion on the part of the littoral state, over this
portion of the sea, as that their ships may be excluded from it, and
that, without any open legislation, or notice to them or their
subjects, the latter may be held liable to the local law, I ask,
first, what proof there is of such assent as here asserted; and,
secondly, to what extent has such assent been carried? a question
of infinite importance, when, undirected by legislation, we are
called upon to apply the law on the strength of such assent.   It
is said that we are to take the statements of the publicists as conclusive proof of the assent in question, and much has been said
to impress on us the respect which is due to their authority, and
that they are to be looked upon as witnesses of the facts to which
they speak, witnesses whose statements, or the foundation on
which those statements rest, we are scarcely at liberty to question.
I demur altogether to this position.   I entertain a profound respect for the opinion of jurists when dealing with the matters of
juridical principle and opinion, but we are here dealing with a
question not of opinion but of fact, and I must assert my entire
liberty to examine the evidence and see upon what foundation
these statements are based.   The question is not one of theoretical opinion, but of fact, and, fortunately, the writers upon whose

1876

THE QUEEN
v.
KEYN.

Cockburn, C.J.

statements we are called upon to act have afforded us the means of testing those statements by reference to facts. They refer us to two things, and to these alone—treaties and usage. Let us look a little more closely into both.

First, then, let us see how the matter stands as regards treaties. It may be asserted, without fear of contradiction, that the rule that the sea surrounding the coast is to be treated as a part of the adjacent territory, so that the state shall have exclusive dominion over it, and that the law of the latter shall be generally applicable to those passing over it in the ships of other nations, has never been made the subject-matter of any treaty, or, as matter of acknowledged right, has formed the basis of any treaty, or has even been the subject of diplomatic discussion. It has been entirely the creation of the writers on international law. It is true that the writers who have been cited constantly refer to treaties in support of the doctrine they assert. But when the treaties they refer to are looked at, they will be found to relate to two subjects only—the observance of the rights and obligations of neutrality, and the exclusive right of fishing. In fixing the limits to which these rights should extend, nations have so far followed the writers on international law as to adopt the three miles range as a convenient distance. There are several treaties by which nations have engaged, in the event of either of them being at war with a third, to treat the sea within three miles of each other's coasts as neutral territory, within which no warlike operations should be carried on; instances of which will be found in the various treatises on international law.

Thus, for instance, in the treaties of commerce, between Great Britain and France, of September, 1786; between France and Russia, of January, 1787; between Great Britain and the United States, of October, 1794, each contracting party engages, if at war with any other nation, not to carry on hostilities within cannon-shot of the coast of the other contracting party; or, if the other should be at war, not to allow its vessels to be captured within the like distance. There are many other treaties of the like tenor, a list of which is given by Azuni (vol. ii. p. 78); and various ordinances and laws have been made by the different states in order to give effect to them.

1876

THE QUEEN
v.
KEYN.

Cockburn, C.J. :

Again, nations, possessing opposite or neighbouring coasts, bordering on a common sea, have sometimes found it expedient to agree that the subjects of each shall exercise an exclusive right of fishing to a given distance from their own shores, and here also have accepted the three miles as a convenient distance.   Such, for instance, are the treaties made between this country and the United States in relation to the fishery off the coast of Newfoundland, and those between this country and France in relation to the fishery on their respective shores; and local laws have been passed to give effect to these engagements.

But in all these treaties this distance is adopted, not as matter of existing right established by the general law of nations, but as matter of mutual concession and convention.   Instead of upholding the doctrine contended for, the fact of these treaties having been entered into has rather the opposite tendency: for it is obvious that, if the territorial right of a nation bordering on the sea to this portion of the adjacent waters had been established by the common assent of nations, these treaty arrangements would have been wholly superfluous.   Each nation would have been bound, independently of treaty engagement, to respect the neutrality of the other in these waters as much as in its inland waters.   The foreigner invading the rights of the local fisherman would have been amenable, consistently with international law, to local legislation prohibiting such infringement, without any stipulation to that effect by treaty.   For what object, then, have treaties been resorted to?   Manifestly in order to obviate all questions as to concurrent or conflicting rights arising under the law of nations. Possibly, after these precedents and all that has been written on this subject, it may not be too much to say that, independently of treaty, the three-mile belt of sea might at this day be taken as belonging, for these purposes, to the local state.   But it is scarcely logical to infer, from such treaties alone, that, because nations have agreed to treat the littoral sea as belonging to the country it adjoins, for certain specified objects, they have therefore assented to forego all other rights previously enjoyed in common, and have submitted themselves, even to the extent of the right of navigation on a portion of the high seas, and the liability of their subjects therein to the criminal law, to the will of the local

1876

THE QUEEN
v.
KEYN.
Cockburn, C.J.
sovereign, and the jurisdiction of the local state. Equally illogical
is it, as it seems to me, from the adoption of the three-mile
distance in these particular instances, to assume, independently of
everything else, a recognition, by the common assent of nations, of
the principle that the subjects of one state passing in ships within
three miles of the coast of another shall be in all respects subject
to the law of the latter. It may be that the maritime nations of
the world are prepared to acquiesce in the appropriation of the
littoral sea; but I cannot think that these treaties help us much
towards arriving at the conclusion that this appropriation has
actually taken place. At all events, the question remains, whether
judicially we can infer that the nations who have been parties to
these treaties, and still further those who have not, have thereby
assented to the application of the criminal law of other nations
to their subjects on the waters in question, and on the strength of
such inference so apply the criminal law of this country.

The uncertainty in which we are left, so far as judicial knowledge is concerned, as to the extent of such assent, likewise presents,
I think, a very serious obstacle to our assuming the jurisdiction
we are called upon to exercise, independently of the, to my mind,
still more serious difficulty, that we should be assuming it without
legislative warrant.

So much for treaties. Then how stands the matter as to usage,
to which reference is so frequently made by the publicists in support of their doctrine? When the matter is looked into, the only
usage found to exist is such as is connected with navigation, or
with revenue, local fisheries, or neutrality, and it is to these alone
that the usage relied on is confined. Usage as to the application
of the general law of the local state to foreigners on the littoral
sea there is actually none. No nation has arrogated to itself the
right of excluding foreign vessels from the use of its external
littoral waters for the purpose of navigation, or has assumed the
power of making foreigners in foreign ships passing through these
waters subject to its law, otherwise than in respect of the matters
to which I have just referred. Nor have the tribunals of any
nation held foreigners in these waters amenable generally to the
local criminal law in respect of offences. It is for the first time
in the annals of jurisprudence that a Court of justice is now called

1876

THE QUEEN
v.
KEYN.

Cockburn, C.J.

upon to apply the criminal law of the country to such a case as the present.

It may well be, I say again, that—after all that has been said and done in this respect—after the instances which have been mentioned of the adoption of the three-mile distance, and the repeated assertion of this doctrine by the writers on public law, a nation which should now deal with this portion of the sea as its own, so as to make foreigners within it subject to its law, for the prevention and punishment of offences, would not be considered as infringing the rights of other nations. But I apprehend that as the ability so to deal with these waters would result, not from any original or inherent right, but, from the acquiescence of other states, some outward manifestation of the national will, in the shape of open practice or municipal legislation, so as to amount, at least constructively, to an occupation of that which was before unappropriated, would be necessary to render the foreigner, not previously amenable to our general law, subject to its control. That such legislation, whether consistent with the general law of nations or not, would be binding on the tribunals of this country —leaving the question of its consistency with international law to be determined between the governments of the respective nations— can of course admit of no doubt. The question is whether such legislation would not, at all events, be necessary to justify our Courts in applying the law of this country to foreigners under entirely novel circumstances in which it has never been applied before.

It is obviously one thing to say that the legislature of a nation may, from the common assent of other nations, have acquired the full right to legislate over a part of that which was before high sea, and as such common to all the world; another and a very different thing to say that the law of the local state becomes thereby at once, without anything more, applicable to foreigners within such part, or that, independently of legislation, the Courts of the local state can proprio vigore so apply it. The one position does not follow from the other; and it is essential to keep the two things, the power of Parliament to legislate, and the authority of our Courts, without such legislation, to apply the criminal law where it could not have been applied before, altogether distinct, which, it is evident, is not always done. It is unnecessary to the defence, and equally so to the decision of the case, to determine whether Parliament has the right to treat the three-mile zone as part of the realm consistently with international law. That is a matter on which it is for Parliament itself to decide. It is enough for us that it has, so far as to be binding upon us, the power to do so. The question is whether, acting judicially, we can treat the power of Parliament to legislate as making up for the absence of actual legislation. I am clearly of opinion that we cannot, and that it is only in the instances in which foreigners on the seas have been made specifically liable to our law by statutory enact- ment that that law can be applied to them.

Let us, then, now see what has been done herein in the way of legislation.

The statutes relating to the sea by which foreigners may be affected may be divided into two classes, those which have no reference to the three-mile zone, and those which have. The latter, again, may be divided into those which expressly refer to the foreigner, and those which are said to do so by implication only. It is desirable to dispose of those first referred to before we come to the statutes which have reference to the three-mile distance. First in order comes the statute of 28 Hen. 8, c. 15, upon which an argument has been founded, resting on a broader basis than that of the modern doctrine, and which, if it could be upheld, would dispense with the necessity of resorting to the theory of the three-mile zone at all. It has been suggested that, independently of any legislation having special reference to the three-mile zone, the statute of Henry VIII., which transferred, as we have seen, the jurisdiction of the admiral to the Courts of common law, had the effect of making foreigners subject to our law for offences committed on foreign ships within the narrow seas; the argument, if I apprehend it rightly, being, first, that the language of the statute being general in its terms, it must be taken to have included foreigners as well as subjects; secondly, that, inasmuch as, at the time when the statute of Henry VIII. was passed, the claim to dominion over the narrow seas was still asserted on the part of the Crown, the jurisdiction given to the admiral by the prior Admiralty Commissions must be taken to have been co-extensive therewith, and such jurisdiction must therefore be considered as having been transferred by the statute.

It is true that the language of the statute is quite general in its terms. After reciting the inconveniences arising from the existing jurisdiction, it enacts that " all treasons, felonies, robberies, murders, and confederacies committed in or upon the sea, or in any haven, river, creek, or place where the admiral or admirals have, or pretend to have"—which has been construed to mean rightfully assert—"jurisdiction, shall be enquired, tried, heard, and determined and judged in such shires and places in the realm as shall be limited by the King's commission, in like form and condition as if such offences had been committed on land." No doubt these words are large enough to include foreigners as well as subjects; but so they are to include the entire ocean as well as the narrow seas. And it cannot be supposed that anything so preposterous was contemplated as to make foreigners liable to the law of this country for offences committed on foreign ships all over the world. The statute must receive a reasonable construction, and the construction put upon it by the highest authorities has always been that all that it effected, or was intended to effect, was, as I have already stated, a transfer of jurisdiction only.

In the Third Institute, cap. 49, p. 112, Lord Coke, speaking of this statute, with reference to the offence of piracy, says:

"This statute did not alter the offence or make the offence felony, but leaveth the offence as it was before this Act, viz., felony only by the civil law, but giveth a mean of trial by the common law."

In Comyns' Digest, title Admiralty, E. 5, it is said:

"This statute does not alter the nature of the offence, which shall be determined by the civil law, but the manner of trial only."

And in Hawkins' Pleas of the Crown (vol. i. s. 2, p. 254) it is said:

"The statute of 28 Hen. 8, c. 15, does not alter the nature of the offence, so as to make that which was before a felony only by the civil law now become a felony by the common law; for the offence must still be alleged as done upon the sea, and is no way cognizable by the common law; but only by virtue of this statute, which, by ordaining that in some respects it shall have the like trial and punishment as are used for felony at common law, shall not be carried so far as to make it also agree with it in other particulars which are not mentioned."
In the same work (vol. ii. p. 354), Hawkins again writes: "The statute 28 Hen. 8, c. 15, altered not the nature of the offence, but only the manner of trial."

1876

THE QUEEN
v.
KEYN.

Cockburn, C.J.

Again, before we can hold the statute, from the generality of its terms, to include foreigners, we have to consider whether, according to the law of nations, the jurisdiction of the admiral over foreigners, in foreign ships, on the high seas, existed when the statute was passed. For where the language of a statute is general, and may include foreigners or not, the true canon of construction is to assume that the legislature has not so enacted as to violate the rights of other nations. In the case of *Le Louis* (1), where, on an appeal from the sentence of a Vice-Admiralty Court, condemning a French ship for being employed in the slave trade and forcibly resisting the King's cruisers, the application of the Slave Trade Act to a foreign ship came into question, Lord Stowell said :

" Neither this British Act of Parliament, nor any commission founded on it, can affect any right or interest of foreigners, unless they are founded on principles and impose regulations that are consistent with the law of nations. That is the only law that Great Britain can apply to them ; and the generality of any terms employed in an Act of Parliament must be narrowed in construction by a religious adherence thereto."

This principle was acted on by Vice-Chancellor Wood, and by the Lords Justices Knight Bruce and Turner on appeal from his decision, in a case of *Cope* v. *Doherty* (2), where the owners of one foreign ship having sued the owners of another for damage done by a collision at sea, on the defendants seeking to take advantage of the limitation of liability established by s. 504 of the Merchant Shipping Act (17 & 18 Vict. c. 104), it was held that, however general in its terms, the enactment did not apply to foreign vessels. Lord Justice Turner says :

" This is a British Act of Parliament, and it is not, I think, to be presumed that the British Parliament could intend to legislate as to the rights and liabilities of foreigners. In order to warrant such a conclusion, I think that either the words of the Act ought to be express, or the context of it very clear."

This being the true rule of construction, we have to consider whether the jurisdiction of the admiral extended over foreigners on the high seas consistently with the rights of other nations, and I take it to be perfectly clear that it did not. Nor could it, consistently with the law of nations, be made to extend to them. For, if there is one proposition of international law more settled and indisputable than another, it is that the ships of each nation

(1) 2 Dodson, 239.   (2) 1 K. & J. 367 ; on appeal, 2 De G. & J. 614.

on the high seas carry the law of their own nation with them, and
that those on board of them are amenable in respect of offences
committed in them (save and except in respect of piracy, which
is an offence against the law of all nations) to the law of such
nation alone: the only exception to this otherwise universal rule
being that the merchant ships of one nation, when in the ports
and waters of another, are subject to the law of the latter. But
this liability is by all jurists treated as the exception to the general
rule. To argue that, because merchant ships and those in them,
when in the waters of another state, are liable to the local law,
this liability can be extended to foreign ships all over the world, is
to make the exception swallow up the rule. And this brings me to
the second branch of the argument, namely, that the jurisdiction
having been asserted as to the narrow seas at the time the statute
passed, it must be taken to have been transferred by the statute.
The answer to such a contention is that, no reference being made
in the statute to this now-exploded claim of sovereignty, we must
read the statute as having transferred—as, indeed, it could alone
transfer—such jurisdiction only as actually existed. Jurists are
now agreed that the claim to exclusive dominion over the narrow
seas, and consequent jurisdiction over foreigners for offences committed thereon, was extravagant and unfounded, and the doctrine
of the three-mile jurisdiction has taken the place of all such
pretensions. In truth, though largely asserted in theory, the
jurisdiction was never practically exercised in respect of foreigners.
The fallacy of such an argument as I have here referred to consists in supposing the jurisdiction to have had a real existence, so
as to be capable of being transferred without being first expressly
created by the statute. And the position contended for labours
under this further difficulty, that it supposes a statutory transfer,
by implication, of a jurisdiction of one extent at the time the
statute was passed, and of another at the present day.

One or two other statutes relating to the sea may be disposed
of in a few words, as having little or no bearing on the question
before us. The Act of 5 Eliz. c. 5, an Act for the protection of
English shipping, after prohibiting, under penalties, the importa-
tion of particular articles in foreign ships, provides (s. 30) that
such of the offences created by the Act as shall be done on the

1876

THE QUEEN
v.
KEYN.

Cockburn, C.J.

main sea, or coasts of the sea, being no part of the body of any
county of this realm, and without the precincts, jurisdiction, and
liberties of the Cinque Ports, and out of any haven or pier, shall
be tried according to the statute of 28 Hen. VIII. If done on the
main sea, or coasts of the sea, within the jurisdiction of the
Cinque Ports, such offence is to be tried before the Lord Warden,
or his lieutenant or judge, or before judges of oyer and terminer,
according to the statute of Henry VIII. It is obvious that this
statute only affects the foreigner who is seeking our shores with
the object of breaking the law.

Coroners for counties, having under the old law no authority to
inquire of matters arising on the sea unless within the body of the
county, are now, by a recent Act of Parliament (6 Vict. c. 12),
enabled, where there is no Admiralty coroner, to hold inquests on
bodies found on the sea. That the Admiralty coroner or the
county coroner is empowered to hold an inquest on a dead body
found floating on the sea, though the body should prove to be that
of a foreigner, can have no bearing on such a question as the
present.

Again, by 7 Geo. 4, c. 38, justices of the peace are empowered
to take any information upon oath touching any treason, piracy,
felony, robbery, murder, conspiracy, or other offence, committed on the sea, or in any haven, river, creek, or place where
the admiral has power or jurisdiction, and to commit or hold to
bail. But this enactment, which is merely in furtherance of the
administration of justice, has no special reference to foreigners,
and would leave the question of jurisdiction to be disposed of by
the Court before which the offence would afterwards come to be
tried.

Two other statutes, passed like the last to further the administration of justice, require to be here noticed. The Merchant
Shipping Act, 17 & 18 Vict. c. 104, s. 521, enacts that

"In all cases where any district, within which any Court, or justice of the
peace, or other magistrate has jurisdiction, either under this or any other Act, or
at common law, for any purpose whatever, is situate on the coast of any sea, or
abutting on, or projecting into any bay, channel, lake, river, or other navigable
water, every such Court, justice of the peace, or magistrate, shall have jurisdiction over any ship or boat being on or lying, or passing off such coast, or being in
or near such bay, channel, lake, river, or navigable water as aforesaid, and over

all persons on board such ship or boat, or for the time being belonging thereto, in the same manner as if such ship, boat, or persons were within the limits of the original jurisdiction of such Court, justice, or magistrate."

The amending Act, 18 & 19 Vict. c. 91, s. 2, contains important provisions with reference to offences committed on the sea. It enacts, that

"If any person being a British subject, charged with having committed any crime or offence on board any British ship on the high seas, or in any foreign port or harbour ; or if any person not being a British subject, charged with having committed any crime or offence on board any British ship on the high seas, is found within the jurisdiction of any Court of justice in Her Majesty's dominions, which would have had cognizance of such crime or offence if committed within the limits of its ordinary jurisdiction, such court shall have jurisdiction to hear and try the case, as if such crime or offence had been committed within such limits."

British subjects may thus be tried by the ordinary Courts of this country for offences committed on board any British ship on the high seas, or in any foreign port or harbour, as if the offence had been committed within the limits of the ordinary jurisdiction of such Courts; but when the section proceeds to deal with those who are not British subjects, it confines their liability to cases in which the crime has been committed on board a British ship on the high seas, and the offender is found within the jurisdiction of a Court of justice in this country, which would have cognizance of the offence if it had been committed within its ordinary jurisdiction.

It thus appears—1st. That the jurisdiction now exercised by justices and coroners over matters occurring on the high seas is superadded by statute to their ordinary functions by special statutory authority. 2nd. That no distinction is made or suggested between one part of the high sea and another. 3rd. That, while provision is made for trying, wherever he may be found, a foreigner who has committed a crime on board a British ship, no provision is made for the case of a foreigner who has committed a crime on board a foreign ship, however near it may have been to the British shore. In the case in which there is undoubted jurisdiction over a foreign ship, namely, where it is within a port or harbour of this country, no such provision was necessary, and none is made; the enactment being designed for cases where the offender, at the time of committing the offence, is beyond the reach of the officers of justice.

1876

THE QUEEN
v.
KEYN.

Cockburn, C.J.

I pass on to the statutory enactments relating to foreigners within the three-mile zone. These enactments may be divided, 1st, into those which are intended to protect the interests of the state and those which are not; 2nd, into those in which the foreigner is expressly named, and those in which he has been held to be included by implication only.

Hitherto, legislation, so far as relates to foreigners in foreign ships in this part of the sea, has been confined to the maintenance of neutral rights and obligations, the prevention of breaches of the revenue and fishery laws, and, under particular circumstances, to cases of collision. In the two first the legislation is altogether irrespective of the three-mile distance, being founded on a totally different principle, namely, the right of a state to take all necessary measures for the protection of its territory and rights, and the prevention of any breach of its revenue laws.

This principle was well explained by Marshall, C.J., in the case of *Church* v. *Hubbard.* (1) The action was on a policy of insurance, on a vessel named the *Aurora,* in which there was a stipulation that the insurer should not be liable if the vessel, which was insured on a voyage to a port in Brazil, should be seized for violation of the Portuguese revenue laws. She was, in fact, engaged on a smuggling adventure, and was seized at a distance of five leagues from the Portuguese coast. An action having been brought to recover for the loss of the vessel, the stipulation in the policy was made the ground of defence. It was urged in answer that the stipulation must be taken to have had reference to a lawful seizure; whereas here the seizure had been illegal, by reason of its having taken place more than three miles from the coast, and, therefore, out of the jurisdiction of the Portuguese authorities. But the defence prevailed.

Marshall, C.J., in giving the judgment of the Court, says:—

"That the law of nations prohibits the exercise of any act of authority over a vessel in the situation of the *Aurora,* and that this seizure is, on that account, a mere marine trespass, not within the exception, cannot be admitted. To reason from the extent of protection a nation will afford to foreigners to the extent of the means it may use for its own security, does not seem to be perfectly correct. It is opposed by principles which are universally acknowledged. The authority

(1) 2 Cranch, (U.S.) 234.

of a nation within its own territory is absolute and exclusive. The seizure of a
vessel within the range of its cannon by a foreign force is an invasion of that
territory, and is a hostile act which it is its duty to repel." But its power to
secure itself from injury may certainly be exercised beyond the limits of its
territory. Upon this principle the right of a belligerent to search a neutral
vessel on the high seas for contraband of war is universally admitted, because the
belligerent has a right to prevent the injury done to himself by the assistance
intended for his enemy : so, too, a nation has a right to prohibit any commerce
within its colonies. Any attempt to violate the laws made to protect this right,
is an injury to itself which it may prevent, and it has a right to use the means
necessary for its prevention." These means do not appear to be limited within
any certain marked boundaries, which remain the same at all times and in all
situations. If they are such as unnecessarily to vex and harass foreign law by
commerce, foreign nations will resist their exercise. If they are such as are
reasonable and necessary to secure their laws from violation, they will be submitted to.

"In different seas," continues the Chief Justice, "and on different coasts,
a wider or more contracted range, in which to exercise the vigilance of the government, will be assented to. Thus, in the Channel, where a very great part of the
commerce to and from all the north of Europe passes through a very narrow sea,
the seizure of vessels on suspicion of attempting an illicit trade must necessarily
be restricted to very narrow limits; but, on the coast of South America, seldom
frequented by vessels but for the purpose of illicit trade, the vigilance of the
government may be extended somewhat further; and foreign nations submit to
such regulations as are reasonable in themselves and are really necessary to secure
that monopoly of colonial commerce which is claimed by all nations holding
distant possessions."

"Indeed, the right given to our own revenue cutters to visit vessels four
leagues from our coasts, is a declaration that, in the opinion of the American
government, no such principle as that contended for has a real existence."

To this class of enactments belong the Acts imposing penalties
for the violation of neutrality, and the so-called "hovering Acts,"
and Acts relating to the Customs. Thus the Foreign Enlistment
Act (33 & 34 Vict. c. 90), which imposes penalties for various acts
done in violation of neutral obligations, some of which are applicable to foreigners as well as to British subjects, is extended in s. 2
to all the dominions of Her Majesty, "including the adjacent
territorial waters."

By the Act of the last session, 39 & 40 Vict. c. 36, for the consolidation of Acts relating to the Customs, it is enacted by s. 179,
embodying the provisions of s. 212 of the previous Act of 16 & 17
Vict. c. 107,

"That, if a foreign-vessel, belonging in part to any of Her Majesty's subjects,
or having half the persons on board subjects of Her Majesty, is found within four
leagues of the coast between the North Foreland and Beachy Head, or within

eight leagues of any other part of the coast; or if a foreign vessel having one or
more of Her Majesty's subjects on board, is found within three leagues, or a
foreign vessel, irrespectively of having any British subject on board, is found
within three miles of the coast, conveying spirits, tea, or tobacco, otherwise than
in vessels or packages of certain specified dimensions, the articles in question as
well as the vessel itself are made liable to forfeiture; and every person who shall
be found or discovered to have been on board any ship or boat liable to forfeiture as aforesaid, within three leagues of the coast if a British subject, or within
one league if a foreigner, or on board any vessel in Her Majesty's service, or on
board any foreign post-office packet employed in carrying mails between any
foreign country and the United Kingdom, having on board any spirits or tobacco
in such packages as aforesaid, or any tobacco stalks, tobacco stalk flour, or snuff
work, shall forfeit a sum not exceeding one hundred pounds; and every such
person may be detained and taken before any justice to be dealt with as hereinafter directed, provided that no person shall be detained whilst actually on board
any vessel in the service of a foreign state or country."

In this section the legislature has also gone so far as to enact
that any ship or boat liable to seizure or examination under this
or any Act for the prevention of smuggling—which would include
any foreign vessel within the respective limits above mentioned—
not bringing to, when required by any vessel employed for the
prevention of smuggling, may be fired into.

It thus appears, no doubt, that, so far as the civil consequences
of smuggling are concerned, the legislature has gone the length
of making foreign vessels and goods liable to forfeiture within the
three-mile distance, irrespectively of their having any of the
Queen's subjects on board. And when, by s. 235, personal penalties are imposed for breaches of the Act, while British subjects
found in any ship liable to forfeiture within the distances specified
in the section, are liable to the penalties imposed by the Act,
foreigners are made so only when found in such vessels within a
league of the coast. We have, therefore, here an application of
the penal law to foreigners within the three-mile zone: but, as I
have already observed, a nation is entitled to take such measures
as it may deem necessary for the protection of its revenue, within
a reasonable distance from its shores; and Parliament may have
deemed the three miles a reasonable distance within which to
make foreigners amenable to penalties under the customs-laws,
without at all assuming that the foreigner within the three-mile
zone should be subjected generally to the criminal law.

The other enactments affecting foreign ships, or foreigners in

1876

THE QUEEN
v.
KEYN.

Cockburn, C.J.

such ships, occur in the Merchant Shipping Acts, statutes passed for the government of the mercantile marine. The original Act, 17 & 18 Vict. c. 104, is divided into separate parts, and nothing relating to foreign ships occurs in the three first parts. Part IV., commencing at s. 291, relates to "safety and the prevention of accidents," and is applicable to British ships only, with the exception of foreign steamships carrying passengers between places in the United Kingdom, foreign steamers having, by a statute passed shortly before, been authorized to be employed in the coasting trade of this country. Important regulations with reference to navigation are made by the Act, and parties neglecting them are subjected to penalties; but although the observance of these regulations on the part of foreign vessels is as essential to the safety of the navigation as the observance of them by British vessels, the latter alone are named, and the statute is silent as to the observance of them by foreign vessels even within the three miles.

Part IV. of the Merchant Shipping Act has received its completion in the Merchant Shipping Acts Amendment Act of 1873, 36 & 37 Vict. c. 85, and the Amendment Act of the last session of 1876, 39 & 40 Vict. c. 86. By s. 16 of the former, very stringent provisions are made as to the duties of masters of vessels in cases of collision; and very serious consequences, some of them of a penal character, attach to non-performance. A master under such circumstances is to stay by the other vessel, and render every practicable assistance which may be necessary for its safety compatible with that of his own, and to give the master of the other vessel the necessary information to identify his own. If he fails in either of these particulars, the collision is to be presumed to have arisen through his neglect or default. So far the enactment is general. But, when the statute goes on to enact that, if the master fails herein, he shall be guilty of a misdemeanor, it confines the enactment to the master of British vessels.

The Merchant Shipping Acts Amendment Act, 36 & 37 Vict. c. 85, as also the Act of the last session (39 & 40 Vict. c. 86), which make it a misdemeanor to send to sea an unseaworthy ship—and provide that a ship about to sail from any part of the United Kingdom, if, by reason of her defective condition, or over-

1876
THE QUEEN
v.
KEYN.
Cockburn, C.J.
loading, or improper loading, unsafe, may be provisionally detained in order to be surveyed, and, if found unfit, may be finally
detained by order of the Board of Trade—confines the former
enactment to British ships alone. The latter is applied to foreign
ships, but only where the foreign ship has taken in her cargo or
any part of it in a British port.

With regard to the "liability of shipowners," which forms the
subject of Part IX. of the first-mentioned Act, the enactments
being general in their terms, without any specific reference to distance, it has been held by judicial construction that the limitation
on such liability created by s. 503 applies to damage done to
foreign vessels by collision if occurring within the distance of
three miles from the coast. But, where it has been so held, the
foreign vessel has been seeking the redress afforded by British law,
in a British Court, in respect of damage done by a British ship.

The strongest instance of legislation relating to foreign shipping,
is the provision in this part of the Act, which, in s. 527, enacts
that,

" Whenever any injury has, in any part of the world, been caused to any property belonging to Her Majesty or to any of Her Majesty's subjects by any foreign
ship, if at any time thereafter such ship is found in any port or river of the United
Kingdom or within three miles of the coast thereof, it shall be lawful to the judge
of any Court of record in the United Kingdom, or for the judge of the High Court
of Admiralty, or in Scotland the Court of Session, or the sheriff of the county
within whose jurisdiction such ship may be, upon it being shewn to him by any
person applying summarily that such injury was probably caused by the misconduct or want of skill of the master or mariners of such ship, to issue an order
directed to any officer of customs, or other officer named by such judge, requiring
him to detain such ship until such time as the owner, master, or consignee thereof
has made satisfaction in respect of such injury, or has given security, to be
approved by the judge, to abide the event of any action, suit, or other legal proceeding that may be instituted in respect of such injury, and to pay all costs and
damages that may be awarded thereon; and any officer of customs or other officer
to whom such order is directed shall detain such ship accordingly."

In one respect this enactment is independent of the three-mile
principle, as it extends the liability to seizure for damage done to
British property by a foreign ship in every part of the world. But
it is undoubtedly a strong assertion of dominion over foreign ships,
and is a striking instance of the adoption of the three-mile principle. It may, however, be doubted whether the enactment would
apply to a ship on a foreign voyage. The authority is to "detain,"

not seize, and would, therefore, seem applicable only to a vessel
voluntarily seeking our waters otherwise than for the purpose of
passage, and so bringing itself within our jurisdiction. Moreover,
the purpose is to obtain satisfaction, not to punish. There is here
no application of the criminal law to those on board.

The enactments relating to pilotage are general in their terms,
making no distinction between British and foreign ships. The
compulsory obligation to take a pilot would, no doubt, attach to a
foreign vessel seeking or being within our ports. But in the case of
The Girolamo (1), Sir John Nicholl expressed great doubt whether
the same rule would apply to a foreign vessel leaving our waters
on a foreign voyage.

These being the instances in which alone the legislature has
applied the principle of the three-mile jurisdiction, it is apparent
that, with the exception of the penalties imposed for violation of
neutral duties or breaches of the revenue or fishery laws, there
has been no assertion of legislative authority in the general application of the penal law to foreigners within the three-mile zone.
The legislature has omitted to adopt the alleged sovereignty over
the littoral sea, to the extent of making our penal law applicable
generally to foreigners passing through it for the purpose of navigation. Can a court of justice take upon itself, in such a matter,
to do what the legislature has not thought fit to do—that is, make
the whole body of our penal law applicable to foreign vessels within three miles of our coasts? It is further apparent from these
instances of specific legislation that, when asserting its power to
legislate with reference to the foreigner within the three-mile
zone, Parliament has deemed it necessary, wherever it was thought
right to subject him to our law, expressly to enact that he should
be so. We must take this, I think, as an exposition of the opinion
of Parliament that specific legislation is here necessary, and consequently, that without it the foreigner in a foreign vessel will not
come within the general law of this country in respect of matters
arising on the sea.

Legislation, in relation to foreign ships coming into British ports
and waters, rests on a totally different principle, as was well explained by Dr. Lushington, in the case of *The Annapolis.* (2) A

(1) 3 Hagg. Adm. 169.   (2) Lush. Adm. 295.

collision having taken place in the Mersey, between the *Annapolis*, an American ship, and the *Johanna Stoll*, a Prussian barque, and the Court, assisted by the Trinity Masters, having decided on the facts that the *Annapolis* was alone to blame, the owners of that vessel claimed immunity, on the ground that the vessel had been in charge of a pilot who had been taken on board, in compliance with the local pilot Acts, which required that a pilot should be taken on board by all vessels entering the Mersey, off a station called Point Lynas, and the pilot had been taken on board accordingly, at a distance of more than three miles from the shore. To this defence it was answered, on behalf of the owners of the damaged vessel, that the having a pilot on board was a good defence only where taking a pilot was compulsory by Act of Parliament; but that here there was no such compulsion, as Parliament had no power to legislate in respect of foreign vessels at a greater distance than three miles from the coast. But this was held not to apply to a vessel voluntarily seeking a British port.

" The Parliament of Great Britain, it is true," says Dr. Lushington, " has not, according to the principles of public law, any authority to legislate for foreign vessels on the high seas, or for foreigners out of the limits of British jurisdiction; though, if Parliament thought fit so to do, this Court, in its instance jurisdiction at least, would be bound to obey. In cases admitting of doubt, the presumption would be that Parliament intended to legislate without violating any rule of international law, and the construction has been accordingly. Within, however, British jurisdiction, namely, within British territory, and at sea within three miles from the coast, and within all British rivers intra fauces, and over foreigners in British ships, I apprehend that the British Parliament has an undoubted right to legislate. I am further of opinion that Parliament has a perfect right to say to foreign ships that they shall not, without complying with British law, enter into British ports, and that if they do enter they shall be subject to penalties, unless they have previously complied with the requisitions ordained by the British Parliament; whether those requisitions be, as in former times, certificates of origin, or clearances of any description from a foreign port, or clean bills of health, or the taking on board a pilot at any place in or out of British jurisdiction before entering British waters. Whether the Parliament has so legislated is now the question to be considered."

That I may not be thought to have left any material part of this inquiry untouched, I proceed to consider the few judicial decisions which, in addition to those already adverted to, have been pronounced in connection with this subject, in order to see whether authority can be gathered from them for application of the law as contended for.

The case of *The Twee Gebroeders* (1) has been much relied on, as shewing that the doctrine of the three-mile zone was recognised and acted upon by Lord Stowell in that case. The question was as to the validity of the capture of a ship by the boats of a ship of war, the legality being disputed on the ground that, though the capture had taken place on the high sea, the ship itself, by the boats of which it had been effected, had been lying in Prussian waters at the time of the capture.

1876

THE QUEEN
v.
KEYN.

Cockburn, C.J.

"I am inclined to think," says Sir William Scott, "on an inspection of the charts, and on hearing what has been urged, that she was lying within the limits to which neutral immunity is usually conceded. She was lying in the eastern branch of the Eems, within what may, I think, be considered as a distance of three miles at most from East Friesland. An exact measurement cannot easily be obtained, but in a case of this nature in which the Court would not willingly act with an unfavourable minuteness towards a neutral state, it will be disposed to calculate the distance very liberally, and more especially as the spot in question is a sand covered with water only on the flow of the tide, but immediately connected with the land of East Friesland, and, when dry, may be considered as making part of it. I am of opinion that the ship was lying within those limits in which all direct hostile operations are by the law of nations forbidden to be exercised."

Lord Stowell certainly here seems to have considered—though it was scarcely necessary to the decision of the case before him, as the place in question at low water became part of the adjacent land, that, to the extent of three miles, the sea adjoining the shore of a neutral state must be considered as neutral water. But it should be remarked that the three-mile distance had at this time been adopted in a series of treaties (as has already been mentioned) as the extent of neutral waters. It by no means follows that the great jurist would have held it to be part of the territory of the neutral state to the extent to which the doctrine now contended for would carry it. It is plain to any one who carefully peruses the judgment of Lord Stowell that that judgment was carefully confined to the matter of neutrality. Speaking of neutral waters, he says, "Such waters are considered as the common thoroughfare of nations, though they may be so far territory as that any actual exercise of hostility is prohibited therein."

In the case of *The Brig Ann* (2), by an Act of Congress an embargo had been laid on "all ships and vessels in the ports and

(1) 3 C. Rob. 162.   (2) 1 Gallison 62.

1876

THE QUEEN
v.
KEYN.

Cockburn, C.J.

places within the limits and jurisdiction of the United States."
The vessel had been seized by the collector of the port of Newburyport, and libelled in the district court, for having sailed on a
voyage to Jamaica, contrary to the Act. It appeared that the
brig had arrived off the port and anchored within two or three
miles of the shore; and, after taking in provisions, stores, and
water, had sailed with cargo for Jamaica. On her return to the
United States, she was seized as has been stated. Story, J., in
delivering judgment, says:

"As soon as the *Ann* arrived off Newburyport, and within three miles of the
shore, it is clear that she was within the acknowledged dominion of the United
States. All the writers upon public law agree that every nation has exclusive
jurisdiction to the distance of a cannon-shot or marine league over the waters
adjacent to its shores"—for which position, however, he cites no other
authority than that of Bynkershoek—"and this doctrine," he continues,
"has been recognised by the Supreme Court of the United States"—(for which
he cites the case of *Church* v. *Hubbard* (1), which case has been
already referred to, and which, as we have seen, proceeded on a
totally different principle). "Such waters," Justice Story adds,
"are considered as part of the territory of the sovereign." "The *Ann* was
certainly in a place within the jurisdiction of the United States."

This, it is true, was the decision of a single judge, but it was
that of a very eminent jurist, whose opinion is entitled to great
respect. But it is to be observed that the ship in question was an
American ship which owed obedience to the American law.

In the case of *The Leda* (2), the three-mile distance was held
to be included in a provision in s. 460 of the Merchant Shipping Act (17 & 18 Vict. c. 104) as to disputes arising with respect
to salvage in "the United Kingdom." Distinguishing salvage as
referred to in this section from assistance rendered to any vessel
stranded on the shore, or in any way in distress on the shore of
any sea or tidal water within the limits of the United Kingdom,
provided for by s. 458, Dr. Lushington, in giving judgment, says:

"Then arises another question,—what are the limits of the United Kingdom,
according to the intention and true construction of the statute? Now, the only
answer I can conceive to that question is—unfortunately, it is one which must
be answered somehow or other—the land of the United Kingdom and three
miles from the shore. Such I apprehend to be the utmost extent to which I
can go; for, neither in law nor in common parlance, is the high sea at a greater
distance from shore than three miles called the United Kingdom."

(1) 2 Cranch (U.S.), 234.   (2) Sw. Adm. 42.

We have here to a certain extent a judicial recognition of the three-mile principle, but the decision had not, it should be observed, any reference at all to foreign ships.

The application of this statute, when a foreigner resorts to the Courts of this country for redress, may be said to rest on a different principle. In the case of *The Vernon* (1), Dr. Lushington held that foreigners resorting for redress, in cases of collision, to the Courts of this country, must be bound by the regulations as to pilotage by reason of their seeking the protection of English law. A Norwegian vessel, the *Alsen*, had been damaged in a collision with the *Vernon*, an English vessel, and it had been decided by Trinity Masters that the *Vernon* was alone to blame, through the fault of the pilot who had charge of the ship. The defence was, that at the time of the collision the *Vernon* had had a pilot on board, in conformity with the Pilotage Acts. To this it was answered on the part of the plaintiffs, that a foreign shipowner could not be prejudiced by the obligation of the British owners, the defendants, to take a pilot, by the English law. But it was held that a foreigner resorting to a local Court for redress must take the remedy according to the lex fori, as being the only law which that tribunal is authorized to administer; consequently, that what would have been a good defence to the foreign vessel, if defendant in the suit, was equally a defence to the owner of a British vessel when sued by the owner of the foreign ship.

"Upon the general principles of international law," says Dr. Lushington, "whoever sues in the court of any country must take the remedy which the law of that country allows. If a contract is made abroad, it may be expounded by the law of the country where it was made, or by the law of the country where it is to be executed; but where a remedy is sought to be obtained, the party must take it according to the law of that country in which it is to be enforced."

In the case of *General Iron Screw Colliery Co.* v. *Schurmanns* (2) it was, however, held, without recurrence to the principle of the foregoing decision, that the limitation on the liability of a shipowner in a case of collision, created by s. 504 of the Merchant Shipping Act (17 & 18 Vict. c. 104), applied to a case of damage done by a British to a foreign vessel, where the collision occurred within three miles of the English coast. Wood, V.C., who, in the

(1) 1 Wm. Rob. 316.   (2) 1 J. & H. 180.

prior case of *Cope* v. *Doherty* (1), had, as we have seen, held, where one foreign ship had been damaged by another on the ocean, that the statute did not apply, on the ground that the foreign ship could not be abridged of its rights by an Act of the British legislature, here held that the statute took effect, the collision having happened within the three miles, although no mention of the three-mile distance is made in the enactment in question. He says:—

"As to the question, how far our legislature could properly affect the rights of foreign ships within the limits of three miles from the coast of this country, there can be no possible doubt that the water below low-water mark is part of the high seas. But it is equally beyond question that for certain purposes every country may, by the common law of nations, legitimately exercise jurisdiction over that portion of the high seas which lies within the distance of three miles from its shores. Whether this limit was determined with reference to the supposed range of cannon, on the principle that the jurisdiction is measured by the power of enforcing it, is not material, for it is clear, at any rate, that it extends to the distance of three miles; and many instances may be given of the exercise of such jurisdiction by various nations. This being so, one would certainly expect that that recognised limit would be the extent of the jurisdiction over foreign ships which the Merchant Shipping Act would purport to exercise. In dealing with so large a subject, the natural desire of the legislature would be to exert all the jurisdiction which it could assert with a due regard to the rights of other nations." Further on he says: "Authorities have been cited to the effect that every nation has the right to use the high seas, even within the distance of three miles from the shore of another country; and it was contended that it was not legitimate to interfere with foreigners so using this portion of the common highway, except for the bonâ fide purposes of defence, protection of the revenue, and the like. It is not questioned that there is a right of interference for defence and revenue purposes; and it is difficult to understand why a country, having this kind of territorial jurisdiction over a certain portion of the high road of nations, should not exercise the right of settling the rules of the road in the interests of commerce. An exercise of jurisdiction for such a purpose would be, at least, as beneficial as for purposes of defence and revenue."

There is here, no doubt, a clear recognition of the three-mile principle for certain purposes; but, as in the preceding case, the foreigner was seeking redress by the application of the local law. The question was as to the construction of an Act of Parliament, and whether the Act, general in its terms, included a foreign vessel within the three-mile distance, and the language of the learned Vice-Chancellor is certainly very far from saying that the sea in question, without the intervention of the legislature, is to be taken

(1) 4 K. & J. 367; 2 D. & J. 614.

to be the territory of the local state for all purposes whatsoever, so that, independently of legislation, the local law will apply universally within it.

The decision just cited would, however, appear to be scarcely reconcilable with those of Lord Stowell and Sir John Nicholl in former cases. In the case of *The Carl Johann*, referred to by Sir John Nicholl in the case of *The Girolamo* (1), where a Swedish vessel had run down an English one, and the registrar's report as to the amount of the damage was objected to, on the ground that the amount of the damage as reported exceeded the value of the ship and freight, to which, by the Act then in force, 53 Geo. 3, c. 159, the liability of the shipowner was limited, Lord Stowell held—

"That the new rule introduced by 53 Geo. 3 was one of domestic policy and that with reference to foreign vessels, it only applied to cases where the advantages and disadvantages of such a rule were common to them and to British vessels; that if all states adopted the same rule, there would be no difficulty, but no such general rule was alleged; that if the law of Sweden adopted such a rule it would apply to both countries, but that Sweden could not claim the protection of the statute without affording a similar protection to British subjects."

He therefore dismissed the petition on behalf of the *Carl Johann*, and finally condemned her owners to make good the damage reported.

"This judgment," says Sir John Nicholl, observing upon it, "appears to be a direct authority that these Acts, however binding in the municipal courts, may, possibly in this Court, as between subject and subject, cannot be set up by a foreign ship in this jurisdiction."

In the case of *The Nostra Signora de los Dolores* (2), Lord Stowell held that foreigners, when suing British subjects in the Court of Admiralty, on a claim arising out of and depending on the law of nations, were not bound by our municipal law.

A suit having been instituted to obtain restitution and damages for the illegal capture of a Spanish ship by an English privateer, it appeared that the name of a deceased party, whose representative was a defendant in the suit, though he was in fact a part owner, had not been put on the register in conformity with the Act 26 Geo. 3, c. 60. An objection having been taken

(1) 3 Hagg. Adm. 186–7.   (2) 1 Dodson, 290.

to the liability on this ground, Lord Stowell, in giving judgment, says:

"It is certainly true that the Act of Parliament, commonly called Lord Liverpool's Act (26 Geo. 3, c. 60), makes it necessary that the name of the owner should appear in the register; and it has been decided in a variety of cases, and is to be taken as clear and established law, that third parties, if British subjects, have no claim on any but the person registered as owner. But I am yet to learn that this rule of law is applicable to foreigners, who are not bound by the municipal regulations of this country. This is a question of the law of nations; and the party complainant, being a foreigner, comes to a Court which has to administer that law. The statute was] passed for reasons of domestic policy, and all its regulations are of a domestic description. Being a British statute, it may well bind all the subjects of this country, because it emanates from an authority which all British subjects are bound to obey; but, as against the subjects of other countries, it has no such force; nor has any authority been cited, either from the decisions of the Courts of Common Law or of Chancery, to shew that it has been so considered. I do not recognise the applicability of those cases which have been determined between British subjects to such a case as this, which is founded on the law of nations, is brought on the complaint of a person not subject to our laws, and is to be tried in a Court whose duty it is to administer the law of nations."

Another case referred to as a judicial recognition of the three-mile zone is that of *Reg.* v. *Lesley.* (1) In this case, the defendant, a British subject and master of a British ship, was indicted for the false imprisonment of certain persons, Chilian subjects, whom, under a contract with the Chilian government, he had taken on board his ship, then lying within a mile of the town of Valparaiso, and conveyed as prisoners to Europe. It was held that, for so much of the imprisonment as took place in the Chilian waters, the defendant, having acted by the authority of the Chilian government—the acts of which towards its own subjects must be taken to be lawful—could not be held liable; but that for its continuance when beyond those waters, the imprisonment there being without lawful authority, he was liable to be convicted. It was assumed on the argument before us that, as the vessel in question was lying a mile from the shore, the Court, in *Reg.* v. *Lesley* (1), must have proceeded on the recognition of the three-mile principle; but no reference to this principle is made throughout that case. It was not disputed on either side that the place in question was within Chilian territory. In the contract

(1) Bell, Cr. C. 220.

betwéen the Chilian government and the defendant, the ship is to sail from the "port of Valparaiso." In one of the counts of the indictment the place is described as the "port of Valparaiso." The probability is that, though a mile from the shore, the place where the ship lay was within the port. No question was raised as to it, and the three-mile jurisdiction is nowhere referred to. The case is therefore no authority for the doctrine contended for.

In addition to the foregoing authorities, one or two judicial, or, perhaps, I should rather say extra-judicial, dicta are also cited as giving authority to the doctrine. In the case of the *Forty-nine Casks of Brandy* (1), in which there was a claim on the part of the lord of a manor to wreck beyond the limits of the shore as against the Crown, Sir John Nicholl says:

"As between nation and nation, the territorial right may, by a sort of tacit understanding, be extended to three miles. But that rests on different principles, protection to fishing, to coast trade, danger from hostilities. But no one ever heard of the body of a county extending three miles into the sea."

This can scarcely be deemed an authority for the position that all persons within the three miles, whether subjects or not, are amenable to the criminal law.

In *Gammell* v. *Commissioners of Woods and Forests* (2), in the House of Lords, in which the exclusive right of the Crown to the salmon fishery on the coast of Scotland was in question, Lord Wensleydale uses the expression,

"That it would be hardly possible to extend fishing seaward beyond the distance of three miles, which, by the acknowledged law of nations, belongs to the coast of the country—that which is under the dominion of the country by being within cannon range—and so capable of being kept in perpetual possession."

But this was said in order to meet a difficulty, suggested by Lord Cranworth, as to the distance to which the claim to such a fishery might be extended. It was wholly unnecessary to the question before the House, which had reference to an alleged right of the Crown of Scotland, as one of its prerogatives, to the ex- clusive right to the fishing for salmon off the coast of that country, and had nothing whatever to do with distance or sove- reignty over a territorial sea. Still, it shews that Lord Wensley- dale had adopted as law the rule commonly received among the foreign jurists.

(1) 3 Hagg. Adm. 259.   (2) 3 Macq. 465.

1876

THE QUEEN
v.
KEYN.

Cockburn, C.J.

" Within British jurisdiction," says Dr. Lushington, in the case of *The Annapolis* (1), "namely, within British territory, and at sea within three miles from the coast, and within all British rivers intra fauces, and over foreigners in British ships, I apprehend that the British Parliament has an undoubted right to legislate." I can only cite this as a dictum of the learned judge, as it was unnecessary to the decision, which, as we have seen, had reference to foreign ships entering British ports, and thereby voluntarily subjecting themselves to British law and the jurisdiction of British courts. At the same time I have no desire whatever to quarrel with this position, as it amounts only to an assertion of the power of legislation, which, as I have more than once observed, is not involved in the present controversy.

In the case of the *Whitstable Fishers* (2), a question having arisen as to the validity of an alleged grant by the Crown of an oyster fishery in the bed of an arm of the sea, Erle, C.J., observes:

"The soil of the sea-shore to the extent of three miles from the beach is vested in the Crown, and I am not aware of any rule of law which prevents the Crown from granting that which is vested in itself."

The learned Lord Chief Justice overlooked the fact that the time when the grant was supposed to have been made was centuries before the idea of a three-mile belt of sea had been thought of; but the observation shews that the principle had been adopted by him.

On the other hand, in the case of *The Saxonia* (3), it was held by the Judicial Committee of the Privy Council, upholding a decision of Dr. Lushington, in a case of collision occurring in the Solent, within three miles of the shore, that, as foreign ships had the right of navigating through this water, such a ship passing through it was not affected by the rules as to navigation established by the Merchant Shipping Act. This case is a very strong authority for the position that a foreign vessel having a right of passage within three miles of the shore, and not being bound to a British port, cannot be held liable under the local law by an English Court.

(1) 1 Lush. Adm. 306.   (2) 11 C. B. (N.S.) 387.
                    (3) 1 Lush. Adm. 310.

One common observation arises on all these decisions, though, perhaps, not on all these dicta. They all arise on the construction of Acts of Parliament. In no instance has the judge been called upon to decide how far without legislation the law of this country can be applied to foreigners on the littoral sea, which is the question we are called upon to decide. They are, therefore, but of little avail to the decision of this question.

Taken together, decisions and dicta no doubt shew that the views and opinions of the foreign jurists as to a territorial sea have been received with favour by eminent judicial authorities of this country, and that the doctrine respecting it has been admitted in the construction of statutory enactments; but none of them go the length of establishing, or even suggesting, that, independently of statute, the criminal law of England is applicable to the foreigner navigating these waters.

But the difficulties which stand in the way of the prosecution are not yet exhausted. A technical difficulty presents itself, which appears to be of a formidable character. Assuming everything, short of the ultimate conclusion, to be conceded to the prosecution—granting that the three-mile zone forms part of the territory or realm of England, and that without parliamentary interference the territorial sea has become part of the realm of England, so that jurisdiction has been acquired over it, the question arises—In whom is the jurisdiction? The indictment alleges that the offence was committed on the high seas. To support this averment the place in question must still remain part of the high sea. But if it is to be held to be the high sea, and so within the jurisdiction of the admiral, the prosecution fails, if the admiral never had jurisdiction over foreigners in foreign ships, the proof of which totally fails, and the negative of which, I think, must be considered as established : and no assent on the part of foreign nations to the exercise of dominion and jurisdiction over these waters can, without an Act of Parliament, confer on the admiral or any other judge of this country a larger jurisdiction than he possessed before. If the littoral sea is to be considered territory—in other words, no longer high sea—the present indictment fails, and this, whether the part in question has become part of a county or not. The only distinction known to the law of England, as regards the sea, is between such part of the sea as is within the body of a county and such as is not. In the first there is jurisdiction over the foreigner on a foreign ship; in the other, there is not. Such a thing as sea which shall be at one and the same time high sea and also part of the territory of the realm, is unknown to the present law, and never had an existence, except in the old and senseless theory of a universal dominion over the narrow seas.

To put this shortly. To sustain this indictment the littoral sea must still be considered as part of the high seas, and as such, under the jurisdiction of the admiral. But the admiral never had criminal jurisdiction over foreign ships on the high seas. How, when exercising the functions of a British judge, can he, or those acting in substitution for him, assume a jurisdiction which heretofore he did not possess, unless authorized by statute? On the other hand, if this sea is to be considered as territory, so as to make a foreigner within it liable to the law of England, it cannot come under the jurisdiction of the Admiralty.

In the result, looking to the fact that all pretension to sovereignty or jurisdiction over foreign ships in the narrow seas has long since been wholly abandoned—to the uncertainty which attaches to the doctrine of the publicists as to the degree of sovereignty and jurisdiction which may be exercised on the so-called territorial sea—to the fact that the right of absolute sovereignty therein, and of penal jurisdiction over the subjects of other states, has never been expressly asserted or conceded among independent nations, or, in practice, exercised and acquiesced in, except for violation of neutrality or breach of revenue or fishery laws, which, as has been pointed out, stand on a different footing —as well as to the fact that, neither in legislating with reference to shipping, nor in respect of the criminal law, has parliament thought proper to assume territorial sovereignty over the three-mile zone, so as to enact that all offences committed upon it, by foreigners in foreign ships, should be within the criminal law of this country, but, on the contrary, wherever it was thought right to make the foreigner amenable to our law, has done so by express and specific legislation—I cannot think that, in the absence of all precedent, and of any judicial decision or authority applicable to

1876

THE QUEEN
v.
KEYN.

Cockburn, C.J.

the present purpose, we should be justified in holding an offence, committed under such circumstances, to be punishable by the law of England, especially as in so holding we must declare the whole body of our penal law to be applicable to the foreigner passing our shores in a foreign vessel on his way to a foreign port.

I am by no means insensible to the argument ab inconvenienti, pressed upon us by the Solicitor General. It is, no doubt, desirable, looking to the frequency of collisions in the neighbourhood of our coasts, that the commanders of foreign vessels, who, by unskilful navigation or gross want of care, cause disaster or death, should be as much amenable to the local law as those navigating our own vessels, instead of redress having to be sought in the, perhaps, distant country of the offender. But the remedy for the deficiency of the law, if it can be made good consistently with international law—as to which we are not called upon to pronounce an opinion—should be supplied by the action of the legislature, with whom the responsibility for any imperfection of the law alone rests, not by a usurpation on our part of a jurisdiction which, without legislation, we do not judicially possess.

This matter has been sometimes discussed upon the assumption that the alternative of the non-exercise of jurisdiction on the part of our Courts must be the total impunity of foreigners in respect of collision arising from negligence in the vicinity of our coast. But this is a mistaken view. If by the assent of other nations the three-mile belt of sea has been brought under the dominion of this country, so that consistently with the right of other nations it may be treated as a portion of British territory, which, of course, is assumed as the foundation of the jurisdiction which the Courts of law are here called upon to exercise, it follows that Parliament can legislate in respect of it. Parliament has only to do so, and the judges of the land will, of course, as in duty bound, give full effect to the law which Parliament shall so create. The question is, whether legislative action shall be applied to meet the exigency of the case, or judicial authority shall be strained and misapplied in order to overcome the difficulty. Every such usurped exercise of judicial power is, in my opinion, a violation of fundamental principles, and in the highest degree unconstitutional. The responsibility is with the legislature, and there it must rest.

1876
THE QUEEN
*.
KEYN.
Cockburn, C.J.

Having arrived at this conclusion, it becomes necessary to consider the second point taken on the part of the Crown, namely, that though the negligence of which the accused was guilty occurred on board a foreign ship, yet, the death having taken place on board a British ship, the offence was committed within the jurisdiction of a British Court of justice. This is the point insisted on by my Brothers Denman and Lindley, with the somewhat hesitating and reluctant assent of the Lord Chief Justice of the Common Pleas. I find myself compelled to dissent altogether from their opinion. In considering this question it is necessary to bear in mind—which I am disposed to think has not always been done—that we must deal with this part of the case without any reference to the theory of the three-mile zone, and (as was very properly admitted by the Solicitor General) as though the two ships had met, and the occurrence had happened, on the ocean.

The argument rests mainly on the authority of *Reg.* v. *Coombe* (1), in which, on a trial for a murder under an Admiralty commission, it was held by all the judges that, where a shot had been fired from the shore at a person in a vessel on the sea, and had killed him, as the death took place on the sea, the offence was properly cognisable under an Admiralty commission.

The case of the *United States* v. *Davis* (2) is, in like manner, an authority in favour of the view that where a person, firing a gun from a ship, kills a person on board another ship, the offence is in point of law committed on board the latter. Indeed this case goes much further than *Reg.* v. *Coombe* (1), as it was held that, the two ships having been lying in the waters of a local state, the person causing the death under such circumstances was amenable to the local law alone, and not to that of the country to which his ship belonged. The defendant was indicted before a circuit court of the United States for manslaughter. He was the master of an American ship, lying in the harbour of Raiatia, one of the Society Islands. A disturbance having arisen on board the ship, the defendant took his gun in hand, and the gun going off— whether fired purposely or not was uncertain—a man on board another vessel was unintentionally killed. The Court held, on

(1) 1 Lea. Cr. C. 388.   (2) 2 Sumner, 482.

1876

THE QUEEN
v.
KEYN.

Cockburn, C.J.

the authority of *Coombe's Case* (1), that the offence, if any, had been committed on board a foreign vessel in the jurisdiction of a foreign government, and that an American court had, therefore, no jurisdiction to try him.

The ratio decidendi in these cases does not appear in the reports; and it becomes desirable, therefore, to see by what principle the decision in such a case should be governed.

Now, homicide, whether it takes the form of murder or of manslaughter, necessarily involves two things essentially distinct—the act of the party killing, as the cause of the death, and the death of the party killed, as the effect of such act. Both are necessary to constitute the crime. But it is obvious that the act of the party killing may take place in one jurisdiction, the death of the party killed in another. A person may be wounded on the sea, and may die on the shore, or vice versâ. He may be wounded in England; he may die in Scotland. In which is the offence committed? As the blow was struck in the one, while the death, without which the offence is not complete, took place in the other, I answer, in neither; and the old authorities who held at common law, before the difficulty arising from divided jurisdictions had been got over by express legislation, that where the wound was inflicted on the sea, and the person struck died on the shore, or vice versâ—or where the wound was inflicted in one county, and the death took place in another—the offender could be tried in neither, because in neither had the entire offence been committed —reasoned, in my opinion, logically, and, in point of principle, rightly. These cases are not, however, in point to the one before us, and, if I advert to them, it is only to clear the way as I advance. We have, in this instance, not the case of the blow or wound in one jurisdiction, and the death in another; but, as in *Reg.* v. *Coombe* (1), one in which the act causing the death begins in one jurisdiction and extends into another, in which it inflicts the blow or wound, from which, as its cause, death ensues. When a man strikes a blow with a club, or inflicts a wound by the thrust of a sword, or the stab of a knife, or blows out another's brains by putting a pistol to his head, the act takes effect immediately. If he hurls a stone, or discharges a bullet from a gun or pistol at

(1) 1 Lea. Cr. C. 388.

1876

THE QUEEN
v.
KEYN.

Cockburn, C.J.
another person, at a distance, the instrument he uses passes from
him; the stone or bullet, having left his hand, has to make its
way through a given space before it strikes the blow it is intended
to inflict. But the blow is as much the act of him who casts the
stone, or fires the gun, as though it had taken effect immediately.
In such a case the act, in lieu of taking effect immediately, is a
continuing act till the end has been effected, that is, till the
missile has struck the blow, the intention of the party using it
accompanying it throughout its course. The act must be taken
to be the act of the party in the effects it was intended to produce, till its agency has become exhausted and its operation has
ceased. When, therefore, a person being in one jurisdiction fires
a shot at a person who is in another, as was the case in *Reg.* v.
Coombe (1), it may well be held that the blow struck by the
bullet is an act done in the jurisdiction in which the bullet takes
effect. Whether the converse of the proposition will equally
hold—whether it can equally be said that the continuing act is
not done in the jurisdiction in which it originates, and in which
the missile is set in motion—in other words, whether the case of
United States v. *Davis* (2) was rightly decided, is a different question, as to which I do not think it necessary now to express an
opinion beyond saying that, should the question arise, it would be
deserving of very serious consideration. It is enough for the present
purpose to say that *Reg.* v. *Coombe* (1) was, in my opinion, rightly
decided; and I think the same principle would apply where the
master of a vessel purposely ran down another, and by so doing
caused the death of a person on board. For, though his immediate act is confined to running his ship against the other, it is,
nevertheless, his act which causes the ship run down to sink. It
is as much his act which causes the death of the person drowned,
as though he had actually thrown such person into the water. If,
therefore, the defendant had purposely run into the *Strathclyde*, I
should have been prepared to hold that the killing of the deceased
was his act where the death took place, and, consequently, that
the act—in other words, the offence of which he has been convicted—had been committed on board a British ship. Whether
the same principle would apply to a case of manslaughter, arising

(1) 1 Lea. Cr. C. 388.   (2) 2 Sumner, 482.

from the running down of another ship through negligence, or to a
case where death is occasioned by the careless discharge of a gun,
is a very different thing, and may, indeed, admit of serious doubt.
For, in such a case, there is no intention accompanying the act
into its ulterior consequences. The negligence in running down
a ship may be said to be confined to the improper navigation of
the ship occasioning the mischief; the party guilty of such negligence is neither actually, nor in intention, and thus constructively,
in the ship on which the death takes place.

But let us assume the contrary: let us take the drowning of the
deceased to have been the act of the defendant done on board a
British vessel. Is this conclusive of the question? By no means.
The subtle argument which would extend the negligence committed
in one ship to another in which it produces its effect, finds its
appropriate answer in reasoning, which, though perhaps also
savouring of subtlety, is yet directly to the purpose, and must not
be overlooked. For the question is—and this appears to me to
have been lost sight of in the argument—not whether the death of
the deceased, which no doubt took place in a British ship, was the
act of the defendant in such ship, but whether the defendant, at
the time the act was done, was himself within British jurisdiction.
But, in point of fact, the defendant was, at the time of the occurrence, not on board the British ship, the *Strathclyde*, but on a
foreign ship, the *Franconia.* And here we must remember that,
ex hypothesi, we have to deal with the case on the assumption that
both the vessels were on the high seas, and not in British waters.
But, though, as we have just seen, an act, begun in one place or
jurisdiction, may extend into another, it is obvious that the person
doing such continuing act cannot himself be at the time in both.
A man who, being in field A, throws a stone at another, who is in
field B, does not thereby transfer himself to the latter. A man
who fires a shot from the shore at one who is on the sea still
remains on the shore, and vice versâ. One who, from the bank of
a river dividing two territories, fires a rifle shot at a person on the
opposite side, cannot be said to be in the territory where the shot
strikes its object. One who from the deck of a vessel, by the discharge of a gun, either purposely or through negligence, kills or
wounds another, is not thereby transported from the deck of his

own vessel to that of the other. But, in order to render a foreigner liable to the local law, he must, at the time the offence was committed, have been within British territory if on land, or in a British ship if at sea. I cannot think that if two ships of different nations met on the ocean, and a person on board of one of them were killed or wounded by a shot fired from the other, the person firing it would be amenable to the law of the ship in which the shot took effect. According to the doctrine of Lord Coke in *Calvin's Case* (1), protection and allegiance are correlative: it is only where protection is afforded by the law that the obligation of allegiance to the law arises; or, as I prefer to put it, it is only for acts done when the person doing them is within the area over which the authority of British law extends, that the subject of a foreign state owes obedience to that law, or can be made amenable to its jurisdiction. But for the opinion expressed by my Brother Denman, I should have thought it beyond all dispute that a foreign ship, when not in British waters, but on the high seas, was not subject to our law. Upon this point I had deemed all jurists unanimous, and could not have supposed that a doubt could exist. Upon what is the contrary opinion founded? Simply upon expediency, which is to prevail over principle. What, it is asked, is to happen if one of your officers, enforcing your revenue laws, should be killed or injured by a foreigner on board a foreign ship? What is to happen if a British and foreign ship meeting on the ocean, a British subject should be killed by a shot fired from the foreign ship? In either of such cases would not the foreigner guilty of the offence be amenable to the English law? Could it be endured that he should escape with impunity? If brought within the reach of a British Court of justice, could he not be tried and punished for the offence, and ought he to be permitted to escape with impunity, or ought he not to be tried and punished for such offence? My first answer is, that the alternative is fallacious. He will not escape with impunity. He will be amenable to the law of his own country, and it is not to be presumed that the law of any civilized people will be such, or so administered, as that such an offence should escape without its adequate punishment. As regards the

(1) 7 Co. Rep.

amenability of the offender under such circumstances to our law, it will be time enough to determine the question when the case arrives. If the conviction and punishment of the offender can only be obtained at the sacrifice of fundamental principles of established law, I, for one, should prefer that justice should fail in the individual case, than that established principles, according to which alone justice should be administered, should be wrested and strained to meet it. I think, therefore, that it is not enough that the running down the *Strathclyde*, and so causing the death of the deceased, can be said to have been the act of the defendant on board the latter vessel, unless it can be made out that the defendant was also on board of it. But the defendant certainly was not actually, nor do I think—no intention on his part having accompanied the act—he can be said to have been, in any sense, constructively, on board the *Strathclyde*. If, therefore, his own vessel was not within British waters, but on the high seas, he owed no obedience to the law of this country, and cannot be punished for an infraction of it.

In the case of *United States* v. *Davis* (1) no such difficulty presented itself. Both ships were in the harbour, and therefore in the water of the local state, and the defendant was consequently amenable to the local law.

I am aware that this view is not in accordance with the decision in the American case of *Adams* v. *The People.* (2) In that case a fraud had been committed at New York by the defendant, a citizen of the state of Ohio, and residing in it, through an agent, at New York, who was wholly innocent and ignorant of the fraud. The accused set up as a defence that he was a citizen of another state, and residing in it when the alleged offence was committed, and therefore not subject to the law of New York; but the objection was overruled, on the ground that a criminal act done through the instrumentality of an innocent agent is in law the act of the principal, who may therefore be held to have committed the offence in the state in which the act was done, and, being found in that State, will be liable to be there tried and punished.

But the judgment in that case which, by the way, is remarkable for much loose reasoning and idle talk about the law of nature, is

(1) 2 Sumner, 482.   (2) 1 Comst. (N.Y.) 173.

1876

THE QUEEN
v.
KEYN.

Cockburn, C.J.

not, to my mind, at all satisfactory. It entirely overlooks what, in my view, is the turning 'point in the case, namely, that though the act of the accused had been committed within the jurisdiction, the defendant, being a foreigner, and having been out of the jurisdiction when the act was done, owed no allegiance to the law of New York, and was not punishable under it.

Both exceptions taken on the part of the Crown to the general rule that a foreigner, committing an offence out of the jurisdiction of a country which is not his own, cannot be brought to trial in the Courts of the former, thus failing, it appears to me that the general rule must prevail, and that the defendant, having been a foreign subject, on board a foreign ship, on a foreign voyage, and on the high seas at the time the offence was committed, is not amenable to the law of this country; that there was, therefore, no jurisdiction to try him, and that, consequently, the conviction was illegal and must be quashed.

In the conflict of opinion which unfortunately exists it is a great satisfaction to me to be able to add that the late Mr. Justice Archibald, whose death the whole profession, and especially those who had the advantage of his intimacy. or acquaintance, must deeply lament, and whose loss, as a most learned, enlightened, able, and conscientious judge, the public has so much reason to regret, having seen my proposed judgment, communicated to me his entire concurrence, both in the conclusion at which I had arrived, and the grounds on which it is founded. His opinion, as he is no more, cannot of course be of any avail to the defendant; but as, without it, the majority of the Court are of opinion that the conviction should be quashed, it must be quashed accordingly.

Lush, J.

LUSH, J. I have already announced that, although I had prepared a separate judgment, I did not feel it necessary to deliver it, because, having since perused the judgment which the Lord Chief Justice has just read, I found that we agreed entirely in our conclusions, and that I agreed in the main with the reasons upon which those conclusions are founded. I wish, however, to guard myself from being supposed to adopt any words or expressions which may seem to imply a doubt as to the competency of Parliament to legislate as it may think fit for these waters. I think that usage and the common consent of nations, which constitute international law, have appropriated these waters to the adjacent State to deal with them as the State may deem expedient for its own interests. They are, therefore, in the language of diplomacy and of international law, termed by a convenient metaphor the territorial waters of Great Britain, and the same or equivalent phrases are used in some of our statutes denoting that this belt of sea is under the exclusive dominion of the State. But the dominion is the dominion of Parliament, not the dominion of the common law. That extends no further than the limits of the realm. In the reign of Richard II. the realm consisted of the land within the body of the counties. All beyond low-water mark was part of the high seas. At that period the three-mile radius had not been thought of. International law, which, upon this subject at least, has grown up since that period, cannot enlarge the area of our municipal law, nor could treaties with all the nations of the world have that effect. That can only be done by Act of Parliament. As no such Act has been passed, it follows that what was out of the realm then is out of the realm now, and what was part of the high seas then is part of the high seas now; and upon the high seas the Admiralty jurisdiction was confined to British ships. Therefore, although, as between nation and nation, these waters are British territory, as being under the exclusive dominion of Great Britain, in judicial language they are out of the realm, and any exercise of criminal jurisdiction over a foreign ship in these waters must in my judgment be authorized by an Act of Parliament.

POLLOCK, B., and FIELD, J., concurred in the judgment of Cockburn, C.J.

Conviction quashed.

Solicitor for the prosecution: *Solicitor to the Treasury.*
Solicitors for defendant: *Stokes, Saunders, and Stokes.*

1877
Jan. 16.

STRINGER, Appellant; SYKES, Respondent.

*Turnpike—Locomotive—Construction of Wheel—Width of Shoes or other bearing
Surface—24 & 25 Vict. c. 70, s. 3.*

By the Locomotive Act (24 & 25 Vict. c. 70), s. 3, every locomotive used on a
highway and drawing any waggon, shall have the wheels cylindrical and smooth
soled, or used with shoes or other bearing surface of a width not less than nine inches.
An engine was so used, which had its wheels fitted with shoes four and a half inches
broad, placed parallel to one another, and three inches apart, and bolted obliquely
across the whole breadth of the wheel; so that when a length of less than nine
inches of one shoe was in contact with the ground the deficiency was made up
by the length of contact of the next shoe with the ground:—

Held, that, the bearing surface not being continuous, the engine was not in
conformity with the Act.

This was a case stated by justices of the West Riding of Yorkshire.

The appellant was convicted for using, on a highway, a locomotive the wheels of which were not constructed in conformity with
the statute 24 & 25 Vict. c. 70, s. 3. (1)

At the hearing it was proved that the appellant was the owner
of an engine which was being used, on the 20th of October, to
draw trucks on a highway. (2) The front wheels of the engine
were smooth and nine inches broad. The hind wheels were
eighteen inches broad across what in smaller wheels would be the
tire, and they had flat bars, known by the name of shoes, bolted
obliquely across the whole breadth of the wheel. These shoes

---

(1) 24 & 25 Vict. c. 70, s. 3, "Every
locomotive propelled by steam or any
other than animal power, not drawing
any carriage, and not exceeding in
weight three tons, shall have the tires of
the wheels thereof not less than three
inches in width; and for every ton or
fractional part thereof additional weight
the tires of the wheels thereof shall be
increased one inch in width; and every
locomotive drawing any waggon or
carriage shall have the tires of the
wheels thereof not less than nine inches
in width; but no locomotive shall exceed seven feet in width or twelve tons

in weight, except as hereinafter provided; and the wheels of every locomotive shall be cylindrical and smooth
soled, or used with shoes or other bearing surface of a width not less than nine
inches; and the owner or owners of
any locomotive used contrary to the
foregoing provisions shall for every such
offence, on summary conviction, forfeit
any sum not exceeding 5l. . . ."

(2) The case set out the evidence,
from which, and from inspection of the
model produced in Court, the description
has been drawn up.

were four and a half inches broad, and three quarters of an inch
thick, and were placed parallel to one another, the distance between
them being three inches. In any position of the wheel a portion
of the surface of one or of two of these shoes would be in contact
with the ground. From the oblique position in which they were
placed it was possible for the length of the contact between the
ground and any one shoe to be ten and a half inches in length, and
whenever, by the revolution of the wheel, the contact was reduced
below nine inches, a second shoe came into contact with the
ground, so that the added lengths of contact with the ground
never amounted to less than nine inches.

At the hearing the respondent contended that the Act required
that the wheels of such an engine should be smooth soled or used
with shoes or other bearing surface of a continued bearing width
of nine inches, and not that interstices of three inches, more or
less, should intervene between each of the shoes.

On behalf of the appellant it was contended that the wheels
were in accordance with the statute, and were cylindrical, and had
a bearing surface of more than nine inches, taking the measurement across the wheels, adding together, when necessary to make
up the nine inches, the bearing surfaces of two shoes that would
bear upon the ground at one time.

The justices convicted the appellant, being of opinion that the
hind wheels of the engine were not constructed in accordance with
the statute, and that the so-called shoes were not such as were
contemplated by the Act.

The question for the Court was whether the justices were right.

Forbes, for the appellant. The engine of the appellant is within
the terms of the Act, which says nothing about the pressure being
continuous or unbroken. The case shews that there is a bearing
surface at any moment of nine inches, and that is all that is
required.   The word "width" is used three times in this section,
and on each occasion in relation to the line of contact between
the wheel and the ground.

Cave, Q.C. (*Sanderson Tennant* with him), for the respondent.
The shoes on this engine are not nine inches in width, but only
four and a half, and if the nine inches in width is to be measured

along the line of contact between each shoe and the ground, then these are not shoes having a bearing surface of nine inches in width. The bearing surface of nine inches must be continuous, and in estimating it two shoes cannot be taken into account at the same time.

Forbes, in reply.

KELLY, C.B. It appears to me that this conviction should be affirmed. The words of the Act do not at first appear ambiguous, though when applied to such a case as the present a doubt may be raised as to their construction. The first part of the section provides for locomotives not drawing any carriage, and it continues, "and every locomotive drawing any waggon or carriage shall have the tires of the wheels thereof not less than nine inches in width," and there width refers to the width of the wheel. After providing that no locomotive should exceed seven feet in width, the section continues, "and the wheels of every locomotive shall be cylindrical and smooth soled:" this standing alone would give a certainty of equal pressure from one side of the wheel to the other, and no question could arise. We have to consider how the legislature has expressed itself when dealing not with cylindrical and smooth-soled wheels, but with wheels used with "shoes or other bearing surface of a width not less than nine inches." I think that means, whatever be the portion of the wheel pressing on the earth, there must be one uniform uninterrupted line from side to side of the wheel. Whether there is really any different effect on a road thus pressed on from what there would be where there is an interruption, I do not undertake to say. In my opinion the object of the section was that the width of the shoes, by which I understand the width from side to side, should not be made up to the requisite nine inches by means of separate portions of pressure, but should be in the case of each shoe an uninterrupted pressure of nine inches. Under these circumstances I think it is safer to adhere to the exact words of the Act, and to take width in its ordinary sense of the breadth or width of the pressure at one time.

CLEASBY, B. If I were prepared to differ from the Lord Chief Baron I should have given my reasons at length, but I cannot properly do so when the conclusion to which they would lead is not made the foundation of a judgment.

Certainly, in the course of the argument I have felt disposed to consider the appellant as in the right; and now, if I were sitting by myself without the assistance of my Lord, I might think that, as there is no exact description in the Act of Parliament of the manner in which the bearing surface of nine inches is to be produced, and the mode adopted does produce a bearing surface of nine inches in width across the wheel, and as I can see no reason why the particular mode is adopted, except that it is a convenient one, there is no infringement of the Act of Parliament. Although I have a doubt on the matter, I do not dissent from the judgment of the Lord Chief Baron, and the judgment will be for the respondent.

Judgment for the respondent.

Solicitors for appellant: *Pitman & Lane.*

Solicitor for respondent: *G. Badham, for J. Marsden, Wakefield.*

THE MANCHESTER, SHEFFIELD, AND LINCOLNSHIRE RAILWAY COMPANY AND THE LONDON AND NORTH WESTERN RAILWAY COMPANY *v.* BROOKS.

Judicature Act, 1873, s. 24, subss. 1, 7, Order XVI., Rules 1, 3—Order XIX., Rule 3—Counter-claim sounding in Damages—Joint Claim and separate Counter-claims.

When two or more plaintiffs sue for a joint claim, the defendant may, under the Judicature Act, 1873, s. 24, subss. 3, 7, Order XVI., Rules 1, 3, 4, 6, 13, and Order XIX., Rule 3, set up against each individual plaintiff separate counter-claims sounding in damages.

Two railway companies having, as joint lessees of a railway, sued for statutory tolls, the defendant set up against each company separate counter-claims for damages in respect of delay in the delivery of goods. The plaintiffs applied under Order XIX., Rule 3, to strike out the counter-claims, but no reasons were alleged why they could not be conveniently disposed of in the action :—

Held, that the counter-claims ought not to be struck out.

THE action was commenced in the District Registry of Manchester in July, 1876.

The statement of claim contained the following allegations:—

1877

MANCHESTER
AND
SHEFFIELD
RAILWAY CO.
v.
BROOKS.

The plaintiff companies are the joint lessees for years of the Oldham, Ashton, and Guide Bridge Junction Railway, and by statute are authorized to levy a reasonable charge for the use of sidings occupied by the consignees of traffic for a longer time than is reasonable. The defendant, a coal dealer, as consignee of traffic, occupied the sidings with waggons of coal for longer times than was reasonable. The plaintiffs claimed 20*l.* 11*s.* 6*d.* as a reasonable charge, being at the rate of 6*d.* per waggon per day.

The statement of defence, besides denying the claim, contained two separate counter-claims, in one of which the defendant claimed 28*l.* 11*s.* from the Manchester, Sheffield, and Lincolnshire Railway Company, on the ground that on several occasions that company had received waggons of coal for delivery to the defendant at Oldham, and had delayed to deliver them, in consequence of which delays the defendant lost various sums, amounting in all to 28*l.* 11*s.* In the other, the defendant claimed 10*l.* 4*s.* 6*d.* from the London and North Western Railway Company for similar delays in respect of coal received by that company for delivery to the defendant at Oldham.

On the plaintiffs' application the Manchester District Registrar made an order to strike out the counter-claims, and this order was rescinded by Grove, J., at chambers, from whose decision the plaintiffs appealed.

Dugdale, for the plaintiffs. The counter-claims are separate against each of the plaintiff companies, and could not therefore have been set up against a joint claim by the two plaintiffs before the Judicature Acts, and the only question is, whether those Acts allow them. The defendant will rely on the Judicature Act, 1873, s. 24, subss. 3, 7, and on Order XIX., Rule 3, but there is nothing in the words or spirit of those enactments warranting such an innovation in the law. Subs. 3 of s. 24 enables the Court to grant to a defendant, in respect of any equitable or legal right, all such relief as might have been granted "in any suit instituted for that purpose by the same defendant against the *same* plaintiff or petitioner;" i.e. it would allow a counter-claim in respect of a right for which the defendant could sue the two plaintiff companies jointly. But the defendant could not sue them jointly in

respect of these counter-claims; he must bring separate actions·
against each, and neither of the plaintiff companies taken singly
is "the same plaintiff" as the two jointly. Order XIX., Rule 3,
does not extend the relief by enacting that a defendant may set
off or set up by counter-claim any right or claim, whether sounding
in damages or not, "against the claims of the plaintiff," for those
general words are qualified by the following: "And such set-off
or counter-claim shall have the same effect as a statement of claim
in a cross-action, so as to enable the Court to pronounce a final
judgment in the same action, both on the original and on the cross-
claim." The cross-actions must be brought against the two plaintiffs separately, and not jointly. The inconvenience of allowing
such counter-claims is manifest; for if the plaintiffs get judgment
for their joint claim, and the defendant gets judgment for either
or both of his separate counter-claims, it will be impossible to say
how much ought to be set off against each plaintiff.

1877

MANCHESTER
AND
SHEFFIELD
RAILWAY Co.
v.
BROOKS.

A. L. Smith, for the defendant. The difficulty suggested will
not arise, for the plaintiffs must know the proportion of the joint
claim to which each is entitled, and can give all the materials for
enabling an account to be taken under the direction of the Court.
The narrow interpretation put by the plaintiffs on the Act and
Rules is inconsistent with the large general words of the Judicature Act, 1873, s. 24, subs. 7, and with Order XVI., Rules 1, 3, 4,
6, 13, which enable persons who claim, or against whom is claimed,
any right "jointly, severally, or in the alternative" to be made
plaintiffs and defendants respectively, and judgment to be given
for one or more of the plaintiffs and against one or more of the
defendants according to their respective liabilities. The object
was to enable Courts of law to determine finally and completely in
the same action all joint and several claims arising between the
same parties or some of them, just as had always been done in
Courts of Equity, and any hardship or abuse may be prevented or
remedied by the ample discretion as to costs and as to joining·or
striking out parties given by Order XVI., Rules 1, 3, 13. If the
plaintiffs' contention be right, any plaintiff might prevent a
counter-claim being raised by joining a fictitious plaintiff.

Dugdale, in reply. The Judicature Act and Rules intended to
allow only counter-claims connected with or relating to the subject-

1877

Manchester
and
Sheffield
Railway Co.
v.
Brooks.

matter of the action, which these are not. The witnesses may be different.

KELLY, C.B. This question is of great importance, and has been very well argued on both sides. I am of opinion that my Brother Grove was right, and the motion must therefore be refused. The plaintiffs, being two railway companies having a joint interest in a railway, sue the defendant for a small sum for tolls incurred in respect of sidings on the railway. The defendant, in his counter-claim, makes two separate and distinct claims, one against each of the plaintiff companies, and alleges that on the whole he is a creditor and not a debtor. The three parties are now before the Court, and if the Court has jurisdiction to determine all claims by the plaintiffs against the defendant, and all counter-claims by the defendant against either or both of the plaintiffs jointly or separately, why in the name of common sense should we refuse to allow the counter-claims and compel the defendant to bring separate actions against each of the plaintiff companies? To see whether we have jurisdiction we must look at the Judicature Acts and Rules. By Order XIX., Rule 3, of the Rules of Court, 1875, a defendant in an action may set up, by way of counter-claim, a claim for unliquidated damages. The defendant here claims unliquidated damages for non-delivery of coals. Then we come to the question of parties, and without referring to the terms of the Acts and Rules, it is enough to say that the Court has large powers of joining plaintiffs and defendants, and if parties are improperly joined the Court can strike them out. Then the question is, these claims being separate against each of the two plaintiff companies, has the Court jurisdiction to deal with them in this action? It is clear that it has. Without going through all the sections and rules which have been referred to, it is enough to read sub. 7 of s. 24 of the Judicature Act, 1873, by which the Court in every cause or matter shall have power to grant and shall grant "all such remedies whatsoever as any of the parties thereto may appear to be entitled to, in respect of any and every legal or equitable claim properly brought forward by them respectively in such cause or matter; so that, as far as possible, all matters so in controversy between the said parties respectively may be com-

pletely and finally determined, and all multiplicity of legal proceedings concerning any of such matters avoided." I consider
this to be one of the most salutary enactments in the Judicature
Acts, and the present case comes within the express words and the
very spirit of that section. I think, therefore, that the present
counter-claims may and ought to be finally determined in this
action.

1877

MANCHESTER
AND
SHEFFIELD
RAILWAY CO.
v.
BROOKS.

POLLOCK, B. I am of the same opinion. This question has
nothing to do with the law of set-off, which is the creature of
statute, and which has always been a matter of considerable tech-
nicality. It is a question of counter-claim, and it is quite clear
that under the Judicature Acts and Rules the Court has power to
allow the counter-claims. The district registrar struck out the
counter-claims under the latter part of Order XIX., Rule 3, which
says that "the Court or a judge may, on the application of the
plaintiff before trial, if in the opinion of the Court or judge such
set-off or counter-claim cannot be conveniently disposed of in the
pending action, or ought not to be allowed, refuse permission to
the defendant to avail himself thereof." There are no doubt cases
in which that power of refusal ought to be exercised. Here, however, the subject-matters of the counter-claims are not only of the
same kind as those of the claim, but almost correlative. It is not
improbable that the same officers of the company may be called
as witnesses in the counter-claims as in the claim. In such a case
a court of equity would allow the counter-claims, and we ought to
allow them. I think the registrar was wrong in deciding that
the counter-claims could not be conveniently disposed of in this
action.

Motion refused.

Solicitors for plaintiffs: *Cunliffe & Beaumont, for R. Lingard-
Monk, Manchester.*

Solicitors for defendant: *Chester & Co., for J. H. McEwen,
Manchester.*

1876
Dec. 19.

[IN THE COURT OF APPEAL.]

ROSE *v.* THE NORTH EASTERN RAILWAY COMPANY.

Railway Company—Negligence—Evidence—Station.

A railway train drew up at a station with two of the carriages beyond the platform. The servants of the company called out to the passengers to keep their seats, but were not heard by the plaintiff and other passengers in one of these carriages. After waiting some little time, and the train not having put back, the plaintiff got out, and in so doing fell and was injured; for which injury she brought an action against the company :—

Held, reversing the decision of the Exchequer Division, that there was evidence of negligence on the part of defendants to go to the jury.

ACTION against the defendants, for damages for injury to a passenger, owing to the negligence of defendants' servants.

At the trial at the Newcastle spring assizes, 1877, before Mellor, J., it appeared that the plaintiff was a third-class passenger to Washington, by a train of the defendants. The train was unusually long and full, in consequence of there being a bazaar at Washington; and some of the carriages, in one of which the plaintiff was, overshot the platform. The station-master was attending to another train, but a clerk and a porter were attending to this train, and called out to the passengers to keep their seats; the plaintiff, however, and those in the carriage with her did not hear it. After waiting some little time, the plaintiff, on the advice of another passenger, seeing the passengers in the other carriages getting out, and assisted by a friend, got out of the carriage, and in so doing fell to the ground and was injured. She lived at Washington, and admitted in her evidence that, on previous occasions, when some of the carriages had overshot the platform, the train had been backed to the platform. In this instance the train was not backed at all.

A verdict was taken by consent for the plaintiff for 100*l.*, with leave to the defendants to move to enter a nonsuit.

The defendants moved accordingly, and judgment was given for them, on the ground that there was no evidence of negligence to go to the jury. (1)

(1) The following are the judgments of the Court (Ex. D. May 15, 1876):—

KELLY, C.B. I forbear to advert to any of the cases which have been cited, because, in the first place, no principle of general application is to be

The plaintiff appealed.

Digby Seymour, Q.C., and *G. Bruce,* for the plaintiff, relied on

1876

ROSS
v.
NORTH
EASTERN
RAILWAY CO.

deduced from any of them, or, as it seems to me, from the whole of them taken together. Each case of this nature must depend upon its own peculiar circumstances; and in this case, looking at the evidence on the one side and on the other, I think the defendants are entitled to judgment.

First of all, the mere fact, taken by itself, that a railway train overshot the platform is not evidence of negligence. Were it otherwise, it would be necessary that every platform in England should be of length equal to that of any train which might arrive at that platform. Then, what is the next circumstance? When the train, or a portion of it, had overshot the platform, was there any invitation, or any act done which amounted to an invitation, to the plaintiff then and there to alight? Not only is there no evidence of any act done, or of any words spoken which might have been construed into an invitation or encouragement to the plaintiff to alight, but it is clear that one of the porters of the company called out, and it is not said that he did not call out in an audible voice, "Keep your seats," although there is no evidence that it was heard by the plaintiff, and, perhaps, there is evidence that the plaintiff did not hear it. Then what further evidence is there in the case? The plaintiff admits that on other occasions the train had backed, and there is no evidence of any one single passenger who had passed the platform, and who intended to alight at that station, remaining in the carriages or in the train at the time when the train proceeded on its journey. Under these circumstances, the fair inference on the whole case is, that, unless the passengers in the foremost part of

the train had all got out without waiting for the train to back, it would have been put back in order that they might alight in safety. Taking all these circumstances together, unless the mere facts of the train passing the platform and the passengers getting out without any express or implied invitation to alight, and without waiting for the train to be put back, amount to negligence on the part of the defendants, there is really no evidence of negligence in this case at all. I, myself, in exceptional cases, may perhaps sometimes relax the rule that it is for the plaintiff always to make out his case, and I am generally in favour of a plaintiff who has received an injury from an accident on a railway. But if this case had been left to the jury upon the question of negligence I think it would have been greatly straining the principles of justice as applicable to cases of this nature. Therefore, although I shall always feel for a person who has met with an injury upon a railway, I am bound to say that in this case there is no evidence of negligence, and the consequence is, that there ought to be judgment for the defendants.

CLEASBY, B. I am quite of the same opinion. What is the alleged negligence here? Not merely overshooting the platform. That is not negligence, both for the reason given by the Lord Chief Baron, and also because in many cases the weather and other causes may make it impossible to calculate exactly where a train will come to a stand. However, it is not contended that the mere overshooting the platform, taken by itself, amounts to negligence; but it is said that there is negligence in the case, inasmuch as the

Bridges v. *North London Ry. Co.* (1); *Robson* 'v. *North Eastern Ry. Co.* (2); and referred to *Siner* v. *Great Western Ry. Co.* (3)

Herschell, Q.C., and *Wilberforce,* for the defendants.

COCKBURN, C.J. This (if I may say so without disrespect to the learned judges in the Court below) appears to me to be the clearest of all possible cases, and I am of opinion that the judgment of the Court below ought to be reversed. I quite agree with what was said, that the mere fact of the end of a train passing the platform, where the passenger can safely alight, is not of itself evidence of negligence, for it is impossible always to regulate the speed of the train, and sometimes the platform may not be long enough. But when this happens, it becomes the duty of the company to take measures for the safety of the passengers in the carriages beyond the platform. They are not to be exposed to unnecessary danger; the train may be backed, and in the meantime the passengers may be warned to keep their seats until it is backed. If, being so warned, they choose to get out and expose themselves to unnecessary danger, that is their fault, and in such circumstances the company would not be liable. But if that course is not adopted, and the train does not back, the passengers should be asked if they will alight, and the porters should assist them in

---

train had overshot the platform under such circumstances as to induce the passengers to believe that the train had come to a final stop, and that they were to get out, and that this, coupled with the dangerous egress, is sufficient to establish a case of negligence. But on looking at the facts, we find that, in the first place, there was a calling out by the porters that the passengers were to keep their seats, and that, on other occasions the train, when it had overshot the platform, had been put back. The plaintiff may not have heard the porters, but the porters could do no more than call out. They could not insure the attention and the hearing of the passengers. Therefore, it appears to me that the reasons given in *Robson* v.

North Eastern Ry. Co. (2 Q. B. D. 85) do not apply to this case. One can see clearly how this accident happened. The plaintiff, instead of acting on her own judgment, acted on the advice of the other passengers, and they assisted her so clumsily that the accident happened. At all events, without putting it upon that ground, the other grounds are sufficient. The case of negligence on the part of the company fails in its foundation, and, therefore, nothing remained which could properly go to the jury.

Judgment for the defendants.

---

(1) Law Rep. 7 H. L. 213.
(2) 2 Q. B. D. 85.
(3) Law Rep. 4 Ex. 117.

getting out,—such of them at least as may require such assistance, —at all events, something should be done to prevent their incurring unnecessary danger. It is not enough that the train has come to a standstill, and the porters call out "Keep your seats," unless the train is afterwards backed or something is done. If the porter did, as he said, call out "Keep your seats," he·did not do it so as to be heard in the plaintiff's carriage, nor was he near enough for her to speak to him or for him to speak to her, and even if he did so call out, it would have been of no use, as the train was not backed, and no assistance was offered. Under these circumstances, what were the passengers to do? Can it be said that they were to sit still and be carried on to the next station, perhaps forty or fifty miles off, and then be liable to be called upon to pay the full fare for the whole distance, and to be exposed to various inconveniences—can that be seriously contended? If the passenger is satisfied that the train is going on, and there is apparently no alternative but to get out, he must do as best he can. Of course, if he is careless in getting out and is thereby injured, it is his own fault, but if he does his best and yet sustains injury, the company will not have done what was incumbent on them to do, and will be liable. Here the company's men did nothing to obviate inconvenience and danger. I do not think that this case depends upon any authorities; but in *Bridges* v. *North London Ry. Co.* (1) it was decided that all such questions are for the jury. We have not now to determine whether the jury would have been right in finding for the plaintiff, but merely whether there was sufficient evidence to go to the jury, and upon that question we can have no difficulty in saying that there was such evidence, and that, therefore, the judgment ought to be reversed.

BRETT, J.A. The only question before us is whether there ought to be a nonsuit on the ground that there was not any evidence of negligence for the jury to consider. It seems to me that there was, for it does not appear that the company's men gave any attention at all to the two carriages which had gone beyond the platform, and that alone, under the circumstances, was some evidence of negligence. There was for many years a differ-

1876

ROSE
v.
NORTH
EASTERN
RAILWAY Co

(1) Law Rep. 7 H. L. 213.

1876

Ross
v.
North
Eastern
Railway Co.

ence of opinion as to how much ought to be left to the jury in these cases and how much the judge ought to take upon himself. That question was determined by the Court of Error in favour of the jury. (1) But it being still disputed, the matter came before the House of Lords in *Bridges* v. *North London Ry. Co.* (2), where it was decided that the question whether what was reasonable was done either by the company or by the passenger, is mainly a question for the jury, and that, the matter being one in the common affairs of life, the judges are not the authorities to decide what is or is not reasonable. Then in the case of *Robson* v. *North Eastern Ry. Co.* (3), a judge, who certainly was as disposed as any judge could be to keep these matters in the hands of the judges, held that the question in that case was for the jury. That case was affirmed by this Court upon appeal (4), and it must now be taken that the decision of such questions is mainly for the jury, and very seldom for the judge.

AMPHLETT, J.A. I am of the same opinion. As I was one of the judges who decided the case of *Robson* v. *North Eastern Ry. Co.* (4), I have not much to add. Previously to *Bridges' Case* (2), there had been a great difference of opinion among the judges as to whether, in a certain state of facts, negligence or not was a question for the judge or for the jury to decide; but the mode of dealing with such cases has now been settled by the decision of the House of Lords. The question came before the Court of Appeal in *Robson* v. *North Eastern Ry. Co.* (4), a case which more than covered this case, and the only real argument was whether the plaintiff here had acted unreasonably in getting out when, if she had remained, she might have been carried on. I entirely agree that the judgment of the Exchequer Division ought to be reversed.

Judgment reversed, and entered for the plaintiff.

Solicitors for plaintiff: *Pattison, Wigg, & Co.*
Solicitors for defendants: *Williamson, Hill, & Co.*

(1) *Cockle* v. *London & South Eastern Ry. Co.*, Law Rep. 7 C. P. 321.

(2) Law Rep. 7 H. L. 213.

(3) Law Rep. 10 Q. B. 271.

(4) 2 Q. B. D. 85.

1877
Feb. 9

[IN THE COURT OF APPEAL.]

COHEN v. THE SOUTH EASTERN RAILWAY COMPANY.

Railway Company—Carriers by Steamer—Passenger's Luggage—Conditions as to Non-liability—Railway and Canal Traffic Act, 1854 (17 & 18 Vict. c. 31) s. 7—Regulation of Railways Act, 1868 (31 & 32 Vict. c. 119) s. 16— Contract in one country to be performed in another, governed by which Law.

Luggage carried for a passenger without extra charge is within s. 7 of the Railway and Canal Traffic Act, 1854, which enacts that a railway company " shall be liable for the loss of or injury to any horse, cattle, or other animals, or to any articles, goods, or things, in the receiving, forwarding, or delivering thereof, occasioned by the neglect of such company or its servants, notwithstanding any notice or condition made and given by such company in anywise limiting such liability ;" and the provisions of that section are extended, by s. 16 of the Regulation of Railways Act, 1868, to the traffic on board steamers belonging to or used by railway companies authorized to have and use them.

Plaintiff was an English subject, and defendants were an English railway company subject to the English statutes as to railways, and authorized to have and work steamers between Boulogne and Folkestone. Plaintiff took a ticket at an office of the defendants in Boulogne, for a through journey from Boulogne to London, by defendants' steamer to Folkestone, and thence by their railway to London. On the ticket was: " Each passenger is allowed 120 lbs. of luggage free of charge." " The company is in no case responsible for luggage of the passenger travelling by this through ticket of greater value than 6*l.*" Plaintiff had a box with her, which was given in charge of defendants' servants, and in transferring it from the boat to the train it fell into the sea, owing to the negligence of defendants' servants, and the contents were damaged to the amount of 73*l.* :—

Held, affirming the judgment of the Exchequer Division, that, assuming the contract to be governed by English law, the condition on the ticket was void by reason of the above sections, and defendants were liable for the loss.

Quære, whether the contract was governed by English or French law, or partly by one and partly by the other.

Stewart v. *London and North Western Ry. Co.* (3 H. & C. 135) overruled.

SPECIAL CASE stated in an action for damage to the personal luggage of the plaintiff's wife, while being carried by the defendants as a passenger from Boulogne to London.

Plaintiff is a British subject domiciled in England.

Defendants are a railway company incorporated by Acts of Parliament; by virtue of which they work a railway from Folkestone to London; and they are authorized by other Acts to build, buy, or hire, and use and work steam-vessels between Boulogne in

France, and Folkestone, and by virtue of those Acts they own certain vessels, and are carriers by them of passengers and their luggage and other goods between the above ports.

In April, 1875, plaintiff's wife being about to return from a visit in France, her son, Mr. S. Cohen, who had been resident and carrying on business at Boulogne for rather more than a year, obtained for her, at her request, at the defendants' office in Boulogne, and paid for a first-class ticket from Boulogne to London.   On the ticket was printed the following :—

"Each passenger (1st class) is allowed to take 120 lbs. of luggage free of charge.

"The South Eastern Railway Company is not responsible for loss, or detention of, or injury to, luggage of the passenger travelling by this through ticket, except while the passenger is travelling by the South Eastern Railway Company's trains or boats, and in this latter case only when the passenger complies with the bye-laws and regulations of the company, and in no case for luggage of greater value than 6*l.*"

Defendants do not offer passengers any alternative terms, other than the above, upon which their luggage may accompany them, and be carried in the same boat and train as themselves.

Amongst Mrs. Cohen's luggage was a box, which was given in charge to a servant of defendants to register it for London, which was accordingly done, and it was placed with the rest of the passengers' luggage on board the steamboat; and a registration ticket for it was given to Mr. S. Cohen.

On the arrival of the vessel at Folkestone, the box, while being transferred from boat to train, fell into the sea, owing to the negligence of defendants' servants, and the contents were damaged by sea-water to the amount of 73*l.*

The above statement of facts was submitted to a French avocat to act as arbitrator as to the French law, and he found: "That, according to the French law, and under the circumstances, the company is responsible for the injuries which have happened by their neglect and default to the plaintiff's box.   The conditions of non-liability printed on their ticket delivered cannot in any way relieve the company from the responsibility resting upon them."

The question for the Court was whether the plaintiff was entitled to recover.

The Exchequer Division having already given judgment for the plaintiff on demurrers raising the same points (1), formal judgment was given in this case also for the plaintiff.

The defendants appealed.

Jan. 22, *Feb.* 9. *Willis* and *Bremner* for the defendants. [They argued, first, that the contract was governed by English law; on this point they cited *Peninsular, &c., Co.* v. *Shand* (2); *Lloyd* v. *Guibert* (3); *Robinson* v. *Bland.* (4)] Secondly, assuming the contract to be governed by English law, the defendants are not liable. In the first place, it must not be assumed that, as regards passengers' luggage, the defendants are common carriers; but if they were, this condition on the ticket would be a contract, and not a mere notice within the Carriers Act, 1 Wm. 4, c. 68: see *Van Toll* v. *South Eastern Ry. Co.* (5), where it was held that the delivery of a ticket with a condition bound the person taking it. In *Talley* v. *Great Western Ry. Co.* (6) it was treated by Willes, J., in a considered judgment of the Court, as a moot point "whether the liability in respect of passengers' luggage is as stringent as that in respect of the ordinary carriage of goods, and whether there be any larger obligation in respect of goods carried with passengers than in respect of the passengers themselves to whom they are accessory;" and the cases pro and contrà are collected. It is to be observed that nothing was paid in respect of the plaintiff's luggage; and Lord Holt decided in two cases— *Middleton* v. *Fowler* (7), and *Upshare* v. *Aides* (8)—that the owner of a stage carriage was not responsible for luggage carried for a passenger gratuitously, though it might be otherwise if the luggage were paid for.

[MELLISH, L.J. Is not the sum paid as the fare of the passenger paid partly for the luggage he is allowed to carry with him?]

(1) 1 Ex. D. 217, 223.
(2) 3 Moo. P. C. (N.S.) 272.
(3) Law Rep. 1 Q. B. 115.
(4) 2 Bur. 1077.

(5) 12 C. B. (N.S.) 75; 31 L. J. (C.P.) 241.
(6) Law Rep. 6 C. P. 44, 50–51.
(7) 1 Salk. 282.

(8) Com. Rep. 25.

T 2

1877

COHEN
v.
SOUTH
EASTERN
RAILWAY CO.

There can be no liability, except upon a separate payment. If the company were liable as common carriers, then this anomaly would follow, that if a passenger were killed and his luggage burnt by an accident, occurring without any want of care on the part of the company, the executors could maintain an action for the loss of the luggage, but not for the death. But, assuming the defendants to be primâ facie under some liability, it is said on behalf of the plaintiff, and it was so decided on the demurrers in the Court of Exchequer, that the condition on the ticket does not protect the defendants, but is void by the joint effect of s. 7 of the Railway and Canal Traffic Act, 1854 (17 & 18 Vict. c. 31), and s. 16 of the Regulation of Railways Act, 1868 (31 & 32 Vict. c. 119). (1) First, s. 7 does not extend to passengers' luggage. By s. 1 "traffic" includes passengers and their luggage; but s. 7 does not contain the word "traffic," and there is no definition of "goods." Passengers' luggage is not received, forwarded, and delivered in the same way as goods or cattle are, and it was not intended to include such incongruous things in one enactment. Moreover, passengers' luggage was not within the mischief intended to be remedied by the enactment, which was caused by such cases as *Carr* v. *Lancashire and Yorkshire Ry. Co.* (2) and *Austin* v. *Manchester, &c., Ry. Co.* (3) *Zunz* v. *South Eastern Ry. Co.* (4) and *Macrow* v. *Great Western Ry. Co.* (5) were cited for the plaintiff in the court below, but they neither of them decide that passengers' luggage is within s. 7. On the other hand, *Stewart* v. *London and North Western Ry. Co.* (6) is a direct authority for the defendants that it is not within the section; for that case is really not distinguishable from the present; the fact that a passenger took a ticket by an excursion train, by which he was allowed to take a smaller amount of luggage with him free of extra charge than by an ordinary train, cannot make any difference in principle. Secondly, s. 16 of 31 and 32 Vict. c. 119, does not incorporate the whole of the previous Act, but only the first six sections, viz. those sections which apply to the equality of charges, &c. The

(1) The sections are set out 1 Ex. D. 218, n.
(2) 7 Ex. 707; 21 L. J. (Ex.) 261.
(3) 10 C. B. 454; 21 L. J. (C.P.) 179.
(4) Law Rep. 4 Q. B. 539.
(5) Law Rep. 6 Q. B. 612.
(6) 3 H. & C. 135; 33 L. J. (Ex.) 199.

first part of s. 16 shews this. The Irish case of *Moore* v. *Midland Ry. Co.* (1) was cited as an authority on this point for the plaintiff, but that case has been since overruled by *Doolan* v. *Midland Ry. Co.* (2), and the latter case is a distinct and deliberate decision that s. 16 does not incorporate s. 7 of the former Act, so as to make the provisions of s. 7 applicable to a contract for the conveyance of goods by steamer.

Bray, for the plaintiff, was not called upon.

MELLISH, L.J. I am of opinion that the judgment of the Exchequer Division ought to be affirmed.

The plaintiff's wife was a passenger who took a ticket at Boulogne, that is, her son went and got a ticket for her, to travel from Boulogne to London, via Folkestone, by the South Eastern Company's steamer from Boulogne to Folkestone, and by their railway from Folkestone to London. There was a provision on the ticket which excluded the liability of the company for the loss of passengers' luggage, if the value of the luggage exceeded a certain sum. This lady's box, by the carelessness of the company's servants, was dropped into Folkestone Harbour and the contents were greatly damaged. It was as clear a case of loss by carelessness as a case could be, and the question is, whether the company is liable.

The first question that arose was, by what law the case was to be governed. It was found by a French advocate,—and there is not the least doubt that the French law is so,—that by the law of France a carrier cannot protect himself from the consequences of his own negligence by putting on his ticket anything of that kind. Therefore, if the contract is to be governed by the law of France the plaintiff is entitled to succeed. But it was argued by the defendants' counsel that it is not governed by the law of France. We have not heard the argument on the other side, and therefore it would not be right that we should express any very confident opinion upon that point; and in fact it is not necessary to express any opinion whether the case is governed by the law of France or England. I confess for my own part that, the contract being made by an English passenger with an English railway

(1) Ir. Rep. 8 C. L. 232.   (2) Ir. Rep. 10 C. L. 47, 82.

company regulated by English law, I should have supposed that it ought to be governed by the law of England, and be taken as made with regard to the law of England. And the more so for this reason, that Parliament having passed Acts to regulate the traffic by both railways and steamboats, when the steamboats belong to the railway company, and there being certain clauses in those Acts for the protection of passengers, I should not be willing to think that the railway company could escape from the stringency of those Acts by having a booking-office in a foreign country, the object being to carry a variety of traffic which was intended to be regulated by Parliament by sea and by land.

The question, however, that we propose to decide is not whether the law of England or France regulates the contract, but whether the Railway and Canal Traffic Acts extend to this particular case; and I will assume in favour of the defendants that English law does apply generally to such a contract. Then the first question is, whether s. 7 of the Railway and Canal Traffic Act applies to passengers' luggage. On the first occasion we heard a very elaborate argument to shew that it did not apply to passengers' luggage; and it was said that the contract for a passenger's luggage was not a contract for the carriage of goods by a common carrier. In the cases cited (1) that very learned judge, Lord Holt, seems to have thought that a coachman who carried some luggage for a passenger by the coach, was a mere gratuitous bailee, and not only was not liable as a carrier, but was not liable to take that degree of care which a bailee for hire would have to take. It was said, and I think, very possibly, said correctly, that that might probably be explained by the modes of carriage which existed at the time of Lord Holt, with which we are very imperfectly acquainted. But I cannot doubt the least, when a railway passenger or steamboat passenger pays a certain sum to the company for the carriage of himself and his luggage, that his luggage is carried for reward just as much as if he sent his goods by a goods train. You cannot settle the precise sum paid respectively for the carriage of the passenger and for the carriage of the luggage. But as the passenger was entitled for the fare he paid to carry a certain amount

(1) See *Middleton* v. *Fowler* (1 Salk. 282), and *Upshare* v. *Aidee* (Com. Rep. 25).

of luggage, it seems to me absurd to say that the company are
gratuitous bailees; and if they are not gratuitous bailees, it necessarily follows that they must be liable for the loss by carelessness.
Whether they are common carriers subject to the liabilities in
respect of carrying passenger traffic, I do not think it necessary to
determine; but upon the authorities cited to us upon the first
occasion, it seems to me that they are subject to the liabilities of
common carriers for the loss of passengers' luggage; but, at any
rate, whether they are liable as common carriers or not, they are
liable for the loss of passengers' luggage caused by their own or
their servants' negligence.

Then the question is this: does s. 7 of the Railway and Canal
Traffic Act apply? It is this: "Every such company shall be
liable for the loss of or for injury done to any horses, cattle, or
other animals, or to any articles, goods, or things, in the receiving,
forwarding or delivering thereof, occasioned by the neglect or
default of such company or its servants, notwithstanding any
notice, condition, or declaration made and given by such company
contrary thereto, or in anywise limiting such liability." It seems
to me that passengers' luggage comes within the plain words of
that section. It is said that passengers' luggage is not "articles,
goods, or things;" but it seems to me passengers' luggage must be
articles, goods, or things, and come within those plain words; and
it is not because in other sections of the Act, or, possibly, in some
other Act, the legislature may have used the word "luggage"
when they intended to speak of the luggage of a passenger, that it
can be said that the words "articles, goods, or things" are not
sufficient in their generality to include passengers' luggage. They
are clearly sufficient. Then is not passengers' luggage "articles,
goods, or things received, forwarded, or delivered" by the company or its servants? The passenger delivers his luggage to
the company's servants, and therefore they receive it; and they
carry it to the place where the passenger wishes to arrive, and
when he arrives at his destination the luggage is delivered to him
again. Therefore they do for reward enter into a contract to
receive, and forward, and deliver that luggage; and it seems to
me that it comes within the plain words. And it not only comes
within the words, but it comes within the mischief which the Act

contemplated; because, it is obvious that if the company choose to insert at the back of their ticket some regulation that they will not be answerable for the loss of passengers' luggage by themselves or their agents, it comes within the mischief which the Act contemplated. The passenger has no remedy, unless he gives up his journey altogether; he has no choice. Therefore it comes within the mischief, and the Act says the company shall not put unreasonable conditions of that kind upon persons who have no power to resist. Therefore it comes directly within the words, and directly within the mischief; and s. 7 ought to be construed to include passengers' luggage.

Then the next question is, whether 31 & 32 Vict. c. 119, s. 16, includes that provision of the Railway and Canal Traffic Act so as to apply it not only to the carriage 'by railway, but to carriage by steamer. It seems to me that this is a still plainer question, except for the doubt thrown upon it by the Irish case. (1) But the words are so clear that there can be no doubt about it: "The provisions of the Railway and Canal Traffic Act, 1854, so far as the same are applicable, shall extend to the steam vessels and to the traffic carried on thereby." Those words in their plain and natural meaning incorporate s. 7, as well as every other section of the Act. Then why should it be excepted? The only reason is that this clause is not contained in a separate section by itself, but is contained at the end of s. 16; and therefore it is said that it is to be confined to the subject-matter to which the previous parts of s. 16 relate. I am not aware that there is any such rule of construction of an Act of Parliament. If some absurdity or inconvenience followed from holding it to apply to the whole Act, it might be reasonable to confine the incorporation to clauses relating to some particular subject-matter; but if there is no inconvenience from holding that the incorporation includes s. 7 as well as the other sections, we ought to hold that it does. For my own part, so far from thinking there is any inconvenience, I think the direct contrary; because, inasmuch as the passenger takes one ticket, and the company enters into one bargain for the carriage both by railway and by steamboat, it would be most inconvenient that the company should be at liberty to put conditions

(1) *Doolan* v. *Midland Ry. Co.*, Ir. Rep. 10 C. L. 47.

of this kind quà the steamboat, and not be able to put conditions quà the railway. The consequence would be that, if a passenger started and delivered his luggage to the railway company, and then arrived at the end of the journey and the luggage was not forthcoming, and nobody knew where it was lost, he would not be able to recover, because he could not prove whether it was lost during the railway passage or whether it was lost during the sea passage. Nothing can be more convenient, as it appears to me, than that the section should apply to both.

Then, it may be observed, the legislature foresaw that injustice might be done to the company in respect of carriage by sea; they are liable to accidents and losses by the dangers of the sea to which they are not liable by land, and if they were subject to a carrier's liability for loss of luggage, which we assume they would be, it would be hard upon them; therefore the legislature has expressly provided for that by another clause; they can, by putting up a notice in the office, save and protect themselves against those extraordinary liabilities against which parties protect themselves by the ordinary bill of lading, that is, against losses by the dangers of the sea, &c. (1) Therefore they can protect themselves from losses by the dangers of the seas; but having so treated the liability by sea, the legislature says that they shall not be subject to the same rule when they carry by railway, and they cannot put unreasonable conditions upon a passenger which shall prevent the passenger recovering for the loss of his luggage.

In my opinion, therefore, assuming in favour of the defendants that this case is to be decided according to the law of England, the judgment of the Court below is perfectly right and ought to be affirmed.

BAGGALLAY, J.A. If this contract is to be construed according to the law of France it is admitted that the plaintiff is entitled to recover from the defendants in respect of the subject-matter of the action. As to whether it should be construed according to the law of France or England I desire not to express any decided opinion, though it appears to me, as at present advised, that there is much to be said in favour of it being construed according to the law of

1877

COBEN
v.
SOUTH
EASTERN
RAILWAY CO.

(1) Sect. 14 of 31 & 32 Vict. c. 119.

1877

Cohen
v.
South
Eastern
Railway Co.

France. This case has been argued upon the assumption that it is to be construed according to the law of England, and I entirely assent to the observations of the Lord Justice in that view of the case. I agree in the conclusion at which he has arrived as to the liability of the company in respect of the subject-matter of the action, and I assent entirely to the observations he has made, and the reasons assigned. I do not think it necessary in that view of the case to add anything to what he has said.

Brett, J.A. If we had thought ourselves bound to hold that there was a difference between the English law and the French law, I foresaw some considerable difficulty in determining whether such a contract was a French or an English one; not so much in this case as in cases which it is obvious must arise every day. In this case the ticket is taken at Boulogne, and all that has to be done is to be performed on an English steamer and on an English railway. But in cases which occur every day, the ticket is taken in Paris, and the first part of the journey is performed on a French railway; the ticket is taken in Paris at an office, as everybody knows, held by the South Eastern Company, and on the head of the ticket, like this we have now before us, is South Eastern Railway Company; therefore, the first part of the journey is performed under a contract made between the South Eastern Company in Paris and an Englishman; but the first part of the journey is to be carried out and performed on a French railway, and the two following parts on an English steamer and on an English railway respectively; and unless you could say that the three were entirely separate contracts, we should be called upon to say what law was to govern the first part of the journey, and whether that first part of the journey was to be ruled by the French law, and the other two by the English law. I, therefore, should find considerable difficulty in saying whether the contract as to the first part of the journey was to be considered as a French contract or an English one. However, it seems immaterial to consider that question, inasmuch as we are about to hold that the law of England and France as to the matter now before us is precisely the same. If you take the contract to be a French one as a whole, then it seems obvious that the com-

1877

COHEN
v.
SOUTH
EASTERN
RAILWAY CO.

pany could not do what they have tried to do by this ticket. I am inclined to think that the contract is an English one; but whether that part of it which has to be performed in France must, in strictness, be said to be performed according to French law, I know not. At all events, I should say that this particular contract is an English contract to be performed according to the English law.

If that is so, then comes the question whether, first of all, the case is within s. 7 of the Railway and Canal Traffic Act. To say that a passenger's luggage is in any sense part of a passenger himself, seems to be absurd, and to say that a passenger's luggage is not " articles, goods, or things," seems to be equally absurd. To say that a company do not receive a passenger's luggage in a different way from that in which they receive the passenger himself, seems to me to shut one's eyes to what goes on before one's eyes every day. If you go to Charing Cross Station you know very well that you yourself will be put in one part of the train, and you will not be allowed to take your luggage with you. If you proposed to take your luggage with you, they would tell you you shall not. They take your luggage from you, and they give you not only a ticket to represent yourself but a ticket with a different number to represent your luggage; they take your luggage away if you book it through, and they tell you you are not to have it until you get to the other end, and you shall not have it then unless you can shew the ticket with the number on it they have given to you. Therefore, they do receive the passenger's luggage; they undertake to deliver it at the other end, and they carry it in the meanwhile. It is an article or a thing of which they have taken charge, which they undertake to carry, and for the carriage of which they make you pay. Therefore, it seems to me impossible to say that it is not within the very words of this s. 7.

Then, if it is within the words of s. 7 whilst on the railway, comes the question whether it is not to be under the same rule whilst it is on board the steamer. I entirely agree with the Lord Justice that it is not possible to say that those words of s. 16 of the other Act do not incorporate the whole of this s. 7, and make it applicable to the carriage on board the steamer.

Against this decision there are two cases, and one is a case in the Irish Court of Exchequer Chamber: *Doolan* v. *Midland Ry. Co.* (1) I do not recollect exactly how far that case decided the present point. If it is a decision contrary to our present judgment, then I can only say with deference I do not agree with it. We are bound here to act upon our own view, and we must act here in the way I have explained. Then there is another case of *Stewart* v. *London and North Western Ry. Co.* (2) in England, which is said to be a direct authority in favour of the defendants. That was the case of an excursion train, and Baron Bramwell, in the Court below, feeling that he must not overrule a case in a Court of co-ordinate jurisdiction, went through the other process, which is never very difficult to an ingenious mind, that is, where you do not like a case and must not overrule it, you distinguish it. That process he performed with his usual skill. But, sitting here, I do not think one is bound to undertake that task. I think one may fairly say at once that one does not agree with *Stewart* v. *London and North Western Ry. Co.* (2) I cannot see any difference between that case and this, although in that case it was an excursion train. If a railway company choose to take a man's luggage away from him and take it in charge themselves, it seems to me it is no less an article or thing carried by the railway because the train is an excursion train. I, therefore, with great deference, do not agree with that case, and think it ought to be overruled.

Judgment affirmed.

Solicitor for plaintiff: *H. J. Coburn.*
Solicitor for defendants : *W. R. Stevens.*

(1) Ir. Rep. 10 C. L. 47.   (2) 3 H. & C. 135 ; 33 L. J. (Ex.) 199.

GATTY v. FRY.

Cheque—Post-dated Cheque to Bearer—Knowledge of Holder—Admissibility in Evidence—Stamp Act, 1870 (33 & 34 Vict. c. 97), ss. 17, 48, 54.

1877
Jan. 27.

A stamped cheque payable to bearer, but post dated, is admissible in evidence in an action brought, after the date of the cheque, by the holder, although he took with knowledge of the post dating, since, under the Stamp Act, 1870, the test of admissibility is whether the instrument appears, when tendered in evidence, to be sufficiently stamped.

THIS was an action in the county court of Westminster.

The plaintiff sued as holder of a cheque for 20l. 10s., drawn by the defendant, and made payable to bearer. The cheque was drawn in the month of May, 1876, but dated the 10th of July, 1876. Between these dates it came into the possession of the plaintiff as holder for value, and he consequently took it with knowledge that it was post dated. The cheque, which bore a penny stamp, was presented after the 10th of July, but not paid, and this action was then brought.

The judge of the county court was of opinion that the cheque was invalid and could not be received in evidence, and he therefore entered a verdict for the defendant, but gave the plaintiff leave to move to enter the verdict for the amount of the claim.

A rule was obtained accordingly, against which

Tatlock shewed cause. The document is not sufficiently stamped. By the Stamp Act, 1870 (33 & 34 Vict. c. 97), s. 48, "bill of exchange" includes "cheque," and the stamp on a bill of exchange payable on demand is, by the schedule to the Act, a penny. But this being post dated was not payable on demand, and was liable to an ad valorem stamp as a bill of exchange. Without that stamp, under ss. 17, 54 (1), it cannot be given in evidence or

(1) By 33 & 34 Vict. c. 97, s. 17, "Save and except as aforesaid, no instrument executed in any part of the United Kingdom, or relating, wheresoever executed, to any property situate, or to any matter or thing done or to be done in any part of the United Kingdom, shall, except in criminal pro-ceedings, be pleaded or given in evidence, or admitted to be good, useful, or available in law or equity, unless it is duly stamped in accordance with the law in force at the time when it was first executed."

By s. 54, "Every person who issues, indorses, transfers, negotiates, presents

1877
——
GATTY
v.
FRY.

made available in any way. [He referred to *Whistler* v. *Forster* (1); *Bull* v. *O'Sullivan* (2); *Austin* v. *Bunyard* (3); *Forster* v. *Mackreth.* (4)]

Geary, in support of the rule. The only objections to a post-dated cheque are statutory. All the Acts prior to the Stamp Act, 1870, have been repealed, and that Act contains nothing to affect the validity of such a cheque.

[CLEASBY, B. I cannot doubt that if the cheque had been taken without notice after the day on which it is dated it would have been valid. The question you have to consider is raised by Blackburn, J., in *Austin* v. *Bunyard* (3), whether notice makes a difference.]

Even if at the time that case was decided the cheque would have been invalid, it is not so now. A post-dated cheque to " order " is valid, though taken with knowledge: *Emanuel* v. *Robarts* (5); and no sound distinction can be drawn on this point between a cheque payable to " order " and one to " bearer."

Cur. adv. vult.

Jan. 30. The judgment of the Court was read by

CLEASBY, B. This case was argued before my Brother Pollock and myself. The only question is, whether a cheque payable to bearer, which was, in fact, post dated to the knowledge of the person receiving it, and suing upon it, was receivable in evidence. The Stamp Act now in force is 33 & 34 Vict. c. 97, most of the earlier Acts, including s. 13 of 55 Geo. 3, c. 184, by which the question raised by this case was formerly affected, being repealed by 33 & 34 Vict. c. 99.

By s. 17 of 33 & 34 Vict. c. 97, no document which is not pro-

---

for payment, or pays, any bill of exchange or promissory note liable to duty and not being duly stamped, shall forfeit the sum of 10*l.*, and the person who takes or receives from any other person any such bill or note, not being duly stamped, either in payment, or as a security, or by purchase or otherwise, shall not be entitled to recover thereon,

or to make the same available to any purpose whatever."

(1) 14 C. B. (N.S.) 248; 32 L. J. (C.P.) 161.

(2) Law Rep. 6 Q. B. 209.

(3) 6 B. & S. 687; 34 L. J. (Q.B.) 217.

(4) Law Rep. 2 Ex. 163.

(5) 9 B. & S. 121.

1877

GATTY
v.
FRY.

perly stamped is receivable in evidence ; and by s. 54 a person who receives a bill of exchange not duly stamped, cannot recover upon it or make it available for any purpose whatever.

The term " bill of exchange " includes a cheque (s. 48) ; and by the statute a bill of exchange payable on demand is liable to a duty of 1*d*.

The question, therefore, is, whether, if upon the face of the instrument the stamp is sufficient, as was the case here, since the cheque, at the time of the trial, was payable on demand, it cannot be used in evidence, because, in fact, when it was given, being post dated, it was not then payable. We think this case is concluded by authority, and that in considering whether the stamp is sufficient we must look at the instrument itself alone. The authorities are, *Williams* v. *Jarrett* (1) ; *Whistler* v. *Forster* (2) ; *Austin* v. *Bunyard.* (3)

Any other conclusion would have introduced the greatest difficulty in the administration of justice, and before a judge could determine whether the stamp was sufficient, the trial would be interrupted by collateral inquiries as to facts accompanying the giving of the instrument. What the Act requires is that a particular instrument, which means the paper with certain things written upon it, shall have a particular stamp applicable to that instrument, and not to that instrument coupled with other circumstances.

The only reason for reserving our judgment in a case otherwise so clear was the concluding sentence in the judgment of Blackburn, J., in *Austin* v. *Bunyard* (3), in which he intimates an opinion that probably the knowledge of the person that a cheque was post dated when he took it might make a difference. But this would not shew that the instrument itself was improperly stamped, but that a different instrument ought to have been drawn with a different stamp. The consideration that the revenue might be defrauded by what was done has nothing to do with the admissibility of the instrument. Legislation might prevent this, but such legislation, if directed to admissibility of the instru-

(1) 5 B. & Ad. 32.   (3) 6 B. & S. 687; 34 L. J. (Q.B.)
(2) 14 C. B. (N.S.) 248; 32 L. J.   217.
(C.P.) 161.

ment, would cause great inconvenience. The authorities are also decisive upon this view of the case. [See those already referred to, and *Emanuel* v. *Robarts.* (1)]

This rule will, therefore, be made absolute, and with costs.

Rule absolute.

Solicitors for plaintiff: *Darley & Cumberland.*
Solicitor for defendant: *H. Wickens.*

MONCK *v.* HILTON.

Rogue and Vagabond—Spiritualism—Palmistry or Otherwise—5 Geo. 4, c. 83, s. 4.

The appellant was convicted by justices under 5 Geo. 4, c. 83, s. 4, which makes punishable as a rogue and vagabond "every person . . . using any subtle craft, means, or device *by palmistry or otherwise* to deceive and impose on any of His Majesty's subjects." In a case stated for this Court, the justices found as a fact that the appellant attempted to deceive and impose upon certain persons by falsely pretending to have the supernatural faculty of obtaining from invisible agents and the spirits of the dead answers, messages, and manifestations of power, namely, noises, raps, and the winding up of a musical box:—

Held, that the means used by the appellant came within the words "by palmistry or otherwise," and that the conviction was right.

CASE stated by justices under 20 & 21 Vict. c. 43.

1. At a petty sessions for the borough of Huddersfield, in the county of York, on the 11th of November, 1876, Francis Ward Monck, the appellant, was charged by the respondent, under s. 4 of 5 Geo. 4, c. 83, with having, on the 23rd of October, 1876, at Huddersfield, unlawfully used certain subtle craft, means, and devices, by palmistry and otherwise, to deceive and impose on certain of Her Majesty's subjects, to wit, Hepplestone, Bedford, Lodge, and others, contrary to the statute. The charge was heard, and the appellant was convicted of the said offence and adjudged, as a rogue and vagabond, to be committed to the House of Correction at Wakefield to hard labour for three calendar months.

2. Upon the hearing it was proved, on the part of the respondent, and found as a fact that the appellant had agreed with one

(1) 9 B. & S. 121.

1877

MONCK
v.
HILTON.

Hepplestone, at the request of the latter, to give two spiritualistic séances at Hepplestone's residence, in Huddersfield, for two pounds each; that, in pursuance of this agreement, the appellant held two séances at Hepplestone's residence on the 22nd and 23rd of October, 1876. At the latter of such séances, in respect of which no money was paid, Hepplestone, Lodge, and others were present, and were directed by the appellant to place their hands upon the table around which they were seated, and their feet under their chairs, after which he said, "We spiritualists have to be very guarded in consequence of the Slade case. Some call it psychic force, some animal magnetism, some legerdemain, some conjuring, some one thing, and some another. I call it spiritualism; but you must judge for yourselves." There was no light in the room except that given by a single gas jet, and, during what were termed the "manifestations" the gas was turned almost out. The alleged "manifestations" were the following:—

(a.) Raps were heard under the table, whereupon the appellant said, "They are soon here to-night, the conditions are very favourable."

(b.) The appellant placed a small tambourine upon a musical instrument called "Fairy Bells," and then put it on the table at a little distance from himself. The instrument was then observed to move towards the appellant, who inquired whether the company had seen it move, whereupon one of them asked him to request the spirit to move it in the opposite direction, to which the appellant replied, "We had better take the manifestations exactly as they come," and that it could not be done. He was asked "Why?" and he answered, "I don't know how it is done."

(c.) A small musical box was handed round to the company, who examined it. It was then placed by the appellant about half a yard in front of himself on the table. He said the spirits were able to play it. He then placed a wooden box over it, and invited the company to ask it questions, and said that one sound would signify "No," and three sounds "Yes." Some questions were asked and certain sounds were heard, but these sounds occasionally were as many as five or six at a time. One of the company directed the appellant's attention to the fact that the musical box, which had been placed under the wooden box, was not wound up, whereupon the appellant said that the spirits could not only play, but wind it up.

(d.) A hand appeared above the table immediately on the left side of the appellant, who put the tambourine to it, and the fingers of the hand tapped it. The fingers did not move separately. The hand was not like a human hand, but like a wax hand which had been rubbed with oil and phosphorus. After a short time the hand disappeared before the table. One of the witnesses was of opinion that the hand was like one of the kid-glove hands found in the appellant's possession.

(e.) Two or three slates were placed by the appellant upon the table. He said they would receive messages from departed spirits. A small piece of pencil was placed by him upon one of the slates. He took hold of one corner of the slate, and a lady took hold of another corner of it. It was then held under the table, and whilst it was there the lady remarked that she felt a great pressure upon it. One of the company asked for a message from some departed one. After the slate had been held under the table about a couple of minutes, it was brought forth and was found to contain, in very crabbed, singular writing, the words, " Oh ! for a Lodge in some vast wilderness." Another message was then asked for, and the appellant and the same lady again held the slate under the table. The lady remarked that she felt a warm hand, whereupon the appellant said, " Well, you're sure it's not my hand ?" She replied, " No, I am not." When the slate was again produced there was a button upon it, and the following message, " Good night, Philemon. Saml.," the appellant having previously stated that his spirit-guide was Samuel Wheeler. It was proved that a scratching on the slate was heard at the same time that the lady felt a warm hand against her own. The button above mentioned was taken off the lady's dress ; she stated that it was pulled from her dress rather violently.

(f.) One of the notes of the piano which was in the room sounded. A lady was then asked by the appellant to sit on the lid of the piano. She did so, and the same note sounded. It was proved that the appellant was close to the piano at the time. Lodge then asked the appellant if the spirit would play some other note. The appellant stamped ; whereupon Lodge asked, " That's you,

doctor, isn't it?"   And he said, "Yes." Lodge then asked, "Will 1877
you kindly play a note lower?" Then came another stamp with Monck
v.
Hilton.
the appellant's foot, which signified "No."

3. Whilst these manifestations were being produced there were
two boxes in the room belonging to the appellant. When the
manifestations were concluded Lodge asked to be allowed to search
the appellant, who declined, and eventually ran away and escaped
out of the house. He left certain boxes, which were subsequently
examined, and in them were found, amongst other things, kid-glove
hands, stuffed and having elastic attached to them, linen with faces
faintly sketched upon it, white gauze, thread, thin wire, a number
of slates and pencils, a musical box, a musical album, and a long
rod divisible into small lengths.

4. It was proved, on behalf of the appellant, that he had had
rooms at a certain house in Bristol for the last four years; that
articles similar to some of those found in his possession had been
openly used by him in his public lectures, shewing how conjurers
produced manifestations similar to those of spiritualism. It was
contended on the part of the appellant that the Vagrant Act was
intended to apply to gipsies and other wandering and homeless
vagabonds, and that this was no offence within the meaning of
s. 4 of 5 Geo. 4, c. 83, and the case of *Johnson* v. *Fenner* (1) was
cited in support of this view.

The justices, however, being of opinion that the evidence brought
the case within the operation of s. 4, gave their determination
against the appellant.

The question of law arising on the above statement for the
opinion of the Court, therefore, is, whether the justices were correct
in their view of the law that the appellant was a rogue and vagabond within the meaning of s. 4 of 5 Geo. 4, c. 83, he having, in
their opinion, upon the evidence before them, attempted to deceive
and impose upon Her Majesty's subjects by using subtle craft,
means, and devices.

If the Court should be of opinion that the conviction was legally
and properly made, and the appellant is liable as aforesaid, then
the conviction is to stand; otherwise the conviction is to be
quashed.

(1) 33 J. P. 740.

Jan. 29. *H. Matthews, Q.C.* (*Lockwood* with him), for the appellant. The justices have found, as a fact, that the appellant attempted to deceive by using subtle craft, &c., omitting the all-important words "by palmistry or otherwise." The appellant waives any technical objection, and only desires to raise the question whether the case as stated, and the facts as found, will properly support a conviction under 5 Geo. 4, c. 83, s. 4. (1) The appellant's performances were not "palmistry" which, as defined by Cowel's Law Dictionary, is "a kind of divination practised by looking upon the lines and marks of the fingers and hands. This was practised by the Egyptians mentioned in the statute (1 Ph. & M. c. 4), and there misprinted *palmystry*." Other dictionaries give similar definitions. The words "or otherwise" must mean "or other acts of the same kind as palmistry," according to the well-known rule of construction that "where a particular class of persons or things is spoken of, and general words follow, the class first mentioned is to be taken as the most comprehensive, and the general words treated as referring to matters ejusdem generis with such class:" Broom's Leg. Max. 5th ed. p. 651, and the cases there cited.

[POLLOCK, B., referred to *Watson* v. *Martin* (2), where it was held that persons tossing halfpence and betting on "heads" or "tails," were not playing or betting . . . . at or with any table or instrument of gaming, at any game, or pretended game of chance," within 5 Geo. 4, c. 83, s. 4.]

The words "or otherwise" would include such arts as physiognomy, chiromancy, and perhaps, rhabdomancy, i.e., divination by a rod or wand: see Sir T. Brown's Pseudodoxia Epidemica, or Vulgar Errors, bk. 5, ch. 23, p. 316 (ed. 1672). The question is concluded by the only authority on the present words, viz., *John-*

---

(1) By that section, "Every person . . . . pretending or professing to tell fortunes or using any subtle craft, means, or device by palmistry or otherwise to deceive and impose on any of his Majesty's subjects . . . shall be deemed a rogue and vagabond within the true intent and meaning of this Act; and it shall be lawful for any justice of the peace to commit such offender (being thereof convicted before him by the confession of such offender or by the evidence on oath of one or more credible witness or witnesses) to the house of correction, there to be kept to hard labour for any time not exceeding three calendar months. . . ."

(2) 34 L. J. (M.C.) 50.

son v. *Fenner* (1), where a man exhibited bags containing what were apparently silver half-crowns, and sold them for 1*s.* each, the bags really holding only halfpence, and it was held by Cockburn, C.J., Mellor and Hannen, JJ., that this case was not within s. 4. The 5 Geo. 4, c. 83, is the last of a series of statutes directed, not against such practices as the appellant's, but against vagrancy, and primarily against the Egyptians : see 22 Hen. 8, c. 10 ; 1 & 2 Ph. & M. c. 4 ; 5 Eliz. c. 20 ; and 17 Geo. 2, c. 5, s. 2, which was aimed against "all persons pretending to be gipsies, or wandering in the habit or form of Egyptians, or pretending to have skill in physiognomy, palmistry, or like crafty science, or pretending to tell fortunes, or using any subtil craft to deceive and impose on any of His Majesty's subjects." Those words were altered in 3 Geo. 4, c. 40, s. 3, and the latter again by the present statute 5 Geo. 4, c. 83, s. 4, the former statutes being all repealed. None of these deal with conjuration, witchcraft, sorcery, or the calling up of evil spirits. Such offences are punishable under a different series of statutes : 33 Hen. 8, c. 8 ; 1 Edw. 6, c. 12 ; 5 Eliz. c. 16 ; 1 Jac. 1, c. 12 ; 9 Geo. 2, c. 5, ss. 3, 4. In 3 Co. Inst. c. 6, p. 43, "Felony by conjuration, witchcraft, sorcery, or inchantment" is fully discussed. See also Lilly's Life of Himself, ed. 1774, p. 107, with an account of his own trial for astrology, and Cowel's Law Dictionary, as to the distinction between conjuration and witchcraft. Since the last of that series, 9 Geo. 2, c. 5, is still in force, and the appellant might have been convicted under it, the legislature cannot have intended to create an additional punishment by the Vagrant Act, 5 Geo. 4, c. 83, which was aimed against the wandering and homeless, and is not applicable to a man who has, like the appellant, lived for four years in the same house. Secondly, the justices took a wrong view of the facts. The appellant pretended nothing, but desired the spectators to judge for themselves.

Poland, for the respondent. In the appellant's construction, the word "otherwise" means "in the same way," or has no meaning at all. But some meaning must be given to the word "other" : see *Bows* v. *Fenwick* (2), and the clause is manifestly aimed, not at any definite class of impostors, but at all who craftily deceive

(1) 33 J. P. 740.   (2) Law Rep. 9 C. P. 339.

simple people by fortune-telling, or by pretending to have super-human knowledge or power. This is the essence of the offence, and within this the appellant comes. It is no answer to this to say that the offence is indictable under another statute, for many of the offences punishable under the Vagrant Act are undoubtedly indictable under other statutes. "Palmistry" is used by good writers in the sense of a trick with the hand : see Worcester's Dictionary ; Addison, in the *Spectator* (vol. ii. No. 130), humorously speaks of pocket-picking by beggars as "a kind of palmistry at which this race of vermin are very dexterous." To "palm" means to trick.

Matthews, Q.C., replied.

Our. adv. vult.

Feb. 6. The following judgments were read :—

CLEASBY, B. It is first necessary to consider what the exact question for our determination is. This must be clearly under-stood, as there appeared at first to be a difficulty, though of a technical nature, from the terms in which the magistrates had found the facts, and if they had only found that the defendant used artful devices with intent to deceive without themselves forming any conclusion as to the means used, there would have been an ob-jection to the case coming before us on appeal. But it is to be taken, and the words properly bear that meaning, that the magis-trates have found that the means set forth in the case were the means used, and to which their express finding applies.

The question, then, before us arises in this way. The magis-trates have found as a fact that the appellant used subtle craft, means, and devices, by the means stated, to deceive and defraud Her Majesty's subjects. They have also found as a conclusion of law that the means used bring the case within the statute, and they then ask our opinion upon the correctness of this conclusion upon the matter of law—whether the findings of fact bring the case within the statute. We have nothing to do with the correctness of the conclusions of fact arrived at by the magistrates. They can only ask our opinion upon matters of law, and we must take the conclusions of fact as found by them. It is right to add, in order to prevent misapprehension, that there was overwhelming evidence to warrant their conclusions.

1877

MONCK
v.
HILTON.

Now as regards the act of the defendant and the means used by him. We are not called upon to express any opinion upon the subject of spiritualism generally—whether there does exist any real power in a medium (as he is called) of the nature set up, or whether its existence is a mere delusion. Such a subject would be a very improper one for argument and decision in a court of law. But it does not arise in the present case, because we have it found as a fact that the appellant was an impostor in pretending to make use of it. The only question, then, is, whether in this particular case the means used by the appellant are within the words "palmistry or otherwise" in the Act in question. We must first see what the means used were. There is a séance for which he is to receive 2l. He calls himself a spiritualist; the room is darkened; raps are heard, and he says, "They are soon here to night, the conditions are very favourable." They then go through the performances described in paragraph 2, and it is sufficient to say that he pretends to exercise the peculiar and supernatural power of obtaining answers and manifestations of power from invisible agents, or "spirits," as he calls them.

We have to determine whether this brings the case within the 4th section of 5 Geo. 4, c. 83. That section enumerates a great number of offences which make a person liable to be punished as a rogue and vagabond. And the second of the enumerations is as follows :—"Every person pretending or professing to tell fortunes, or using any subtle craft, means, or device by palmistry or otherwise to deceive and impose on any of His Majesty's subjects." The appellant could not properly be regarded as a person professing to tell fortunes, and was not so charged, and the argument before us was that the words "palmistry or otherwise" must be read as pointing to palmistry which, it was said, was well known to signify forming conclusions from the lines of the hands, and other similar pretensions, such as physiognomy, &c.

It was first contended, and I think with success, that the Act of Parliament could not be read as if the words "by palmistry or otherwise" were omitted altogether, so as to make it apply to all subtle devices used to deceive and impose on Her Majesty's subjects. Some effect must always be given to all the words in a statute creating an offence. But it was further contended that the words

" or otherwise " following a particular word, " palmistry," must be read as having reference to arts or pretensions of the same description as palmistry, according to a general rule of construction limiting the effect of general words following a particular description. As to the general rule, no authority was necessary, but a case was referred to in which the Court of Queen's Bench, in construing the statute and section in question, held that the words " or otherwise " must have a limited signification, and were not applicable to the case of a man wagering with people upon tricks of sleight of hand, and so deceiving and defrauding them. The case is *Johnson* v. *Fenner*. (1)

In such a case no peculiar power is pretended like telling fortunes, or palmistry, to impose upon the credulous, but a great skill of manipulation and sleight of hand, and persons are found confident enough to back their eyesight against the skill and dexterity of the performer. This is so different an act from the acts particularised in the clause that a Court would properly hold that you could not apply general words to so very different a thing. But in the present case we are dealing with an impostor exercising a power by a pretended intercourse with the invisible world, a peculiar power belonging to himself. In construing the clause in question we are entitled to consider the whole of it. We are not construing such words as "palmistry and any other art" standing by themselves, a case to which the argument used would more closely apply. The clause includes all persons who pretend to tell fortunes (which imports that deception is practised by doing so), or use subtle devices, by palmistry or otherwise, to defraud.

Now the present case is clearly brought within the words " by palmistry or otherwise " taken in their natural sense. But the appellant seeks to limit this natural sense by construction, that is, by applying the rule of construction referred to. It appears to me that it would be going beyond any application of this rule to hold that the words "or otherwise" (which in their usual sense introduce something new and different), taken in connection with the rest of the clause, only apply to modes of deception of any precise class or genus, if such there be, of which palmistry can be said to be

(1) 33 J. P. 740.

1877

MONCK
v.
HILTON.

an instance. It may be quite right to hold that the words do not
apply to anything in its character and pretences entirely different
from fortune telling and palmistry. But I cannot regard the arts
and pretences of the appellant as so entirely different. Something
besides fortune telling and palmistry must be held as included, or
you must reject the words " or otherwise," which cannot be done.
And I could not myself fix upon any crafty devices more properly
coupled for punishment with those of fortune-telling and palmistry
than those set forth in the case as practised by the appellant.

The learned counsel for the appellant referred to very early
statutes shewing that the offence of palmistry and the pretending to hold intercourse with spirits had formerly been treated as
totally different offences with very different punishments, which
was no doubt the case. Palmistry was at one time practised by
gipsies and persons leading a vagabond life, and the legislation
was directed against them. But the idea of leading a wandering
and vagabond life is not now at all an ingredient in the description of a rogue and vagabond, as is obvious by reading the enumeration in s. 4. The statute 5 Geo. 4, c. 83, repeals all the former
statutes relating to rogues and vagabonds, and forms itself the
legislation on the subject, and enacts in substance that by doing
certain things, or neglecting certain duties, a man shall be in the
same predicament as rogues and vagabonds, and dealt with as such.
Whatever an offender's position may be under other Acts of Parliament not relating to rogues and vagabonds, if he comes within
the enumeration in s. 4 he is properly punished as a rogue and
a vagabond.

For the reasons above given, I think the appellant was properly
dealt with by the magistrates as a rogue and vagabond, and that
the conviction must be affirmed, and of course with costs.

POLLOCK, B. In my judgment the justices were correct in the
view of the law which they took when they found the appellant
in this case to be a rogue and vagabond within the meaning of the
statute 5 Geo. 4, c. 83, s. 4.

The first matter material to consider is, what was it that the
magistrates found in fact ? Taking the evidence which they have
set out in the case coupled with their finding, the only fair con-

clusion to be drawn is that they found that the appellant did attempt to deceive and impose upon the persons named in the charge, and that the means by which he so attempted was not by mere slight of hand, dexterous manipulation of instruments, or illusion of the eye or ear such as is practised by a conjuror or ventriloquist, but that in addition to and accompanied with the exercise of physical dexterity, the appellant so conducted himself as to assume the power of communicating with and calling in the aid of unseen spirits who could do certain acts and produce certain results, such as the winding-up and playing upon a musical box and the communication of messages from persons who had died. We have therefore a craft, means, and device which is beyond that of physical dexterity, and a professed dealing with some spiritual agency which is enacted, not for the mere purpose of individual experiment or so-called scientific pursuit, but to deceive and impose on others. And the only remaining question is whether this is within the scope of the statute.

The words of the Act are, "Every person pretending or professing to tell fortunes, or using any subtle craft, means, or device, by palmistry or otherwise, to deceive and impose on any of His Majesty's subjects." And the well-known rule of construction was urged upon us that in giving effect to the words "or otherwise" we must read the statute as if it had used the words "by palmistry or other acts of a like kind." The principle upon which this rule is founded is thoroughly established, and the only difficulty which arises is in the mode and extent of its application to the provision in question. If the only words were, "any person pretending by palmistry or otherwise to deceive," the argument would have greater force, but the language whence the scope and intent of the section are to be gathered is much wider, and to get at this we must look back to the words preceding "palmistry." These shew that the character of the act which is made an offence is assuming a special power beyond the ordinary limits of human agency. This is indicated by the first offence specified—"professing to tell fortunes."

Those which follow are of a like character, "using any subtle craft, means, or device, by palmistry *or otherwise* to deceive," &c. The general character of the means or device is sufficiently indicated by the earlier words, and to read the word "otherwise" as limiting the means to acts which must necessarily be similar to palmistry, would, in my judgment, wrest from the statute its spirit and expressed intention. Reading it as a whole, I should take the word "otherwise" not as limiting the earlier words, but as enlarging the word "palmistry," and providing against the professing to tell fortunes, or using craft, means, or device to deceive, whether by palmistry or by contrivances to deceive other than palmistry, provided they are of the same general character as is indicated by the earlier words of the section.

It is unnecessary now to say what other means or devices may come within the statute; but as to this I should guard myself against being supposed to hold that there might not be cases in which the means used were legerdemain, ventriloquism, or the like, and yet that they were included. Whether they would or would not be included must depend upon many circumstances, one very important one being the profession of the performer, and another being the education and means of knowledge possessed by the audience. For instance, persons at the present day hearing an ordinary ventriloquist would hardly say he intended to deceive or impose upon them, but it well might have been in time past, and might be now, that a ventriloquist should endeavour to impose on others by leading them to think that he could carry on a conversation with a relation who had died, and who, when spoken to by him, answered from a chest or closet. Whether this were so or not would be a question of fact for the decision of the magistrates. So would it be in the case of a juggler or conjurer; it would be for the tribunal before which the question was tried to say whether the performer merely backed his skill and agility against the quickness and accuracy of the eyes and ears of those present, as was clearly the case in *Johnson* v. *Fenner*, which was cited before us from 33rd Just. of the Peace, 740, or whether he intended to convey the impression that he was dealing with or assisted by any supernatural agency. In the present case the finding by the magistrates is conclusive, and well supported by the evidence before them.

Our attention was very properly called by Mr. Matthews, on behalf of the appellant, to the fact that the statute in question is only the last of a series commencing so far back as 22 Hen. 8, c. 10, all of which profess to deal with jugglers and persons pretending to have skill in physiognomy, palmistry, or like crafty science, whereas there has long existed a parallel set of statutes beginning with 33 Hen. 8, c. 8, and ending with 9 Geo. 2, c. 5, s. 4, whose expressed object is to deal with persons using, practising, or exercising any invocation or conjuration of an evil spirit; and he argued that the offence of the appellant, if any, came more properly within the scope of these latter statutes. The offences dealt with by these statutes are fully explained by Lord Coke in his treatise on 1 Jac. 1, c. 12 (3rd Inst. 44), and include what in more modern days is commonly called witchcraft, and it is to be observed that by these the dealing with the supernatural is itself made an offence, apart from any deceiving or imposing on others. It may be that the appellant, by doing what he did, brought himself within these Acts, but it is unnecessary to decide this, and one would pause before seeking to put in force criminal statutes pointing to an offence practically obsolete; but even were his acts within the existing statute against witchcraft, it by no means follows that when he used devices to deceive and impose on others he was not liable under the Act in question.

I think, therefore, that the conclusion at which the magistrates arrived is within the statute, and that there is no ground for disturbing the conviction.

Conviction affirmed with costs.

Solicitor for appellant: *W. M. Miller.*
Solicitors for respondent: *Layton & Jaques,* for *C. Mills, Huddersfield.*

*Practice—Costs on Payment into Court—Common Law Procedure Act, 1852,
s. 73—Rules of Court, 1875, Order XXX., Rules 1, 2, 3, 4.*

In an action for work, labour and materials, the writ claimed a balance of
373*l*. The defendant paid 200*l*. into court under Order XXX., Rule 1, and gave
notice in Form 5, Appendix B, that "that sum is enough to satisfy the plaintiffs' claim." The plaintiffs took it out under Order XXX., Rule 3, but did not
give the notice under Order XXX., Rule 4, or any other notice. The cause was
afterwards referred, under the Common Law Procedure Act, 1854, to the certificate of an arbitrator, "the costs of the cause to abide the event." No pleadings were ever delivered on either side. The arbitrator, after hearing the parties,
gave his certificate that the 200*l*. paid into court was enough to satisfy the plaintiff's claim. The master having taxed the plaintiffs' costs against the defendant
up to the time of their taking the money out of court, and having from that
point taxed the defendant's costs against the plaintiffs :—

Held, that as the 200*l*. had been paid in generally, and the event of the reference was that the plaintiffs recovered nothing beyond the amount paid into court,
the plaintiffs were not entitled to any costs, and the defendant was entitled to
her costs of suit from the commencement, and that the taxation must be reviewed
accordingly.

THE action was for work, labour, and materials supplied by the
plaintiffs, who were builders. The writ was issued for the balance
of a statement of account rendered, and amount of other work
executed, 1023*l*., less a payment of 650*l*., leaving a balance of
373*l*., which the plaintiffs also claimed on an account stated. On
the 21st of December, 1875, a master's order was made that
unless the parties agreed on an arbitrator, the cause should be
referred to one of the masters, "the costs of the cause to abide
the event," the costs of the reference to be in the discretion of
the master. On the 19th of February, 1876, the defendant paid
200*l*. into court, and gave notice in Form 5, Appendix B., "that
that sum is enough to satisfy the plaintiffs' claim," and obtained a
receipt from the proper officer. Shortly after the plaintiffs took
the 200*l*. out of court, under Order XXX., Rule 3, but did not
give the notice in Form 6, Appendix B., or any other notice.
On the 13th of March, Pollock, B., made an order that the order
of the 21st of December, 1875, be varied, and that the cause be
accordingly referred to the certificate of S. under 17 & 18 Vict.
c. 125, with all the powers as to certifying and amending of a

judge at nisi prius, "the costs of the cause to abide the event," the costs of the reference to be in the discretion of the arbitrator. No pleadings were ever delivered on either side. After hearing both parties S., on the 31st of August, gave his certificate that the 200*l.* paid into court was enough to satisfy the plaintiffs' claim, and directed that each party should bear his own costs of the reference, and that the costs of the certificate should be divided equally between the parties.

On the 29th of September, the defendant signed judgment for her costs, and on taxation the master, under Rule 12 of Reg. Gen. H. T. 1853, taxed the plaintiffs' costs against the defendant up to the time of their taking the money out of court, and from that point taxed the defendant's costs against the plaintiffs.

The defendant took out a summons to review the taxation, and Hawkins, J., having refused to make an order, the defendant now moved by way of appeal.

M'Leod, for the defendant. The plaintiffs are not entitled to their costs unless some statute or rule gives them. Rule 12 of Reg. Gen. H. T., 1853, does not give them, because that only applies to "money paid into court in respect of any particular sum or cause of action in the declaration." The 200*l.* was paid in to the entire cause of action, and taken out by the plaintiffs, but not in satisfaction. For that reason the plaintiffs are not entitled to any costs under s. 73 of the Common Law Procedure Act, 1852, and the defendant is entitled to all her costs under that section and under the terms of the order of reference, the event having been decided in her favour. (1) Before the Judicature

(1) By s. 73 of the Common Law Procedure Act, 1852, "The plaintiff, after the delivery of a plea of payment of money into court, shall be at liberty to reply to the same by accepting the sum so paid into court in full satisfaction and discharge of the cause of action in respect of which it has been paid in, and he shall be at liberty in that case to tax his costs of suit, and in case of non-payment thereof within forty-eight hours, to sign judgment for his costs of suit so taxed; or the plaintiff may reply that the sum paid into court is not enough to satisfy the claim of the plaintiff in respect of the matter to which the plea is pleaded; and in the event of an issue thereon being found for the defendant the defendant shall be entitled to judgment and his costs of suit."

By Reg. Gen. H. T. 1853, R. 12, "When money is paid into court in respect of any particular sum or cause of action in the declaration, and the plaintiff accepts the same in satisfac-

Acts a defendant might always pay money in generally, and put the plaintiff to the alternative of taking it out in satisfaction, or proceeding for more: *Rumbelow* v. *Whalley* (1), following *Harrison* v. *Watt*. (2) The Judicature Acts, have not altered this

tion, the plaintiff, when the costs of the cause are taxed, shall be entitled to the costs of the cause in respect of that part of his claim so satisfied up to the time the money is so paid in and taken out, whatever may be the result of any issue or issues in respect of other causes of action ; and if the defendant succeeds in defeating the residue of the claim he will be entitled to the costs of the cause in respect of such defence commencing at ' Instructions for Plea,' but not before."

By Order XXX., Rule 1, of the Rules of Court, 1875, " Where any action is brought to recover a debt or damages any defendant may, at any time after service of the writ and before or at the time of delivering his defence, or by leave of the Court or a judge at any later time, pay into court a sum of money by way of satisfaction or amends. Payment into court shall be pleaded in the defence, and the claim or cause of action in respect of which such payment shall be made, shall be specified therein."

Rule 2 : " Such sum of money shall be paid to the proper officer, who shall give a receipt for the same. If such payment be made before delivering his defence, the defendant shall thereupon serve upon the plaintiff a notice that he has paid in such money, and in respect of what claim, in the Form No. 5 in Appendix B hereto."

Rule 3 : " Money paid into court as aforesaid may, unless otherwise ordered by a judge, be paid out to the plaintiff or to his solicitor on the written authority of the plaintiff. No affidavit shall be necessary to verify the plaintiff's signature to such written authority unless specially required by the officers of the court."

Rule 4 : " The plaintiff, if payment into court is made before delivering a defence, may within four days after receipt of notice of such payment, or if such payment is first stated in a defence delivered, then may, before reply, accept the same in satisfaction of the causes of action in respect of which it is paid in ; in which case he shall give notice to the defendant in the Form No. 6 in Appendix B hereto, and shall be at liberty in case the sum paid in is accepted in satisfaction of the entire cause of action to tax his costs, and in case of non-payment within forty-eight hours to sign judgment for his costs so taxed."

By Rule 28 of the Rules of the Supreme Court, 1875 (Costs), " Special Allowances and General Provisions," " the rules, orders, and practice of any Court whose jurisdiction is transferred to the High Court of Justice or Court of Appeal, relating to costs, and the allowance of the fees of solicitors and attorneys, and the taxation of costs, existing prior to the commencement of the Act, shall, in so far as they are not inconsistent with the Act and the Rules of Court in pursuance thereof, remain in force and be applicable to costs of the same or analogous proceedings, and to the allowance of the fees of solicitors of the Supreme Court, and the taxation of costs in the High Court of Justice and Court of Appeal."

(1) 16 Q. B. 397; 20 L. J. (Q.B.) 262.

(2) 16 M. & W. 316; 17 L. J. (Ex.) 74.

privilege. Form 5, Appendix B., recognises it by allowing the defendant to pay money in, either generally or in satisfaction of a particular cause of action.

J. Robins, for the plaintiffs. The plaintiffs were compelled to bring an action, and have recovered 200*l*. In justice, they ought to have their costs of obtaining the 200*l*. The action is for a liquidated demand, and the defendant could not, before the Judicature Acts, have paid in a smaller sum in satisfaction of a larger; such a plea would have been demurrable: *Tattersall* v. *Parkinson*. (1) Order XXX., Rule 1, though making it possible to pay money into court without pleadings, does not make that a good payment now which would have been bad before. The taxation was right, and ought not to be disturbed.

KELLY, C.B. I pronounce no opinion as to what our decision ought to have been if the cause had proceeded to trial, or been brought before the arbitrator upon the ordinary statements of claim and defence. In that case the pleadings might have raised a different question, and I desire that my decision shall not be applied to a case in which there are pleadings.

The facts are simple, and, so far as I know, the point raised under the Judicature Acts is new. [After stating the facts, as above, his Lordship proceeded.] There being no pleadings, and the 200*l*. having been paid into court in respect of the whole cause of action, the question is whether the plaintiffs are entitled to have their costs taxed against the defendant from the commencement of the action down to the time of taking the money out of court, it being admitted that from that point the defendant is entitled to her costs against the plaintiff. I think they are not. Two cases were cited, in each of which the plaintiff was held entitled to his costs down to the time of the payment into court. In the first, *Harrison* v. *Watt* (2), decided in 1847, the action was debt for goods sold and delivered. The defendant pleaded, except as to 15*s*., parcel of the moneys claimed, never indebted; secondly, as to the 15*s*., payment into court of 15*s*. The replication joined issue on the first plea, and as to the second, the plaintiff accepted the 15*s*. in satisfaction of the causes of action as to

(1) 16 M. & W. 752; 16 L. J. (Ex.)   (2) 16 M. & W. 316; 17 L. J. (Ex.)
196.   74.

which it was paid in, and prayed judgment for his costs in that behalf. At the trial the jury found that the defendant never was indebted except as to the 15s., and the Court held that the plaintiff was entitled to his costs on the plea of payment into court.

That decision was followed in *Rumbelow* v. *Whalley* (1), decided in 1851. That was an action of debt for work and labour. The defendant pleaded, except as to 10l., parcel, &c., never indebted, and as to the 10l., payment into court of 10l. 1s. The plaintiff joined issue on the plea of never indebted, and as to the payment into court, accepted the sum paid in, and prayed judgment for his costs in that respect. The result of the trial was that the plaintiff recovered nothing more than the money paid into court, but it was held that he was entitled to all his costs as to the causes of action to which the plea of payment into court was pleaded, up to and including the payment into court; it being admitted that the defendant was entitled to his costs subsequent to the payment into court. In both those cases the plaintiff, by accepting the payment in satisfaction of the causes of action in respect of which it was paid in, acquired a vested right to the costs, and nothing occurred to divest him of that right.

The principle of those cases, and of others to the same effect was carried out by the legislature in the Common Law Procedure Act, 1852, s. 73, and Rule 12 of Hilary Term, 1853, which left untouched the principle that where a plaintiff accepted the sum paid into court in satisfaction of the cause of action in respect of which it was paid in, he was entitled to his costs in respect of those causes of action up to the time the money was paid in and taken out.

Then come the Judicature Acts and Rules, and by Order XXX., Rule 1, a defendant may pay money into court to any action for debt or damages. If there is a statement of defence "the claim or cause of action in respect of which such payment shall be made shall be specified therein." Then, by Rule 2, " If such payment be made before delivering his defence the defendant shall thereupon serve upon the plaintiff a notice that he has paid in such money, and in respect of what claim, in the Form No. 5 in Appendix (B.) hereto." In the present case the defendant, on paying the 200l. into court,

(1) 16 Q. B. 397; 20 L. J. (Q.B.) 262.

gave the notice provided in that Form, that the 200*l.* " is enough to satisfy the plaintiff's claim," and obtained a receipt from the officer in accordance with Rule 2. Rule 3 provides that money so paid into court may be paid out to the plaintiff, and the present plaintiffs took the 200*l.* out of court under that Rule. Rule 4 provides that if payment into court is made before delivering a defence, the plaintiff " may, within four days after receipt of notice of such payment, . . . accept the same in satisfaction of the causes of action in respect of which it is paid in ; in which case he shall give notice to the defendant in the Form No. 6 in Appendix (B.) hereto ; and shall be at liberty, in case the sum paid in is accepted in satisfaction of the entire cause of action, to tax his costs, and in case of non-payment within forty-eight hours, to sign judgment for his costs so taxed." Now if the plaintiff had given the notice in that form, he would have acquired a vested right to the costs up to the time of payment into court, of which nothing that might happen afterwards could deprive him. But he did not do that : he did not accept the 200*l.* in satisfaction of the cause of action in respect of which it was paid in, and the element was wanting which was the foundation of the two cases I have referred to, and of the provisions of the Common Law Procedure Act, 1852, and the Rules founded thereon, and also of the Rules made under the Judicature Acts. If a plaintiff proceeds as the plaintiffs here did he takes his chance, and if the event is determined against him 'the defendant is entitled to judgment and costs, and the plaintiff loses the right which he might have secured. This is my decision on the circumstances of this case, there being no pleadings and nothing to insulate the payment into court to any particular sum or cause of action.

HUDDLESTON, B. I am of the same opinion. It is clear that the defendant is entitled to her costs, whichever way you look at it. Mr. Robins urged that the discretion over costs given to the Court by Order LV. ought to be exercised in the plaintiff's favour, because the plaintiff shewed he had the right to bring an action, for he recovered 200*l.* That is a captivating way of putting the case, but when the facts and letters are looked at, they shew that if any discretion should be exercised, it ought to be in the contrary direction.

Then as to the question of law. The order of Pollock, B., drawn up by consent, was that the costs of the cause should "abide the event." What was the event? The plaintiff's claim was for 373*l.* a balance for work, labour, and materials, after giving credit for payment of a large sum. The defendant paid into court 200*l.*, and alleged that that was enough to satisfy the plaintiff's claim. The "event," then, was whether 200*l.* was sufficient to satisfy the plaintiff's claim. Upon that "event" the defendant succeeded, having satisfied the arbitrator that the plaintiff was not entitled to more than 200*l.*

Under the old practice a defendant could pay money into court only at the time of pleading, but by Order XXX., Rule 1, a defendant may pay it in before delivering his defence. If there had been pleadings, the cause of action in respect of which the payment was made would have been specified. But that stage was never reached. The plaintiffs might have taken out a summons to require the defendant to specify the cause of action in respect of which the 200*l.* was paid in, but I do not think I should have made any order upon such a summons, because the notice given under Form 5 (Appendix B.) was sufficiently specific; the money was paid in satisfaction of the whole cause of action. The plaintiffs, then, not having chosen to proceed in the way pointed out by Rule 4, went on at their peril. Rule 28 of the Rules of the Supreme Court, 1875 (Costs), "Special Allowances and General Provisions," shews that the old practice as to costs is still in force where not inconsistent with the new Acts and Rules.

The old practice is very clearly stated by Patteson, J., in the considered judgment of the Court in *Rumbelow* v. *Whalley*. (1) That case was decided upon a Rule of Trinity Term, 1 Vict., which was identical with s. 73 of the Common Law Procedure Act, 1852. In that judgment it is said, "By the language of this rule it is plain that it contemplates the payment into court either in respect of the whole causes of action or in respect of a part only of them selected by the defendant; and in either case it gives the plaintiff his costs of suit if he accepts the money so paid into court in discharge. It is equally clear that it gives the defendant his costs of suit only where the plaintiff replies damages or debt

(1) 16 Q. B. 397; 20 L. J. (Q B.) 262.

1877
Langridge
v.
Campbell.

to a greater amount, and there is an issue thereon, that is, on such allegation of greater amount . . . . It comes to this, therefore, that whenever the only question intended to be raised by the pleadings is the amount of the original debt the defendant can put the plaintiff to the alternative of accepting in discharge of his whole demand whatever sum the defendant chooses to pay into court, or proceeding for more at the risk of the costs of the suit. But whenever the original debt is larger than the sum which the defendant chooses to pay into court as a balance, and thus he is obliged to plead an affirmative plea or pleas to reduce that original debt to such balance, he necessarily insulates the sum so paid in from the rest of the declaration, and so entitles the plaintiff to accept it in discharge of the causes of action in respect of which it is paid into court, and to receive all costs of suit thereon."

That language equally applies to s. 73 of the Common Law Procedure Act, 1852. The defendant put the plaintiffs to the alternative of accepting the 200*l.* in discharge of their whole demand, or proceeding for more at the risk of the costs of the suit. Then it was said that Rule 12 of Hilary Term, 1853, applied. No question could arise under that rule, because the money was paid in generally, and not "in respect of any particular sum or cause of action in the declaration."

The question before us must be decided upon the Judicature Acts and Rules, and upon such of the principles previously existing as have not been altered. The money having been paid in generally, the plaintiffs take issue, the event being whether the 200*l.* was sufficient to satisfy the plaintiffs' claim or not. The plaintiffs assert that it was not, and fail, and therefore must pay the defendants' costs of the suit.

> *Order absolute to review the taxation and to disallow the plaintiffs' costs, and to allow the defendant her costs of suit from the commencement.*

Solicitors for plaintiffs: *Bicknell and Horton.*
Solicitors for defendant: *Tatham, Oblein, & Nash.*

1877
Jan. 16.

[IN THE COURT OF APPEAL.]

GREAVES v. GREENWOOD AND OTHERS.

Inheritance—Pedigree—Heir-at-Law—Claim through a Female—Evidence to prove Extinction of superior Lines of Descent—3 & 4 Wm. 4, c. 106, ss. 7, 8.

At the trial of an action for the recovery of land, in 1876, it was proved by the plaintiff that J. F. W. died seised in fee, without issue, and intestate, in 1868 ; that all the descendants of his paternal grandfather, J. W., were dead, and that the plaintiff was the heir-at-law of the paternal grandmother. On the death of the intestate in 1868 advertisements were published in the London and provincial newspapers, for the heir-at-law of J. F. W., describing his father and grandfather and the property. Several persons came forward, and, besides the plaintiff, no one was able to establish any relationship except the defendants, who were co-heiresses of the mother of J. F. W., and to whom the tenants of the property had attorned. Deeds, wills, and documents were put in evidence, in which no mention was made of any person who would have been of nearer kin than the plaintiff, beyond those whose deaths were proved. The defendants proved that the paternal great-grandfather had, besides J. W., another son, N. W., born in 1717, and also a sister, a Mrs. M., both of whom were alive in 1755, and that the paternal great-grandmother's maiden name was S. B. But no further evidence as to N. W., Mrs. M., or the B. family was given :—

Held, that there was evidence on which the jury might properly find for the plaintiff.

Richards v. *Richards* (15 East, 294, n.) commented on.

ACTION to recover possession of three houses in Manchester.   Ex. D.

At the trial before Brett, J., at the Manchester Spring Assizes, 1876, the plaintiff proved that John Frederick Winterbottom, the purchaser, died in 1868, seised in fee of the houses in question, leaving no issue and intestate as to this property. The paternal grandfather of J. F. Winterbottom was John Winterbottom, of Manchester. He had numerous descendants, and the death of all of them was proved. The plaintiff claimed and proved his title as heir-at-law to the paternal grandmother, the wife of John Winterbottom, the plaintiff being the great-grandson and heir-at-law of her father, Joseph Greaves. Wills and other documents were put in evidence, in which no mention was made of the existence of any person who would have been of nearer kin than the plaintiff, beyond those whose deaths were proved. J. F. Winterbottom died entitled also and intestate as to some Yorkshire property, and at his death advertisements were inserted, by direction of his widow, in the London and Leeds and Huddersfield newspapers, for the heir-at-law of John Frederick Winterbottom, describing his extraction and the property, and giving the names of his father and grandfather. Several persons came forward (some from the neighbourhood of Manchester), but no one was able to establish any relationship, except the plaintiff, who took possession of the Yorkshire property, and the three defendants who appeared to defend as landlords, to whom Greenwood and the other defendants, tenants in possession, had attorned. The defendants were the co-heiresses of the mother of J. F. Winterbottom.

On the part of the defendants, deeds, wills, and certificates were put in, from which it appeared that the father of John Winterbottom, the grandfather, was James Winterbottom, and he had another son, Nathaniel, born about 1717 and alive in 1755; and he had also a sister, a Mrs. Moult, who was a widow and alive in 1755. It was also shewn that the wife of James Winterbottom was Sarah Bent. Nothing further was proved as to Nathaniel Winterbottom, Mrs. Moult, or the Bent family.

The defendants contended that the plaintiff was bound to give some evidence as to the extinction of those three lines of descent, which were preferable to his own. The Judge overruled the objection.

It was agreed that the jury should find a verdict for the plaintiff, and judgment be entered accordingly, leave being reserved to move to enter judgment for the defendants, if the Court should be of opinion that there was no evidence upon which the jury could properly find for the plaintiff, the Court to have power to draw inferences of fact consistent with the jury having so found.

June 19, 1876. *Herschell, Q.C. (Gully, W. Barber,* and *A. Dixon,* with him), for the defendants, moved accordingly.

C. Russell, Q.C., Taylor, and *Aspland,* for the plaintiff.

BRAMWELL, B. I think that our judgment must be for the plaintiff. The question is, whether there was evidence to go to the jury upon which they might properly find for the plaintiff. I

think there was. If the plaintiff had simply proved his pedigree,
I think that there would have been a case for the jury, but it
would have been a case with which the jury, as reasonable men,
would have said they were not satisfied. On the other hand,
supposing that the plaintiff had shewn that the paternal grandfather was illegitimate and had exhausted the descendants of
that ancestor, he would have shewn conclusively that he was
heir. But having shewn his own title, is he bound to shew nega-
tively that there were no persons who could claim a nearer heirship than that which, to some extent, he has proved? I confess
I have considerable misgiving whether he is. I doubt very much
whether a person is bound to prove a negative in cases of this
description. The common expression is, that the plaintiff must
exhaust the possibility that there are other heirs, and give some
negative evidence to shew that there are no descendants entitled
in preference to himself. But I cannot help thinking that the
expression must mean that, if this is not done, the jury will be
directed, as reasonable and prudent men, to say that they are not
satisfied with the case made out. In this particular case, no doubt,
there is very great difficulty in supposing that this plaintiff really
is the heir, because it is a condition of things which can hardly
exist unless we suppose there is some interruption in the pedigree,
such as bastardy. But I think if the Act 3 & 4 Wm. 4, c. 106,
s. 7, is ever to be applied, it must be applied where one is satisfied,
from no one appearing, that no nearer heir to the deceased can be
found than the person making the claim. I think there is great
weight in the argument that this is a possessory action only, and
that another person may, at any future time, if he can make out
a title, come forward and displace this plaintiff. I doubt, therefore, very much whether there is any necessity for a man to do
more than trace his heirship, and, for prudence and safety's sake,
exhaust the possibility of near heirship of modern existence, which
he can reasonably be expected to do; but when he gets beyond
living memory, and beyond his dealing with it in any way, I
doubt whether he is bound to do more than say that he knows
nothing about it.

1877
GREAVES
v.
GREENWOOD.

Now, in this case the plaintiff has exhausted all the persons whom reasonably he could be expected to exhaust; but then it is shewn that 120 years ago there were certainly persons in existence, none of whom, we can suppose, are alive now, but each of whom might have married and had children. It is a possibility, no doubt, but I think that the plaintiff is entitled to say, "That is a possibility which I am not called upon to negative, or, if I am, I am not called upon to negative it further than this, by shewing that inquiry has been made for them, and they have not been heard of." Whether, if there had been any affirmative evidence on the part of the defendants to make one think that such descendants might be in existence, whether in that case, the plaintiff's evidence would have been sufficient to satisfy a jury I do not know; nor whether they might not think that he ought to have made some further inquiries. That is not the question now. Advertisements were put in the papers eight years before the trial, and no claimant has appeared. Is not that, reasonably, all the negative evidence that a person making such a claim can give? It seems to me that it is. And I cannot help thinking that there is something in this, that the defendants are not entirely strangers, but are persons who, to a certain extent, must be taken to be setting up an heirship, though not so near to the deceased man as the plaintiff.

In the first place, therefore, I doubt very much whether any evidence is necessary on the part of the plaintiff, beyond proof of heirship, to go to the jury. He is not called upon to negative what, for convenience' sake, I will call a nearer heirship. But, supposing he is called upon to negative it, I think he has done so, because he has given evidence, where it was possible to do so, that is to say, as to things existing within the time of living memory; and he has given negative evidence of no claim being made by descendants of those who are shewn to be in existence at a time so remote, that it is presumably impossible to give distinct evidence of their death without issue. I think, therefore, that if he is called upon to give such negative evidence, he has done it.

So much for the reason of the thing. But, in addition to that, it does seem to me that the case of *Doe* v. *Wolley* (1), cannot be distinguished from the present case. There it was shewn that there were several brothers between the person from whom the intestate was descended and the brother through whom the plaintiff claimed; of course it was possible that all those brothers might have married and had children, and there was not a particle of evidence given in that case to negative their having done so, except the fact that no such issue had appeared and claimed, and that there were certain instruments put in evidence in which no mention was made of any such posterity.. Here also were such instruments; but it was said that it would not be reasonable to expect that any mention should be made in them of the descendants of Mrs. Moult or Nathaniel Winterbottom, but I do not know that in *Doe* v. *Wolley* (1) it would have been more reasonable to suppose so. I think, therefore, that that case is really in point. The case of *Richards* v. *Richards* (2) was referred to, which is, "In ejectment the lessor of the plaintiff claimed as heir by descent, and shewed the death of his elder brothers, but not that they died without issue:—*Curia*, this must likewise be proved." That may be taken to be right, it being a matter reasonably within the capability of proof by the plaintiff, not being without the time of living memory, and the persons who were dead being his elder brothers only; I should, with all respect, therefore, say that what the Court said so far was right, for it was a thing which the plaintiff could prove, and if he does not prove it the jury would say they were not satisfied that he is the heir. So in this particular case negative evidence as to the more recent relatives is necessary, and that has been given. The note goes on to say, "The plaintiff must remove every possibility of title in another person." But that cannot possibly be correct. There must be some inaccuracy, for all the plaintiff can be called upon to do is to give evidence to shew that it is improbable there are any preferable descendants. With respect to this. note, which is very short, I must say that I differ from it, except as to the first part of it. I think, upon the whole, that in this case the plaintiff is entitled to our judgment.

(1) 8 B. & C. 22.   (2) 15 East, 294, n.

1877

GREAVES
v.
GREENWOOD.

AMPHLETT, B.   I entirely agree with the judgment of my
Brother Bramwell.

Motion refused.

The defendants appealed.

C. A.

Jan. 16.   *Herschell, Q.C.,* and *W. Barber (Gully,* with them), for
the defendants.   By 3 & 4 Wm. 4, c. 106, s. 7 (1) the heir through
a female paternal ancestor cannot inherit until the male paternal
ancestors are shewn to have failed.   The plaintiff is no doubt heir
of the paternal grandmother, and, as such, has a better title than
the defendants, who claim under the mother; but before he can
recover and turn out the defendants, who are in possession, he must
shew that there are no heirs of the grandfather in existence, or, at
all events, none discoverable by inquiry.   The onus is on the plaintiff, and he has not proved the failure of such heirs.   He has not
made sufficient inquiry.   It was not necessary for the defendants to
give any evidence, but they did prove that there had been relations
of the paternal grandfather who might have left descendants.   It
was no part of the defendants' duty to find out such descendants,
who could of course recover against both plaintiff and defendants,
but they have a right to call on the plaintiff to prove his own title,
and to shew that there are no such persons.   The defendants are
in possession, and it is not enough for the plaintiff merely to prove
that he was the heir of the grandmother, and so has a better title
than the defendants, who are heirs of the mother.   In order to
recover he must shew an absolute title.   There is no presumption
in his favour: *Doe* v. *Wolley* (2); *Doe* v. *Deakin* (3); 1 Tayl. Ev.
§ 156; *Richards* v. *Richards.* (4)   The rule is well shewn in
the American case of *Emmerson* v. *White.* (5)   If the plaintiff re-

(1) 3 & 4 Wm. 4, c. 106, s. 7:
"None of the maternal ancestors of the
person from whom the descent is to
be traced, nor any of their descendants,
shall be capable of inheriting until
all his paternal ancestors and their
descendants shall have failed; and no
female paternal ancestor of such person,
nor any of her descendants, shall be
capable of inheriting until all his male
paternal ancestors and their descendants

shall have failed; and no female maternal ancestor of such person nor any of
her descendants, shall be capable of inheriting until all his male maternal
ancestors and their descendants shall
have failed."

(2) 8 B. & C. 22.
(3) 3 C. & P. 402.
(4) 15 East, 294, n.
(5) 9 Foster, New Hampshire Rep.
(1854) 482.

covers and compels the tenants to pay rent, the heir of Nathaniel Winterbottom may by-and-bye appear and compel the tenants to pay over again.

C. Russell, Q.C., and *Aspland*, for the plaintiff. If the defendants succeed, the 7th section of the Act will become all but nugatory, as it will be impossible for any one to succeed as an heir through a female, unless one of the male ancestors was a bastard; for in no other case can it be shewn positively that there are no heirs of a male paternal ancestor: Hubback on Succession, p. 227. The Act must mean that unless an heir is forthcoming he must be presumed not to exist. Inquiry has been made, and persons came to claim, but failed; and what more could the plaintiff do? All that the defendants have done is to shew that, 120 years ago, persons existed who may have left descendants, of whom, however, no trace is found.'

Herschell, Q.C., in reply.

COCKBURN, C.J. I think that the judgment of the Court below should be affirmed. I quite agree in the position taken by Mr. Herschell, that there is no presumption in a matter of this kind. If it is proved that long ago a man died, and there is nothing to shew whether he died with issue or without issue, I agree in the American doctrine that there is no presumption either way. But then comes the question whether there was here, independently of any presumption, evidence proper for the consideration of a jury that the male paternal line of the Winterbottoms had become extinct, and that, consequently, the heir on the female side was entitled. Now, it appears that the grandfather of John Frederick Winterbottom, who has died intestate as to the property sought to be recovered in this action, had a brother, Nathaniel, who was born in 1717, and there is therefore a good presumption that he has long since been dead. But the question arises whether Nathaniel had any issue. Granting that there is no presumption either way, how is the fact to be ascertained? It might be ascertained by positive evidence, such as an entry in a register, or in a will, or other instrument, in which reference was made to him as having children or not having children; but there is no such evidence. We have, however, this evidence:

1877

GREAVES
v.
GREENWOOD.

there is a large property in various counties, the subject-matter of inquiry and of dispute; the widow of the man last seised, with the honest desire of ascertaining whether he had any heir, and if so, who that heir was, caused advertisements to be inserted in the general and local papers, with a view of ascertaining whether any male heir or any heir of the male line could be found; and it is clear that these advertisements were circulated to a considerable extent, because we have the fact proved that numerous persons came forward, each endeavouring to make out his right to be considered and dealt with as the heir, but all of them failed to establish their relationship. This, I agree, is by no means conclusive. The real heir may still be somewhere, ignorant of this inquiry, ignorant of these claims, ignorant of all that has taken place. But as a century and a half has elapsed since the man was born, as to whom the inquiry whether he had children or not is made, and as there is not any trace of any issue of his, and as nothing of such issue was known to any member of the family, or to any of the relations, and as, after an advertisement of this kind, no one has come forward who has been able to substantiate his claim, I cannot say— however inconclusive such proof may be—that there was not some evidence on which the jury might act. It is difficult to believe, after all that has taken place, all that has been known upon this subject, including the trial of this ejectment, that if there were any persons who could have made out their claim as being the descendants of Nathaniel Winterbottom, they would not have come forward. It is just possible, no doubt, that there may be some person in existence who could make out his claim, but I think the jury may very properly have looked at the case in the way in which I have put it, using their common sense. A property of this sort does not usually go begging. Every one of the name of Winterbottom is put on the qui vive to see if it is not possible to make out a descent from Nathaniel Winterbottom. I cannot say, therefore that there was no evidence to go to the jury, and I think the decision of the Court below must stand. That is all we have to determine. We have not to determine what we should have done as jurymen, nor what we should have done if we had had to sum up the case to the jury; all we have to determine is, was there evidence proper for their consideration?

BAGGALLAY, J.A. I am of the same opinion. A reasonable
interpretation must be given to the 7th section of 3 & 4 Wm. 4,
c. 106; and if the interpretation which has been put forward is
to be adopted as regards the failure of all paternal ancestors and
their descendants, it would be impossible for a descendant of a
maternal ancestor to succeed, except in the case of some paternal
ancestor being illegitimate.   It would be necessary to go back
to the very remotest antiquity before it could be said that the
paternal line was exhausted. I think the true meaning of the
section is that, when there is no reasonable possibility of ascertaining that there are descendants from the paternal ancestors—
I mean, of course, a reasonable possibility, after due and sufficient
investigation and inquiry,—and what may be a due and sufficient
investigation must depend on the circumstances of the case,—
then descendants of the maternal ancestors must be sought for.
In the present case all the descendants of paternal ancestors who
have been born within 150 years have been exhausted. The
intestate was the last of those descendants. Therefore, we are
considering a case in which certainly there has been a very full
and very complete investigation.

It may be, no doubt, that, if we were to go back further, relations of females in the paternal line might be discovered, from
whom it is suggested that there may be a descendant. It is
suggested also that, as it has been proved that there was one
Nathaniel, who was a descendant of a paternal ancestor and was
born as long ago as the year 1717, it is possible that there
may be some descendants of his still alive. I think the facts
which are proved, of the birth of this Nathaniel in 1717 and of
his being alive in the year 1755, if we proceeded no further in
the investigation (although it is no very important element for our
consideration), are evidence to be considered. But we have also
this additional fact. The intestate having died eight years before
the trial, an advertisement was published in different papers, calling
on the heir-at-law of this intestate to come forward, particularizing
not only the intestate himself but his father and grandfather, and
particularizing also where the property was situate. Those were all
circumstances tending in themselves to induce persons, who might
think that they might be or were the relatives of the intestate, to

1877

GREAVES
v.
GREENWOOD.

come forward and shew whether there was a failure of descendants of paternal ancestors. All those were facts for the consideration of the jury. I am bound to say that in this case I should have been quite as well satisfied if, upon the evidence which was before them, the jury had come to the conclusion that the plaintiff had not established his case as heir-at-law; but that was for the jury to decide, and it is not for me to express an opinion. If, then, there was evidence for them to consider, and on which they might find a verdict, we cannot on any ground which has been urged before us, disturb it. I think the decision at which the Court of Exchequer have arrived is, on the whole, correct, and must be affirmed.

BRETT, J.A. I am of the same opinion. It seems to me that we are not called upon or bound to lay down any new rule as to the law of inheritance. I agree that, inasmuch as the plaintiff was bringing an action of ejectment, it lay upon him not merely to prove that he was what may be called the nearest relation, but to prove that he was the heir-at-law; and I agree that, as he was claiming through a maternal ancestor, it was necessary that there should be at the trial reasonable evidence that the paternal line was exhausted, and also that the superior maternal lines were exhausted. But the question is whether there was such reasonable evidence on both points as ought to have been left to the jury. If there was not, I, who tried the case, ought to have nonsuited the plaintiff. The point of time in the trial, which we are bound to consider, is not the end of the plaintiff's case, unless the defendant proposes to leave the case there. If the defendant adduces evidence, the question will then properly arise whether the plaintiff ought to be nonsuited. If, by any addition which the defendant makes to the case, he shews that there is no reasonable evidence of the exhaustion of the paternal line and of the superior maternal lines, then he may be entitled to a nonsuit, but if there is reasonable evidence there cannot be a nonsuit. Now, upon the question whether there was reasonable evidence in this particular case, it is quite unnecessary to consider what was the evidence in any other case. It seems to me that a great many circumstances were proved here which are material. It is material that there have been

1877

GREAVES
v.
GREENWOOD.

claims made not only as to this property which is in dispute, but as to other property belonging to the same intestate. The defendants were also members of the family, and came forward claiming as heirs-at-law. Now I think it is but reasonable to assume that they must then have made some inquiry into the family history, because it was necessary for them to do so in order to see if they could support a claim to the Yorkshire property as against the present plaintiff. Then there has been this litigation, and the plaintiff has inquired into the family history, and having gone through the family for more than 100 years, he has certainly exhausted, within that 100 years, all the family of whom he could find any trace, and having done that, he has gone to the female ancestor through whom he claims. It is also very material to consider the inquiry made by the widow of the intestate. It is clear that she (who had herself made no claim) meant that those inquiries should be honestly made. She employed a firm of solicitors well known and of the highest respectability, who put in those advertisements which, under the circumstances, must, I think, be taken to have been entirely honest, and intended to find out who was the heir-at-law. It may be that a better form of advertisement might be suggested, or that a fuller form might have been used; but we are not here deciding upon the sufficiency of the form, but whether there was evidence proper to be left to the jury, and sufficient to enable them to decide whether reasonable inquiries were made by means of those advertisements or by other means. It was for them to say whether the advertisements were or were not sufficient, and I think they might properly come to the conclusion that they were. Then on the trial the defendants shew the closeness of the inquiries they had made made by going beyond the 100 years, and shewing the existence of this Nathaniel Winterbottom. No doubt it was in one sense skilful on their part to stop at Nathaniel, and to make no further inquiry as to whether he had any issue, or had ever been married. But I cannot say that it would have been good tactics to have stopped there if the defendants could have shewn that Nathaniel had issue. I agree with Sir George Bramwell that we should require the plaintiff to give more evidence of a negative as to occurrences within the last century than we should require as to occurrences before the last century, because he would have easier means of proving a negative. I think that that is not an artificial distinction, but is a good and practical view of what you would reasonably expect a man to do; therefore, it would have been to the advantage of the defendants if they could have shewn that Nathaniel was a married man and had children of that marriage, but they advisedly stopped short of that. Then we have the fact that, notwithstanding the advertisements, no single claimant has come forward to say that he is the representative of Nathaniel.

Taking all those circumstances into consideration, the jury would have been, in my judgment, justified in saying that they were satisfied that there was no descendant of Nathaniel. If that is so, we have got rid of the Winterbottom family, and are driven to the Bents and Moults. I do not think it necessary to go back 150 years to get rid of those lines of descent. Nothing is proved with regard to them by either side, and I think we cannot expect the plaintiff to go back for that purpose. In my mind, the objection to Mr. Herschell's argument throughout is that it goes too far; it is a solid objection to that argument that according to it no person claiming through a maternal line can succeed unless he exhausts all the male paternal ancestors who ever existed. That cannot be the meaning of this statute. If the evidence goes back as far as the evidence did in this case, that is to say, for 150 years, that is sufficient. And unless something is shewn to throw doubt upon the want of appearance of any descendants, it is not enough to say by way of argument, because the argument is equally conclusive on the other side, that there must be other people either on the paternal or maternal lines. Of course there must be, but they have gone into the vast multitude of the world, so that they cannot be taken notice of. Therefore I think that this judgment should be affirmed.

Judgment affirmed.

Solicitors for plaintiff: *Torr & Co.*
Solicitors for defendants: *Currie, Williams, & Co.*

[IN THE COURT OF APPEAL.]   1877
                                                            Jan. 31.

THE HONDURAS INTER-OCEANIC RAILWAY COMPANY *v.* LEFEVRE AND TUCKER.

Pleading—Joinder of Defendants—Alternative Relief—Rules of Court, 1875, . *Order XVI., Rules* 3, 6.

In an action brought by a company against L. and T., the claim stated that L., through T., who professed to be, and in fact was, the agent of L., contracted to take a certain number of debentures in the plaintiff company, which contract L. had failed to perform ; and that L. denied that T. was authorized by him to make the contract. The plaintiffs prayed for specific performance of the contract or for damages against L. ; or in the alternative, if it should appear that T. had no authority to act as L.'s agent, then for specific performance and damages against T.

T. having applied to have judgment entered up in his favour, or to have his name struck out as defendant :—

Held, affirming the decision of the Exchequer Division, that, under the circumstances stated in the claim, the plaintiffs were entitled to join L. and T. as defendants, and to claim alternative relief against them under Order XVI., Rules 3, 6.

THIS was an appeal from an order of the Exchequer Division (Kelly, C.B., and Cleasby, B.)

The plaintiffs were a limited company, having their principal registered offices at Westminster. Before the coming into operation of the Judicature Acts the plaintiffs commenced an action in the Court of Exchequer against the defendant, C. J. Lefevre. The declaration contained several counts, founded on promises made by Lefevre, by himself or his agents, to subscribe certain large sums for debentures in the plaintiff company, in consideration of the plaintiff company proceeding to an allotment of the shares and debentures applied for by the public.

The defendant Lefevre pleaded several pleas traversing the allegations in the declaration, and the plaintiffs joined issue on the 31st of May, 1876.

The plaintiffs subsequently applied, by summons in Chambers, under Order XVI., Rule 13, to add as a defendant, J. Tucker, who had acted, or professed to act, as the agent of Lefevre in the business. The matter was afterwards brought before the Divisional Court, when the Court made an order giving the plaintiffs leave to add Tucker as defendant, and to commence their pleadings de novo, they paying Lefevre's costs up to that time.

The plaintiffs accordingly issued a fresh writ under the new practice against Lefevre and Tucker, and filed a statement of claim on the 8th of November, 1876. This statement was afterwards amended and, as amended, stated (inter alia) as follows: That the directors, finding the money subscribed by the public not sufficient to enable them to proceed with their undertaking, proposed to abandon it, and that the defendant Lefevre, through the defendant Tucker, who stated that he had authority, and which authority he then, in fact, had from the defendant Lefevre so to do, promised the company that, in consideration of their allotting such debentures and shares as had been or might be applied for, and proceeding with their undertaking, and also delivering to the defendant Tucker, on behalf of the defendant Lefevre, debentures to the amount of 10,000*l.* in blank, the defendant Lefevre would subscribe, or procure to be subscribed, the sum of 80,000*l.* on the security of the debentures of the company or otherwise.

That the company allotted the debentures and shares, and in all respects performed their part of the contract, but the defendant Lefevre refused to subscribe or procure the sum of 80,000*l.*, or any amount of money.

That Tucker represented to the plaintiffs, at the time of making the promises, that he had authority to make them on behalf of Lefevre, but that Lefevre now asserted that Tucker had no such authority from him, and refused to perform his promise on that ground; that the plaintiffs relied on the representations of Tucker, and that, in the event of Lefevre being held not liable, on the ground that Tucker had no such authority as he represented himself to have, the plaintiffs would claim from Tucker the damages claimed in the prayer.

The plaintiffs prayed for specific performance of the contract, or damages against Lefevre; and in the event of its being held that Lefevre was not liable, on the ground that Tucker was not authorized as his agent, then for specific performance of the contract or damages against Tucker.

The defendant Tucker then applied to the judge in chambers to have judgment entered up in his favour on the admissions in the

1877

HONDURAS
RAILWAY CO.
v.
TUCKER.

pleadings, and the summons was referred to the Court. The matter was heard on the 16th of January, 1877, when the defendant Tucker moved the Court either to enter up judgment in his favour under Order XL., Rule 11, or to strike his name out of the record under Order XVI., Rule 13.

- The Court refused either relief, and Tucker appealed.

Pollard, for the defendant, Tucker. Tucker has been made a defendant under the notion that this can be done under the 3rd or 6th Rule of Order XVI. (1) But the 3rd Rule does not apply to cases where the relief prayed in one alternative is inconsistent with the relief prayed in the other; nor does either Rule apply to cases where the grounds of action against the two defendants are distinct. In such cases the plaintiff must still bring separate actions as under the old practice. Before the passing of the Judicature Acts a bill which prayed inconsistent relief against two defendants was demurrable : *Clark* v. *Lord Rivers*. (2) And in *Evans* v. *Buck* (3) the Master of the Rolls held that the old rule still prevailed. In the present case the plaintiffs pray relief against Lefevre, if he is liable under the contract; then they pray relief on totally inconsistent grounds against Tucker. It would be very inconvenient and almost impossible to try a double issue like this at one trial. Moreover, the causes of action in the two cases are different. The claim against Lefevre is based on his contract; the claim against Tucker is based on tort, for his misrepresentation of his authority, and the measure of damages may be different in the two cases : *Randell* v. *Trimen*. (4) If the wide construction of

---

(1) Order XVI., Rule 3, is as follows: "All persons may be joined as defendants against whom the right to any relief is alleged to exist, whether jointly, severally, or in the alternative. And judgment may be given against such one or more of the defendants as may be found to be liable according to their respective liabilities, without any amendment."

Rule 6: "Where, in any action, whether founded upon contract or trover, the plaintiff is in doubt as to the person from whom he is entitled to redress, he may in such manner as hereinafter mentioned, or as may be prescribed in any special order, join two or more defendants to the intent that, in such action, the question as to which, if any, of the defendants is liable, and to what extent, may be determined as between all parties to the action."

(2) Law Rep. 5 Eq. 91.
(3) Weekly Notes, 1876, p. 305.
(4) 18 C. B. 786; 25 L. J. (C.P.) 307

the 3rd Rule contended for is the true one, there was no occasiou for the 4th Rule, nor for the special mention of bills of exchange in it.

If the Court should be of opinion that Tucker's name ought not to be struck out, he is entitled to judgment under Order XL., Rule 11, on the ground that in the statement of claim there is no allegation that Tucker had no authority : *Oxenham* v. *Smythe.* (1) On the contrary, there is an express allegation that he had authority. He is therefore entitled to judgment as if he had demurred : *Gilbert* v. *Smith.* (2)

Watkin Williams, Q.C. (*Tindal Atkinson* with him), for the plaintiffs. All the rules under Order XVI. ought to be read together. Rule 3 relates to the joinder of defendants in the original writ, Rule 6 to the addition of defendants by amendment after the action has commenced, and Rules 14, 15, and 16 shew how that is to be done. Rule 6 bears the same relation to Rule 3 as Rule 2 does to Rule 1. It is clear, from the 17th, 18th, and 19th Rules, that the legislature contemplated very complex actions being tried under this Order. The rules are made to prevent the failure of justice which sometimes took place in such cases as the present, where the plaintiff proceeded, first, against the principal and then against the agent, and was baffled in both actions by the impossibility of shewing whether the agent had authority or not. No inconvenience can arise out of the application of the rule to such a case as the present, because the Court has full power to direct how the action shall be tried, or to make such other order as may be right: *Benecke* v. *Frost.* (3) The new rules only put actions on contracts on the same footing as actions on tort were formerly; when an action for an assault, for instance, was brought against several persons, if the plaintiff proved his case against one, it was sufficient to sustain the action. Tucker contends that the rules only apply to alternative relief in respect of the same cause of action; but there are no words in the rule to limit their application. It can make no practical difference that the measure of damages in the case of the two defendants is

(1) 6 H. & N. 690; 31 L. J. (Ex.) 110.   (2) 2 Ch. D. 686.
(3) 1 Q. B. D. 419.

1877

HONDURAS
RAILWAY CO.
v.
TUCKER.

different. In almost all cases of alternative relief this must be the case.

Pollard, in reply, referred to *Jenkins* v. *Hutchinson.* (1)

COCKBURN, C.J. I am of opinion that this appeal must be dismissed. It is not necessary to decide whether the case falls within the 3rd Rule of Order XVI. My impression is that it does not, but that that Rule is confined to cases in which a plaintiff has a right of action at his option against either of two parties, as, for instance, against a principal debtor and his surety. But it is enough for the present purpose to say that it is within the 6th Rule. This rule, I think, is applicable to actions which have been already commenced, as well as to those in which the plaintiff is in doubt on commencing the action; and if, after having brought the action, the plaintiff is in doubt whether he has made the right person defendant, he may apply to the Court, under Rule 13, and obtain permission to add another defendant. When I say that the 6th Rule is applicable, I must be understood as limiting my opinion to such circumstances as exist here. I do not say that in every case in which a plaintiff may have a cause of action against A. or B. in the alternative, he would be entitled to join them as defendants. I think it very doubtful whether if the redress claimed against them differed in substance he would be entitled to join them. On that, however, I pronounce no opinion. But here we have a claim for redress against two persons arising out of a common transaction, to which both of them are alleged to have been parties—against the one as principal if the agent had authority to bind him, against the other who professed to be an agent, if he acted without authority. What the plaintiffs complain of is the non-performance of a contract. If their claim is against Lefevre it is because the contract is broken; if it is against Tucker it is also because the contract has failed and remains unfulfilled. The only difference is that, although the redress claimed is the same, if there had been separate actions the process would have been different in the two actions. In the one it would have been on the contract; in the other on the special ground that the defendant professed to have authority which he had not, and so

(1) 13 Q. B. 744.

the contract failed. But whatever course was pursued the redress
would, in both cases, have been for damages arising out of non-
performance of the contract.

Therefore I think that the case is within Order XVI., Rule 6,
and that the defendant, Tucker, is not entitled to have his name
struck out. The appeal must be dismissed with costs.

MELLISH, L.J. I am of the same opinion. The rules ought to
be interpreted fairly to carry out the intention of the legislature
in making them. There can be no question that the intention of
the legislature was that it should not be necessary for a plaintiff
to bring an action first against A., and then against B., and to run
the risk of the jury taking a contrary view of the evidence in the
two cases, but that he should have both defendants before the
Court at once, and try it out between them. The only question
is whether the case can be brought within the words of the 6th
Rule. In my opinion, if we give the ordinary meaning to the
words, this case is within the rule. The action is on a contract.
The plaintiffs complain of a breach of it, and claim specific performance against Lefevre, whom they allege to be the principal;
and then they allege that Lefevre denies that Tucker was authorized as his agent to make such a contract, and that if he was
not authorized then Tucker is liable. Therefore, the plaintiffs
are in doubt which person to proceed against. If Tucker was
Lefevre's agent, then they claim against Lefevre, if not, then
against Tucker, on account of the contract not being performed.
I think that such a case is within the plain meaning of the words
of the rule. I think the plaintiffs are not concerned to enter into
the contest between them. They have a right to make out their
case against one or the other.

BAGGALLAY, J.A. I am of the same opinion.

BRAMWELL, J.A. I am also of the same opinion. In all litigation the question arises who is to be plaintiff and who is to be
defendant. Rule 1 of Order XVI. says that any number of plaintiffs may be joined, and the relief claimed may be different for
different plaintiffs; for it may be alleged to exist either jointly,
severally, or in the alternative. Then the joinder of defendants is
provided for by Rule 3, which says that all persons may be joined

as defendants against whom the right to any relief is alleged to exist, either jointly, severally, or in the alternative.

Coupling this with what is said about plaintiffs in Rule 1, it comes to this, that you may have as many plaintiffs as you like claiming in the alternative, and by Rule 3, as many defendants as you like, against whom relief is claimed in the alternative. If Rule 3 is not wide enough to include this case, I think it is included in Rule 6. There is some colour for saying that Rule 6 refers to Rule 3; but I think it was not intended to apply only to actions already commenced. It appears to me impossible to suppose that the legislature would say: First bring your action, and then if any doubt arises in the course of the action whether you have the proper defendant, ask leave of the Court to add another defendant. It seems to me more probable that the words "in any action" are equivalent to "any intended action." I think that the rule shews that alternative relief of different kinds may be given against alternative defendants.

Appeal dismissed.

Solicitors for plaintiffs : *Mercer & Mercer.*
Solicitor for defendant: *R. Reece.*

MURPHY, APPELLANT; MANNING AND ANOTHER, RESPONDENTS.

Cruelty to Animals—Cutting Cocks' Combs—12 & 13 Vict. c. 92, s. 2.

Upon an information against the respondents, under 12 & 13 Vict. c. 92, s. 2, for cutting the combs of cocks, evidence was given that the operation caused very great pain, and was inflicted in order to fit the birds for one or other of two purposes; cock-fighting or winning prizes at exhibitions. The magistrates having referred to the Court the question whether the case was one of the class contemplated by the statute :—

Held by Kelly, C.B., that the respondents did, as a matter of fact, "cruelly ill-treat, abuse, or torture the birds ;" that, as a matter of law, the act could not be justified by the purpose of cockfighting, and that the respondents ought to have been convicted.

By Cleasby, B. (without expressing any opinion upon the facts), that neither the purpose of cockfighting nor that of winning prizes at exhibitions would prevent the case from being within the statute.

CASE stated under 20 & 21 Vict. c. 43.

At a petty sessions at Sittingbourne, in Kent, on the 17th of

January, 1876, two informations were preferred by the appellant Murphy, inspector to the Rochester and Chatham branch of the Royal Society for the Prevention of Cruelty to Animals; (1.) against Manning, veterinary surgeon, for having, on the 20th of November, 1875, at Rainham, unlawfully and · cruelly ill-treated three cocks; and (2.) against Sayer, the owner of the cocks, for unlawfully causing them to be so ill-treated contrary to 12 & 13 Vict. c. 92, s. 2. (1)

The appellant stated that on the 27th of November he went to Sayer's house, and saw three bantam cocks. Their combs had been cut off as closely as it could be done, and there were unhealed scabs, the effect of a wound, on their heads. Sayer said he had been told at the Crystal Palace that unless the combs were off he could obtain no prizes, which was the only reason for having it done. The next day the appellant saw Manning, and asked him as to the cutting of the combs, and he said he did it at Sayer's request for the purpose of exhibition. The appellant asked Manning if he did not consider it caused pain. Manning replied that there was a measure of pain, but he did not think it very great, it was soon over; the birds winced their heads during the cutting, and bobbed them two or three times when cut. He mentioned that he had been in the habit of doing it more or less for forty years past. On cross-examination, appellant said he could not say whether the birds were cocks or cockerels; he took them to be full-grown birds.

The police-constable stated that they looked as though they had been just recently cut. They were full-grown birds, duck-winged.

James Broad, a member of the council of the Royal College of Veterinary Surgeons, stated that in his opinion great pain was caused to cocks in cutting their combs. The removal did not prevent the cock from suffering disease; the only object was for fighting purposes, he knew of no other cause for cutting them.

(1) 12 & 13 Vict. c. 92, s. 2: "If any person shall, from and after the passing of this Act, cruelly beat, ill-treat, over-drive, abuse, or torture, or cause or procure to be cruelly beaten, ill-treated, over-driven, abused, or tortured, any animal, every such offender shall, for every such offence, forfeit and pay a penalty not exceeding five pounds."

On cross-examination he admitted that he had never done it himself nor seen it done; that it might be done in a minute. There was no portion of the comb without a nerve which communicated with the spinal cord; it was a tissue of bloodvessels.

W. H. Jones, a member of the College of Veterinary Surgeons, stated that in his opinion the cutting would cause pain. There were nerves separated in the cutting off the comb. The fact of their wincing shewed this. On cross-examination he admitted that he had never cut a comb or seen it done, and that blood was no proof of pain. He had studied the habits of fowls.

Frederick Crook, one of the judges of the Crystal Palace Poultry Show, stated that it was detrimental to a cock to cut its comb. It depended upon the class in which a bird was entered, whether or no it would disqualify the bird. There were exhibition classes in which it was the practice to "dub" birds, and there were also classes in which it was the practice not to have them "dubbed."

Harrison Weir, an animal painter and artist, said he had spent a good deal of time in studying the habits of birds and animals, and, in his opinion, "dubbing" spoiled the look of the bird, and must be very painful. He would not interfere with nature.

For the respondents, it was contended, that the combs were cut for the purpose of their being exhibited, and that it was clear, from the evidence of Mr. Crook, that the practice was for game cocks to be dubbed; that, so far from the operation of dubbing being cruel, it was for the real benefit of the birds themselves, inasmuch as in case they quarrelled or fought with one another in the fowl-pen or yard, they could not pull one another by the comb, in which way they often injured themselves; and that such an act did not come within the statute.

George Barker, who was a veterinary inspector to the corporation of Gravesend, and had had sixteen years' experience in veterinary matters, said, that cutting the comb of a game cock would decidedly not create much pain. He called a comb a fleshy excrescence, and said it had never been proved that it contained nerves communicating with the brain. He considered it an advantage to game birds to have their combs cut, as it prevented their fighting with one another. He said it was an ordinary practice to do it in farm yards in Lincolnshire, where he had cut hundreds; it took a quarter of a minute, and the bird would eat directly, and did not appear to suffer. The comb, in his opinion, did not contain a nerve vein; there were blood-vessels. In frosty weather the comb gets frost-bitten. He did not consider it cruelty.

The justices, being of opinion that the offences charged were not of the class contemplated by the statute, dismissed the informations.

The question for the Court was, whether their decision was right.

Waddy, Q.C. (*Morton Smith* with him), for the appellant. Webster's Dictionary defines " cruelly " as " with cruelty," and " cruelty " as a " barbarous deed, any act of a human being which inflicts unnecessary pain." Is the operation of dubbing unnecessary pain? If it is, then it is cruel. It is admitted that the pain can be inflicted for only two purposes, viz., to prepare the birds for exhibition, and to render them less likely to be injured when fighting. Cock-fighting is illegal, and therefore there is no necessity that the birds should be prepared against contingencies which could not happen in lawful course. As to the other point, the Court will not say that it is right that pain should be inflicted simply to satisfy some arbitrary requirement of people who wish to see the birds exhibited in a particular shape. Suppose there was a prize for one-eyed dogs. Would a man be justified in putting out one eye of his dog to qualify it for exhibition? If people cannot obtain prizes without cutting the combs of these cocks, they must go without prizes, or they must get the regulations altered; it is none the less cruelty because they only conform to the rules of an exhibition. In 5 & 6 Wm. 4, c. 59, s. 2, upon which the section in question is based, there appears another word which is purposely left out of the present statute—the word " wantonly." Wightman, J., in *Budge* v. *Parsons* (1), said, " the cruelty intended by the statute is the unnecessary abuse of the animal." It was not necessary that the birds should be exhibited, or if exhibited that their combs should be cut any more than their neck should be broken. Trimming sheep, by cutting off their tails for sale at fairs, would be

(1) 3 B. & S. 382, at p. 385.

within the statute. The castration of horses would not, because
that is not done for mere profit.

1877

MURPHY
v.
MANNING.

[KELLY, C.B. The act may be cruel in the sense that it gives
pain: yet the cruelty may be legalised by reference to the object
with which it is inflicted.]

To justify the pain it must be for the necessary use of the
animal. No one can say that it is for the necessary use of the
animal that it should be exhibited. Take the case of terriers used
for ratting. Would it be lawful to cut the ears of terriers that
they might not be worried or laid hold of by rats? or because a
person could not obtain prizes unless the ears were so cut?

Biron, for the respondents. The question whether dubbing is
cruelty or not is one entirely of fact for the magistrates, and they
having given their decision, this Court cannot review it. But if
that question be open it is clear that the mere infliction of pain
per se is not within the statute, else to flog a restive horse would
be cruelty. The question is whether the pain inflicted is of such
a degree as to amount to cruelty; but that is a question not of
law but of fact, for the decision of the justices. But even if it
were for the Court to decide as a matter of law whether this
dubbing is cruelty or not, it does not at all follow that it is cruelty
within the meaning of the penal statute because the act done
inflicted a certain amount of pain. And it is the amount that is
here in controversy. Two gentlemen called in support of the
informations were of opinion that the amount of pain inflicted by
the cutting of the combs was very considerable; a veterinary
inspector, called for the respondents, gave it as his belief that the
pain was very slight indeed, for the reason that the birds would
eat within a minute or two of the operation being performed upon
them. According to the appellant's argument, one would imagine
that dubbing was the only operation performed upon cocks; but
there is another, called "caponising," which is infinitely more
barbarous, but which enables the bird to put on flesh, and to become more adapted for the table. No one can say that this is for
the bird's advantage, though it may be for the benefit of the con-
sumer. But it must be taken that the justices exercised a fair
judgment; and that they came to the conclusion that so far from

dubbing being cruel it was really for the benefit of the birds, as it prevented them from hurting each other when fighting as much as they would otherwise do. It is said to be illegal for cocks to fight ; but game cocks do fight in the farmyard ; and if they can injure each other more with their combs uncut than when dubbed, surely it is humane to deprive them of the power to mangle each other. By an operation, which is over in half a minute, a bird for its whole life may be saved the risk of being mangled. If this operation be not done with a reckless, foolish purpose, but with a bonâ fide intention of improving the bird, then it is not cruelty within the statute. The ears of foxhounds are rounded to make them more comfortable in the pursuit of game. They are less likely to be caught in the brambles when going through the woods at full speed. The appellant must go further than shewing that, in the strictest sense of the words, the pain inflicted by dubbing is not necessary for the good of the animal or the use of man ; he must shew that the act was purposeless, and without any ulterior intention to benefit the bird, or to make it more happy in after life or more useful to mankind.

Waddy, Q.C., in reply. Admittedly the dubbing was not performed to benefit the birds, but simply to put money in the shape of prizes into some one's pocket.

KELLY, C.B.   I do not hesitate to say that I am most clearly of opinion that the decision of the magistrates was wholly incorrect, and that the respondents ought to have been convicted. The first question is, Is it cruel to cut the combs of these cocks ? Now I admit there are some acts which are cruel in the extreme, and no legislation can make them otherwise, yet they are perfectly lawful and not within the Act, because they are done for some lawful purpose—as, for instance, the cutting of horses. The purpose and object may be such as to legalise acts which would otherwise be within the statute. So as to the much milder operations upon sheep and dogs, and many other cases which might be put. But I do not enter into those questions now. It is enough to deal with cases when they arise. The present case, with which alone

I deal, is one which causes not only pain, but torture. No one
can doubt that to do it is to "cruelly ill-treat, abuse, and torture"
the animal. One witness treats it as a light matter. I disregard his
evidence altogether. I entirely believe the evidence of the
member of the Royal College of Veterinary Surgeons, who said it
gave great pain. In cross-examination he asserted, and, I should
say, was proud to assert, that he had never himself done it. The
excision of the nerves from the animal's head must cause harrow-
ing pain. We cannot define the measure, but it must be very
severe. There is the obvious and visible effect of the operation on
the bird. He winces, and throws his head up and down. The fact
that it is done quickly does not make any difference. Let any one
try to hold his hand over a flame for two seconds, and I think he
would say that half a minute, not to say a minute, was a long time
for an operation of this kind. Then the question is, is there any
purpose or reason which can legalise or justify an act of such
extreme barbarity? To my mind the object, as shewn by the
whole of the evidence, is that the animals may be used for cock-
fighting. This, which once was legal, is now illegal. Taking off
the combs makes them more fit for fighting. It is cruelty, and
an abuse and ill-treatment—the very words in the Act. As it
does not better fit the animal for the use of man or for any other
lawful or proper purpose, it is wholly unjustifiable, and is a criminal
act which comes within the statute.

CLEASBY, B. The magistrates have, as I understand, found the
facts, and referred to us as a matter of law whether the case is
within the statute. If, instead of stating the case in that way, they
had found as their conclusion of fact that pain was not inflicted
under such circumstances, or to such an extent as to amount to
cruelty, there would have been no case for us to consider. But
they have not so stated the case; therefore I think they have not
drawn that conclusion. They thought, however, that the purpose
for which the act was done was such that it was one of a class
of cases not within the statute, and upon this they ask our
opinion. I do not agree in that conclusion.

Undoubtedly every treatment of an animal which inflicts pain,
even the great pain of mutilation, and which is cruel in the

1877

MURPHY
v.
MANNING.

ordinary sense of the word, is not necessarily within the Act.
Many cases were put in the course of the argument in which it is
clearly not so. Whenever the purpose for which the act is done
is to make the animal more serviceable for the use of man the
statute ought not to be held to apply. As was said by Wightman, J., in *Budge* v. *Parsons* (1), the cruelty intended by the
statute is the *unnecessary* abuse of the animal. Neither cock-
fighting, nor the chance of a prize at an exhibition, is such a
purpose as prevents the word "cruel," as used in the Act, from
applying.

*Case remitted to the magistrates with
this opinion.*

Solicitor for appellant : *Leslie.*

Solicitor for respondents: *Dollman, for Hayward, Rochester.*

SKEET *v.* LINDSAY.

Statute of Limitations—Acknowledgment of Debt—Implied Promise to pay.

The defendant, whose debt to the plaintiff was barred by the Statute of Limitations, wrote to the plaintiff within six years before action the following letter :
"I return to Shepperton about Easter. If you send me there the particulars of
your account with vouchers, I shall have it examined and cheque sent to you for
the amount due; but you must be under some great mistake in supposing that
the amount due to you is anything like the sum you now claim :"—

Held, that the debt was revived, as the request to be furnished with an account
with vouchers at a particular time and place did not negative the implied promise
to pay arising from the admission of a balance due.

DEMURRER to a replication.

The claim was debt for horse hire and hay and straw supplied by
the plaintiff to the defendant in 1868. The defence was the Statute
of Limitations, to which the plaintiff replied that the case was
taken out of the statute by the following note, written by the
defendant within six years of action brought and signed by him :
"Your note and its inclosure have been forwarded to me here.
I return to Shepperton about Easter. If you send me there
the particulars of your account with vouchers, I shall have it

(1) 3 B. & S. 382, at p. 385.

1877

Skelt
v.
Lindsay.

examined and cheque sent to you for the amount due; but you
must be under some great mistake in supposing that the amount
due to you is anything like the sum you now claim."

Demurrer.

Jan. 25. *J. Brown, Q.C.* (*A. L. Smith* with him), for the defendant. The letter shews nothing more than that the defendant was
willing to pay conditionally, but the condition has not been performed. [He referred to *Smith* v. *Thorne* (1); *Chasemore* v.
Turner (2); *In re River Steamer Co., Mitchell's Claim* (3); *Hales*
v. *Stevenson* (4); *Quincey* v. *Sharpe* (5).]

J. O. Griffits, Q.C. (*Wilberforce* with him), for the plaintiff. The
whole of the letter must be taken together, and it shews an admission of an outstanding account, which raises an inference of a
promise to pay. To this promise the request to be furnished with
vouchers is not a condition, but only suggests a mode of arriving at
the balance. [He referred to *Prance* v. *Sympson* (6); *Sidwell* v.
Mason (7); *Colledge* v. *Horn* (8); *Gardner* v. *M'Mahon* (9).]

J. Brown, Q.C., in reply.

Cur adv. vult.

Jan. 30. CLEASBY, B., read the following judgment. This case
was argued before me. The only question is whether a particular
letter set out in the reply is such an acknowledgment of a debt as
takes the case out of the operation of the Statute of Limitations.
In the excellent argument which took place before me the only
question argued was that to which the case is properly reduced.
That question was whether, coupled with an absolute acknowledgment of a debt, there is in the present case such a conditional
promise to pay as negatives the promise which would be implied
from an absolute acknowledgment of a debt taken by itself.

It was very properly not contested that an absolute acknowledgment of a balance has the same effect, so far as the present
question is concerned, as the acknowledgment of a particular sum.
It was also not contested that it is settled conclusively by the

(1) 18 Q. B. 134.
(2) Law Rep. 10 Q. B. 500.
(3) Law Rep. 6 Ch. 822.
(4) 7 L. T. (N.S.) 317; 8 L. T.
(N.S.) 798.
(5) 1 Ex. D. 72.
(6) Kay, 678.
(7) 2 H. & N. 306; 26 L. J. (Ex.) 407.
(8) 3 Bing. 119.
(9) 3 Q. B. 561.

1877

SKEET
v.
LINDSAY.

authorities on the subject, beginning with *Tanner* v. *Smart* (1), that an absolute acknowledgment of the debt by itself is sufficient, because you may imply from it an unconditional promise to pay the debt, but an absolute acknowledgment of the debt coupled with anything which shewed that the debtor only promised to pay it on a particular event happening, or a particular condition being performed, is not sufficient to revive the original debt payable on request.

The law on the subject is most clearly summed up by Mellish, L.J., *In re River Steamer Co.*, *Mitchell's Claim* (2): "There must be one of these three things to take the case out of the statute. Either there must be an acknowledgment of the debt, from which a promise to pay is to be implied, or secondly, there must be an unconditional promise to pay the debt, or thirdly, there must be a conditional promise to pay the debt, and evidence that the condition has been performed."

Many cases have arisen in which the question decided has been whether particular words constituted such a conditional promise as to negative the promise which would be implied from an unqualified acknowledgment. Instances may be put on both sides which would be clear. If the words used were that the debtor would pay if he recovered from an illness and could attend to business, or if he succeeded in a law suit in which he was engaged, such words would import that in those events only a fresh promise to pay was made, and there would be no implied promise to pay on request; but if the words were that he would look over the account and pay when he met his creditor on the next market day, these words would not import that he would only pay in that event, and the original promise would be revived.

Among the cases referred to in the course of the argument are *Hales* v. *Stevenson* (3), *Chasemore* v. *Turner* (4), *Sidwell* v. *Mason* (5), *Gardner* v. *M'Mahon* (6), *Quincey* v. *Sharpe*. (7)

When the question is, what effect is to be given to particular words, little assistance can be derived from the effect given to

(1) 6 B. & C. 603.
(2) Law Rep. 6 Ch. at p. 828.
(3) 7 L. T. (N.S.) 317; 8 L. T. (N.S.) 798.
(4) Law Rep. 10 Q. B. 500.
(5) 2 H. & N. 306; 26 L. J. (Ex.) 407.
(6) 3 Q. B. 561; 26 L. J. (Ex.) 407.
(7) 1 Ex. D. 72.

1877

Skeet
v.
Lindsay.

other words in applying a principle which is admitted. A similar question to the present one was much considered in the above cited case of *Chasemore* v. *Turner* (1) on appeal, where there was difference of opinion among the judges, Lord Coleridge differing from the rest of the Court. But there was no difference as to the rule to be applied. The difference was more as to the meaning of the words used than the legal effect of them, if the meaning was ascertained. The words in that case were, " The old account between us which has been standing over so long has not escaped our memory, and as soon as we can get our affairs arranged we will see you are paid; perhaps, in the meantime, you will let your clerk send me an account of how it stands." It is not surprising that there was a difference of opinion. Lord Coleridge thought those words imported a condition that the affairs were arranged, but the majority of the Court, consisting of five judges, thought that those words did not in any reasonable sense express an intention of the defendant that the plaintiff should not be paid unless the affairs were arranged. They considered that the non-happening of such an event as the arrangement of the affairs was not contemplated, but the happening of that event was assumed, and then a convenient time pointed out for the payment. This case was certainly as near the line as any one which has been so decided, and the judges considered it so.

But the present case appears to me a much clearer one. The words are, " I return to Shepperton about Easter. If you send me there the particulars of your account with vouchers, I shall have it examined and cheque sent to you for the amount due; but you must be under some great mistake in supposing that the amount due to you is anything like the sum you now claim."

The latter part is a clear and absolute acknowledgment of a balance being due. Does the former part upon any reasonable construction import that the balance is only to be paid in case the plaintiff sends to Shepperton (where the defendant was to return about Easter) the particulars with vouchers? Is it not rather a mode of arriving at the correct balance, which the defendant engages absolutely to pay? It appears to me that the latter is the proper effect to be given to it, and that there is not such a

(1) Law Rep. 10 Q. B. 500.

condition imported as to negative the promise to be implied from the absolute acknowledgment.

The learned counsel relied upon the form of the sentence being in express terms a condition commencing with the word " if." But we must, in giving the proper effect to a passage, look not at the form so much as to the substantial meaning of the language.

For the above reasons I think the acknowledgment is sufficient, and the plaintiff entitled to judgment and with costs.

Judgment for the plaintiff.

Solicitors for plaintiff: *Worthington, Evans, & Cook.*
Solicitors for defendant : *Trinders & Curtis Hayward.*

———

Feb. 13.

HAND v. HALL.

Lease—Option to Lessee to continue Holding beyond Three Years—Statute of Frauds (29 Car. 2, c. 3) ss. 1, 2—8 & 9 Vict. c. 106, s. 3.

A lease, not under seal, for an original term of less than three years, whether by parol or in writing, is invalid, if it gives a right to the lessee to continue the holding beyond three years from the making of the lease.

THIS was an action to recover one quarter's rent, alleged to be due under an agreement signed by both the plaintiff and defendant, but not under seal, of which the following is the material portion :—

"1876. Jan. 26.

"Memorandum.—Samuel Hand agrees to let, and John William Hall agrees to take the Large Room on the south end of the Exchange, Wolverhampton, from the 14th day of February, next, until the following Midsummer twelve months, and with right at end of that term for the tenant, by a month's previous notice, to remain on for three years and a half more. The rent for such term (original or renewed) to be at the rate of 120*l.* a year."

The defendant did not enter under this agreement, which contained other terms on which questions were raised to which it is not necessary to refer. At the trial before Brett, J., at the Staffordshire Summer Assizes, 1876, it was admitted that if the defendant was liable, a quarter's rent was due, and, thereupon,

judgment was entered for the plaintiff, leave being reserved to
move to set it aside, and enter judgment for the defendant.

Feb. 13. *H. Matthews, Q.C.,* and *Baldock Stone,* moved accordingly. They contended first that this was an agreement for a
lease, and not itself a lease, and that as no possession had been
taken under it, an action for rent would not lie; and secondly,
that if the memorandum was a lease it gave the tenant a right to
a term of more than three years, and not being by deed was
invalid.

J. J. Powell, Q.C. (*Underhill* with him), for the plaintiff, contended that the memorandum was a lease for a term not exceeding three years from the making thereof, and was within the exception of s. 2 of the Statute of Frauds.

H. Matthews, Q.C., in reply.

Cur. adv. vult.

Feb. 15. The judgment of the Court (Cleasby and Pollock, BB.)
was delivered by

CLEASBY, B. This action was brought to recover rent under a
lease. The plaintiff and defendant had both executed a document
not under seal purporting to be a lease. There had been no
occupation under it, but the time for payment of a quarter's rent
had expired.

There were two defences: one on the document itself, and the
other on matter extrinsic: first, that by the effect of the Statute
of Frauds and the Statute 8 & 9 Vict. c. 106, s. 3, it was not a
valid lease; second, that the plaintiff, who was himself a lessee,
had no title to grant the lease intended, and that the defendant,
before entry and before commencement of the intended term,
avoided the lease on that ground.

The question which arises on the first defence set up is, whether
the lease which was signed is a lease not exceeding three years.
If it is a lease not exceeding three years, then no writing was
necessary to make it valid, and the statute does not apply. But
if it exceeded three years, then it is not within the 2nd section of
the Statute of Frauds, a writing was necessary under the 1st
section, and a deed is now necessary.

We have, therefore, to construe the lease in question. No

authority was cited to us upon this part of the case, and we are aware of none from which we can derive much assistance. The conclusion, however, we have arrived at is that we cannot consider this as a lease not exceeding three years. A lease not exceeding three years, in our opinion, must be a lease not giving a right (independent of the lessor) exceeding three years. We think a demise for three years, and for three years longer, at the option of the lessee, could not be said to be a lease not exceeding three years, and would not be valid if by parol only.

It is true that in the present case the lease is not in the above terms, but the tenant acquires under it a right at his own option by a month's notice to continue it on. If that is given the tenant still holds under the original demise—there is no further act of the lessor.

The question decided in the present case appears to be a technical one, viz., that a deed is necessary where there is a writing. But we are bound to give effect to the objection, because we are in effect deciding to what extent a lease by parol only is binding, a question affecting the title to property to a considerable extent.

The case of *Crosby* v. *Wadsworth* (1) is so different from the present that it cannot be referred to as an authority; but Lord Ellenborough's language, in speaking of the 1st and 2nd sections of the Statute of Frauds, is deserving of notice. He says (p. 610): "The leases, &c., meant to be vacated by the 1st section must be understood as leases of the like kind with those in the 2nd, but which conveyed a larger interest to the party than for a term of three years." In the present case a larger interest was conveyed than for a term of three years.

The above conclusion makes it unnecessary to consider the other question, because, in our opinion, the foundation of the plaintiff's claim for rent fails, and there must be judgment for the defendant.

Judgment for the defendant.

Solicitors for plaintiff: *Gregory, Rowcliffes, & Rawle, for Manby,* Wolverhampton.

Solicitors for defendant: *Pickett & Mytton, for T. W. Hall,* Bilston.

(1) 6 East, 602.

1877
Jan. 30.

BROADHEAD v. HOLDSWORTH.

Vaccination—Certificate that Child has had Smallpox—Vaccination Act, 1871
(34 & 35 Vict. c. 98), ss. 7, 15.

By the Vaccination Act, 1871, s. 7, every certificate of a child being unfit for, or insusceptible of, successful vaccination shall be transmitted to the vaccination officer under a penalty on failure to do so. The Poor Law Board, under the authority of s. 15 of the Act, issued a form of certificate expressed in the alternative, either that the child had been not less than three times unsuccessfully vaccinated and was insusceptible of vaccination, or that the child had already had smallpox :—

Held, that a parent to whom a certificate that the child had already had smallpox was given, and who failed to forward it to the vaccination officer, was not liable under s. 7.

CASE stated by justices for the borough of Huddersfield, in the West Riding of the county of York.

On the 2nd of June, 1876, the appellant laid an information under 30 & 31 Vict. c. 84, s. 31 (1), that he had reason to believe that a child under the age of fourteen years, residing within the Huddersfield Poor Law Union, had not been successfully vaccinated ; that he had duly given the respondent, as the father of the child, notice to procure its being vaccinated, and that such notice had been disregarded.

(1) 30 & 31 Vict. c. 84, s. 31: "If any registrar or any officer appointed by the guardians to enforce the provisions of this Act shall give information in writing to a justice of the peace that he has reason to believe that any child under the age of fourteen years, being within the union or parish for which the informant acts, has not been successfully vaccinated, and that he has given notice to the parent or person having the custody of such child to procure its being vaccinated, and that this notice has been disregarded, the justice may summon such parent or person to appear with the child before him at a certain time and place, and upon the appearance, if the justice shall find, after such examination as he shall deem necessary, that the child has not been vaccinated, nor has already had the smallpox, he may, if he see fit, make an order under his hand and seal directing such child to be vaccinated within a certain time; and if at the expiration of such time the child shall not have been so vaccinated, or shall not be shewn to be then unfit to be vaccinated, or to be insusceptible of vaccination, the person upon whom such order shall have been made shall be proceeded against summarily, and unless he can shew some reasonable ground for his omission to carry the order into effect, shall be liable to a penalty not exceeding twenty shillings."

Upon the hearing it was proved by the respondent that his child had then already had the smallpox, and the justices thereupon discharged the respondent.

It was, however, contended on behalf of the appellant that although the defendant had not been found guilty of the offence of not taking or causing to be taken his child to be vaccinated, he was yet guilty of an offence by not transmitting a certificate of the fact of such child having had the smallpox according to form "C," in the schedule to the general order of the Local Government Board issued on the 30th day of November, 1871, and the appellant sought to have the respondent convicted upon the ground of the non-transmission of such a certificate, relying upon the 4th paragraph of 34 & 35 Vict. c. 98, s. 11 (the Vaccination Act, 1871). (1)

The justices were of opinion that in point of law the respondent was not required, either by the principal or the amending Act, to transmit a certificate of the fact of his child having had smallpox, since s. 7 of 34 & 35 Vict. c. 98 only requires certificates of a child being "unfit for, or insusceptible of, successful vaccination" to be transmitted by the parent to the vaccination officer, and does not in terms extend to the case of a child having had smallpox, and that as the penalty is imposed upon those only who act in contravention of the last-mentioned section, the respondent was not guilty of any offence. (2)   They, therefore, ordered him to be discharged.

(1) 34 & 35 Vict. c. 98, s. 11: "Where a person is charged with the offence of neglecting to take or cause to be taken any child to be vaccinated, and on the defence made by such person it appears to the justices having cognizance of the case that such person is not guilty of such offence, but has been guilty of the offence of not transmitting any certificate required by the principal Act or this Act with respect to the vaccination of such child, the justices may convict such person of the last-mentioned offence in like manner as if he had been charged therewith."

(2) 34 & 35 Vict. c. 98, s. 7: "Every certificate of a child being unfit for or insusceptible of successful vaccination, if given by a public vaccinator, shall, instead of being delivered by him to the parent, be transmitted by such public vaccinator, and if given by any other medical practitioner shall be transmitted by the parent of such child to the vaccination officer, in like manner as if it was a certificate of successful vaccination. . . . Every person who acts in contravention of or fails to comply with any provision of this section shall be liable on summary conviction to a penalty not exceeding twenty shillings. . . ."

The question of law arising was, whether the justices were right in deciding that the Vaccination Acts did not impose any penalty upon persons who fail to transmit to the vaccination officer a certificate of a child having had smallpox.

Sir H. S. Giffard, S.G. (*S. Romilly* with him), for the appellant. The object of the Acts is that all certificates should be forwarded to the proper officer for registration, and the power given to the Poor Law Board, by s. 15 of the Vaccination Act, 1871, to alter the forms formerly in use, under which the respondent would have been liable, cannot be taken to override this.

Poland, for the respondent. The decision of the justices is correct, and the respondent cannot be convicted under s. 7 for not sending a certificate that he does not possess. [He was then stopped.]

CLEASBY, B. I think our judgment should be for the respondent. It seems to me that the legislation on this point is imperfect, and that this is a *casus omissus,* which we cannot supply in an enactment creating an offence. The principal thing to look at is s. 7 of 34 & 35 Vict. c. 98, in order to see what the real meaning of the words is, where we find it enacted that every certificate of a child being unfit for or insusceptible of vaccination is to be forwarded to the vaccination officer. The certificate to this effect is to be transmitted by the parent to the officer. There is a peculiarity in this respect, that there was a form given in the schedule to the former Act of Parliament (1) which made the certificate of having had smallpox conclude with the words, "and I am of opinion that such child is insusceptible of successful vaccination." There might be a difficulty in this conclusion, and power was given to the Poor Law Board to alter the forms. When we look at the alteration, there seems to be no doubt in the case. The place where the alteration is to come in is indicated by a figure, referring to a note in the margin in the form C, which is now before me, issued by the Poor Law Board. The concluding part of that form runs thus, "(has been   times unsuccessfully vaccinated by me, and is in my opinion insusceptible of successful

(1) The Vaccination Act, 1867 (30 & 31 Vict. c. 84).

vaccination), *or* (has already had smallpox)," and the note in the margin is, " strike out the words which do not apply to the case." There must be a certificate in one form or the other, either that the child is insusceptible of successful vaccination by reason of not less than three trials having been made to vaccinate it, or else that the child has had the smallpox. The latter certificate, which rightly omits the insusceptibility to vaccination, we are asked to include in the 7th section by extending its construction. The respondent has not such a certificate as that mentioned in s. 7, but something quite different, and that being so, he cannot be punished for not transmitting that which he has not.

POLLOCK, B.   I am of the same opinion.

Judgment for the respondent.

Solicitors for appellant: *Shum, Crossman, & Crossman, for John Sykes & Son, Huddersfield.*

Solicitors for respondent: *Layton & Jaques, for Mills & Bilby, Huddersfield.*

STAPLES *v.* YOUNG.

Costs—County Court Act, 1867, *s.* 5—*Judicature Act,* 1873, *s* 67, *Order XIX., Rule* 3, *Order LV.*

In an action tried by a jury, in which the plaintiff proves a claim but a counter-claim of less amount is proved by the defendant, the plaintiff recovers judgment for the balance only, and if no order as to costs is made, the plaintiff's right to costs under the County Court Act, 1867, and Order LV. of the Judicature Acts, must be decided with reference to that balance, and not to the amount of the claim proved.

THIS was an action for the balance of purchase-money on the sale of the good-will and stock of a business, in which the plaintiff claimed 26l. 13s. The defendant set up a set-off and counter-claim for money expended by him in repairs, on an agreement that the plaintiff should repay him, and for unliquidated damages for breach of a representation amounting to a warranty by the plaintiff on the sale of the business, with regard to the average gross receipts. The plaintiff replied, denying the case set up in defence.

At the trial before Grove, J., the jury found that the balance claimed by the plaintiff was due; they also found the allegations of the counter-claim proved, and assessed the sum due to the defendant for the work done at 3*l.* 1*s.* 6*d.*, and the sum due to him on the claim for unliquidated damages at 20*l.* On these findings the learned judge directed the judgment " to be entered accordingly," and declined to make any order as to costs.

The plaintiff applied to a master at Chambers to have his costs taxed against the defendant, which was refused, and on appeal to a judge at Chambers the order of the master was confirmed. This was an appeal from the judge's decision.

C. Dodd, for the plaintiff, contended that he was entitled to his costs from the defendant. The judgment was entered for 26*l.* 13*s.* for the plaintiff, and for 23*l.* 1*s.* 6*d.* for the defendant, and the plaintiff has recovered the former amount, and no certificate under the County Court Act, 1867, is required. The counter-claim is in the nature of a cross action. Admitting that a liquidated set-off must be deducted in estimating what amount a plaintiff recovers, there would be a hardship in so doing in the case of an unliquidated debt, because the plaintiff cannot know the amount that will be recovered against him, and therefore cannot tell whether he ought to bring his action in the superior court or not. At all events, the Court should now give a certificate under Order LV.

R. V. Williams. Order XIX., Rule 3, deals with set-off and counter-claim on the same footing, and so does Order XXIL, Rule 10, which directs that if the balance is in favour of the defendant, the Court may give him judgment. By Order LV., in default of direction by the judge or Court, the costs follow the event, but that must be taken with the limitations produced by the reservation in s. 67 of the Judicature Act, 1873, of the sections of the County Court Act, 1867, applying to costs. It cannot be that both plaintiff and defendant get judgments—one or other must recover the balance which is in his favour.

C. Dodd, in reply.

CLEASBY, B. .It appears to me that the order should stand. The jury have found in favour of the plaintiff on his claim, and in favour of the defendant on his counter-claim, and the learned judge who tried the cause has directed judgment to be entered accordingly. The question arises, What has the plaintiff recovered

in his action within the meaning of the County Court Act, 1867,
s. 5? The words of the Act deprive the plaintiff in a superior
court of his costs of suit "if he shall recover a sum not exceeding twenty pounds" in an action founded on contract, unless
he obtains a certificate. By Order XIX., Rule 3, a defendant
may set off or set up by way of counter-claim any right or claim,
whether such set-off or counter-claim sound in damages or not;
and such set off or counter-claim shall have the same effect as a
statement of claim in a cross action, so as to enable the Court to
pronounce a final judgment in the same action, both on the original and on the cross claim; and then by Order XXII., Rule 10,
from which we may derive some assistance, the defendant, if the
balance is in his favour, may have judgment for such balance.
Can we say here, looking at those rules, that the plaintiff has
recovered the full amount of the claim that he proved, and that
the defendant has recovered the amount of the counter-claim that
he set up, or must we say that the plaintiff has recovered the
balance? It seems to me that the latter view is the right one,
and that by it only can we give to the counter-claim the same
effect as to a statement of claim in a cross action and give a final
judgment on both the original and cross claim. The intention
and words of the rules are, that the final judgment is to be founded
on the result of both original and cross claim taken together and
treated as arising in the same action. Order XXII., Rule 10,
provides for the opposite case, where the balance is in favour of the
defendant, for in such cases the Court may give judgment for the
defendant for such balance. That judgment would be a judgment
in the action, and the defendant would recover, not in his counter-
claim, but in the action to the extent of the balance. Then we
have to see what is the effect of the provision as to costs in
Order LV. By the Judicature Act, 1873, s. 67, the provisions of
the County Court Acts relating to costs are incorporated. The provision in Order LV. is that in any action or issue tried by a jury,
which clearly includes cases in which a counter-claim is set up
in an action, the costs shall follow the event, unless, upon application made at the trial for good cause shewn, the judge before whom
such action or issue is tried, or the Court, shall otherwise order.
When the Act says that costs shall follow the event, it cannot

mean that in every instance when the successful party gets any sum of money, however small, he shall necessarily have his costs, but that they shall be regulated by the event. This conclusion might operate to produce hardship in case of a claim and a new counter-claim which the plaintiff in commencing his action could not anticipate, in which case, after a long inquiry, he might only recover a small sum, when in commencing his action for a substantial claim he was not aware of the counter-claim, as he would have been aware of a set-off. This, however, is obviated by the discretionary power of the Court or judge to deal with costs. We are asked in this case to exercise that discretionary power. But here, at least, the claim and counter-claim arose out of the same transaction, and I think we should not interfere.

POLLOCK, B. I am of the same opinion. I think it clear that the judge at the trial might have dealt with the costs under Order LV.; but as he has not done so, the question is what is the strict right of the plaintiff? It is clear that set-off was always treated as a reduction of damages, one of the best proofs of this being that the plaintiff, if he so chose, might elect to deduct the set-off and take a verdict for the balance, whereby the defendant would be barred in respect of his claim on the set-off. Then the question is whether, under the Judicature Acts, a counter-claim is to be treated for this purpose as though it were a set-off. The argument is that it should be treated not as though it were merely advanced in reduction of damages, but as a distinct matter, although for motives of convenience and otherwise the two actions are tried together. It seems to me that the intention of the statute with regard to the trial and the result of it in the matter of costs was to place counter-claim and set-off on the same footing. There is one judgment, and that is for the balance; and I think that, inasmuch as the provisions as to costs in actions in which relief could be obtained in the county court are reserved in the Judicature Acts, the plaintiff in this case gets no costs.

Rule refused with costs.

Solicitor for plaintiff: *Miller.*
Solicitors for defendant: *Ingle, Cooper, & Holmes, for H. Howard, Greenwich.*

1877

Feb. 15.

THE MAYOR, &c., OF PENRYN *v.* HOLM.

Duchy of Cornwall—Right to foreshore in Cornwall—Charter of 11 *Edw.* 3—
21 & 22 *Vict. c.* 109.

The charter of 11 Edw. 3, as interpreted by 21 & 22 Vict. c. 109, conveyed to
the Duke of Cornwall all the rights of the Crown in the foreshore of the county of
Cornwall, and not merely the foreshore attached to the manors granted by the
charter.

THIS was an action of trespass and ejectment tried at Bodmin
before Amphlett, B., at the summer assizes, 1876.

It appeared at the trial that the defendant had built a boathouse
on a part of the foreshore of Penryn Harbour, in the county of
Cornwall, from which the plaintiffs sought to eject him as a
trespasser.

The plaintiffs were the mayor, aldermen, and burgesses of
Penryn, and they claimed the foreshore under a conveyance from
the Ecclesiastical Commissioners of England.

The title of the Ecclesiastical Commissioners was twofold.
They claimed, first, as grantees of the foreshore under a conveyance
from the Duke of Cornwall, dated the 18th of July, 1865, which
purported to convey the rights of the Duke of Cornwall to the
foreshore in question; and, secondly, they claimed as successors
and representatives of the See of Exeter, and thus as lords of the
manor of Penryn. The second of these claims depended on
various charters from the Crown to the bishops of Exeter, but the
consideration of this derivative title became immaterial. The
claim through the Duke of Cornwall arose under the charter of
11 Edw. 3, which has the force of an Act of Parliament. (1) By
that charter certain castles, manors, and other things were granted
to Edward the Black Prince, who had recently been created Duke
of Cornwall. Among other things granted were seventeen manors
by name in the county of Cornwall with their appurtenances; the
manor of Penryn not being one of those named. There was
further granted "all the profits of our ports, within the same

(1) See preface to the *Prince's Case,*   of *Rowe* v. *Brenton·* a translation of the
8 Co. Rep. 1, and see also 3 M. & R.   charter is set out at length.
474, where in an Appendix to the case

county of Cornwall, to us belonging, together with wreck of the
sea, as well of whales and sturgeon and other fishes which do
belong to us by reason of our prerogative, as whatsoever other
things belong to such wreck of the sea, with the appurtenances in
all our said county of Cornwall." (1)

Some years back questions arose between the Crown and the
duchy of Cornwall as to whether the mines and minerals lying
under the seashore between high and low water marks within the
county of Cornwall, and under the estuaries and tidal rivers
within the same county, and under the open sea below low water
mark, adjacent to but not in or part of the same county, were
respectively the property of Her Majesty the Queen in right of
her Crown, or of the Prince of Wales in right of his duchy of
Cornwall, and such questions were referred to Sir John Patteson.
The statute 21 & 22 Vict. c. 109 was passed to give effect to the
award made in pursuance of this reference. By that statute, by
sects. 1 and 2, it is enacted and declared that minerals under the
seashore between high and low water marks in Cornwall are, as
between the Queen and the Prince of Wales, vested in the latter
"in right of the duchy of Cornwall as part of the soil and territorial possessions of the said duchy," and that minerals below
low water mark under the open sea adjacent to, but not part of,
Cornwall are vested in the Queen in right of her Crown as part of
the soil and territorial possessions of the Crown, and by sect. 3
Her Majesty and her lessees are to have liberty to work such last-
mentioned minerals through the lands of the duchy, and by sect. 9
the rights of all other persons are reserved.

The Ecclesiastical Commissioners claiming the foreshore of the
harbour of Penryn as lords of the manor and representing the
See of Exeter, obtained (to prevent disputes) from the duchy a
grant, as above-mentioned, of that foreshore amongst other things,
and they granted it to the mayor, aldermen, and burgesses of
Penryn.

The defendant set up no title in himself, and the learned judge
being of opinion that the claim of the plaintiffs through the duchy
was made out, directed a verdict for the plaintiffs, reserving to the
defendant leave to move to set aside this verdict and enter it for

(1) Quoted from 3 M. & R. at p. 477.

MAYOR OF
PENRYN
v.
HOLM.

himself, on the ground that the plaintiffs had failed to make out
their title.

Feb. 10. *Kingdon, Q.C.*, moved accordingly. He contended
that the charter of Edward III. had only conveyed to the Duke
of Cornwall the manors named in it, and the rights appurtenant
to them and the royal prerogatives in relation to them, and that it
was not intended to pass all the prerogatives of the Crown within
the county. The grant of a manor with wreck of the sea may
pass the foreshore attached to that manor: *Attorney-General* v.
Jones (1), but cannot do more. The statute 21 & 22 Vict. c. 109,
goes no further, and must be construed as applying only to the
manors named in the charter, and the words in the statute shewing that the Duke of Cornwall held the minerals " as part of the
soil " confirm this view.

C. Vivian (with him *A. Charles* and *Hugh Neville*), for the
plaintiffs. The words relating to the prerogatives of the Crown
in the charter are perfectly general, and cannot be cut down as
suggested. The statute is declaratory, and puts a wide construction on the charter, declaring that the foreshore belongs to the
Duke of Cornwall "as part of the soil and territorial possessions
of the duchy." This construction is confirmed by the fact that
the statute gives rights of access to the Crown to work the mines
below low water mark, which would not have been necessary had
the foreshore been vested in the Crown.

. *Kingdon, Q.C.*, in reply.

Cur. adv. vult.

Feb. 15. The judgment of the Court (Cleasby and Pollock, BB.)
was delivered by

CLEASBY, B. We had brought before us in this case a question
of a very general nature, which it seems has never formed the
subject of discussion before.

The defendant had taken possession of a small piece of land on
the foreshore of a creek of the sea, adjoining the parish of Budock
in the county of Cornwall. The claimants who derive title from
the duchy of Cornwall brought the present action to dispossess

(1) 2 H. & C. 347 ; 33 L. J. (Ex.) 249.

him, and the defendant set up the defence that nothing had taken place to deprive the Crown of its prima facie ownership, and vest it in the Duke of Cornwall. There can be no question that the ownership of the foreshore is prima facie in the Crown, and the case for the plaintiffs was rested upon this, that by the effect of the charter, or Act of Edward III., creating the duchy, and an Act of 21 & 22 Vict. c. 109, the right of the Crown was transferred to the Duke of Cornwall. The charter, or Act of Edward III., is set out at length in the *Prince's Case* (1), in which it was decided that this charter had all the effect of an Act of Parliament. Certain manors, seventeen in number, are assigned to the duchy, and there then follow words of a very general and comprehensive nature as follows :—" Also the profits of all the ports within the same our county of Cornwall to us belonging, together with wreck of the sea, as well of whales and sturgeon and other fishes which do belong to us by reason of our prerogative, and whatsoever belongs to any wreck of the sea, with the appurtenances in our said county of Cornwall." (2) The land in question is not within the specified manors.

Now upon the above words, which give such extensive rights, including wreck of the sea, over the whole duchy, a question might, no doubt, be raised whether they could have the effect of passing the whole foreshore of the duchy, and if the question turned wholly upon the construction of this charter, whatever evidence of uniform enjoyment or of other relevant matters was produced, there still might remain a difficulty. But the Act of Parliament referred to was passed for the express purpose of putting an end to any dispute between the Crown and the duchy regarding the foreshore within the duchy. It begins by reciting that questions had arisen inter alia as to whether the mines and minerals lying under the seashore, between high and low water marks, within the county of Cornwall, were the property of Her Majesty in right of her Crown, or of the Prince of Wales in right of his duchy of Cornwall, and that such questions had been referred to Sir John Patteson for his decision. It then recites that Sir John Patteson had decided that the right to all mines and minerals lying under the seashore between high and low water

(1) 8 Co. Rep. 1.   (2) Quoted from 8 Co. Rep. 8 b.

marks was vested in the Prince, as part of the soil and territorial possessions of the duchy. It further recited that it was intended that a bill should be submitted to parliament for the purpose of obtaining the sanction and ratification of the said reference and award. The recitals have only been referred to so far as they relate to the right in question. We have then by clause 1 the following enactment so far as it relates to the same right: " That all mines and minerals lying under the seashore between high and low water marks, within the said county of Cornwall, and under estuaries and tidal rivers and other places (below high water mark), even below low water mark, being in and part of the said county, are, as between the Queen's Majesty in right of her Crown on the one hand, and His Royal Highness Albert Edward, Prince of Wales and Duke of Cornwall, in right of his duchy of Cornwall, on the other hand, vested in his said Royal Highness Albert Edward, Prince of Wales and Duke of Cornwall, in right of the duchy of Cornwall as part of the soil and territorial possessions of the said duchy." The argument of the learned counsel for the defendant was that this enactment could not be construed to vest the whole foreshore of Cornwall in the duchy, but must be limited in its operation to the foreshore adjoining those manors which had been made his property by the charter. It might possibly have been reasonable so to limit the reference and award and enactment, but throughout the subject-matter is, "the seashore between high and low water marks within the county of Cornwall." It is impossible to cut down such clear words as those of the award, namely, "all mines and minerals lying under the seashore between high and low water marks within the county of Cornwall," and make them signify a certain portion in connection with certain manors. There is really no reason for doing so, as the duke had clearly other rights, such as wreck of the sea, extending over the whole county. The 1st section deals only with the mines and minerals under the foreshore, but by the 8th section, which is an interpretation clause, mines and minerals are to comprehend all sub-strata and the soil under which they are, so that they include the foreshore.

The decision rests upon this: the prima facie title to the foreshore everywhere is in the Crown. The effect of the charter and the Act of Parliament is to transfer the title to the Duke of Cornwall of the foreshore in the county of Cornwall. The plaintiffs claim under the duchy of Cornwall, and therefore establish a primâ facie case, and the defendant has no answer. Resting, therefore, on the primâ facie case, the consequence is that the action was maintainable, and the judgment will be for the plaintiffs.

1877
MAYOR OF
PENRYN
v.
HOLM.

Judgment for the plaintiffs.

Solicitors for plaintiffs: *Gregory, Rowcliffes, & Rawle, for G. A. Jenkins, Penryn.*

Solicitors for defendants: *Harris & Powell, for R. Dobell, jun., Truro.*

[IN THE COURT OF APPEAL.]

March 7.

HOLLOWAY *v.* YORK.

Practice—Transfer of Action to Chancery Division—Rules of Court—
Order LI., rule 2.

W. contracted to purchase a property, and paid a deposit. He afterwards gave notice to rescind the contract on the ground of the vendor's delay in making out a title, after which he took proceedings for the liquidation of his affairs. His trustee commenced an action in the Exchequer Division against the vendor for a return of the deposit, and for damages. The vendor delivered a counter-claim for specific performance, insisting that there had not been any such delay as to entitle the purchaser to rescind :—

Held, reversing the decision of the Exchequer Division, that as there was a question to be tried, which was not a question for a jury, and if the vendor succeeded upon it he would be entitled to relief, for giving which the Chancery Division alone had the requisite machinery, the action ought to be transferred to that Division.

J. H. WILSON agreed to buy from the defendant York a certain freehold property for 500*l.*, and paid him a deposit of 30*l.*

Wilson afterwards took proceedings for the liquidation of his affairs by arrangement, and Holloway, his trustee, commenced an action in the Exchequer Division to recover the deposit and damages. The statement of claim alleged that all conditions were performed, and that all things were done and happened, and that all times elapsed to entitle Wilson to have a title made out to the property pursuant to the agreement. That the defendant did not make out, and was unable to make out a title; that Wilson therefore became entitled to rescind, and did rescind the agreement, and became entitled to have the deposit returned. The plaintiff claimed the deposit and the expenses of investigating the title.

The defendant, in his statement of defence, stated, by way of counter-claim, that he had delivered an abstract of title; that requisitions had been made which he answered. That on the 10th of April, 1876, Wilson sent in further requisitions, one of which was for evidence of the death of a person who died in America, with a notice at the foot that if the requisitions were not satisfied within six weeks the purchaser would rescind, and that on the 26th of May, the evidence not having been furnished, the plaintiff's solicitors gave notice to the defendant that the contract was at an end. That the defendant used all diligence in procuring the evidence, procured it by the latter part of September, 1876, and on the 27th gave the plaintiff notice, but plaintiff refused to complete. The defendant claimed to have the contract specifically performed, and for that purpose to have the action transferred to the Chancery Division.

The defendant took out a summons to have the action transferred to the Chancery Division. Huddleston, B., refused to make any order, and this decision was affirmed by the Exchequer Division. The defendant appealed.

C. Herbert Smith, for the defendant. This case is governed by *Hillman* v. *Mayhew.* (1) The defendant wants the remedies which the Chancery Division only can give, a resale at the purchaser's expense, with liberty to prove against his estate for the deficiency.

Warton, for the plaintiff. The purchaser is entitled to recover his deposit: *Moeser* v. *Wisker* (2); the vendor having been guilty of such default as entitled him to rescind, and there is no case for specific performance. The plaintiff wishes for a jury, and the case can be best tried where it is.

MELLISH, L.J. There is a question to be tried which is a question of equity, and not a matter for a jury. If the vendor succeeds on the trial of this question the Chancery Division is the only one that has the requisite machinery for giving him the

(1) 1 Ex. D. 132.   (2) Law Rep. 6 C. P. 120.

relief to which he will be entitled. I am of opinion that the action ought to be transferred.

JESSEL, M.R. I am of the same opinion, and for the same reasons.

, BAGGALLAY, L.J., concurred.

Decision reversed.

Solicitor for plaintiff: *J. J. Rae.*
Solicitor for defendant: *W. C. Smith.*

[IN THE COURT OF APPEAL.]

BLAKE, APPELLANT; BEECH, RESPONDENT.

Practice—Appeal in Criminal Matter—Judicature Act, 1873 (36 & 37 *Vict.* c. 66), *s.* 47.

A judgment of the Court of Appeal from Inferior Courts, against the validity of a conviction, under 16 & 17 Vict. c. 119, s. 3, for keeping a common gaming-house, on a case stated under 20 & 21 Vict. c. 43, is a judgment of the High Court in a criminal matter from which, by s. 47 of the Judicature Act, 1873, there is no appeal.

THE COURT OF APPEAL from Inferior Courts gave judgment in favour of the appellant on an appeal against a conviction, in a penalty under 16 & 17 Vict. c. 119, s. 3, for keeping a common gaming-house, on a case stated under 20 & 21 Vict. c. 43 (see 1 Ex. D. 320). The respondent obtained leave to appeal, and the appeal was brought before the Judicature Amendment Act of 1876 was passed.

R. G. Arbuthnot for the respondent, in support of the appeal. It is disputed whether the appeal in cases like this is not taken away by s. 47 of the Judicature Act, 1873. In *Howes* v. *Board of Inland Revenue* (1), the appeal was heard, but not in *Reg.* v. *Steel* (2), and *Reg.* v. *Fletcher.* (3) This is a penal, but is not a criminal matter, and the respondent has leave to appeal; nor is this a case in which the judgment is final, so that the right of appeal would not be

_____

(1) 1 Ex. D. 385.   (2) 2 Q. B. D. 37.

(3) 2 Q. B. D. 43.

1877

BLAKE

v.

BEECH.

taken away by s. 20 of the Act of 1876 (39 & 40 Vict. c. 59), supposing that Act to apply to an appeal brought before it passed.

Baylis, Q.C., and *T. W. Wheeler,* for the appellant, were not
called upon.

LORD COLERIDGE, C.J. Without pronouncing any opinion upon
the second point, it is clear that we have no jurisdiction in this
case. *Reg.* v. *Fletcher* (1) is exactly in point, that this is a judgment in a criminal matter within s. 47 of the Judicature Act,
1873.

BRAMWELL and BRETT, L.JJ., concurred.

Appeal dismissed.

Solicitors for appellant: *Chester, Urquhart, & Co., for H. M.
Richardson, Bolton.*

Solicitors for respondent: *Gregory & Co., for Hall, Bolton.*

April 26.   WILSON AND ANOTHER *v.* FINCH HATTON.

*Landlord and Tenant—Lease of a Furnished House—Implied Condition of
Fitness for Occupation.*

In an agreement to let a furnished house there is an implied condition that the
house shall be fit for occupation at the time at which the tenancy is to begin, and
if the condition is not fulfilled the lessee is entitled thereupon to rescind the
contract.

The defendant agreed to rent the plaintiffs' furnished house for three months
from the 7th of May, but having at the beginning of the intended tenancy
discovered that the house was, owing to defective drainage, unfit for habitation,
refused to occupy. The plaintiffs repaired the drains, and on the 26th of May
tendered the house in a wholesome condition to the defendant, who refused to
occupy or to pay any rent. The plaintiffs having sued for the rent and for use
and occupation :—

Held, that the state of the house at the beginning of the intended tenancy
entitled the defendant to rescind the contract, and that he was not liable for the
rent or for use and occupation.

Smith v. *Marrable* (11 M. & W. 5; 12 L. J. (Ex.) 223), approved.

THIS was an action to recover the sum of 450 guineas, being the
rent of a furnished house in Wilton Crescent, under an agreement,
by which the defendant agreed to hire the plaintiffs' house from

(1) 2 Q. B. D. 43.

the 7th of May to the 31st of July, 1875. The plaintiffs also claimed the same sum for use and occupation of the house.

The statement of defence alleged that the agreement was made upon the implied condition that the house should be fit for habitation, and that owing to the bad state of the drains, it was not fit on the 7th of May. The occupation was also denied.

At the trial before Quain, J., in Middlesex, at the Hilary Sittings, 1876, it appeared that the defendant, acting for the Dowager Countess of Winchelsea, agreed to take the house from the plaintiffs, who as trustees of a Mrs. Hale, were owners thereof. The agreement contained provisions to the effect that the rent should be paid in two equal instalments, one on the first day and the other on the last day of the tenancy; that the plaintiffs should keep the premises in good substantial repair, and that the defendant should deliver them up at the end of the tenancy in as good a state as he had received them, reasonable wear excepted.

Before the agreement was signed the defendant wrote to the plaintiffs' agent to make inquiries as to the state of the drains. The agent wrote in reply that " Mrs. Hale believes the drainage to be in perfect order."

On Saturday, the 8th May, the tenant's coachman brought her horses to the stable, and she herself arrived from the country with her servants and personal luggage; but as she perceived an unpleasant smell in the house she declined to occupy the house, and had her horses taken out of the stable. A builder examined the house at the request of the tenant on the following Monday, and she then wrote to the plaintiffs' agent to say that she would not occupy the house.

The inspector of nuisances for the district also visited the house on the Monday, and inspected the premises, when he discovered that the drains, which were old brick drains, were much out of repair; that there was a cesspool under the pantry, and a considerable amount of stagnant sewage matter under the basement floor. The defendant thereupon gave notice to the plaintiffs that he should decline to occupy the house at all. The sanitary authorities gave the plaintiffs formal notice to repair the drains, and these repairs having been effected, the house was tendered to the defendant in a wholesome condition on the 26th of May. He, however, declined to enter and occupy, or to pay any rent.

Quain, J., told the jury that there was an implied condition in an agreement for the letting of a furnished house, that it should be fit for occupation, and asked them whether this house was so fit on the 7th of May. The jury answered this question in the negative, and the learned judge entered the verdict for the defendant, leave being reserved to the plaintiffs to move to set aside the verdict and enter it for them, on the ground that there was no implied term or condition that the premises were to be fit for habitation, and further that the premises being put in such a condition by the 26th of May, the plaintiffs were entitled to the rent.

April 26. (1) *J. Brown, Q.C.,* and *Trevelyan,* moved accordingly. In the absence of misrepresentation or fraud the landlord was not bound to inform the tenant of that which he could by inspection discover for himself. The intending lessee of a house does not trust to the lessor's judgment, but inspects it himself, or by his agent. The condition of the premises, therefore, is as much within his knowledge as within that of the lessor, and there is, therefore, no implied covenant such as the defendant wishes to introduce here: *Francis* v. *Cockrell* (2), per Kelly, C.B. The case of hiring a house resembles that of a buyer who inspects goods, and buys them on his own judgment, in which case there is no implied warranty, according to the first rule laid down in *Jones* v. *Just.* (3) A tenant examines the house and can satisfy himself as to its condition, and make such stipulations as seem necessary: *Keates* v. *Earl Cadogan.* (4) *Smith* v. *Marrable* (5) will be relied on by the defendant, but that case may be distinguished on the ground that the defect was in the furniture, and not in the house; and also, because the agreement in that case did not contain the express provisions that are found here. *Smith* v. *Marrable* (5), however, has been so much doubted even if not overruled, that it cannot now be considered good law. Parke, B., who was a party to the decision, questioned its autho-

---

(1) The motion was originally made on the 10th of May, 1875; but the Court, which then consisted of two judges only, desired that the case should be argued again before three judges.

(2) Law Rep. 5 Q. B. 501, at p. 506.
(3) Law Rep. 3 Q. B. 197, at p. 202.
(4) 10 C. B. 591; 20 L. J. (C.P.) 76.
(5) 11 M. & W. 5; 12 L. J. (Ex.) 223.

rity in giving judgment in *Sutton* v. *Temple* (1), and he also stated in *Hart* v. *Windsor* (2) that the cases on which the decision in *Smith* v. *Marrable* (3) proceeded could not be supported, and were not law. This view is confirmed by the remarks of Coltman, J., in *Surplice* v. *Farnsworth* (4); and the observations of Erle, J., in *Heard* v. *Camplin* (5), shew that he did not consider *Smith* v. *Marrable* (3) to be good law. It was clearly stated by the Court in *Searle* v. *Laverick* (6) that in the ordinary case of lessor and lessee there is no implied covenant that the building shall be fit for the purpose for which it is let. The American cases confirm the authority of the decisions in *Sutton* v. *Temple* (1) and *Hart* v. *Windsor* (2), and shew that the defendant is, at all events, bound to pay the rent claimed, and to bring a cross action to recover the damages, if any, caused by the plaintiffs' default: *Westlake* v. *De Graw* (7); *Dutton* v. *Gerrish* (8); *Foster* v. *Peyser* (9); *McGlashan* v. *Tallmadge.* (10) The Irish case of *Murray* v. *Mace* (11) is to the same effect. Even if it could be said that in some cases there might be an implied covenant, that contention is excluded here by the fact that there is in this agreement an express covenant by the plaintiffs to keep the premises in repair, so that all implied covenants are excluded: *Line* v. *Stephenson* (12): for by the terms of such a covenant the plaintiffs would be bound to put them into repair: *Payne* v. *Haine.* (13) Moreover, if there was an implied condition such as the defendant contends for, it is not more than a covenant, and it is not a condition precedent, so that it does not go to the whole consideration for the agreement, and does not give the defendant a right to rescind the contract, but only to sue for damages, or to recover the expenses which have been caused by the breach of the covenant, according to the well known rule in *Pordage* v. *Cole.* (14)

(1) 12 M. & W. 52; 13 L. J. (Ex.) 17.

(2) 12 M. & W. 68; 13 L. J. (Ex.) 129.

(3) 11 M. & W. 5; 12 L. J. (Ex.) 223.

(4) 8 Scott, N. R. 307, at p. 316; 13 L. J. (C.P.) 215.

(5) 15 L. T. (O. S.) 437.

(6) Law Rep. 9 Q. B. 122, at p. 131.

(7) 25 Wendell, 669.

(8) 63 Massachusetts, 89.

(9) 63 Massachusetts, 243.

(10) 37 Barbour, 313.

(11) Ir. Rep. 8 C. L. 396.

(12) 4 Bing. N. C. 678; 7 L. J. (C.P.) 263.

(13) 16 M. & W. 541; 16 L. J. (Ex.) 130.

(14) 1 Wms. Saund. p. 320, c.

A. L. Smith (with him *McIntyre, Q.C.*), for the defendant. The rule as to warranties which are implied by law is well expressed in *Redhead* v. *Midland Ry. Co.* (1) by M. Smith, J., who says that they are founded on the presumed intention of the parties to the contract. The cases cited for the plaintiffs may be distinguished on the broad ground that they relate to demises of real property, and therefore they do not overrule *Smith* v. *Marrable.* (2) The tenant did not get what she had bargained for, viz., a habitable house for the whole term. [He was then stopped.]

KELLY, C.B. We have allowed some argument to be addressed to us by the counsel for the defendant, not because we entertained any real doubt upon the question raised in this case, but because of the general importance of the points involved, and because of the comments which have been made at various times on the law as laid down in the case of *Smith* v. *Marrable.* (2) The question we have to determine is whether, on an agreement of this nature, which is an agreement for the letting and hiring of a house, in what is considered a fashionable district, at a high rent for three months at the height of the season, if the house prove not merely not habitable and not reasonably fit for occupation, but in some respects so unsuitable for the accommodation of those who intend to occupy it, that they could not reside in it, even for one night, without danger to their health, whether, I say, in such a case the hirer of that house is at liberty to consider the agreement at an end, to throw the house up altogether, and to resist all demands for rent. Is there, in short, in an agreement such as this, an implied condition that the house is reasonably fit for habitation, so that the intending tenant can safely enter into his tenancy on the day on which that tenancy begins? In the first place, we shall do well to consider what is in the contemplation of both parties at the time they enter into the contract.

In the case now before us, a lady, who generally resides in the country, is about to come to town for the season, and she enters into negotiations for the occupation of a house for the season. It is clear that she intends to have immediate possession of the house,

(1) Law Rep. 4 Q. B. 379, at p. 392.   (2) 11 M. & W. 5; 12 L. J. (Ex.) 223.

1877

WILSON

v.

FINCH

HATTON.

for she sends her carriage and horses into the stable, some of her servants arrive, and she herself comes to the house with a considerable quantity of personal luggage on the very day on which her tenancy began. It is, therefore, abundantly clear that it was in the contemplation of both parties that the house should be ready for her entry and for occupation by her.

I now proceed to consider whether both parties to this agreement intended that the house should be fit for occupation, that is, that it should be reasonably healthy, and so not dangerous to the life of those inhabiting it. I think that it is quite manifest that they did so intend; and, indeed, one of the letters of the lady who intended to occupy the house (and she is practically the defendant) mentions the subject of drainage. Is it not, then, clear, that the tenant is entitled to find the drains in such a condition that she and her family and servants can safely enter and live in the house? However, on the contrary, when she entered she found that there were strong and noisome odours in the house, and that there was, under the rooms in the basement, a deposit of filth and fœcal substance, which it was absolutely necessary to remove before the house could be safely occupied by any one. Without doubt, a person who so enters under such an agreement as this on furnished premises in the condition just described may at once throw up the lease and decline to pay any rent under it. Can it be that the lessee would be bound to give notice of the defects in the house to the lessor, and then to procure another temporary residence, and wait there until the lessor had completed the alterations necessary to render the house healthy? I am of opinion that if such were the law of England it is time that it should be altered; but the law is not so, and the principle on which the true law rests is plain. For in a case such as the present, the lessee does not get that for which she contracted; for if she contracted for a house to be ready for occupation on the 7th of May, and she does not get a house until the 26th, she clearly is offered something substantially different from that which was contracted to be given.

The recent case of *Tully* v. *Howling* (1), which was decided in the Court of Appeal, laid down clearly that where a plaintiff agreed to charter a ship for twelve months, and the owner

(1) 2 Q. B. D. 182.

1877

WILSON
v.
FINCH
HATTON.

was unable to supply a ship until two months after the time agreed on for the commencement of the contract, the charterer was entitled to repudiate the contract, and this on the clear ground that in all contracts which are to be mutually performed, the party who claims the performance must be ready to perform his part of the contract, and cannot compel the other party to take something substantially different from that which was contracted to be given.   The same reason, when applied to the present case, shews clearly that the lessee of this house is entitled to repudiate the lease because she did not get what she contracted for.   The contract was for the use of the house for three months, and what was offered was a house for three weeks less than that time, whereas the lessee was entitled to occupy that house for every hour of the three months.

It is contended on behalf of the plaintiffs, that there is no implied warranty or condition that a furnished house shall be fit for the purpose for which it is let; but all the cases cited are cases of agreements for the letting and hiring of real property.   Now the circumstances in which furnished houses are, and those in which real property is, demised, differ very greatly.   Where real property, such as a house and lands, is taken by a tenant in a state so dilapidated as to require a large expenditure of money to put it into repair, to hold that the contract contained an implied condition that the lessor should put such premises into repair, would be clearly contrary to the intention of the parties.   When, however, a person takes a furnished house for a brief period of time it is clear that he expects to find it reasonably fit for occupation from the very day on which he intends to enter, and the lessor is well aware that this is the view entertained by the tenant.   If indeed this were not so, what limit could be imposed to the time during which the tenant might be kept out of possession, and how long would he have to wait while the value of his tenancy was daily diminishing? It is then said that the tenant in this case could have gone to an hotel, and could have recovered the amount of the expenses there incurred from the plaintiffs; but I am of opinion that she is not to be forced to do this, and to be compelled to sue the plaintiffs as well as to suffer the loss of that for which she had contracted, and for which she would, according to this contention, be paying rent.

With regard to the exclusion of all implied conditions by the express agreement to keep in repair, I think that as there is no express contract here to put the premises into good repair, that argument is not well founded, and that the plaintiffs cannot be entitled to recover on that ground. I may say that, although I was quite prepared to hold on the ground of reason and common sense, that the defendant was not liable in this action, still I listened carefully to the facts of each case cited, in order that I might notice whether any of them were cases of furnished houses; but none of those cited did relate to furnished houses, with the exception of the case of *Smith* v. *Marrable* (1), which is a decision in favour of the defendant, and directly opposed to the contention of the plaintiffs. Now, I am prepared to hold that the law as laid down in that case is good and sound law, and I may add that, although some discussion may have taken place about that case, and although some doubts may have been thrown on the law as there propounded by judges of learning and eminence, still, I have no hesitation in holding that it is an implied condition in the letting of a furnished house, that it shall be reasonably fit for habitation. I am therefore of opinion that, both on the authority of *Smith* v. *Marrable* (1), and on the general principles of law, there is an implied condition that a furnished house shall be in a good and tenantable condition, and reasonably fit for human occupation from the very day on which the tenancy is dated to begin, and that where such a house is in such a condition that there is either great discomfort or danger to health in entering and dwelling in it, then the intending tenant is entitled to repudiate the contract altogether. Consequently, this motion must be refused, and the judgment of the Court must be for the defendant.

POLLOCK, B. If this were the case of an agreement for the letting of real property, the well-established rules of law would apply, and they would force us to hold that the tenant could not succeed in this case; but although in the case of a furnished house many of the incidents which attach to a demise of realty may be applicable, inasmuch as the rent does in a sense, issue out of the realty, still the rent paid for a furnished house such as this

(1) 11 M. & W. 5; 12 L. J. (Ex.) 223.

is not merely rent for the use of the realty, but a sum paid for the accommodation afforded by the use of the house, with all its appurtenances and contents, during the particular period of three months for which it is taken.

This is a contract for the occupation of a house and furniture for a named three months. Looking at the subject-matter, it is clear that such a contract does not come within the rules laid down in the judgment in *Jones* v. *Just* (1); but still some of the incidents of this contract are analogous to those of the cases of the supply of chattels there discussed, and it may therefore be observed that the defect was in this case latent, and that the defendant may be held to have relied with reason on the assurance of the lessors as to the condition of the house.

Apart, however, from authority, it is, I think, clear, that the plaintiffs have not supplied to the tenant that which both parties intended they should supply. The tenant then has done what she was entitled to do, as she repudiated the contract without delay, and she is not to be compelled to enter on the tenancy and then to sue the plaintiffs in a cross action for damages.

The cases which refer to real property do not govern this contract; but *Smith* v. *Marrable* (2) furnishes us with an authority for our decision. In my opinion, that case has been hardly treated, for the judgment has never been overruled, and is now good law. It is true that Parke, B., did rest his own judgment in banc in part on the authorities which relate to demises of real property, and therefore he did in the more recent case of *Hart* v. *Windsor* (3) retract so much of his judgment as was founded on those cases; but the rest of the judgment remains untouched, and the real principle of the case is unassailed, and I think unassailable; for, as is said in the judgment of Lord Abinger (4): "A man who lets a ready-furnished house, surely does so under the implied condition or obligation that the house is in a fit state to be inhabited." It has been assumed, too, that it was the furniture and not the house that was infested; but it would seem that that was not the case, and that the animals were found in both.

(1) Law Rep 3 Q. B. at p. 202.
(2) 11 M. & W. 5; 12 L. J. (Ex.) 223.
(3) 12 M. & W. 68; 13 L. J. (Ex.)
(4) 11 M. & W. at p. 9.
129.

It was next argued that there could be no implied condition or warranty, because there was an express proviso that the premises should be kept in good repair. The answer to that contention is, that the immediate cause of the evil complained of was the sewage matter which had collected under the floor, and not the structural want of repair which led to the leakage, whence the bad smells arose.

Then it was said that this condition is not a condition precedent, but a covenant, and that the case was thus brought within the well known doctrine contained in *Boone* v. *Eyre* (1), and, therefore, as the breach does not go to the whole consideration, it does not entitle the tenant to reject the tenancy in *toto*, but only gives her a remedy on the covenant, and entitles her on entry to bring an action for damages for the delay. The answer to this argument is, I think, the same as the answer to the first part of the plaintiffs' contention, and as the Lord Chief Baron has so fully dealt with that, I do not think it necessary to go over the ground again; for I think it is clear that the tenant was entitled to reject the contract at once, and was not bound to wait until the premises were put into proper repair. I therefore agree that the judgment of the Court must be for the defendant.

HUDDLESTON, B. I am of the same opinion. There was here an agreement made, terms settled, and an entry under that agreement. On first entering the lessee found a state of affairs which the witnesses at the trial described as dangerous to health, and the jury found that the premises were unfit for occupation.

I think it is clear that there is in such a contract as this an implied condition that the furnished house agreed to be let and taken shall be reasonably and decently fit for occupation. For this there is the good authority of *Smith* v. *Marrable* (2), where Lord Abinger says, with excellent sense, "no authorities are wanted, and the case is one which common sense enables us to decide."

Now this doctrine has never been overruled, and Lord Abinger adhered to it in *Sutton* v. *Temple* (3), and in *Hart* v. *Windsor*. (4)

(1) 1 H. Bl. 273, n.   (3) 12 M. & W. 52; 13 L. J. (Ex.) 17
(2) 11 M. & W. 5; 12 L. J. (Ex.)   (4) 12 M. & W. 68; 13 L. J. (Ex.)
223.   129.

1877

WILSON
v.
FINCH
HATTON.

In the American case of *Dutton* v. *Gerrish* (1), Shaw, J., says that in the case of furnished rooms in a lodging house, let for a particular season, a warranty may be implied that they are suitably fitted for such use. *Searle* v. *Laverick* (2) was decided on another point, and *Smith* v. *Marrable* (3) was consequently not cited; but in the nisi prius case of *Campbell* v. *Wenlock* (4) it was discussed and approved. I am of opinion, therefore, that we are justified on principle, authority, and justice in holding that there is a condition in a lease of a furnished house that it is fit for living in, and that the defendant in this case was justified in repudiating this house and in refusing to pay any rent.

Motion refused and judgment for the defendant.

Solicitors for plaintiffs: *Combe & Wainwright.*
Solicitors for defendant: *Parker & Burne.*

May 5.

ORAM *v.* BREAREY.

Prohibition—Want of Jurisdiction in Inferior Court—Application by Defendant —Salford Hundred Court of Record Act, 1868 (31 & 32 Vict. c. cxxx.).

Sect. 7 of the Salford Hundred Court of Record Act, 1868, enacts that "No defendant shall be permitted to object to the jurisdiction of the Court otherwise than by special plea, and if the want of jurisdiction be not so pleaded the Court shall have jurisdiction for all purposes":—

Held, that the section did not oust the jurisdiction of the superior courts to restrain by prohibition, and that a defendant who was sued in the Salford Court, for a matter over which that Court had no jurisdiction, might himself apply to a superior court for a writ of prohibition.

Jacobs v. *Brett* (Law Rep. 20 Eq. 1) approved.

THIS was a rule calling on the plaintiff to shew cause why a writ of prohibition should not issue to stay all further proceedings herein in the court of record for the hundred of Salford, on the ground that that Court had no jurisdiction. The matter came before Field, J., at chambers, who refused to make the order, and the defendant appealed from that decision.

The court for the hundred of Salford is regulated by 31 & 32 Vict. cxxx. (local), which gives jurisdiction in personal actions

(1) 63 Massachusetts, 89, at p. 94.   (3) 11 M. & W. 5; 12 L. J. (Ex.) 223.
(2) Law Rep. 9 Q. B. 122.   (4) 4 F. & F. 716.

where the debt or damage sought to be recovered does not exceed 50*l.* if the cause of action arise within the hundred. The affidavit of the defendant (which was not contradicted) shewed that the cause of action did not arise within the hundred of Salford, where neither the plaintiff nor the defendant resided or carried on business. The defendant had not raised the objection to the jurisdiction of the Court by plea as provided by the 7th section of the Act. (1)

1877

ORAM
v.
BREAREY.

Firth, for the defendant. The section of the local Act is analogous to sect. 15 of the Mayor's Court Procedure Act, 1827, 20 & 21 Vict. c. clvii., and its effect is to prevent the defendant from taking, in the Court itself, an objection to the jurisdiction otherwise than by plea, but not to prevent prohibition issuing from this Court, and the application for prohibition may be by the defendant himself: *Jacob* v. *Brett.* (2) [He referred also to *Hawes* v. *Paveley* (3), *Mayor of London* v. *Cox.* (4)]

Henn Collins, contrà. The section here is wider in its terms than the 15th section of the Mayor's Court Procedure Act, and expressly gives jurisdiction unless the objection is taken by plea. Further, *Manning* v. *Farquharson* (5) has not been overruled, although the decision of the Master of the Rolls in *Jacobs* v. *Brett* (2) is inconsistent with it. The decision is spoken of with approval in the considered judgment of the Exchequer Chamber in *Cox* v. *Mayor of London.* (6)

Firth, in reply, referred to *Bridge* v. *Branch.* (7)

POLLOCK, B. I think, both on principle and authority, the defendant is entitled to stay these proceedings by prohibition. It is admitted in this case that the Salford Hundred Court would have no jurisdiction at common law, and therefore it would be the duty of this Court to interfere: *Worthington* v. *Jefferies.* (8) But it is said that s. 7 of the local Act shews that the local Court has

(1) 31 & 32 Vict. c. cxxx. s. 7, "No defendant shall be permitted to object to the jurisdiction of the Court otherwise than by special plea, and if the want of jurisdiction be not so pleaded the Court shall have jurisdiction for all purposes."

(2) Law Rep. 20 Eq. 1.
(3) 1 C. P. D. 418.
(4) Law Rep. 2 H. L. 239.
(5) 30 L. J. (Q. B.) 22.
(6) 32 L. J. (Ex.) 282.
(7) 1 C. P. D. 633.
(8) Law Rep. 10 C. P. 379.

jurisdiction, there being no special plea by the defendant raising the objection to the jurisdiction.

No rule is better understood than that the jurisdiction of a superior court is not to be ousted unless by express language in, or obvious inference from, some Act of Parliament. Here there is no expression to oust the jurisdiction of the superior court, and no inference can be drawn that that was intended. We give full force to the words of the statute by holding that its effect is that, in the local court, the defendant can only take exception to the jurisdiction by special plea. The case is very similar to the cases decided on the Mayor's Court Act, and in my opinion the words "if the want of jurisdiction be not so pleaded the Court shall have jurisdiction for all purposes," do not add to the effect of the preceding words, but only make them more clear. As to the authorities, it is admitted that the current of modern cases is in favour of the defendant. We are pressed with the case of *Manning* v. *Farquharson* (1) on the ground that it has not been reversed, although it has been subject to an adverse decision of the Master of the Rolls, and also in consequence of the mode in which it was spoken of in the considered judgment of the Exchequer Chamber in *Cox* v. *Mayor of London.* (2) As to its being an authority, if that case and *Jacobs* v. *Brett* (3) stood alone, I think we should be entitled to give preference to the latter, as, since the decision of the former case, much more light has been thrown on the subject. Then, as to the judgment of the Exchequer Chamber in *Cox* v. *Mayor of London* (2), that was reversed in the House of Lords; and the opinion of Willes, J., who gave the answers to the questions put to the judges, was against the case of *Manning* v. *Farquharson.* (1) It is, therefore, open to us to deal with this matter as a question of principle, and so regarding it, I consider the defendant is entitled to his prohibition.

HUDDLESTON, B., concurred.

Rule absolute.

Solicitors for plaintiff: *Pritchard, Englefield, & Co.*
Solicitors for defendant: *Berry & Binns, for W. Briggs, Derby.*

(1) 30 L. J. (Q. B.) 22.   (2) 32 L. J. (Ex.) 282.
(3) Law Rep. 20 Eq. 1.

1877
June 2.

[IN THE COURT OF APPEAL.]

GARNET *v.* BRADLEY.

Practice—Costs—Slander—Judicature Act, 1875—*Order LV.*—" *Costs shall follow the event.*"

None of the statutes as to costs are repealed by Order LV., and it must be read with reference to them. When, therefore, the proviso says that on a trial by jury the costs shall follow the event, it must be taken to mean that the costs will follow as regulated by the statutes, if any, applicable to the case.

The plaintiff, in an action of slander, recovered one farthing damages. The judge made no order as to costs, and no certificate was given:—

Held, reversing the judgment of the Exchequer Division (by Bramwell and Brett, L.JJ., Kelly, C.B. dissenting), that the plaintiff was not entitled to costs.

Parsons v. *Tinling* (2 C. P. D. 119) overruled.

IN an action of slander tried before a jury the plaintiff recovered one farthing damages. The judge made no order as to costs. No certificate was applied for.

The master taxed the plaintiff his full costs on the authority of *Parsons* v. *Tinling*. (1) The defendant appealed from the master to a judge at chambers, and the judge referred the matter to the Court. The Exchequer Division, acting on the same authority, refused to review the master's taxation.

The defendant appealed.

May 18. *Lawrance, Q.C.,* and *Bigham*, for the defendant. The question is, what construction is to be put on the words "costs shall follow the event" in Order LV. ? (2) The true construction of those words is, that costs shall follow the event subject to the operation of the statutes that are in force respecting costs. There are no express words in Order LV., which repeal the existing

(1) 2 C. P. D. 119.

(2) Order LV.: Subject to the provisions of the Act, the costs of and incident to all proceedings in the High Court shall be in the discretion of the Court; but nothing herein contained shall deprive a trustee, mortgagee, or other person of any right to costs out of a particular estate or fund to which he would be entitled according to the rules hitherto acted upon in courts of equity: provided that where any action or issue is tried by a jury the costs shall follow the event, unless upon application made at the trial, for good cause shewn, the judge before whom such action or issue is tried or the Court shall otherwise order.

1877

GARNET
v.
BRADLEY.

statutes on costs; neither. can it be said that those statutes, including 21 Jac. 1, c. 16, and 3 & 4 Vict. c. 24, are repealed by implication; for Order LV. is not manifestly repugnant to these provisions. As they are not repealed they must be viewed as controlling Order LV. *Evans* v. *Rees* (1) and *Marshall* v. *Martin* (2) are authorities to shew that where the words of two Acts of Parliament are affirmative the latter does not repeal the former. It follows, therefore, that, under 21 Jac. 1, c. 16, and 3 & 4 Vict. c. 24, the plaintiff having recovered only one farthing damages and the judge not having certified, the plaintiff is not entitled to costs. *Parsons* v. *Tinling* (3) no doubt will be relied on by the other side, but that case is not binding on this Court, and this appeal is brought in effect to reverse that decision, the present case having been decided in deference to that authority.

Mellor, Q.C., and *Dugdale,* for the plaintiff. The intention of the legislature was to make one simple and uniform rule as to costs. In changing the system of judicature they have altered the law of costs, the object being to assimilate the practice as to costs in the Common Law and Chancery Divisions: to effect this all the previous statutes have been swept away. By the enacting part of Order LV. the costs are in the discretion of the Court. Then comes the proviso, which says where any action is tried by a jury the costs shall follow the event unless the judge shall otherwise order. All previous statutes as to costs are, therefore, repealed, and the new law is contained in Order LV.

[BRETT, L.J. How do you deal with the rule mentioned in the judgment of Grove, J., in *Parsons* v. *Tinling* (4): "That when there is no repeal by affirmative words in a subsequent Act of the provisions of previous Acts, the subsequent Act does not operate to repeal those provisions unless it is inconsistent with them."]

The words of Order LV. are inconsistent with the statutes of 21 Jac. 1, c. 16, and 3 & 4 Vict. c. 24. The words are, "the costs shall follow the event." If the 3 & 4 Vict. c. 24, is in force, and the judge had certified the plaintiff would not get his costs, as under the statute of 21 Jac. 1, c. 16, he would only get so much costs as the damages given would amount to, and the costs would

(1) 9 C. B. (N.S.) 391; 30 L. J. (C.P.) 16.   (3) 2 C. P. D. 119.
(2) Law Rep. 5 Q. B. 239.   (4) 2 C. P. D. at p. 123.

not follow the event. As pointed out by Lord Coleridge, C.J., in
Parsons v. *Tinling* (1), the other side contend " that the true construction of the proviso is that the words shall follow the event
mean shall follow the event according as before the Act they
would or would not have done so. This would require a very
considerable interpolation of words in the order." It must also
be noticed that the words of Order LV. are "subject to the
provisions of this Act." Those words apply to the proviso as well
as to the enacting part. This has reference to s. 67 of the Judicature Act of 1873, and shews that the Order LV. is applicable to
all actions except those mentioned in that section. Any other
construction would render these words unmeaning; and s. 67 does
not apply to actions of slander. *Parsons* v. *Tinling* (2) is well
decided; and the Exchequer Division were right in their decision
that the plaintiff is entitled to costs.

Lawrance, Q.C., in reply.

Cur. adv. vult.

June 2. The following judgments were delivered :—

BRAMWELL, L.J. I am about to deliver the judgment of my
Brother Brett and myself. We are of opinion that this appeal
must be allowed. The question is whether 21 Jac. 1, c. 16, s. 6, is
repealed by Order LV. of the Judicature Act, 1875. We are of
opinion that it is not. No doubt that order in terms includes all
costs in all cases, and leaves them to the discretion of the Court,
while 21 Jac. 1, c. 16, s. 6, says the plaintiff recovering less than
40s. in an action of slander shall recover no more costs than
damages; and it is a rule that posterior laws repeal prior ones
to the contrary. But that rule is subject to a qualification excel-
lently, as it seems to me, expressed by Sir P. B. Maxwell in his book
on the interpretation of statutes. He says, at p. 157, under the
heading "Generalia specialibus non derogant," "It is but a particular application of the general presumption against an intention
to alter the law beyond the immediate scope of the statute to say
that a general Act is to be construed as not repealing a particular
one by mere implication. A general later law does not abrogate
an earlier special one. It is presumed to have only general cases

_____

(1) 2 C. P. D. at p. 121.   (2) 2 C. P. D. 119.

in view, and not particular cases, which have been already provided for by a special or local Act, or, what is the same thing, by custom. Having already given its attention to the particular subject, and provided for it, the legislature is reasonably presumed not to intend to alter that special provision by a subsequent general enactment, unless it manifests that intention in explicit language." He cites his authority. Thence the maxim above quoted. During the argument I had a doubt, not as to the existence of this rule, but as to its applicability, whether it could be said there was a general rule as to costs, whether the law of costs was not made up of special rules. I am satisfied that doubt was wholly unfounded. There was a very plain general rule, viz., at common law the costs followed the event for plaintiff or defendant; in equity they were in the discretion of the Court. There were special exceptions, as in the case before us. The object of the Order was not to repeal such special laws, but to provide a general law in lieu of the two general laws existing before the fusion of the two jurisdictions.

We are assisted in coming to this conclusion by the following considerations. If 21 Jac. 1, c. 16, s. 6, is repealed, so is what remains of the statutes, 43 Eliz. c. 6, and of 22 & 23 Car. 2, c. 9. So is 3 & 4 Vict. c. 24. So are those statutes which give double costs to the magistrates and others, which, though modified by Sir F. Pollock's Act (5 & 6 Vict. c. 97), practically remain in force to give more than " the costs " to a defendant. Since that Act many have been passed giving double costs, see 8 & 9 Vict. c. 100, s. 105. Are they repealed? So, if I am not mistaken, would be repealed the City Small Debts Act, 15 & 16 Vict. c. lxxvii., in its provisions as to costs in superior Courts. So would s. 3 of 3 & 4 Vict. c. 24, entitling a plaintiff to costs in a case of a trespass after notice. So also the provisions of statutes giving costs to defendants held to bail for too much. So where an action is brought on a judgment where no costs are recovered, unless specially ordered. So in many other instances, as in patent cases. In the same Session in which the Judicature Act, 1875, was passed, the Marine Mutiny Act was previously passed, giving treble costs in certain cases, repeated doubtless since annually. Was that provision in the Marine Mutiny Act repealed? It may be said that this multiplicity of cases shews the desirability of some compendious and general rule. No doubt that would be desirable, as put by Lord Coleridge (1), but we cannot agree that the legislature intended to repeal these enactments, having the particular objects they had, and we do not think the words used are sufficient to do so. It has been asked what is the use of s. 67 of the Act of 1873 if this argument is right. We think, if not necessary, it was introduced ex majori cautelâ. But it seems to us to alter the law. It would be difficult to say that the provisions in the County Court Acts as to costs of actions in the superior Courts, now applied to actions for slander, breach of promise, &c. No assistance can be got from the proviso to Order LV. We cannot see its object. It is said that the Court could exercise its discretion according to the Act repealed by the Order. But, in the first place, to do that, all the benefit of simplicity would be lost. But, further, the Court has only a discretion over *the* costs, meaning ordinary costs; it could, therefore, not give double, or extra, or full costs. We are, therefore, with all deference to the Court below, of opinion that the judgment should be reversed.

KELLY, C.B. This is one of those cases which, it appears to me, may be decided either way without any departure from the true principle of construction applicable to Acts of Parliament.

The Order LV. upon the Judicature Act, 1875, is express to the effect that " the costs of and incident to all proceedings in the High Court shall be in the discretion of the Court." This is the governing rule prescribed on the subject of costs, as to all causes, suits, and ´proceedings whatsoever, and this enactment ought to prevail unless some exception is to be found in the Act or in the rules expressly to a contrary effect. It is introduced by the words " subject to the provisions of the Act," and the first qualification immediately follows, and relates to the right of mortgagees and others to costs out of a particular estate; and this has no bearing upon the question in this case. The next and remaining exception is the proviso, " that where any action or issue is tried by a jury the costs shall follow the event," with the qualification that this shall be so unless the judge who tries the case shall other-

(1) In *Parsons* v. *Tinling*, 2 C. P. D. at p. 121.

wise order. So that here again the principal enactment prevails, that the costs in all cases shall be in the discretion of the Court with the single exception of the above proviso, that in cases tried before a jury "the costs shall follow the event." The question, therefore in this cause is, upon the meaning of the words "shall follow the event." If the meaning be, as it is generally understood to be, simply that when the plaintiff obtains the verdict, the plaintiff shall be entitled to the costs of the cause, unless the judge shall otherwise order (and no such order has been made by the judge), the judgment below must be affirmed. If, on the other hand, the meaning is that the event shall include the operation of Lord Denman's Act (3 & 4 Vict. c. 24), and the Act of 21 Jac. 1, c. 16, and other Acts of Parliament, which affect the right of the plaintiff to costs, independently of the exercise of the discretion of the judge, then the plaintiff in this case is not entitled to his costs.

I cannot say that it would be unreasonable or plainly contrary to any established principle of construction to take the latter view of the meaning of this rule. But it appears to me first, that the general intent of the Judicature Acts and of this rule so expressly declared as above, that the costs of all proceedings whatsoever should be in the discretion of the judge, ought to prevail; and I can imagine no reason why whether a particular case may be within Lord Denman's Act, or the statute of James, or not, the discretion of the judge to determine the question of costs should be taken away. If he thinks that it is a case which ought to come within Lord Denman's Act or within the statute of James, or any other particular Act, touching the costs of a cause, he may make an order to the same effect, as if the statutes were unrepealed.

But, further, the reference in s. 67 of the Act, 1873, to the County Court Acts though not conclusive, seems to me to favour the construction which I would put upon the rule in question; not only upon the doctrine "Exceptio unius est exclusio alterius," but because it shews that where, as in the case of the county courts, it is thought right to take away the discretion of the judge, an express provision is found to that effect.

The rule adverted to during the argument, by my Brother Brett, that a general enactment does not repeal the provisions of parti-

1877

GARNET
v.
BRADLEY.

cular statutes, unless by express words, is no doubt sound doctrine; but if the meaning which I put upon the words " shall follow the event," be the true meaning, they do expressly repeal all those provisions in Acts of Parliament relating to costs (except the re-enactment of the County Court Acts), as effectually as if the words had been "the costs shall be payable to the party who recovers the verdict." On these grounds, I think the decision of Lord Coleridge and the Court of Common Pleas (1) was right, and that the judgment of the Court of Exchequer ought to be affirmed; but as the majority of the Court are of a contrary opinion, that judgment must be reversed.

Judgment reversed.

Solicitor for plaintiff: *C. Butcher.*
Solicitors for defendant : *Stevens & Co.*

HAND v. HALL.

Landlord and Tenant—Agreement, Construction of—Demise, Actual or Contingent—Option to Lessee to continue holding for Three Years beyond a Demise for a Year—Statute of Frauds (29 Car. 2, c. 3), s. 1, 2; 8 & 9 Vict. c. 106, s. 3.

The plaintiff and defendant entered into the following agreement not under seal : " Jan 26. Hand agrees to let, and Hall agrees to take, the large room, &c., from 14th February next until the following Midsummer twelve months, and with right at end of that term for the tenant, by a month's previous notice, to remain on for three years and a half more:"—

Held, reversing the judgment of the Exchequer Division, that the agreement was divisible, and contained an actual demise for a term less than three years, with a superadded stipulation, that the defendant at his option should have a renewal of the tenancy, and that, as to the actual demise, it need not be under seal pursuant to 8 & 9 Vict. c. 106, s. 3.

APPEAL by the plaintiff from the judgment of the Exchequer Division in favour of the defendant, ante, p. 318.

Powell, Q.C., and *Arthur Underhill* for the plaintiff. The

(1) In *Parsons* v. *Tinling,* 2 C. P. D. 119.

question is, whether the document is a lease for more than three years; the Exchequer Division held, in effect, that it is, and not being under seal, is invalid. That decision is erroneous. The document contains two distinct agreements; the first part is an actual demise from the 14th of February till the following Midsummer twelvemonths; the latter part is a contract that, at the option of the tenant, on a notice given by him, he may remain in possession; it is, in effect, a contract for the renewal of the term. Non constat, that the defendant will ever exercise his option to have a renewal. In *Rollason* v. *Leon* (1) the defendants, by a contract dated January, agreed to let, and the plaintiffs to take, a mill and premises for the period of three years from Lady Day then next, a lease for the same to be executed as soon as possible, subject to the permission of the landlord; and the defendants also agreed to let, and the plaintiff to take, the mill from the date of the agreement up to Lady Day then next, Channell, B., says, "The parties here intended to provide for two periods of time— one to Lady Day, the other from three years from that time— at all events, there was an actual demise till Lady Day." In the present case there is an actual demise until Midsummer, and then a contract for the renewal of the term; and although that part of the agreement may be void, the first part, which creates an actual demise, is perfectly good. It is true that there has been no occupation; the plaintiff, however, seeks to recover the rent not by reason of occupation, but under the demise. The document shews that the intention of the parties was that one should let, and the other take, the premises; the words create a present demise, and the plaintiff is entitled to recover the rent: *Fergusson* v. *Cornish*. (2)

Francis, for the defendant. The question is, what right does the memorandum of agreement give the defendant? It confers on him a right to continue tenant for a longer period than three years. If so, under 29 Car. 2, c. 3, ss. 1, 2, and 8 & 9 Vict. c. 106, s. 3, the agreement, not being by deed, is void. The term is not an absolute present demise. The agreement is dated the 26th of January, and the term is to begin on the 14th of February, and

(1) 7 H. & N. 73; 31 L. J. (Ex.) 96.   (2) 2 Burr. 1032.

then, on the tenant giving a notice, he is to continue his holding under the right originally given by this document. He requires no fresh document or title, but he holds on under the same document and title for a period greater than three years. The document, therefore, confers an interest for a longer period than three years, and ought to have been by deed. The agreement cannot be divided into two parts; it is one entire agreement creating one term only. Secondly, there is an implied agreement for title; the plaintiff had no power to grant the lease (1); the defendant has a right, therefore, to rescind the contract.

[LORD CAIRNS, C. The defendant cannot set up that defence where there is an actual demise; before the Judicature Acts the remedy would have been by action, and now it may be stated by way of counter-claim, but that has not been done in this case.]

Powell, Q.C., was not heard in reply.

LORD CAIRNS, C. The document we have to construe in this case runs thus: "Hand agrees to let, and Hall agrees to take, the large room on the south end of the Exchange, Wolverhampton, from the 14th February next until the following Midsummer twelve months." Stopping there, there can be no doubt that those words are words of present demise, and if the document had contained those words only, the defendant would have become tenant from the 14th of February to the following Midsummer twelve months. The document, however, goes on: "with right at the end of that term for the tenant, by a previous month's notice, to remain on for three years and a half more." By this latter part of the agreement an option is given to the defendant, and must be exercised by him before it can be said that any interest has passed to him. It is a stipulation that at his option, on a notice given to the plaintiff, he shall not be disturbed for three years and a half. Whereas there is not anything to be done by the tenant in the first part of the agreement to create a demise, in the second part something has to be done by him before that part takes effect, and until that is done it is impossible to tell whether a tenancy

(1) The plaintiff held under a lease which contained a covenant not to underlet.

shall come into force or not. I think, therefore, that it is absolutely necessary to divide the contract into two parts. I think the agreement is an actual demise, with a stipulation superadded, that if at his option the tenant gives the landlord a notice of his intention to remain, he shall have a renewal of his tenancy for three years and a half.

With all respect for the judgment of the Court below, s. 1 of the Statute of Frauds does not apply, nor has 8 & 9 Vict. c. 106 any application to this case.

With regard to the other point. Here there is an actual demise. If the plaintiff's title is defective, it would not entitle the defendant to rescind the contract. If any objection of that nature exists, it must be set up as a cross claim. The demise cannot be got rid of by simply giving a notice to rescind the contract.

I am, therefore, of opinion that the judgment of the Court below should be reversed.

COCKBURN, C.J., and BRETT, L.J., concurred.

Judgment reversed.

Solicitors for plaintiff: *Gregory, Rowcliffes, & Rawle, for Mamby, Wolverhampton.*

Solicitors for defendant: *Pickett & Mytton, for T. W. Hall, Bilston.*

[IN THE COURT OF APPEAL.]

1877
June 21.

FRANCES HENRIETTA NORMAN v. VILLARS.

Husband and Wife—Status of Wife after Decree Nisi for dissolution of Marriage, and before Decree Absolute.

The status of a married woman is not affected by the pronouncing of a decree nisi for the dissolution of the marriage. She continues to be subject to all the disabilities of coverture until the decree is made absolute.

Action for taking goods of the plaintiff. Plea: coverture of plaintiff at the time of the alleged taking and of plea pleaded. Prior to the alleged taking a decree nisi had been pronounced for the dissolution of the plaintiff's marriage, which was made absolute after plea and before the trial:—

Held (reversing the judgment of the Exchequer Division), that the plaintiff was still a married woman notwithstanding the decree nisi, and that the plea was proved.

Prole v. *Soady* (Law Rep. 3 Ch. 220) distinguished.

WRIT, dated the 4th of February, 1875.

Declaration, that the defendant broke and entered divers rooms of the plaintiff, and seized and took divers goods of the plaintiff.

Plea, dated March 24th, 1875: that at the time of the committing the alleged grievances in the declaration mentioned the plaintiff was, and still is, married to and the wife of George Lewis Norman, who is still living.

Issue joined.

The action was brought to recover the value of furniture and other goods of the plaintiff, which had been illegally seized by the defendant on the 6th of January, 1875. The plaintiff was a married woman; but prior to that date proceedings had been taken in the Divorce Court by the plaintiff against her husband; and on the 18th of November, 1874, a decree nisi had been pronounced for the dissolution of the marriage. The decree was in the usual form: "That the marriage" between, &c., "be dissolved by reason of the respondent's adultery and cruelty unless sufficient cause be shewn to the Court why this decree should not be made absolute within six months from the making thereof." That decree was made absolute on the 25th of May, 1875.

The trial took place before Huddleston, B., at the sittings in

2 E 2   4

London after Trinity Term, 1875, on a day subsequent to the 25th of May.

The learned judge directed a nonsuit, on the ground that the plaintiff being married when the action was brought the husband ought to have been joined, giving leave to move to enter a verdict for the plaintiff for 25*l.*, at which the jury assessed the damages.

On motion in the Exchequer Division, the Court (Kelly, C.B., Pollock and Huddleston, BB.) gave judgment for the plaintiff, being of opinion that the case was governed by *Prole* v. *Soady.* (1)

The defendant appealed.

Talfourd Salter, Q.C., and *Keogh*, for the defendant. The defendant is entitled to succeed on the plea of coverture. The plaintiff was still a married woman at the date of the writ, for the marriage is not dissolved until the decree has been made absolute. On this point *Hulse* v. *Hulse* (2) is conclusive. It was there held that adultery committed by the petitioner during the currency of the decree nisi was adultery committed " during the marriage," and entitled the Court to refuse to finally dissolve the marriage under 20 & 21 Vict. c. 85, s. 31. The case of *Grant* v. *Grant* (3) is to the same effect. There the petitioner having died before the decree nisi had been made absolute, the question was raised whether the Court had power to vary the marriage settlement under 22 & 23 Vict. c. 61, s. 5, by which section they are empowered to do so only after a *final* decree for dissolution. And the Court held that they had no jurisdiction, for one of the parties having died the suit had abated, and therefore the decree could not be made absolute, and that until it was made absolute there was no final decree. In *Ousey* v. *Ousey* (4) Sir James Hannen expresses the same opinion that the final decision of the Court by which the marriage is dissolved is the decree absolute, not the decree nisi. It will, however, be urged upon the other side, on the authority of *Prole* v. *Soady* (1), that, even if the decree nisi does not of itself put an end to the marriage, still when once it has been made absolute the dissolution relates back to the date of the decree nisi. But though the decree absolute may have a

(1) Law Rep. 3 Ch. 220.   (3) 31 L. J. (P. & M.) 174.
(2) Law Rep. 2 P. & D. 259.   (4) Law Rep. 1 P. D. 56, at p. 62.

retrospective effect for some purposes, it is not retrospective in the sense that it alters the status of the wife in the interval, so as to entitle her to sue during that period as a feme sole ; any more than an order obtained under 20 & 21 Vict. c. 85, s. 21, by a married woman, deserted by her husband, for the protection of her property acquired since desertion is retrospective so as to entitle her to maintain an action commenced before the date of the order for injuries to such property : *Midland Ry. Co.* v. *Pye.* (1)

McLeod and *Safford,* for the plaintiff. The plea of coverture was not proved, for the decree had been made absolute before the trial, and thereupon the dissolution related back to the date of the decree nisi, which was prior to that of the commencement of the action. On that point *Prole* v. *Soady* (2) is conclusive. There a married woman being entitled to a fund in court, joined with her husband in assigning the fund by way of mortgage as security for a loan. Soon afterwards a decree nisi was pronounced for the dissolution of the marriage, and before it was made absolute, Stuart, V.C., on the application of the assignee ordered payment of his debt out of the fund in court. Subsequently to the date of that order the decree was made absolute. On appeal Cairns, L.J., reversed the Vice-Chancellor's order, on the ground that the decree for the dissolution of marriage on becoming absolute took effect from the date of the decree nisi, and that consequently the order made in the interval was of no avail to reduce the fund into possession.

[LORD CAIRNS, L.J. I cannot see that that decision has any application to the present question. It does not in any way determine the status of the wife during the currency of the decree nisi.]

After the decree has been made absolute the wife is only under one disability, namely, that she cannot marry again within the period of appeal. But the legislature by prohibiting marriage impliedly gives her all the other rights of a feme sole. Then, since the decree absolute is made on precisely the same evidence as the decree nisi, it is to be inferred that the legislature intended to give the wife upon the pronouncing of the decree nisi all the rights of a feme sole except that of marriage.

(1) 10 C. B. (N.S.) 179; 30 L. J. (C.P.) 314.   (2) Law Rep. 3 Ch. 220.

court to the wife's credit after a decree nisi had been pronounced for the dissolution of the marriage. It is one thing for a court of equity to refuse to allow a husband, after a decree nisi has been pronounced, to reduce his wife's choses in action into possession, and thereby defeat her right of survivorship; it is quite another thing to say that the decree nisi alters the status of the parties.

I am of opinion then that until the legislature otherwise orders, the status of a married woman remains the same until the decree is made absolute.

BAGGALLAY, L.J. This action was properly brought if the plaintiff had lost her former status. That depends on whether the decree nisi had the effect of changing her status. I am of the same opinion as the Lord Chancellor that there is no effective decree until it has been made absolute.

BRETT, L.J. In this action the judge at the trial nonsuited the plaintiff on the ground that the action was improperly brought in her sole name, she being still a married woman at the time of the action brought. I should certainly have thought that the more proper course would have been to direct a verdict for the defendant on the ground that the plea was proved.

The question here depends upon what was the effect of the decree nisi, which was still running at the date of the plea. It was argued that the decree nisi by itself gave the wife the rights of a feme sole. I am however of opinion that that is not the case. In the first Divorce Act (20 & 21 Vict. c. 85) there was but one decree, absolute in the first instance, upon the pronouncing of which decree the wife at once acquired all the rights of a feme sole (with the one exception of re-marriage within the period limited for appeal). These rights, however, were not given by the Act, but arose as common law rights upon the change of the status. Afterwards the legislature, thinking it too abrupt a course to dissolve the marriage by a single decree, by 23 & 24 Vict. c. 144, altered the procedure, and substituted two decrees, one nisi, the other absolute. But the two decrees together are substituted for the single decree under the former Act, not the decree nisi alone. The form of the decree nisi is this "that the marriage be dissolved unless cause be shewn"—not why it should be set aside—but "why it should not be made absolute." Until the decree is made absolute therefore there is no decree at all. On this point I think the case of *Hulse* v. *Hulse* (1) is decisive.

But it was urged that when once the decree was made absolute there is a relation back of the dissolution to the date of the decree nisi, and therefore that as here the decree was made absolute before the trial the plaintiff ought to be considered as having been a feme sole at the time of the grievances committed and action brought. But I do not think that there is any relation back in that sense. There are obvious reasons 'for holding, as was held in the case of *Prole* v. *Soady* (2), that the decree when made absolute relates back so as to avoid any act done by the husband in the interval, for the purpose of reducing his wife's choses in action into possession; but I do not think that it relates back so as to alter the wife's status in that interval, or that the above case is any authority for such a proposition.

Judgment reversed.

' Solicitor for plaintiff: *S. J. Debenham.*
Solicitor for defendant: *W. H. Roberts.*

HORWELL *v.* LONDON GENERAL OMNIBUS COMPANY, LIMITED,
Re THE LONDON TRAMWAYS COMPANY, LIMITED.

April 10;
May 9.

Practice—Claim by Defendant against Third Party in Action of Tort—Joinder of Third Party—Order XVI., rr. 17, 18, 19.

In an action of tort for injury sustained by the plaintiff through the defendants' negligence, the defendants obtained an order under Order XVI., Rule 17, that third parties who it was alleged through their negligence had caused the injury should be added as defendants:—

Held, by Cockburn, C.J., Kelly, C.B., and Bramwell, L.J. (Brett, L.J., dissenting) reversing the decision of the Exchequer Division, that the defendants were not entitled to have such third persons made parties to the action.

THE statement of claim stated that the plaintiff was a passenger on an omnibus of the defendant, and whilst the omnibus was proceeding along the Walworth Road, the defendants by

(1) Law Rep. 2 P. & D. 259.   (2) Law Rep. 3 Ch. 220.

their servant the driver, so negligently drove the horses that the omnibus came into collision with a van standing by the side of the road, and in consequence of the collision the plaintiff was thrown from the omnibus and severely injured.

The statement of defence contained a denial of the negligence, and also a statement that the accident could not have been avoided by any reasonable care of the defendants, but was owing to the imperfect state in which the rails of the London Tramways Company, Limited, were kept, and for which they alone were responsible.

On the 15th of December, 1876, the defendants applied for and obtained a master's order to join the London Tramways Company as third parties to the action under Order XVI., Rule 17, of the Judicature Act, 1875. In support of the application for the order an affidavit was made on behalf of the defendants stating " that the case for the defendants was that the collision took place through the negligence of the London Tramways Company in not keeping their tramway lines in the Walworth Road in proper repair."

On the 19th December, 1876, the order of the 15th of December was served on the London Tramways Company, together with a notice, which, after stating that the action had been brought by the plaintiff against the defendants for injury caused by an omnibus of the defendants coming into collision with a van, and that the collision happened through the neglect and default of the London Tramways Company, Limited, in not keeping their rails on a level with the road, and in proper condition as required by the statutes of the tramways company, alleged, " if you wish to dispute your liability you must cause an appearance to be entered for you within eight days after service of this notice ; in default of your so appearing you will not be entitled in any future proceeding between the defendants and yourself to dispute the validity of the judgment in this action whether obtained by consent or otherwise."

The London Tramways Company, Limited, did not cause an appearance to be entered, but took out a summons before the master to rescind the order of the 15th of December, and the master, on the 6th of January, rescinded the order with costs.

The defendants then appealed from the master's order of the 6th of January to Field, J., who confirmed that order, and dismissed the appeal with costs. The defendants appealed to the Exchequer Division.

April 10. *Talfourd Salter, Q.C.,* and *Finlay,* for the defendants. *Kemp, Q.C.,* and *E. Clarke,* for the London Tramways Company.

POLLOCK, B. The question in this case is whether an order refusing to make the London Tramways Company defendants, should be rescinded, and I am of opinion that it should. The question turns on the construction of Order XVI., Rule 17. The first words of the rule point to the decision of some common fact which should govern subsequent litigation, as when there are a vendor, vendee and subsequent purchasers, so that in determining their rights inter se, it might be desirable to determine once for all the conditions of the original sale. These, however, are not the only cases which are dealt with. There were many instances in which a number of defendants could be brought before a Court of Equity on a surmise that their interests might be affected by the litigation going on; while this course could not be pursued by a court of law. We have, therefore, this Rule referring to remedy over or relief (which is not sought here), but adding a more general power, which is thus expressed: "Where, from any other cause, it appears to the Court or a judge that the question in the action should be determined not only as between the plaintiff and the defendant, but as between the plaintiff and defendant, and any other person, or between any or either of them, the Court or a judge may, on notice being given to such last-mentioned person, make such order as may be proper for having the question so determined." I am well aware of the difficulties when other parties than the original litigants are summoned before the Court, but no such difficulties arise here. It seems to me that the word "question" in the rule does not mean, as has been suggested, "issue," but subject-matter of the action. The Rule should be treated in the broadest way, subject to the exercise of discretion on the points I have already referred to.

The defendants here say that they can shew that they were innocent agents in inflicting the injury complained of, and that the

1877
HORWELL
v.
LONDON
OMNIBUS Co.

tramways company are legally liable. In my judgment, this is a question within the meaning of the rule, which it is desirable to determine in the action.

HAWKINS, J. I am of the same opinion. The question whether the tramways company caused the injury to the plaintiff, is a question in the cause. Then is it fit that it should be determined not only as between the plaintiff and the defendant, but as between the plaintiff and any other person? It seems to me that it is fit it should be determined between the plaintiff and the tramways company in this action, because the effect of doing so will be to prevent multiplicity of actions, and to give the plaintiff his remedy against one or other of the defendants, whichever is in fault. I think it is in our power to make the order asked for, and as a matter of discretion that we ought to make it.

Master's order of Jan. 6 set aside.

The London Tramways Company, Limited, appealed.

May 9. *Kemp, Q.C.,* and *E. Clarke,* for the London Tramways Company. The defendants cannot join the Tramways Company as third parties to this action. These proceedings are instituted by the defendants alone, and the plaintiff is no party to them. The defendants are therefore endeavouring to force the plaintiff to sue third parties as defendants, against whom he has not thought it right to proceed. The plaintiff, if he pleased, might have in the first instance joined both defendants. The object of the legislature, as appears from Order XVI., Rules 17, 18, and 19 (1),

---

(1) Order XVI., Rule 17: Where a defendant is, or claims to be, entitled to contribution, or indemnity, or any other remedy or relief over against any other person, or where from any other cause it appears to the Court or a judge that a question in the action should be determined not only as between the plaintiff and the defendant, but as between the plaintiff, defendant, and any other person, or between any or either of them, the Court or a judge may, on notice being given to such last-mentioned person, make such order as may be proper for having the question so determined.

18. Where a defendant claims to be entitled to contribution, indemnity, or other remedy or relief over against any person not a party to the action, he may, by leave of the Court or judge, issue a notice to that effect, stamped with the seal with which writs of summons are sealed. A copy of such notice shall be filed with the proper officer, and served on such person

1877

HORWELL
v.
LONDON
OMNIBUS Co.

is that where there is a substantial question which may be determined in the action not only between the plaintiff and the defendant, but also between the defendant and a third party, that question is not to be tried twice over: *Swansea Shipping Co.* v. *Duncan & Co.* (1). Here the question between the plaintiff and the defendants is, have the defendants been guilty of negligence? It is not competent for the defendants to say the tramways company have been guilty of negligence; to say so is, in truth, an argumentative way of saying that they the defendants have not been guilty of negligence. The case does not fall within Rule 17, for it is not a question to be determined between the plaintiff and the defendant and any other person. " A question in the action " means a material question in the original action. Whether the tramways company have been guilty of negligence, is not a question in the original action.

[BRAMWELL, L.J. If the tramways company are joined, can the plaintiff be compelled to serve them with a statement of claim ?]

It would be strange if the plaintiff could be compelled to sue a defendant against whom he might believe he had no cause of action, and, if he failed, to pay the costs. The notice served upon the tramways company is a notice framed under Rule 18, which cannot under any circumstances be applicable. Assuming that this case fell within the second part of Rule 17, the notice would

according to the rules relating to the service of writs of summons. The notice shall state the nature and grounds of the claim, and shall, unless otherwise ordered by the Court or a judge, be served within the time limited for delivering his statement of defence. Such notice may be in the form and to the effect of the form No. 1 in Appendix B hereto, with such variations as circumstances may require, and therewith shall be served a copy of the statement of claim, or if there be no statement of claim, then a copy of the writ of summons in the action.

19. When under rule 17 of this order it is made to appear to the Court or a judge, at any time before or at the trial, that a question in the action should be determined not only as between the plaintiff, and the defendant, but as between the plaintiff and the defendant, and any other person, or between any or either of them, the Court or a judge, before and at the time of making the order for having such question determined, shall direct such notice to be given by the plaintiff at such time and to such person, and in such manner as may be thought proper, and if made at the trial, the judge may postpone such trial as he may think fit.

(1) 1 Q. B. D. 664.

1877

HORWELL
v.
LONDON
OMNIBUS CO.

have to be given under Rule 19, and by that Rule the judge "shall direct such notice to be given by the plaintiff." The notice is bad in form, and has been given by the wrong party.

Talfourd Salter, Q.C., and *Finlay,* for the defendants. The decision of the Exchequer Division is right. The case comes strictly within Order XVI., Rule 17. It is not contended that the first part of Rule 17 is applicable, but the defendants rely on the second part. The words are, "Where from any other cause it appears to the Court or judge that a question in the action should be determined," the judge can make an order to have the question so determined. This language is very large, and includes the question which incidentally arises in the present case. The words are not if "at the trial of the issue between the plaintiff and defendant," but where from any cause it appears that there is a question in the action "not only as between the plaintiff and the defendant, but as between the plaintiff and the defendant and any other person, or between any and either of them;" the object being, as stated in *Swansea Shipping Co.* v. *Duncan* (1), that in no instance shall a question in dispute be twice tried. The question here is whether the defendants or the tramways company have been guilty of negligence. With regard to the costs incurred by the plaintiff of having the tramways company added as defendants, they would be reserved until after the trial and dealt with by the judge; any difficulty that may be supposed to arise as to the pleadings and subsequent proceedings, would be regulated by Rule 21. This is a beneficial enactment, saving the expense of a double trial; it is not prejudicial to the plaintiff, and ought to receive a liberal construction. With regard to the notice, if it is informal the objection to it is not insuperable, it might be amended. If the defendants are entitled to have the tramways company added as a third party, the Court will not, because the notice given is informal, refuse the application.

Kemp, Q.C., in reply.

BRETT, L.J. In this case, as I understand it, an action was brought by the plaintiff against the omnibus company: a statement of claim was delivered, and a statement of defence was put

(1) 1 Q. B. D. 664.

in, containing an allegation that the omnibus company were not the persons liable to the plaintiff, because they said in the trans-action on which the plaintiff's claim was founded, a third person was implicated, namely, the tramways company ; and that, upon a true investigation of facts, it would turn out there had been no negligence on the part of the omnibus company, although, in fact their omnibus had been in collision with a van, but that the negligence, and the only negligence, was on the part of the tramways company. There would, therefore, be a question raised in the inquiry, which inquiry would embrace one transaction in which all the three parties are alleged to have been implicated and at which they were all present. A question would have been raised in the inquiry as to whether it was the omnibus company's servants who were negligent, or the tramways company's servants who were negligent, or both.

Now it seems to me, that upon that state of facts arising, either the plaintiff was at liberty to apply to the Court to join the tram-ways company as defendants, or that the omnibus company, the original defendants, might make the application; at all events, they might inform the Court of the facts, and leave the Court to determine whether the tramways company should be added as a party to the action.

I am of opinion that the case is within Order XVI., Rule 17. I apprehend that the great and fundamental object of the Judi-cature Act, and of the Rules and Orders which have been made under it, was that upon an inquiry into any transaction one trial should make an end of the whole contest in it between all the parties, and that larger power was to be given under the new Act to the new Court than was before possessed either by the common law courts or by the Court of Equity, the great object being that there should be one litigation only, and that all persons who might be implicated in the transaction which was the cause of the litigation should, if the Court thought fit, be brought in as parties, and that there should be only one inquiry amongst them all, which should be final. At the present day the judgment is not to be given in the form in which it was given under the old pro-cedure. All judgments are to be decrees, and where there is to be a decree, although there are many parties to the action, a decree may be as between the plaintiff and some of the defendants, or as between the defendants amongst themselves.

In this case, if the plaintiff had been so pleased, under Order XVI., Rule 3, he might have joined both these defendants and he might, having so joined them, have framed the statement of the claim in the alternative, that is, he might have alleged that both the defendants have been guilty of negligence, or he might have alleged either one defendant or the other has been guilty of negligence, and if the plaintiff had so brought his action originally, most of the difficulties, as it seems to me, which have been suggested, must have occurred in that action. The question for the jury, if it came to be tried by a jury, would be as between the plaintiff and the first defendant, was that defendant guilty of negligence, or as between the plantiff and the second defendant, if the first was not guilty of negligence, was the second guilty of negligence? It is an alternative case. The decree would have been in favour of the plaintiff, either against both defendants, if both were guilty of negligence, or against one of them, and there would have been a decree in favour of the other. Under those circumstances, if the plaintiff had sued them in the alternative, if he succeeded against both, he would have his costs against both. If he succeeded against only one he would have had his costs against that one, but the other would have had his costs against the plaintiff. However, the plaintiff did not take that course, but it appearing afterwards there might be an alternative case, it seems to me clear and obvious under the second part of Rule 17 that the plaintiff might have come to the Court and asked for an order to bring in the tramways company, and make the tramways company a defendant, and what is more, to make the tramways company an alternative defendant. If that had been so, and the Court had thought fit to make such an order, then the position of things would have been just the same as if the tramways company had been brought in originally as an alternative defendant.

The question now raised before us is, whether, upon the facts being made known to the Court by the omnibus company, the case is brought within Rule 17. Now, under the first part of Rule 17, it is obvious that the second defendant is brought in as

1877

HORWELL
v.
LONDON
OMNIBUS Co.

a party to the action not by the plaintiff, but by the first defendant. It has been held in the case that has been cited (1) that the second defendant is not brought in so as to be bound as between him and the first defendant on every question that arises in the action, but supposing he is brought in, the first ·defendant saying he has a claim over against him, then the whole of that question as to the claim may or may not be decided in the action, but there being one question in the action which is common to that whole case, the second defendant is allowed to be brought in. I think that Rule 17 does not limit the application to one to be made on the part of the plaintiff. I think the first defendant may rightly make such an application. Then it is said that " the question in the action " must be a question in the original action. I apprehend the real meaning of the words " a question in the action," means a question which will arise in the inquiry, and not a question which is either an issue or a question within the original action. If we look at Rule 13, we find this phraseology: " That the name or names of any party or parties, whether plaintiffs or defendants, who ought to have been joined, or whose presence before the Court may be necessary in order to enable the Court effectually and completely to adjudicate upon and settle all the questions involved in the action, be added." That is, where there are many defendants or where there are many plaintiffs; all the questions which are involved in the inquiry as between them all, and that phrase " a question in the action " never was meant to be confined to an issue in the action, and never intended to be confined to a question which would be only a question between the original plaintiff and the original defendant. In fact that phrase, it must be noticed, is applicable to the first part of Rule 17 as well as to the second, and it is applicable to the case where it is admitted the question is between the two defendants.

If that be so, it being a question in the action, that question is to be determined, not only " as between the plaintiff and the defendant," that is, the original plaintiff and the original defendant, " but as between the plaintiff and defendant and any other person," that is, any other person who may be brought in, " as between

(1) *Swansea Shipping Co.* v. *Duncan,* 1 Q. B. D. 664.

any or either of them." I can give no meaning to such words
following the other words, but to say it may be a question between
the plaintiff and the defendant, or either of them, or a question
between two defendants or between any or either of them. Therefore, if the question be said to be between the two defendants, it
is a question which under Rule 17 may be determined.

Now Rule 17 is divided into two parts. The mode in which it
is to be carried out, if the case comes under the first part, is by
means of Rule 18; on that part of the case I have nothing to add.
If it comes under the second part, then it is to be carried out by
means of Rule 19. By that rule, the Court or judge has power to
make an order and to direct such notice as he may think fit to
be given. I apprehend that includes an order to give a notice
to the third party to come in as a defendant. If the third party
is brought in as a defendant, then his difficulties are said to arise.
Supposing a defendant is brought in, it is said the plaintiff will
admit the second defendant's statement, but that is so unlikely to
happen that I do not think it ought to be dealt with. Why
should a plaintiff, as a mere matter of conscience, as it is said,
and not being able to appreciate all the facts, admit that a person
who is alleged to be negligent towards him, and against whom if
negligence be proved, he would have a valid claim—why should
he admit that he has no claim against that defendant?

If a defendant be brought in and appears as a defendant, whether
the plaintiff gives evidence against him or not, he will be a defendant on the record, and the plaintiff will give such evidence as
he is advised. He will give evidence in order to fix the first
defendant. He may fail in that, or he may make a primâ facie
case. But the first defendant, either by cross-examination of the
plaintiff's witnesses or by bringing witnesses of his own, will shew
that the second defendant was the person guilty of negligence,
which negligence injured the plaintiff. I see no difficulty whatever in making a decree under these circumstances that he should
be liable to the plaintiff; and more than that, if the evidence came
out to the satisfaction of the tribunal that the first defendant was
not negligent, but that the second defendant was, then it seems to
me the decree ought to be, and would be, that the second defendant
is liable to the plaintiff, and must pay the plaintiff's costs. The

1877

HORWELL
v.
LONDON
OMNIBUS Co.

first defendant, upon that assumption, would be found not to be liable, but the plaintiff, therefore, would have erred in bringing his action against the first defendant; then the plaintiff would be bound to pay the costs of the first defendant, but he would receive his costs of the trial from the second defendant.

Now supposing, in that given case, the first defendant was found to be a person guilty of negligence, and the second defendant was found to be not guilty, if the plaintiff had taken no action at all against the second defendant, and had confined himself at the trial to his original ground that he only charged the first defendant, then the first defendant would have to pay the costs of the plaintiff, the second defendant would be held harmless. How must he be indemnified? Why, as it seems to me plainly, by the person who brought him in, and not by the plaintiff who had taken no action against him. Under those circumstances I see nothing in the law which would prevent the Court from making, and the Court, in the exercise of a proper judicial discretion, ought to make, and I have no doubt the Court would make, the proper order as to costs, namely, under those circumstances the person who brought in the second defendant would have to pay the costs to the second defendant.

I know not the practice in Chancery, but I believe where there were several defendants, if a new set of defendants were brought in in consequence of some statement made on the part of first defendants, and upon the hearing it should have been found they ought not to have been so brought in, and that statement ought not to have been made, I believe that the order as to costs would have been made as between the plaintiff and those defendants who were liable to the plaintiff and as between the defendants where one set of defendants, by wrong statements, had caused others to be summoned as parties to the suit. Whether that be so or not, it seems to me that is a power which is given by this present statute. It seems to me to hold otherwise would be to do away with and abrogate one of the great and substantive objects of the statute and of the rules; for if these defendants could not be brought in, there might be two inquiries in the same transaction. The plaintiff would be put to sue the present defendants, and if he failed against them, he might bring another suit against the second defendants, and if it be held that even if the second defendants be brought in, no decree could be made against them on the part of the plaintiff, then there must be two inquiries with the same transaction, the very thing which this statute and these rules were framed to obviate.

I am, therefore, of opinion this case is within the second part of Rule 17; that the first order of the master was properly made, and if that order had been carried out by a proper notice, then the notice which should have been given under that order was a simple notice to the second defendants to come in and appear as defendants. The notice given has added something more, but it contains a notice to the tramways company to come in and appear as defendants, and I do not think the good part of the notice given, which is in obedience to the order, which I apprehend is a proper order, is vitiated by something being added to the notice which does not apply to the present case.

I am, therefore, of opinion the first order of the master was right, and the order of the Divisional Court setting aside the second order of the master, was also right.

BRAMWELL, L.J. I regret that I cannot agree with my Brother Brett. Let us see who are the parties concerned. There is the plaintiff, the omnibus company, and the tramways company. We may leave out the tramways company, for the tramways company do not desire to be added as defendants. We may leave out the plaintiff, because he does not desire that the tramways company should be added, and, it may be observed, if he desired the tramways company should be defendants in this action he might have made them so originally, or have got them added under the Rule 13 to which my Brother Brett has referred. The only remaining party, therefore, whose interests are in question is the omnibus company. Let us see whether any good will be done to the omnibus company by the addition of the tramways company as defendants. To my mind it is really demonstrable that none will be. The case will be tried, and the plaintiff will either get a verdict against the omnibus company, or the omnibus company will get a verdict against the plaintiff. Let us suppose the plaintiff gets a verdict against the omnibus company, what is to become of the

1877

HORWELL
v.
LONDON
OMNIBUS Co.

tramways company if they are added? I suppose there would be no finding at all about them, or it may be found they were guilty of negligence too, and that the joint negligence caused the accident. What good will that do to the omnibus company? There is no contribution amongst wrong-doers. Suppose the plaintiff gets a verdict against the omnibus company, and nothing is said about the tramways company, what good will that do to the omnibus company? Now take the case the other way. Suppose the omnibus company gets a verdict, what good will it have done to the omnibus company to have added the tramways company? I can see none. The tramways company ought certainly not to be added as defendants unless it will do the omnibus company some good. To my mind it is an injustice to the plaintiff that the tramways company should be added as defendants.

There is another observation I have to make. In my judgment, this is not a case in which a question arises between the tramways company and any other party : it is not a question in the action. The question in the action is, did the omnibus company by their negligence cause this damage to the plaintiff? As I said before, that might be by their sole negligence or by their negligence conjointly with the tramways company. Any judge who directed the jury properly would tell them it is not a question in the action whether the tramways company were guilty of negligence, but what he would say to them would be this : The plaintiff has to make out his case. The defendants have not got to make out any answer to it. If the plaintiff makes out that the omnibus company have been guilty of negligence, you will find a verdict for him. The omnibus company tell you it was not their fault, but it was the fault of the tramways company. If they prove this, then you will find it was not the fault of the omnibus company ; but, whether the tramways company were guilty of negligence or not, the only question is, was the omnibus company guilty of negligence which caused this mischief? Now that would be the question which any judge could properly leave to the jury.

Now it has been said the case comes under the second part of Rule 17 : " Where from any other cause it appears to the Court or judge that a question in the action should be determined, not only as between the plaintiff and defendant, but as between the plain-

tiff, defendant, and any other person." It is said that if this case
is not within that clause, those words have no meaning : with great
submission it is not so. I can conceive a case where they will
have an ample meaning. It is to be remembered these words
do not apply to the second part of the rule only, but are applicable also to " where a defendant claims to be entitled to contribution and indemnity "—that is to the first part of Rule 17. Take
this case. An action is brought against a surety for the default of
his principal in paying money, upon which the surety says the
verdict may go against me. I may have to pay the plaintiff, and
when I apply to my principal he will say, " I have paid the
money." That is a question to be determined between the principal and surety ; it is a question in the action. As to the rele-
vancy of these words, as it seems to me, one might retort this sort
of case : A man brings an action for assault and battery against
A. The night is dark, and all the plaintiff knows is that he has
been beaten, and he believes A. beat him ; on which A., under the
ingenious style of pleading, adopted in this case, first denies the
assault, and then he adds, " The defendant also says that it was B.
that beat the plaintiff." Thereupon, according to the contention
of the defendants, as I understand it, A. would have a right to
add B. as a defendant, and would say the question in the case is
whether B. beat the plaintiff. So it is in a sense, but it is not a
question in the action, and the judge would be quite right in telling the jury it was not the question. He would be entitled to say
the question is, did A. beat the plaintiff ? If you are satisfied it
is B., you will not find it is A., but the question for you is whether
A. did it. Could it be contended for a moment under Rule 17, if
a man brings an action for assault against A., that A. can say it
was B. or fifty other people ? Say there was a crowd ; could he
say that it was any one of the crowd rather than A. ? As well as I
understand the rule, it is not applicable to such a case as this,
and one can test it in this way. Let us suppose the case goes
down for trial. Let us suppose the jury acquit the omnibus company and find the tramways company liable. There is no declaration, no claim for damages, nothing in the case, by which the
plaintiff can recover against the tramways company. I do not
mean to say it might not be so moulded ; but I say, adding the

1877

HORWELL
v.
LONDON
OMNIBUS Co.

tramways company as defendants, makes the plaintiff a plaintiff in an action in the alternative which he has not chosen to be. I confess that I think this is a plain case, and that the order of the Divisional Court was wrong, and ought to be reversed.

KELLY, C.B. But for the opinion of Brett, L.J., and the decision of the Exchequer Division, I should not have entertained a doubt as to this case. It is only necessary to look at the statement of defence, and to construe the rules and orders with reference to the joinder of parties to see that the case before us is clearly not within Order XVI., and the rules contained in it. The plaintiff alleges that the defendants, by their servants, so negligently drove an omnibus upon which the plaintiff was riding, that he was thrown off, and sustained injuries. The defendants allege that they were not guilty of negligence, but that the tramways company were guilty. They now seek to make the tramways company a party to the action, and they rely upon Order XVI., Rule 17, but that rule has no application to this case. If the defendants cannot support their case under either Rule 18 or Rule 19 they must fail. I will first comment upon Rule 18. It only applies to cases "where a defendant claims to be entitled to contribution indemnity, or other remedy or relief over against any person not a party to the action." Is this a case of contribution? Clearly it is not. If the plaintiff fails there is an end of the case, but suppose that he establishes that the defendants were guilty of negligence, and recovers damages against them ; the defendant cannot claim contribution from the tramways company, for the defendants and the tramways company would both be wrong-doers, and it is clear that there is no contribution between wrong-doers. The word contribution would also include a case where the members of a co-partnership are sued for goods sold, and where they have a dormant partner who ought to bear a portion of the price; for if the action succeeds against the original defendants they would be entitled to call upon him to pay a share of the money recovered from them.

Is it a case of indemnity? By "indemnity" the legislature perhaps intended to provide for a case where a surety is sued alone, and he is desirous of making the principal debtor a party to the proceedings. Then does this case come within the words "other remedy or relief over against any person not a party to the action." That will apply to a case where an action is brought for the breach of warranty upon the sale of goods by sample, and the defendant alleges that he bought the goods by sample under a similar warranty; in that case, under these words the defendant will be entitled to make his vendor a party to the action, and, if the plaintiff succeeds, to recover from him by reason of breach of warranty. But in the present case the defendants, by their notice, allege that the accident happened through the neglect of the tramways company; if they prove that at the trial the action will fail, but if it is not proved the plaintiff will be entitled to recover damages from them; but in either case they will not be entitled to any remedy or relief from the tramways company.

I will now turn to Rule 19. That rule refers to Rule 17 in express terms, and provides that where it is made to appear that a question in the action should be determined not only as between the plaintiff and the defendant, but as between the plaintiff and the defendant and any other person, or between any or either of them, the Court or a judge shall direct notice to be given by the plaintiff. These words show that the rule was intended to have a much more extended operation than Rule 18, but it is to be put in force at the instance of the plaintiff. Where it shall be made to appear to the Court or judge that by introducing another party to the record the plaintiff could sustain a claim either conditionally or in the alternative, in that case an order may be obtained to make that party a defendant, and the question between the plaintiff and the defendant may be raised and determined. In the present case, if the plaintiff had ascertained after he had brought the action that the tramways company had caused the omnibus to strike against the van, then he might have obtained an order under Rule 19 to make the tramways company defendants; but I repeat it must have been obtained at the instance of the plaintiff. The second defendants would be then compelled to plead to the statement of claim, and the action would proceed against both. At the trial the plaintiff might succeed against one and fail against the other, or he might succeed as to both, or fail against both, but whatever might be the result, all the questions between the parties would be determined. Even if this case could be brought within any of these rules, to join the tramways company as a party to this action would be a useless proceeding. The circumstance that the tramways company are made a party to the action will not assist the case for the defendants, for if it was the negligence of the tramways company that caused the accident it is perfectly immaterial, so far as the defendants are concerned, whether the tramways company are or are not parties to the action. I therefore think that the decision of the Exchequer Division must be reversed.

COCKBURN, C.J. The result of the discussion has removed from my mind any trace of doubt as to this case not being within Rule 17 of Order XVI. Rule 17 is divided into two parts, and it has two different purposes. The first part embraces cases in which a defendant has a claim to contribution or indemnity from some third party or parties. It is clear that in this case the defendants, the Omnibus Company, have no claim to contribution, indemnity, or any other remedy or relief over against the Tramways Company. The second part relates to cases where it appears to a Court or judge that "a question in the action should be determined, not only as between the plaintiff and the defendant, but as between the plaintiff, the defendant, and any other person, or between any or either of them." In which case, "the Court or a judge may on notice being given to such last-mentioned person make such order as may be proper for having the question so determined." This can scarcely be intended to apply to the case in which a plaintiff desires to introduce a third party, because by the third rule of this order the plaintiff has the option where he has an alternative remedy, or believes he has a case against two persons, jointly or severally, to make those persons defendants in the alternative; and if he omits to introduce the second defendant, but afterwards has reason to think that he ought to include him he may apply to amend his statement of claim and bring in the other defendant. The provision must refer to an application by a defendant to join a third party as defendant. But even if it could be held that that part of the rule would enable a defendant to introduce a third party as a defendant in the alternative, it appears to me

1877

HORWELL
*.
LONDON
OMNIBUS CO.

repugnant to every principle of law and every notion of common
sense, that a man can be forced to be a plaintiff against his
will, and be thus forced to sue another party whom he does not
desire to sue, and whom he has not made a defendant, by a
proceeding had behind his back without his being served with a
proper notice upon a summons or rule. If it were possible that
a defendant could compel a plaintiff to proceed against a second
defendant as well as against himself, at least it must be a preliminary condition that the plaintiff should be heard to object to
such a proceeding. It may be that there is no case against the
third party; it may be that to add him as a defendant will delay
the plaintiff's case and put him to expense and inconvenience.
Is it to be said that he is not to be heard, and that the defendant
can have it in his power to introduce a third party in the action
in despite of the plaintiff, who is the dominus litis, and has the
conduct and management of the case, and is entitled to conduct it
in his own way, and in the manner most consistent with his own
interest? But what satisfies me that this rule will not apply to
the present case is this, that there is the difference in the process
in a case where a defendant seeks to bring in a third party, and
where the plaintiff seeks to bring in a third party. When a defendant seeks to bring in a third party without making the
plaintiff party to the proceeding, Rule 18 provides for the mode
in which notice shall be given, namely, by the defendant himself.
If the plaintiff is the party making the application, then the plaintiff is to give notice to the intended additional defendant.

Again, if a person not a party to the action is proceeded against
under Rule 18, he may enter an appearance in the action if he
chooses. What if he does not? Is it that "in default of his so
doing he shall be deemed to be a party to the cause, and liable
to have judgment go against him by default? Not at all: "he
shall be deemed to admit the validity of the judgment obtained
against such defendant, whether obtained by consent or otherwise." Manifestly shewing, that so far as the defendant is concerned, the only case in which he can bring in a third party without making the plaintiff a party to such proceeding is where that
third party has an interest in defeating the plaintiff's claim against
the first defendant, inasmuch as if the plaintiff succeeds against

such defendant, he (the third party) will be liable to the latter. 1877
For which reason if he does not come in and assist in that respect HORWELL
he is to be bound by the judgment, and cannot afterwards dispute *v.*
LONDON
it, if liable to the action for contribution or indemnity, or other OMNIBUS Co.
relief, which the first defendant would have against him.

The whole scope of this legislation is simply that if the plaintiff
is uncertain as to which of two parties he shall proceed against,
he is entitled to make them both defendants. Being plaintiff,
and making them both defendants, he becomes liable in costs to
the one against whom he failed to succeed. But where the defendant is allowed to bring in a third party, is not where he may
be able to say, "I have not committed this wrong, but another
has;" but where the verdict obtained against him by the plaintiff
entitles him to found upon it proceedings against a third party.
But he can bring in the third party only when the third party
chooses to come in and be a third party. If he does not so choose,
then Rule 20 says he shall be bound for ever and conclusively
by the verdict which the plaintiff has obtained against the defendant to whom he is liable for contribution. This satisfies my
mind that this is not a case which could be brought under Rule
17, at all events, unless the plaintiff was brought before the
Court or a judge to be heard as to how far it was consistent with
justice and his interest that he should be compelled to admit
a second defendant. I doubt very much whether another defendant could be forced upon him, though he was heard and had an
opportunity of saying what he had to say against the course of
proceeding. It is, at all events, clear to my mind that to make
him liable by the mere action of the defendant to have another
person introduced into the action whom he did not want to have
introduced there, and which might involve him in very serious
inconvenience and possibly questions of costs, is a thing perfectly
out of the question. Therefore, even supposing this case to be
within Rule 17, the fact that the plaintiff was not made a party
is to my mind utterly fatal to the whole proceeding. Besides
which, looking to the particular nature of this proceeding, there
is the additional circumstance that if negligence is proved against
the defendant company it could do them no good to shew negligence in a third party. If negligence can be shewn against them,

the negligence of others will avail them nothing; if the negligence cannot be made good against them they will require no further assistance.

Therefore looking at the matter merely as one of discretion, there was here an absence of the discreet exercise of the authority of the Court, even if they had any such authority under Rule 17, in allowing the tramways company to be added as defendants. It can be of no avail to the other defendants, and to do it without giving the plaintiff an opportunity of being heard against it was a mistaken proceeding, and one which we cannot uphold. I am, therefore, of opinion that this order must be set aside.

Order of the Divisional Court reversed.

Solicitors for defendants: *Stevens, Wilkinson, & Harries.*
Solicitor for the London Tramways Company: *H. C. Godfray.*

Feb. 14.   [IN THE COURT OF APPEAL.]

WOODLEY v. THE METROPOLITAN DISTRICT RAILWAY COMPANY.

*Master and Servant—Negligence—Sub-Contractor under Railway Company—
Common Employment.*

The plaintiff, a workman in the employ of a contractor engaged by the defendants, had to work in a dark tunnel rendered dangerous by the passing of trains. After he had been working a fortnight he was injured by a passing train. The jury found that the defendants in not adopting any precautions for the protection of the plaintiff had been guilty of negligence:—

Held, by the majority of the Court of Appeal (Cockburn, C.J., Mellor and Grove, JJ.), reversing the decision of the Court of Exchequer, that the plaintiff having continued in his employment with full knowledge, could not make the defendants liable for an injury arising from danger to which he voluntarily exposed himself:

Held by Mellish, and Baggallay, L.JJ., dissenting, that the plaintiff, as servant to the contractor and not to the defendants, had entered into no contract with the latter which would modify the ordinary duty of those who carry on a dangerous business to take reasonable precaution that no one should suffer personal injury from the manner in which it is carried on; and that no such contract should be inferred from the plaintiff remaining in his employment.

THIS was an action tried before Kelly, C.B., at the Middlesex sittings for Hilary Term, 1874. The action was to recover damages for injuries received by the plaintiff through the alleged negligence of the defendants under the circumstances narrated in the judgments of the Court of Appeal. A verdict was found for the plaintiff for 300*l*., leave being reserved to the defendants to move to enter a verdict for the defendants or a nonsuit. A rule nisi was accordingly applied for and obtained, on the ground that there was no breach of duty on the part of the defendants towards the plaintiff which caused the injury to him. Against this rule the plaintiff shewed cause, and it was discharged by a judgment of the Court of Exchequer (Kelly, C.B., Cleasby and Amphlett, BB. (1)), in Michaelmas Term, 1874.

The defendants appealed to the Court of Appeal.

1877

WOODLEY
v.
METRO-
POLITAN
DISTRICT
RAILWAY CO.

(1) The following were the judgments in the Court below :—

KELLY, C.B., after stating the facts of the case, continued :—This is an action against a railway company in which a rule has been obtained by Mr. Thesiger to enter a verdict for the defendants, the jury having found a verdict for the plaintiff with 300*l*. damages. It appears to me, upon the facts of this particular case, the plaintiff is entitled to retain his verdict, and that the rule ought to be discharged.

It was an action against the Metropolitan District Railway Company by a workman who had been employed, not by the defendants, but by a contractor engaged by the defendants, to execute certain works in a tunnel very near to one of the metropolitan stations, and the defendants were charged with negligence, amongst other things, in not having provided somebody who should look out with a view to warn the workmen in this tunnel against approaching trains.

Now, the circumstances of the case appear to be these :—The plaintiff had been employed to assist in the execution of certain works in this tunnel, which was dark. It appears that while the plaintiff was at work a train rapidly approached, came upon the spot, ran against him, threw him down and inflicted the injuries upon him of

which he complains in this action. It appeared that the train in question came along the railway by means of a curve, and that the curve terminated only within some twenty or thirty yards, or thereabouts, of the spot at which the plaintiff was working, so that he could not see the train approaching until it was within the distance of twenty or thirty yards, coming on rapidly. I do not propose to lay down any general rule upon the subject : certainly not to hold that in all cases where work is done in a dark tunnel and by a stranger, not a servant of the company, or by some one who has no connection with the company, it is the duty of the company to employ a look-out man to see when trains are approaching, and warn the workmen against any mischief arising ; I do not say that there may not be many such cases in which no such duty is or ought to be imposed on the railway company. But in the circumstances of this particular case in which a train was approaching which the workman had no means of either seeing or hearing in time to enable himself to get out of the way, and so to avoid the mischief, the question arose, upon which we have now to deliver an opinion, whether it was not the duty of the company to have stationed a look-out man at the corner of the curve to have

1877

WOODLEY
*.
METRO-
POLITAN
DISTRICT
RAILWAY CO.

1875. Feb. 24. *Cave, Q.C.,* and *F. M. White,* for the defendants.
Francis, for the plaintiff.

[The following cases were cited: *Seymour* v. *Maddox* (1); *Inder-maur* v. *Dames* (2); *Morgan* v. *Vale of Neath Ry. Co.* (3); *Wiggett* v. *Fox* (4); *Bilbee* v. *London, Brighton, and South Coast Ry. Co.* (5); *Skelton* v. *London and North Western Ry. Co.* (6);

---

warned the workman, who might then have avoided all danger. It appeared on some former occasion, and on some other part of the same railway, a look-out man had been employed, though no doubt that might have been done ex majori cautela, and it appeared also that after this accident had occurred a look-out man was thenceforth employed at the spot in question. Under these circumstances, and dealing only with the facts of this particular case, I am of opinion the the jury were fully justified in finding that it was the duty of the company to have provided a look-out man, and so prevented the mischief which actually occurred. That being so, it appears to me that the verdict ought not to be disturbed, and that the rule should be discharged.

CLEASBY, B. I am not about to express an opinion at variance with that which has been given by the Lord Chief Baron, but I may add that this case has been much considered, and the delay in delivering the judgment has arisen perhaps in a great measure from my having felt a good deal of difficulty upon this ground—the plaintiff appeared to me to expose himself voluntarily, that is, as a man who was paid for the work he was doing, and to expose himself voluntarily to a known danger, the danger being that he is to work in a tunnel near to a curve where trains are passing every six minutes, and therefore the risk which he appears to take upon himself is not always being prepared to get out of the

way as each train comes. As to that I cannot help thinking, for his own safety, he would necessarily rely very much upon himself, and that placing himself voluntarily in that position, incurring that risk voluntarily, he cannot complain if the consequence is that in a particular case he is not prepared to get out of the way, and the train comes against him. One might apply the maxim, Volenti non fit injuria: he takes the risk upon himself, and there is no wrong if the consequence arises which is likely to arise upon his taking it. But my learned Brothers in this case see sufficient evidence to shew that by the conduct of the defendants, and I may say the improper conduct, the plaintiff was exposed to greater dangers than those which he took upon himself in the way I have mentioned: and if that be so, then it follows he has a right to complain.

AMPHLETT, B. I agree in the judgment delivered by my Lord in this case, limiting it, as he has done in his judgment, to the particular circumstances of the case, and laying down no general rule.

Rule discharged.

(1) 16 Q. B. 326; 20 L. J. (Q.B.) 327.

(2) Law Rep. 1 C. P. 274; Law Rep. 2 C. P. 311.

(3) Law Rep. 1 Q. B. 149.

(4) 11 Ex. 832.

(5) 18 C. B. (N.S.) 584; 34 L. J. (C.P.) 182.

(6) Law Rep. 2 C. P. 631.

Paterson v. *Wallace* (1); *Bartonshill Coal Co.* v. *Reid* (2); *Holmes*
v. *Clarke* (3); *Watling* v. *Oastler.* (4)]

1877

WOODLEY
v.
METRO-
POLITAN
DISTRICT
RAILWAY CO.

Cur. adv. vult.

1877. Feb. 14. THE COURT (Cockburn, C.J., Mellish and
Baggallay, L.JJ., Mellor and Grove, JJ.), having differed in
opinion, the following judgments were read by Baggallay, L.J.:—

COCKBURN, C.J. In this case, which was an action to recover
damages for an injury sustained by the plaintiff from one of the
defendants' trains having struck him while at work on their
premises, the jury found for the plaintiff with 300*l.* damages;
but a rule was obtained, on leave reserved, to enter a verdict for
the defendants, on the ground that the plaintiff having voluntarily exposed himself to the danger, the defendants were not
bound to adopt precautionary measures for his protection.

The facts of the case were as follows:—The plaintiff was a
workman in the employ of a contractor engaged by the defendants to execute certain work on a side wall on their line of railway in a dark tunnel. Trains were passing the spot every ten
minutes, and the line being there on a curve, the workmen would
not be aware of the approach of a train till it was within twenty
or thirty yards of them. The space between the rail and the wall,
on which the workmen had to stand while at work, was just sufficient to enable them to keep clear of a train when sensible of its
approach. The place in question was wholly without light. No
one was stationed to give notice of an approaching train. The
speed of the trains was not slackened when arriving near where
the men were at work, nor was any signal given by sounding the
steam whistle. It is unnecessary to say that the service on which
the plaintiff was thus employed was one of extreme danger.
While he was reaching across the rail to find a tool he had laid
down a train came upon him suddenly, and struck and seriously
injured him.

It appeared that on a previous occasion, when similar work was
being done, a look-out man had been stationed to give warning of
approaching trains, but this precaution had been discontinued.

(1) 1 Macq. H. L. Cas. 748.   (3) 7 H. & N. 937; 31 L. J. (Ex.) 356.
(2) 3 Macq. H. L. Cas. 266.   (4) Law Rep. 6 Ex. 73.

1877

Woodley
v.
Metro-
politan
District
Railway Co.

Under these circumstances I have no hesitation in saying that, morally speaking, great culpability attached to the defendants for having omitted to adopt any precautionary measures to lessen as much as possible the danger to which the plaintiff and his fellow-workmen were exposed. The jury have found that they were herein guilty of negligence, and, according to the recent decision of the House of Lords in *Bridges* v. *North London Ry. Co.* (1), the question of negligence, if there is any evidence to go to the jury, is for the jury and not for the Court. But in this case I am bound to say that, in my view, so far as the question of negligence was concerned, not only was there evidence to go to the jury, but the verdict was in this respect perfectly right. Whether, notwithstanding that the injury to the plaintiff was caused by the negligence of the defendants, the latter are in point of law liable is a different question, and one on which I have had considerable difficulty in making up my mind.

If the plaintiff, in doing the work on the railway, is to be looked upon as the servant of the company, the decision of the Court of Exchequer in his favour cannot, as it seems to me, be upheld. It could not be said that any deception was practised on the plaintiff as to the degree of danger to which he would be exposed. He must be taken to have been aware of the nature and character of the work and its attendant risks when he entered into the employ of the contractor for the job in question, or at all events he must have become fully aware of it as soon as he began to work. If he had been misled in supposing that precautionary measures such as the dangerous nature of the service rendered reasonably necessary would be taken, he had a right to throw up his engagement and to decline to go on with the work; and such would have been his proper course. But with a full knowledge of the danger, he continued in the employment, and had been working in the tunnel for a fortnight when the accident happened. A man who enters on a necessarily dangerous employment with his eyes open takes it with its accompanying risks. On the other hand, if the danger is concealed from him and an accident happens before he becomes aware of it, or if he is led to expect, or may reasonably expect, that proper precautions will

(1) Law Rep. 7 H. L. 213.

1877

Woodley
v.
Metro-
politan
District
Railway Co.

be adopted by the employer to prevent or lessen the danger, and from the want of such precautions an accident happens to him before he has become aware of their absence, he may hold the employer liable. If he becomes aware of the danger which has been concealed from him, and which he had not the means of becoming acquainted with before he entered on the employment, or of the want of the necessary means to prevent mischief, his proper course is to quit the employment. If he continues in it, he is in the same position as though he had accepted it with a full knowledge of its danger in the first instance, and must be taken to waive his right to call upon the employer to do what is necessary for his protection, or in the alternative to quit the service. If he continues to take the benefit of the employment, he must take it subject to its disadvantages. He cannot put on the employer terms to which he has now full notice that the employer never intended to bind himself. It is competent to an employer, at least so far as civil consequences are concerned, to invite persons to work for him under circumstances of danger caused or aggravated by want of due precautions on the part of the employer. If a man chooses to accept the employment, or to continue in it with a knowledge of the danger, he must abide the consequences, so far as any claim to compensation against the employer is concerned. Morally speaking, those who employ men on dangerous work without doing all in their power to obviate the danger are highly reprehensible, as I certainly think the company were in the present instance. The workman who depends on his employment for the bread of himself and his family is thus tempted to incur risks to which, as a matter of humanity, he ought not to be exposed. But looking at the matter in a legal point of view, if a man, for the sake of the employment, takes it or continues in it with a knowledge of its risks, he must trust to himself to keep clear of injury.

But it may be said the plaintiff was not in the service of the defendants at all. He was on their premises not only on lawful business, but it may be said by their invitation, as he was working under a contractor employed by them to do the work in question. He sustained the injury complained of through what the jury have found to have been negligence on the part of the company,

1877

WOODLEY
*.
METRO-
POLITAN
DISTRICT
RAILWAY Co.

he is therefore entitled to damages. But this reasoning appears to me to be fallacious. That which would be negligence in a company, with reference to the state of their premises or the manner of conducting their business, so as to give a right to compensation for an injury resulting therefrom to a stranger lawfully resorting to their premises in ignorance of the existence of the danger, will give no such right to one, who being aware of the danger, voluntarily encounters it, and fails to take the extra care necessary for avoiding it. The same observation arises as before: with full knowledge of the manner in which the traffic was carried on, and of the danger attendant on it, the plaintiff thought proper to remain in the employment. No doubt he thought that by the exercise of extra vigilance and care on his part the danger might be avoided. By a want of particular care in depositing one of his tools he exposed himself to the danger, and unfortunately suffered from it. He cannot, I think, make the company liable for injury arising from danger to which he voluntarily exposed himself. The contractor, the immediate employer of the plaintiff, undertook to execute work which he knew would be attended with danger in the circumstances under which it was to be executed. The plaintiff as his servant did the same. They are in a very different position from that in which they would have stood had they been at work on the defendants' premises in ignorance of the danger.

The conclusion, therefore, at which I have arrived, I must say with much regret, as I think the conduct of the defendants open to great reprehension, is that the judgment of the Court of Exchequer is wrong and must be reversed.

MELLISH, L.J. The course which the argument in this case has taken makes it desirable to consider, in the first place, whether railway companies are under any obligation to take reasonable care that the servants of contractors, who are brought on the line for the purpose of repairing the works of the railway, do not suffer personal injury from the passing trains. In the Court below it seems to have been taken for granted that railway companies were under such an obligation, but it is now contended that they are under no such obligation, and that the servant of the contractor, if he does not like to incur the risk of being run over, must throw up his employment with his master, and that however great may be the risk to which he is exposed, and however great may be the negligence of the arrangements of the railway company with respect to the running of their trains, he has no action against the railway company for any injury he may suffer. Now there can be no doubt that by the law of this country every person who carries on a dangerous trade is bound to take reasonable care that no other person (not being his own servant) suffers a personal injury from the manner in which his trade is carried on. No one has a right to carry on his trade in such a manner as is likely to cause personal injury to others. This liability is not founded on contract. It may be modified or taken away by contract, but it is founded on the right which is inherent in every one, not to be subject to personal injury from the wrongful or careless act of another. In the case of a servant who enters into the service of a master who carries on a dangerous trade, the right of the servant to be protected in his person is largely modified by the contract between master and servant. The servant is considered to contract that he will run all the ordinary risks arising from the nature of his master's business and from the regulations under which it is carried on, and all risks arising from the negligence of his co-servants ; but the servant of the contractor enters into no such contract with the railway company, because he enters into no contract with the railway company at all, and his contract with his own master is res inter alios acta, and in my opinion is altogether immaterial. I am unable to discover any principle by which railway companies are freed from the liability of taking reasonable care that the servants of contractors are not injured by the passing trains. I think the company is entitled to assume that contractors' labourers who are brought on their line to do repairs are persons who have reasonable nerve and reasonable skill in avoiding danger; but if the company's arrangements are such that persons who have as much nerve and as much skill in avoiding danger as it can be expected contractors' labourers would have are nevertheless exposed to an undue risk of personal injury, I think that the company are liable for any personal injury they may in consequence suffer. The work which the plaintiff in this

1877

WOODLEY
v.
METRO-
POLITAN
DISTRICT
RAILWAY Co.

1877

WOODLEY
&
METRO-
POLITAN
DISTRICT
RAILWAY Co.

case was employed to do was not in itself dangerous at all. It was disagreeable work, because it was to be performed in a dark and dirty tunnel; but the danger to which the plaintiff was exposed arose entirely from the act of the company in running their trains, and it is because the danger arose from the act of the company, that the company were the persons upon whom the duty lay to see that the trains were run in such a manner and with such precautions that the servants of the contractors, who were working in the tunnel with the leave and for the benefit of the company, were exposed to no undue risk.

This being, in my opinion, the nature of the liability of the company, I have next to consider whether there was any evidence that the plaintiff, on the occasion in question, was, through the negligent arrangements of the company, exposed to a greater risk of personal injury than he ought to have been, and I agree with the Court below there was such evidence. The question I have to decide is not whether I myself, if I had been on the jury, should have found that the company's arrangements were negligent, but whether there was evidence from which a jury might reasonably so find. This question mainly depends upon the degree of skill and nerve in avoiding passing trains which may reasonably be expected from a bricklayer's labourer in a dark tunnel. This is obviously a question of fact, on which it is utterly impossible to lay down any rule of law. The jury, under the direction of the judge, have found that under all the circumstances of the case, the darkness of the tunnel, there being a curve at the place the plaintiff was working so that an approaching train could not be seen, the noise of the work and of trains passing on the other side making it difficult to hear an approaching train, the plaintiff was not sufficiently protected from the risk of personal injury. The jury have also expressed an opinion that the proper precaution to have been taken was for the company to have placed a man to warn the workmen when a train was coming. I am quite unable to say whether this would have been a proper or a sufficient precaution, but I cannot hold that the conclusions to which the jury have come on pure questions of fact, on which it seems to me some men might reasonably come to one conclusion and some to another, were so wrong that the Court is entitled to enter a verdict for

1877

WOODLEY
v.
METRO-
POLITAN
DISTRICT
RAILWAY Co.

the defendants on the ground that there was no evidence to go to the jury.

It was argued, however, strongly on the part of the defendants, that as the plaintiff had been working in the tunnel for a fortnight, though not at the spot at which he was working when the accident happened, and knew that the company were running their trains as usual without taking any precautions for the protection of the workmen in the tunnel, he must be taken to have assented to the trains being so run, and on that account cannot recover. This, as I understand, is the objection which made Baron Cleasby doubt in the Court below whether the rule should not be made absolute to enter a verdict for the defendants. Now this defence in substance amounts to a defence of leave and licence, and it is possible that, though the plaintiff has not bound himself by any contract with the defendants to take upon himself all risk arising from the passing trains, yet he may have licensed the defendants to run their trains as usual without taking any precautions to protect him, and it is necessary to consider whether it was proved that he did so.

Is it, then, a necessary inference in point of law from the fact of the plaintiff having worked in the tunnel for a fortnight without making any objection, and without abandoning his service with his master, that he consented to the company's running their trains as usual without taking any precautions for the safety of the workmen in the tunnel? In my opinion it is not. In the first place it is by no means certain that the plaintiff, an ordinary bricklayer's labourer, understood at all what the extent of the risk was which he was running, or what the precautions were which were reasonably necessary. In the next place, assuming that he did understand what the risk was which he was running, and that he knew that the workmen in the tunnel were not reasonably protected, it seems to me it would be extremely unjust to hold that he was obliged either at once to quit his master's employment or else to lose his right of action against the railway company for negligently running over him. I think he is entitled to say, "I know I was running great risk, and did not like it at all, but I could not afford to give up my good place from which I get my livelihood, and I supposed that if I was injured by their

1877

WOODLEY
*.
METRO-
POLITAN
DISTRICT
RAILWAY Co.

carelessness I should have an action against the company, and that
if I was killed my wife and children would have their action also."
Suppose this case : a man is employed by a contractor for cleansing
the street, to scrape a particular street, and for the space of a
fortnight he has the opportunity of observing that a particular
hansom cabman drives his cab with extremely little regard for the
safety of the men who scrape the streets.   At the end of a
fortnight the man who scrapes the streets is negligently run over
by the cabman.   An action is brought in the county court, and
the cabman says in his defence : "You know my style of driving,
you had seen me drive for a fortnight, I was only driving in my
usual style." "Yes, but your usual style of driving is a very
negligent style, and my having seen you drive for a fortnight has
nothing to do with it."   It will not be disputed the scraper of the
streets in the case I have supposed is entitled to maintain his
action, and in my opinion his case does not differ from the case
we have to determine, there being no contract between the
defendants and the plaintiff any more than between the cabman
and the scraper of the streets.   On the whole, I am of opinion
that the judgment of the Court below ought to be affirmed.

BAGGALLAY, J.A.   I agree with Lord Justice Mellish in thinking
that the judgment of the Court below should be affirmed.

In the view which I take of the case the plaintiff cannot be
regarded as a servant of the company ; he was the servant of the
contractor ; and at the time when the accident occurred he was
upon the premises of the company in the course of fulfilling, on
behalf of his employer, a contract in which his employer and the
company were jointly interested : he was there upon lawful business, and not upon bare permission.   If this be the true view of
the case, it appears to me that it cannot be distinguished, in
principle, from that of *Indermaur* v. *Dames* (1), and that there
was a duty imposed by law on the company either to avert the
danger or to give the plaintiff reasonable notice of it, so that he
might protect himself.

Was there then, in fact, neglect on the part of the company in
either of these respects?   I fully assent to the view that the

(1) Law Rep. 1 C. P. 274; Law Rep. 2 C. P. 311.

1877

WOODLEY
v.
METRO-
POLITAN
DISTRICT
RAILWAY Co.

company had a right to expect that the contractor's labourers would be men possessed of a reasonable amount of skill in the performance of their duties, of knowledge of the ordinary risks to which their employment exposes them, and of prudence in avoiding the dangers to which they were subjected; but the circumstances of the present case were very peculiar; the accident which occurred to the plaintiff was not occasioned by the work upon which he was engaged, as by the falling of any portion of the brickwork, or the giving way of a scaffold, but by the company running their trains at the time when that work was going on; the real question is whether the company's train was run in such a manner, and with such precautions, that the plaintiff was not exposed to any undue risk; and this was essentially a question for the jury. As has been stated by the Lord Justice, it is impossible to lay down any general rule of law applicable to cases of this description; each must depend upon its own circumstances. The jury found a verdict for the plaintiff; the learned judge by whom the case was tried was not dissatisfied with that verdict, and the Court of Exchequer have concurred in it. So far as I am competent to form an opinion from the materials before us, I agree with the jury in thinking that reasonable precautions were not taken by the company for the protection of the plaintiff. Whether the jury were right or not in the opinion which they expressed as to what would have been a sufficient precaution, it is immaterial to consider.

It was contended on the part of the company that they were under no obligation to adopt measures for the protection of the servants of a contractor against the careless or negligent acts of their own servants; that the plaintiff, and other persons similarly situated, must enter upon such employment at their own risk, and that unless they were willing to do so they should refuse to be so employed. If this is the true state of the law the company would probably be entitled to have the judgment of the Court below reversed; but I cannot adopt this view, concurring as I do most entirely in the reasons assigned by Willes, J., in delivering the judgment of the Court in the case of *Indermaur* v. *Dames* (1), to which I have already alluded.

(1) Law Rep. 1 C. P. 274; Law Rep. 2 C. P. 311.

1877

WOODLEY
v.
METRO-
POLITAN
DISTRICT
RAILWAY Co.

MELLOR, J. I am of opinion that the judgment of the Court of Exchequer must be reversed.

The defendants can only be made liable on the proof of some negligent conduct on their part which occasioned the accident by which the plaintiff was injured, and I can discover none.

The Lord Chief Baron in his judgment suggests, and it is upon this matter alone that he relies as the foundation of the liability of the defendants, that it was reasonable for the jury to hold that there was an obligation and duty imposed upon the company, in this case for the preservation of human life, to have stationed a man at the bend of the curve who would have been enabled, on the approach of the train, to have warned the workman, and enabled him to escape danger. Whether any such precaution, even were it possible, would have been of any practical value may be doubtful, considering the number of trains passing in the tunnel, but, if it were, I can see no ground for inferring such an obligation and duty to have existed under the circumstances on the part of the company. Whether it might have been a prudent thing for the contractor to have stipulated for additional precautions, when he undertook the repair of the tunnel, is quite a different question, but I can see no implied obligation on the part of the company, at their expense, to employ such a person, as the Lord Chief Baron referred to. No such person was, in any sense, necessary for the proper and ordinary working of the defendants' trains, or conducting their business, and it is not suggested that there was anything done by the company or omitted by the company, in the mode of working their trains or carrying on their business, of an unusual character, or in any respect differing from the course of working which they had used during the period of the plaintiff's employment, and it seems to me that in principle, so far as the liability of the defendants is concerned, the case does not differ from that of *Ellis* v. *Great Western Ry. Co.* (1) It is now completely settled that a master is not liable to one servant for the consequences resulting from the negligence of a fellow-servant in the course of the same employment, on the ground that the servant undertakes as between himself and his master the natural risks and perils incident to the performance of his duty,

(1) Law Rep. 9 C. P. 551.

1877

WOODLEY
v.
METRO-
POLITAN
DISTRICT
RAILWAY Co.

and the presumption is that such risks are considered in the wages: *Morgan* v. *Vale of Neath Ry. Co.* (1) When, therefore, the contractor in this case undertook to perform the work in question, and in the performance of which the plaintiff was engaged at the time of the accident, it is reasonable to assume that the character and nature of the work was duly considered and included in the price paid for it; and if the plaintiff thought that there was danger of an unusual character in the nature of the work, he ought either to have stipulated with his master or the company to provide some additional means or precautions against such possible danger, or, as he was better able to judge than they whether the work could safely be performed without additional precautions, he ought to have refused the task unless they were provided.

Now, whether the master has done anything which may make him liable as between himself and the plaintiff we are not concerned to decide. *Priestly* v. *Fowler* (2), which is a leading case on the subject, has a strong bearing upon this state of things, and throws light upon the principle upon which this case may be decided. In that case it was said by Lord Abinger, in delivering the judgment of the Court, "The mere relation of master and servant can never imply an obligation on the part of the master to take more care of the servant than he may reasonably be expected to do of himself. He is, no doubt, bound to provide for the safety of the servant in the course of his employment to the best of his judgment, information, and belief. The servant is not bound to risk his safety in the service of his master, and may, if he thinks fit, decline any service in which he reasonably apprehends danger to himself, and in most cases in which danger may be incurred, if not in all, he is just as likely to be acquainted with the probability and extent of it as his master."

In the present case the plaintiff had probably the same opportunity of judging of the possible danger as his master had, and might have declined the work, and refused to undertake it, without additional precautions being taken or means provided by his master, but, as it appears to me, that was a matter affecting his relation with his master, and not in any way affecting the duty of the company.

(1) Law Rep. 1 Q. B. 149.   (2) 3 M. & W. 1.

1877

WOODLEY
v.
METRO-
POLITAN
DISTRICT
RAILWAY Co.
I think that the company can in no respect be said to be guilty of negligence. They conducted the business in the ordinary way, and the accident did not occur through any misconduct or mis-management on their part. I think that the plaintiff, who must be presumed to know the ordinary traffic of the company, and the limited space within which he had to work, came within the maxim, Volenti non fit injuria, and has, at all events, no remedy against the defendants.

BAGGALLAY, J.A.   Mr. Justice Grove has not written a separate judgment, but he agrees in that of Mr. Justice Mellor, and, as the majority of the Court are in favour of the appellants, the form of the judgment will be to enter the verdict for the defendants.

Judgment to enter the verdict for the defendants.

Solicitor for plaintiff: *D. Aston.*
Solicitors for defendants: *Burchells.*

[IN THE COURT OF APPEAL.]

THE ATTORNEY GENERAL *v.* CHARLTON AND OTHERS.

Succession Duty—Predecessor—General Power of Appointment—Succession Duty Act, 1853 (16 & 17 Vict. c. 51), ss. 2, 4.

S., tenant for life in possession, and W., his eldest son, tenant in tail in re-mainder, of certain estates, by deed of the 22nd of March, 1854, barred the entail, and settled the estates to such uses as they should jointly appoint. By deed of the 23rd of March, 1854, they jointly appointed the estates (in the event which happened) to such uses as they should jointly appoint, and in default, to the use that W. should, during the joint lives of himself and S., receive a yearly rent-charge, and subject thereto to S. for life, with remainder to W. for life, with remainder to the first and other sons of W. in tail male, with remainder to such uses as S. and his second son, T., should jointly appoint, and in default of appoint-ment to T. for life, with remainders over. W. died in 1864, without issue, and without the joint power of S. and W. having been exercised. In 1866 S. and T. by deed appointed the estates (subject to S.'s life estate, and in the events which happened) to the use that, after the decease of S., A., his wife, should, if she should survive him, receive during her life a yearly rent-charge, and, subject thereto, that the estates should go to the use of D., the daughter of T., during so much of a certain period as she should live. S. died in 1873, leaving A. surviving him; and D. came into possession of the estates:—

Held, by Cockburn, C.J., James and Brett, L.JJ. (Bramwell, L.J., dissenting), reversing the decision of the Exchequer Division, that, solely, on the authority of *Attorney General* v. *Floyer* (9 H. L. C. 477; 31 L. J. (Ex.) 404), the case fell within s. 2 of the Succession Duty Act, 1853, and that A. and D. took their annuity and life interest respectively, as successions derived from W. as the donor of the power, and that the duties payable in respect of their successions were to be calculated on their respective lives, according to their respective relationship to W.

Lord Braybrooke v. *Attorney General* (9 H. L. C. 150; 31 L. J. (Ex.) 177), *Attorney General* v. *Floyer* (9 H. L. C. 477; 31 L. J. (Ex.) 404), and *Attorney General* v. *Smythe* (9 H. L. C. 497; 31 L. J. (Ex.) 404), discussed.

INFORMATION, claiming succession duty, stating the following facts :—St. John Charlton, being tenant for life in possession, and William Charlton, his eldest son, being tenant in tail in remainder, of certain estates, by a deed of the 22nd of March, 1854, barred the entail, and resettled the estates to such uses as St. John Charlton and William Charlton should jointly appoint, and in default of appointment, to the use of St. John Charlton for life, with remainder to William Charlton in tail male. By deed of the 23rd of March, 1854, St. John Charlton and William Charlton, in exercise of the above joint power, appointed the estates to such uses as they should jointly appoint, and, in default, to the use that William Charlton should during the joint lives of himself and St. John Charlton receive a yearly rent-charge of 800*l.*, and subject thereto to St. John Charlton for life, with remainder to William Charlton for life, with remainder to the first and other sons of William Charlton in tail male, with remainder to such uses as St. John Charlton and Thomas Charlton (St. John Charlton's second son, who afterwards assumed the name of Meyrick), should jointly appoint, and in default to Thomas Charlton for life, with remainder to his first and other sons in tail male, with remainders over.

William Charlton died in 1864, during his father's lifetime, without issue, and without the joint power of appointment vested in him and his father, by the deed of the 23rd of March, 1854, having been exercised.

By an indenture of the 16th of February, 1866, St. John Charlton and Thomas Meyrick appointed the estates, subject to the life estate of St. John Charlton, to the use that after the death of St. John Charlton, Anne Charlton (his wife) should, if she survived him, receive a yearly rent-charge of 1700*l.*, and, subject

1877

thereto, and in the events which happened, that the estates should go to the use of Dora, the daughter of Thomas Meyrick, during so much of a certain period as she should live.

St. John Charlton died on the 23rd of February, 1873, leaving his wife, Anne, surviving him ; and Dora Meyrick thereupon came into possession of the estates.

The information prayed that it might be declared that Anne Charlton was liable to pay succession duty at the rate of 1 per cent. in respect of her rent-charge of 1700*l.*, as a succession derived by her from William Charlton, her son, and that Dora Meyrick was liable to pay succession duty at the rate of 3 per cent. in respect of her life estate, as a succession derived by her from William Charlton, her uncle ; but that, if the Court should be of opinion that the power of appointment, under which the above interests were limited, ought to be deemed a general power within the meaning of s. 4 of the Succession Duty Act, 1853, then that duty was payable at the rate of 2 per cent. in respect of the interests so appointed, as a joint succession derived by St. John Charlton and Thomas Meyrick, by reason of the exercise by them of such power. (1)

The Exchequer Division (2) held, distinguishing the cases of *Lord Braybrooke* v. *Attorney General* (3), and *Attorney General* v. *Floyer* (4), that the Crown was only entitled to succession duties on the footing of St. John Charlton and Thomas Meyrick being the predecessors, and that consequently the duties payable were, 1 per cent. by Anne Charlton on a moiety of her rent-charge, as derived from her son, and 1 per cent. by Dora Meyrick on her life interest, either moiety being derived from her grandfather and father respectively.

The Attorney General appealed.

This appeal was part heard on the 19th and 20th of January, 1877, when it was adjourned. It was re-argued on the 31st of

---

(1) In this latter case the information further prayed for a second duty upon the successions derived by Anne Charlton and Dora Meyrick respectively upon the death of St. John Charlton, but the

claim was not pressed by the counsel for the Crown in argument.

(2) 1 Ex. D. 204.

(3) 9 H. L. C. 150; 31 L. J. (Ex.) 177.

(4) 9 H. L. C. 477; 31 L. J. (Ex.) 404.

May and the 1st of June, 1877, the Court being differently constituted.

May 31, June 1.   *Gorst, Q.C.*, and *W. W. Karslake* (*Sir John Holker, A.G.*, with them), for the Crown.   This case falls under s. 4 of the Succession Duty Act (1), and upon the true construction of that section the interests of Anne Charlton and Dora Meyrick are liable respectively to a duty of 1 per cent. on one moiety and 3 per cent. on the other moiety.   By that section, where a person has a general power of appointment, taking effect upon the death of a person dying after the commencement of the Act, he shall, upon his exercising such power, be deemed to be entitled, at the date of such exercise, to the interests thereby appointed as a succession derived from the donor of the power.   Here the power was a general power, which took effect, i.e., became exercisable (vide *In re Lovelace* (2)) upon the death of William, the eldest son, which death occurred after the commencement of the Act.   By virtue of s. 4, therefore, St. John, the father, and Thomas the

---

(1) By s. 2 of the Succession Duty Act, 1853 (16 & 17 Vict. c. 51), "Every past or future disposition of property, by reason whereof any person has or shall become beneficially entitled to any property or the income thereof upon the death of any person dying after the time appointed for the commencement of this Act, either immediately or after any interval, either certainly or contingently, and either originally or by way of substitutive limitation, and every devolution by law of any beneficial interest in property, or the income thereof, upon the death of any person dying after the time appointed for the commencement of this Act, to any other person, in possession or expectancy, shall be deemed to have conferred or to confer on the person entitled, by reason of any such disposition or devolution, a succession; and the term "successor" shall denote the person so entitled ; and the term "predecessor" shall denote the settlor, dis-

poner, testator, obligator, ancestor, or other person from whom the interest of the successor is or shall be derived."

By s. 4: "Where any person shall have a general power of appointment, under any disposition of property, taking effect upon the death of any person dying after the time appointed for the commencement of this Act, over property, he shall, in the event of his making any appointment thereunder, be deemed to be entitled, at the time of his exercising such power, to the property or interest thereby appointed as a succession derived from the donor of the power; and where any person shall have a limited power of appointment, under a disposition taking effect, upon any such death, over property, any person taking any property by the exercise of such power shall be deemed to take the same as a succession derived from the person creating the power as predecessor."

(2) 4 De G. & J. at p. 351.

second son, the donees of the power, upon their exercising the
power, became, at the date of such exercise, namely, in 1866,
entitled to the interests thereby appointed, namely, the annuity
of Anne and the life interest of Dora expectant on the death of
St. John, as a succession derived from the donor of the power.
It will be observed that though s. 4 says that the person exercising a general power is to be deemed to have had a succession, it does not say who is to pay the duty upon it, or when. At
this point three questions arise:—1. At what rate is the duty
payable upon the successions of St. John and Thomas? 2. When
is it payable? 3. By whom? The answer to the first question
depends upon this, Who was the donor of the power? That is
determined by the authority of *Lord Braybrooke* v. *Attorney
General* (1), and *Attorney General* v. *Floyer* (2), which cases go to
shew that William the tenant in tail was the sole donor, for the
power was created wholly out of the estate tail, and not at all at
the expense of the life estate of the father. Therefore, upon the
exercise of the power by St. John and Thomas in 1866 a duty
became due, at that date, at the rate of 1 per cent. on a moiety of
Anne's annuity and on a moiety of Dora's life interest respectively,
as a succession derived by St. John from his son William, and at
the rate of 3 per cent. on the other moieties of the annuity and
life interest respectively as a succession derived by Thomas from
his brother. Next, when did such duty become payable? A distinction is here to be drawn between the time at which the duty
becomes due, and the time at which it becomes payable. The
duty no doubt became due, i.e. a liability to duty attached to the
property in 1866 at the date of the exercise of the power, under
s. 4, but it did not become payable until the time pointed out by
s. 20, by which section the duty is to be paid "at the time when
the successor, or any person in his right, shall become entitled in
possession to his succession." In this case that did not happen
till 1873, when St. John the father died. The duty then became
payable in 1873. But by whom was it payable? The answer is
given by the same section, s. 20. The duty is to be paid by the
"successor or any person in his right," that is to say, in the case

(1) 9 H. L. C. 150; 31 L. J. (Ex.)   (2) 9 H. L. C. 477; 31 L. J. (Ex.)
177.   404.

of a succession arising upon the exercise of a general power, the successor is to pay if he appoints to himself, but if he appoints to third persons, then those third persons are to pay, here Anne and Dora. This argument is, however, no doubt open to the objection that it points to a double duty being payable, viz. the duty above mentioned upon the fictitious succession of St. John and Thomas, and a second duty upon the actual succession of Anne and Dora on the death of St. John; and the Court would naturally be averse to allowing a claim of double duty. But the difficulty may be got over by praying in aid the latter half of s. 15: "Where any succession shall, before the successor shall become entitled thereto in possession, have become vested by any title not conferring a new succession, then the duty shall be paid as if no such derivative title had been created." But what is the meaning of the words "not conferring a new succession?" They must mean "not involving a new death." Now here there was no new death involved in the appointment, for the subject of the appointment was itself a reversion; Anne and Dora, therefore, took their respective interests "by a title not conferring a new succession." By virtue, then, of that 15th section, they will only have to pay duty upon the succession of St. John and Thomas.

But upon the argument for the Crown upon this point it must be admitted that the case of *Attorney General* v. *Upton* (1) is adverse. There a testator devised an estate to his wife, remainder to such uses as she should appoint. The wife exercised the power in favour of the testator's nephew. Now if the argument on s. 15 is right, no duty would have been payable by the nephew at all, for, first, he was not liable, as standing in the widow's shoes, to any duty in respect of her succession under s. 4 upon the exercise by her of the general power of appointment, for the donor of the power was her husband, and no duty is payable on the succession of a wife to her husband; and secondly, he would not have been liable to pay duty as on his own succession, for he took the property "by a title not conferring a new succession," the subject of the power being a reversion. The Court, however, there held that duty was payable. But the answer is that the attention of the Court was not directed to s. 15 at all.

(1) Law Rep. 1 Ex. 224.

1877

ATTORNEY
GENERAL
v.
CHARLTON.

If however, the case does not come under s. 4, but under s. 2, the duty will be payable at a different rate, for, though the predecessor remains the same, the successors are different. The predecessor is by s. 2 the settlor, who, on the authority of the cases in the House of Lords above referred to, is William, the donor of the power. The successors are the persons " beneficially entitled," Anne and Dora. The rate, then, at which duty would be payable by them under s. 2 would be 1 per cent. on the annuity of Anne as a succession derived from her son, and 3 per cent. on the life estate of Dora as a succession derived from her uncle.

Fox Bristowe, Q.C., and *G. Law (Spencer Butler* with them), for the defendants. If this case can be brought under s. 2, then the Court need not go further to fulfil the requirements of the Act. And upon the defendants' construction of that section the predecessors are St. John and Thomas, and therefore the duty payable by Anne will be 1 per cent. on a moiety of her annuity as derived from her son, and nothing on the other moiety as derived from her husband, and the duty payable by Dora will be 1 per cent. on the whole of her interest as derived from lineal ascendants. The claim of duty is referrable to the person or persons from whom the bounty is immediately derived. For take the case of a purchase, with a power of appointment given by the conveyance; on that power being subsequently executed by the purchaser in favour of his son, would the son have to pay 10 per cent. succession duty as successor to the vendor, the creator of the power? Surely not—but if not, why not? Because it is from the father and not the vendor that the son derives the bounty. From whom was the bounty in the present case derived? From St. John and Thomas, the donees of the power, for they were the absolute owners of the estate after the death of William. They then were the predecessors. And the cases of *Lord Braybrooke v. Attorney General* (1) and *Attorney General v. Floyer* (2) are not opposed to this contention, for those cases are distinguishable in this material particular, that there the persons who executed the powers were also the persons who created them. All that those cases decide is, as was suggested by Lord Justice Mellish on the

(1) 9 H. L. C. 150; 31 L. J. (Ex.)		(2) 9 H. L. C. 477; 31 L. J. (Ex.)
177.

1877

ATTORNEY
GENERAL
v.
CHARLTON.

first hearing of this appeal in January last (1), that where the father, tenant for life, and the son, tenant in tail, join in barring the entail, and resettle the estate to the father for life, remainder to such uses as they shall jointly appoint, and subsequently execute the power, the deed creating the power and the deed executing it are to be treated as one and the same deed, in which case their joint effect amounts merely to a disposition by the tenant in tail. The use of two deeds instead of one is a mere conveyancing operation, to enable the son more conveniently to dispose of his interest. The bounty which in such case the appointee receives is derived wholly from the tenant in tail; he therefore is to be regarded as the person making the disposition. The cases of *Attorney General* v. *Floyer* (2) and *Attorney General* v. *Braybrooke* (3) turned not upon s. 2, but on s. 12, the House of Lords treating the son (who before was tenant in tail), on his coming into possession, as a person "taking a succession under a disposition made by himself." Here, however, the case is very different—here the two deeds are not to be treated as one—for the tenant in tail does not, as there, give the power to the father and himself, but to the father and the second son, who, being third persons, may be treated as being in the same position as purchasers for value. Nor can any distinction be taken that that which was given to them was only a general power and not the fee. They are given what is practically the absolute interest in the property, an interest which they could sell in the market, for there is no implied trust that the donees should exercise the power in favour of the donor's wishes. St. John and Thomas, therefore, being the absolute owners of the estate, are the persons from whom the bounty was derived, and are, consequently, to be regarded as the predecessors. The distinction between the House of Lord's cases and the present may be shortly stated thus: where the tenant in tail, donor of the power, is also the sole donee or one of the donees of the power, the creation of the power is to be disregarded, as a mere piece of conveyancing machinery, and he

(1) The case was originally part heard at the Hilary Sittings, when the late Lord Justice Mellish was a member of the Court.

(2) 9 H. L. C. 477; 31 L. J. (Ex.) 404.

(3) 9 H. L. C. 150; 31 L. J. (Ex.) 177.

is to be treated as sole predecessor; but where he is not one of the donees, then the donees, the power being a general power, become a fresh stock of descent, and they are to be regarded as the predecessors, not the tenant in tail: *Attorney General* v. *Upton*. (1) If, however, this case falls under s. 4, then it is governed by *Upton's Case* (1), for here, as there, the donor and donees of the power are distinct persons. As regards the rate at which the duty would in such case be payable, the effect would be the same as if it fell under s. 2.

Gorst, Q.C., in reply.

Cur. adv. vult.

June 30. The following judgments were delivered:—

Bramwell, L.J.

BRAMWELL, L.J. I think that this case should be governed by s. 4; that Thomas Meyrick is liable to a duty on the property he with his father appointed, to be calculated on his life at the time of his father's death; that Mrs. Charlton, is liable to no duty, at least not to the Crown; and that Dora Meyrick is liable to no duty, except as being in possession of the estate.

In considering questions under this statute, it must be remembered that the substance of the thing is to be looked at, and not our technical modes of transferring property. It must also be remembered that we are to look to see from whose bounty the succession is derived, the legislature intending that the duty should be varied according to the nearness in relationship, thinking, no doubt, that the more remote the relationship the less is the right to expect a benefit, and consequently the less the hardship in paying for it. Sects. 2 and 4 must be read together. They may be described thus: Sect. 4 deals with powers general and limited. Sect. 2 with other modes of transfer, including devolution. Whether s. 2 would have included transfers by powers if s. 4 had not existed, it is not necessary to determine, but it is obvious that the words of s. 2 are not words such as would be used in speaking of powers. "Every disposition of property by reason whereof any person shall become beneficially entitled to any property upon the death of any person," are the words in relation to this matter. Now, it is not necessary to say whether

(1) Law Rep. 1 Ex. 224. .

"beneficially interested" means "in possession." With submission to the Master of the Rolls (1), I should have thought not.
I should think they meant beneficially as distinguished from
merely "legally," not only because that is the ordinary meaning of
those words, but because provision is afterwards made for the consequences of estates becoming estates in possession which were not
so at first: and see per Lord Wensleydale in *Lord Braybrooke's
Case*. (2)   But whatever is the meaning of those words, it seems
clear that a person having a limited power of appointment otherwise than to himself cannot in any sense be said to be beneficially
entitled to the property he can appoint.   Indeed it may happen
that, owing to ulterior limitations for default of appointment his
interest may be not to exercise the power.

Limited powers seem, therefore, clearly not within the words of
this section, besides being provided for by s. 4.   Then why should
general powers be ?   The words of s. 2 are not apt and appropriate
words.

A man, having a general power of appointment, and appointing
to himself and a vendee, is not accurately described by calling
him a person "beneficially entitled to property immediately or
after any interval, certainly or contingently," for this obvious
reason, among others, that he may not choose to exercise the
power.   I do not forget my own argument, that we must look to
the substance of the matter; and it may be that if s. 4 were not
there, rather than that estates created under a power of appointment, general or limited, and the donees of such powers should
escape, they should be held to be included in s. 2.   But s. 4 is
there, and its words are plain: "Where any person shall have a
general power of appointment, under any disposition of property,
taking effect upon the death of any person, over property, he shall,
in the event of his making any appointment thereunder, be
deemed to be entitled at the time of his exercising such power to
the property or interest thereby appointed, as a succession derived
from the donor of the power."   The words of this clause are plain,
and, to my mind, the reasons.   A general power of appointment
is the same as a gift or devise to the extent of the power.   A gift

(1) See *Fryer* v. *Morland*, 3 Ch. D.   (2) 9 H. L. C. 150; 31 L. J. (Ex.)
at p. 683.   177.

1877

ATTORNEY
GENERAL
v.
·CHARLTON.

·Bramwell, L.J.

or devise in fee is not distinguishable in substance from a power to appoint in fee. The mere gift or devise of the power before its exercise does not create a succession, because it may never be exercised, or when exercised may be exercised over part of the estates only, or for a limited interest. Some confusion arises in this case from Mrs. Charlton and Miss Meyrick being relations of the donees of the power, and being gratuitous appointees. But the case is the same as though the appointee had been a stranger who had given 500,000l. for the estate. Suppose the father and Mr. Meyrick had had an estate in fee in reversion, instead of this power of appointment, they would undoubtedly have had a succession. Then suppose they had had a power of appointment, and for default of appointment an estate in fee, they would undoubtedly have had a succession. Suppose they sold the estate, but conveyed by the exercise of their power, would they have lost their succession? or pay a different duty to what they would if they conveyed by an exercise of the power? Then suppose, as is the case, that they have only a power, is there any difference in results, when there is none in substance but only in words? An estate devised or granted does not vest unless the devisee or grantee chooses to take it; so a power does not create a succession till the donee chooses to execute it. This case is within the very words of the section; the father and Mr. Meyrick had a general power of appointment, under a disposition of property, taking effect on the death of the elder son, over property, and they have made an appointment under the power. To what case does s. 4 apply if not to this? Mr. Bristowe could give no answer to that question. No injustice is done by this construction. Mr. Meyrick ought to pay a duty; he with his father has in substance had a succession on his brother's death. He and his father have given the property away; but suppose they had sold it? What is the difference between what has happened and what would have happened if instead of a general power of appointment his father and he had had an estate in fee, and had disposed of it as they have disposed of their power? Whatever question his father's death may give rise to, would equally arise if they had had an estate in fee. Whatever question may be made owing to Mrs. Charlton and Dora Meyrick being gratuitous appointees, might be made if Dora

1877

ATTORNEY
GENERAL
v.
CHARLTON.

Bramwell, L.J.

Meyrick had been a gratuitous grantee in fee of the estate, whether charged or not with an annuity to Mrs. Charlton, or if she had been a grantee for value with or without the charge of the annuity. As between her and her father different questions might arise as to the ultimate incidence of the duty, to what would arise between him and a purchaser for value. I should suppose that if she accepts the estate she accepts cum onere, while a purchaser would be entitled to have it free from encumbrance. So as to Mrs. Charlton, it may be that Miss Meyrick might well be entitled to say that if she is liable to the duty because she has accepted the estate, Mrs. Charlton must bear a proportionate part of it. But it is not necessary to determine this. The same question would arise if the father and Mr. Meyrick had had an estate in fee, and had granted it for the same estates and interest as they have created by the exercise of their power. Suppose the father and Mr. Meyrick had purchased the power of appointment from the father and William for 500,000l., what would be the case? Mrs. Charlton and Dora would not be successors on its exercise, any more than a vendee would, but the father and Mr. Meyrick would be. It matters not that they are gratuitous donees of the power. Then it is asked, suppose Mr. Meyrick had died before his father, would there have been any such duty? I ask, suppose they had had an estate in fee, would there have been? and I answer in both cases No, because there would have been no enjoyment. Then it is asked, would Miss Meyrick in that case be liable to a succession duty? I answer No. Upon which it is said that there would be a death, a succession, and no duty. I protest against having to answer all these possible cases, and content myself with asking in return, what would be the case if Mr. Charlton and Mr. Meyrick had had an estate in fee. If I understand s. 15 no duty would be payable. Mr. Charlton and Mr. Meyrick would never have enjoyed, and Miss Meyrick would take by a conveyance inter vivos. The all-important thing is to bear in mind the rule that this general power of appointment when acted on is the same as an estate to the same extent as is created by the exercise of the power. This opinion is, to my mind, much confirmed by s. 33. I suppose that would apply to a case, among others, where a man had an estate for life with a power of appointment beyond his life

1877

ATTORNEY
GENERAL
v.
CHARLTON.

Bramwell, L.J.

and exercised it. Then he would pay no duty on its exercise. The Crown is not wronged by this construction. *There are not two enjoyments or two deaths.* If Mr. Charlton and Mr. Meyrick had appointed to Mr. Meyrick for life with remainder to Miss Meyrick, then Mr. Meyrick would be subject to a duty and so would Miss Meyrick on his death. I am of opinion, therefore, that the Crown is not entitled to two duties, but is entitled to a duty from Mr. Meyrick, and that as, according to *Lord Braybrooke* v. *Attorney General* (1) and *Attorney General* v. *Floyer* (2), he and his father derived their succession from William Charlton, the father's moiety is derived from his son William, and Mr. Meyrick's from his brother. I should have thought therefore that the duty should be charged, 1 per cent. on one moiety, and 3 per cent. on the other, averaging therefore 2 per cent. The calculation should, I think, under s. 21, be on the life of Mr. Meyrick. Again I say I treat the case as though he and his father had had an estate in fee and had granted it as they have. That is the key to all difficulties. The father is dead. But suppose he and Mr. Meyrick had appointed to a vendee for value and divided the price, whatever would be true then is true now. I should have thought it right then to say that the Crown was entitled to duty at the rate of 2 per cent. were it not for the case of *Attorney General* v. *Floyer* (2), where, on a case not distinguishable in principle, as I think, the Crown was held entitled to 3 per cent. I say not distinguishable in principle, though it was in fact. For here the donees of a general power of appointment appoint *to a stranger to the power*; there they appointed to one of themselves. The 4th section was never mentioned in the arguments or judgment. In my opinion the question there, as here, turned on the 4th section. If *Attorney General* v. *Floyer* (2) governs this case, then Mr. Meyrick is liable to a duty of 3 per cent. Anyhow, I think the decree of the Court below cannot be supported. I think that decree is fundamentally wrong in treating Miss Meyrick and Mrs. Charlton as successors. *Upton's Case* (3) is distinguishable from this. There the donee of the general power exercised it so

as to create a succession on *her* death, and she was treated as predecessor in that succession. *She never enjoyed under the power.*
Here the donees exercise it so as to create an estate which is in
possession during the life of one of them as it turns out, and
create no new succession.

Had they exercised it in Miss Meyrick's favour on Mr. Meyrick's
death, then she would have been a successor to him alone or to
him and his father, while he would have been liable as a successor
for his life estate.   I think, then, the decree cannot stand, that
Attorney General v. *Floyer* (1) is an authority that 3 per cent. is
the duty, but with all submission, I think that the statute makes
it 2 per cent. only.   I have thought it my duty to express this
opinion because (I hope I shall not be thought presumptuous) I
entertain it strongly, justified by the opinions of the Lord Chief
Justice and my Brother Brett, and because I think cases of this
sort cannot be properly considered without regard to s. 4, whether
to ascertain who is the successor or what is the duty.

JAMES, L.J. I am myself unable to find any difference in any
material fact between the case before us and the cases in the
House of Lords. The only distinction that was suggested is that
in those cases the donors of the power were the same as the
donees of the power, i.e., the tenant for life and the eldest son,
and that · here the donees were the tenant for life and the second
son. To my mind that creates no more difference in law than the
fact that the names are different does. That being so, I consider
myself not merely at liberty, but bound to follow the decisions of
the House of Lords implicitly, and not to exercise my own judgment at all. On a question whether under particular circumstances
a succession duty of 1 per cent., or 2 per cent., or 3 per cent., is
payable, and on whose life to be calculated, the decision of the
final Court of Appeal is one which I am well content to accept,
thankful for being relieved from all duty except obedience, and
from all responsibility.

Under that decision the duty will be calculated on the lives of
the appointees of the power according to their relationship to the
eldest son.

(1) 9 H. L. C. 477 ; 31 L. J. (Ex.) 404.

1877

ATTORNEY
GENERAL
v.
CHARLTON.

James, L.J.

I consider the House of Lords to have disregarded the 4th clause—whether rightly or wrongly, or whether with or without sufficient consideration, it is not for me to say. They have spoken —the matter is for me ended.

With a view to other cases, I will, however, make one observation on the 4th clause. In this Act of Parliament I am not aware of any clause where it is necessary to read a singular word for plural, and I am of opinion that in this case the context requires us to confine the singular to the singular. A joint power of appointment is, in my opinion, an entirely different thing in intention and practical operation from a general and absolute power of appointment in one individual. In the latter case it is really and practically the equivalent of property—when exercised the property becomes assets. In the other case it is what it purports to be—a form of remoulding a settlement according to the exigencies of the family. Such a case as is suggested of a joint power of appointment with a limitation to the two donees as joint tenants never, I should think, has occurred, and never will, I imagine, occur in any settlement. It may possibly have occurred in conveyances of partnership property, but those things are outside the purview of this Act.

Cockburn, C.J.

COCKBURN, C.J. I am of opinion that the judgment of the Exchequer Division should be reversed. If, indeed, the matter were res integra, I should entirely concur in the view taken by Lord Justice Bramwell, that this case came within the 4th section of the Succession Duty Act, and that, on the true construction of that section, the result arrived at by the Exchequer Division could be upheld, though not on the grounds on which the decision of that Court proceeds; but the question at issue appears to me to be concluded by the authority of the cases of *Attorney General* v. *Floyer* (1) and *Attorney General* v. *Smythe* (2), with the decision in which cases the judgment appealed against appears to me to be incapable of being reconciled.

In addition to these cases, the decision of the House of Lords in *Lord Braybrooke* v. *Attorney General* (3), was also relied upon by

(1) 9 H. L. C. 477; 31 L. J. (Ex.)   (2) 9 H. L. C. 497; 31 L. J. (Ex.)
404.   404.

(3) 9 H. L. C. 150; 31 L. J. (Ex.) 177.

the counsel for the Crown as an authority in their favour; but I
think that the latter case may well be distinguished from the one
before us. In *Lord Braybrooke* v. *Attorney General* (1), there was
a devise by a distant relative, Lord Howard de Walden, the first
Lord Braybrooke, to Richard Aldworth Neville, afterwards second
Lord Braybrooke, for life, remainder to his eldest son, Richard
Neville, for life, remainder to the sons of Richard Neville, successively, in tail male. Richard Aldworth Neville having died,
Richard Neville, the third Lord Braybrooke, then being tenant for
life in possession, and his eldest son Richard Cornwallis Neville,
being tenant in tail in expectancy on the death of his father, barred
the entail, and, subject to the life estate of the father, conveyed to
trustees to hold to such uses as the father and son should appoint,
and in default of such appointment to such uses as the son, if he
survived, should appoint; and in default of such appointment to
the son for life, with remainder to his sons in tail male. By a
subsequent deed, in execution of the power of appointment by the
father and the son, the estate was limited to the father for life,
with remainder to the son for life, remainder to the sons of the
latter successively in tail male. On the son, the fourth Lord
Braybrooke, coming into possession on the death of his father, the
question arose whether the succession duty was to be paid on the
footing that his estate had been derived from the appointment of
his father and himself, or from the original devise. It was held by
the House of Lords that, notwithstanding the subsequent estates
created by disentailing the original estate, by the creation of the
power and the appointment under it, yet, for the purpose of fixing
the amount of duty, the succession must be taken to have been
acquired under the original devise, and not under the appointment. And the decision is obviously just. One who, under the
disposition from which he derives an estate, is liable to a given
amount of duty, cannot be permitted, by a subsequent disposition
of it by himself, to take by the appointment, under a power
created by himself, of a person nearer in relationship than the
original disponer, and so diminish the duty. It was observed by
Lord Kingsdown that "as regards the reversion the son took
nothing from the father." "It was a disposition made by the son

(1) 9 H. L. C. 150; 31 L. J. (Ex.) 177.

1877

ATTORNEY
GENERAL
v.
CHARLTON.

Cockburn, C.J.

of an estate which he previously held." Besides this, it was pointed out by Lord Campbell that the case fell directly within the 12th section of the Succession Duty Act; for the succession was created out of the estate tail, not out of the estate for life, and was therefore the act of the tenant in tail entitled in expectancy on the death of the tenant for life. It was, therefore, directly within the 12th section, which was obviously passed to meet such a case. "The object of the 12th section," says Lord Campbell, "was to prevent any one with a vested estate tail in remainder, from diminishing by his own act the rate of succession duty to which he would be liable if he did not deal with the estate till it vested in possession."

From the foregoing case, however, the case before us is distinguishable with reference to its facts, inasmuch as it is not the case of an estate derived from a stranger, and therefore primarily liable to succession duty as such. St. John Charlton, being tenant for life in possession, and William Charlton, his eldest son, being tenant in tail in remainder, of certain estates, by a deed of the 22nd of March, 1854, barred the entail and settled the estates to such uses as they should jointly appoint, and in default of appointment to the use of St. John Charlton the father for life, with remainder to William Charlton the son in tail male. By a deed of the 23rd of March, in exercise of the power, they appointed the estates to such uses as they should jointly appoint, and in default of appointment to St. John Charlton for life, with remainder to William Charlton for life, with remainder to his sons in tail male, with remainder to such uses as St. John Charlton and his second son Thomas (who afterwards assumed the name of Meyrick) should jointly appoint, and in default of appointment to Thomas for life, with remainder to his sons in tail male, with remainders over. William Charlton having died in 1864 without issue, and without the power of appointment vested in him and his father having been exercised, St. John Charlton and his son Thomas Meyrick, in exercise of their joint power, appointed the estates, subject to the father's life estate, and in the events which happened, to the use that after the death of St. John Charlton, Ann his wife, if she survived him, should receive a yearly rent-charge of 1700*l.* and subject thereto to the use that Mary Rhoda should, in certain events which have not yet happened, receive a yearly rent-charge of 1000*l.*, and subject to these rent-charges that the estates should go to the use of Dora, the daughter of Thomas Meyrick, during so much of a certain period as she should live. St. John Charlton died in 1873, his wife Ann surviving him, and Dora, the daughter of Thomas, came into possession. Upon this state of facts it was contended for the Crown that for the purpose of assessing the succession duty payable under s. 2 of the Act of 1853 (the section, as it was said, properly applicable), by Ann Charlton and Dora Meyrick respectively, their successions must be taken to be derived from William Charlton, the donor of the power, as their predecessor, and not from St. John Charlton and Thomas Meyrick, as their predecessors, within the meaning of the section.

If I had had to deal with this case independently of authority, I should have been prepared to hold that, even assuming the case to be within the 2nd section, the succession was derived by the appointment of the father, St. John Charlton, and Thomas Meyrick, his son; but the cases of *Floyer* (1) and *Smythe* (1) seem to me to be directly in point and fatal to this view.

In *Attorney General* v. *Floyer* (1) Henry Bankes devised certain estates to trustees to the use of his eldest son Henry for life, with remainder to the use of his first and other sons in tail male. Afterwards, in 1810, Henry the son, and William John, his eldest son, being then respectively tenant for life and tenant in tail in expectancy, suffered a recovery, and settled the estates to the use of such persons as they should jointly appoint, and, in default of appointment, to Henry the father for life, remainder to such uses as William John, if he survived his father, should appoint. In 1821 the father and son executed a joint deed of appointment, by which, after a recital that Henry the father was seised of other estates, and that it would be convenient that all the estates should be held under one settlement, and that the father and son had agreed to join in settling the estates, and for that purpose had agreed to execute their joint power of appointment, they proceeded to appoint the estates settled in 1810 to Henry the father in fee simple, the others to such uses as they should jointly

(1) 9 H. L. C. 477; 31 L. J. (Ex.) 404.

appoint, in default to the father for life, remainder to the son
William John for life, remainder to his sons in tail male, remainder to George, the eldest brother of William John, and his other
brothers successively, in tail male. The joint power was never
exercised. William John survived his father, but died unmarried,
whereupon George, his brother, came into possession.

The first question in the case was as to the rate of duty which
George was to be charged with on this succession. But a further
question presented itself. George Bankes having become tenant
for life ˙in possession, and his eldest son, Edmund George, being
tenant in tail in expectancy, by a deed executed by both, Edmund
George the son, with the assent of his father as protector of the
settlement, disentailed the settled estates, and conveyed them to a
trustee, upon such uses as the father and son should jointly appoint,
and in default of such appointment to the uses of the prior settlement. A deed of appointment followed immediately afterwards,
executed by the father and son, whereby the settled estates were
conveyed to such uses as the father and son should appoint, and in
default of appointment to trustees to pay certain annuities, and,
subject thereto, to the use of George the father for life, remainder
to trustees for the use of Edmund George the son for life, with
remainder to his sons in tail male. Both in the settlement of
1821 and in the later one a power was reserved to George Bankes
the father to charge the estates for the benefit of his younger
children. This he accordingly did by his will. He died after the
Succession Duty Act had come into operation, but when one
instalment only of the duty on account of his succession had
become payable. Three per cent. was claimed on it, as on a succession derived from his brother William John. Three per cent.
was also claimed on the succession of Edmund George, as one
created by his own disposition, and therefore chargeable under
s. 12 of the Act. The Court of Exchequer, however, held that
Henry and William John were the joint predecessors of George,
and, this being so, that his succession was chargeable with a duty
of 1 per cent. on half the property, as having been derived from
his father, and 3 per cent. on the other half, as derived from his
brother. For the like reason they held that the succession of
Edmund George was chargeable with duty at the same rate. As

regards the succession of the younger children of George, they held that, the interest being derived from their father, a duty of 1 per cent. only was payable.

But the House of Lords (Lords Cranworth and Wensleydale) reversed this decision, holding that William John Bankes, the brother of George, had been sole predecessor of the latter, and that consequently a duty of 3 per cent. was payable in respect of the whole. As regards the duty payable on the succession of Edmund George, they held that he took under his own disposition, on a succession derived from William John, his uncle, and consequently was liable to a duty of 3 per cent. As to the younger children of George, they held that (except as to certain estates brought into settlement by their grandfather, Henry Bankes, on which a duty of 1 per cent. only would be chargeable) the succession was derived from their brother Edmund George, and was consequently liable to a duty of 3 per cent.

The principle of this decision, as explained by Lord Cranworth, was that, in order to see who is the settlor within the 2nd section of the Act, that is to say, the settlor "from whom the interest of the successor is derived," we must inquire, not who are the parties by whose conveyance the estate has been created, but who is the party out of whose estate the interest has been derived, and that it matters not whether the disposition be made under the disentailing deed itself or under a joint power of appointment created by such deed.

Observing on the decision in the *Braybrooke Case* (1), Lord Cranworth says: "The ground of the decision evidently was that, although the estate of the son arose under a joint power of appointment made by his father and himself, and although therefore the father was in a sense one of the settlors, yet he was not a settlor from whom the interest or any part of the interest of the son, in his character of successor, was derived. And the decision shews that, in order to ascertain who is the settlor within the 2nd section, i.e. the settlor "from whom the interest of the successor is derived," we must inquire, not who are the parties by whose conveyance the estate has been created, but who is the conveying party out of whose estate the interest in question has been derived."

(1) 9 H. L. C. 150; 31 L. J. (Ex.) 177.

And his Lordship further adds: "The decision in the *Braybrooke Case* (1) necessarily leads to the conclusion that the settlor, within the true meaning of the 2nd section, must be a settlor out of whose estate the succession is derived, and so that, though the act of the father in making the appointment was necessary to the creation of the portions, yet as they did not to any extent come out of his estate, he was not the settlor within the meaning of the statute." Lord Wensleydale also observes that "the decision in *Lord Braybrooke's Case* (1) is in effect that, if the tenant in tail in remainder joins with the tenant for life in executing a general power of appointment to another, the interest of the appointee is derived from the tenant in tail in remainder, and must be charged with succession duty accordingly."

In the case of *Attorney General* v. *Smythe* (2) Sir Edward Joseph Smythe, being seised in fee of certain estates, settled the estates to himself for life, with remainder to his first and other sons in tail male. On his eldest son Edward Joseph Smythe coming of age, the father and son executed a disentailing deed, by which the estates were conveyed to such uses as they should jointly appoint, and in default of appointment to remain to the uses of the prior settlement. Immediately afterwards, on the marriage of the son, articles were executed to which the father and son were parties, by which it was agreed that the property should be conveyed to the use of Sir Edward Joseph Smythe the father for life, remainder to the son for life, remainder to the first and other sons of the marriage in tail male, remainder to the use of Richard Peter Carrington, the second son of Sir E. J. Smythe, and his sons in tail male, with a like remainder to Charles Frederick, the third son of Sir Edward. The eldest son, Edward Joseph Smythe, died without issue. Thereupon Sir Edward Joseph and his then eldest son, Richard Peter Carrington, executed a deed disentailing the estates, and conveying them to such uses as they should jointly appoint, and in default to such uses as were then subsisting. Subsequently, in execution of this power, they appointed the estates to Sir Edward Joseph for life, remainder to the son, Richard Peter Carrington, for life, and to his

(1) 9 H. L. C. 150; 31 L. J. (Ex.)   (2) 9 H. L. C. 477; 31 L. J. (Ex.)
177.   404.

1877

ATTORNEY
GENERAL
v.
CHARLTON.

Cockburn, C.J.

sons in tail male; remainder to Charles Frederick for life, with remainder to his sons in tail male.   Richard Peter Carrington died, like his elder brother, without issue, whereupon Charles Frederick succeeded.   The Court of Exchequer held, as in the preceding case, that the succession was to the father and the brother, and that the duty payable was consequently 1 per cent. on the one half and 3 per cent. on the other half.   But the House of Lords again held that the entire succession was derived from the brother, and that consequently 3 per cent. was payable on the whole.

I am at a loss to see the distinction between these cases and the present, though I would gladly do so if I could.   I cannot disguise my regret at the construction put upon the statute by the House of Lords, which, even assuming the 2nd section to have been applicable to the case, I cannot but think to have been altogether contrary to the spirit of the Act.   Technically speaking, there can be no doubt that when tenant for life and tenant in tail in expectancy join in disentailing an estate, and conveying it anew, it is only to the disentailing part of the proceeding that the concurrence of the tenant for life is necessary or operative. The estate once disentailed, the new disposition of it is the act of the remainderman whose estate in remainder has become enlarged from an estate tail into an estate in fee simple.   But in effect these successive settlements and re-settlements of estates are neither more nor less than a mode of transmitting family estates from father to son, according to the ordinary principles of succession, with the least possible danger of these estates being alienated, and so lost to the family.   Each tenant in tail in his turn, with the consent of his father the tenant for life, gives up his estate tail, and is content to take an estate for life, while he so settles the succession as that his eldest son shall take an estate for life, with remainder to his issue in tail, the effect of which is to secure the estate to the family for at least another generation.   At the same time care is always taken in such a settlement that the younger sons who were in remainder in the previous settlement shall have estates in remainder in the event of the failure of issue of the eldest son.   No one can fail to see that while, in a technical sense, the future estates created by such a settlement are carved out of the estate in fee, which thus becomes at the disposal of the son, in reality the dominant party is the father, who concurs in the disentailing of the estate, only in order to enable his son to make the necessary settlement on his marriage, and who, as the condition of his doing so, stipulates for the conveyance of the newly created estate to specified uses.

Now a leading principle of the succession duty being that on a succession in the direct descending or ascending line a duty of 1 per cent. only shall be chargeable, it certainly seems inconsistent with common sense [to say, where a younger son, who under a prior setttlement would, on his elder brother having died without issue, have succeeded his father as tenant in tail in remainder, now succeeds, in consequence of his elder brother having died, to his father in the possession of the paternal estate, under a settlement to which the father was a party, and in which the interests of all the sons were equally intended to be secured, that because, with a view to the more convenient transmission of the estates, the latter have for a moment been vested in the deceased brother, the younger son shall be held to take them as a succession to the brother, who never in fact possessed them, and not from the father, whom he in fact immediately succeeds, is certainly a very striking anomaly.

It was said by Lord Campbell, then Lord Chancellor, in the *Braybrooke Case* (1), that "this statute, which by the same enactment imposes a tax on successions in every part of the United Kingdom, is to be construed, not according to the technicalities of the law of real property in England or in Scotland, but according to the popular use of the language employed." But, unfortunately, his Lordship, in applying the statute, took the narrowest and most technical view of it. Well might Baron Amphlett say, with reference to the case before us, "No one can doubt that, in a popular sense, and according to the ordinary notions of mankind, the interests of these defendants would be considered as derived from the makers of the settlement of 1866, who had in themselves, without the control of any other person, full and entire dominion over the estates. It never could have occurred to any one not versed in the technicalities of English law that we were

(1) 9 H. L. C. 150; 31 L. J. (Ex.) 177.

to look back through the title for the predecessor, until we come to some person or other out of whose estate, as contradistinguished from power, the interest of the successor was derived. Observe, too, that it is theoretically possible that you might have to travel back for centuries before you could find such a predecessor, for there is nothing contrary to law in carrying on an estate from one generation to another ad infinitum by the successive creation of general powers. Of course no one would seriously contend that we were to go back in that way through several generations to find the predecessor, but the alternative is that you must take a person with only a power as predecessor."

But while I fully enter into this view, and concur in this reasoning on the general question, I am unable to follow the reasoning by which it is attempted to distinguish the case before us from the cases of *Floyer* (1) and *Smythe* (1). It matters not that the estates were created under a joint power of appointment. The rule once established that the case falls within the 2nd section, and that the succession is to be sought, not in the party creating the interest, but in the estate out of which the interest is created, and that the disentailed estate is to be held exclusively in him who before was tenant in tail, it becomes indifferent whether the new estates are created by the latter, or by virtue of a power created by the disentailing deed. Besides, in both the cases referred to, the successions had been created under a joint power of appointment, as in the present case.

The other ground taken in the judgment below, namely, that the joint power to appoint was purchased by the father, St. John Charlton, does not make the estate out of which the succession was derived any the less the estate of William, previously the tenant in tail. Moreover, there was equally consideration moving from the father in the case of *Attorney General* v. *Floyer*. (1) For new estates were there brought into the settlement executed between Henry Bankes and William John Bankes in 1821.

I entirely agree with Lord Justice Bramwell, that the cases in the House of Lords came under the 4th section, and not the 2nd section, of the Succession Duty Act, and that a duty of 1 per cent. was all that was under the circumstances payable. But I

(1) 9 H. L. C. 477; 31 L. J. (Ex.) 404.

am bound by the authority of the decisions referred to, however
fatally wrong I may deem them to be, and must therefore concur
in reversing the decision of the Exchequer Division in the present
case.

BRETT, L.J.   I have heard this case argued twice—once in the
Exchequer, and a second time in this Court.   I have not been able
to see any distinction between *Attorney General* v. *Floyer* (1) and
this case.   If, however, this case is to be treated as coming under
s. 2, then I can see no case to which s. 4 can apply.

> *Judgment reversed and entered for the Crown accordingly.*

Solicitor for the Crown : *Solicitor to Inland Revenue.*
Solicitors for Defendants : *Law, Hussey, & Halbert.*

[IN THE COURT OF APPEAL.]

DIGGLE *v.* HIGGS.

*Gaming—8 & 9 Vict. c. 109, s. 18—Money deposited with Stakeholder when
recoverable—Wager.*

An agreement to walk a match for 200*l.* a side, the money being deposited
with a stakeholder, is a wager, and null and void under 8 & 9 Vict. c. 109, s. 18.
And the deposit of the money is not a subscription or contribution for a sum of
money to be awarded to the winner of a lawful game within the proviso of that
enactment: and although the winner of the match cannot sue the loser or the
stakeholder to recover the stakes, yet a depositor may maintain an action to
recover back the share deposited by him with the stakeholder.

The plaintiff and one S. agreed to walk a match for 200*l.* a side, and each
deposited 200*l.* with the defendant to be paid to the winner.   S. won the match.
The plaintiff, after the determination of the match, but before the money was
paid over to S., demanded the sum deposited by him from the defendant :—

Held, that the plaintiff was entitled to recover his share of the deposit from
the defendant.

Batty v. *Marriott* (5 C. B. 818) overruled.

ACTION to recover from the defendant the sum of 200*l.*

At the trial before Huddleston, B., at the Manchester Spring
Assizes, 1877, the following facts appeared in evidence :—

On the 28th of July, 1876, the plaintiff and one Simmonite
entered into the following agreement, which was signed by both

(1) 9 H. L. C. 477; 31 L. J. (Ex.) 404.

parties:—"Articles of agreement between Simmonite and T. Diggle, to walk at Higginshaw Grounds, Oldham, on the 19th of October, 1866, for 200*l.* a side.   T. Diggle to receive 100 yards start in one mile.   25*l.* a side down in the hands of C. Higgs, stakeholder; second deposit, 25*l.* each, to be made on August 5, at Unwin's, up to 9 o'clock; third deposit of 50*l.* each on September 16; and the final 100*l.* each to be made at 12 o'clock, the day of walking.   The men to be on their marks at 10 o'clock. All the money to be deposited in C. Higgs' hands.   Perkins referee, and C. Higgs final stakeholder and pistol-firer.   Either parties not agreeing to these articles to forfeit the money down."

Pursuant to this agreement the defendant received 200*l.* down from each of the competitors.   On the 19th of October the walking match took place, and the referee, Perkins, decided that Simmonite had won the match.   On the 21st of October, before the defendant had paid over the stakes to Simmonite, the plaintiff's solicitor gave the defendant a written notice not to pay Simmonite, and demanded a return of the sum of 200*l.* deposited by the plaintiff with the defendant.   Subsequently the defendant, pursuant to the referee Perkin's decision, paid the whole of the 400*l.* to Simmonite.

These facts being admitted, after argument, the learned judge, on the authority of *Batty* v. *Marriott* (1), directed the judgment to be entered for the defendant, on the ground that the case was within the proviso in s. 18. (2)

Edwards, Q.C., for the plaintiff.   The question is whether the plaintiff having demanded the sum deposited with the defendant

(1) 5 C. B. 818.

(2) By 8 & 9 Vict. c. 109, s. 41, all contracts or agreements, whether by parol or in writing, by way of gaming or wagering, shall be null and void; and no suit shall be brought or maintained in any court of law or equity for recovering any sum of money or valuable thing alleged to be won upon any wager, or which shall have been deposited in the hands of any person to abide the event on which any wager shall have been made; provided always that this enactment shall not be deemed to apply to any subscription or contribution, or agreement to subscribe or contribute for or towards any plate, prize, or sum of money to be awarded to the winner or winners of any lawful game, sport, pastime, or exercise.

as stakeholder before he has paid it over, but after the event has happened, can recover it back. According to the authorities it is clear that he can. In *Hastelow* v. *Jackson* (1) Bayley, J., says: "If a stakeholder pays over money without authority from the party and in opposition to his desire he does so at his peril." That statement of the law was approved of in *Hampden* v. *Walsh* (2), and that case is a direct authority for the plaintiff. By 8 & 9 Vict. c. 109, s. 18, all contracts by way of gaming or wagering are null and void, and it makes no difference in the present state of the law whether the wager is legal or illegal, even assuming a foot-race to be a legal game, the plaintiff having demanded his deposit before it was paid over is entitled to recover it from the defendant. *Batty* v. *Marriott* (3) is, no doubt, an authority for the defendant, but that case was disapproved of in the Court of Appeal in *Batson* v. *Newman*. (4) It will be contended for the defendant that the payment of the money to the defendant is "a subscription or contribution for or towards any plate, prize, or sum of money to be awarded to the winner of a lawful game, sport, pastime, or exercise" within the meaning of the proviso in s. 18. But in this case the agreement between the parties is a wager; the one bets the other that he will beat him in a walking-match; the persons who deposit the money are personally interested in an event which is uncertain; it is a wager between the two persons, and not within the proviso. *Varney* v. *Hickman* (5), *Martin* v. *Hewson* (6), and *Graham* v. *Thompson* (7) are also authorities to shew that the plaintiff is entitled to recover back the money deposited.

C. Russell, Q.C., and *Crompton*, for the defendant. The agreement between the plaintiff and Simmonite is not a wager, and the money paid to the defendant is a subscription towards a sum of money to be awarded to the winner of a lawful game within the proviso in s. 18. The plaintiff therefore cannot recover in this action. This question has been decided in *Batty* v. *Marriott*. (3) It was there held that a foot race was a legal game, and that a sum of money which each of two persons deposited with a stake-

(1) 8 B. & C. at p. 225.   (4) 1 C. P. D. 573.
(2) 1 Q. B. D. 189.   (5) 5 C. B. 271; 17 L. J. (C.P.) 102.
(3) 5 C. B. 818.   (6) 10 Ex. 737; 24 L. J. (Ex.) 174.
                (7) 2 Ir. Rep. C. L. 64.

1877

DIGGLE
v.
HIGGS.

holder to abide the event of a foot-race to be run between them was a subscription for a sum to be awarded to the winner of a lawful game. *Batson* v. *Newman* (1) is distinguishable. There there was a bet between two persons that a horse would cover a certain distance in a given time; it was a race against time; it is clear that was not a lawful game. The earlier decisions proceeded on the ground that a stakeholder is in the position of an agent or arbitrator; he receives the money in that character, his authority may be revoked before the event has happened, but a revocation is too late after it has come off. A walking match is not unlawful, and a subscription of money to be paid to the winner clearly comes within the proviso. Two persons may subscribe towards a sum of money, and the circumstance that there are only two persons who subscribe, and that they are competitors, does not make it the less a subscription. The words of the proviso are " subscription or contribution." Subscription would include the money of competitors, be they two or more, and contribution would be the money received from third persons. After the event has come off the defendant holds the money not for the persons who have deposited it, but for the winner; the winner alone, if anybody, can sue for it. If the winner cannot sue, neither can the plaintiff, for the second clause of s. 18 provides that no suit shall be brought for recovering any sum of money which shall have been deposited in the hands of any person to abide the event on which the wager shall have been made. No doubt *Varney* v. *Hickman* (2) and *Martin* v. *Hewson* (3) have decided that that clause relates to the case where a winner brings an action against a loser, seeking to recover the wager from the loser; but in *Savage* v. *Madder* (4) Martin, B., expresses an opinion that no action of any kind can be brought with respect to betting contracts, the object of the Act being to prevent trials in courts of law with respect to betting transactions, and in *Hampden* v. *Walsh* (5) the Court seem to invite a review of these decisions in a Court of Appeal. In all the cases in which the money has been recovered back, except *Varney* v. *Hickman* (2), the games were illegal.

(1) 1 C. P. D. 573.   (3) 10 Ex. 737; 24 L. J. (Ex.) 174.
(2) 5 C. B. 571.   (4) 36 L. J. (Ex.) 178.
             (5) 1 Q. B. D. 189.

Edwards, Q.C., was not heard in reply.

LORD CAIRNS, L.C. The first question which we must ask ourselves is, was this contract a wager? It seems to me beyond a
doubt that it was a wager; it was a wager between two men for a
walking match. They agreed to walk at the Higginshaw grounds
for 200*l.* a side; it is not the less a wager because the money was
deposited with the defendant as stakeholder. When the wager
was decided, the winner would be paid the 200*l.* deposited by the
loser, and receive back his own 200*l.* Now upon that, what is the
construction of s. 18 of 8 & 9 Vict. c. 109? Is a contract of this
kind excepted by the proviso? We start with this, that the contract was clearly a wager, and was within the first part of the section.
That section says all contracts and agreements, whether by parol or
in writing, by way of gaming or wagering, shall be null and void;
and then there is a proviso which follows upon an intervening
sentence in these words: "And no suit shall be brought or maintained in any court of law or equity for recovering any sum of
money or valuable thing alleged to have been won upon any
wager, or which shall have been deposited in the hands of any
person to abide the event on which any wager shall have been
made." Then comes the proviso on which this question mainly
rests: "Provided always that this enactment shall not be deemed
to apply to any subscription or contribution or agreement to
subscribe or contribute for or towards any plate, prize, or sum of
money to be awarded to the winner or winners of any lawful game,
sport, pastime, or exercise."

It is clear that there may be in scores of forms "subscriptions,
or contributions" towards a plate or prize without there being any
wager, and I cannot read this proviso, which has a natural and
intelligible meaning, in a different way, and one which would have
the effect of neutralising the enactment. The legislature, I think,
never intended to say that there should be no action brought to
recover a sum of money which shall have been deposited in the
hands of any person to abide the event on which any wager shall
have been made, and yet that if the wager is in the form of a subscription or contribution the winner may recover it. I read the
proviso thus: Provided that so long as there is a subscription

which is not a wager the second part of the section shall not apply to it. There is no authority in favour of the view of the defendant except *Batty* v. *Marriott* (1), and if that authority is to be followed it cannot be denied it is a very strong authority for the defendant. What the Court had in their minds in that case was the question whether the game was a lawful or an unlawful game, and having come to the conclusion that it was a lawful game, they were of opinion that there was nothing in the case which was struck at by the Act of Parliament, and that the Act was only intended to strike at unlawful games. That view seems to me to be erroneous, and I think that the Court overlooked the first part of the section, which applies to all contracts, lawful or unlawful, by way of gaming or wagering. When *Batson* v. *Newman* (2) came before this Court, although there was a certain degree of difference between that case and *Batty* v. *Marriott* (1), yet it is obvious that *Batty* v. *Marriott* (1) did not meet with approval. I cannot follow that case. I therefore think that although there was a deposit of money, the contract in this case was a wager, and that all the consequences which are imposed by s. 18 on contracts by way of wagering follow.

Then it is said that this is an action by a party to the contract, and that he has revoked the authority given to the defendant to pay over the money, on the ground that the contract is void, and that s. 18 has taken away his right to maintain an action under that part of the section which says no suit shall be brought for recovering money which shall have been deposited in the hands of any person to abide the event on which any wager shall have been made." On that I must observe, that in *Hampden* v. *Walsh* (3) the Queen's Bench Division appeared to have been of opinion that an action under similar circumstances could be maintained; and in *Batty* v. *Marriott* (1) the objection was not taken. Be that as it may, I am of opinion that that objection cannot be maintained. The section amounts to this: all contracts by way of gaming and wagering are null and void; and then, dealing with those contracts, it says that no action shall be brought with respect to them: that is to say, all gaming contracts are void,

(1) 5 C. B. 818.   (2) 1 C. P. D. 573.
          (3) 1 Q. B. D. 189.

and the winner of the game or wager shall not maintain a suit against his antagonist or the stakeholder. This construction makes one member of the section in unison with the other. What legal right there may be to recover back money paid under a contract that is void, the statute leaves it untouched. The decision of the learned judge was wrong, and I think that the judgment ought to be entered for the plaintiff.

COCKBURN, C.J. I think that the judgment in this case ought to be entered for the plaintiff. I concur in thinking that the agreement is substantially a wager. I further think that the case is not protected by the proviso at the end of s. 18. In my opinion that proviso was intended to meet the case of bonâ fide contributions to a prize to be given to the winner in some lawful competition, but not to money deposited by way of wager. I confess I entertain considerable doubt on the other question. If it were res integra I should have thought that this action was excluded by the provision in s. 18, which says that no suit shall be brought to recover any sum of money which shall have been deposited in the hands of any person to abide the event on which any wager shall have been made. I think that what the statute was intended to effect there was that whereas, but for the statutory provision, after the event had come off a winner might insist on having the money paid to him, or, before the event, the person who had deposited the money might have recovered it back from the stakeholder, the statute was intended to strike at all wagers : it was intended to hit both these possibilities, in order that the time of the Court should not be taken up with litigation of this sort. The intention was that the man who won the wager should not recover the stakes, or the man who had deposited his money get it back again; that neither the one nor the other should receive any assistance from the courts, but should get their money as best they could. But whatever may be my own opinion, this point has been before two courts; once before the Court of Common Pleas in *Varney* v. *Hickman* (1), and again before the Court of Exchequer in *Martin* v. *Hewson* (2), and both courts put a construction on this enactment contrary to the view I entertain.

(1) 5 C. B. 271; 17 L. J. (C.P.) 102.   (2) 10 Ex. 737; 24 L. J. (Ex.) 174.

I am not desirous to disturb the law as thus settled, and I do
not wish to take further time to consider the question.

BRAMWELL, L.J.   I agree in opinion with the Lord Chancellor.
I think the construction put upon this section is the right one.   I
only wish to add that the clause of s. 18, that " no suit shall be
brought for recovering money won upon a wager " is unnecessary,
and might have been left out of the statute; it seems to me to
be wholly superfluous.   I think the judgment entered for the
defendant wrong, and that the plaintiff is entitled to recover his
deposit from the defendant.

Judgment reversed and entered for the plaintiff.

Solicitors for plaintiff: *Richards & Walker, for Mellor, Oldham.*
Solicitors for defendant: *Singleton & Tattershall.*

[IN THE COURT OF APPEAL.]

THOMPSON v. THE SUNDERLAND GAS COMPANY.

Gasworks Clauses Act, 1847 (10 *Vict.* c. 15) *ss.* 6, 7—*Powers of Gas Company
to break up Soil and lay down Pipes—Buildings.*

By s. 6 of 10 Vict. c. 15, the undertakers are authorized to open and break up
the soil and pavement of the several streets within the limits of their special Act
and to lay down pipes for supplying gas.   Sect. 7 provides " that nothing herein
shall authorize the undertakers to lay down or place any pipe or other works, into,
through, or against any building, or in any land not dedicated to the public use,
without the consent of the owners and occupiers thereof . . .

A road passed alongside the plaintiff's premises, and over certain arches
occupied by him as cellars.   The defendants, a company constituted under a
local Act incorporating 10 Vict. c. 15, in opening and breaking up the soil of the
road for the purpose of laying down gas-pipes, damaged the arches :—

Held, that the arches were buildings within s. 7, and that the defendants could
not justify breaking through them.

THE statement of claim, amongst other things, stated that the
plaintiff was the owner of a certain ship-building yard, situate on
the side of a certain public road, which road passed over several
arches belonging to and possessed by the plaintiff, and occupied
and used by him as store rooms in connection with his business as
a shipbuilder; that the defendants, in laying down certain gas-

pipes, opened up and excavated the public road and dug trenches
therein, and so negligently conducted the laying down the gas-
pipes that the arches were greatly damaged by the defendants
having broken and cut up the brickwork of the top of the arches,
whereby they were rendered unfit for use.

' The statement of defence, amongst other things, alleged that the
defendants, under the powers of certain Acts of Parliament, took
up and excavated the public road to replace certain gas-pipes, and
in performing the work in a proper and careful manner, and in order
to avoid injuring a certain wooden casing placed under the public
road by the plaintiff, laid their gas-pipes at a level which made it
necessary to take off the top bricks of one of the arches, and to lay
pipes thereupon; and that the same was done by them in careful
and proper execution of the powers under their Acts of Parliament
and without negligence.

At the trial, before Lopes, J., at the Durham Spring Assizes,
1877, it was proved that the road in question passed alongside the
plaintiff's premises, and over arches which belonged to the plaintiff,
and which opened out into his yard; that they had doors attached
to them, and were used by the plaintiff as stores or cellars. There
was no evidence to shew how the arches came to be under the
road, or when they were first used as cellars, but it appeared that
some cottages had formerly been erected near to this spot, and it
was suggested that the arches had been used as cellars by the
occupiers. It was also proved that the defendants, in laying down
gas-pipes, opened the soil of the road, and broke in the crown of
the arches, thereby causing an injury to the amount of 25l.

The defendants, who were a gas company incorporated under
20 & 21 Vict. c. vii., with which 10 Vict. c. 15 was incorporated,
contended that their acts were lawful and justified by s. 6 (1)

---

(1) By 10 Vict. c. 15, s. 6, the undertakers, under such superintendence as
hereinafter specified, may open and
break up the soil and pavement of the
several streets and bridges within the
limits of the special Act, and may open
and break up any sewers, drains, or
tunnels within or under such streets or
bridges, and lay down and place within
the same limits pipes, conduits, service

pipes, and other works, and from time
to time repair, alter, or remove the
same, and also make any sewers that
may be necessary for carrying off the
washings and waste liquids which may
arise in the making of the gas; and for
the purposes aforesaid may remove and
use all earth and materials in and under
such streets and bridges, and they may
in such streets erect any pillars, lamps,

1877

THOMPSON
.v.
SUNDERLAND
GAS CO.

of 10 Vict. c. 15. The jury having negatived any negligence on the part of the defendants in laying down the pipes, the learned judge directed the judgment to be entered for them.

M'Clymont, for the plaintiff. The judgment is wrongly entered for the defendants. At common law the surface of the road alone is dedicated to the public, not the soil underneath the road; the defendants would have no right to break through the arches and destroy the plaintiff's property. They claim to justify their acts under 10 Vict. c. 15, s. 6. Assuming that the defendants have power under that section to open and break up the soil of the street or road for the purpose of laying down their pipes, s. 7 prohibits them from laying down their pipes into, through, or against any buildings or in any land not dedicated to the public use, without the consent of the owner. It is admitted that the consent of the owner has not been obtained; the arches which have been interfered with are cellars in the possession of the plaintiff, and although they are underneath the soil are buildings within the meaning of s. 7.

Herschell, Q.C., and *Shield,* for the defendants. If the cellars are buildings within s. 7, and the case is not within s. 6, then the defendants would be powerless to lay down pipes for the purpose of supplying gas in this part of their district, and great inconvenience would be caused to the public. Sect. 6 gives the defendants

and other works, and do all other acts which the undertakers shall from time to time deem necessary for supplying gas to the inhabitants of the district included within the said limits, doing as little damage as may be in the execution of the powers hereby or by the special Act granted, and making compensation for any damage which may be done in the execution of such powers.

By s. 7: Provided always that nothing herein shall authorize or empower the undertakers to lay down or place any pipe or other works into, through, or against any building, or in any land not dedicated to the public

use, without the consent of the owners and occupiers thereof: except that the undertakers may at any time enter upon and lay or place any new pipe in the place of an existing pipe in any land wherein any pipe hath been already lawfully laid down or placed in pursuance of this or the special Act, or any other Act of Parliament, and may repair or alter any pipe so laid down.

By s. 2: The expression "the undertakers" shall mean the persons by the special Act authorized to construct the gasworks.

By s. 3: The word "street shall include . . . . road."

1877

THOMPSON
v.
SUNDERLAND
GAS CO.

power to break up the soil of streets or roads within the limits of their Act for the purpose of laying down pipes, and this necessarily gives them power to interfere with the arches or cellars that may be underneath. If, in exercising their powers, the defendants have broken the crown of the plaintiff's arches he is not without his remedy; he is entitled under the same section to compensation for the damage that has been done him, but he cannot bring an action of trespass against the defendants. Buildings in s. 7 must be construed to mean buildings on the surface of the land, and not buildings that are underground.

M'Clymont was not heard in reply.

LORD CAIRNS, L.C. This case raises a very simple question upon the construction of ss. 6 and 7 of 10 Vict. c. 15. The defendants, the gas company, were exercising, as they thought right, the powers given to them by their Act of Parliament, and supposing they had parliamentary powers for what they did, the jury have found that there was no negligence in the exercise of those powers. If they had, therefore, on the construction of this Act of Parliament, parliamentary powers for what they did, there is an end of the case, and they are right: if on the other hand they had not parliamentary powers for what they have done they are in the wrong, and the plaintiff is entitled to judgment, and it is agreed that the damage which he has sustained in respect of this part of the case is 25*l*.

Now what the gas company have done is this: they were laying pipes under a road, the road was in part supported by brick arches, which were underneath, and the company in laying their pipes opened the soil of the road, and came down upon those brick arches and broke into them to some extent, and in breaking into the arches caused the injury, the damages of which were assessed at 25*l*. Now, s. 6 of the Gas Clauses Act, which is incorporated with the special Act (20 & 21 Vict. c. vii.), gives the undertakers certain powers with regard to streets and bridges. The powers it gives them are these: [The Lord Chancellor read s. 6.] Now, there is no doubt this section confers very large powers. The place where they are to be exercised is in and under the soil and pavement of the streets and bridges, and the assumption of the

1877

THOMPSON
v.
SUNDERLAND
GAS CO.

legislature seems to me to .have been this: that you may take a street or a bridge—and street, by the interpretation clause, is extended so as to mean "any square, court, or alley, highway, lane, road, or thoroughfare"—that you may take a street under these meanings as being something which is dedicated to the public, and primâ facie having nothing under it but valueless soil and materials, and that, at all events, to the extent to which a gas company might naturally have to go down into the earth they may safely be trusted to go down under a highway or thoroughfare of this description, removing the soil and reinstating it, doing as little damage as they can. If the matter had stood there, and in going down under a street the gas company had come upon an archway: possibly a question might arise whether an archway of that kind, comes under the words " earth and materials," and could be removed or interfered with. My own impression is—it is not necessary to decide it—that if the case stood on s. 6 there would be an absolute power under this section to open the soil and to lay pipes.

But s. 7 seems to me to make this case clear beyond all doubt. It is a proviso engrafted on s. 6, although it is a separate section. It provides: " That nothing herein "—that is, in the 6th section— " shall authorize or empower the undertakers to lay down or place any pipe or other works into, through, or against any building." Now I am not considering at this moment whether the archway is a building or not. Assume it to be a building. The learned counsel argued that a building within s. 7 must mean a building upon the soil of the road. I do not know on what principle we are to put that limited construction on a word that is perfectly general in the statute. You have s. 6 authorizing you to do works under a street, inter alia, and you have s. 7 saying, by way of proviso, that shall not authorize you to interfere—and they use a simple word—with any building. I want to know on what principle that is not to include, as the words would naturally include, a building if there be a building under a road. It seems to me perfectly clear that there can be no principle whatever to authorize us so to limit s. 7. And I must say that reason and common sense seem to me to go entirely with that construction. We know there are many houses which have important parts of the building under a footway or a road. But the question remains, was this in fact a building? Now the place was one or more arches. The history of those arches is not very clear. They may originally have been placed there because it was the most convenient way of supporting the road, or it may be that when the road came to be made or came to be supported, the owner of the soil may have thought it a convenient thing to have arches so that he might use them; but whether they were made mainly for the support of the road, or for the convenience of the land-owner at the same time that they were supporting the road, they have been used by the landowner as stores or cellars, doors having been placed upon them, and in other respects just as you might use a building which has been constructed for the specific purpose of being used as a store. They are not the natural formation of the ground under the road; they are artificial, they are the con-struction of man, they are the putting together of bricks and mortar, and being used for the purpose for which they are used, I am at a loss to conceive why they are not to be included under the word building. In my opinion they clearly are build-ings within the meaning of the words of the Act of Parliament.

The result of that, therefore, is, that there was not parliamen-tary power without the consent of the owner to interfere with these buildings, and having interfered with them, the defendants exceeded their parliamentary powers, and were trespassers. The damage having been assessed at 25*l.*, for that sum the plaintiff must have judgment.

COCKBURN, C.J. I concur in the result at which the Lord Chancellor has arrived, though not altogether upon the same grounds; for I think, on the true construction of s. 6, that what was done here by the gas company was beyond the power conferred by that section. I think the power thence derived is limited to opening and breaking up the soil and pavement of streets and bridges in the strict sense of the term; and that whatever else is referred to in respect of sewers, drains, and tunnels, must be taken as subordinate to the exercise of the power as so limited. The power being thus limited to the soil of the street or bridge, I cannot think that anything which does not properly constitute

1877

THOMPSON
v.
SUNDERLAND
GAS CO.

the soil is within the power. Suppose there were no building there, but that the question was as to the use of the soil of the street, I think it would be necessary to consider to what depth the soil of the street can be said to extend, as the power of using the soil for the purpose of laying their pipes extends only to what can properly be called the soil of the street. But whether or not that is the right construction of s. 6, as I think it is, I agree in the view which the Lord Chancellor has expressed as to the operation of s. 7 of the statute. I think this was a building within the meaning of that section. I must altogether reject the contention of Mr. Shield that the term "building" in s. 7 has reference only to buildings that are upon the surface of, and not beneath the street. The fact pointed out by the Lord Chancellor of there being so many instances in which part of a house itself is under the street makes it monstrous to suppose that a gas company might deal with such portions of a man's house with a total disregard of the injurious consequences that might result to him. The legislature meant that a company should divert the course of their pipes so as to avoid these parts of houses. I agree that if arches were made solely for the purpose of supporting the road— if that was their primary origin, or their sole use—it might be a question whether such arches could be held to be buildings within the meaning of s. 7, although their artificial construction by the hands of man renders them distinguishable from the soil of a street or bridge. Here in fact, these arches had apparently been used as long as the road or street had been in existence for the purposes of the owner of the soil as buildings. I think there is reason to suppose that they were originally cellars which belonged to the houses which have stood there as far back as the evidence goes, and for some time past they have been used as subsidiary to the premises of the plaintiff which adjoin. I think they were buildings as distinguishable from mere constructions to support the road, and therefore that they were buildings within s. 7, and as such within the protection of it. I agree with the Lord Chancellor that there ought to be judgment for the plaintiff to the extent of 25*l.*, which is the amount of damage occasioned by this act of the defendants.

BRAMWELL, L.J. I am of the same opinion. It is not denied
that this was a building, and not the material of the road. If the
road had been taken away, it would have left nothing but a building, and it was not the less a building by reason of the road going
over it. Then Mr. Shield's contention that the statute meant
buildings above ground really is an impossible one. I will not
attempt to add to the reasons which the Lord Chancellor has given
why the legislature could not have meant so, but I content myself
with saying it is an impossible construction, because Mr. Shield's
argument is this, that s. 7 means "nothing herein contained
shall authorize or empower the undertakers to lay down or place
any pipe or other works into, through, or against any building"
above ground. That is how he reads it. But when you look at
s. 6, the only authority they have is to lay pipes underground.
Therefore, it would come to this: s. 6 says you may place pipes
underground, but s. 7 says you shall not place them in a building
above ground. That cannot very well be. I say no more upon
that. Upon the other point, I agree with the Lord Chief Justice.
I will say one word, and one word only upon it, because it is not
necessary for the purposes of to-day. It seems to me under this
Act of Parliament there is power given to the undertakers or the
gas companies to acquire an easement or right of occupancy, but
apparently never upon the terms of their paying for it. It is
always something that is gratuitous. It seems to me that makes
it almost certain that the legislature did not mean that anything
in which the landowner had a beneficial occupancy should be
interfered with. What the legislature had in view was this:
the soil of a public road where such mains are generally laid is of
very little value to its owner; it is no use to anybody but to the
public as a road, but nevertheless if the gas company would have
had to pay for a right to put their gas pipes there, the result
would have been that they would have had to pay a price for that
which was of no value. Therefore the legislature enacted that
the comparatively worthless ownership should be disregarded. 1
think that is the scheme of the Act. And I think that is corrobo-
rated by the words that they may open the soil and pavement of
the several streets, and may take away the materials. I think

the contention that they may not only take away the materials, but may do more, viz., that they may abridge the amount of enjoyment which a man has in his cellars is an impossible contention. I think, therefore, that the judgment should be for the plaintiff for 25*l*.

1877

THOMPSON
v.
SUNDERLAND
GAS CO.

Judgment reversed, and entered for the plaintiff.

Solicitor for plaintiff: *John Tucker.*
Solicitors for defendants: *Johnson & Weatherall.*

————

[IN THE COURT OF APPEAL.]

June 6.

FRIEND *v.* THE LONDON, CHATHAM, AND DOVER RAILWAY
COMPANY.

*Practice — Discovery — Privileged Documents — Report of Examination of
Plaintiff by Medical Man—Regulation of Railways Act (31 & 32 Vict.
c. 119), s. 26.*

Where, on an action against a railway company to recover damages for injuries sustained by the defendants' negligence, the plaintiff is examined by medical men employed on the defendants' behalf, the reports sent by the medical men to the defendants are privileged from inspection, provided that the examination and reports were procured by the defendants' solicitor, or at his instance, for the purpose of enabling him to give advice to the defendants with reference to the action, and of assisting him generally in the conduct of the legal proceedings.

It is immaterial that the judge's order under which the plaintiff was examined was drawn up with the words "and by consent" struck out, as a judge has no jurisdiction to make an order in that form except under 31 & 32 Vict. c. 119, s. 26, and the plaintiff must be treated as if he had submitted voluntarily to the examination.

THIS was an action to recover damages for personal injuries caused by the defendants' negligence.

The defendants, in order to ascertain the extent of the plaintiff's injuries, procured a judge's order, that they should be at liberty to have him examined by their medical men.

It did not appear on the face of the order that the medical men were not to be witnesses on either side, nor was there any reference to the Regulation of Railways Act, 31 & 32 Vict.

1877

FRIEND

v.

LONDON,
CHATHAM,
AND DOVER
RAILWAY Co.

c. 119 (1); but the words "and by consent" in the ordinary printed form at the head of the order were struck out.

The plaintiff was examined under the order, and the medical men sent reports of the examination to the defendants. Upon an order for discovery, the defendants, in their affidavit of documents, which was unanswered by the plaintiff, objected to produce these reports, on the ground that they were "communications written at the instance and for the use of the solicitor of the defendants, for the purpose of the legal proceedings in this action, and of giving advice to the defendants with reference to the same." Lush, J., at chambers, made an order for the inspection of the reports, which order was afterwards set aside by the Exchequer Division.

The plaintiff appealed.

H. T. Cole, Q.C., for the plaintiff. The order for the examination of the plaintiff must have been made under the Regulation of Railways Act, 31 & 32 Vict. c. 119, s. 26, for the words "by consent" are struck out, and it is only by virtue of that section that a court has power in such a case to make an adverse order. But if the order was made under that section then the plaintiff is entitled to see the medical men's reports. If it was not made under that section, then, as the plaintiff submitted to be examined under an order improperly made, the plaintiff is still entitled to inspection, for there must have been an implied undertaking to let the plaintiff see the result. The case of *Baker* v. *London and South Western Ry. Co.* (2), is a distinct authority in favour of making the order for inspection in this case. [He also referred to *Anderson* v. *Bank of British Columbia.*] (3)

Harrison, Q.C., for the defendants. The reports are privileged, the defendants' affidavit bringing them within the exception to the rule in *Bustros* v. *White.* (4) The case of *Pacey* v. *London Tram-*

(1) By 31 & 32 Vict. c. 119, s. 26: "Whenever any person injured by an accident on a railway claims compensation on account of the injury, any judge of the court in which proceedings to recover such compensation are taken . . . . may order that the person injured be examined by some duly qualified medical practitioner named in the order, and not being a witness on either side."

(2) Law Rep. 3 Q. B. 91.

(3) 2 Ch. D. 644.

(4) 1 Q. B. D. 423.

ways Co. (1), in which a similar affidavit was made, is conclusive of the whole question, and shews that there is no such implied undertaking to shew the results of the examination as is contended for by the other side.

1877

FRIEND
v.
LONDON,
CHATHAM,
AND DOVER
RAILWAY Co.

[COCKBURN, C.J. Surely there is this distinction between that case and the present, that there the examination was by consent of the parties, whereas here it was under an order purporting to be adverse.]

That can make no difference in this case, for the examination was at all events practically by consent. The order was not made under the Regulation of Railways Act, for had it been it would have referred to that Act, and also it would have appeared on the face of it that the medical men were not witnesses on either side. Moreover, s. 26 of that Act is practically a dead letter; it is never resorted to. But if the order was not made under that Act, then it is immaterial that the words " and by consent," are struck out, for the judge at chambers had no power to make such an order. The plaintiff, therefore, the order being a nullity, must be treated as in exactly the same position as if he had voluntarily submitted to the examination without any order being made. There is, therefore, no distinction between that case and the present.

[He also referred to *Cossey* v. *London, Brighton, and South Coast Ry. Co.* (2); *Skinner* v. *Great Northern Ry. Co.* (3); and *Woolley* v. *North London Ry. Co.* (4)]

COCKBURN, C.J. I think that the defendants' affidavit, which is unanswered, and therefore must be assumed to be true, brings this case within the exception to the general rule mentioned in *Bustros* v. *White.* (5) The defendants intended that the medical men should make the examination merely with the view of informing their solicitor.

BRAMWELL, L.J. I am of the same opinion. The case of *Pacey* v. *London Tramways Co.* (1), appears to me to be conclusive of the whole question.

(1) See note at end of the case.   (3) Law Rep. 9 Ex. 298.
(2) Law Rep. 5 C. P. 146.   (4) Law Rep. 4 C. P. 602.
                    (5) 1 Q. B. D. 423.

1877

FRIEND
v.
LONDON,
CHATHAM,
AND DOVER
RAILWAY CO.

BRETT, L.J. Upon the unanswered affidavit, it must be taken that the examination and reports were made at the request of the defendants' solicitor. That being so, I am clearly of opinion that the reports were privileged documents. *Pacey* v. *London Tramways Co.* (1) is directly in point, and no distinction can be taken that in that case the plaintiff consented to the examination, and that here he was examined under an adverse order. The learned judge had no power to make such an order; the plaintiff, therefore in submitting to it, must be treated as if he had consented to the examination.

Appeal dismissed.

Solicitors for plaintiff: *Myers, Meakin, & Hall.*
Solicitor for defendants: *White.*

(1) 1876. May 17. [IN THE COURT OF APPEAL.]
PACEY *v.* LONDON TRAMWAYS COMPANY.

Action to recover damages for injuries caused by the defendants' negligence. After claim made, but before action brought, the plaintiff had voluntarily submitted to be examined by the defendants' medical officer, who sent a report of the examination to the defendants' solicitors. Upon an order for discovery of documents being made, the defendants in their affidavit discovered the report, but objected to produce it, on the ground that it was "a communication from the defendants' medical adviser to the defendants' solicitors made at the request of such solicitors after receipt of notice of the plaintiff's claim, and the same was so made in view of the litigation then apprehended in respect of such claim, and of the evidence to be adduced on behalf of the defendants in defence thereto."

On the hearing of a summons for inspection of the report, Pollock, B., refused to make an order. And the Exchequer Division on appeal from the judge, held, following the prior decisions of that Court, that the judge was right in so refusing, at the same time however, intimating that, but for those decisions, they should have considered the plaintiff entitled to the inspection prayed.

The plaintiff appealed.

W. H. Clay, for the plaintiff.
Waddy, Q.C., for the defendants.

The COURT (Jessel, M.R., Lord Coleridge, C.J., Mellish, L.J., and Denman, J.), held that under the circumstances stated in the defendants' affidavit, the report was privileged.

Appeal dismissed.

Solicitors for plaintiff: *J. G. & P. Vanderpump.*
Solicitors for defendants: *Ashurst, Morris, & Co.*

[IN THE COURT OF APPEAL.]   1877
June 13.

ATKINSON *v.* THE NEWCASTLE AND GATESHEAD WATERWORKS
COMPANY.

*Public Statutory Duty, Breach of, when Actionable—Waterworks Clauses Act,
1847—10 Vict. c. 17, ss. 42, 43.*

The mere fact that the breach of a public statutory duty has caused damage
does not vest a right of action in the person suffering the damage against the
person guilty of the breach; whether the breach does or does not give such right
of action must depend upon the object and language of the particular statute.

By the Waterworks Clauses Act, 1847, the undertakers are: (1) to fix and
maintain fire-plugs; (2) to furnish to the town commissioners a sufficient supply
of water for certain public purposes; (3) to keep their pipes to which fire-plugs
are fixed at all times charged with water at a certain pressure, and to allow all
persons at all times to use the same for extinguishing fire without compensation;
and (4) to supply to every owner or occupier of any dwelling-house, having paid
or tendered the water-rate, sufficient water for domestic purposes.

By s. 43 a penalty of 10*l.* (recoverable summarily before two justices, who may
award not more than half the penalty to the informer and are to give the remainder to the overseers of the parish), is imposed on the undertakers for the
neglect of each of the above duties, and for the neglect of (2) and (4) they are
further to forfeit to the commissioners or ratepayer a penalty of 40*s.* a day, for each
day during which such neglect continues after notice in writing of non-supply.

The plaintiff brought an action for damages against a waterworks company
for not keeping their pipes charged as required by the Act, whereby his premises
situate within the limits of the defendants' Act were burnt down:—

Held (reversing the decision of the Court of Exchequer), that the statute gave
no right of action to the plaintiff.

Couch v. *Steel* (3 E. & B. 402, 23 L. J. (Q. B.) 121), questioned.

DECLARATION: That by 26 Vict. cxxxiv. (incorporating the
Waterworks Clauses Act, 1847, 10 Vict. c. 17) (1), the defendants

(1) The material sections of 10 Vict.
c. 17, are:—

Sect. 42: "The undertakers shall at
all times keep charged with water,
under such pressure as aforesaid (which
by s. 35 is such a pressure as will make
the water reach the top storey of the
highest houses within the limits), all
their pipes to which fire-plugs shall be
fixed, unless prevented by frost, unusual
drought, or other unavoidable cause or
accident, or during necessary repairs,
and shall allow all persons at all times
to take and use such water for extinguishing fire, without making compensation for the same."

Sect. 43: "If, except when prevented
as aforesaid, the undertakers neglect or
refuse to fix (s. 38), maintain, or repair
(s. 39) such fire-plugs, or to furnish to
the town commissioners a sufficient
supply of water for the public purposes aforesaid (which by s. 37 are the
cleansing of sewers, supplying of baths

were incorporated with certain powers of taking land and supplying
and maintaining waterworks; that the plaintiff was the owner and
occupier of a dwelling-house, timber-yard, and saw mills situate
within the limits prescribed by the defendants' Act for the supply
of water by the defendants, and was under the provisions of the
said Act, and the Waterworks Clauses Act, 1847, entitled, for
reward to be paid by him to the defendants in that behalf, to a
supply of water by the defendants, and had complied with all the
provisions of the said Acts in order to entitle him to such supply
for domestic and other purposes; that the defendants had laid
down pipes near to the dwelling-house, &c., of the plaintiff for the
purpose of supplying water according to the said Acts, and had
fixed to such pipes fire-plugs; that nevertheless the defendants,
neglecting their duty in that behalf, did not at all times, and
especially at the time of the breaking out on the dwelling-house,
&c., of the plaintiff of the fire hereinafter mentioned, keep charged
with water their pipes to which fire-plugs had been fixed, under
such pressure as by the defendants' Act and the Waterworks
Clauses Act, 1847, was required, although the defendants were
not prevented from so doing by frost, unusual drought, or other
unavoidable cause or accident, or by the doing of necessary
repairs. That, during the time the pipes, with the said fire-plugs
affixed thereto, were so laid as aforesaid, a fire broke out in the
timber-yard and saw mills of the plaintiff, and by reason of the

---

and wash-houses, and other public purposes not including the extinguishing
of fire), upon such terms as shall have
been agreed on or settled as aforesaid,
or if, except as aforesaid, they neglect
to keep their pipes charged under such
pressure as aforesaid (s. 42), or neglect
or refuse to furnish to any owner or
occupier entitled under this or the
special Act to receive a supply of water
during any part of the time for which
the rates for such supply have been
paid or tendered (s. 53), they shall be
liable to a penalty of 10l., and shall
also forfeit to the town commissioners,
and to every person having paid or
tendered the rate, the sum of 40s. for
every day during which such refusal or
neglect shall continue after notice in
writing shall have been given to the
undertakers of the want of supply."

By s. 85, the clauses of the Railway
Clauses Consolidation Act, 1845 (8 Vict.
c. 20), with respect to the recovery of
damages and penalties are to be incorporated; and by s. 145 of 8 Vict. c. 20,
penalties are recoverable by summary
proceeding before two justices, who by
s. 150 may award not more than one
half the penalty to the informer, and
shall award the remainder to the overseers of the parish.

defendants not having charged the pipes under such pressure as aforesaid, a proper supply of water could not be procured for the purpose of extinguishing the fire, and in consequence thereof the timber-yard and saw mills were burnt down, and the plaintiff was greatly damaged.

Demurrer and joinder.

The Court of Exchequer held the declaration good (1) on the authority of *Couch* v. *Steel* (2).

The defendants appealed.

C. Russell, Q.C. (*G. Bruce* and *Shield* with him), for the plaintiff. (3) The fact of the imposition of a penalty, recoverable by a common informer, for the breach of the duty, does not deprive the plaintiff, who has suffered special damage from the defendants' neglect, of his common law remedy by action for compensation. *Couch* v. *Steel* (2) is a direct authority in favour of the plaintiff's right to maintain this action. Lord Campbell there lays it down that the " right by the common law to maintain an action on the case for special damage sustained by the breach of a public duty is not taken away by reason of the statute which creates the duty imposing a penalty recoverable by a common informer for neglect to perform it though no actual damage is sustained by any one." For the penalty given by the statute is applicable only to the public wrong, not to the private damage. And the case of *Stevens* v. *Jeacocke* (4) is not against the plaintiff's contention, for that case is distinguishable on the ground pointed out by Lord Campbell in *Couch* v. *Steel* (2), that no duty was there imposed by the statute on the defendant, he was only prohibited from exercising the right of fishing to the same extent that he had it at common law.

Sir John Holker, A.G., and *Herschell*, Q.C. (*Crompton* with them), for the defendants. The remedy for the defendants' neglect to discharge the duty imposed upon them by s. 42 is confined to the recovery of the penalty, whether damage is caused by that neglect or not. The Court must look at the particular Act to see what

(1) Law Rep. 6 Ex. 404.
(2) 3 E. & B. 402; 23 L. J. (Q.B.) 121.
(4) 11 Q. B. 731; 17 L. J. (Q.B.) 168.

(3) There being a cross appeal on another point, the plaintiff began.

was the intention of the legislature. The only authority for the plaintiff's contention is the case of *Couch* v. *Steel.* (1) But the authorities there relied on in support of the decision in that case do not warrant it. That case is inconsistent with *Stevens* v. *Jeacocke* (2), which was improperly distinguished from it by Lord Campbell. There is no difference between a duty not to do a thing, and a duty to do a thing as far as regards their character as duties. Yet that was the only distinction drawn by the Court.

G. Bruce, in reply. Here the duty, for the breach of which the plaintiff sues, was not a duty created for the benefit of the public generally, but only of persons living in a particular district, only those persons whose houses are near enough to the pipes in question to derive advantage from the water in such pipes in the event of fire. But where a statute imposes a duty for the benefit of a class of persons, any member of that class who is injured by a breach of such duty must have a remedy by action, if there is no penalty given specially to him, otherwise the statute would be a dead letter. Here there is no penalty given to the person injured, therefore the action lies. There is *a* remedy given by the Act no doubt, but not a remedy to the person aggrieved in the sense of compensation for injury.

LORD CAIRNS, L.C. In considering the sufficiency of this declaration, we may, as I pointed out in the course of the argument, reject at once all that part of it which relates to the supply of water for reward, for the breach alleged is not dependent on the payment of money. It is a breach of a duty to keep certain pipes, to which fire-plugs are fixed, charged with water at a certain pressure, a duty which is not made, by the Act creating it, to depend in any way upon the payment of money by anybody. That duty of so keeping the pipes charged arises under s. 42 of the Waterworks Clauses Act, 1847, by which it is enacted that "the undertakers shall at all times keep charged with water, under such pressure as aforesaid (which by s. 35 is such pressure as will make the water reach the top storey of the highest house within the limits), all their pipes to which fire-plugs shall be fixed, ... and shall allow all

(1) 3 E. & B. 402; 23 L. J. (Q.B.) 121.

(2) 11 Q. B. 731; 17 L. J. (Q.B.) 163.

1877

ATKINSON
v.
NEWCASTLE
WATER-
WORKS Co.

persons at all times to take and use such water for extinguishing fire without making compensation for the same." Now in my judgment the general scheme of these waterworks clauses, and of any Act in which they are incorporated, would appear to be this: A waterworks company, proposing to supply water to a town, apply to parliament' for powers to take certain springs and land, and to charge rates for the supply of water, in consideration of which powers being granted them they enter into certain obligations. Besides general obligations to supply the town commissioners with water for public purposes, they enter into certain special obligations as to fire-plugs, viz., to keep the pipes connected with those plugs charged with water at a certain pressure, and to allow all persons—not any particular persons, or owners of particular houses, but *all* persons—at all times to take water for the purpose of extinguishing fire without making compensation for it. The object for which the water is in such case to be used is a public object, and to effect that object the company are willing to accept the obligation to allow any person to take any quantity of water gratuitously, and further to keep the pipes from which that water is to be taken charged at such a pressure that the water so taken may be most effectively employed.

That this creates a statutory duty no one can dispute, but the question is whether the creation of that duty gives a right of action for damages to an individual who, like the plaintiff, can aver that he had a house situate within the company's limits and near to one of their fire-plugs, that a fire broke out, that the pipes connected with the plug were not charged at the pressure required by the section, and that in consequence his house was burnt down. Now, à priori, it certainly appears a startling thing to say that a company undertaking to supply a town like Newcastle with water, would not only be willing to be put under this parliamentary duty to supply gratuitously for the purpose of extinguishing fire an unlimited quantity of water at a certain pressure, and to be subjected to penalties for the non-performance of that duty, but would further be willing in their contract with parliament to subject themselves to the liability to actions by any number of householders who might happen to have their houses burnt down in consequence; and it is, à priori, equally improbable that parliament

1877

ATKINSON
v.
NEWCASTLE
WATER-
WORKS CO.

would think it a necessary or reasonable bargain to make. In the
one case the undertakers would know beforehand what they had
to meet as the consequence of their 'neglect, they would come
under definite penalties; in the other they would virtually become
gratuitous insurers of the safety from fire, so far as water is capable
of producing that safety, of all the houses within the district over
which their powers were to extend.

It is, however, necessary to look at the 43rd section, which imposes the penalty for the breach of the duty in question. That
section deals with four classes of neglect, the neglect to fix, maintain, or repair fire-plugs, the neglect to furnish the town commissioners with a sufficient supply of water for public purposes, the
neglect to keep the pipes charged under the required pressure, and
the neglect to 'furnish any owner or occupier with the supply of
water to which he is entitled. For each of those four classes of
neglect the company is visited with a penalty of 10l. And in two
of them, the second and fourth, the company is also to forfeit to
the commissioners or the ratepayer 'aggrieved a further penalty of
40s. a day for every day during which the neglect continues after
notice in writing given to the company. Now, why is it that in
some cases there is a penalty which is to go into the pocket of the
persons injured, and not in the case of neglecting to keep the
pipes fixed to the fire-plugs charged under the proper pressure?
The reason is obvious. In the former cases it is convenient to
give a penalty to the individual, in the latter case it is not. In the
cases of the town commissioners and the owners or occupiers
asking for and not getting their proper supply of water, you have
a person or persons known and determined to whom the penalty
may be given, but in the case of neglect to keep the pipes properly
charged there is no particular person whom you can single out
beforehand, and say that in the event of a breach, he is to be entitled to the penalty. In that case then the only guarantee taken
by parliament for the fulfilment of the obligation, an obligation
which has the appearance of being imposed for the benefit of the
public, is what I may term the public penalty of 10l. Apart,
then, from authority, I should say, without hesitation, that it was
no part of the scheme of this Act to create any duty which was to
become the subject of an action at the suit of individuals, to create
any right in individuals with a power of enforcing that right by

action; but that its scheme was, having laid down certain duties, to provide guarantees for the due fulfilment of them, and where convenient to give the penalties, or some of them, to the persons injured, but, where not convenient so to do, there simply to impose public penalties, not by way of compensation, but as a security to the public for the due performance of the duty. To split up the 43rd section, and to say that in those cases in which a penalty is to go into the pocket of the individual injured there is to be no right of action, but that where no penalty is so given to the individual there is to be a right of action, is to violate the ordinary rule of construction. There being here in a certain number of cases a penalty which the plaintiff himself admits excludes the right of action, the conclusion is irresistible that in the remaining cases also in the same section the legislature intended to give no right of action.

Now that would have been my opinion apart from authority. Is there then any authority which compels me to depart from that opinion? The only case which was cited to us in support of the plaintiff's contention was that of *Couch* v. *Steel*. (1) There a seaman of a merchant ship sued to recover damages for injuries sustained by him by reason of the omission of the defendant, a shipowner, to provide proper medicines for the ship's company. The declaration in that case was not framed upon any Act of Parliament, but on the argument of the demurrer one of the Merchant Shipping Acts was referred to as creating a duty in the shipowner to provide certain medicines for the benefit of the crew, and the case was put by counsel very much as if there had been a parliamentary obligation to provide a greatcoat or some specific chattel for each particular member of the ship's crew. The same Act which created the duty to provide the medicines imposed a penalty recoverable by a common informer for the omission to perform that duty; but it was there held that, notwithstanding the imposition of the penalty, an action lay at the suit of any one of the crew suffering special damage from such omission. With regard to that case, and the effect of that particular Act, I will say this, that if the matter were brought before this Court for review I should like to take time to consider

1877

ATKINSON
v.
NEWCASTLE
WATER-
WORKS CO.

(1) 3 E. & B. 402; 23 L. J. (Q.B.) 121.

whether, with reference to that particular Act, that case was
rightly decided. I will not go further than that, for it is unnecessary here to enter into that question, the Act of Parliament
under which the present action is brought being of a widely
different character, and one which is open to observations which
would not apply to the Merchant Shipping Act which was before
the Court in *Couch* v. *Steel.* (1)   But I must venture, with great
respect to the learned judges who decided that case, and particularly to Lord Campbell, to express grave doubts whether the
authorities cited by Lord Campbell (2) justify the broad general
proposition that appears to have been there laid down,—that,
wherever a statutory duty is created, any person, who can shew
that he has sustained injuries from the non-performance of that
duty, can bring an action for damages against the person on
whom the duty is imposed. I cannot but think that that must,
to a great extent, depend on the purview of the legislature in
the particular statute, and the language which they have there
employed, and more especially when, as here, the Act with which
the Court have to deal is not an Act of public and general policy,
but is rather in the nature of a private legislative bargain with a
body of undertakers as to the manner in which they will keep up
certain public works. The case of *Couch* v. *Steel* (1), therefore, is
no authority to regulate our decision in the present case. I am
of opinion, therefore, that the declaration discloses no cause of
action, and that the judgment of the Court of Exchequer must
be reversed.

COCKBURN, C.J.   I am of the same opinion. Notwithstanding
the great respect that I entertain for the judges who decided the
case of *Couch* v. *Steel* (1), I must say that I fully concur with
the Lord Chancellor in thinking, that the question, whether that
case was rightly decided, is one which is open to very grave
doubts. That question, however, is one which it is unnecessary
to entertain here, for the present case is clearly distinguishable.
The Act of Parliament on which that case turned was a public
general Act applicable to all the Queen's subjects; here we are
dealing with certain obligations imposed by the legislature upon

(1) 3 E. & B. 402; 23 L. J. (Q.B.)   (2) 3 E. & B. at p. 411; 23 L. J.
121.   (Q.B.) at p. 125.

a private company, as the conditions upon which parliament granted them the powers under which they carried out their undertaking; and I think that such an Act of Parliament as this is liable to a much more limited and strict interpretation than that which can be put upon one which is applicable to all the subjects of the realm. I entirely agree with the Lord Chancellor in the conclusion at which he has arrived, that the particular Act which we have now before us does not by implication give to persons, who may be injured by the breach of the duties thereby imposed, any remedy over and above those which it gives in express terms. If, therefore, any person is injured by a breach of such duty, he must have recourse to the statutory remedy, and cannot maintain an action for damages.

BRETT, L.J. On the true construction of this statute it is plainly the intention of the legislature that the only remedy for such a breach of duty as the present should be the recovery of the penalty. I am, therefore, of opinion, that the demurrer must be allowed. It is unnecessary to determine here whether *Couch* v. *Steel* (1) was properly decided upon the particular Act under which the action in that case was brought; I am, however, bound to say that I entertain the strongest doubt whether the broad rule there enunciated can be maintained, the rule, that is to say, that, where a new duty is created by statute, and a penalty is imposed for its breach, which penalty is to go to the person injured by such breach, the penalty, however small and inadequate a compensation it may be, is in such a case to be regarded as indicating an intention on the part of the legislature that there should be no action by such person for damages, but that, where a similar duty is created, and a similar penalty imposed which is not to go to the person injured, then the intention is that he is to have a right of action. I do not think that that proposition can be supported.

Judgment reversed.

Solicitors for plaintiff: *Walters & Gush, for Chartres & Youll,* Newcastle-upon-Tyne.

Solicitors for defendants: *Williamson, Hill, & Co.*

(1) 3 E. & B. 402; 23 L. J. (Q.B.) 121.

1877
June 28.

In the Matter of an Application by TOOMER and Others *v.* THE LONDON, CHATHAM, AND DOVER RAILWAY COMPANY and THE SOUTH EASTERN RAILWAY COMPANY.

Railway Commissioners—Jurisdiction of, to make Orders requiring two Companies to act jointly—Order for Penalties—Prohibition—Regulation of Railways Act, 1873 (36 & 37 Vict. c. 48), ss. 6, 11, 26—Railway and Canal Traffic Act, 1854 (17 & 18 Vict. c. 31), ss. 2, 3.

The Railway Commissioners, under 36 & 37 Vict. c. 48, made an order requiring the C. and the S. E. Railway Companies to make arrangements and to afford facilities for the transference of traffic from the line of one company to the other; to arrange the arrivals of their trains at a junction in a particular manner, and directing the C. Company to run trains over a disused branch line; and, upon non-compliance with the order, made a further order imposing penalties upon both companies for their disobedience :—

Held, that the first order was invalid, and that a prohibition must be granted to restrain the commissioners from enforcing it; for, assuming that they had jurisdiction to require each company separately to give facilities according to its powers, they were not entitled to order two companies to act jointly in doing what neither could do separately.

Quære, whether, if the first order had been valid, the commissioners had, under s. 6, jurisdiction to impose penalties for non-compliance with it.

Rule obtained by the London, Chatham, and Dover Railway Company, calling on Toomer and others (the applicants to the Railway Commissioners in a complaint against the Chatham and the South Eastern Railway Companies) to shew cause why a writ of prohibition should not issue, to prevent the Railway Commissioners from enforcing two orders made by them on the 6th of January and the 14th of March, 1877, and from taking any further proceedings to compel the Chatham Company to run trains between Strood and Chatham.

The facts upon the affidavits were that in December, 1876, Toomer and certain other persons resident in the neighbourhood of Strood made a complaint to the Railway Commissioners, under the Regulation of Railways Act, 1873. (1)

---

(1) 36 & 37 Vict. c. 48, s. 6: " Any person complaining of anything done or of any omission made in violation or contravention of s. 2 of the Railway and Canal Traffic Act, 1854, or of s. 16 of the Regulation of Railways Act, 1868, or of this Act, . . . may apply to the commissioners . . . and they shall have and may exercise all the jurisdiction conferred by s. 3 of the Railway and Canal Traffic Act, 1854, on the several courts and judges empowered

1877

TOOMER
v.
LONDON,
CHATHAM,
AND DOVER
RAILWAY CO.

The commissioners delivered a judgment on this complaint on the 6th of January, 1877. The following abstract of the judgment shews the grounds of the application and the nature of the relief sought:—

This is a complaint against the Chatham and the South Eastern Railway Companies for not establishing a proper through service viâ Strood Junction for traffic requiring to pass over a portion of each company's railway, and for not availing themselves of the junction for the interchange of passenger traffic. The railways of the two companies form at Strood a continuous line of communication. A short branch diverges out of the Chatham railway just north of the railway bridge over the Medway, and connects with the Strood station on the North Kent Line of the South Eastern Railway. This branch, which is seventeen chains in length, makes it practicable for through traffic to be interchanged by the two companies without break of railway, and was

---

to hear and determine complaints under that Act, and may make orders of like nature with the writs and orders authorized to be issued and made by the said courts and judges ; and the said courts and judges shall, except for the purpose of enforcing any decision or order of the commissioners, cease to exercise the jurisdiction conferred on them by that section."

Sect. 11 recites, explains, and amends s. 2 of the Railway and Canal Traffic Act, 1854, with reference to " the due and reasonable receiving, forwarding, and delivering of through traffic."

Sect. 26: " Any decision or any order made by the commissioners for the purpose of carrying into effect any of the provisions of this Act, may be made a rule or order of any superior Court, and shall be enforced either in the manner directed by s. 3 of the Railway and Canal Traffic Act, 1854, as to the writs and orders therein mentioned, or in like manner as any rule or order of such Court. . . .

" The commissioners shall, in all proceedings before them under ss. 6, 11, 12, and 13 of this Act, and may if they think fit in all other proceedings before them under this Act . . . state a case in writing for the opinion of any superior Court determined by the commissioners upon any question which in the opinion of the commissioners is a question of law.

" The Court to which the case is transmitted shall hear and determine the question or questions of law arising thereon, and shall thereupon reverse, affirm, or amend the determination in respect of which the case has been stated, or remit the matter to the commissioners with the opinion of the Court thereon, or may make such other order in relation to the matter, and may make such order as to costs as to the Court may seem fit, and all such orders shall be final and conclusive on all parties. . . . . Save as aforesaid, every decision and order of the commissioners shall be final."

1877
———
TOOMER
v.
LONDON,
CHATHAM.
AND DOVER
RAILWAY Co.
for some time used for that purpose. It was part of the main
line of the East Kent (now the Chatham) Railway until that company obtained access to London by a route independent of the
North Kent Line, when this portion of the line ceased altogether
to be used for passenger traffic. The applicants, however, who
desire to use the lines of these two companies as a continuous line,
complain of having to walk or drive between the Strood station of
the South Eastern Railway and Chatham station of the Chatham
Company, and of having also to re-book at those stations; they
complain further of the unreasonable delay attending through
journeys from the trains not being run to suit each other, and
their times therefore not corresponding, and they find not less
fault with the way of carrying through goods traffic.

We entertain no doubt that the particular accommodation sought
for, the working, that is, of a train service to connect the railways,
is one which it is an obligation on the companies to provide.

It does not appear that except by arrangement the South
Eastern Company could run to Chatham or upon the line branch-
ing off from Strood station; but the East Kent Railway Act, 1853,
gives, by s. 39, the Chatham Company power to use the Strood
station of the South Eastern Company as fully as if it was their
own.

The commissioners accordingly made the following order, dated
the 6th of January, 1877:—

"We do order and enjoin the Chatham and the South Eastern
Companies to make arrangements and afford all due facilities and
conveniences for the Strood station of the South Eastern Company
on and from the 1st day of February next, being the place where
through traffic of any description may be transferred to and from
the North Kent Railway from and to the Chatham Railway and
the Chatham Company, to convey without delay all such traffic by
railway between Chatham and Strood stations.

"Provided always, that if at any time the two companies prefer
that the Chatham station of the Chatham Company shall be the
place where such traffic shall be transferred or exchanged, and
shall make all suitable and convenient arrangements, as well with
regard to transfer at the Chatham station as to conveyance by

1877

TOOMER
v.
LONDON,
CHATHAM,
AND DOVER
RAILWAY CO.

rail between the Chatham and Strood stations, such arrangements may be put in operation in lieu of those to be made pursuant to this part of our order, and in such case from and after the date of their coming into operation and during their continuance this part of our order, so far as such arrangements may differ from. it as regards the Chatham Company being the particular company to convey between Chatham and Strood, and as regards Strood station being the place of exchange between the two companies, shall to that extent be in abeyance.

"And we order and enjoin the South Eastern and the Chatham Companies so to arrange the arrival and departure of their respective trains as that for up through journeys each day there shall be four departures of trains from Strood within half-an-hour of the arrivals of trains at Chatham, and for down through journeys four departures of trains from Chatham within half-an-hour of the arrivals of trains at Strood, and we order the Chatham Company to convey by railway between Chatham and Strood stations passengers and luggage travelling by any of such trains at times to fit the arrivals and departures of four other up and four other down trains run on the North Kent line by the South Eastern Company."

The commissioners, on the 9th of February, on the application of the Chatham Company, extended the time for compliance with this order to the 1st of March.

The companies not having obeyed this order, application was made to the commissioners, and they made an order on the 14th of March, of which the following is the material part:—

We decide that the Chatham Company and the South Eastern Company have respectively failed to obey our orders of the 6th day of January and the 9th day of February, 1877, and that no sufficient reason has been shewn by the Chatham Company or the South Eastern Company for such failure to obey our orders. And we do order the Chatham Company to pay into court, to abide our ultimate decision in the matter of this application, the sum of 60*l.* for every day after the 31st day of March instant that the Chatham and Dover Company shall fail to obey our orders dated the 6th day of January and the 9th day of February, 1877. And we do order the South Eastern Railway Company to pay into court, to abide our ultimate decision in this matter, the sum of 15*l.* for

           EXCHEQUER DIVISION.

1877

Toomer
v.
London,
Chatham,
and Dover
Railway Co.

every day after the 31st day of March that the South Eastern Company fail to obey our orders of the 6th day of January and 9th day of February, 1877.

June 21, 22. *Thesiger, Q.C.*, and *Willis, Q.C.* (with them *Jeune*), for the applicants, shewed cause. The Railway Commissioners have jurisdiction to compel companies to conform to every part of s. 2 of the Railway and Canal Traffic Act, 1854, as explained and extended by s. 11 of the Railways Regulation Act, 1873, and are authorized to make them work their lines so as to give the public "all reasonable facilities according to their respective powers" (17 & 18 Vict. c. 31, s. 2); and this applies in an especial sense to cases of through traffic; for this purpose, therefore, they have power to point out and specify the particular facilities which the public ought to enjoy: *Innes* v. *London, Brighton, and South Coast Ry. Co.* (1). The reason why the Court did not interfere with the numbers of trains that stopped at a station in the Caterham case was that it was not proved to them that the convenience of the public was not consulted: *Caterham Railway* v. *London, Brighton, and South Coast Ry. Co.* (2); whereas here the commissioners have expressly found that sufficient accommodation is not afforded to the public, and their finding is conclusive (36 & 37 Vict. c. 48, s. 26). A junction between two lines makes them a continuous line, the lines of the Chatham and South Eastern Railways come, therefore, under s. 2 of the Railway and Canal Traffic Act, and it is competent to the commissioners to make an order requiring both companies to use their respective powers in forwarding through traffic: *Local Board of Uckfield* v. *London, Brighton, and South Coast Ry. Co.* (3)

All the jurisdiction of the Court of Common Pleas has been transferred to the commissioners by s. 6 of the Railways Regulation Act, 1873, and the courts of law have ceased to exercise jurisdiction in these matters; so that the commissioners have power to enforce their own orders by penalties, while the courts of law only retain the procedure and machinery by which, if necessary, such penalties may be levied.

(1) 2 Nev. & Macn. 155.   (2) 1 C. B. (N.S.) 410; 26 L. J. (C.P.) 16.
                  (3) 2 Nev. & Macn. 214.

1877

TOOMER
v.
LONDON,
CHATHAM,
AND DOVER
RAILWAY CO.

Pope, Q.C., and *W. G. Harrison, Q.C.* (with them *Moulton*), for the
Chatham Company, in support of the rule. The commissioners
had power, without doubt, to entertain the question brought before
them by the complaint of the applicants: but they exceeded their
jurisdiction in making the order of the 6th of January. This order
requires the Chatham Company to give facilities off their own line,
that is, to use running powers over the line of another company,
to run trains between two stations belonging to two different companies, to do that which they cannot do without the concurrence
of the South Eastern Company, so that this order attempts to do
that which the Court of Appeal in Chancery has declined to do:
Powell Duffryn Steam & Coal Co. v. *Taff Vale Ry. Co.* (1) The
commissioners have no power to frame a time table, to arrange
the traffic, to direct how the facilities the public desire are to be
given, they cannot make an order which would require the construction of new works, and so might necessitate the raising of
new capital. They have no jurisdiction to decide whether their
orders have been obeyed, and their powers were exhausted when
they had made their first orders; they have no power to make an
order for penalties, the only orders that they can make are orders
by way of injunction, as provided by s. 3 of the Railway and Canal
Traffic Act, 1854, which defines the jurisdiction now transferred to
the commissioners; the enforcement of orders made by the commissioners remain with the courts of law, as provided by s. 26 of
the Regulation of Railways Act, 1873, so that the order of the
14th of March was ultrà vires.

Willis, Q.C., in reply.

Cur. adv. vult.

June 28. The judgment of the Court (Cleasby, B., and
Hawkins, J.) was read by

CLEASBY, B. In this case a question of some difficulty has been
brought before us in the form of an application for a prohibition
to the Railway Commissioners restraining them from taking further
proceedings to enforce certain orders made by them.

The Railway Commissioners now exercise by virtue of 36 &
37 Vict. c. 48, the jurisdiction possessed by the Court of Common

(1) Law Rep. 9 Ch. 331.

1877

Toomer
v.
London,
Chatham,
and Dover
Railway Co.

Pleas under the Railway and Canal Traffic Act, 1854. The exercise of this jurisdiction was from the beginning considered as attended with much difficulty (see Mr. Justice Cresswell's remarks in *Ransom* v. *Great Eastern Ry. Co.* (1)), and the difficulty is not diminished when we have to consider the extent to which it ought to be and can legally be exercised.

There must be some limit to its exercise, and as there is no absolute right to an appeal (for sect. 26 of the Act only gives a right to a case upon questions which in the opinion of the commissioners are questions of law), the proceeding by prohibition seems to be the proper mode of calling in question the legality of an order.

It is contended by the Chatham Company (a name by which we will for convenience call the London, Chatham, and Dover Railway Company) that the commissioners have gone beyond their jurisdiction in making two orders upon them and the South Eastern Company of the 6th of January, 1877, and the 14th of March, 1877.

The principal question arises upon the order of the 6th of January, which is as follows :—

"And we order and enjoin the Chatham and Dover Company and the South Eastern Company to make arrangements and afford all due facilities and conveniences for the Strood Station of the South Eastern Company, on and from the 1st day of February next, being the place where through traffic of any description shall or may be transferred to and from the North Kent Railway, from and to the London, Chatham, and Dover Railway, and the Chatham and Dover Company to convey without delay all such traffic by railway between Chatham and the said Strood Station: Provided always, that if at any time the said two companies prefer that the Chatham Station of the Chatham and Dover Company shall be the place where such traffic shall be exchanged or transferred, and shall make all suitable and convenient arrangements as well with regard to transfer at the Chatham Station as to conveyance by rail between the Chatham and Strood Stations, such arrangements may be put in operation in lieu of those to be made pursuant to this part of our order, and in such case from and after

(1) 1 C. B. (N.S.) 437 : 26 L. J. (C.P.) 91.

1877

TOOMER
v.
LONDON,
CHATHAM,
AND DOVER
RAILWAY Co.

the date of their coming into operation and during their continuance this part of our order, so far as such arrangements may differ from it as regards the Chatham and Dover Company being the particular company to convey between Chatham and Strood, and as regards Strood Station being the place of exchange between the companies, shall to that extent be in abeyance."

Then there follows a further order upon the South Eastern Company and the Chatham Company to arrange the arrivals and departures of their trains at Strood in a particular manner, and an order upon the Chatham Company to convey by railway between Chatham station and Strood certain passengers.

A further question is also raised upon the order of the 14th of March, viz., the authority of the commissioners under the 6th section of the Act to enforce orders made by them, which is undoubtedly a proper case for prohibition if any real question arises as to that authority. But the first question was that upon which the principal argument was addressed. It arises upon the 2nd and 3rd sections of the Railway and Canal Traffic Act, 1854. The 2nd section directs what railway companies shall do, and the 3rd section provides the means to be resorted to upon a complaint of default.

Now we have nothing to do with the reasonableness of the conclusion arrived at by the commissioners as to the default of either the Chatham or the South Eastern Companies in not affording due facilities, and obstructing the public on a continuous line of railway. The question brought before us was not the competency of the commissioners to entertain those matters and form conclusions upon them, which could not be questioned. The question brought before us was the competency of the commissioners to entertain an application which resulted in the order of the 6th of January, and the question may be tested properly by considering whether if the application had been in the terms of the order it was one which the commissioners could properly entertain, not being an application against the companies for each of them to give facilities, or do something which it was in their own power to do, but an application against the two companies to act jointly in doing what neither could do separately, as for example, to enter into arrangements for making Strood a station for the transfer of traffic, and

1877

Toomer
v.
London,
Chatham,
and Dover
Railway Co.
to make jointly a time-table of particular traffic. When the obligation to give facilities, &c., is enlarged in this way, Mr. Justice Cresswell might well have said the question assumes a very complicated and difficult character. Considering the application in this way, both my Brother Hawkins and myself think that it is one thing to call upon each company, according to its powers, to give certain facilities, and a different thing to call upon them to act jointly in any way. A little consideration will shew how different the two things are. The former can be done by each acting independently in the exercise of its own powers. The latter is something which is not properly within the exercise of the powers of each acting independently, and the attempt to carry it into effect would lead to frequent disputes, and is not really as certain and final as an order ought to be professing to enjoin a particular thing. This is not intended as an objection to the order on a matter of form, but has reference to the application for such an order being in substance an application which the commissioners cannot entertain. We had the advantage of a very full and able argument upon the matter. And the conclusion at which we have arrived is, that in making the order of the 6th of January, the commissioners have exceeded their jurisdiction. We were called upon by the learned counsel who shewed cause against the rule, if our decision was in favour of a prohibition, only to order a declaration in prohibition, and formerly we should unquestionably have done so. But now that our order can be considered on appeal, in the same manner as if the question were raised upon the record, we see no reason for doing this. It would lead to great delay, and with a penalty of 60l. a day running, such delay ought to be prevented, unless some advantage is to be derived from it. We do not see how the question can be better raised than on the present application. We therefore feel bound to act upon the conclusion at which we have arrived and to direct the prohibition to issue. The Queen's Bench Division has, we understand, acted upon this view and declined to order a declaration in prohibition for the purpose of raising a question of difficulty and importance. (1)

The prohibition will be against taking any further proceedings to enforce the order of the 6th of January. This disposes of the

(1) See *Serjeant* v. *Dale*, 2 Q. B. D. at p. 568.

case before us, and the other question, viz., the validity of the order of the 14th of March (on the supposition of the order of the 6th of January being legal) is not properly before us for decision, but the prohibition may go in the form asked by the rule, so far as regards the restraining the commissioners from enforcing or taking further proceedings to enforce the orders of the 6th of January and the 14th of March, 1877, but not further to restrain them generally from compelling the Chatham Company to run trains between Chatham and Strood. We cannot decide beforehand that no order could under any circumstances be legally made directing such trains to run.

As regards the costs of this application, we see no ground for saying that the application actually made to the commissioners was an improper one, and as the commissioners have made the order complained of, there is no sufficient reason for making the original applicants pay the costs of setting it aside. There will therefore be no order for costs.

Rule absolute.

Solicitor for applicants: *Howard Russell, Gravesend.*

Solicitor for London, Chatham, and Dover Railway Company: *White, Victoria Station.*

1877

TOOMER
v.
LONDON,
CHATHAM,
AND DOVER
RAILWAY CO.

BISSICKS *v.* THE BATH COLLIERY COMPANY, LIMITED.
EX PARTE BISSICKS.

Sheriff—Levy under fi. fa.—Poundage and Fee—29 Eliz. c. 4—1 Vict. c. 55.

A sheriff's officer in the execution of a warrant of fi. fa. went with another man to the debtor's house, shewed him the warrant, and demanded payment, and told him that in default of payment the man must remain in possession and further proceedings be taken. The debtor then paid the sum demanded in the warrant, which included poundage and officer's fee:—

Held, that there had been in substance a levy, and that the sheriff was entitled to poundage and fee, though there had been no sale.

Nash v. *Dickinson* (Law Rep. 2 C. P. 252), and *Roe* v. *Hammond* (2 C. P. D. 300), not followed.

IN this case judgment had been given against the plaintiff with costs, which were taxed at 23*l.* 19*s.* 2*d.* A writ of fi. fa. having been delivered to the sheriff of Bristol, his officer, accompanied by another man, proceeded with the warrant to the plaintiff's

shop, where he found the plaintiff and told him he had a warrant
to execute a writ of fi. fa. for 28*l.* 7*s.* 2*d.* The plaintiff being
then engaged in serving a customer the officer waited about a
quarter of an hour till the plaintiff was at liberty, and then explained the nature of the warrant, and read over the principal
parts to him. The plaintiff took the various items down in
writing, and the officer then told him that he required immediate payment, otherwise further proceedings would be taken
and the man must remain in possession. The plaintiff then asked
the officer into his counting-house, took out a cashbox and paid
him the 28*l.* 7*s.* 2*d.*, which was made up as follows: taxed costs,
23*l.* 19*s.* 2*d.*; costs of execution, 1*l.* 15*s.*; interest, 1*s.*; poundage,
1*l.* 6*s.*; levy fees, 1*l.* 6*s.*

An order having been obtained calling on the sheriff to shew
cause why he should not return the 2*l.* 12*s.* illegally received by
him for poundage and fees,

M'Kellar, for the sheriff, contended that he was entitled to both
poundage and fees, since what was done amounted to a levy, or
at all events to a seizure, which was sufficient. He referred to
29 Eliz. c. 4, by which poundage is granted; 43 Geo. 3, c. 46,
s. 5; Common Law Procedure Act, 1852, s. 123; *Rex* v. *Jethe-
rell* (1); *Graham* v. *Grill* (2); *Rawstorne* v. *Wilkinson* (3); *Colls*
v. *Coates* (4); *Miles* v. *Harris* (5), per Willes, J.; *Rex* v. *Robinson* (6); *Hutchins* v. *Scott* (7); *Masters* v. *Lowther* (8); and to *Nash*
v. *Dickinson* (9), which was distinguishable since it did not appear
there were any goods to seize, and the money was paid under
protest.

F. M. White, Q.C., for the plaintiff. *Miles* v. *Harris* (5) decided
that the sheriff is not entitled to poundage unless he has sold,
though there may have been an actual seizure—per Erle, C.J.,
and Willes, J. (10). Here there was not even a seizure. *Nash* v.

(1) Parker, 177.
(2) 2 M. & S. 298.
(3) 4 M. & S. 256.
(4) 11 A. & E. 826; 9 L. J. (N.S.)
(Q.B.) 232.
(5) 12 C. B. (N.S.) at p. 559; 31
L. J. (C.P.) 361.

(6) 2 C. M. & R. 334.
(7) 2 M. & W. 809.
(8) 11 C. B. 948; 21 L. J. (C.P.)
130.
(9) Law Rep. 2 C. P. 252.
(10) 31 L. J. (C.P.) at p. 362.

Dickinson (1) is a direct authority that under circumstances like the present the sheriff is not entitled to poundage. There is no appreciable distinction, and that case must be overruled if the sheriff is to be held entitled. In *Roe* v. *Hammond* (2) it was held that the sheriff who has seized but not sold is not entitled to poundage, the Court following an anonymous case cited from Lofft, where it was said in the King's Bench, "It seems on inquiry into the practice the sheriff cannot have poundage till the goods are sold." As to the sheriff's fee of 1*l.* 1*s.* which is granted under 1 Vict. c. 55, it is not due till the warrant is executed. In the Table of Fees (2 Ch. Arch. Pr. 1777, 12th ed.) it is expressed, "To the bailiffs for executing warrants on . . . . fi. fa. . . . . 1*l.* 1*s.*" In the form given for writs of fi. fa. in the Judicature Act, 1875, Appendix F, 1, the sheriff is commanded that of the goods and chattels of —— he "cause to be *made* the sum of £ —." In *Masters* v. *Lowther* (3) Jervis, C.J., said that where the goods are released without execution being executed no poundage is payable. The writ is not wholly executed till the goods are sold and the proceeds handed over: *Harrison* v. *Paynter* (4).

COCKBURN, C.J. The question is whether the writ of fi. fa. was executed. If it was the sheriff is entitled to the poundage and fees; if it was not executed he is not entitled. The case of *Nash* v. *Dickinson* (1), though the facts are not precisely the same, is substantially a decision upon this point. But in matters of practice the decisions of one Court are not binding upon the others, unless the practice has become so settled that it ought not to be shaken. In my opinion it is enough if the sheriff's officer goes down to the premises with the warrant and gets payment. He can only receive payment by virtue of the warrant, which is his authority, and the debtor can make a valid payment only under the warrant; and if the debtor in order to avoid the inconvenience of a levy and sale prefers to pay the money, I think the sheriff's officer is not only authorized but bound to accept it. But is he therefore to lose his remuneration? It is a great

1877

BISSICKS
v.
BATH COLLIERY CO.

---

(1) Law Rep. 2 C. P. 252.
(2) 2 C. P. D. 305.
(3) 11 C. B. at p. 958.

(4) 6 M. & W. 387; 9 L. J. (N.S.)
Ex. 169.

relief to the debtor to have the matter settled as early as possible. If we were to say that it is only by a levy and sale that the officer earns his remuneration, then in every instance the officer would have to insist on the whole performance being gone through, and that would cause great inconvenience.

We must look to see if the writ has been *virtually* executed. The officer comes and says, "I have a warrant to seize your goods for a certain sum, which must be paid or further proceedings will be taken." They go through the items together, and the debtor voluntarily hands over the money to the officer, being under an obligation to him for his courtesy in giving as little trouble as possible, and then the debtor dishonourably turns round and refuses to pay his fees. I think therefore that the sheriff is entitled to these sums, and that the decision of *Nash* v. *Dickinson* (1) was on insufficient grounds. I say nothing about *Bos* v. *Hammond* (2) because that decision appears to have been founded on an anonymous case in Lofft's Reports, which is not sufficient to support it.

CLEASBY, B. It is of no use attempting to define a levy, but I think in this case there was in substance an actual levy, and if so, the sheriff is entitled to his poundage and fees.

Solicitors for plaintiff: *Mead & Daubeny.*
Solicitors for sheriff: *Guscott, Wadham & Daw, for Wadham, Chilton, & Green—Armytage, Bristol.*

   (1) Law Rep. 2 C. P. 252.   (2) 2 C. P. D. 300.

[IN THE COURT OF APPEAL.]

SPICE *v.* BACON.

*Innkeeper's Liability—26 & 27 Vict. c. 41, ss. 1 and 3 —Sufficiency of Notice
limiting Liabilty.*

By s. 1 of 26 & 27 Vict. c. 41, no innkeeper shall be liable to make good to any
guest of such innkeeper any loss of or injury to property brought to his inn . . .
to a greater amount than the sum of 30*l.*, except in the following cases : Where
such property shall have been stolen, lost, or injured, through the wilful act, default, or neglect of such innkeeper, or any servant in his employ . . . . Sect. 3
requires the innkeeper to exhibit a copy of s. 1 in a conspicuous part of the hall
or entrance to his inn, otherwise he cannot claim the protection of s. 1.

The defendant, an innkeeper, caused a paper which purported to be a copy of
s. 1 of 26 & 27 Vict. c. 41, to be exhibited in the hall or entrance to his inn, but
the paper was unintentionally misprinted, and the sentence stood : " Where such
property shall have been stolen, lost, or injured through the wilful default or
neglect of such innkeeper or any servant in his employ."

The plaintiff, while a guest at the defendant's inn, had stolen from his bedroom
at night property amounting to the value of 119*l.* :—

Held, that, the notice contained no statement which admitted the continuance
of the common law liability for the goods or property stolen, lost, or injured
through the wilful act of the innkeeper or his servant, and therefore did not
protect the defendant.

THE statement of claim alleged, that the plaintiff on the 15th
of November, 1875, was received by the defendant, who was the
innkeeper of the the the Old Ship Hotel at Brighton, and lodged as a
guest in the inn for reward payable by the plaintiff in that behalf
to the defendant, and a certain bedroom in the inn was set apart
by the defendant for the use of the plaintiff while lodging in the
inn. On the night of that day, the plaintiff slept in the bedroom,
and while he slept certain goods and money of the plaintiff which
he had brought with him to the inn and had placed in the bedroom, to wit, a gold watch and chain with a compass attached, a
gold diamond ring, signet ring, a case of instruments, a purse containing 5*l.* in gold and some silver, were stolen and carried away
from the bedroom ; and that the goods and money were stolen
and lost by reason of the default and neglect of the defendant
and his servants, in permitting persons of dishonest character to
frequent the inn.

The statement of defence, amongst other things, alleged that the notices, which are required under 26 & 27 Vict. c. 41, s. 3 (1), to be exhibited in order that the defendant might be entitled to the benefit of that Act, were duly exhibited in the manner provided thereby, when the goods and money were brought by the plaintiff to the hotel; and that by reason of the provisions of the Act the defendant was not liable to a greater extent than the sum of 30*l.*, and that he had paid this sum into court.

The plaintiff replied, that under the circumstances set forth in the statement of claim, the defendant was not protected by the statute, and that the sum of 30*l.* was not sufficient to satisfy his claim.

At the trial, before Kelly, C.B., at the London sittings, on the 14th of February, 1877, the following facts were proved. The plaintiff was a guest at the hotel kept by the defendant, and while there, during the night of the 15th of November, 1875, the articles and money mentioned in the statement of claim, were stolen from his bedroom while he slept. The defendant had caused a copy of s. 1 of 26 & 27 Vict. c. 41, to be exhibited as required by the third section of the same Act, in a conspicuous part of the hall or entrance to his inn; but the copy was unintentionally misprinted, and the sentence stood: "Where such property shall have been stolen, lost, or injured, through the wilful default or neglect of such innkeeper or any servant in his employ."

At the trial, the plaintiff contended that the variance between the first section and the copy exhibited, was a substantial variance, and disentitled the defendant to the protection of the Act. He also contended that the loss was caused by the wilful act of the defendant and his servants.

The defendant contended that the plaintiff's loss was caused by

(1) By 26 & 27 Vict. c. 41, s. 1, no innkeeper shall, after the passing of this Act, be liable to make good to any guest of such innkeeper any loss of, or injury to, goods or property brought to his inn .... to a greater amount than the sum of 30*l.*, except in the following cases: that is to say, (1) where such goods or property shall have been stolen, lost, or injured, through the wilful act, default, or neglect of such innkeeper or any servant in his employ.... By s. 3, every innkeeper shall cause at least one copy of the first section of this Act, printed in plain type to be exhibited in a conspicuous part of the hall or entrance to his inn, and he shall be entitled to the benefit of this Act in respect of such goods or property only as shall be brought to his inn while such copy shall be so exhibited.

his own negligence. The jury found a verdict for the defendant, and Kelly, C.B., subsequently directed judgment to be entered for the plaintiff. (1)

1877

SPICE
v.
BACON.

Grantham, Q.C., and *J. H. Johnstone,* for the defendant, contended that the printed paper purporting to be a copy of s. 1 of 26 & 27 Vict. c. 41, was substantially a copy of that section, that the error was a mere verbal error unintentionally made, not designed to mislead, and could not mislead any one, and that there had been a compliance with the statute, and that the defendant was protected.

Herschell, Q.C., and *G. Bruce,* for the plaintiff, contended that the defendant was not entitled to the protection of the statute, for the omission from the copy of the word "act" altered the sense of the sentence, and that it was, therefore, a substantial and material variance: that its omission appeared to limit the liability of the innkeeper, and, if the notice had correctly stated the statute, he could claim an exemption from liability although the goods had been stolen by his servants.

J. H. Johnstone was heard in reply.

LORD CAIRNS, L.C. We do not entertain any doubt as to the effect of the notice under the statute. I regret coming to the conclusion which I feel obliged to come to upon that point, because I have not the least doubt that there was a bonâ fide intention on the part of the defendant to give a notice which was an exact compliance with the statute, and that the omission which was relied upon has occurred entirely per incuriam; but it has occurred, and we must deal with the notice as it stands.

Now at first it rather appeared that it might be looked upon as if there had been an omission of a word not material to the sense, and I certainly should not be prepared to hold that, if a paper had been put up in an inn, which was intended in good faith to be a copy of the section of the statute, and that all that could be said

---

(1) The Court of Appeal reverses this judgment and entered the judgment for the defendant, on the ground that on the facts proved in evidence the jury were warranted in finding that there was such negligence or absence of care on the part of the plaintiff as disentitled him to recover in the action.

of it in opposition to its being a copy was that a word or two words which were not material to the sense and to the operation of the statute had been omitted, the paper had ceased to be, or failed to be, a copy within the meaning of the statute. But the word which is here omitted is the word " act," and the sentence, which should have run: " Stolen, lost, or injured, through the wilful act, default, or neglect of such innkeeper, or any servant in his employ," runs: " Stolen, lost, or injured through the wilful default or neglect of such innkeeper or any servant in his employ." There is, therefore, nothing in the notice—no statement—which admits the continuance of the common law liability for the goods or property which shall have been stolen, lost, or injured through the wilful act of the innkeeper or any servant in his employment. The result of that is this: if it could be supposed that, in a case like the present, the goods were actually stolen by a servant in the employment of the innkeeper, the notice, as it now runs, would be a notice asserting that the common law liability had ceased even in that case. It would be a notice not admitting the continuance of the common law liability, where what had led to the loss of the goods had been the act of a servant in the employ of the innkeeper.

It is sufficient to say if that be so, the omission here entirely alters the operation of the section of the statute. The notice is, therefore, not a notice stating the law in the way the first section of the statute states it. I feel obliged, I repeat reluctantly, to hold that the claim for protection under the statute fails, and that the case must be dealt with as if the statute never had passed.

COCKBURN, C.J. I concur in the view which has been just stated by the Lord Chancellor.

I quite concur in thinking that if this were a mere clerical error, we might hold the notice sufficient to meet the requirement of the Act, as still being a copy; but when we find an omission of that which is material, with a view to a clear and distinct statement of the rights and liabilities of the parties respectively, we have an omission which is far beyond a mere clerical error. It is an omission of a substantial part of the notice. When we have an omission of a material and really substantial part of the notice required by statute, I cannot think it a copy sufficient to satisfy the requirements of the Act.

BRAMWELL, L.J. I concur that on this point our judgment must be for the plaintiff.

Judgment accordingly.

Solicitor for plaintiff: *S. R. Hoyle.*

Solicitors for defendant: *Stibbard & Cronshey, for Woods & Dempster, Brighton.*

THE GENERAL STEAM NAVIGATION COMPANY *v.* THE LONDON AND EDINBURGH SHIPPING COMPANY.

Practice—Costs of Successful Party in Actions for Collision between Ships— Judicature Act, 1875, Order LV.

In an action in the Exchequer Division, tried by a jury, for damages caused by the collision of the defendants' ship with the plaintiffs' ship, the defendants raised several grounds of defence, but succeeded only on the ground that the collision was caused by the negligence of the pilot, whom they were compelled by law to employ. The plaintiffs afterwards, under the Judicature Act, 1875, Order LV., applied to the Exchequer Division for an order depriving the defendants of costs, on the ground that in the Probate, Divorce, and Admiralty Division a defendant under similar circumstances is entitled to no costs:—

Held, that, whether the Exchequer Division had or had not power to make such an order, it ought not to be made, for the rule which prevails in the Probate, Divorce, and Admiralty Division does not extend to the other Divisions.

THIS action was for damages caused by the defendants' vessel negligently coming into collision with the plaintiffs' vessel in the Thames. The statement of defence alleged: first, that the plaintiffs' vessel was in fault for neglecting to have the regulation light; secondly, that the collision was not caused by the negligence of those in charge of the defendants' vessel, but was, so far as they were concerned, an inevitable accident; thirdly, that if the collision was caused by the negligent navigation of the defendants' vessel, it was solely the fault of the pilot who was acting in charge of the defendants' vessel under circumstances and within a district such as to render the employment of a duly qualified pilot compulsory by law.

At the trial before Kelly, C.B., at Guildhall, the defendants abandoned the first two grounds of defence, and relied on the

1877

General
Steam Navi-
gation Co.
v.
London and
Edinburgh
Shipping Co.

third, upon which the jury found a verdict for the plaintiffs, leave being reserved to the defendants to move to enter judgment for them, on the ground that in the position in which the defendants' ship was the employment of a pilot was compulsory by law. This question having been argued, the Exchequer Division, on the 29th of May, 1877, ordered judgment to be entered for the defendants upon the point reserved.

The plaintiffs moved for an order directing that the defendants be not entitled to recover any costs of defence from the plaintiffs but pay their own, on the ground that the defendants had failed on all the grounds of defence other than that of compulsory pilotage, and had succeeded only on the latter; and also directing that the defendants pay the plaintiffs their costs on the issues on which the latter had succeeded.

Butt, Q.C., and *R. E. Webster,* for the plaintiffs, in support of the motion. The Court has the same power to make the order asked for, as the judge who tried the cause would have had "at the trial for good cause shewn." This power is conferred by the Judicature Act, 1875, Order LV. (1) The plaintiffs had no opportunity of making this application at the trial, for they obtained the verdict, and could not foresee that judgment would be eventually entered for the defendants. Assuming, then, that the Court has the power, the plaintiffs must shew "good cause" why the Court should make the order. The "good cause" is furnished by the universal practice which prevailed in the Admiralty Court and now prevails in the Probate, Divorce, and Admiralty Division, that where in actions for collision the defendant raises several defences and succeeds only on that of compulsory pilotage, he shall get no costs. The reason for that rule is probably that the master is primâ facie responsible for the injury, and till the action is tried the plaintiff has no means of discovering who really is responsible. That practice was sanctioned by the Privy Council, and has now been affirmed by the Court of

(1) Order LV.: "Subject to the provisions of the Act, the costs of and incident to all proceedings in the High Court shall be in the discretion of the Court; . . . . Provided that where any action or issue is tried by a jury, the costs shall follow the event, unless upon application made at the trial for good cause shewn the judge before whom such action or issue is tried or the Court shall otherwise order."

Appeal in *The Daois*. (1)   That case was an appeal from the Probate   1877
Division and Admiralty Division, but since the Judicature Act
there is but one Court of Appeal from all the Divisions, and the
object of that Act was to render the practice uniform in all the
Divisions.   This Division is therefore bound by that case.

Murphy, Q.C., and *Bray*, for the defendants were not heard.

GENERAL
STEAM NAVI-
GATION CO.
v.
LONDON AND
EDINBURGH
SHIPPING CO.

KELLY, C.B.   This is an application by the plaintiffs for an
order under Order LV. of the Rules of Court, 1875, directing that
the defendants be not entitled to their costs on the issue of compulsory pilotage.   No application was made to me at the trial
upon this question, probably because at the trial the verdict was
entered for the plaintiffs.

It is quite clear that any application to the judge under Order
LV. must be made at the trial, and for good cause shewn, and as
no such application was made to me at the trial, I have no power
now to deprive the defendants of costs.   But it is contended that
under the last words of Order LV., " the Court " has after the
trial such a power substantially and quite independently of the
question whether any application was made to the judge at the
trial, and whether he granted or refused it.   That contention
raises a question of great nicety and importance, upon which, as
it is not necessary to give any decision, I express no opinion.

But supposing the Court has such a power, upon what ground
are we asked to deprive the defendants of their costs?   For centuries, the law and practice of all the Courts at Westminster,
have been this, that the party who succeeds in obtaining the
verdict is entitled to costs unless he be deprived by some statute,
or by a judge under some statutory power such as that given by
Order LV.   This being so, I think we ought not to deprive the
successful defendants of their costs unless some good cause can be
shewn; without which I could not have made the order at the
trial.   The only cause now shewn is the practice which always
prevailed in the Admiralty Court while it existed as a separate
court, and which now prevails in the Probate, Divorce, and Admiralty Division—that where an action is brought for damages
caused by the collision of the defendants' ship with the plaintiffs'
ship, and the defendant pleads several defences, and succeeds only

(1) Weekly Notes, 1877, p. 93.

1877

GENERAL
STEAM NAVI-
GATION CO.
v.
LONDON AND
EDINBURGH
SHIPPING CO.

on the defence that the damage was caused by the negligence of the pilot whom the defendant employed under the Acts relating to compulsory pilotage, the defendant is entitled to no costs.

It appears from *The Daoiz* (1), that the Court of Appeal has held that that well established rule should prevail, and we are asked to treat that decision as binding on us, on the ground that the Court of Appeal from the Admiralty Division is also the Court of Appeal from the Exchequer Division. It is no doubt desirable that the legislature should interpose to assimilate the practice of the several Divisions, and to make the practice of the Admiralty Division conformable to that of the other divisions in this respect, or to make the practice of the other divisions conformable to that of the Admiralty Division. That has been done by the legislature in the Judicature Act, 1873, s. 25, sub-s. 9, which enacts that " in any cause or proceeding for damages arising out of a collision between two ships, if both ships shall be found to have been in fault, the rules hitherto in force in the Court of Admiralty, so far as they have been at variance with the rules in force in the courts of common law, shall prevail." Under that enactment the law and practice of the Admiralty Court, which were that in such causes each party should bear the losses equally, are imposed upon the other divisions where the law and practice were different. But that could be done by the act of the legislature alone. There is then no ground for the order we are now asked to make except the practice of the Admiralty Division.

It has been urged that other defences having been raised, on which the plaintiffs have succeeded, they are entitled to the costs of those issues. It is premature to express any opinion on that point. If on taxation the master refuses to tax the plaintiffs' costs on any issues on which they are entitled to their costs, that taxation can be reviewed. I think, therefore, that no good cause has been shewn why we should deprive the defendants of their costs, and that this application must be refused.

HUDDLESTON, B. Upon the first question, whether the Court has the power to grant the present application, I have no doubt that it has the power, and I arrive at this conclusion both from the words of Order LV. and on authority. Under Order LV. an

(1) Weekly Notes, 1877, p. 98.

order to deprive the successful party of costs may be made (as I read it) either by the judge who tries the cause, if an application is made to him at the trial and good cause be shewn, or, where no application has been made at the trial, by the Court sitting, not on appeal, but as the Court to which the application is made, and the Court will then decide on the merits. The only authority on the matter is *Baker* v. *Oakes* (1), where Cockburn, C.J., and Brett, L.J., two of the three judges of the Court of Appeal, seemed to adopt this view, and the third, Amphlett, L.J., neither assented nor dissented. During the argument (2), Brett, L.J., says the rule gives the Court power "if the judge at the trial made no order," and Cockburn, C.J., in his judgment (3), says: "The defendant had omitted to make any application as to costs to the judge at the trial, but it was still open to him to have applied to the Court."

But on the second question the plaintiffs have not shewn any reason on the merits for the present application. If I thought the decision of the Court of Appeal in *The Davis* (4) was intended to lay down a rule for all the divisions, I should follow it as binding on us, though I should be much disinclined to depart from the general rule as to costs which prevails in all the divisions except the Admiralty Division. But I do not consider that decision binding on us. The Master of the Rolls there said that the rule acted on in the Admiralty Court ought to be applied in the Court of Appeal, but I read that as meaning in cases of appeal from the Admiralty Division, and he does not suggest that it ought to be applied in the other divisions, and I think that if the Court of Appeal had the present case on appeal from the Exchequer Division, they would adopt the practice of the Exchequer Division. That decision is, therefore, not binding on us, and if so I see no reason for deviating from the well established rule, that the successful party is entitled to costs.

Motion refused.

R. E. Webster applied for leave to appeal, which was refused.

Solicitor for plaintiffs: *W. Batham.*
Solicitor for defendants: *Thomas Cooper.*

(1) 2 Q. B. D. 171.   (3) 2 Q. B. D. at p. 174.
(2) 2 Q. B. D. at p. 173.   (4) Weekly Notes, 1877, p. 93.

1877

GENERAL
STEAM NAVI-
GATION Co.
v.
LONDON AND
EDINBURGH
SHIPPING Co.

1877
May 31.

THE WEST OF ENGLAND AND SOUTH WALES DISTRICT BANK *v.*
THE CANTON INSURANCE COMPANY.

Practice—Discovery and Inspection—Marine Insurance—Ship's Papers.

An action having been brought on a policy of marine insurance by the mortgagees of 32-64ths of the ship and it appearing that the plaintiffs had no ship's
papers, but that the ship had been sailed by the mortgagor, who was the
managing owner, and who had since died, the defendants applied for an order
that not only the plaintiffs but the mortgagor or his representatives, and also all
persons interested in the proceedings and in the insurance on the ship, should
produce upon oath the ship's papers, and that in the meantime all the proceedings
should be stayed:—

Held, that the old practice had not been superseded by the Judicature Act,
1875, Order XXXI., rules 11–18, and that the defendants were entitled to the
order, which must remain in force until, at all events, the plaintiffs had satisfied
the Court that they had applied to the mortgagor and done all in their power
to produce the ship's papers.

THIS was an action on a voyage policy of insurance on the ship
Monarch, made in March, 1876, by the plaintiffs, who were
mortgagees, not in possession, of 32-64ths of the ship. The ship
was lost on the voyage insured, having been sailed by the mortgagors, who were the managing owners, and who had since died.
After the statement of claim had been delivered, the defendants
took out a summons requiring the plaintiffs to shew cause why
they "and all parties interested" should not produce to the
defendants all the ship's papers. Upon the hearing at chambers,
Denman, J., made an order in December, 1876, for a stay of proceedings until the ship's papers should be produced by the plaintiffs, but struck out the words "and all parties interested."

The defendants gave notice of motion to vary the order of Denman, J., by directing "that not only the plaintiffs, but the mortgagors of the ship, or their representatives, and also all persons
interested in these proceedings and in the insurance on the ship
Monarch, do produce upon oath the documents referred to in the
order of Denman, J., and that they, as well as the plaintiffs, should
also account for all such documents as were once, but are not now,
in their or either of their possession or power."

An affidavit in opposition was made to the effect that the plaintiffs had no ship's papers.

1877

WEST OF
ENGLAND
BANK
v.
CANTON
INSURANCE CO.

C. Bowen, for the defendants, in support of the motion. The defendants are entitled to see all the ship's papers, i.e., the protests, surveys, log books, &c., and all documents which can throw light on the accident to the ship, for without these they cannot prepare their defence. The plaintiffs being bare mortgagees, not in possession, cannot have these papers, which must be in the possession or power of the mortgagors as managing owners, or of their representatives. The plaintiffs have a right to see these papers, and can obtain production of them from the mortgagors by taking out a summons under s. 48 of the Common Law Procedure Act, 1854. In actions on marine policies, the practice has been for many years to require production of the ship's papers by the plaintiffs and all persons interested in the proceedings, in the insurance, and in the ship.

Pollard, for the plaintiffs. No case has gone the length now contended for. The practice has been confined to cases where other persons besides the plaintiff were interested in the action or in the insurance. It is not pretended that any person is interested except the plaintiffs in the present action or in this insurance. But whatever the practice was it is superseded by the Judicature Act, 1873, Order XXXI. Rules 11–17 of that Order provide for discovery on oath and inspection of documents. Rule 18 enacts that, except in the case of documents referred to in the pleadings or affidavits of the party against whom the application is made, an application for inspection shall be founded upon an affidavit shewing of what documents inspection is sought, and that they " are in the possession or power of the other party." The defendant's proper course is to wait till the plaintiffs make their affidavit as to documents, and then upon proper affidavits to, as it were, surcharge the plaintiffs as to particular documents alleged to be in their "possession or power." The Court cannot order a party to an action to give inspection of documents not in his possession or power: *Fraser* v. *Burrows* (1). Still less have they power to stay

(1) 2 Q. B. D. 624.

1877

WEST OF
ENGLAND
BANK
v.
CANTON
INSURANCE Co.

proceedings as now asked for.　The defendants themselves can proceed under s. 48 of the Common Law Procedure Act, 1854, but they have no right to compel the plaintiffs to do so.

KELLY, C.B.　I think that the order prayed for on the part of the defendants ought to be made, and upon the materials now before us.　I regret that the notice of motion prays for an order in this peculiar and unsatisfactory form, viz., that the action shall be stayed—not till the plaintiffs shall have satisfied the Court that they have resorted to all reasonable, lawful, and practicable means in their power to produce, or cause to be produced, the ship's papers—but that the action shall be stayed till they have caused or procured affidavits to be made by a number of other persons over whom they may possess no control.　I regret that the form is in those terms ; but as it appears to be the form in which in actions of this kind orders have been made at chambers for a very long time, I think we shall be doing no injustice by making this order absolute, and if the plaintiffs on another occasion apply to us shewing that there is an absolute impossibility on their part in complying with the order, we may then consider what it is our duty to do.

CLEASBY, B.　I am certainly not prepared to say that the old practice, which is confined to actions on marine policies, is superseded by the Judicature Act.　I am quite sure I have made this order at chambers myself more than once since the passing of the Judicature Act.　That being so, the question which arises here is this : The interest of the plaintiffs is that of bare mortgagees.　They have nothing to do with the sailing of the ship ; they merely have an interest in the ship itself.　The ship is lost ; they bring this action.　Is the underwriter entitled to call upon them not only to make an affidavit and to produce that which they have—which is nothing, from their interest being such as I have mentioned—but to cause these papers to be produced upon affidavit by the mortgagor, who by permission of the mortgagee has sailed the ship, and who, I assume, would be the person in possession of all the ship's papers ?　I do not say that the mortgagees would

be *bound* to produce through the mortgagor all those papers—we
do not decide that, but at all events they cannot say, " We will
do no more than make an affidavit that we have no papers our
selves, or none under our actual control." No; they must go
further, and endeavour to comply with the practice in substance;
that is to say, they must endeavour to produce the ship's papers;
they must satisfy us that they have made application to the
mortgagor, and have done what they can to place the defendant in
the position of knowing what his defence to the action is.

1877

Wᴇsᴛ ᴏғ
Eɴɢʟᴀɴᴅ
Bᴀɴᴋ
v.
Cᴀɴᴛᴏɴ
Iɴsᴜʀᴀɴᴄᴇ Co.

*Order absolute, in the terms of the notice
of motion.*

Solicitors for plaintiffs : *Lyne & Holmans.*
Solicitors for defendants : *Freshfields & Williams.*

The Mode of Citation of the Volumes in the *Three Series* of the LAW REPORTS, commencing January 1, 1876, will be as follows :—

In the First Series,
1 Ch. D.

In the Second Series,

1 Q. B. D.   1 Ex. D.
1 C. P. D.   1 P. D.

In the Third Series,
1 App. Cas.

INDEX.

DISCOVERY - - - - 437, 472
    See PRACTICE. 9, 10.

ESTREATED RECOGNIZANCE - - 47
    See ATTACHMENT.

EVIDENCE—Of negligence - - 243
    See RAILWAY COMPANY. 2.

—— To prove extinction of superior lines of
descent - - - - 289
    See DESCENT.

FORESHORE—Right to - - 328
    See CORNWALL.

FRAUDS, STATUTE OF - 30, 318, 355
    See LANDLORD AND TENANT. 2, 3, 4.

GAMING—8 & 9 *Vict.* c. 109, s. 18—*Money deposited with Stakeholder when recoverable—Wager.*] An agreement to walk a match for 200*l.* a side, the money being deposited with a stakeholder, is a wager, and null and void under 8 & 9 Vict. c. 109, s. 18. And the deposit of the money is not a subscription or contribution for a sum of money to be awarded to the winner of a lawful game within the proviso of that enactment: and although the winner of the match cannot sue the loser or the stakeholder to recover the stakes, yet a depositor may maintain an action to recover back the share deposited by him with the stakeholder.—The plaintiff and one S. agreed to walk a match for 200*l.* a side, and each deposited 200*l.* with the defendant to be paid to the winner. S. won the match. The plaintiff, after the determination of the match, but before the money was paid over to S., demanded the sum deposited by him from the defendant:—*Held*, that the plaintiff was entitled to recover his share of the deposit from the defendant.—*Batty v. Marriott* (5 C. B. 818) overruled. DIGGLE *v.* HIGGS C. A. 422

GASWORKS CLAUSES ACT, 1847 (10 *Vict.* c. 15), *ss.* 6, 7—*Powers of Gas Company to break up Soil and lay down Pipes—Buildings.*] By s. 6 of 10 Vict. c. 15, the undertakers are authorized to open and break up the soil and pavement of the several streets within the limits of their special Act, and to lay down pipes for supplying gas. Sect. 7 provides " that nothing · herein shall authorize the undertakers to lay down or place any pipe or other works, into, through, or against any building, or in any land not dedicated to the public use, without the consent of the owners and occupiers thereof . . ."—A road passed alongside the plaintiff's premises, and over certain arches occupied by him, as cellars. The defendants, a company constituted under a local Act incorporating 10 Vict. c. 15, in opening and breaking up the soil of the road for the purpose of laying down gas-pipes, damaged the arches :—*Held*, that the arches were buildings within s. 7, and that the defendants could not justify breaking through them. THOMPSON *v.* THE SUNDERLAND GAS COMPANY
    [C. A. 429

HEIR-AT-LAW - - - - 289
    See DESCENT.

HIGHWAY—Surveyor - - 21
    See JURISDICTION. 2.

HUSBAND AND WIFE—*Status of Wife after Decree Nisi for dissolution of Marriage, and before Decree Absolute.*] The status of a married woman

HUSBAND AND WIFE—*continued.*
is not affected by the pronouncing of a decree nisi for the dissolution of the marriage. She continues to be subject to all the disabilities of coverture until the decree is made absolute.—Action for taking goods of the plaintiff. Plea : coverture of plaintiff at the time of the alleged taking and of plea pleaded. Prior to the alleged taking a decree nisi had been pronounced for the dissolution of the plaintiff's marriage, which was made absolute after plea and before the trial :—*Held* (reversing the judgment of the Exchequer Division), that the plaintiff was still a married woman notwithstanding the decree nisi, and that the plea was proved.—*Prole v. Soady* (Law Rep. 3 Ch. 220) distinguished. NORMAN *v.* VILLARS C. A. 359

IMPLIED CONDITION—Fitness for occupation
    See LANDLORD AND TENANT. 1. [336

IMPLIED PROMISE TO PAY - - 314
    See LIMITATIONS, STATUTE OF.

IMPRISONMENT FOR DEBT - - 47
    See ATTACHMENT.

INHERITANCE - - - - 289
    See DESCENT.

INNKEEPER—26 & 27 *Vict.* c. 41, *ss.* 1 *and* 3 —*Sufficiency of Notice limiting Liability.*] By s. 1 of 26 & 27 Vict. c. 41, no innkeeper shall be liable to make good to any guest of such innkeeper, any loss of or injury to property brought to his inn . . . . to a greater amount than the sum of 30*l.*, except in the following cases : Where such property shall have been stolen, lost, or injured, through the wilful act, default, or neglect of such innkeeper, or any servant in his employ . . . . s. 3, requires the innkeeper to exhibit a copy of s. 1, in a conspicuous part of the hall or entrance to his inn, otherwise he cannot claim the protection of s. 1.—The defendant, an innkeeper, caused a paper which purported to be a copy of s. 1 of 26 & 27 Vict. c. 41, to be exhibited in the hall or entrance to his inn, but the paper was unintentionally misprinted, and the sentence stood : " Where such property shall have been stolen, lost, or injured through the wilful default or neglect of such innkeeper or any servant in his employ."—The plaintiff, while a guest at the defendant's inn, had stolen from his bedroom at night property amounting to the value of 119*l.* :—*Held*, that the notice contained no statement which admitted the continuance of the common law liability for the goods or property stolen, lost, or injured through the wilful act of the innkeeper or his servant, and therefore did not protect the defendant. SPICE *v.* BACON - C. A. 463

JOINDER OF DEFENDANTS - - 301
    See PRACTICE. 9.

JOINT CLAIM AND SEPARATE COUNTER-CLAIMS - - - - 243
    See PRACTICE. 8.

JURISDICTION—*Central Criminal Court—Admiralty—Territorial Waters—Offence within Three Miles of English Coast—Manslaughter*—15 *Ric.* 2, c. 3—28 *Hen.* 8, c. 5—39 *Geo.* 3, c. 37—4 & 5 *Wm.* 4, c. 36, *s.* 22—7 & 8 *Vict.* c. 2.] The prisoner was indicted at the Central Criminal Court for manslaughter. He was a foreigner and in command of a foreign ship, passing within three miles of the shore of England on a voyage to a foreign port; and whilst within that distance his ship ran into a British ship and sank her, whereby a passenger on board the latter ship was drowned. The facts of the case were such as to amount to manslaughter by English law :—Held, by the majority of the Court (Cockburn, C.J., Kelly, C.B., Bramwell, J.A., Lush and Field, JJ., Sir R. Phillimore, and Pollock, B.; Lord Coleridge, C.J., Brett, and Amphlett, JJ.A., Grove, Denman, and Lindley, JJ., dissenting), that the Central Criminal Court had no jurisdiction to try the prisoner for the offence charged.—By the whole of the majority of the Court, on the ground that, prior to 28 Hen. 8, c. 15, the admiral had no jurisdiction to try offences by foreigners on board foreign ships, whether within or without the limit of three miles from the shore of England; that that and the subsequent statutes only transferred to the Common Law Courts and the Central Criminal Court the jurisdiction formerly possessed by the admiral; and that, therefore, in the absence of statutory enactment, the Central Criminal Court had no power to try such an offence.—By Kelly, C.B., and Sir R. Phillimore, also, on the ground that, by the principles of international law, the power of a nation over the sea within three miles of its coasts is only for certain limited purposes; and that parliament could not, consistently with those principles, apply English criminal law within those limits.—Held, contrà, by Lord Coleridge, C.J., Brett and Amphlett, JJ.A., Grove, Denman, and Lindley, JJ., on the ground that the sea within three miles of the coast of England is part of the territory of England; that the English criminal law extends over those limits; and the admiral formerly had, and the Central Criminal Court now has, jurisdiction to try offences there committed although on board foreign ships.—By Lord Coleridge, C J., and Denman, J., on the ground that the prisoner's ship having run into a British ship and sank it, and so caused the death of a passenger on board the latter ship, the offence was committed on board a British ship, and, therefore, the Central Criminal Court had jurisdiction. THE QUEEN v. KEYN C. C. R. 63

2. —— Justices—Wilful or malicious Injury to Property — Surveyor of Highways — Removal of Obstruction and Nuisance to Highway — 24 & 25 Vict. c. 97, s. 52.] The respondent was the occupier of a residence which communicated with an adjoining highway by means of a gateway; an inclosed drain and brickwork were put down at the gateway for the purpose of convenient access to the respondent's residence, and also for the purpose of allowing the free passage water running by the side of the highway. The drain and brickwork, with the earth covering the same, formed a nuisance and obstruction to the highway. The appellant, being surveyor of highways for the parish within which the respondent's residence was situate, took up and removed the drain and the brickwork, and in so doing damaged them. The appellant having been charged upon an information before justices with committing damage, injury, and spoil upon the respondent's property, against the provisions of 24 & 25 Vict.

c. 97, s. 52, they found that the appellant acted bonâ fide, but that he did not do the act complained of under a fair and reasonable supposition that he had a right to do it, and they convicted him of the offence charged :—Held, that the conviction was wrong, and that the information ought to have been dismissed: for the appellant was not a private individual, but the surveyor of highways having a control over, and an interest in, the drains laid for carrying off the water, and that in dealing bonâ fide with the drains he was not guilty of wilful or malicious damage.—Semble, that, as the appellant, according to the finding of the justices, acted bonâ fide, they ought, upon the facts stated, also to have found that he acted under a fair and reasonable supposition that he had a right to do what was complained of in the information.—White v. Feast (Law Rep. 7 Q. B. 353) distinguished. DENNY v. THWAITES

[C. A. 21

—— Railway Commissioners - - 450
See RAILWAY COMPANY.

KNOWLEDGE OF HOLDER - - 285
See CHEQUE.

LANDLORD AND TENANT— Lease of a Furnished House—Implied Condition of Fitness for Occupation.] In an agreement to let a furnished house there is an implied condition that the house shall be fit for occupation at the time at which the tenancy is to begin, and if the condition is not fulfilled the lessee is entitled thereupon to rescind the contract.—The defendant agreed to rent the plaintiff's furnished house for three months from the 7th of May, but having at the beginning of the intended tenancy discovered that the house was, owing to defective drainage, unfit for habitation, refused to occupy. The plaintiffs repaired the drains, and on the 26th of May tendered the house in a wholesome condition to the defendant, who refused to occupy or to pay any rent. The plaintiffs having sued for the rent and for use and occupation :—Held, that the state of the house at the beginning of the intended tenancy entitled the defendant to rescind the contract, and that he was not liable for the rent or for use and occupation.—Smith v. Marrable (11 M. & W. 5; 12 L. J. (Ex.) 223), approved. WILSON v. FINCH HATTON - - - - - 326

2. —— Agreement, Construction of — Demise, Actual or Contingent—Option to Lessee to continue holding for Three Years beyond a Demise for a Year—Statute of Frauds (29 Car. 2. c. 3), s. 1, 2; 8 & 9 Vict. c. 106, s. 3.] The plaintiff and defendant entered into the following agreement not under seal : " Jan. 26. Hand agrees to let, and Hall agrees to take, the large room, &c., from 14th February next until the following Midsummer twelve months, and with right at end of that term for the tenant, by a month's previous notice, to remain on for three years and a half more :"—Held, reversing the judgment of the Exchequer Division, that the agreement was divisible, and contained an actual demise for a term less than three years, with a superadded stipulation, that the defendant at his option

PLEADING - - - **242, 301, 365**
See PRACTICE. 8, 8, 11.

POOR-RATE—*Mode of rating Property occupied by a public Body for public Purposes—Rateable Value ascertained by actual Profit—Occupier subject to statutory Restrictions.*] Where land is used for a public purpose, and the occupiers thereof are prevented by statute from deriving the full pecuniary benefit which it is capable of producing, the land is to be rated to the poor with reference to the amount of profit actually made, and not with reference to the amount which might be earned by the occupiers if they were not subject to restrictions.—The local board of health for W. erected and occupied works for the purpose of supplying the inhabitants thereof with water. The works were situate within the parish of C. In order to benefit the inhabitants of W., the local board made the scale of charges so low, as to leave a profit far less than would have accrued to a company carrying on the works as a commercial undertaking. In adopting the scale of charges above mentioned, the local board intended to carry out those provisions of the Public Health Act, 1848, the object of which was to insure a supply of water at a low price for sanitary purposes. The assessment committee of the D. union, within which the parish of C. was situate, by a valuation list assessed the local board at a rateable value of 1400*l.*, based upon the amount which might have been earned by a trading company carrying on the waterworks for their own benefit; the local board claimed to be assessed at a rateable value of 540*l.*, based upon the profit actually earned by them :—*Held*, affirming the judgment of the Court of Appeal from inferior Courts, that the assessment of 1400*l.* was wrong, and that the local board were liable to be assessed at 540*l.* only; for, under the provisions of the Public Health Act, 1848, they could not make rates of an amount more than sufficient to enable them to maintain the waterworks, and they could be lawfully assessed only with reference to the profit actually earned. CORPORATION OF WORCESTER *v.* DROITWICH ASSESSMENT COMMITTEE - **49**

POST-DATED CHEQUE - - - **265**
See CHEQUE.

POUNDAGE AND FEE - - - **459**
See SHERIFF.

PRACTICE—*Appeal in Criminal Matter—Judicature Act,* 1873 (36 & 37 *Vict. c.* 66), *s.* 47.] A judgment of the Court of Appeal from inferior Courts, against the validity of a conviction, under 16 & 17 *Vict. c.* 119, *s.* 3, for keeping a common gaming-house, on a case stated under 20 & 21 *Vict. c.* 43, is a judgment of the High Court in a criminal matter from which, by *s.* 47 of the Judicature Act, 1873, there is no appeal. BLAKE *v.* BEECH - - - - - C. A. **335**

2. —— *Award—Signing Judgment—Judicature Act,* 1873 (36 & 37 *Vict. c.* 66), *s.* 22—*Order XL., Rule* 3.] A verdict having been taken, subject to a reference, before the Judicature Act came into operation, the arbitrator had power to direct a verdict for either party, the award was not made until after the Act came into operation :—*Held*, that judgment on the award could be signed without obtaining an order of the Court or of a judge.—*Semble*, per Brett, J.A., that where the award, made under a reference since the Act,

is final and conclusive on the parties, judgment may be signed on the award, though no direction to that effect is given in the order of reference or in the award; and it is not necessary to set down the action on motion for judgment under Order XL., Rule 3. LLOYD *v.* LEWIS - - C. A. **7**

3. —— *Claim by Defendant against Third Party in Action of Tort—Joinder of Third Party —Order XVI., rr.* 17, 18, 19.] In an action of tort for injury sustained by the plaintiff through the defendants' negligence, the defendants obtained an order under Order XVI., Rule 17, that third parties who it was alleged through their negligence had caused the injury should be added as defendants :—*Held*, by Cockburn, C.J., Kelly, C.B., and Bramwell, L.J. (Brett, L.J., dissenting), reversing the decision of the Exchequer Division, that the defendants were not entitled to have such third persons made parties to the action. HOSWELL *v.* LONDON OMNIBUS COMPANY - C. A. **365**

4. —— *Costs—County Court Act,* 1867, *s.* 5—*Judicature Act,* 1873, *s.* 67, *Order XIX., Rule* 3, *Order LV.*] In an action tried by a jury, in which the plaintiff proves a claim, but a counterclaim of less amount is proved by the defendant, the plaintiff recovers judgment for the balance only, and if no order as to costs is made, the plaintiff's right to costs under the County Court Act, 1867, and Order LV. of the Judicature Acts, must be decided with reference to that balance, and not to the amount of the claim proved. STAPLE *v.* YOUNG - - - - **394**

5. —— *Costs on Payment into Court—Common Law Procedure Act,* 1852, *s.* 73—*Rules of Court,* 1875, *Order XXX., Rules* 1, 2, 3, 4.] In an action for work, labour, and materials, the writ claimed a balance of 373*l.* The defendant paid 200*l.* into court under Order XXX., Rule 1, and gave notice in Form 5, Appendix B, that "that sum is enough to satisfy the plaintiffs' claim." The plaintiffs took it out under Order XXX., Rule 3, but did not give the notice under Order XXX., Rule 4, or any other notice. The cause was afterwards referred, under the Common Law Procedure Act, 1854, to the certificate of an arbitrator, "the costs of the cause to abide the event." No pleadings were ever delivered on either side. The arbitrator, after hearing the parties, gave his certificate that the 200*l.* paid into court was enough to satisfy the plaintiffs' claim. The master having taxed the plaintiffs' costs against the defendant up to the time of their taking the money out of court, and having from that point taxed the defendant's costs against the plaintiffs :—*Held*, that as the 200*l.* had been paid in generally, and the event of the reference was that the plaintiffs recovered nothing beyond the amount paid into court, the plaintiffs were not entitled to any costs, and the defendant was entitled to her costs of suit from the commencement, and that the taxation must be reviewed accordingly. LANGRIDGE *v.* CAMPBELL - - - - - **281**

6. —— *Costs of Successful Party in Actions for Collision between Ships—Judicature Act,* 1875, *Order LV.*] In an action in the Exchequer Division, tried by a jury, for damages caused by the collision of the defendants' ship with the

PRACTICE—*continued.*

plaintiffs' ship, the defendants raised several grounds of defence, but succeeded only on the ground that the collision was caused by the negligence of the pilot, whom they were compelled by law to employ. The plaintiffs afterwards, under the Judicature Act, 1875, Order LV., applied to the Exchequer Division for an order depriving the defendants of costs, on the ground that in the Probate, Divorce, and Admiralty Division a defendant under similar circumstances is entitled to no costs:—*Held*, that, whether the Exchequer Division had or had not power to make such an order, it ought not to be made, for the rule which prevails in the Probate, Divorce, and Admiralty Division does not extend to the other Divisions. The GENERAL STEAM NAVIGATION COMPANY v. THE LONDON AND EDINBURGH SHIPPING COMPANY - - **467**

7. —— *Costs—Slander—Judicature Act, 1875 —Order LV.—" Costs shall follow the event."*] None of the statutes as to costs are repealed by Order LV., and it must be read with reference to them. When, therefore, the proviso says that on a trial by jury the costs shall follow the event, it must be taken to mean that the costs will follow as regulated by the statutes, if any, applicable to the case.—The plaintiff, in an action of slander, recovered one farthing damages. The judge made an order as to costs, and no certificate was given: —*Held*, reversing the judgment of the Exchequer Division (by Bramwell and Brett, L.JJ., Kelly, C.B., dissenting), that the plaintiff was not entitled to costs.—*Parsons v. Tinling* (2 C. P. D. 119) overruled. GARNET v. BRADLEY - C. A. **349**

8. —— *Counter-claim—Judicature Act, 1873, s. 24, sub-ss. 1, 7, Order XVI., Rules 1, 3—Order XIX., Rule 3—Counter-claim sounding in Damages — Joint Claim and separate Counter-claims.*] When two or more plaintiffs sue for a joint claim, the defendant may, under the Judicature Act, 1873, s. 24, sub-ss. 3, 7, Order XVI., Rules 1, 3, 4, 6, 13, and Order XIX., Rule 3, set up against each individual plaintiff separate counter-claims sounding in damages.—Two railway companies having, as joint lessees of a railway, sued for statutory tolls, the defendant set up against each company separate counter-claims for damages in respect of delay in the delivery of goods. The plaintiffs applied under Order XIX., Rule 3, to strike out the counter-claims, but no reasons were alleged why they could not be conveniently disposed of in the action:—*Held*, that the counter-claims ought not to be struck out. THE MANCHESTER, SHEFFIELD, AND LINCOLNSHIRE RAILWAY COMPANY AND THE LONDON AND NORTH WESTERN RAILWAY COMPANY v. BROOKS - - **243**

9. —— *Discovery and Inspection—Marine Insurance—Ship's Papers.*] An action having been brought on a policy of marine insurance by the mortgagees of 32-64ths of the ship, and it appearing that the plaintiffs had no ship's papers, but that the ship had been sailed by the mortgagor, who was the managing owner, and who had since died, the defendants applied for an order that not only the plaintiffs but the mortgagor or his representatives, and also all persons interested in the proceedings and in the insurance on the ship,

PRACTICE—*continued.*

should produce upon oath the ship's papers, and that in the meantime all the proceedings should be stayed:—*Held*, that the old practice had not been superseded by the Judicature Act, 1875, Order XXXI., rules 11-18, and that the defendants were entitled to the order, which must remain in force until, at all events, the plaintiffs had satisfied the Court that they had applied to the mortgagor and done all in their power to produce the ship's papers. WEST OF ENGLAND BANK v. CANTON INSURANCE COMPANY - - **472**

10. —— *Discovery—Privileged Documents— Report of Examination of Plaintiff by Medical Man—Regulation of Railways Act* (31 & 32 Vict. c. 119), s. 26.] Where, on an action against a railway company to recover damages for injuries sustained by the defendants' negligence, the plaintiff is examined by medical men employed on the defendants' behalf, the reports sent by the medical men to the defendants are privileged from inspection, provided that the examination and reports were procured by the defendants' solicitor, or at his instance, for the purpose of enabling him to give advice to the defendants with reference to the action, and of assisting him generally in the conduct of the legal proceedings. —It is immaterial that the judge's order under which the plaintiff was examined was drawn up with the words "and by consent" struck out, as a judge has no jurisdiction to make an order in that form except under 31 & 32 Vict. c. 119, s. 26, and the plaintiff must be treated as if he had submitted voluntarily to the examination. FRIEND v. THE LONDON, CHATHAM, AND DOVER RAILWAY COMPANY - - - - C. A. **437**

11. —— *Joinder of Defendants — Alternative Relief—Rules of Court, 1875, Order XVI., Rules 3, 6.*] In an action brought by a company against L. and T., the claim stated that L., through T., who professed to be, and in fact was, the agent of L., contracted to take a certain number of debentures in the plaintiff company, which contract L. had failed to perform; and that L. denied that T. was authorized by him to make the contract. The plaintiffs prayed for specific performance of the contract or for damages against L.; or in the alternative, if it should appear that T. had no authority to act as L.'s agent, then for specific performance and damages against T.—T. having applied to have judgment entered up in his favour, or to have his name struck out as defendant:— *Held*, affirming the decision of the Exchequer Division, that, under the circumstances stated in the claim, the plaintiffs were entitled to join L. and T. as defendants, and to claim alternative relief against them under Order XVI., Rules 3, 6. THE HONDURAS INTER-OCEANIC RAILWAY COMPANY v. LEFEVRE - - - C. A. **301**

12. —— *Transfer of Action to Chancery Division—Rules of Court—Order LI., rule 2.*] W. contracted to purchase a property, and paid a deposit. He afterwards gave notice to rescind the contract on the ground of the vendor's delay in making out a title, after which he took proceedings for the liquidation of his affairs. His trustee commenced an action in the Exchequer Division against the vendor for a return of the deposit, and

SALE OF GOODS—*Construction — Cargo.*] The plaintiffs sold to the defendant "a cargo of from 2500 to 3000 barrels (seller's option) American petroleum . . . . to be shipped from New York . . . . and vessel to call for orders off coast for any safe floating port in the United Kingdom, or on the Continent between Havre and Hamburg, both inclusive (buyer's option)." The plaintiffs chartered a vessel, on which were placed 3000 barrels of petroleum, and a bill of lading was signed making them deliverable to the plaintiffs; but as this quantity did not constitute a full cargo, 300 additional barrels were placed on board, which were marked with a different mark, and for which a separate bill of lading was signed. The plaintiffs gave notice to the defendant of the shipment of the 3000 barrels, and were ready to order the vessel from its port of call to any port of delivery within the contract, and there to deliver to the defendant the 3000 barrels and to take the 300 barrels themselves, or to deliver to the defendant at any such port 2750 barrels as the mean between 2500 and 3000, but the defendant refused to accept either the 3000 barrels or any other quantity. The plaintiffs having brought an action for non-acceptance:—*Held*, affirming the decision of the Exchequer Division, that, on the true construction of the contract, "cargo" meant the entire load of the vessel which carried it; that the defendant was therefore not bound to accept part of a cargo; and that the action was not maintainable. BORROWMAN *v.* DRAYTON - - C. A. 15

SALFORD HUNDRED COURT OF RECORD ACT, 1868 (31 & 32 Vict. c. cxxx.) - 346
  See PROHIBITION.

SHERIFF—*Levy under fi. fa.—Poundages and Fees —29 Eliz. c. 4—1 Vict. c. 55.*] A sheriff's officer in the execution of a warrant of fi. fa. went with another man to the debtor's house, shewed him the warrant, and demanded payment, and told him that in default of payment the man must remain in possession and further proceedings be taken. The debtor then paid the sum demanded in the warrant, which included poundage and officer's fee.—*Held*, that there had been in substance a levy, and that the sheriff was entitled to poundage and fee, though there had been no sale. *Nash* v. *Dickinson* (Law Rep. 2 C. P. 252), and

SHERIFF—*continued.*
Roe v. *Hammond* (2 C. P. D. 300), not followed. BISSICKS *v.* THE BATH COLLIERY COMPANY, LIMITED. EX PARTE BISSICKS - - 459

"SIC UTERE TUO UT ALIENUM NON LÆDAS"
  See WATER. 1. [1

SUCCESSION DUTY—*Predecessor—General Power of Appointment—Succession Duty Act,* 1853 (16 & 17 *Vict. c.* 51), *ss.* 2, 4.] S., tenant for life in possession, and W., his eldest son, tenant in tail in remainder, by deed of the 22nd of March, 1854, barred the entail, and settled the estates to such uses as they should jointly appoint. By deed of the 23rd of March, 1854, they jointly appointed the estates (in the event which happened) to such uses as they should jointly appoint, and in default, to the use that W. should, during the joint lives of himself and S., receive a yearly rent-charge, and subject thereto to S. for life, with remainder to W. for life, with remainder to the first and other sons of W. in tail male, with remainder to such uses as S. and his second son, T., should jointly appoint, and in default of appointment to T. for life, with remainders over. W. died in 1864, without issue, and without the joint power of S. and W. having been exercised. In 1866 S. and T. by deed appointed the estates (subject to S.'s life estate, and in the events which happened) to the use that, after the decease of S., A., his wife, should, if she should survive him, receive during her life a yearly rent-charge, and, subject thereto, that the estates should go to the use of D., the daughter of T., during so much of a certain period as she should live. S. died in 1873, leaving A. surviving him; and D. came into possession of the estates :—*Held*, by Cockburn, C.J., James and Brett, L.JJ. (Bramwell, L.JJ., dissenting), reversing the decision of the Exchequer Division, that, solely, on the authority of *Attorney General* v. *Floyer* (9 H. L. C. 477; 31 L. J. (Ex.) 404), the case fell within s. 2 of the Succession Duty Act, 1853, and that A. and D. took their annuity and life interest respectively,

SUCCESSION DUTY—*continued.*
as successions derived from W. as the donor of the power, and that the duties payable in respect of their successions were to be calculated on their respective lives, according to their respective relationship to W.—*Lord Braybrooke* v. *Attorney General* (9 H. L. C. 150; 31 L. J. (Ex.) 177), *Attorney General* v. *Floyer* (9 H. L. C. 477; 31 L. J. (Ex.) 404), and *Attorney General* v. *Smythe* (9 H. L. C. 497; 31 L. J. (Ex.) 404), discussed. THE ATTORNEY GENERAL v. CHARLTON C. A. 396

TURNPIKE—*Locomotive—Construction of Wheel —Width of Shoes or other bearing Surface—*24 & 25 *Vict c.* 70, *s.* 3.] By the Locomotive Act (24 & 25 Vict. c. 70), s. 3, every locomotive used on a highway and drawing any waggon, shall have the wheels cylindrical and smooth soled, or used with shoes or other bearing surface of a width not less than nine inches. An engine was so used, which had its wheels fitted with shoes four and a half inches broad, placed parallel to one another, and three inches apart, and bolted obliquely across the whole breadth of the wheel; so that when a length of less than nine inches of one shoe was in contact with the ground the deficiency was made up by the length of contact of the next shoe with the ground :—*Held*, that the bearing surface not being continuous, the engine was not in conformity with the Act. STRINGER v. SYKES 240

UNION OF BUILDINGS - - - 39
   See METROPOLITAN BUILDING ACT.

VACCINATION—*Certificate that Child has had Smallpox—Vaccination Act,* 1871 (34 & 35 *Vict. c.* 98), *ss.* 7, 15.] By the Vaccination Act, 1871, s. 7, every certificate of a child being unfit for, or insusceptible of, successful vaccination shall be transmitted to the vaccination officer under a penalty on failure to do so. The Poor Law Board, under the authority of s. 15 of the Act, issued a form of certificate expressed in the alternative, either that the child had been not less than three times unsuccessfully vaccinated and was insusceptible of vaccination, or that the child had already had smallpox :—*Held*, that a parent to whom a certificate that the child had already had smallpox was given, and who failed to forward it to the vaccination officer, was not liable under s. 7. BROADHEAD v. HOLDSWORTH 321

VAGRANCY ACT—*Rogue and Vagabond—Spiritualism—Palmistry or Otherwise—*5 Geo. 4, c. 83, s. 4.] The appellant was convicted by justices under 5 Geo. 4, c. 83, s. 4, which makes punishable as a rogue and vagabond " every person . . . using any subtle craft, means, or device *by palmistry or otherwise* to deceive and impose on any of

VAGRANCY ACT—*continued.*

His Majesty's subjects." In a case stated for this Court, the justices found as a fact that the appellant attempted to deceive and impose upon certain persons by falsely pretending to have the supernatural faculty of obtaining from invisible agents and the spirits of the dead answers, messages, and manifestations of power, namely, noises, raps, and the winding up of a musical box :—*Held,* that the means used by the appellant came within the words " by palmistry or otherwise," and that the conviction was right. MONCK *v.* HILTON - **268**

VIS MAJOR—Proximate cause of damage -   **1**
   See WATER.

WAGERING   -   -   -   -   **423**
   See GAMING.

WATER—*Liability of Owner for Escape of Water —Vis major or Act of God proximate Cause of Damage—Maxim Sic utere tuo ut alienum non lædas.*] One who stores water on his own land, and uses all reasonable care to keep it safely there, is not liable for damage effected by an escape of the water, if the escape be caused by the act of God, or vis major; e.g., by an extraordinary rainfall, which could not reasonably have been anticipated, although, if it had been anticipated, the effect might have been prevented.—On the defendant's land were ornamental pools containing large quantities of water. These pools had been formed by damming up with artificial banks a natural stream which rose above the defendant's land and flowed through it, and which was allowed to escape from the pools successively by weirs into its original course. An extraordinary rainfall caused the stream and the water in the pools to swell so that the artificial banks were carried away by the pressure, and the water in the pools, being thus suddenly let loose, rushed down the course of the stream and injured the plaintiff's adjoining property. The plaintiff having brought an action against the defendant for damages, the jury found that there was no negligence in the maintenance or construction of the pools, and that the flood was so great that it could not reasonably have been anticipated, though if it had been anticipated the effect might have been prevented :—*Held,* affirming the judgment of the Court of Exchequer, that this was in substance a finding that the escape of the water was caused by the act of God, or vis major, and that the defendant was not liable for the damage.—*Rylands v. Fletcher* (Law Rep. 3 H. L. 330) distinguished. NICHOLS *v.* MEESLAND C.A. **1**

WATERWORKS CLAUSES ACT, 1847 — *Public Statutory Duty, Breach of, when Actionable*—10 Vict. c. 17, ss. 42, 43.] The mere fact that the

WATERWORKS CLAUSES ACT, 1847—*continued.* breach of a public statutory duty has caused damage does not vest a right of action in the person suffering the damage against the person guilty of the breach ; whether the breach does or does not give such right of action must depend upon the object and language of the particular statute.—By the Waterworks Clauses Act, 1847, the undertakers are: (1) to fix and maintain fire-plugs ; (2) to furnish to the town commissioners a sufficient supply of water for certain public purposes ; (3) to keep their pipes to which fire-plugs are fixed at all times charged with water at a certain pressure, and to allow all persons at all times to use the same for extinguishing fire without compensation ; and (4) to supply to every owner or occupier of any dwelling-house, having paid or tendered the water-rate, sufficient water for domestic purposes.—By s. 43 a penalty of 10*l.* (recoverable summarily before two justices, who may award not more than half the penalty to the informer and are to give the remainder to the overseers of the parish), is imposed on the undertakers for the neglect of each of the above duties, and for the neglect of (2) and (4) they are further to forfeit to the commissioners or ratepayer a penalty of 40*s.* a day, for each day during which such neglect continues after notice in writing of non-supply.—The plaintiff brought an action for damages against a waterworks company for not keeping their pipes charged as required by the Act, whereby his premises situate within the limits of the defendants' Act were burnt down :— *Held* (reversing the decision of the Court of Exchequer), that the statute gave no right of action to the plaintiff.—*Couch v. Steel* (3 E. & B. 402, 23 L. J. (Q. B.) 121), questioned. ATKINSON *v.* THE NEWCASTLE AND GATESHEAD WATERWORKS COMPANY   -   -   -   C. A. **441**

WHEEL—Construction of   -   -   -   **240**
   See TURNPIKE.

WIDTH OF SHOES—Locomotive engine—Turnpike   -   -   -   -   **240**
   See TURNPIKE.

WILFUL INJURY TO PROPERTY -   -   **31**
   See JURISDICTION. 2.

WORDS—" Cargo "   -   -   -   **15**
   See SALE OF GOODS.

—— " Company in no case responsible for luggage of passenger of greater value than 6*l.*"
   See RAILWAY COMPANY. 1.   [**253**

—— " Costs to abide the event "   -   **231**
   See PRACTICE. 5.

—— " Costs shall follow the event "   -   **349**
   See PRACTICE. 7.

—— " Palmistry or otherwise "   -   **268**
   See VAGRANCY ACT.

END OF VOL. II.

Lightning Source UK Ltd.
Milton Keynes UK
UKHW012250110219
337137UK00006B/892/P